BizTalk™ Server 2000: A Beginner's Guide

CLEMENS F. **VASTERS**

Osborne/**McGraw-Hill**

New York   Chicago   San Francisco
Lisbon   London   Madrid   Mexico City
Milan   New Delhi   San Juan
Seoul   Singapore   Sydney   Toronto

2/23/03 Comp USA 19.99

Osborne/**McGraw-Hill**
2600 Tenth Street
Berkeley, California 94710
U.S.A.

To arrange bulk purchase discounts for sales promotions, premiums, or fund-raisers, please contact Osborne/**McGraw-Hill** at the above address. For information on translations or book distributors outside the U.S.A., please see the International Contact Information page immediately following the index of this book.

BizTalk™ Server 2000: A Beginner's Guide

1234567890 DOC DOC 01987654321

ISBN 0-07-219011-6

Publisher
Brandon A. Nordin
Vice President & Associate Publisher
Scott Rogers
Editorial Director
Tracy Dunkelberger
Project Editor
Janet Walden
Acquisitions Coordinator
Emma Acker
Technical Editor
Steve Wright
Copy Editor
Chrisa Hotchkiss

Proofreader
John Schindel
Indexer
Claire Splan
Computer Designers
Carie Abrew, Melinda Moore Lytle,
Kelly Stanton-Scott
Illustrators
Michael Mueller, Alex Putney,
Beth E. Young
Cover Design
Amparo del Rio
Series Design
Peter F. Hancik

This book was composed with Corel VENTURA™ Publisher.

ABOUT THE AUTHOR

Clemens F. Vasters is cofounder and chief technical officer of newtelligence AG, a German developer services company focusing on XML, BizTalk, and the Microsoft .NET Framework. Before starting newtelligence AG with two partners in the summer of 2000, he was director of research at a major German financial software provider from 1997 and, before that, development director at a financial software company in New York, NY starting 1995. Clemens has developed applications for the Microsoft Windows OS family since 1990 and has used COM and ODBC for business applications since 1992. He is coauthor of the Microsoft .NET Developer Tools Readiness Kit developed for Microsoft Consulting Services, and teaches Microsoft .NET technologies to Microsoft Partners, CTEC trainers, and Enterprise Consultants at workshops in the United States, Asia, and Europe. In addition, he is a frequent speaker at major international developer conferences. And in his free time he takes care of the aliens that landed in his backyard three years ago.

AT A GLANCE

Part I   **Electronic Information Exchange**

▼ 1   A Brief History of Electronic
       Data Interchange   3
▼ 2   Federated Services:
       The Connected Economy   17
▼ 3   Data Formats   33
▼ 4   Microsoft .NET   67

Part II   **BizTalk Overview and Concepts**

▼ 5   Introducing BizTalk Server 2000   83
▼ 6   BizTalk Ideas and Concepts   103
▼ 7   BizTalk Server Messaging Terminology   125
▼ 8   BizTalk Messaging Concepts   139
▼ 9   BizTalk Orchestration Concepts   155
▼ 10 BizTalk Messaging Tools Overview   175

Part III	BizTalk Architecture and Components	
▼ 11	BizTalk Messaging Architecture	203
▼ 12	BizTalk Orchestration Architecture	247

Part IV	Architecting, Designing, and Configuring BizTalk Server 2000 Solutions	
▼ 13	Finding and Defining the Solution Architecture	261
▼ 14	Creating Orchestration Schedules	271
▼ 15	Creating Document Specifications	317
▼ 16	Mapping Documents	359
▼ 17	Configuring the Application	403
▼ 18	Testing and Troubleshooting BizTalk Messaging	439

Part V	Administering BizTalk Server 2000	
▼ 19	Installing BizTalk in a Production Environment	463
▼ 20	Programmatic Application Deployment and Configuration	487
▼ 21	Tracking Documents	511

Part VI	Extending BizTalk Server 2000: The Basics	
▼ 22	Custom Parsers and Serializers	533
▼ 23	Writing Application Integration Components	591
▼ 24	Writing Custom Functoid Containers	607

Part VII	Appendixes	
▼ A	BizTalk Schema	621
▼ B	ISO 6523 Codes	627

| | Index | 633 |

CONTENTS

Acknowledgments   xv
Introduction. xix

Part I

Electronic Information Exchange

▼ 1   A Brief History of Electronic Data Interchange   3

Castrum Novaesium   4
Electronic Data Interchange   5
The eXtensible Markup Language   9
Enterprise Application Integration Worries 12
    The Common Object Request Broker Architecture 12
    Java 13
    The Component Object Model 14
EDI Meets XML Meets EAI 14

▼ 2   Federated Services: The Connected Economy 17

B2B Is a Reality 18
Web Services 22
Security and the Electronic Signature 23
    Privacy 24
    Integrity 24

Authenticity   25
Redefining Document   26
    Challenges   26
    Benefiting from B2B Requires Flexibility   28
Heterogeneous System Landscapes   28
    Centralized Data Processing   29
    Collaboration Is the Key   29
    Agile Information Anywhere and Anytime   30
Document Standardization   31
    Standards Bodies   31
    Industry Consortia   31
    The United Nations   31
    XML Communities   32

▼ 3   Data Formats   33
ANSI X12   34
    X12 Syntax and Structure   35
    X12 Semantics   38
    X12 Transaction Sets   38
UN/EDIFACT   40
    UN/EDIFACT Syntax and Structure   40
    UN/EDIFACT Semantics   42
SWIFT/ISO 15022   43
    SWIFT Syntax and Structure   44
    SWIFT Semantics   46
XML   46
    XML Document Syntax   46
    XML Namespaces   48
    DTD and Schema   49
    XML References: XPath, XPointer, and XLink   57
    XSLT   62
    SOAP/XMLP   66

▼ 4   Microsoft .NET   67
The .NET Framework   68
    The Common Type System   69
    Comprehensive XML Support   70
    Common Language Runtime   70
    .NET Framework Library   71
The .NET Enterprise Servers   73
    Windows 2000 Server   74
    Microsoft Application Center 2000   76

Microsoft SQL Server 2000   76

Microsoft Exchange Server 2000   77

Microsoft SharePoint Portal Server 2000   77

Microsoft Host Integration Server 2000   78

Microsoft Commerce Server 2000   78

Microsoft Internet Security and Acceleration Server 2000   . .   79

Part II

BizTalk Overview and Concepts

▼ 5 Introducing BizTalk Server 2000   83

What BizTalk Server Does and Doesn't Do   84

BizTalk Server Editions   86

What's in the Box?   87

Installing BizTalk Server   89

Preinstallation Tasks   89

Installing the Server   90

▼ 6 BizTalk Ideas and Concepts   103

Document-Driven Systems   104

Rapid Adaptation and Short Turnaround Times   106

The BizTalk Community—BizTalk.org   107

The BizTalk Framework   108

The Simple Object Access Protocol   110

BizTalk Messages   113

▼ 7 BizTalk Server Messaging Terminology   125

Organizations and Applications   126

Organization Identifiers   126

The Home Organization   127

Application Identifiers   127

Document Definitions   128

Ports   129

Messaging Ports   129

Transports   130

Destination Identifier   131

Envelopes   132

Encryption, Signature, and Encoding   132

Channels   133

Envelope Definition   137

Distribution Lists   138

▼ **8**   BizTalk Messaging Concepts   139
   BizTalk Messaging Service   140
      BizTalk Queues in Detail   140
      Receive Functions   143
   BizTalk Interchange Application   144
      COM+ in a Nutshell   145
      Submitting Documents   146
   Document Routing   148
      Routing Fundamentals   148
      Channel Selection   149
      Channel Filters   153
      Open Destination Routing   153

▼ **9**   BizTalk Orchestration Concepts   155
   A Common Language for Developers and Analysts   157
   From Drawings to Applications   166
      Ports   168
      BizTalk Messaging Integration   170

▼ **10** BizTalk Messaging Tools Overview   175
   BizTalk Editor   176
   BizTalk Mapper   181
   BizTalk Messaging Manager   184
      The Configuration Assistant   191
      The BizTalk Direct Integration Tool   193
   BizTalk Administrator   193
   BizTalk Document Tracking   196

Part III

BizTalk Architecture and Components

▼ **11** BizTalk Messaging Architecture   203
   The Architectural Big Picture   204
   The BizTalk Management Database   206
      Administration Object Tables   207
      Messaging Object Tables   217
   The Shared Queue Database   234
   The BizTalk Document Tracking Database   234
   Document-Processing Pipeline Components   234
      Pipeline Components Under the Hood   237
      How the Pipeline Works   239

▼ **12** BizTalk Orchestration Architecture 247

    Orchestration Schedules and XLANG 248

    How to Run Schedules 251

        A Brief Moniker Lesson 251

    Schedules as Components 254

    About Properties, Constants, and the Nonexistence of Variables . 255

    Hydration and Dehydration 257

Part IV

Architecting, Designing, and Configuring BizTalk Server 2000 Solutions

▼ **13** Finding and Defining the Solution Architecture 261

    Managing Complexity 263

        Short-Track Analysis Principles 263

        Collecting Requirements 268

        Requirements Analysis 269

▼ **14** Creating Orchestration Schedules 271

    Introducing Orchestration Designer 272

        Visio for Beginners 272

    Defining the Business Flow 274

    Defining Ports 279

        Shaping the Data Flow 306

        A Generic Component for Loopback Channels 309

    Long-Running Transactions 310

▼ **15** Creating Document Specifications 317

    Review 318

        Document Definition Concepts 318

        BizTalk Editor 318

    Defining XML Documents 320

        Root Elements: The Reference Tab 321

        The Declaration Tab 323

        Creating Records 324

        Defining Fields 326

        Completing and Testing the Sample 332

        Creating Specifications from Templates 337

        Inferring Schema from Documents 339

    Defining EDI Documents 340

        UN/EDIFACT Heaven 341

        UN/EDIFACT Hell 351

Defining Flatfile Documents 355
  Defining Delimited Flatfile Streams 356
  Defining Positional Flatfile Streams 358

▼ 16 Mapping Documents 359
  BizTalk Mapper 360
  Mapping Fundamentals 360
    Mapping Fields 364
    Mapping Records 368
    Understanding Functoids 373
  Mapping Documents 388
  More Mapping Examples 400

▼ 17 Configuring the Application 403
  BizTalk Messaging Manager 404
  Defining Applications and Organizations 405
  Creating Ports 407
  Creating Channels 411
  Creating Loopback Ports 419
  Completing the Sample Configuration 421
  Implementing Advanced Features 429
    Certificates for Signatures, Encryption, and HTTPS 431
    Implementing the Sender of a Secure Connection 432
    Setting up HTTP Receive Capabilities 435
    Implementing the Receiver Side of a Secure Connection . . . 436
  Sending Functional Acknowledgments and Receipts 436

▼ 18 Testing and Troubleshooting BizTalk Messaging 439
  Avoiding Messaging Problems Before They Happen 440
    Validating Standards-Based Document Specifications 443
    Validating Custom Document Specifications 447
    Testing Document Specifications and Document Maps . . . 448
    Simulating Routing 449
    Testing in Realistic Deployments 450
  Finding and Isolating Messaging Errors 451
    Parsing Stage Errors 454
    Channel Selection Stage Errors 457
    Document Validation and Mapping Stage Errors 458

Part V

Administering BizTalk Server 2000

▼ **19** Installing BizTalk in a Production Environment 463
Considerations for Planning Deployments 464
Performance Considerations 465
Scaling BizTalk Systems 469
Security Considerations 472
Automated Deployment 483

▼ **20** Programmatic Application Deployment and Configuration 487
The BizTalk Configuration Object Model 488
The Configuration Object Model's Configuration Object . . 490
Managing Ports 492
Managing Channels 498
Using Windows Management Instrumentation 502
The WMI API in Brief 503
BizTalk WMI Classes 504

▼ **21** Tracking Documents 511
The Document Tracking Database 512
The Document Tracking Tool 528

Part VI

Extending BizTalk Server 2000: The Basics

▼ **22** Custom Parsers and Serializers 533
Implementing a Custom Parser 534
How BizTalk Parsers Plug into BizTalk 535
The Job 536
The Parser Code 542
Writing Custom Serializers 575
How BizTalk Serializers Plug into BizTalk 576
The Serializer Code 576

▼ **23** Writing Application Integration Components 591
Writing Simple Integration Components 593
Writing Pipeline Components 595

▼ **24** Writing Custom Functoid Containers 607

Writing Functoid Scripts 608

Implementing Functoid Containers 613

Part VII

Appendixes

▼ **A** BizTalk Schema 621

▼ **B** ISO 6523 Codes 627

Index 633

ACKNOWLEDGMENTS

For the last six months of my life, I have lived half of my time inside the BizTalk Server product box and the other half inside the .NET Framework SDK. If I had known about the depth and complexity of the BizTalk product when I agreed to write this book, the book would probably not exist. While I was writing this, I also co-authored the Microsoft .NET Developer Tools Readiness Kit, a developer education toolkit on .NET now used by Microsoft Consulting Services and training partners worldwide. So, in addition to the masses of information that I gathered and put into this book, I also took a very deep look at the Microsoft .NET Framework and related technologies, and I have been teaching developers on .NET technologies in Europe, the U.S., and Asia, as well as speaking at several major Microsoft conferences.

Doing all these things at the same time and staying focused would certainly not have been possible without Patricia's great support and tolerance over the past couple of months, when I spent virtually every hour at home "click-clacking" on my notebook. *Danke, Danke, Pat! Ich liebe Dich.*

My partners and colleagues at newtelligence AG were also a tremendous help by generously tolerating my split attention on what needed to be done at our company and what was needed to get this book done. To Bart DePetrillo, Achim Oellers, Jörg Freiberger, Jörg Hermann, Christiane Vasters, Karlheinz Näser, Ute Welzel, Patricia Näser, Andreas Zehmisch: *Besten Dank.*

BizTalk™ Server 2000: A Beginner's Guide has my name on the cover, but getting a book on the shelves is truly a team effort. This book is also proof that "virtual workgroups" that only collaborate through the Internet do actually work great.

I would like to thank Tracy Dunkelberger, editorial director at Osborne/McGraw-Hill for initiating and coordinating this project and for convincing me that it would be a good idea to write this book. Ross Doll, Emma Acker, Janet Walden, and Chrisa Hotchkiss did an awesome job in keeping me on track with the content and schedules, organizing the logistics, querying consistency, and turning "Clemens English" into actual English. Thank you all, you were a fantastic team to work with. At the same time I don't want to forget all the people that worked behind the scenes to turn the plain text, sketches, and screenshots into the format that this book has now. Thanks.

Steve Wright, my technical editor for this book and a great software developer and architect, played a more than excellent "devil's advocate" on every little technical aspect of this book and caught a lot of bugs and inconsistencies that are just as inevitable in writing books as in writing code. And Steve made sure that I really covered all necessary aspects whenever I overlooked a feature or behavior. Thank you, Steve.

Of course it would be difficult to write a book on the first version of a product just by browsing the publicly available documentation and working with it, especially because of the great number of changes from the beta version to the release version. BizTalk Server 2000 was released by Microsoft in January of this year, after I was already working on this book. A big "thank you" to Simon Sparks, who got me onto the BizTalk track to begin with, to Tilo Böttcher from Microsoft Germany for keeping me updated in the early stages of this book project, and to Scott Woodgate from the BizTalk product group for answering questions on some of the more non-obvious issues.

I would also like to thank Compaq Computer Corporation for letting me use their EDIFACT partner agreements (used for exchanging supply chain information with their suppliers) as the basis for my examples in the EDI sections of this book.

Und: Das Buch gäbe es natürlich ganz und gar überhaupt so überhaupt nicht, wenn meine Eltern nicht wären. Meine Mutter Eva-Maria, meine Stiefmutter Gisela und der „Meister" Richard Vasters. Danke für alles. Vielen Dank auch an Dominik, Christiane, Sarah, Andreas, Bianka, David, Karin und „Onkel" Dietmar und natürlich ganz besonders auch an „Omi" Adelheid Klein besonders dafür, daß Ihr toleriert habt, daß ich mich in der letzten Zeit so selten habe blicken lassen. Ein ganz dicker Dank natürlich auch an die Seite meiner „besseren Hälfte", Karlheinz und Karin.

And a big "thank you" to everybody else, too numerous to mention here, who helped me with this project in one way or another by publishing information on the Web, answering questions, or providing other support.

Last but not least, I'd like to thank *you* for buying and reading this book. I hope you like it and I would love to hear whether you do or don't. There is nothing that cannot be improved, but nothing can be improved without constructive feedback.

Clemens F. Vasters
Cofounder and CTO, newtelligence AG, Germany
clemensv@newtelligence.com

May 2001

INTRODUCTION

t's big, it's pricey, and for most people it's one of the most confusing Microsoft product releases in recent years.

Unlike most of its siblings in the .NET Enterprise Server family, Microsoft BizTalk Server 2000 is not just a new version of a well-known product like Commerce Server (the successor of Site Server Commerce), Host Integration Server (formerly known as SNA Server), or of the Microsoft product with the longest product name ever, Internet Security and Acceleration Server 2000, which is a major upgrade from Microsoft Proxy Server 2.0.

The primary reason why BizTalk causes so much confusion is that it is the first product that was specifically designed for needs of large corporations ("the enterprise") and it aims to compete in an area that has been traditionally dominated by large-scale Unix systems and mainframes: electronic data interchange, or EDI.

EDI is the moniker that generally describes the exchange of digital documents on private networks between banks, large manufacturing and trading companies and their suppliers and customers, or between government agencies. Long before "being connected" inspired the thinking and dreams of today's Internet entrepreneurs and users, the Global 2000 corporations had networks in place that allowed (and still allow) automated, secure, and reliable interchange of documents, purchase orders, or money transfers. Or, as a 75-year-old mainframe veteran from Houston, who I recently had the pleasure to have a long conversation with, put it (with a thick Texan accent and a cigar): "That Internet thing adds no value whatsoever!" Now I beg to differ on the "whatsoever" part, but, in essence, the rise of the Internet has indeed not had the sweeping impact on the EDI space that it had on most other aspects of computing.

One of the reasons for this is certainly that the complex EDI data formats like ANSI X12, ISO15022, and UN/EDIFACT do not have the appeal and simplicity of HTML or XML. They require a long time to understand, are narrowly standardized, and are very expensive to implement and deploy. Consequently, they have been mostly ignored by the majority of the technology companies competing to secure their spot in the Internet marketplace.

Really only since the "B2B" buzzword became a popular term in 1998, have more companies (and investors) jumped to find and develop "new and innovative" solutions to connect businesses and provide integration solutions through Internet-based data exchange. Except for using a public IP network and coming up with "proactive, innovative, revolutionary" solutions that attracted venture capitalists like a lit open window lures mosquitoes, the gentleman from Texas is indeed right in a lot of ways.

With the advent of Microsoft BizTalk, a lot of things may now be changing.

EDI solutions have traditionally been developed as individually tailored in-house solutions for large corporations. The tool and infrastructure software makers for EDI have therefore had a rather narrow market with financially solid clients, a traditional sales force, and long established and strong customer relationships.

Microsoft now enters the EDI space with its huge marketing punch and literally millions of well-educated developers and consultants at their partner firms and enables all of them to provide solutions that leverage decades of real, working B2B experience through EDI.

But not only does BizTalk open up the EDI space to Windows and Internet developers, it is also an elegant and flexible bridge from EDI to the rapidly expanding new world of data interchange and processing: XML.

In most publications, including much of Microsoft's own marketing material, BizTalk is portrayed as Microsoft's XML data exchange server, and BizTalk is indeed internally fully based on the XML standard. However, reducing BizTalk to an XML-only product misses the mark. With Microsoft BizTalk you can implement pure XML document interchange solutions just as well as it allows you to build EDIFACT or X12-only applications or any combination of all these document formats.

BizTalk is a huge product that can hardly be covered in a single book in all of its detailed facets (at least not in a somewhat educational way) and the full background information for many of the standards that you will see mentioned and explained here fills several bookshelves alone.

This book will introduce you to the philosophy and functionality of Microsoft BizTalk Server 2000 and will provide you with what you need to know to start building BizTalk solutions. It's a "beginner's guide"—for EDI developers entering the XML world and for Internet developers stepping up to EDI.

Who Should Read This Book

This book is for BizTalk beginners from both the EDI space and the Internet world, who want to build cross-organization integration solutions, and for readers who want to learn about how to use BizTalk Server 2000 to integrate enterprise systems across platforms using XML.

It aims to provide a comprehensive and comprehendible introduction to Microsoft BizTalk and its vision for IS/IT managers, as well as an explanation of the core concepts and procedures for BizTalk administrators, operators, and developers.

You will find that, although Microsoft BizTalk Server 2000 is tightly integrated with the Windows 2000 operating environment and has native support for Windows properties such as the Microsoft MessageQueue and COM components, BizTalk is a very open solution that can exchange documents with any endpoint, no matter whether it runs Windows or any other operating system.

Even if your organization has not deployed any of the Microsoft BackOffice or .NET Enterprise Server products or does not even have Windows NT or Windows 2000 Servers in production use, you still will find BizTalk to be a great integration solution for your corporate IT resources through its support for a wide range of document formats and communication protocols.

How You Should Read This Book

The simple answer would be to start at the front and read straight through to the back, but that may actually not be the optimal path for you.

Depending on your background, you may actually find some of the introductory material contained in this book to be too long, too short, or outright superfluous. XML developers may yawn at the five hundredth introduction to XML, while EDI experts will find an introduction to a format that they've been using for the past 20 years not very educating. If that is the case, this part is not for you, but the respective other one certainly is.

In addition, you may find that there is a lot of theory and little hands-on material in the first two parts of the book. If you zip right into Part III and beyond, you will see why: BizTalk's complexity is overwhelming. The introductory matter is written to make the sometimes dry, theoretical background more tangible, in order to make it easier for you to chew and swallow.

The book is organized in six main parts, as described in the following sections.

Part I: Electronic Information Exchange

This first part goes back into the history of document exchange and introduces its basic principles and terminology in a very non-technical way.

Furthermore, you will learn about the origins of electronic data interchange (EDI) and the eXtensible Markup Language (XML), and we will explore the Microsoft vision of "federated services," for which Microsoft BizTalk Server plays a central role.

We will also explore the most popular document formats from both the Internet world (XML) and the EDI space (X12, EDIFACT) to give everyone a solid basis to start from.

Part II: BizTalk Overview and Concepts

Because of BizTalk's complexity and the novelty of its concept, this part is dedicated to the terminology, philosophy, and concepts of Microsoft BizTalk Server 2000.

You will learn about the core ideas behind BizTalk Server and the BizTalk Framework, and we will go into detail on what the terms "Messaging" and "Orchestration" mean in the BizTalk context.

Since BizTalk is a core element of the Microsoft .NET architecture, we will also take a look at the overall .NET vision and will figure out where and how BizTalk's features fit into .NET's big picture.

Part III: BizTalk Architecture and Components

In the third part, we will dig into BizTalk Server's architecture, and you will learn how all the concepts that have been presented in the previous parts fit into the product. You will get to know the BizTalk components and how data and documents are routed and stored.

Part IV: Architecting, Designing, and Configuring BizTalk Server 2000 Solutions

Building BizTalk solutions is a collaborative process of business analysts, administrators, and developers. This part of the book describes in depth how to create BizTalk solutions.

We will first explore how you can capture the business needs in a short-track requirements analysis and how to transfer them into an architectural approach.

That in hand, we proceed to implement the requirements using Orchestration schedules, document definitions, and messaging configurations.

Part V: Administering BizTalk Server 2000

BizTalk is an administration-centric product. If you need to deploy and operate BizTalk Server solutions, you will find this part useful, as it covers how to configure the product, supervise its operations, and diagnose problems.

Part VI: Extending BizTalk Server 2000: The Basics

The last main section of the book addresses how to extend BizTalk Server with your own extensions such as serializers and parsers, your own communication protocols, or custom functoid containers. A word of warning: This is "wear hard-hats at any time" developer territory.

PART I

Electronic Information Exchange

CHAPTER 1

A Brief History of Electronic Data Interchange

Unlike most of its siblings from the Microsoft .NET Enterprise Server family, Microsoft BizTalk Server 2000 (BTS) is not a product that you can install, configure, and run within a few hours, and it is not as instantly usable for end-user scenarios as Microsoft Exchange Server 2000 for electronic mail and collaboration tasks, or SharePoint Portal Server 2000 for corporate intranet portals and document sharing. Instead, Microsoft BizTalk Server 2000 is one of the first Microsoft products specifically designed for the needs of enterprise customers, who want to leverage the power and benefits of direct business process and systems integration across corporate boundaries. As such, BizTalk is much more of a development and integration toolkit than a "traditional" server product that supplies end-user applications like Microsoft Internet Explorer, Microsoft Outlook, or your internal line-of-business applications with data or documents. From the corporate end-user's perspective, BizTalk is a "stealth" product that silently and powerfully forwards digital documents between applications and business partners, but will go largely unnoticed by many users.

The fact that BizTalk is a product that acts much in the background and has no flashy "end-user ready" interfaces and does not do live streaming media should not distract you from a very important fact: Microsoft BizTalk Server 2000 is one of the centerpieces of Microsoft's .NET strategy and Microsoft's central hub for digital business document exchange.

Because BizTalk is not a "plug-and-play" product, the first part of this book is entirely dedicated to providing you with the necessary background and reasoning for why electronic document interchange is important for your business and how the web services paradigm that is part of Microsoft's third-generation Internet vision will change the way electronic business is conducted.

CASTRUM NOVAESIUM

We're starting our exploration of Microsoft BizTalk Server 2000 at a very unlikely place and a very unlikely time: Castrum Novaesium, A.D. 50. To maintain an iron grip on their empire, the Roman emperors and their administrative apparatus had a system that could be met in its speed and efficiency only in the late nineteenth century: the *cursus publicus,* or Roman postal service.

Castrum Novaesium was a Roman military settlement on the west shore of the Rhine River, located on the territory of the modern city of Neuss, Germany. Messages from Rome could reach the local commander in as little as eight to ten days and those from the province governors within only a day or two, traveling at speeds of up to 270 km per day. This speed enabled the Romans to quickly learn about problems in their colonies and to order redeployment of troops within a matter of days—much faster than any of their adversaries.

Another pillar of Rome's success was their bureaucracy. Organizational orders and military messages were strictly formalized and brief, expressed in a very logical and unambiguous language: Latin. The orders were transported using the reliable military postal system and were uniquely signed and authenticated.

If the Novaesium commander encountered problems with the Germanic barbarians on the other side of the Rhine river, he could efficiently ask for help and quickly receive it. This advantage was essential not only to maintain power, but also just to stay alive. At the same time, Roman citizens could maintain a most enjoyable life back home due to the efficiency of the administration and tax collection system in place even at their remotest provinces—enabled by a sophisticated communication system.

The organizational level of the Roman postal system was hardly met, well into the nineteenth century. However, the diplomatically correct formalization of letters—along with the strict distinction between address and handling information, content, and signature to guarantee secrecy and authenticity—are still important to governments today. Are you surprised that we're going to rediscover all of these features when we explore electronic data interchange (EDI), eXtensible Markup Language (XML), Simple Object Access Protocol (SOAP), and BizTalk Messaging?

But wait—reliable, quick, and secure messaging isn't everything. Orders and organizational measures that are triggered by incoming messages must be carried out in a well-defined and orderly fashion.

In times of crisis, like heavy losses of soldiers in battle or poor farm seasons in the homeland, emperors appeased the Roman citizens not only through *panem et circencis* (bread and games), but also by increasing the tax deeds of the provinces. Fulfilling such a vital, central role required the emperors to orchestrate all of the empire's resources by giving orders and setting up procedures: military camps had to be put on higher alert to avert uprisings in the conquered territories, special envoys were sometimes sent to assist and supervise the effort, and local governors had to execute the orders thoroughly with their local forces.

However, once the mandated taxation level was established, the empire had to be flexible enough to reallocate resources and switch organizational structures quickly to conquer and assimilate more territories to further enhance Rome's wealth. If the empire had a static, military structure optimized only for rapid expansion, it would have suffered the same quick collapse as all those later attempts to conquer the known world. The Romans were successful through communication and orchestration of all their resources—for more than five centuries.

BizTalk will neither enable you to conquer the known world nor guarantee you a successful business for the next few centuries; however, its Orchestration features will allow you to adjust your document-driven business processes quickly to meet changing needs. With BizTalk, you can visually create dynamic workflow schedules instead of writing and maintaining static and manually coded (and therefore expensive) programs or batch jobs. Its messaging features will let you accept and deliver messages from your outposts and allies and act rapidly when the volume or shape of the information changes, or when you need to add new corporate settlements or partners to your information flow.

ELECTRONIC DATA INTERCHANGE

Let us move on to some more recent history and enter the electric age.

The telegraph's immediate predecessors—light-signal towers—had been used in England and France since the late eighteenth century. They allowed quick relay of manually keyed signals from hilltop to hilltop. But the Morse telegraph, which started spreading quickly in Europe and North America in the 1840s, was a truly revolutionary invention. It allowed information to travel at the speed of light end-to-end and at an affordable cost.

This innovation made the telegraph one of the earliest and most important commercial applications of electricity for communications. Because commercial success spawns competition and money, only roughly 30 years after the invention of the telegraph, Phillippe Baudot invented a five-bit code that was used for transmitting character information between machines. His invention combined the typewriter and the telegraph and later became commonly known as the teletypewriter, Teletype, or Telex.

The Teletype and Telex systems grew to span the world in the early twentieth century and became ubiquitous in the 1940s, allowing businesses to communicate and exchange information at 150 Baudot, or 30 characters per second, allowing a full page of information to be transmitted in about two minutes.

While Telex allowed the transfer of typed documents between locations, it was still a paper-to-paper technology that was not really designed for exchanging raw data. The need to exchange raw data grew with the increasing use of digital computer systems in commerce. Large international corporations like retailers, transportation providers, and manufacturers started to establish direct data links between systems in the mid-1960s. They were driven by the vision of the "paperless office" and more reliable communication that eliminated human error in transferring printouts manually from one system into other systems.

Although these first steps of electronic data interchange (EDI) proved to be efficient, they were proprietary. Thus, they were costly to implement and nearly impossible to deploy across a large number of organizations. Recognizing this, the Accredited Standards Committee X12—a standards institution under the umbrella of ANSI, appointed by EDI vendors and users—moved to standardize the EDI space.

As a result, the ANSI ASC X.121 (ANSI X12) standard was established, which has been the dominant EDI document format for the past three decades. The following is a sample purchase order document as it looks when expressed in ANSI X12 ("transaction set" 850):

```
ISA*00*    *00*    *01*003897733    *12*PARTNER
ID*980923*1804*U*00200*000000002*0*T*@
GS*PO*MFUS*PARTNER ID*19980924*0937*3*X*004010
ST*850*0001
BEG*00*SA*4560006385**19980923
CUR*BY*USD
TAX*1-00-123456-6
FOB*DF***02*DDP
ITD*01*ZZ*****45*****NET 45 - Payment due 45 days from Document Date
TD5*Z****Ship via Airborne
N9*L1**SEE FOLLOWING TEXT
```

```
MSG*PLEASE CONFIRM PRICE IF NOT CORRECT.
N9*L1**SEE FOLLOWING TEXT
MSG*THANKS, BILL 281-555-5555
N1*BT**92*USA1
N1*BY*BLUEWAY SAMPLE CORPORATION*92*MFUS
PER*BD*PETE WELLDONE
N1*SE*PARTNER COMPANY NAME*92*0010001000
N1*ST*Blueway Sample Corporation*92*0000002924
N3*24500 F.D.R. Drive 290
N4*New York*NY*10004*US
PO1*00010*3300*EA*0.888*CT*BP*123456-123*EC*AM*VP*123456*123
PID*F****LOGO, 2000,MC-R6
SCH*3300*EA***002*19981101
CTT*1
SE*23*0001
GE*1*2
IEA*1*000000002
```

ANSI X12 also forms the basis for the international UN/EDIFACT (United Nations Directories for Electronic Data Interchange for Administration, Commerce, and Transport) standard, whose definition started in 1985. UN/EDIFACT has been officially phasing out ANSI X12 since 1995; however, the ANSI X12 standard remains so popular in the United States that the final normative adoption of UN/EDIFACT instead of ANSI X12 is postponed year by year by year. The fact that the United Nations is developing a technology standard clearly signals the importance of EDI in international commerce.

The following document is also a purchase order. It is expressed as a UN/EDIFACT "ORDERS" message that is compliant to the standards release S93A (directory release D93A):

```
UNB+UNOB:1+003897733:01:1234567+PARTNER ID:ZZ+000101:1050
+00000000000916++ORDERS'
UNH+1+ORDERS:S:93A:UN'
BGM+221+P1M24987E+9'
DTM+4:20000101:102'
FTX+PUR+3++GENERAL PURCHASE ORDER INSTRUCTION'
RFF+CT:123-456'
RFF+CR:1'
NAD+SE+10025392::92++SUPPLIER NAME'
CTA+SR+:STEVE'
NAD+BT+B2::92++BLUEWAY SAMPLE CORPORATION+P O BOX 901000
+NEW YORK+NY+10013000+US'
NAD+BY+MFUS::92++BLUEWAY SAMPLE CORPORATION'
CTA+PD+:JANE EGGLAND-FULTON'
NAD+ST+CM6::92++BLUEWAY SAMPLE CORPORATION+CCM6 RECEIVING DOCK:20555
```

```
SH 249+NEW YORK+NY+10034+US'
TAX+9+++++3-00105-5135-3'
CUX+2:USD:9'
PAT+1++1:1:D:45'
PAT+22++1:1:D:30'
PCD+12:2'
TDT+20++++:::AIRBORNE'
LOC+16+BLUEWAY DOCK'
TOD+2+NS+:::ORIGIN COLLECT'
LIN+000001++107315-001:BP'
PIA+1+AA:EC+123456:VP'
IMD+F+8+:::PART DESCRIPTION INFORMATION'
QTY+21:10000000:PCE'
DTM+2:20000301:102'
FTX+PUR+3++LINE ITEM COMMENTS'
PRI+CON:50'
TAX+7++++:::100'
MOA+124:100'
UNS+S'
UNT+31+1'
UNZ+1+000000000000916'
```

Before the Internet even left the educational space, value-added networks (VANs)—operated by providers such as IBM, GEIS, and AT&T—have been connecting the Global 2000 companies, reliably carrying EDI messages, optimizing collaboration, and reducing costs in international business.

In finance, EDI plays such a central role that the global financial system wouldn't function without it. The Society for Worldwide Interbank Financial Telecommunications (SWIFT) was initiated by seven major international banks in 1974 to overcome the speed, format, and security limitations of the Telex system. The society established the SWIFT messaging system in 1977, when it started operations with 230 banks from five countries.

SWIFT defines a large number of standard messages based on the ISO 7775 standard, which covers most aspects of interbank communications. (ISO 7775 is currently being phased out by the incremental ISO 15022 standard.) One of the better-known SWIFT messages is MT940, the "customer account statement" message that can be imported by most business accounting systems.

Here is a sample SWIFT message:

```
{1:F01BANKBEBBAXXX2222123456}
{2:I100BANKDEFFXXXXU3003}
{3: {113:9601}{108:abcdefgh12345678}}
{4:
:20:PAYREF- TB54302
:32A:910103BEF1000000,
```

```
:50:CUSTOMER NAME
AND ADDRESS
:59:/123-456-789
BENEFICIARY NAME
AND ADDRESS
-}
{5:{MAC:41720873} {CHK:123456789ABC}}
```

SWIFT's rock-solid, secure network carries over 3 million messages a day with an uptime consistently exceeding 99.99 percent a year. It is so reliable that SWIFT takes full responsibility for messages once they have been accepted and are transmitted over its network.

Ninety percent of U.S. Fortune 500 companies use UN/EDIFACT or X12 solutions, with similar adoption levels in Europe. Roughly only 6 percent of all other companies in the world are EDI enabled. However, over one hundred thousand businesses in the United States use an EDI solution of some sort to communicate with their customers, suppliers, or financial service providers.

THE EXTENSIBLE MARKUP LANGUAGE

While EDI was bred in the domain of global corporations, the eXtensible Markup Language (XML) is the child of the personal information technology space. Ever since Apple invented the legendary Apple II and IBM introduced the PC (with the short-sighted intent of creating a smarter mainframe terminal), the development of personal computers and their software was mainly driven by consumers and small businesses.

Most of today's software developers grew up with PCs or desktop workstations using Microsoft's DOS, Windows, or some variant of UNIX. The PC revolution concentrated on the desktop, providing personal or group-enabled network solutions for businesses, home organizations, and entertainment.

The desire for information, natural human curiosity, and the potential for entertainment were also the driving forces for the rise of the Internet. Conceived in the 1970s, the Internet became a universal network for educational institutions around the world throughout the 1980s with the emergence of Hypertext Markup Language (HTML). HTML combines a reduced text layout description variant of the Structured General Markup Language (SGML), a document description and definition language developed for the publishing and printing industry, and the simple concept of the hyperlink to provide navigable (clickable) pointers between documents. No longer an overly complex tool only for computer geeks, the Internet grew rapidly in the educational and scientific sector with the popularity of the HTML-based World Wide Web. In 1994, the Internet finally exploded like a giant supernova into the commercial space.

HTML is a simple, text-based format with just a handful of syntactical elements that allow you to define the layout of text documents. HTML was originally developed in conjunction with the Hypertext Transfer Protocol (HTTP) to allow international scientists to efficiently access the large amounts of research data that the Swiss nuclear research lab CERN produces every day.

HTML's simplicity and platform-independence enables users to easily publish their ideas and access others' ideas without requiring them to install specialized applications—except a single, simple HTML viewer-application: a browser. With hyperlinks, all of this information can be woven together to create an informational web. What a phenomenal idea. It's so phenomenal that it created an entire new industry—driven by enthusiastic PC-agers.

Take the simplicity and the most fundamental text notation of HTML, introduce some more consistency, and then drop all of the hypertext layout elements in favor of a mechanism to allow everyone to come up with their own set of elements, and you get XML. The following is a sample XML data stream:

```xml
<?xml version="1.0" encoding="iso-8859-1" ?>
<CustomerData>
    <Customer ID="1234567">
        <Name>newtelligence AG</Name>
        <Contacts>
            <Contact>
                <Name>Vasters</Name>
                <FirstName>Clemens</FirstName>
                <Position>CTO</Position>
            </Contact>
            <Contact>
                <Name>DePetrillo</Name>
                <FirstName>Bart A.</FirstName>
                <Position>
                    Director Intl. Business Development
                </Position>
            </Contact>
        </Contacts>
        <MailAddress>
            <Country>DE</Country>
            <PostalCode>41352</PostalCode>
            <City>Korschenbroich</City>
            <Street>Gilleshütte 99</Street>
        </MailAddress>
    </Customer>
</CustomerData>
```

Traditional EDI formats structure their content either by using predefined positions or by using certain—often user-defined—delimiter characters. Common to all EDI data formats is that external documentation is required to understand, parse, and write any EDI document. XML is not only much simpler, but it is also very self-descriptive.

In fact, the revolution that HTML sparked for human-readable interactive text and information is synonymous with what XML is doing for data. XML is a young standard: the base specification was standardized in 1998, and a lot of the more advanced specifications advanced to the standard-equivalent recommendation level only by the end of 2000.

XML has rapidly grown beyond the simple set of text formatting rules defined in the XML 1.0 recommendation issued by the World Wide Web Consortium (W3C). Therefore, XML is attractive for virtually every aspect of computing and is growing more popular even in areas traditionally covered by EDI. Every advanced XML feature in the following list has no equivalent match in any of the popular EDI formats. The XML format is clearly superior in terms of syntax and universal applicability.

▼   Namespaces allow you to merge multiple sets of semantics into a single document. XML documents can carry additional user-defined data and control information at any place, without violating the semantics and integrity of a standardized specification.

■   Schema allows you to narrowly define the structure of an XML document in XML itself, making the XML documents and their definitions entirely self-contained. Schema also specifies a rich set of standard data types that can be user-refined with precise constraints or grouped into arbitrarily complex types.

■   The XML Information Set defines an abstraction of the XML data format, providing you with a standardized in-memory representation of XML documents; it enables the creation of a unified programming interface for XML documents: the XML Document Object Model (DOM).

■   XBase and XLink allow you to define precise locations and cross-references between any element inside or across documents. The XPath language, which builds on these standards, is a powerful language for expressing queries into XML documents.

■   Stylesheets provide you with a standardized mechanism to define transformation rules between different document types (schemas). They also provide a way to augment XML data with formatting hints for improved presentation to human readers.

▲   The Simple Object Access Protocol (SOAP) and the upcoming XML Protocol (XMLP) (which is based on the SOAP proposal) specify a standard envelope and transport bindings so that you can move XML data between systems in a standardized way.

In contrast, all common EDI standards define only the core construction rules for messages. They also have truckloads of static data dictionaries, expressed in a nonstandardized mix of tabular field definitions and prosaic explanations that define the permitted records, fields, and their relationships.

None of the XML specifications depends on a certain platform or implementation. Because simplicity is a fundamental principle of the core XML standard, all of the aforementioned specifications are designed in the same spirit. Consequently, any software development organization can easily implement XML and all of its facets on every plat-form and any device, ranging from large mainframe systems to portable phones or "wearable computers."

ENTERPRISE APPLICATION INTEGRATION WORRIES

Simplicity sets XML apart from all other previous attempts to establish standardized ap-plication-to-application data interchange, recently more often referred to as enterprise application integration (EAI). Before XML became popular, the integration technologies developed in the 1990s were basically divided into four different camps, which were rap-idly drifting away from each other with only incomplete and brittle bridging technolo-gies between them.

All of these technologies provide remote access to business logic services (objects) and provide ways to publicize and find these services on networks. They also provide ad-ditional services for, amongst others, authentication, authorization, privacy, and transac-tion support.

The EDI space is one of the camps, without necessarily being aware of it. EDI tradi-tionally has been a mainframe computer domain that everyone had to integrate toward and that would typically not actively integrate other systems' data formats and transport protocols. Mainframe systems are simply at the top of the food-chain.

Most other enterprise systems are being developed based on one of three fiercely competing technology sets (which are the other camps): the Common Object Request Broker Architecture (CORBA) from the Object Management Group (OMG), Java from Sun Microsystems, and the Component Object Model (COM) from Microsoft.

All three technologies are used to *build* enterprise applications, and they or their suc-cessors will continue to be predominant choices for that task in the future. However, none of them will ever become the predominant *integration* solution that they were envi-sioned to be. The single, dominant integration technology will likely be based on XML and simple, open protocols like SOAP that any software vendor can easily imple-ment—and which leverage the equally open Internet infrastructure and protocol suites.

To underline this point, let's take a quick look at CORBA, Java, and COM.

The Common Object Request Broker Architecture

The Common Object Request Broker Architecture (CORBA) was crafted in the early 1990s and has more recently been amended with the Internet Inter-Orb Protocol (IIOP). The CORBA specification is a joint effort by a consortium of well over 300 companies (the Object Management Group) to establish a standard for remotable object implementations.

The CORBA architecture has successfully provided interoperability and infrastruc-ture for object-based solutions in many industries. CORBA object request brokers (ORBs) are popular on UNIX systems because this operating environment does not have a native object model like the Windows operating system family. Hence, ORBs fulfill much the same role in UNIX or in heterogeneous environments as COM does in the Windows world. CORBA-based systems have been successfully implemented in many industries—from trade to aerospace—and do especially well wherever object-oriented systems with many "live" objects need to be tightly integrated with each other.

However, CORBA suffers the same fate as many architecture-focused approaches defined by industry consortia: it has long lacked full standardization in many of its core elements, leaving fundamental aspects to the software vendors implementing the specification. This problem creates many incompatibilities, especially on the server-implementation side. Any CORBA-based application is locked to the object request broker's vendor and that product's specific enhanced features that fill the void left undefined in the core specification.

In addition, CORBA is extremely complex. The specification effort is driven by many cooperating organizations; however, only a small number of companies are actually capable of implementing a reasonably complete CORBA infrastructure form. Because the investments to create reliable CORBA implementations are substantial and most vendors' target markets are rather small, CORBA products are typically quite expensive.

On the other hand, affordable and even free CORBA implementations do exist. However, they also come with support options that are equivalent to their pricing. And that is usually not acceptable for systems on which you want to run the lifeline of your business.

CORBA's standardized wire protocol is IIOP. While you can implement IIOP independently of a compliant ORB product, it still exhibits most of the complexity issues of the core specification, making it similarly difficult to implement and understand.

The large number of companies supporting CORBA and the number of products implementing the specification appear to confirm the success of that initiative. In reality, the implementations are not necessarily compatible where it matters: on the server. Consequently, your code is locked into a single vendor's product and the platform support is limited to the platform support of that vendor.

Speaking of platforms and CORBA, it's time to move on to the third camp: Java.

Java

For many people, Sun Microsystem's Java is the poster child of the "open systems" idea. While the Java programming language is its most visible part, the Java Virtual Machine (JVM) is the heart of this technology. JVM is a software-based virtual CPU that executes a special command-set, called *bytecode*. JVM is designed to be implemented on top of existing platforms; therefore, Java programs can theoretically be moved between those platforms without changes or, as Sun puts it, "write once, run everywhere."

In reality, the quality of Java applications heavily depends on that of the underlying virtual machine and its capabilities. In addition, the Java model is built on the vision that all services available to a Java application are also written in Java and are therefore agile between platforms. Herein lies the problem. To leverage the power and features of the underlying operating environment, like the high volume transaction capabilities of IBM's OS/390 or the scalability of Sun's own Solaris platform, Java applications need to make direct calls into the underlying platform using Java's raw native interface (RNI) bridging technology. Once you go down this path, the platform agility is lost and the platform abstraction layer with its processing overhead becomes more of a hindrance than an advantage.

For EAI tasks and remote access of objects, Java has its own wire protocol, called Remote Method Invocation (RMI). It's not much of a surprise that RMI is just as complex as IIOP or Microsoft's COM wire protocol (discussed in the following section). RMI is also bound to the JVM standards, such as the Java type system; therefore, it is a Java-centric technology.

In addition, RMI is a core part of the Java standard—as such, it is subject to the standards exclusively defined by Sun and their restrictive testing rules. Vendors cannot compatibly enhance or improve RMI without risking their license being revoked by Sun. In the Java world, Sun decides what is Java, they decide who implements Java, and they ultimately decide who they drag to court if a company decides to improve Java beyond Sun's vision.

The Component Object Model

The Microsoft Component Object Model (COM) was created in 1992 as the fundamental technology for Microsoft's document integration technology, Object Linking and Embedding (OLE). Since it hit the market in its finalized version in 1993, COM has undergone a lot of changes—many of them changes of name. You may know COM under its cover names OLE, OCX, ActiveX, DCOM, or COM+. Microsoft marketing is really good at obfuscating the roots of a technology by giving it a new name on every day it's not raining in Redmond—which, as people say, is a major event in the Seattle area.

From a developer perspective, the fundamental principles of COM haven't really changed since then. But under the hood, the COM functionality and the services available to COM components have grown and improved so much that it became the most commercially successful component and object technology on the market today. However, COM suffers from many of the same limitations as CORBA.

Like CORBA, COM is too complex to implement independently. In fact, while COM's wire protocol has been openly documented as an Internet draft, only a single implementation has ever gotten anywhere near commercial quality, and it even used the Microsoft source code as the starting point: Software AG's DCOM for UNIX, called EntireX. The little-known Microsoft product COM for Solaris is essentially a Microsoft-branded version of the Software AG porting effort. However, none of these ports really did have any substantial commercial success on non-Microsoft platforms.

While the vendor lock-in issue is not obvious in the CORBA space, it is clearly visible with COM. If you commit to COM, you commit to one of the Microsoft platforms. This also means that if you commit to COM, you can talk only to Microsoft platforms.

EDI MEETS XML MEETS EAI

Now that you know the history of EDI and XML and understand the problems with the most widely used enterprise integration technologies, you can clearly see that XML has striking advantages over EDI and the most common EAI technologies. XML-based data exchange protocols are obviously better suited to integrate solutions across organization and platform boundaries than any of the 1990s favorites.

The simplicity and openness of XML is the key factor.

Application integration either of the CORBA, Java, or COM integration models works only if all potential peers can be expected to support that technology in both implementation model and wire protocol. In reality, this was always a very optimistic, marketing-driven wish at best.

The adoption of EDI found its natural barriers in IT budgets. The most widely used EDI standards are too complicated and costly to implement and maintain on a large scale and, at the same time, too static because they do not allow businesses to adjust to rapidly changing needs without violating the narrowly defined standards.

Through simplicity and openness, XML enables broader adoption of electronic data exchange by making it less expensive. XML also allows tighter integration of systems across all platforms. It is simple enough to be directly implemented on any platform and any device, and it is agnostic to all the established rivaling camps.

If you are a developer who has grown up on Microsoft technologies and you haven't been involved in EDI projects (which is the case even for a lot of seasoned software architects), you are unlikely to be familiar with the terminology and complexity that BizTalk brings to the Windows platform from the EDI space. If you have developed EDI applications and are now eyeing BizTalk as an alternative to your current infrastructure, you will be confronted with a lot of Windows-specific terminology and acronyms, like COM, ASP, IIS, or WSH.

Maybe you are confused about BizTalk after browsing the available marketing material. If so, join the club of developers who come from a different background, speaking a different language, and who now meet to build solutions by using a product that bridges the gap between both worlds. Now that you understand the roots of both EDI and XML, you are ready to start your journey of Microsoft BizTalk Server.

CHAPTER 2

Federated Services: The Connected Economy

This chapter explains the reality of business-to-business (B2B) data exchange today. The interactive Web is often an inadequate tool for providing integration and optimization for business processes that cross organization boundaries. True systems integration over the Internet is possible only through noninteractive, programmable services—web services—that allow partners to query information from each other and act as mailboxes for business documents. This chapter will cover the following topics:

▼ **B2B is a reality**   The B2B information exchange, which was one of the big buzz terms of the financial markets before the Internet stock shakeout, did not appear overnight or within the last couple of years as many of the Internet startups want to make people believe. It is a very real asset of today's economy, but the marketed Internet B2B vision, which is most often associated with Internet-based marketplaces and interactive catalogs, unfortunately fails to deliver on its promises.

■ **Web services**   The web services paradigm allows business process integration on a systems level; it does not require human interaction or switches between different media.

■ **Security and electronic signature**   For systems integration and reliable electronic document transfers to replace our paper-based business communications, security, privacy, and, most importantly, authenticity must be guaranteed for data that is being exchanged between partners.

■ **Redefining document**   With the web services paradigm and a working authenticity and security infrastructure, the term "document" will become synonymous with "electronic documents" in daily business, and not with the image of paper.

■ **Heterogeneous system landscapes**   Delivery on this promise will be possible only if the technology is platform- and base-technology-agnostic. Any approach for integration and ubiquitous data exchange that depends on certain base technology prerequisites like operating systems or specific hardware has failed in the past and will fail in the future.

▲ **Document standardization**   When we exchange documents electronically, we must have standards. Unlike people, computers cannot guess content from a business document. Computers must have clear rules that dictate how and where to find information. Document standardization efforts attempt to create such definitions.

B2B IS A REALITY

Frankly speaking, the distinction between the "old" and the "new" economy is pretty senseless. Much the same can be said about the current fascination with B2B marketplaces and the attempts of web directories or web auction sites to catch the big corporate fishes. Let's sharpen our senses here. As the established corporations and the Internet upstarts converge on a common network with common standards, the phrase "connected economy" makes a lot more sense than trying to distinguish between the "old" and the "new" economy.

Looking at the old and the new schools from an information-technology perspective, we really see a difference only in where the people driving the companies come from and what their backgrounds are. The new companies are technology focused, and most of their senior management and technical staff has grown up in the PC age. On the other hand, a lot of senior personnel in the older companies have been raised with a completely different mindset, being focused on the now and not necessarily on what the future will bring in the next several years. The focus is on measurable results, not so much on a promise of even better results later. If we look at the technology, both the new and the old schools perform a lot of tasks similarly. It's just that the old school has some 30 years of working B2B experience with rock-solid, established (and therefore boring) systems, while the new school has innovative and productive tools that offer quick solutions.

The second-generation Internet—which is so dominated by the World Wide Web that the terms have become synonymous—enables virtually everyone to easily access a vast array of information, to shop for products and services online, or to be entertained by interactive games and multimedia experiences.

In business, the Web has brought buyers and suppliers closer together than ever. Through a single point of origin, virtual vertical marketplaces can provide market transparency and cost efficiency for corporate procurement. Some business models are even only possible on the Internet, and they have grown and were field-tested in business-to-consumer and consumer-to-consumer relations. Forward or reverse auctions, ad hoc buyer communities, and knowledge exchanges are quickly gaining ground in the B2B space.

While all of this sounds attractive, many B2B marketplaces that were launched with high hopes in the last two years have already collapsed or will fold in the near future, burning millions of invested capital. Why? Business processes do not work the way the Web works.

The interactive Web is a great tool for publishing and finding information, as well as for interactively researching business opportunities both from a buyer and supplier perspective. The web-based B2B exchanges work for finding, comparing, and acquiring auxiliary goods like small tools and office materials. They also fill a gap between buyers and sellers that do not have a common process for exchanging information. Instead, they provide something like an interactive, lightweight electronic data interchange (EDI) mechanism. In the long run, the interactive Web is completely inadequate for integrating large-scale business processes.

Imagine a buyer at a fictitious automotive supplier firm called PowerMech, which manufactures the mechanics for the roof of a convertible sports car. In the manufacturing process of products as complicated as cars, the chain of buyers and suppliers is actually quite long because special engineering and processing skills are needed at every step. Therefore, this specialized firm needs to buy its steel-cast elements from another specialized engineering firm, whose foundry partner actually turns blocks of raw steel into the required elements.

The whole supply chain functions perfectly until the foundry suddenly experiences financial troubles and deliberately breaks the contract with the steel-cast engineering firm to fulfill a series of more lucrative orders with higher margins—to stay in business. Let's ignore the legal battles that may ensue—they will not solve the buyer's sudden, urgent, and very real problems in the just-in-time supply chain to which she is bound.

The primary problem is that market transparency isn't necessarily desirable in the manufacturing industry. One of the flaws of the B2B marketplace's vision is that it assumes that buyers and sellers are seriously limited in their ability to compete on a world-wide scale. Because there was no efficient way to make price information available to a wide range of potential buyers from the seller side or to have a comprehensive overview of the potential suppliers from the buyer side, the market was not transparent to either side. Each specialized marketplace aims to add this transparency to a specific industry. The goal is that vendors from all stages of the manufacturing chain can both obtain pricing information from all possible suppliers and offer goods to all potential buyers. The marketplace itself does charge commission for transactions executed through its system.

In short, this is what the business vision of virtually every B2B marketplace tells us. The flaw is that the customers' culture and reality is not taken into account. The supply chains in manufacturing and even in service-oriented businesses are tightly integrated. Switching between suppliers is not as easy as buying a different brand of orange juice the next time you go to the grocery store. Knowledge and quality often count more than price—and, for that matter, even physical inspection of the manufacturing sites by trusted partners often counts more. Suppliers are highly unlikely to allow all or any of their channels to be made transparent to the world through a public B2B exchange. To maintain the relationship with long-time buyers, manufacturers may not even want to advertise their products, or they may even be contractually prohibited to do so.

The PowerMech buyer knows that she cannot solve the problem alone because she doesn't know who the qualified foundries are. Furthermore, she cannot assess whether any foundry has the specific engineering knowledge required to specify, produce, and quality test the machinery parts in question.

The buyer is under serious time pressure, with just two weeks of supplies remaining until the problem stops production at the car-maker's factory. This leaves little time to find a new supplier, build new casting tools, and fully restart the quality assurance (QA) process. Unless her current, immediate supplier finds a new foundry directly, the buyer must now locate a supplier with a qualified foundry that can work off the same tools—effectively having compatible machinery.

Even if that should succeed, the buyer must also organize the tools to be transported from the old foundry to the new location through her two suppliers without disclosing either identity. Their mutually knowing each other could adversely affect competition down the road. Could this problem be solved using an interactive B2B web marketplace?

If you are buying only a few parts externally, you may be tempted to give such a marketplace a try, but think of having to coordinate the acquisitions process for thousands of parts with dozens of suppliers where the same situation as in the example presented can occur. As a representative of a manufacturing company that depends on external suppliers, the reality is that you must maintain long, trust-based relationships and have alternatives in place in case a supplier fails to deliver. Successful companies have their network of suppliers already in place and will remain hesitant to switch suppliers. The "federated services" vision that is part of the Microsoft .NET strategy and aims on tightly integrating such partner networks builds on that reality.

The usual buzz about the B2B moniker appears to assume that the world economy just started to exist last week. However, the federated service idea reflects the reality of existing and incrementally growing business relationships that need to be optimized instead of constantly being rebuilt or reestablished.

In the PowerMech example, the buyer must be able to access from all of her suppliers the precise, up-to-date information on available production capacity and the type of machinery at their backend facilities—without necessarily forcing her suppliers to disclose their partner's identity at the other end. A foundry has a very precise, day-to-day overview of its production capacity. It knows exactly how much capacity can be expended to certain customers, it can specify production facility, and it can make this information readily available to the supply chain partner.

Consolidating the information from all of their foundry partners and associating their respective production capacities with certain products and buyers, the engineering company that currently supplies PowerMech with the steel-cast parts can now advertise the available alternatives with precise availability and quality parameters. The buyer at PowerMech can query this information from a number of trusted supply sources to find a partner with sufficient and compatible backend production capacity. Then she can make a qualified decision based on both price and a certain level of quality that she expects to receive from the individual suppliers.

Even if a new supplier has been found, the execution of this deal requires the buyer organization to access an additional set of resources. If the parts are transported by ship on free on board (FOB) or free alongside ship (FAS) Incoterms (International Trade Conditions and Terms), clearance at customs and transport from the port must be timed and organized by the buyer organization itself. To secure international transactions, the buyer may also need to acquire a letter of credit (LOC), and at the time of shipment, monetary funds need to be released and transferred at precise times during transit.

EDI users know that the last part of this scenario, order processing—electronically coordinating the shipping of goods and executing payments—is a daily practice. However, they also know that establishing and maintaining links between all those resources is costly and is far from being flexible. While most of these procedures are captured in document standards such as ANSI X12 and UN/EDIFACT, many companies use slightly customized versions or accept only a subset of the standardized information in their procedures.

Some of these customizations aim to eliminate standardized information sets that are not applicable to a specific industry or trade scenario and thus serve to reduce implementation complexity. Others try to add industry-related information that does not readily fit into the standardized framework. These reductions and alternations are the Achilles heel of all of the EDI standard formats.

ANSI X12 and its spawn UN/EDIFACT, as well as the SWIFT interbanking format (based on the ISO 7775/15022 standards) are text-based formats that employ some sort of a mix of delimited and positional fields. Through business-driven adjustments, the applications of some these formats have even become syntactically inconsistent. Chapter 3 discusses these document formats, along with the eXtensible Markup Language (XML) standard, in great detail.

WEB SERVICES

Now consider the PowerMech scenario and imagine how you would attempt to handle the task by using only traditional means: telephone, fax, and probably a computer with an office application suite.

You would likely have some document templates customized for the daily tasks. Based on agreed-upon procedures in your organization and with your external partners, you would then fax the documents to your trading partners or sign and send them by postal mail because a fax is not always recognized as legally binding.

However, if you start to have problems, the communication gets a lot more ad hoc. Once you're notified that your parts supply is going to be cut off immediately, you will likely grab the nearest phone, call your supplier, and have them explain the situation to you.

With your supplier making some desperate excuses and working hard to resolve the situation, your next move may be to send out some informal faxes to other suppliers that can manufacture the same parts. Some of the suppliers may deny the request right away because they are at capacity and cannot handle any more orders; others may ask you to wait a day or two until they have checked with their downstream suppliers.

While you wait for answers, you may want to get a Dun & Bradstreet report and some additional background information from other services or from your industry partners. Once you have received a response and possibly formal offers from all potential suppliers, you can then fall back to the defined process and place a formal order with one of them.

The standard documents that your company exchanges with its partners are usually well-defined, such as orders, invoices, shipping orders, or shipping notifications. But the ad hoc communication queries certain properties of your partner's information pool that you need to know to reach a decision, but which do not really fit into any formal document category and which are not covered by any standardized business transaction.

Returning to the electronic document realm, most formal business transactions are covered and can be performed by using standardized EDI or XML documents. In contrast, using the less formal ad hoc queries into a partner's information pool and combining their results with your own business' decision logic is neither covered by the common standards, nor is the document interchange infrastructure an adequate tool to achieve this. Business processes, decision logic, and other less formal queries can be made accessible to you on the Internet as a Web Service. A *web service* is a callable set of functions that you can invoke via HTTP and that returns XML information.

The third-generation Internet will be much more a Web of services than a Web of interactive information. Interactivity helped the Web gain the popularity that it enjoys today.

But for business, raw information obtained by calling web services that can be processed with your own tools and evaluated with your own business and decision logic is much more valuable than information that can be obtained by interactively navigating the visual Web.

Consequently, the way money is made on the Internet will change significantly. Today, most sites offer their content for free and finance their services through paid advertising, or they regard publishing information as part of their marketing strategy. This model works because people actively navigate through sites. It also works because the information contained on such sites is more or less exclusive to that particular site. If you attempted to collect information from various sites to republish it on your own site (which would violate copyright laws, of course), you would find that parsing the needed information out of HTML is complicated. You would have to adjust your parsers every time the owner of the original site made even minor design corrections.

Web services allow information providers and companies to open up their databases to external clients through callable methods that provide fine-grained access to raw data and specialized business logic. And because raw data is much more valuable, providers will be able to start charging for these services even if the same information has previously been freely accessible via the interactive Web. Electronic document interchange—either using traditional EDI formats or XML and the web services model—go hand in hand in the federated services world.

Because all formal commercial document exchanges require consistent information flow between businesses, they must have reliable, secure channels and standardized business document definitions. Any ad hoc information that you need to reach decisions or any services that allow you to have certain data processed at specialized service providers support your business and help to evaluate business opportunities. Thus, both documents and services are part of your business logic and must be integrated and orchestrated in a flexible way to turn information into business advantage.

SECURITY AND THE ELECTRONIC SIGNATURE

Neither XML nor web services nor the federation of all internal and external services into corporate businesses are the key to establishing a globally connected economy. The most important requirement for a successful transition from paper-based information flow to electronic flow is that privacy, integrity, and authenticity must be guaranteed and verifiable.

Even with current communication technology, important documents are still on paper. They are manually signed, sealed with the corporate stamp, and sent via courier or postal mail. The reason is obvious: without a standardized and trusted security infrastructure, digital information can easily be modified at any time before, after, or during transit. Also, many countries still have problems with the legal proof of digital documents.

The irony here is that most paper documents typically exchanged between businesses are virtually unprotected against fraud. Signatures can easily be forged, company paper can easily be copied, and even if you send letters via certified mail or couriers, you can put any sender's address on the envelope. Try to recall the last time a post office or Federal Express agent asked you for proof of identity. In effect, the information system that we traditionally trust the most for business is just as insecure as the digital realm. However, the threat of fraudulent digital information seems much more real; thus, people and organizations are more aware of it.

For digital document exchange to become popular, the cost-saving and communication optimization advantages must be paired with clear security improvements even over the well-known and established postal system. Some of the issues raised in the following sections may sound paranoid, but you should seriously consider them. Global commerce is not the place where you want to assume everyone out there is playing fair.

Privacy

Documents must be securely encrypted so that only the sender and intended receiver can read their content. Unencrypted documents sent over the Internet or most other communication wires are like postcards. Just like anybody working at a post office can read postcards, anybody working at any waypoint of Internet traffic can potentially wiretap and read that information. Have you ever wondered why international telephone and data traffic is usually routed through just one or two central hubs in a country? This information is served on a silver platter for the national intelligence services. In postal mail, the old water steam trick still works with many envelopes.

Openly developed and thoroughly analyzed digital encryption technology can make a difference here—keeping information private between peers as it should be. Of course, these developments must go hand in hand with legislation. In France, encryption for most private telecommunication purposes is basically prohibited, and strong encryption falls under the same export regulations as nuclear weapons in the United States. In Germany, the free development, use, and export of strong encryption technology is guaranteed even by the constitution.

Integrity

Guaranteeing data integrity is just as important as privacy and authenticity. Documents that are verifiably signed and encrypted must also be protected against modifications in transit or even at the destination. Modifications in transit can occur unintentionally through communication or software errors or may even be made with clear intent.

In case of unintentional changes, simple bit flips in the encrypted data stream may not cause corruption of the entire stream, but just minor (yet significant) changes that remain undetected in the data payload. For intentional changes in transit, imagine a scenario in which strong encryption technology is not legally available and the algorithms that are used are not sufficiently secure. Additional protection must be in place that assures that the data arriving at the destination has not been modified.

Similarly, digital documents must be verifiably protected against alterations at either end. If you send out paper documents, you typically create a copy for your own files and send out the original. In case of legal disagreement between parties, proof of integrity is typically guaranteed by both—the copy and the original being identical in their visual appearance. The same level of trust must be established for digital documents.

Authenticity

The authentication of the data origin is equivalent to the signature you put on paper documents. The personal signature authenticates a paper document through its uniqueness to a specific writer. Likewise, digital signatures authenticate digital documents through their unique association with a specific individual. While a handwritten signature on paper is actually a *biometric* feature of a person—and thus the association between the signature and the person is natural—digital signatures suffer from the limitations of the human/computer interface; therefore, the link between the person and the signature cannot be established immediately.

To establish the same level of trust in the relationship between a person and his or her digital signature, a trusted third party must certify that person or business' identity and the authenticity of the signature. These certificates are issued by trust centers, which verify a person's identity before assigning a unique key. With more countries introducing digital signature legislation, these trust centers become strictly regulated—a key requirement to establish a level of trust that you can rely on for conducting business.

The actual act of signing digital documents is performed with these certificates and "stamp" documents with the association between an individual and a digital signature that the certificate certifies. If you choose an advanced biometric input device like a fin gerprint sensor or even a retina scan, the certificate's "proof of ownership" data is an initial data sample against which you compare the scanning device's input. The same is true for passwords or smart card–based certificate procedures. In both cases, proof of ownership (for example, knowing the password) is the required proof against the certificate system that the user is actually the person to which the certificate applies.

Clearly, biometric input systems provide the greatest reliability and trust. The inherent weaknesses of password-based authentication almost invalidate the entire effort of establishing the trust relationship between an individual and his or her certificate. Most people probably use a spouse's first name or a pet's name as their password if they are not forced to follow certain password creation rules.

Sometimes a system administrator tries to enforce strong passwords: for example, "case-sensitive, alpha *and* numeric *and* with special characters and at least 12 characters in length, alter twice a week." However, he or she just can't beat the sticky note on the monitor. (The average person cannot remember passwords of that complexity.)

But even with a working authentication infrastructure in place, the problems discussed in this book so far raise a completely different issue: who signs digital documents in high-volume systems? Certificates and digital signing capabilities are not necessarily bound to individuals but are issued for corporations or web-site operators—who, in turn, can then issue subcertificates for their divisions, departments, or individual employees.

When planning the security infrastructure, check with your legal department or lawyer to learn the exact regulations for using digital signatures and to find out what consequences and liabilities could arise from incorrect use. Take the German 1997 Digital Signatures Act (*Signaturgesetz*), for example. The issuance of certificates that can be used for signatures is limited to individuals. Such certificates can be issued only by the certification institutions that conform to the regulations of this law, and they require strict supervision of RegTP, the government agency for telecommunication and postal regulations (equivalent to the U.S. FCC).

This law—the first of its kind in the world—strictly translates the handwritten signature concept into the digital domain. Therefore, digital documents must be signed by using an individual's legally compliant certificate. Several other countries have adopted similar laws, including the U.S. E-Sign bill enacted in 2000.

The only acceptable individual's certificates for signing business transactions are those of the managers who typically sign for purchases and release funds for payments, approve execution of substantial client orders, and so on. From a legal standpoint, systems like those implemented with BizTalk would have to use those manager's certificates for signing documents—effectively giving the IT department a blank check to sign any outbound digital document from that department. This is probably not going to be acceptable for all business cases. Clearly, this area requires a lot of organization.

Digital signatures must establish the level of trust that the postal system has traditionally had. From a legal standpoint, digitally signed documents do not yet provide the same level of security as manually signed documents. However, we will get there shortly.

REDEFINING DOCUMENT

The technical prerequisites do exist today to establish a global security framework for digital document interchange. Now we need legislation and international treaties that cover all aspects of the digital signature, along with freedom of encryption to put digital documents on par with their paper-based counterparts.

Today's EDI users overcome this legal dilemma by using strong, extensive bilateral trading partner agreements that govern the mutual data exchange and its legal implications and consequences. However, having corporate lawyers haggling over such agreements for weeks before any transaction can be performed does not aid flexibility. If the benefits of EDI cannot be applied to short-term trade relationships, possibly as short as a single transaction, the overall benefits of focusing on electronic documents quickly evaporate.

Once digital documents are accepted in the world's trade courts as being equivalent to paper documents, and once the standardized and commonly accepted document formats are based on a consistent, simple standard like XML, the definition of "document" and the way documents are handled will change dramatically.

The technical infrastructure is mostly in place, the standardization processes for XML-based documents is underway, and legislature is starting to recognize the importance of this transition. Indeed, we are currently at the beginning of this transition phase. Everyone must start embracing digital documents, even companies that have not been using EDI.

Challenges

With all the technical and legal prerequisites for establishing the connected economy falling into place in the next few years, corporations will face challenges that arise directly from the volume and variety of data that is going to be shared between peers. In today's EDI, data formats are mostly industry-specific, and trade partners can usually focus on their vertical standards. The banking industry uses SWIFT, trade organizations use much of the ANSI X12 or UN/EDIFACT standard transaction messages, and healthcare and many other industries employ some of their own standards that build on the technical infrastructure of XML, ANSI X12, or UN/EDIFACT.

As more companies embrace electronic documents, these "industry islands" will have to make way for a more horizontal approach, where companies need to be able to interact with digital data across industry borders.

The challenges will also rise within those industries that have been using EDI for a long time. Because only the largest companies drive EDI, every industry has only a few key players who narrow down or customize the existing standards to their specific needs, and all of their customers and suppliers must adopt these rules. In a connected economy where virtually every business can become digitally enabled, information exchange will eventually become more democratic and dynamic.

Increasing Rate of Change

Businesses that start exchanging digital information will not necessarily accept being restricted by standards as defined by the common UN/EDIFACT or X12 message formats, or even their XML-based successors. Instead, businesses extend the information sets and tailor them to their own needs, allowing partners to exchange data at the level of detail they are accustomed to from their paper-based processes.

Simply put, the more businesses that adopt electronic document exchange, the more variations of documents will be created and continuously optimized, steadily accelerating the overall rate of change.

Documents Are Digital

With the increasing adoption of digital documents, more information will become exclusively available in digital form. This is already true for many commercial catalogues and will soon be true for all but the most essential documents.

For any business, integrating digital documents into the IT infrastructure is not a matter of strategy or choice: it is a necessity. Not accepting digital documents would be much like not accepting credit cards at a retail store—you just wouldn't survive without it.

Information Is Competitive Advantage

Standardization is the key to the connected economy and a common foundation for how businesses exchange information. However, as stated before, standardization cannot mean restriction. Having information and sharing it with partners that cooperate on common business goals is an important competitive advantage.

An organization must adhere to key standards and must continuously keep track of its most recent revisions. At the same time, it must optimize and expand its own enhancements to these base standards as the business requirements grow.

Information grows out of business needs, and business needs grow out of opportunity. Once business users find out how to reliably exchange data by using tools like BizTalk Server, and once they can use web services to easily tap external information services, IT departments will face a whole new class of creative business requirements. Just wait and see.

Benefiting from B2B Requires Flexibility

One of the real benefits of B2B is establishing new contacts across industry borders, which means to integrate foreign data formats into your own IT landscape. Flexibility is key.

The Web has demonstrated how the ease of creating simple hyperlinks between visual information makes for truly strange bedfellows across industries that would previously never have had the idea of cooperating. Creating a couple of images and hyperlinks is cheap, easy, and much simpler than cross-marketing efforts in the nonvirtual world of "brick and mortar" stores. Today, it is easy and inexpensive to promote a stylish convertible sports car along with a sporty woman's dress that perfectly matches the interior. Throw some cool sunglasses and watches into the mix, and then provide "buy me" clickable links to the music that softly hums in the background while the full-coverage car insurance's special discount rate scrolls smoothly at the bottom of the screen.

In this kind of efficient comarketing, all participants basically pursue their own business. But what if these companies actually want to engage in business with each other? The fashion company's car fleet certainly needs insurance coverage, and the car manufacturer may just decide to give each buyer that pair of sunglasses and the watch for free. Once digital cross-industry marketing becomes digital cross-industry trade, systems must be flexible enough to adopt different standards and other industries' data formats.

HETEROGENEOUS SYSTEM LANDSCAPES

So far, this chapter has approached B2B data exchange only from legal, strategic, and security angles. We have discussed the necessity of compatible and standardized electronic document technologies. However, we have not yet covered today's information technology reality—the legacy systems.

The Internet is dominated by two operating-system families and their underlying compatible hardware: Microsoft Windows NT and Windows 2000 operating systems on the one hand, and several UNIX variants or clones, most prominently Linux, BSD, and Sun Solaris, on the other. EDI systems are typically implemented either on high-end UNIX systems or mainframe systems. The reason is obvious: EDI has grown much in line with the corporate adoption of high-end computer systems.

Chapter 1 already discussed several enterprise application integration (EAI) trends and the problems with those technologies that have all been individually promoted as the "ultimate integration platform." None of them actually lives up to the promise for various reasons. A successful integration technology must be based on much simpler standards that build on an established and accepted infrastructure—such as XML and HTTP bundled into the protocol SOAP, or its likely standardized successor XML Protocol (XMLP).

Centralized Data Processing

Both, the Internet and traditional enterprise solutions employ a centralized data processing model. In the 1980s and much of the 1990s, the PC was often believed to be the final nail in the coffin of the mainframe. The buzz phrase was client/server—the data storage is at some central location but all the processing happens at the desktop.

The Internet changed this entire concept that dominated the PC age for most of its existence. If you have been developing mostly on mainframe systems until now, you will find many well-known concepts from your domain being advertised as new and ground-breaking in the Internet space.

Essentially, the Internet has brought the renaissance of the mainframe model. In their basic principles, web browsers are much like 3270 terminals. Likewise, IBM's IMS and CICS transaction systems provided the functional model for the transaction monitors that power today's Internet systems. The huge difference here is, of course, the motivation to adopt a centralized processing model.

When computers started to gain ground in the corporate world in the 1960s, a single computer filled half a building and was insanely expensive. Although of enormous size, these systems had a main memory of substantially less than a megabyte and a total processing capacity that is easily exceeded a few hundred times by the notebook this book was (mostly) written on. Still, these machines could serve hundreds of concurrent users running multiple applications—through stateless design paired with resource-minded development.

The motivation for centralized processing on the Internet was location and bandwidth. Dynamic, data-centric web sites are typically hosted at a single location, and the available bandwidth was and is relatively thin. Therefore, all processing is typically confined to a single server farm and may need to serve thousands of concurrent users.

So, while we have basically looped back to the centralized processing mindset, the advances in data transmission technology and the consequent gains in bandwidth at affordable cost favor the federated services model.

Collaboration Is the Key

No single organization, no matter what size, can handle all their business tasks without partners. To beat the competition, an integrated network of services—including digital services—is the key factor. The federated services model that unifies electronic document interchange with callable web services is the core building block for effective collaboration in the connected economy.

When digital collaboration becomes one of the most important factors that determines success for an alliance of businesses working hand in hand, there is no room for technological ivory towers and corporate strategies that sit on technology islands, independent of the size of these islands.

If a technology choice for system connectivity is not pervasive and does not allow integration across any type of platform or system implementation, it just does not qualify as a foundation for the connected economy. That said, the Common Object Request Broker Architecture (CORBA), the Component Object Model (COM), and Java will continue to be the foundation for corporate development tools, but the integration technology will be platform- and vendor-agnostic—XML.

Consider the use of the term "cross platform" in this context. The term is typically synonymous with "software that runs on any platform." In that sense, cross-platform software is of little relevance for collaborative systems. What counts is that software integrates perfectly across platforms, independent of the implementation technology used at either end of a communication channel.

If you think that cross-platform–enabled software is truly essential for your business, answer these two questions: How many different platforms do you typically use to run a specific software package in a realistic production environment? How would Sun Microsystems' hardware sales figures look without Java?

Agile Information Anywhere and Anytime

The need for integration becomes even more obvious if we forget about the traditional model of centralized servers and connected desktop workstations. This book was written in the office, on the sofa at home, on planes, and on trains. The only reason most of it was written on a notebook is that it has a reasonably sized keyboard—if voice recognition software would be equivalent to typing in its error rate and level of control, a pocket size device with color display with a microphone would be just as good. Writing books is, of course, a collaborative process. Chapters need to be sent back and forth between the author and the editors and reviewers. And to research details, you must write e-mails to other experts or check information on the Web. An Internet connected pocket device like the one described would perfectly serve the purpose, if the input capabilities were adequate. We are slowly getting to the point where such devices will become available.

Furthermore, if you are on the road in a particular city, your secretary may rearrange your business meetings for you back at the office so you don't have to go from New York's financial area downtown and then to 65th Street for another meeting, just to turn around and go back near Wall Street an hour later. Because you are already in a meeting and your cell phone is off, your secretary can simply update your calendar at the server back home, and your wristwatch or personal digital assistant (PDA) that synchronizes with the server every 15 minutes will let you know of the change.

Although mobile devices and their processors have greatly advanced in the last couple of years, the capacities are still quite limited compared to desktop machines. Pervasive connectivity must reach out to these devices without an always-available humongous software infrastructure in and around them. Also, device manufacturers will not want to limit their reach to a particular fraction of the market that happens to support a specific complex technology set. Again, this is an argument for using the XML standard for communication—the development of pervasive technology needs the promise of thorough market adoption.

DOCUMENT STANDARDIZATION

In Chapter 1, you learned about the significance of technology and document standard-ization. Now you will learn the following: how document standardization works today, why only a customized application of these standards is practically inevitable instead of adoption of the full scale of definitions, and why a global document format standard will probably never exist beyond a set of agreed-upon basic technologies.

Standards Bodies

Only five internationally accepted standards bodies exist that can set IT standards for broad adoption: the International Standards Organization (ISO), the Institute of Electrics and Electronics Engineers (IEEE), the European Computer Manufacturers Association (ECMA), the Internet Engineering Taskforce (IETF), and the World Wide Web Consortium (W3C). However, even if a technology is acclaimed as an international standard, another organization may issue contradictory international standards.

The most accepted standards body is the ISO, a federal system whose members are the formal standards bodies of individual countries, which are typically govern-ment-driven. Because ISO has very strict rules and is also heavily influenced by politics, software vendors evade the complex process by submitting technology proposals to other accepted standards bodies such as ECMA.

Although the standards bodies try to stay out of each other's domains, overlaps are inevitable. Also, local standardization in a single country or even a number of countries may not yield an ISO certification. Due to lack of ISO acceptance, the dominant U.S. ANSI X12 document standard has no formal relevance in Europe.

Industry Consortia

Industry consortia also attempt to achieve technology and document standardiza-tion—driven either by a nonprofit organization founded to enforce standardization among companies or by a single dominant company. Examples include the RosettaNet effort driven by a group of semiconductor manufacturers, the standards of the Automo-bile Industry Action Group (AIAG), or those of the International Air Transport Associa-tion (IATA).

Focusing on their industry, these consortia do not always watch what is happening around them. Naturally, these efforts touch any aspect of their members' businesses, creating overlaps and inconsistencies with other industries' standards.

The United Nations

As you already learned in Chapter 1, in the EDI space, the United Nations actively engages in technology standardization. The UN/EDIFACT standard was developed under the United Nations umbrella and has become the most widely accepted standard for document inter-change. Currently, the United Nations Centre for Trade Facilitation and Electronic Business

(UN/CEFACT), the same UN committee that already drove the UN/EDIFACT effort is driving another XML-focused initiative, called electronic business XML (ebXML), which aims to provide a basic infrastructure for XML-based document interchange. After the successful completion of this effort, the United Nations will probably move on to create standardized document specifications based on XML. Just like UN/EDIFACT, these specifications will focus on international trade.

XML Communities

Pending document standardization from any of the accepted standards bodies, the Internet community keeps moving on its own speed. To achieve at least minimal consensus among companies in the same industry, public XML communities such as BizTalk.org (driven by Microsoft) or XML.org have created XML schema repositories that allow companies to share their document specifications. Of course, such smaller-scale communities also exist on industry-specific technology portals.

The bottom line is that the term "standard" does not represent an absolute measurement of the universality of a specification. Common document specifications and technology standards are of relative value to their users only if concurring standards exist. Because universally accepted, single standards are unlikely to exist for any type of business transaction, a company's software tools must be flexible enough to allow the adoption of *any* standard.

CHAPTER 3

Data Formats

Now that you have learned much about electronic data interchange (EDI) from both a historic and a business-strategy perspective but have only scratched the surface of the technical aspects, this chapter finally gets technical. And this chapter is the last one in this book that does not focus mainly on BizTalk.

Whether you use BizTalk Server for electronic document interchange with outside partners or as an enterprise application integration (EAI) tool, you will have to deal with a variety of data formats. For EDI, you must understand the specifics of the American National Standards Institute (ANSI) X12 standards and/or the United Nations Directories for Electronic Data Interchange for Administration, Commerce, and Transport (UN/EDIFACT). For EAI, you may need to comprehend and handle all sorts of proprietary data streams.

This chapter introduces the ANSI X12 and UN/EDIFACT standards, which are both understood by BizTalk Server. It also presents the Society for Worldwide Interbank Financial Telecommunications (SWIFT) data format, which BizTalk does not support out of the box (and you will see why), but for which we will build a (limited) custom parsing component in Chapter 22.

Regardless of whether you use BizTalk primarily for EDI or EAI, you will always have to use the eXtensible Markup Language (XML). XML is BizTalk's native data format, and it has become the lingua franca for data on the Internet as well. BizTalk Server and its siblings from Microsoft's .NET Enterprise Server family, as well as the new Microsoft .NET development platform, build on XML as their main architectural pillar. This is not only because Microsoft regards XML to be a useful technology, but also because XML is the first integration technology that has been embraced by every major software maker.

Because XML is so significant, this chapter also features an introduction to XML that is much more detailed than the explanation of the other formats. If you consider yourself an XML professional, you can safely skip the last section of this chapter.

ANSI X12

The ANSI Accredited Standards Committee (ASC) X12, chartered in 1979, is the maintainer of the X12 EDI standard, which is used predominantly in North America. X12 is only a normative standard for the United States and has not been promoted to an international standard, unlike its successor, UN/EDIFACT (covered in the "UN/EDIFACT" section later in this chapter), which builds on X12 to some extent.

The X12 standard defines syntax and semantics for business documents. On top of these definitions, it layers a set of universally applicable document definitions for business transactions, such as purchase orders, confirmations, and invoices.

X12 also defines security through the security structures contained in specification X12.58 and the cryptography rules in X12.42. It also provides documents that serve strictly technical purposes. What X12 does not define is the transport. X12 documents are transported on a wide range of media, including floppies and magnetic tape—or, more commonly, through value-added networks (VANs) or peer-to-peer data connections.

X12 Syntax and Structure

The foundation for standardized document exchange is to set common syntax and structure rules. The X12 format defines the following structural elements, as shown in Figure 3-1.

▼ **Data element**   A data element is the most fundamental data structure and represents a single unit of data. X12 supports numeric values, strings, binaries, and alphanumeric strings. Quite a few elements are standardized with semantics

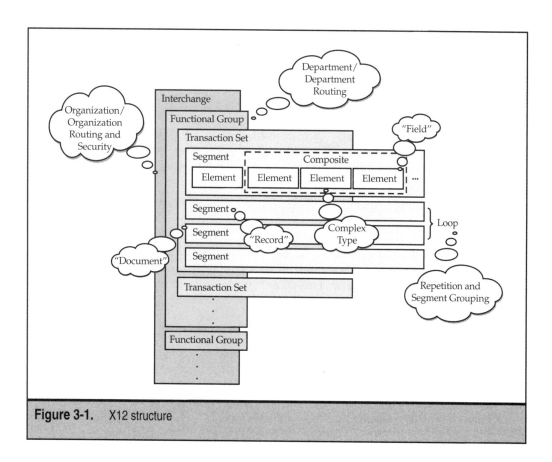

Figure 3-1.   X12 structure

in the data element dictionary, which is defined in X12.3. The basic data types are shown in the following table:

Code	Type
N*n*	Signed numeric type with n decimal places expressed as an integer number without decimal separator. If the data type is N3, the expression 12345 evaluates to 12.345; with the data type N2, it would be 123.45. Consequently, N0 is an integer number.
R	Signed explicit decimal number with decimal point or using IEEE exponential notation.
ID	Special alphanumeric data type for identifiers and reference numbers.
AN	Alphanumeric character string.
DT	Date value using the format CCYYMMDD or (in older versions of the specifications) the Y2K-challenged format YYMMDD.
TM	Time of day in the format HHMM and, optionally, seconds and hundredths of a second.
B	Sequence of binary octets (bytes).

- ■ **Composite data structure** A composite data structure is a complex data type that is a combination of two or more mandatory or optional data elements, separated by a delimiter character (a data element separator). The delimiter can be any character that is guaranteed not to appear in the data.

- ■ **Segment** A segment is the X12 equivalent of a data record. A segment is composed of one or more data elements and/or data structures. Each of these elements is equivalent to a field in a record. A number of standard segments are part of the X12 standard's segment dictionary X12.22. An element separator separates elements of a segment, and a segment terminator terminates the segment. For these separators, the same rules apply as for the component data element separators—they can be any character that does not appear in the data. For the element separator, the most common choice is the asterisk (*) character; for the segment terminator, it is typically a carriage return. Each segment element can be attributed to be mandatory, optional, or conditional. The conditional attribute is applied to two or more elements and defines their relationship more closely, as shown in the following table:

Attribute	Description
P	Inclusive AND condition, called Paired or Multiple. If any of the elements are used, all of this conditional group must be specified.
R	OR condition, called Required. At least one of the conditions must be specified, but it can be any of condition.

Attribute	Description
E	Exclusive OR. Zero or at most one of these elements may be used.
C	Conditional. The first element of the group determines whether the following elements must be present. If the element exists, all others must be there; if the element is missing, the others cannot be specified.
L	List Conditional. Similar to C, but with all other elements having R conditional status. If the first element of the group is present, at least one of the following must be present.

■ **Loop**   A loop is a predefined sequence of segments that groups related information and, depending on the context, may occur multiple times in sequential order in a transaction set. (See the next bulleted item.) While a loop hints at the repetition characteristics only, a loop is just as much a structure of structures that can appear exactly once or at most once in a context. A loop is either unbounded beginning at a user-defined segment with a predefined set of child segments, or it is bounded, in which case, it is explicitly limited by the special X12 segments loop start (LS) and loop end (LE). From a conceptual perspective, a loop is a supersegment that can be documented and referred to as a consistent block.

■ **Transaction set**   A transaction set is a group of segments (that may or may not be contained in loops) that is exchanged between peers. The transaction set definition describes the context and sequence of segments. Note that segments are not necessarily unique within the scope of a transaction set, but they may appear multiple times in a sequence, even with different semantics at every instance. The most common transaction sets required to perform electronic business are part of the X12 core specification's transaction set dictionaries.

■ **Functional group**   All transaction sets that belong to a functional data unit—like multiple requests for quotations that go to a single business unit at a company—comprise a functional group. If you imagine a transaction set as being equivalent to a paper document, the functional group is a binder around multiple such documents, all related to a single business case.

▲ **Interchange**   The interchange is the envelope that you use to mail a binder from one company to another company. The interchange header contains information about origin and destination of the message and authentication data, and it also defines the delimiters for the transaction sets contained in the interchange, as shown in Figure 3-2. The Interchange Control Header (ISA) and Trailer (IEA) are often very specific to the transport medium or network provider because the contained routing information applies only to that provider's network.

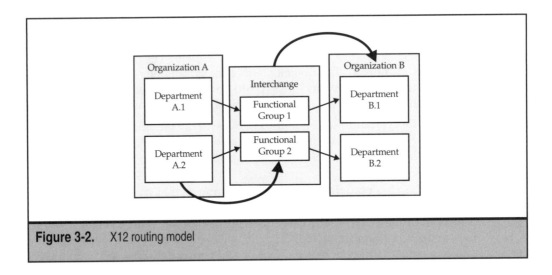

Figure 3-2. X12 routing model

X12 Semantics

As you can tell from the previous section, X12's semantics are contained in three dictionaries that define uniform semantics for data elements, segments, and transaction sets. The term "dictionary" may prompt you to imagine long rows of books on mile-long shelves with endless pages of boring definitions. You are absolutely on target with that thought.

The X12 standard is much more a standard of business semantics than one of nailed-to-the-floor document specifications and related syntax rules. If you sum up the raw essence of the syntax rules, it would not even fill half a page in this book: you have fields, segments, and three types of separators—everything else is really semantics and documented somewhere in X12's dictionaries.

The dictionaries define a large number of common data elements in part X12.3 that can be used within segments, and part X12.22 defines segments that can be included in transaction sets. (See Figure 3-3.)

X12 Transaction Sets

The implementation process for X12 is typically that two partners agree on a trade relationship and define the business needs for their data exchange. Once this is defined, they pick the closest match from the standard transaction sets and investigate which loops and segments are needed to meet the business requirements and determine if any of the segments can be dropped or if data needs to be added. If data is added, it should preferably be added by using one of the predefined segments from the segment dictionary.

Because X12 has been in continued development for quite some time and has incorporated many requirements from all sorts of industries, the X12 dictionaries have grown above and beyond what any single company may ever need. Therefore, X12 transaction

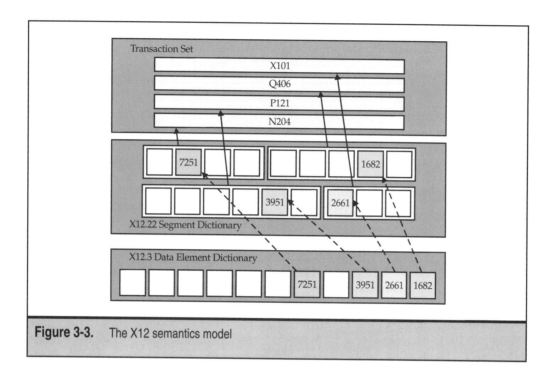

Figure 3-3. The X12 semantics model

sets are never used in reality—they have been drawn up in the committees. ("What is a camel? A horse defined by a committee.") Table 3-1 lists some of the most widely used X12 transaction sets.

TS ID	Purpose
840	Request For Quotation
843	Response To Request For Quotation
832	Price/Sales Catalog
850	Purchase Order
855	Purchase Order Acknowledgment
869	Order Status Inquiry
870	Order Status Report

Table 3-1. Sample X12 Transaction Sets

X12's complexity also explains why the adoption of the standard has been mostly limited to large companies. X12 is applicable only for peer-to-peer data exchange. It is not flexible enough to be used on a large scale and between n:m combinations of peers.

Because the X12 syntax and structure rules do not allow X12 documents to be defined by X12 inherent mechanisms (unlike XML), external data dictionaries, for which no standard for machine-readability exists, are absolutely required to understand and interpret X12 documents. X12 is not self-contained. Therefore, it is virtually impossible to create universally accessible repositories for X12 specifications that could be used by tools to ease the development process and would allow custom definitions to be shared by multiple organizations.

Due to backwards-compatibility considerations for Telex and legacy systems (really old systems), the permissible character set in X12 consists of the uppercase characters A to Z, digits, and some special characters. An extended character set that also includes the lowercase letters is defined but not widely used.

While the lack of lowercase characters causes some collateral damage in formatting, this is mostly acceptable for English-speaking countries. However, these limits are nearly unacceptable for countries like France, Germany, Sweden, Holland, the Czech Republic, Poland, Turkey, Spain, and many other countries that have special variants of Latin characters or diacritic marks as essential elements of their written language. The X12 format is entirely unfit for exchanging natural language information between peers that use any language that does not use the Latin alphabet.

UN/EDIFACT

Recognizing the importance of standards in electronic commerce, the United Nations Center for Trade Facilitation and Electronic Business (UN/CEFACT) has taken on the role of a standards body for electronic documents standards. Through the involvement of the United Nations, the UN/EDIFACT standard has become the dominant data interchange format outside the United States.

UN/EDIFACT was established as an ISO standard in 1987 resulting from a standardization process that combined the U.S. X12 standards with the European Guidelines for Trade Data Interchange (GTDI). And because the UN/EDIFACT standard is a couple of years younger than X12, it shows some improvements over the X12 standard for consistency, takes a more generic approach to data types, and uses easier-to-remember (but still cryptic) alphabetic names for its data elements.

UN/EDIFACT Syntax and Structure

As you can see in Figure 3-4, the fundamental syntax structure of a UN/EDIFACT interchange is somewhat similar to X12. However, these similarities do not suggest that both formats are merely marginally different—they do indeed differ greatly at the detail level.

From a syntax perspective, it is an improvement that delimiters cannot be freely defined on a per-interchange basis in UN/EDIFACT. They are part of the core syntax, allowing for

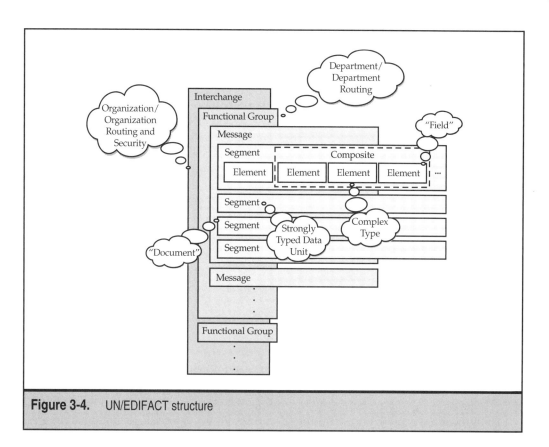

Figure 3-4. UN/EDIFACT structure

more consistency of documents across organizations. Also leading to more consistency is the fact that the data-type set features only three types—alphabetic, alphanumeric, and a single numeric type—mandating that all other data types must be composites of these data types.

UN/EDIFACT builds on the following components:

▼ **Simple data element** A simple data element is the smallest unit in UN/EDIFACT, containing a character sequence representing data. The standard does not explicitly define any data types, but allows definitions to limit the permissible characters to either alphabetic characters, numeric characters, or a combination of both. The representation of numeric data is defined through three simple rules regarding their text representation: no thousands separators are allowed; by default, all numeric values are positive with an optional minus-sign prefix for negative values that does not count for the maximum/minimum length constraints of fields; and, by default, the decimal mark is a comma (,) sign with the alternative period (.) sign being equivalently allowed. The decimal mark is also not counted for maximum/minimum field-length constraints.

- **Composite data element** A composite data element consists of two or more simple data elements separated by a colon (:).

- **Segment** A segment is a well-defined unit of data. However—and this is much unlike X12—UN/EDIFACT segments often have more the character of strongly typed general-purpose data units than of entire data records that describe specifics from a business case. A good example of the general-purpose nature of segments is the date/time container DTM. This segment occurs in a plethora of messages and carries a date/time expression along with very precise information about formatting and semantics. Segments may be repeated either implicitly just through multiple occurrences in a sequence, or explicitly by using indexes. The indexing rules also address nested elements. The inherent support for repetitive elements eliminates the need for X12-style loops.

- **Message** A message is composed from multiple data segments. A message definition specifies a strict, linear sequence of segments. The message itself is the resulting formatted sequence of these segments. Note that the message itself typically exhibits no immediately understandable semantic structure. The UN/EDIFACT INVOIC segment sequence begins with these segments: begin of message (BGM), date/time (DTM), payment instruction (PAI), additional information (ALI), and item description (IMD). So, while UN/EDIFACT is technically more consistent than X12, it lacks X12's data-record style of encoding business data, and the resulting messages are much harder to comprehend.

- **Functional group** A functional group is a sequence of messages of the same message type that share the same origin and destination information. Like X12, functional groups allow routing of information between departments of two organizations, but unlike X12, the message package must be homogenous. The use of functional groups is optional.

- **Interchange** An interchange is the envelope for one or multiple messages or functional groups. The use of messages or functional groups at the interchange level is mutually exclusive. So, in addition to what Figure 3-4 shows, messages may also appear outside and without a functional group, but there cannot be a mix of functional groups and messages at the interchange level. The interchange header contains information about origin and sender organization, as well as authentication and control data.

UN/EDIFACT Semantics

As already stated in the syntax explanation, the segments concept in UN/EDIFACT is much less intuitive than the data record–oriented view in X12 that is used to group data elements into semantically related units. In UN/EDIFACT, these record boundaries exist merely in the message description and cannot be immediately derived from the message structure. (See Figure 3-5.) Messages are just very long sequences of segments, of which any given subsequence may or may not be interrelated.

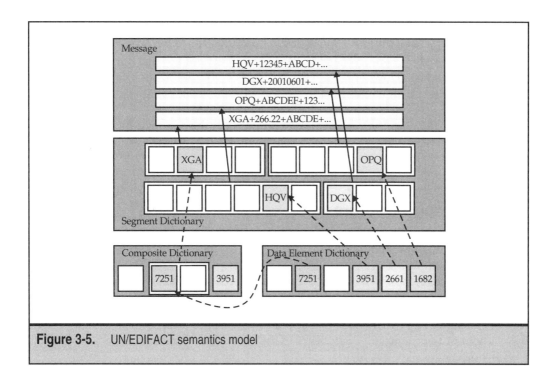

Figure 3-5.   UN/EDIFACT semantics model

X12 has simple and clear data record–style definitions with semantic boundaries. UN/EDIFACT's structural model trades this simplicity for strong semantics for its data elements and segments. This difference is an important distinction in the granularity of semantic expressiveness of segments and thus determines how generic their definition becomes. In X12, segments are very specific and bound to a certain purpose, resulting in large numbers of segment definitions. In UN/EDIFACT, segments are very generic, resulting is fewer segments but with semantics encoded in the data of those generic elements.

The semantics model that is defined in the segment dictionaries is nothing short of impressive, even outright shocking, in its wealth of definitions. The date/time type, for instance, comes with over 450 predefined choices (codes) for what a particular date expression means in the current context and more than 80 choices for the unit of time in which the value is expressed.

So, while X12 gains its semantic context mostly from the segment definitions, UN/EDIFACT employs a lookup-based model. If you see a DTM segment, the code qualifier gives quite a precise hint of its meaning in the context of the entire message.

SWIFT/ISO 15022

The Society for Worldwide Interbank Financial Technology (SWIFT) data exchange standard, formalized as an international standard by the ISO (ISO 7775, recently replaced by

ISO 15022) was established and went into production use before the ASC X12 committee was even formed—in 1977.

The SWIFT format was designed for SWIFT's own network to exchange data between SWIFT partner banks. However, the format has been adopted throughout the financial industry. Chances are high that the stock transactions for your personal portfolio may be routed using the MT5xx family of SWIFT messages.

The MT940 (MT stands for *message type*) format is the best known format outside the financial industry—it's the account statement a bank sends to their customers. Regardless of whether your business handles EDI messages, you are likely to have to import some variant of MT940 into your accounting system.

SWIFT Syntax and Structure

The SWIFT format is strictly sequential and nonextensible. It is also much less complex in its structure and syntax than X12 or UN/EDIFACT—but not necessarily simpler. (See Figure 3-6.)

The structural components of a SWIFT message are the following:

▼ **Basic header block(Block Identifier 1)**   The basic header block is the only mandatory SWIFT header that applies to all user-to-user, user-to-system, and system-to-user messages. It identifies the sender, the application type and protocol, and the current session.

■ **Application header block(Block Identifier 2)**   The application header block identifies and provides information about the message. The application header block differs depending on the message direction. Input headers (seen from the SWIFT system's perspective—so they are outbound from the user's side) describe the type and priority of the message and the recipient's address. Output headers contain the date and the time when the message left the SWIFT network and a message input reference (MIR) that identifies the sender.

■ **User header block(Block Identifier 3)**   This block is available for user-to-user header information and not explicitly defined. However, some standards that build on SWIFT use this header for additional information. The Industry Standardization for Institutional Trade Communications Group (ISITC) uses SWIFT messages to link custodian banks for investment management and uses this header for their message version control structures.

■ **Text block(Block Identifier 4)**   This block contains the body of the message.

▲ **Trailers block(Block Identifier 5)**   Trailer information is either mandated by the system (such as checksum or authentication) or can be added by the user. All trailer information, which is typically a product of message content such as checksums, appears in this block—regardless of which header information it may match.

Each block is enclosed in curly brackets ({}) and always begins with its block identifier code followed by a colon (:).

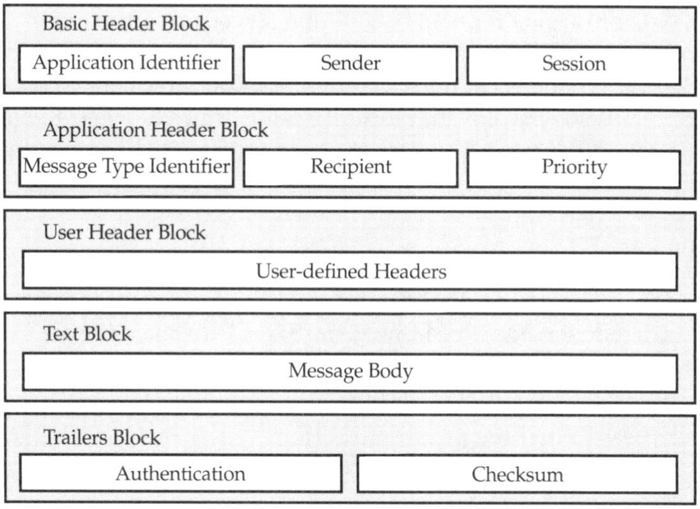

Figure 3-6.   SWIFT format structure

The format for the basic application header blocks is strictly positional. This means that all information contained in these headers is of fixed length and appears at predefined positions. The user headers and trailers and some text blocks may have subordinate blocks that are, again, enclosed in curly brackets and begin with their block identifier followed by a colon.

The text block contains the body of the message. Text blocks are composed of fields, each prefixed with its own field identifier followed by a colon. Fields contain either a single data item or are composed from multiple subfields. While the structure of most text fields with subfields is positional, this model proved to be too limiting for some value and text messages, so they employ a delimited format. And because delimiters are not part of the original design, their use often appears to be quite arbitrary.

The result from these extensions is quite a messy mix of positional elements and a few different delimiter models. In some fields, subfields are delimited using a predefined character or character sequence (such as CR-LF); in others, the delimiter is defined inline—the first delimiter occurrence is declared positional and the character appearing at that position is the delimiter for the rest of the field. Finally, some subfields are identified, prefixed, and delimited by using special subfield identifiers like /OCMT/nnn or /CHGS/nnnn.

Furthermore, other fields exhibit inconsistencies as well. For example, some subfields are defined as positional, with fixed position and length, but their length actually depends on an enumeration. Subfield 3 of text field 61 may have the values C, D, RD, or RC. This field is either exactly one or exactly two characters long, depending on its content.

The bottom line is that while the SWIFT format has a well-defined macro structure, a clearly defined, reliable syntax for fields does not really exist. Consequently, a table-driven approach for parsing SWIFT formats is much harder to implement than for either X12 or UN/EDIFACT. With all the exceptions, defining lookup tables or parameterizations for parsing code becomes so complex that it is ultimately more efficient to hard-code a custom parser for each SWIFT field. This also explains why SWIFT is not supported directly by BizTalk.

SWIFT Semantics

Except for a library of text fields that can be used across several message types and, of course, a standardized message type library, the SWIFT format does not have a semantics model comparable to those of X12 or UN/EDIFACT.

XML

Compared to SWIFT, X12, and UN/EDIFACT, the XML format is really a newborn. The World Wide Web Consortium (W3C), the standards committee that oversees the standardization of web-based technologies, standardized the eXtensible Markup Language only in 1998. The global acceptance of W3C-defined standards is quite interesting and reflects the nature of the Internet, given that it formed out of the Internet-user and infrastructure-provider community and is not a formal government-accredited standards organization such as ISO.

Comparing XML to UN/EDIFACT or X12 is actually somewhat like comparing apples with pears. As we have seen, the EDI standards have very limited syntax rules and provide a very static, nonextensible framework for formulating data in text. On the other hand, both provide huge semantics catalogs, and they provide common electronic definitions for business documents as they are exchanged between parties in digital or paper form all over the world. So UN/EDIFACT and X12 are really mostly about semantics.

In contrast, XML is all about syntax. The XML standards do not mention business semantics or document standardization anywhere in the core specification or in any of the most important extension specifications. However, the XML technology set allows rich augmentation of data, which can be used to leverage the EDI semantics for XML information. The various EDI/XML initiatives actually use this technique to merge the semantic wealth of EDI with the strong syntax of XML.

XML Document Syntax

XML's document syntax is specified in detail in the XML 1.0 specification that can be found at the permanent web location http://www.w3c.org/TR/REC-xml. To understand and use XML, the specification is certainly required reading. Luckily, the specification is written in the spirit of all other W3C documents in that it is mostly easy to understand.

While the specification prominently features its version number in the title, we are quite unlikely to see dramatic changes to the core specification that would cause the major version number to change.

The core syntax principles of XML are so simple that they can be summarized in a few sentences:

▼   *XML is plaintext*. All structural elements and the content of an XML document are machine-readable and can also be intuitively understood by human readers. With the exception of three characters (<, >, &) that can appear only by using special escape sequences, all printable characters can be used with XML; if the Unicode encoding is used, this includes all letters used anywhere in the world.

■   *XML is hierarchical*. All XML documents have a single root and all content is nested in an arbitrary number of levels below this root.

■   *XML data is contained in elements*. XML elements are named data containers that have unique semantics within a certain scope. The data is enclosed between two tags that serve as the element's delimiters. The syntax for the opening tag is "<"+*element-name*+">". The end tag is expressed as "</"+*element-name*+">". The data content of an element can be plaintext or other nested elements. Elements that contain no data can have empty tags that are formulated as "<"+*element-name*+"/>".

▲   *XML elements can have attributes*. Attributes allow you to augment an element with auxiliary data. Attributes appear within the opening tag of an element as name-value pairs.

XML documents that conform to these rules are called *well formed*.

When we compare the XML syntax rules against the EDI formats, it becomes apparent that they elegantly fix one of the core problems: field and composite boundaries and nesting.

X12 and UN/EDIFACT employ a strictly delimited format and feature three different types of delimiters to create a three-level nested structure of segments, fields, and subfields. Both formats cannot easily describe more levels of nesting and are therefore limited in their representation of more complex data. SWIFT is positional by design and therefore has massive problems with variable field lengths. To make variable field lengths possible, various inconsistent extensions have been created on a case-by-case basis that introduce delimiter schemes. SWIFT's problems with complex data are similar to those of UN/EDIFACT.

However, XML has none of these problems. Data can nest in any depth and can therefore be arbitrarily complex. Fields are always of variable length and are enclosed in start and end tags, defining clear boundaries for any field. The disadvantage of this formatting style is size. XML documents carry very explicit information about their structure as part of their data, and the ratio between structural information and payload is often nearly even.

Considering that the capacity of systems to process and store information has grown dramatically only in the past 15 years—while steadily becoming more affordable at the same time—it's no surprise that a format with these features has not been developed or gained popularity earlier. All EDI formats are a testimony of their designer's concern about size. When a standard data link between peers uses a 300 or even 9600 bps modem, size does matter.

XML Namespaces

The core XML document specification focuses strictly on the syntax of XML documents. It also mandates that the tag names of elements must be uniquely assigned to semantics. However, it neither provides a mechanism to qualify these semantics nor provides a way to disambiguate colliding tag names derived from generic common language terms such as "name" that may appear somewhere in a real-world document with two or three different meanings.

The XML namespaces specification (http://www.w3.org/TR/REC-xml-names/) adds these capabilities as an extension to XML. This reflects the extensible nature of the XML language. While namespaces add a whole set of new information to XML documents, all documents with namespace support are fully XML 1.0–compliant and can be read and understood by parsers or readers that may or may not be namespace-enabled.

In a nutshell, *namespaces* are collections of tags that all share a common semantic context. The context is uniquely identified worldwide and is sometimes also defined by a Universal Resource Identifier (URI). A URI can be either a URL—as you may know them from web addresses such as http://www.osborne.com—or a Universal Resource Name (URN) that is prefixed by *urn:* and followed by a unique name.

Each document has a default namespace that may or may not be explicitly defined using an *xmlns* attribute on the root element. Listing 3-1 shows how the default namespace is defined for a document.

Listing 3-1:

```
<?xml version="1.0" encoding="iso-8859-1" ?>
<CustomerData xmlns="urn:schemas-newtelligence-com:customerdata">
    <Customer ID="1234567">
       <Name>newtelligence AG</Name>
       <Address>Gilleshütte 99,Korschenbroich, Germany</Address>
    </Customer>
</CustomerData>
```

Once you need to merge information from multiple sources or merge different types of information into a single document, you need to assign distinct semantics to the elements. If we take the example from Listing 3-1 and add e-mail information to the customer, we might add this to the default namespace, but for the sake of illustration and to keep the example easy, we assume that the customer's e-mail address is enclosed in an Address tag from a special namespace. The resulting document can be seen in Listing 3-2. It shows how the two otherwise colliding fields with the common Address tag name now have distinct semantics.

Listing 3-2:

```
<?xml version="1.0" encoding="iso-8859-1" ?>
<CustomerData xmlns="urn:schemas-newtelligence-com:customerdata"
              xmlns:e="urn:schemas-newtelligence-com:email">
   <Customer ID="1234567">
```

```
     <Name>newtelligence AG</Name>
     <Address>Gilleshütte 99,Korschenbroich, Germany</Address>
     <e:Address>info@newtelligence.com</e:Address>
   </Customer>
</CustomerData>
```

Namespaces can also be used to qualify attributes. In Listing 3-3, we model a ficti-tious, fractional X12 purchase order and apply the semantics of X12 to the document at the same time. The default namespace reflects the structure of the purchase order, while the "x12" namespace refers to the X12 semantics model.

Listing 3-3:

```
<?xml version="1.0" encoding="UTF-16" ?>
<PurchaseOrder xmlns="urn:schemas-newtelligence-com:purchaseorder"
               xmlns:x12="urn:schemas-newtelligence-com:x12">
   <OrderInfo>
       <Purpose x12:ref="BEG01" x12:id="353">00</Purpose>
       <Type x12:ref="BEG02" x12:id="92">NE</Type>
       <OrderNumber x12:ref="BEG03" x12:id="324">
             7728-2777-2001
       </OrderNumber>
       <UserOrderReference x12:ref="REF02" x12:refqualifier="REF01"
                           x12:refselector="EU">
             0027366218-2001
       </UserOrderReference>
       <Department x12:ref="REF02" x12:refqualifier="REF01"
                                   x12:refselector="DP">
           245
       </Department>
       <Date x12:ref="BEG04" x12:id="373">2001-11-19</Date>
   </OrderInfo>
   <Conditions>
       <SalesRequirement x12:ref="CSH01" x12:id="563">N</SalesRequirement>
       <FreightCharge x12:ref="SAC05" x12:refqualifier="SAC01"
                   x12:refselector="C" x12:subqualifier="SAC02"
                   x12:subselector="D240">
           266.90
       </FreightCharge>
   </Conditions>
   <!-- { … remaining data .. } -->
</PurchaseOrder>
```

As you can see, namespaces are a great tool to disambiguate elements and to merge data with technical and semantic augmentation.

DTD and Schema

The core XML specification goes well beyond defining syntax rules. Most of the spec defines and explains the concept of Document Type Definitions (DTD). *Document Type Definitions* allow an XML document to contain its own formatting rules that define which elements and attributes can and must occur at which position, and they also provide a mechanism to specify type information for the contained data. DTDs may also be provided as external documents to create definitions that can be referenced by multiple documents.

This concept offers a major advantage over X12, UN/EDIFACT, and virtually all other traditional EDI standards. These formats require external documents to define their structure, which are not standardized and typically not even machine-readable. So, while DTDs allow software tools to code-generate customized parsers and serializers to transform data into and out of XML, none of the EDI formats allows this procedure to be done in a standardized way.

Even though DTDs are already a great tool, they leave a lot of room for improvement. They are not expressed in well-formed XML but use their own special syntax rules that require special parsing code. Ironically, the DTD syntax is not extensible; it is restricted to the capabilities outlined in the core spec. To overcome these limitations, various XML-based alternatives to DTD have been developed over the years. The most successful was Microsoft and IBM's XML Data proposal to the W3C.

A slimmed-down variant thereof, XML Data Reduced (XDR), is the basis for the BizTalk Schema model. The result of the W3C standardization process that was launched with XML Data as its starting point is the XML Schema Definition (XSD) language, which took well over two years to define and was not available as a standard when BizTalk (or any of its .NET Enterprise Server siblings) was released to manufacturing. Both models allow for a very precise definition of data types, cardinalities, and the overall document structure, and are even better suited for document validation and code generation than the DTD model.

Because all three variants—DTD, XDR, and XSD—are popular and actively used to define business documents, we will look at each a bit more in depth.

DTD

DTDs define the structure of an XML document and, if present, must be defined before any occurrence of markup (tags) in the document.

The following is a sample DTD that illustrates this concept; note that the line numbers are shown only for reference purposes and are not part of the document.

```
01: <?xml version="1.0" encoding="iso-8859-1" ?>
02: <!DOCTYPE Person [
03: <!ELEMENT Person (Name,Address+)>
04: <!ATTLIST Person id  ID #REQUIRED>
05: <!ELEMENT Name (#PCDATA)>
06: <!ELEMENT Address (Street?|City|Country?|Phone*)>
07: <!ATTLIST Address type (home|business|other) #IMPLIED>
08: <!ELEMENT Street (#PCDATA)>
09: <!ELEMENT City (#PCDATA)>
10: <!ELEMENT Country (#PCDATA)>
11: <!ELEMENT Phone (#PCDATA)>
12: ]>
```

```
13: <Person id="28882">
14:     <Name>Paul Jones</Name>
15:     <Address type="home">
16:          <Street>3526 South Beach Walk</Street>
17:          <City>Sunnyville</City>
18:          <Phone>403-555-2727</Phone>
19:          <Phone>403-555-2728</Phone>
20:     </Address>
21:     <Address type="business">
22:          <City>Busytown</City>
23:          <Country>US</Country>
24:     </Address>
25: </Person>
```

This example shows a document describing some personal data. The document root is the <Person> element containing a <Name> element and two <Address> elements with subelements providing street, city, and country data as well as zero or more phone numbers. If we look at DTD, we find these rules encoded into the definition set.

Every document type definition is enclosed in a DOCTYPE declaration. Like all other declarations, the DOCTYPE declaration is enclosed in angle brackets and begins with an exclamation mark before the keyword. In our example, the declaration begins at line 2 and ends at line 12. All declarations of elements and attributes are contained within DOCTYPE using a pair of square brackets. Immediately following the DOCTYPE keyword is the name of the DTD, which is also the name for the root element and must be matched by an element declaration.

This root element is declared on line 3. All elements are declared sequentially and in no particular order (as opposed to hierarchically—order has no significance here). An element declaration begins with the keyword ELEMENT, followed by the element name and the specification of the element content.

The example shows multiple variants of the content declaration. The declarations ANY and EMPTY are not shown. An element declaration for an empty element is formulated like this: <!ELEMENT IAmEmpty EMPTY>. To create a universal container that contains anything, you would express the declaration like this: <!ELEMENT GarbageDump ANY>.

The declaration on line 3 (<!ELEMENT Person (Name,Address+)>) specifies that the Person element must contain the child elements Name and Address in the shown order (the comma separator indicates this), that the Name is mandatory, and that the Address must appear at least once. The cardinality modifiers are suffixes to the element references or to a group of references. If there's no modifier suffix, it means that the element must appear, a question mark (?) suffix means that the element may appear at most once, the asterisk (*) indicates zero or more occurrences, and the plus (+) sign mandates at least one element of the given type to be present.

The element declaration on line 5 (<!ELEMENT Name (#PCDATA)>) contains parsed character data, which may or may not contain additional markup. #PCDATA is the keyword that allows you to specify that an element contains text data.

Attributes for elements are declared using the ATTLIST keyword followed by the element name and a list of attributes. An attribute is declared with its name, the data type, and an optional modifier. The available data types are ID, NMTOKEN, NMTOKENS, ENTITY, ENTITIES, CDATA, or the enumeration type. These types serve mostly structural purposes within XML and are used to enforce certain constraints that allow optimization of XML processing. The ID type may occur only once in an attribute list, and its value must uniquely identify any such element within any document based on this DTD (called a *document instance*). The NMTOKEN type limits the attribute data to valid XML identifiers, and the ENTITY type to references to unparsed entities defined in the DTD.

The only types actually available and useful for data are either CDATA for plain character strings or a sequence of values enclosed in parentheses and separated by the pipe (|) symbol as an enumerated type. The latter is shown on line 7 (<!ATTLIST Address type (home | business | other) #IMPLIED>).

If you want to specify shared external DTDs, you can create a file that contains only the DTD and formulate the DOCTYPE statement as <!DOCTYPE Person SYSTEM "filename.dtd">. The SYSTEM keyword indicates that the following expression is a URI that can and should be resolved by the system to obtain the DTD. You may also encounter such declarations with the PUBLIC keyword; two strings follow the PUBLIC keyword: the public identifier of the DTD, which may or may not be a URI, and the (optional) system identifier that is a URI.

We have not seen entities in the example. *Entities* are somewhat like a macro facility for XML, which allows you to create special escape sequences for common expressions. Entities are not bound to the document structure; they can occur anywhere in the document. XML knows two different entity types. *Internal* entities are declared inline in the document definition, such as <!ENTITY myname "Clemens Vasters"> > They are referenced by using the special sequence *&myname;* anywhere in the document. The string then replaces the reference. *External* entities are constructed much like the external document type references, such as <!ENTITY mydata "http://tempuri.org/mydata.xml">.

Parameter entities (internal or external) are a very special case of definitions. They are used only within DTD sections and are immediately resolved within the DTD.

XDR

DTDs are indeed complex, and their nonintuitiveness does not really fit the simplicity of the remaining XML syntax.

The XML Data Reduced schema language was one of the first attempts aimed to replace the DTD model for defining documents. Unlike the other XML technologies mentioned in this chapter, XML Data Reduced is not a standard. It is an intermediate solution and an open definition provided and used by Microsoft until W3C's XSD Schema effort reaches recommendation (standard) status. The XDR version implemented in BizTalk and other Microsoft products is already a refinement of the original submission to W3C. It includes some of the features of the W3C schema standard for future compatibility and a smooth transition from XDR to XSD. Microsoft has stated many times that they will adopt and migrate toward the XSD schema language across all products.

We will use the same example that we used for the DTD explanation to illustrate XDR Schema. XDR is more intuitive but a lot longer in its expression:

```
01: <?xml version="1.0" encoding="iso-8859-1" ?>
02: <s:Schema xmlns:s="urn:schemas-microsoft-com:xml-data"
03:           xmlns:dt="urn:schemas-microsoft-com:datatypes"
04:           name="Person">
05:   <s:ElementType name="Name" content="textOnly" dt:type="string"/>
06:   <s:ElementType name="Person" content="eltOnly" order="seq">
07:      <s:AttributeType name="id" dt:type="ID" />
08:      <s:attribute type="id" required="yes" />
09:      <s:element type="Name" minOccurs="1" maxOccurs="1" />
10:      <s:element type="Address" minOccurs="1" maxOccurs="*"/>
11:   </s:ElementType>
12:   <s:ElementType name="Street" content="textOnly"
13:                   dt:type="string"/>
14:   <s:ElementType name="City" content="textOnly"
15:                   dt:type="string"/>
16:   <s:ElementType name="Country" content="textOnly"
17:                   dt:type="string"/>
18:   <s:ElementType name="Phone" content="textOnly"
19:                   dt:type="string"/>
20:   <s:ElementType name="Address" content="eltOnly">
21:      <s:element type="Street" minOccurs="0" maxOccurs="1" />
22:      <s:element type="City" minOccurs="1" maxOccurs="1" />
23:      <s:element type="Country" minOccurs="0" maxOccurs="1" />
24:      <s:element type="Phone" minOccurs="0" maxOccurs="*" />
25:   </s:ElementType>
26: </s:Schema>
```

The greatest difference between DTD and XDR is that the latter is expressed using XML. This means that XDR Schemas can use the same extensibility mechanisms that are available for documents and can leverage the namespace features to allow additional augmentation for special purposes. BizTalk's own BizTalk Schema language is in fact an augmented XDR Schema that fully exploits this extensibility.

But let's look at the basics first and read the example schema from top to bottom—just because we can.

This XDR Schema (line 2) that also makes use of the XDR data-type model (line 3) has the name "Person" (4), meaning that its root element is of the corresponding element type defined in this schema. This element type (6)—of course named "Person"—may contain other elements only in the exact sequence shown. In the scope of this element type, an attribute type (7) with the name "id" of the XML ID type is defined. The "Person" element type contains a mandatory attribute (8) of the local attribute type "id" (6) and exactly one child element (9) of the element type "Name", whose element type (5) may contain text data that conforms only to the constraints of the XML Data type "string" and one or more elements (10) of the global type " "Address" (20).

The element type "Address" (20), which may contain only child elements, uses four element types that may all contain nothing but text data of type "string": Street (12), City (14), Country (16), and Phone (18). An element of type "Address" may contain at most one child element of the types "Street" (21) and "Country" (23), must contain exactly one of type "City" (22), and any number of children (24) of type "Phone".

More formally, XDR Schema is typically defined using the elements from the following (incomplete!) table. Note that XDR has a type-definition facility to create your own data types and also allows you to define entities much like DTD. We will skip both feature sets here and focus only on the document structure declaration features to allow this book to fit on an industry-standard shelf.

Schema   Declares and contains an XDR Schema. The namespace for the Schema element must use the qualifier urn:schemas-microsoft-com:xml-data.

Attribute	Description
name	Name for the schema. The name must match an element type declared in the schema, which becomes the root element of any conformant document.
model	"closed" This schema has a closed model. Elements and attributes defined only in this schema can appear in a document that is valid for this schema. "open" This schema's model is open. All declared elements and attributes must be conformant with this schema, but a document can also contain additional data. (This is the default.)

ElementType   Declares an element type. This element may appear either as an immediate child of the Schema element or as a child of another ElementType element.

Attribute	Description
name	Name for the element type. The name identifies this type and is also used as the tag name.
content	"eltOnly" Elements of this type may contain only other elements. "textOnly" Elements of this type may contain only text data. "mixed" Elements of this type may contain both elements and text. "empty" Elements of this type are always empty.
model	"open"/"closed" Semantically equivalent to the Schema element.
dt:type	Data type from a predefined set of types. Includes the XML types, date and time, string, various numeric types, binary, and a UUID.

Attribute	Description
order	"seq" Child elements must occur in the order in which they are declared. "one" At least one of the declared child elements must be used, even if they are all optional by themselves. "all" All child elements must appear and may do so in any order. "many" Any number of elements may appear in any order.

AttributeType   Declares an attribute type either globally as an immediate child of Schema or locally as a child of an ElementType element.

Attribute	Description
Name	Name for the attribute type. The name identifies this type and is also used as the attribute name within elements.
dt:type	Data type (See "ElementType.")
default	Default value for attributes of this type.
required	"yes"/"no" (trivial)

element   Defines an element as an instance of a predefined local or global element type within the scope of the current element type. This element may occur only within ElementType.

Attribute	Description
type	Reference to the *name* attribute of a previously declared ElementType element.
minOccurs	Minimum number of occurrences.
maxOccurs	Maximum numbers of occurrences or an asterisk (*) for infinity.

attribute   Defines an attribute of a previously defined attribute type for the containing element type.

Attribute	Description
type	Reference to the name attribute of a previously declared AttributeType element.
default	Overrides the default value of the base type.
required	Overrides the required status of the base type.

group   Specifies a different order attribute for a group of XDR element declarations. This element is a utility container that is typically used to enforce a sequence for a subset of child elements, that may contain elements only of the "Element" element, and that may be contained only in the ElementType element.

Attribute	Description
order	See "ElementType."

XSD

The XML Schema format—defined by W3C as an evolution of XDR—is still similar to its ancestor, but the committee has done some very good work in creating an even more consistent and extremely powerful data-definition language. We will not discuss XSD in detail here because Microsoft BizTalk Server 2000 currently does not directly support it, but XSD is illustrated to provide completeness of the XML introduction.

```
01: <?xml version="1.0" encoding="iso-8859-1" ?>
02: <xsd:schema xmlns:xsd="http://www.w3.org/2000/08/XMLSchema">
03:   <xsd:element name="Person" type="personType" />
04:   <xsd:complexType name="personType">
05:     <xsd:attribute name="id" type="xsd:id" />
06:     <xsd:sequence>
07:       <xsd:element name="Name" type="xsd:string"/>
08:       <xsd:element name="Address" maxOccurs="*" type="addressType"/>
09:     </xsd:sequence>
10:   </xsd:complexType>
11:   <xsd:complexType name="addressType">
12:     <xsd:sequence>
13:       <xsd:element name="Street" minOccurs="0" type="xsd:string"/>
14:       <xsd:element name="City" type="xsd:string"/>
15:       <xsd:element name="Country" minOccurs="0" type="xsd:string"/>
16:       <xsd:element name="Phone" minOccurs="0" maxOccurs="*"
17:                      type="xsd:string"/>
18:     </xsd:sequence>
19:   </xsd:complexType>
20: </xsd:schema>
21: <Person id="28882">
22:     <Name>Paul Jones</Name>
23:     <Address type="home">
24:         <Street>3526 South Beach Walk</Street>
25:         <City>Sunnyville</City>
26:         <Phone>403-555-2727</Phone>
27:         <Phone>403-555-2728</Phone>
28:     </Address>
29:     <Address type="business">
30:         <City>Busytown</City>
31:         <Country>US</Country>
32:     </Address>
33: </Person>
```

If you put the schema versions XSD and XDR side by side, you would probably first look for the schema name and an unambiguous definition for the root element. However, the XSD designers found that such a declaration is unnecessary.

While XDR is still very closely aligned with the XML document model and mandates three different type models for attributes, elements, entities, and data, XSD is much more generic and can serve as a universal type definition facility for data as such. XSD knows simple types that describe single values and complex types that are composed of multiple embedded types or referenced simple or complex types.

A complex type therefore forms a hierarchy of types, which maps perfectly to the XML document model. If a schema defines multiple global element declarations at the topmost level, any document instance that implements a consistent subset of the schema with any of the global elements as its root is considered valid.

While this may sound strange as compared to the DTD or XDR model, such standalone definitions are actually essential to allow creating XML schemas that do not define entire documents but only fractional augmentations, possibly only a set of attributes (for other, more complete schemas). By not mandating the strict hierarchy of an XML document, XSD also becomes immediately useful as a general-purpose type definition toolset—Microsoft's VisualStudio.NET uses XSD to define and code-generate strongly typed ADO.NET data sets that may actually never deal with document instances.

As indicated, a more detailed discussion of XSD is beyond the scope of this book. The XSD specification documents have a total size of well over 1.5MB and justify more than a single book by themselves.

XML References: XPath, XPointer, and XLink

One of the strengths of XML documents is their hierarchical nature with unlimited levels of nesting. This makes XML documents easy to parse and understand.

However, hierarchical data also has disadvantages. Storing complex data in hierarchical databases (what XML documents are) often causes some degree of information redundancy. If you take a purchase order that mandates specifying both shipping and billing address while the address is actually identical, you must replicate the information and place it into both locations within the hierarchical structure. Because the information is identical, a cross-referencing mechanism that allows shipping and billing address to use the exact same source data is essential to eliminate unnecessary redundancy and enforce identity.

Also, XML data is essentially text only and is not well suited to carry binary information. While all descriptions and pricing information of a product catalog can be perfectly expressed in XML, photographic images of the goods are difficult to embed into such documents. Instead, the images associated with the data can be stored at an external location and be linked to the data.

Finally, if you formulate a purchase order for a particular item in XML, you may want to refer to the exact catalog entry from the original document without replicating that information.

The XML extension specifications XBase, XPath, XPointer, and XLink address these issues.

XLink

Chapter 1 introduced XML with a reference to HTML. While the comparison is accurate for simplicity and syntactical similarities, XML and HTML are actually siblings that are both based on the Standardized General Markup Language (SGML), which is an ISO standard (ISO 8879). As its killer feature, HTML introduced the additional hyperlink feature to create links between or within documents. For XML, links between or within documents are declared by using XML Linking Language (XLink) expressions.

The XLink language defines a set of attributes that can be defined for any XML element and causes this element to be linked to an internal source within the same document or an external source. Because XML is a general-purpose language that may represent application-to-application data as well as application-to-user data, XLink also contains some features that are of interest mostly for interactive applications.

All XLink expressions are attributes identified by using the namespace qualifier http://www.w3.org/1999/xlink. The attribute type qualifies an element either as an extended or simple link or to contain auxiliary data used to construct-extended links. Extended links are extremely powerful in allowing you to group multiple documents' internal and external resources into a single associative group. Arcs can then be defined that specify the traversal rules between elements of the group and provide directionality to links. Simply speaking, *extended links* are formalized, navigable link collections.

The XBase specification (http://www.w3.org/TR/xmlbase) complements XLink by providing base locations (common prefixes) for link targets.

As you can see in Listing 3-4, a simple link is the lightweight version of the extended link. A *simple link* associates an element of the XLink type "simple" with a location identified by its XLink href attribute.

Listing 3-4:

```
<?xml version="1.0" encoding="iso-8859-1" ?>
<People xmlns="urn:schemas-newtelligence-com:people"
            xmlns:xlink="http://www.w3.org/1999/xlink">
   <Person ID="1234567">
      <Name>Peter Smith</Name>
      <Photo xlink:type="simple"
            xlink:href="http://www.newtelligence.com/bts/photo.jpg"/>
   </Person>
   <Person>
      <Name>Ellen Smith</Name>
      <Spouse xlink:type="simple"
            xlink:href="#1234567"/>
   </Person>
</People>
```

The internal link between Ellen Smith and her husband Peter in Listing 3-4 is expressed by using a combination of XLink and XPointer bare names that provide linkable locations based on element identifiers (XML 1.0 attribute ID). We will come back to XPointer, but we must discuss XPath first because that information is necessary to understand XPointer.

XPath

The XML Path Language (XPath) (http://www.w3.org/TR/xpath) serves to address parts or single elements by using navigational paths into the hierarchical structure of XML documents. The simplest expressions are those that navigate into a document by using simple straight paths that traverse the document along the tag names. The expression /CustomerData/Customer/Name applied to the XML document from Listing 3-2 would identify the "Name" element containing the string "newtelligence AG".

But XPath is much richer than this—and more complex.

Any XPath expression is a sequence of relative location paths. Prefixed with a forward slash (/), the relative location path becomes an absolute location part whose traversal begins at the document root. For relative location paths, the navigation begins at the current location. When we discuss XPointer and XSLT in the following section, you will see what significance the current location has in those contexts.

A path is composed from one or more location steps, separated by forward slashes. Each location step navigates into the document and performs a selection of elements, *fragments* (XML subexpressions that are not well-formed documents), or attributes. The next location step operates on the selection produced by the previous step.

Each location step is defined by three parts:

▼ **Axis**   The axis defines where the navigation step should go. If the axis is *child*, navigation is performed on all child elements of a node; if the axis is *parent*, the parent of the current node is inspected.

■ **Node Test**   The node test is an expression that selects a set of nodes by tag name. It can either be a distinct tag name, a wildcard (*), or a node-type selector (e.g., "text()" selects text nodes).

▲ **Predicates**   Predicates are (optional) functions or expressions enclosed in square brackets that allow a precise selection of the nodes found by node-testing on the specified axis.

If we inspect these parts a bit more in depth, the axis model is much richer than you might think. If you consider what you would need beyond the obvious parent, child, self, you may come up with a few more—the following table lists 13:

Axis	Scope
child	All immediate children of the current context.
descendant	All immediate and indirect children in any nesting depth below the current context. This axis selection effectively flattens the entire tree below the current context.
parent	The parent node of the current context.

Axis	Scope
ancestor	All parents and grandparents and their parents above the current context in the hierarchy. This axis always includes the root node. The axis flattens the branch above the current context.
following-sibling	All sibling nodes following the current context node in the document sequence.
preceding sibling	All sibling nodes preceding the current context node in the document sequence.
following	All nodes following the current context node in the document, but not descendants of the current node.
preceding	All nodes preceding the current node in the document sequence, but not any of the ancestors.
attribute	All attributes of the context node.
namespace	The declaring namespace element of the current context.
self	The context node itself.
descendant-or-self	Like descendant, but does include the context node.
ancestor-or-self	Like ancestor, but does include the context node.

If we look at the XML fragment and place the current context at the first Customer element, the axis expressions will resolve as shown here:

```
ancestor              <CustomerData>
self                  <Customer ID="1234567">
child, descendant         <Name>newtelligence AG</Name>
child, descendant         <Address>
descendant                    <Street>Gilleshütte 99</Street>
descendant                    <City>Korschenbroich</City>
descendant                    <Country>Germany</Country>
                          </Address>
                      </Customer>
following-sibling     <Customer ID="3294367">
following                 <Name>G+S GmbH</Name>
following                 <Address>
following                     <Street>Rheydter Strasse 180</Street>
following                     <City>Mönchengladbach</City>
following                     <Country>Germany</Country>
                          </Address>
                      </Customer>
                  </CustomerData>
```

In the second example, we place the current context further down into the document to illustrate the ancestors and preceding axes.

```
ancestor               <CustomerData>
preceding                  <Customer ID="1234567">
preceding                      <Name>newtelligence AG</Name>
preceding                      <Address>
preceding                          <Street>Gilleshütte 99</Street>
preceding                          <City>Korschenbroich</City>
preceding                          <Country>Germany</Country>
                               </Address>
                           </Customer>
ancestor                   <Customer ID="3294367">
preceding-sibling              <Name>G+S GmbH</Name>
self                           <Address>
child                              <Street>Rheydter Strasse 180</Street>
child                              <City>Mönchengladbach</City>
child                              <Country>Germany</Country>
                               </Address>
                           </Customer>
                       </CustomerData>
```

The node test is used in conjunction with the axis selection. The format is axis::node-test. Taking this document as our example, we can now formulate the following expressions:

▼ **child::City**   Resolves to the Element with the content Mönchengladbach

■ **ancestor::CustomerData**   Resolves to the CustomerData root element

■ **preceding::Street**   Resolves to the Street element above this element

■ **Country**   The shorthand form for child::Country

■ **parent::***   Resolves to the parent element (Customer)

▲ **descendant::text()**   Resolves to a collection of text nodes containing {Rheydter Strasse 180, Mönchengladbach, Germany}

If we concatenate these expressions into location paths, we can already select groups of data from XML documents quite precisely. However, axes and node tests can use the document structure only for navigation and selection. Inspecting content is reserved to predicates.

Once the axis and node test has found either a single node or an arbitrarily long list of nodes chosen based on structural aspects, predicates can be used to compute Boolean expressions with predefined functions and relational operators that take the data of these elements as arguments or operands. The predicate itself may use other XPath expressions as arguments.

The following complete XPath expression selects the second Customer element in the second example shown earlier: /descendant::*[@ID="3294367"]. The at (@) sign prefix is used to select attributes instead of elements.

Predicates allow comparisons using all common relational operators by using the C notation style, where not equal is expressed as "!=". Logical expressions may be grouped with parentheses and combined with the logical operators **and**, **or**, and **xor**. All expressions must resolve to either Boolean True or False.

Special cases are predicates that contain only a number, e.g., /CustomerData/Customer[2]. Here, the expression is evaluated as position()='number'. The built-in function *position()* returns the position in the current node set, which has been selected by axis and node test.

The built-in function set contains functions that evaluate the current node set, such as *position()*, *count()*, and *last()*, defines string functions like *concat()*, *contains()*, *starts-with()*, and *substring()*, and even has numeric functions, for example, *sum()*, *floor()*, *ceiling()*, or *round()*. All functions are fully described in section 4 of the XPath specification, which serves well as an easy-to-understand reference.

XPointer

The XPointer language (http://www.w3.org/TR/xptr) is designed to create references into XML documents. It complements XLink, providing a mechanism that allows pointing not only to a document as a whole, but to specific locations inside that document or to a selected range of XML nodes.

To select the range or point location, XPointer uses the XPath syntax. If the document from the second example in the previous section resides at the location http://www.newtelligence.com/bts/fig36.xml, the complete XPointer expression for the second customer would be http://www.newtelligence.com/bts/fig36.xml#xpointer (//Customer [@ID="3294367"]).

Using the id() function that matches attributes of the XML-inherent identifier type, the following expression is equivalent: xpointer(id("3294367")).

XPointer also knows a shorthand form for this expression: the ID itself. So another alternate expression for the same location is the following, which suddenly looks very familiar to people accustomed to the way HTML bookmarks work: http://www.newtelligence.com/bts/fig36.xml#3294367.

Bare names is the feature that uses element identifiers to define such pointers. This feature is a great example of how the XML technologies map perfectly into the established best-practice technologies like HTML and URIs but still preserve their own consistency. As you have seen, the simple syntax from the previous link example builds on the XLink, XPath, and XPointer definitions.

XSLT

The XML Stylesheet Language Transformations (XSLT) standard provides a mechanism to convert one XML document into another XML document or actually into any other text data stream. Because XSLT builds on or complements all of the XML technologies we have discussed up to this point, it is also the most complex and, for many developers, the most feared specification of the XML family.

It also differs greatly from most other XML technologies in that it is *active*. Except XPath and XPointer—which define some basic callable functions to evaluate an expression into a Boolean selection decision for whether to include or exclude data from a query selection—all of XML is static, and it is about declaring, representing, or containing data in well-structured documents or data streams.

In contrast, XSLT is really a functional programming language optimized for document mapping and conversions that is expressed in XML. However, XSLT is not rocket science; it is quite straightforward.

Figure 3-7 shows a simplified illustration of what XSLT does. A source document is passed to an XSLT processor that contains a loaded XSLT stylesheet. The stylesheet is created by using an actual or imaginary schema (hence, the dotted lines around the words in the figure) with which any source document complies. As a result, the stylesheet is actually applicable not only for a single document instance, but can be used to convert any document with a certain structure into another document with a certain different structure, defined by another different schema that may or may not exist as a formal document. Conceptually, both schemas do exist, although they are neither explicitly referenced nor is the schema concept even mentioned anywhere in the XSLT spec. As we will see later in Chapter 16, the BizTalk Mapper tool helps build transformation maps based on this model.

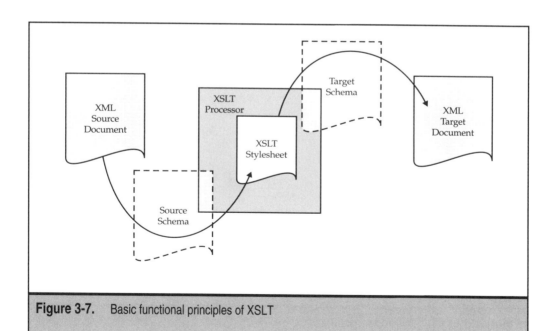

Figure 3-7.   Basic functional principles of XSLT

The organization of XSLT stylesheets conceptually resembles more of a cloud than an XML-ish hierarchy. Figure 3-8 illustrates how elements are mapped from the source into the target schema through processing by one of the templates contained in the stylesheet. Templates are contained in the stylesheet document in no particular order; the XSLT processor loads all templates into memory at the same time and applies them to the source document elements during traversal as it sees them match.

Beginning with a special template that is applied to the entire document by the XSLT processor, the traversal of the source document is driven by the templates. A template contains fragments of the target structure and rules for how content from the source maps into it. If a pattern exists for mapping certain source elements to the target, this pattern is implemented with a new template, which can be applied to matching elements from within any other template.

Figure 3-9 shows a simple stylesheet containing two templates and illustrates how the XSLT processor applies these stylesheets to transform a source document into a target document.

In step 1, the document template (identified by match="/") is applied to the entire document. Note that it is not applied to the root element, but rather, to the edge of the document—if you imagine XML being printed on paper.

When the template is processed (step 2), all of the content that does not qualify to belong to the XSLT namespace is output to the target document. Here, it is an opening and closing tag for an element named "q". The expression xsl:apply-templates belongs to the XSLT namespace and signals to the XSLT processor that the "best-match" templates for each entry of the node set produced by the XPath query "a/b" should be searched and

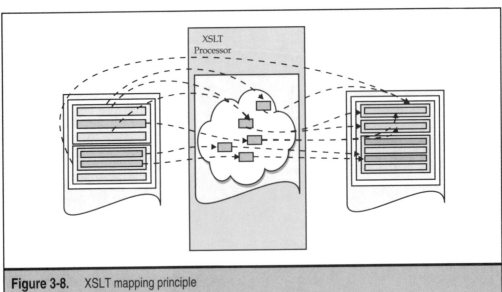

Figure 3-8. XSLT mapping principle

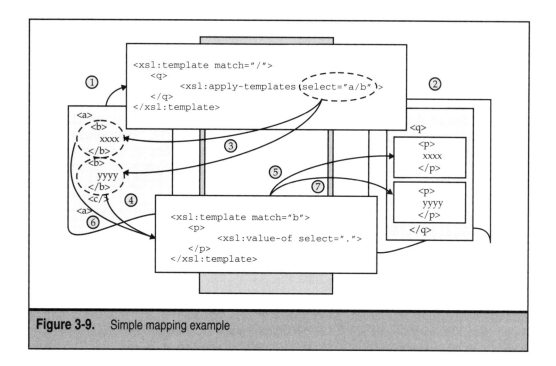

Figure 3-9.   Simple mapping example

used. The results from this query (step 3) are the two "b" elements in the source document, and the best match for both is the template with the attribute match="b".

Consequently, the first element of type "b" is run through the template (step 4), producing the first mapping in the target document (step 5). This is repeated for the second element "b" in steps 6 and 7. Voilá!

The example contains virtually all the "magic" of XSLT—it really is straightforward. Here is the stylesheet in its formal context:

```
<?xml version="1.0" encoding="iso-8859-1" ?>
<xsl:stylesheet version="1.0"
                xmlns:xsl="http://www.w3.org/1999/XSL/Transform">
  <xsl:template match="/">
    <q>
      <xsl:apply-templates select="a/b" />
    </q>
  </xsl:template>
  <xsl:template match="b">
    <p>
     <xsl:value-of select="." />
    </p>
```

```
    </xsl:template>
</xsl:stylesheet>
```

Any stylesheet is qualified by the namespace URI "http://www.w3.org/ 1999/XSL/ Transform" and is enclosed with the tag stylesheet. The namespace prefix *xsl* is used by convention.

Templates are declared with the template element and selected and applied by using the XPath expression contained in the *select* attribute of the apply-templates element. The data from the source document is transferred to the target by using the value-of element, which resolves to a value by extracting the content value of the source element identified by the XPath expression specified in its *select* attribute. In this case, the XPath expression is simply a dot (.) identifying the current element.

The value-of element is just one of a couple dozen functions available in XSLT. You can create elements and attributes, copy whole trees of elements from source to target, and build master stylesheets by including multiple other stylesheets. In addition, starting in the currently developed XSLT version 1.1 and already now in Microsoft's XSLT processor that ships with Microsoft BizTalk Server 2000, you can also create your own script expressions that you can use in the conversion process. You can use these script blocks, expressed in JScript or VBScript (VBScript in the case of BizTalk), to pull multiple elements from the source document together, perform concatenation tasks or calculations on them, and then place them into the target. In BizTalk, we will rediscover them as *functoids*.

For further information on XSLT, take a look at the specification at http://www. w3.org/TR/xslt.

SOAP/XMLP

The Simple Object Access Protocol (SOAP) is the basis for an ongoing standardization process of the XML Protocol (XMLP) activity group within W3C. SOAP is one of the most essential foundations for the Microsoft .NET strategy and also for the BizTalk Framework. SOAP is a transport-independent routing and access protocol for XML. In other words, if XML is a letter, SOAP is the envelope.

We will take a closer look at the BizTalk Framework in Chapter 6 and will discuss SOAP in that context.

CHAPTER 4

Microsoft .NET

Because Microsoft BizTalk Server 2000 is a member of the new Microsoft .NET Enterprise Server product line, it makes sense to fit BizTalk into the big picture of the product family and the overall Microsoft .NET strategy before we go into the product details.

In July 2000, the Microsoft .NET initiative, whose centerpiece is the new .NET Framework development platform, was announced at the already legendary Professional Developer's Conference (PDC2000). Beginning in the mid-1990s, Microsoft began putting an immense amount of resources and money into the new .NET development platform. The results that Microsoft presented at the PDC are currently making big waves throughout the IT industry.

The Microsoft .NET initiative stands on three pillars:

▼　The Microsoft .NET Framework

■　The Microsoft .NET Enterprise Server family

▲　The Microsoft .NET Web Service Building Blocks (code named "Hailstorm")

NOTE:　This chapter looks at the .NET Framework and the .NET Enterprise Servers in detail, but the Hailstorm services are not covered because little information is available yet. In essence, Hailstorm is a set of Simple Object Access Protocol (SOAP) interfaces (web services) that are implemented and hosted by Microsoft (and can be equally implemented and hosted by third parties). Hailstorm provides distributed user authentication via Microsoft's Passport service and provides central repositories for electronic mail, calendars, and other user profiles, which can all be consumed by .NET applications. Essentially, Hailstorm provides a digital wallet in which you can carry personal information, including your address and calendar, and release bits of information to web sites and services as you browse the Web.

Before discussing the server product line and how BizTalk is positioned among its product siblings, we will first explore the new .NET technology set. If you are developing software on any Microsoft platform, .NET will certainly affect your professional life in a big way in the next few years. If you administer Microsoft platform systems, you will have similar exposure to the new technologies for deployment and security that have been reinvented with the .NET Framework.

THE .NET FRAMEWORK

The attendees of PDC2000 and other major Microsoft developer conferences around the world were excited, baffled, and shocked by many of the .NET presentations. They suddenly realized that the paradigm shift between .NET development and Windows development can really only be compared to the transition between MS-DOS and Windows programming. This is great news because it gives Microsoft the opportunity to redesign those programming interfaces—which were long overdue for an overhaul. The bad news is that developers will have to learn a new platform from the ground up.

With such a dramatic shift, Microsoft is certainly taking a huge risk that developers will adopt the new platform. Should that fail, even a giant like Microsoft could find itself in major trouble. When Microsoft is betting the farm on a brand new platform, it is certainly worth taking a closer look at the fundamentals of the .NET Framework, which is the heart of the .NET platform and the entire Microsoft .NET strategy.

The Common Type System

Everything that happens in applications is about data. To allow applications to access types efficiently and with proper semantics, data is usually typed.

The .NET common type system is a specification for a language-independent, object-oriented data-type system that can represent any simple types (numbers, Boolean true/false expressions, and strings) or composed types (classes). All types, from a simple Boolean value to a complex class with nested types, are descendants of the same base type System.Object. This base type allows for a very generic and object-oriented approach to building container classes like arrays or dictionaries, and it provides a very consistent overall infrastructure.

The "object-ness" of all types is one of the fundamental differences from the Java platform, to which .NET is often compared. In Java, simple types like integer numbers are "magic" and not part of the object system. Therefore, they have to be handled differently from all other objects in the language. In .NET, an integer number is just another class in most respects and can therefore be consistently used with generic infrastructure classes. In the new Microsoft C# (C sharp) language (and some other .NET languages), the expression *8.ToString()* is therefore perfectly legal and returns the string "8".

Comparable software environments that share a common base class for each data type, such as the SmallTalk environment, are real heavyweights in terms of memory consumption and management overhead. Because objects are usually by-reference data types that manage their own memory, every class being an object means that each expression causes the allocation of small memory blocks, and references top these blocks that need to be managed.

Because this type of management overhead is clearly not acceptable for an enterprise-quality run-time environment, .NET clearly distinguishes between value and reference data types without breaking the type system's consistency. This allows the memory layout and object management to be optimized in a way that makes .NET's memory and reference management as efficient as that of more traditional development platforms and languages like C or C++.

Although it is implemented through a class, the .NET System.Int32 32-bit-wide integer data type (and all other simple types except strings) is a value type. It is always passed by value in method calls and when assigned to other values. This copy-always behavior allows such types to be embedded into other objects' memory layout because references to them will never be shared.

Implementing this behavior for types is, of course, not a privilege exclusive to the .NET platform designers: it is available to all developers on the platform. (Virtually no behavior in .NET is magic or Microsoft-only.) If a C# developer wants to create a new value type that is always copied and never referenced (and therefore help to improve efficiency when dealing with very small data elements), he or she simply creates a "struct" structure. These structures automatically have the same behavior as the simple .NET types in that they are copy-always and embedded into other object's memory layout, but they can still have methods and most other object capabilities.

Comprehensive XML Support

The .NET Framework is designed to be a platform for services that act both as information hubs and information endpoints. Moreover, the Framework is designed to be portable to operating systems other than Windows, and the .NET Compact Framework is the scaled-down version for handheld devices and other embedded systems. The portability of its design is underlined by the fact that Microsoft has submitted a substantial portion of the run-time specifications, the associated library, and the C# language to the European Computer Manufacturers Association (ECMA) for standardization, which opens the door for virtually anyone to port the run time to other platforms.

To enable the information hub and integration function, the .NET framework "speaks" XML at all levels. The internal data representation for the database access technology (dubbed ADO.NET) is XML. The preferred wire format for calls between remote .NET services is the XML-based SOAP protocol. At development and run time, all .NET configuration files are expressed in XML. And, most importantly, the web services technology set ASP.NET exposes SOAP-compliant web services with metadata expressed in the XML-based Web Service Description Language (WSDL). Therefore, the common type system's core array of data types is very close to those defined in the XML Schema (XSD) standard. This allows seamless serialization of any simple or complex (composed) .NET data type into XML, and it allows a direct backward mapping from XML data onto .NET objects.

Common Language Runtime

The aforementioned services, which are just a minor fraction of the services the .NET Framework provides, are all executed in a managed environment provided by the common language runtime. The common language runtime is an active run-time environment that provides services like memory management (automatic garbage collection—you can simply "forget" objects in memory instead of having to manually free them), metadata reflection (applications can explore their own structure), threading, advanced diagnostics, and many more services.

The common type system and common language runtime are called *common* because they are indeed common to all programming languages targeting the .NET platform. Every language compiler, including the new Microsoft favorite C#, is required to adhere to a certain set of rules (the common language specification) that narrowly specifies how types must be constructed to be legal in the .NET platform. As a result, the .NET Framework has some truly unique advantages: cross-language object inheritance, seamless data exchange, and invocation of code between objects written in any .NET language within the same application and across applications. "Any .NET language" means that you can pick from an impressive lineup from Microsoft and many third-party vendors, including the following: Visual Basic.NET, C#, Microsoft Visual C++ with Managed Extensions, JScript.NET, Perl, Python, SmallTalk, Eiffel#, COBOL, Haskell, Mercury, Scheme, Pascal, Oberon, Java (Microsoft JUMP Toolkit), APL, Standard ML, Objective Camel, and others.

All of these languages do not compile to native code for the platform, but to the Microsoft Intermediate Language (IL). IL is a high-level object-oriented assembly language that is conceptually similar to P-Code or Java bytecode in that it is a machine-independent, machine code–like language. However, the similarities end here. IL is designed to be compiled and not to be interpreted by a virtual machine. Each .NET application therefore goes through two compilation stages: the program is compiled from its native implementation language into IL and then IL is compiled and optimized for the target platform. .NET applications always execute natively as machine code on the platform's processor(s), instead of a virtual processor that has to be managed by an extra software layer implemented on top of the native system processor.

.NET applications will almost always execute faster than Java applications, for instance, because that additional execution layer is never needed. Just In Time (JIT) compilers from several vendors (including Sun) and even dedicated Java-enabled hardware provide a similar mechanism for the Java platform, but their scope is typically limited to optimizing applications at run time. The Sun Java JIT compiler will compile Java bytecode into native code on a per-method-call basis and cache the result for later calls as long as the application runs. However, because the entire Java architecture is built for bytecode interpretation and not for compilation, the .NET option to preJIT an entire application into native code before it is executed does not exist.

A nice side effect of the compile-always paradigm is that no more interpreter languages exist on the .NET platform. Although designed as an interpreter scripting language, JScript.NET is a fully compiled language on the .NET platform, and the .NET Framework even compiles regular expressions and XPath expressions to native code. Consequently, .NET no longer needs nor supports the Visual Basic Scripting Edition (VBScript). On the new platform, all language dialects of Visual Basic converge into a single language and compiler platform: Visual Basic.NET.

.NET Framework Library

All these languages share not only the same run-time environment, but they also share the same run-time library: the .NET Framework library.

Without .NET, development on the Windows platform (and most other platforms as well) is somewhat discriminating no matter which language and implementation techniques you choose. For high-level tasks, you can use scripting languages or optimized high-level languages (like Visual Basic) with highly effective rapid application development environments to achieve quick results. However, as soon as you need to get closer to the metal, you must use a lower-level language like C, which provides a lot more control at the cost of more complex code that may take longer to complete.

So the basic choice to make is ease of development versus raw power. Many projects require both, so you are always caught in a compromise situation because multilanguage projects are very difficult to manage. In .NET, every programming language has equal access to the full functionality of the .NET Framework and the infrastructure. For example, there is nothing (or at least very little) that you can do with C# that you cannot do in Visual Basic.NET.

While the unification of the type systems and the run-time libraries will enable more consistent applications and better integration of code in the long run, adopting the .NET Framework will initially mean that developers face a rather steep learning curve. The .NET Framework library is news for Windows developers in every corner—except the Visual J++ Java developers, who will find some of the library layouts to be suspiciously similar to the Windows Foundation Classes (WFC).

Consequently, Microsoft used the opportunity to unify the access to many of the Windows platform APIs, some of which are showing their age after undergoing multiple revisions. The result is a newly designed, consistent, and fully object-oriented class framework, which will reward the initial learning effort with a much more efficient and more productive development.

Some important elements of the .NET Framework library include the following:

▼ **ADO.NET**   Data access and manipulation infrastructure with managed providers for accessing databases. The OLE Database (OLE DB) managed provider allows access to all databases that have compliant OLE DB providers.

■ **ASP.NET**   The web services (and web site) run-time environment. ASP.NET features Web Forms, which are a brand new approach to web site development. They allow a form-based development paradigm that mirrors the successful Visual Basic model for Windows application forms. Web Forms are compliant with any client-side web browser.

■ **Windows Forms**   The object-oriented wrapper of the Win32 windowing API that provides a unified interface replacing the different APIs of Visual C++ MFC, Visual Basic Forms, and Visual J++ WFC.

■ **GDI+**   The everything-new overhaul of the Windows graphics device interface programming API with up-to-date graphics capabilities and support for current file formats. The GDI+ programming interface is also available as unmanaged code for use outside the .NET Framework.

▲ **.NET Remoting**   The complete replacement for the DCOM wire protocol. It is extensible at all levels and communicates by using the open SOAP protocol when used in conjunction with HTTP over the Internet. When used with straight IP sockets on corporate intranets, .NET Remoting uses a compact binary wire format. Other wire formats and transport options can be developed by third parties and can be plugged into the existing infrastructure.

This everything-new approach does not forget the installed base. The .NET Framework integrates very well with COM+ services, COM components, and unmanaged code through its interoperability services; thus, it allows you to leverage your existing code bases and existing Windows services through the well-established and solid Windows component technologies. Therefore, moving to .NET does not necessarily mean porting to .NET; rather, it means component-oriented migration. It often makes sense *not* to port your existing unmanaged components, but instead integrate them into new .NET solutions through the interoperability interfaces and move them to the .NET platform only when they are due for a major revision.

THE .NET ENTERPRISE SERVERS

The COM interoperability migration path is the same one Microsoft is taking for its own server product line. Despite their family name, none of the .NET Enterprise Servers is based on the .NET Framework technology because the Framework isn't expected to ship until fall of 2001, while all the servers presented in this chapter were already released. Because they are all implemented based on COM+ and Win32, the correct family name would probably be Windows DNA Enterprise Servers. (DNA stands for Digital Network Architecture, and it is a somewhat pointless umbrella term coined by Microsoft marketing for the development technologies that were available on the Windows platform). However, through the comprehensive XML support of most 2000 servers and the .NET Framework's excellent COM+ services integration, the .NET Enterprise Servers provide a great foundation for building .NET Framework applications: the servers carry the .NET label with good reason.

But Microsoft's own servers are not the only ones that provide a good back end for the .NET Framework. The ADO.NET database interface technology uses the existing OLE DB drivers to interface with most modern database systems; furthermore, other server solutions like Software AG's excellent Tamino XML database allow for great integration through the Framework's native XML support. Tamino is especially interesting to look at in conjunction with BizTalk because it is a great XML repository.

A Tamino database behaves like a single huge document. Besides letting you add new XML documents that conform to configured schemas and letting you query for specific documents by index number, the most powerful function is that you can run an XPath query on the database. When you run an XPath query, all document boundaries blur and all data in the database appears to be a single document, which is extremely powerful. If you use this to store incoming XML purchase orders, extracting statistics data for which product is the most popular with your clients is merely a matter of a single query. You don't have to do any mapping to a relational database system to achieve this.

The following sections briefly review each of the server products that are part of the Microsoft .NET Enterprise Server family.

Windows 2000 Server

The most fundamental server is the Windows 2000 Server product (and, of course, the upcoming Windows 2002 Server platform). Windows 2000 is the most stable operating system Microsoft has ever put on the market. Unless you have some really quirky drivers for your hardware, "blue-screen-of-death" experiences with Windows 2000 are extremely rare. The Windows 2000 platform is a solid, multipurpose operating system with multiple services that provide a great foundation for writing network-centric and client/server applications. We will look at only a few of those services here. You can access them all directly from managed code by using .NET Framework classes, and they are the most essential services for building enterprise applications.

Internet Information Server

The Internet Information Server (IIS) 5.0 services (updated to version 6.0 in Windows 2002) are an integral part of Windows 2000. They provide scalable and fast server implementations for HTTP, FTP, and SMTP. Internet Information Server comes with the Active Server Pages (ASP) development platform for web sites, which allows server-side applications to be written using scripting languages like VBScript and Microsoft's implementation of ECMAScript, called JScript.

Internet Information Server is an installation prerequisite for Microsoft BizTalk Server 2000 because it provides BizTalk with the web services infrastructure for much of its management interfaces, and it is also responsible for handling incoming HTTP traffic.

COM+ Component Services

In 1996, Microsoft introduced the Microsoft Transaction Server (MTS) add-on to Windows NT 4.0 (and Windows 9x) through the Windows NT Option Pack. Although the initial release went largely unnoticed outside the developer community and was indeed only part of the free Option Pack update to Windows NT 4.0, Microsoft Transaction Server is undoubtedly one of the most influential and revolutionary products that Microsoft ever released.

Microsoft Transaction Server—which was substantially enhanced and (more appropriately) renamed COM+ Component Services in Windows 2000—is a management and run-time environment for COM-based software components that simplifies deployment of components, has a role-based security model, and provides several run-time services. The most important of these services is automatic transactions. With MTS (Windows 2000 term: COM+ Transactions), components can be configured to support or require transactions. If a component requires a transaction, each database or message queue operation it performs is executed in a transactional manner. That means that all operations either jointly succeed or jointly fail.

The great advantage of COM+ Transactions is that it takes care of the transaction management under the hood, and components do not even need to be aware of the transaction. Before a component is called, COM+ Transactions creates a transactional shell around it (called a *context* in proper terms) or places it into an already-existing context if a transactional component requests services from another transactional component. When none of the components explicitly votes to abort the transaction, COM+ coordinates the committing of changes to all data resources. If a component votes to abort, COM+ will make sure that none of the changes that the transaction made is durable. (This behavior is called *rollback*.)

The automatic transactions programming model has meanwhile been adopted (read: copied) by Sun Microsystems for the Enterprise Java Beans model (Java 2 Enterprise Edition—J2EE), and it is also the fundamental feature of the CORBA Object Transaction System (OTS).

Other COM+ services include COM+ Events, which is a publisher/subscriber disconnected events model, and COM+ Object Pooling, which manages pools of components that can serve requests more quickly. Microsoft BizTalk Server takes advantage of many of the COM+ services, including COM+ Events and COM+ Transactions.

Microsoft Message Queue

Microsoft Message Queue (MSMQ) is another service that is built into Windows 2000 and also developed with the Windows NT 4.0 Option Pack. MSMQ is a powerful message queuing system for building scalable and transactional applications that take advantage of the asynchronous programming model. MSMQ is essential for asynchronous COM+ operations and is also the means by which BizTalk Server integrates its own services.

Although it ships with every copy of Windows 2000 and comes as a free add-on to Windows NT 4.0, Message Queue is one of the most undervalued development tools on the Windows NT and Windows 2000 platforms. Developers (and some architects) have a hard time differentiating between the usage scenarios for synchronous calls to components and those for asynchronous, transactional communication.

Many operations, especially handing information to other systems for further processing, do not require an immediate answer except for "safely dropped off and guaranteed to be delivered." These tasks are perfect candidates for message queuing. Doing everything synchronously is like going to your nearest FedEx agent, handing in an express letter, and sitting in the FedEx office until the letter has not only arrived at the destination, but the answer letter is handed back to you. It would be pretty boring, and you could do a lot of more productive work in the meantime. What's true for you is also true for servers.

BizTalk Server makes it easy to use MSMQ. Also, the BizTalk Orchestration feature that we will explore throughout this book is a real killer application for message queuing because it makes using MSMQ easier than ever before.

Active Directory Services

While it is not really used by Microsoft BizTalk Server 2000, the Active Directory Services feature of Windows 2000 must be included in this list. Active Directory provides a network-wide repository for computers, printers, users, user groups, distribution lists, and virtually any type of custom data class that must be shared across a networked environment. Windows 2000 stores all security- and management-related information in Active

Directory. Some of the .NET Enterprise Servers, most prominently Exchange Server, store almost their entire configuration in Active Directory, allowing for perfect integration of Windows 2000 user and resources management with the server's configuration data.

Windows Management Instrumentation

Windows Management Instrumentation (WMI) is an implementation of the Web-Based Enterprise Management (WBEM) standards that are developed under the auspices of the Distributed Management Task Force (DMTF), which includes companies like Compaq, Intel, BMC, Cisco, and Microsoft.

WMI is a single shopping point for obtaining and modifying configuration information of Windows 2000 systems, from hardware and driver settings to higher-level server software management tasks. In essence, you can manage local and remote Windows 2000 systems through a single interface, independently of where the configuration information is stored. Whether hardware driver settings are stored in the Registry or other configuration data is stored in databases or proprietary application files, WMI makes them all equally accessible.

The core configuration settings of Microsoft BizTalk Server are exposed and programmatically accessible only through WMI. The BizTalk Administration tool that you will learn about later in Chapter 19 uses WMI to access and modify BizTalk Server's settings.

Microsoft Application Center 2000

Application Center 2000 is an extension service for Windows 2000 that provides advanced deployment and diagnostics services for *web server farms* (multiple servers with identical content that share the processing load). It includes features like Component Load Balancing (CLB), which BizTalk can use to load balance calls to its inbound data gateway (called the Interchange component—more on this later in Chapters 8 and 11).

Application Center 2000 is really COM+ on steroids. In fact, many of Application Center 2000's features were initially slated to become an integral part of Windows NT 5.0 (which is now Windows 2000), but they were then moved into the Application Center 2000 product before Windows 2000 was released.

Microsoft SQL Server 2000

Microsoft SQL Server 2000, Microsoft's fast relational database product, is a prerequisite for BizTalk Server 2000, and it is the place where BizTalk stores virtually all data.

Long perceived as a small server that was not ready for serious enterprise use, SQL Server now regularly wins the crown for the highest throughput of the Transaction Processing Council's TPC/C benchmark since it was virtually reimplemented from the ground up in version 7.0.

SQL Server 2000 is a significant update to SQL Server 7.0, which now incorporates new XML capabilities. The SQL Server database engine can evaluate XML data and use XML documents in joins with native SQL Server tables. And through a few simple syntax extensions, SQL Server can now produce XML output instead of the typical rows and columns. This is paired with the Internet Information Server extensions for SQL Server that help produce complex XML documents, complete reports, and web sites directly from within SQL Server. In SQL Server XML Web Release 1, which is a freely download-able extension to SQL Server 2000, additional capabilities like Updategrams are added, which allow databases to be updated using XML documents and without using SQL lan-guage expressions. With these capabilities and a dedicated managed provider imple-mented in the .NET Framework, SQL Server is the most .NET-ready server of the .NET Enterprise Server family.

Microsoft Exchange Server 2000

Microsoft Exchange Server 2000 is Microsoft's e-mail and collaboration server product, which provides comprehensive support for Internet and corporate messaging, scheduling, and conferencing.

The most important new feature that Microsoft Exchange 2000 provides for the .NET technology set is the Web Storage system. The Exchange Web Storage system (which also ships with SharePoint Portal Server) is a database engine that can store arbitrary data like documents, objects, and XML files, and it makes them accessible through various stan-dard protocols. The Web Storage system combines the features of the Web with those of a file system and a database. You can submit and retrieve documents via Web Distributed Authoring and Versioning (WebDAV), you can expose databases via NNTP and make them look like an Internet newsgroup, and you can have databases published via IMAP4 and POP3 protocols so that they act like a user's mailbox. Exchange 2000 uses these fea-tures for the traditional means, but through the web storage's extensibility, applications can leverage these features for virtually any other purpose that developers see fit.

For BizTalk Server 2000, Microsoft Exchange Server 2000 can provide e-mail receive capabilities, which BizTalk does not provide out of the box. Standalone, BizTalk can only send e-mail messages via SMTP but not receive them.

Another integration opportunity, which does require custom development, is to turn electronic documents received by BizTalk Server into human-readable documents, which can then be routed through a decision process by using the Exchange workflow capabili-ties. Once the process is complete, the resulting document can be submitted back into BizTalk for further processing.

Exchange and BizTalk both provide workflow capabilities, which seem to be competing within the same server family. This is confusing at first. In fact, both products have a clearly defined scope and different focus for their workflow capabilities. BizTalk Orchestration workflows aim to integrate and coordinate business processes between applications, while Exchange Server workflows are about e-mail and document routing between people.

Microsoft SharePoint Portal Server 2000

SharePoint Portal Server is Microsoft's new intranet portal server, which serves as a uni-versal index and knowledgebase of the vast amounts of information that exists on corpo-rate servers in digital form. SharePoint is a very smart indexing service that is capable of automatically categorizing documents based on their content after it has learned the criteria for what qualifies a document to belong to a specific category. The learning process happens by example and training. You have SharePoint read a sample of documents that you would put into a certain category, and SharePoint uses that as a pattern for further automatic categorizations.

With these capabilities, SharePoint allows you to categorize content from internal and external sources like Exchange Server, Active Directory, local file systems, and the Web into a single knowledge portal, which can be built by using Digital Dashboard blocks.

Microsoft Host Integration Server 2000

Microsoft Host Integration Server (HIS) 2000 is an updated version of Microsoft SNA Server. It allows you to integrate the Windows 2000 platform with IBM mainframe systems. Therefore, it plays an important role when you want to integrate Microsoft BizTalk with those systems.

Host Integration Server provides, among other bridging technologies, a connection between MSMQ and the IBM MQSeries message queuing services. It allows you to expose host transactions as COM components by using the COM Transaction Integrator (COMTI). This allows almost seamless integration of host systems with BizTalk Server's message queue support and lets you plug host transactions into BizTalk Orchestration without much further programming.

Microsoft Commerce Server 2000

Microsoft Commerce Server 2000 is an e-commerce server solution that provides product catalog services, user profiles, business analysis, and site personalization for e-commerce web sites. Commerce Server 2000 shares some of its architecture with Microsoft BizTalk Server, allowing tight integration of both products.

One scenario for this is a combination of an interactive web shop that is backed by Commerce Server. It is receiving digital purchase orders in EDI or XML formats that BizTalk can forward to Commerce Server and which can therefore be handled by the same order-processing pipeline. In the other direction, Commerce Server can also push information to clients via BizTalk Server as electronic documents. BizTalk Orchestration is also very useful with Commerce Server to coordinate the back end fulfillment processes that result from online orders.

Microsoft Internet Security and Acceleration Server 2000

Internet Security and Acceleration Server (ISA) is Microsoft's firewall and proxy server product, which complements all server products that communicate directly with the Internet. Although Windows 2000 already provides you with basic packet and port filtering capabilities, any corporate network that is directly connected to the Internet must be guarded by an extra firewall that provides a higher level of protection against attacks from the outside. Firewall servers provide a high level of protection against unwanted access from outside intruders by inspecting and filtering all inbound traffic.

In addition to the firewall functionality, ISA comes with improved caching capabilities over its predecessor Microsoft Proxy Server 2.0.

CAUTION: BizTalk Server 2000 should be run behind a firewall if it is connected directly to the Internet. Of course, Microsoft ISA Server is not the only option, and you may indeed go and look for other solutions as well, since ISA Server is relatively new.

Firewalls are products that need time to become really secure because the best testers for firewalls are hackers who want to get to information that they are not supposed to see and who rarely reveal their trade secrets to companies that produce the line of defense against their attacks. For example, Check Point's Firewall-1 has been on the market for several years already and can, in all honesty, be assumed to be more mature than the first generation firewall from Microsoft, although Microsoft has put a lot of energy into getting the first product release right. Nevertheless, ISA is a very serious and very extensible firewall product that will draw a lot of interest from hackers and corporate users alike. It can be expected to harden much faster than any competitor product did in the past.

PART II

BizTalk Overview and Concepts

CHAPTER 5

Introducing BizTalk Server 2000

From Jerusalem's Temple to Britain's Stonehenge, from the Rhine River to the majestic stream of the Nile, the Roman Empire managed to hold a firm grip on its territories for centuries. How? Through efficient communication and orchestration of their resources. This is no different from corporations that want to keep a firm grip on their markets. Universal communication and efficient, agile use of all corporate resources is key for success in business. Microsoft BizTalk Server 2000 is designed as an integration tool that acts as "universal glue" between applications, data sources, and partners that share or exchange information. BizTalk optimizes communication and provides the agility that corporations need in an ever-changing marketplace.

This chapter provides a compact overview on what BizTalk does and doesn't do, explains the different BizTalk Server products editions, and provides a detailed walk-through on how you can install BizTalk Server 2000 on a development machine.

WHAT BIZTALK SERVER DOES AND DOESN'T DO

Although the term "messaging" is used in some context in virtually all of the following chapters, BizTalk is not an autonomous messaging solution in itself. The terms "enterprise integration" and "workflow" also appear quite a few times—again, BizTalk is not some type of object broker or any other universal bridge for all sorts of data transport protocols.

Just as the .NET Enterprise Server family provides building blocks for your own solutions, these products increasingly depend on each other for such building block services. By using these products together, you can count on optimum performance and a maximum feature set instead of having too many functional overlaps between the server products.

Surprisingly, many users still expect server products to be entirely self-contained. The press, on the other hand, has been slamming Microsoft, Corel, and other desktop application vendors for years for not integrating their office applications more. The .NET Enterprise Server family demonstrates that Microsoft takes integration of their server products more seriously than ever, and BizTalk is that case's strongest testimony.

To exchange information using the Internet or other electronic mail services, Microsoft Exchange Server provides excellent, flexible, and very manageable support for X.400, the Simple Mail Transfer Protocol (SMTP), the Messaging Application Programming Interface (MAPI), and other mail transport protocols. To receive messages through HTTP calls or FTP drop-off, Microsoft Internet Information Server (IIS) is the fastest and best integrated choice on the Windows 2000 platform.

For integrating CICS or IMS transactions on host systems by using SNA protocols or IBM's MQSeries, Microsoft Host Integration Server (HIS, formerly SNA Server) and Microsoft Message Queue (MSMQ) are a proven team. Electronic storefronts find excellent infrastructure support to manage catalogues, user profiles, and sequential order processing pipelines in Commerce Server. Finally, the TPC-C (Transaction Processing Council Benchmark C) world-champion SQL Server 2000 is not only extremely fast, but also the most manageable database product on the market.

Consequently, Microsoft BizTalk Server cannot autonomously receive SMTP mail or HTTP packages. Also, it will not talk the LU6.2 IBM host protocol, store data, or run your web portal. If all those servers already do so much of the work and take care of the essentials, what's left? A lot. To understand the whole purpose of BizTalk, the following typical scenarios elucidate the point.

▼ Continuously replicate and import bookkeeping data from independently operating daughter firms that use their own vertical market software solutions. Keep the system open for further acquisitions or other partners. While you're at it, import account statements from a handful of international banks into the accounting system and allow export of money transfer orders.

■ Electronically accept bulk purchase orders from your channel partners as well as many small purchase orders from the web storefront. At the same time, allow purchase orders to be entered by sales personnel in the existing system. Prioritize purchase orders by order volume—biggest first. Daily between 6 and 9 A.M., excluding Sunday, forward orders along with the invoice documents to the external storage and shipping center for disposition and processing. Once shipped, inform the customer by e-mail and drop the invoice into the accounting system.

■ From within a server transaction that backs an intranet application, print electronic forms that serve as legal documents to a printer beside a clerk's web terminal. Data must be transmitted as raw data through low-bandwidth wide area networks (WANs) and merged into predefined document templates near the physical printer. If printing fails, it must be resumed independently of printer queues, possibly on another device. If recovery is impossible, the transaction must be effectively annulled by using a compensating transaction back at the server.

▲ The new sales director has found out that your organization's divisions use four different Customer Relationship Management (CRM) systems. According to the sales director, "Sharing all customer information between all of them shouldn't be that hard. In fact, we're going to reorganize so that we'll distribute the common administrative tasks across the units to focus and save cost—and then we move the case back to the appropriate unit for further handling. I guess you guys call that workflow management." Yes, we do. Sigh!

What do all these scenarios have in common? (The list could go on forever!) They are realistic business problems that require integrative solutions somewhere in the open space between standard software packages. Most of the main functionality will likely be available in one of the products that your organization is already using, but the complete business solution requires custom code that serves as a bridge between those products or performs the additional processing that just cannot be found in any of the off-the-shelf solutions.

Many of these custom solutions involve the parsing of custom data formats that the integrated applications read or write. Or the solutions might involve some sort of X12, UN/EDIFACT, SWIFT, or other common EDI format. While some prebuilt parsing and formatting solutions exist as libraries or components for the more popular formats, the integration code to pass that data between applications is still "hand made."

If you are a developer, you may say, "Code pays my bills: code is good." In reality, all the plumbing in the wasteland between line-of-business applications is not much fun, is very expensive to maintain, and, after all, is not why you became a developer in the first place. There must be about 15,436 different custom-built parsers to import bank account statements into accounting packages—times 1,000 different sources for bugs.

Likewise, a few dozen bridges exist for every software product that spits out any meaningful data that can be fed into SAP R/3 or other Enterprise Resource Planning (ERP) systems. And an army of developers does nothing but struggle to keep these bridging solutions barely synchronized with business requirements.

All integration scenarios include some standard line-of-business applications and a bunch of data formats that carry data between these applications. On top of it all, half of the applications run in your own organization and the others run at trading partner firms. If you look closely, you will discover that the poster argument for object broker systems—enabling tight integration between systems where two applications maintain a very chatty, object-based, continuous hot link—is just not the case in most integration scenarios. Most applications do have distinct import and export interfaces and allow data to be exported only in a certain, consistent state. In addition, most applications just do not feature the type of extensibility that would allow such tight integration; and if they would, the result would quite likely be a monolithic maintenance nightmare. Data is really exchanged between applications and partners in large, consistent chunks—electronic documents.

The systems integration niche is where BizTalk fits in perfectly. BizTalk Server is both an enterprise application integration (EAI) solution to serve as a bridge between business applications and an EDI package to create electronic document communication between partners.

BIZTALK SERVER EDITIONS

BizTalk Server 2000 comes in three flavors. The Enterprise and Developer editions differ only in price and in their license policies. (The Developer version is only for development—go figure.) They both provide unrestricted versions of the products. On the other hand, the Standard Edition supports only a single processor and is restricted to five applications and five external partners. This book makes no general distinction between the three editions. If a certain passage does not apply to the Standard Edition, a note will clearly state this.

Also note the price differences. At the time of product release, the standalone Developer Edition cost U.S.$500, but it also ships automatically through the Microsoft Developer Network's MSDN Professional subscription; the Standard Edition cost U.S.$5,000; and the Enterprise Edition has a Microsoft record price tag of U.S.$25,000 per CPU. These figures are estimated retail prices for the standalone shrink-wrapped box. Expect considerable price breaks for more CPUs or if you are enrolled in a Microsoft volume-licensing program. If you compare these prices to the closest competitors, however, even the Enterprise Edition is a bargain. Competing products easily cost $250 thousand or more.

What's in the Box?

Microsoft BizTalk Server 2000 is actually two servers in one.

First, the BizTalk box contains the BizTalk Messaging Service that is capable of parsing, translating, and routing electronic documents in XML, EDIFACT, X12, and certain flat text-file formats. The software development kit (SDK) portion of the product contains all the necessary libraries and header files to create extensions to parse and write any other data formats.

The BizTalk Server Messaging Manager is the configuration tool for the messaging service. The Messaging Manager serves to create and maintain all messaging definitions and options: ports, channels, organizations and applications, envelopes, document definitions, and distributions lists. (Chapter 7 explores these subjects in more detail.)

The BizTalk Server Document Tracking tool is a web application that allows you to search the BizTalk document tracking database. Optionally, BizTalk keeps track of all routed documents and retains copies of documents in XML or native data formats. You can also track single data items contained in the documents to serve as search criteria within the document-tracking tool.

To supervise the operations of BizTalk Server's messaging service in a production environment, the BizTalk Server Administration tool extends the Microsoft Management Console (MMC). The administration component allows you to inspect and manage the BizTalk work queues and to change the settings for all BizTalk servers and server groups in the production unit.

BizTalk internally handles all documents—regardless of their native format—as XML data streams. The BizTalk Editor serves to create XML Data Reduced (XDR)-based BizTalk Schema specifications for XML documents and all other supported file formats. The document specifications that the Editor creates drive the parsing and serialization engines for EDI formats, and they are the basis for document mapping.

You use the BizTalk Mapper utility to create these mappings. The Mapper allows you to visually create conversion rules that translate any source document to any target document. Because document definitions may differ vastly and data fields rarely map one-to-one even for the same business case, the Mapper features so-called "functoids." Functoids use an intuitive drag-and-drop paradigm to concatenate, split, calculate, and group fields and even allow for intermediate database lookups.

The second server in BizTalk Server is the Orchestration engine.

BizTalk Orchestration is the universal glue for enterprise integration tasks. As you already learned, application integration typically requires a lot of custom code, which is expensive to write and even more costly to maintain. In addition, integration code is the most volatile. Because all links between the larger building blocks of an organization's IT infrastructure reflect the large-scale workflow that is at the heart of the business, all those connections are subject to continuous changes.

Also, these dataflow and workflow specifications may never suffer from translation errors—not the translation errors that are found in code, but the translation errors that occur between the business analysts and the developers. Integration tasks always result from very specific, large-scale business needs. Integration tasks require less design and implementation choices than a line-of-business application, in which many hundreds of detailed requirements must be organized in a software product.

The comparatively few requirements for application integration tasks are of utmost importance. A successful business depends on how purchase orders are received and confirmed, how and when they are submitted into the order pipelines, and how order processing is organized. Because integration is rapid change paired with vital business requirements, business analysts and developers must be able to speak a common language to achieve the desired turnaround times with successful results.

The BizTalk Orchestration language is a simplistic, graphical means of expression for business workflow. A business analyst may not necessarily understand program codes, and developers can easily misinterpret nuances of plain-text descriptions because they lack the necessary business background. Therefore, this language combines ease-of-use and logical expressiveness so that both analysts and developers can understand it. Compared to specialized workflow packages, the BizTalk Orchestration language indeed lacks many of the bells and whistles. But it is still complete and, most importantly, simple— a strong advantage for the tasks at hand.

The BizTalk Orchestration Designer creates *Orchestration schedules*. (That's the BizTalk terminology for workflow definitions.) The Orchestration Designer is an application on top of Microsoft Visio 2000. It requires Visio Service Release 1 (SR-1) to be installed on the machine before the designer can install the BizTalk tools. The Orchestration language, which is discussed in detail in Chapter 9, is a collection of simple Visio shapes contained in two *stencils*. (That's the Visio term for a collection of shapes.)

One stencil contains the flow-control elements that the business analyst uses to describe the requirements and draw the grand picture of the application flow. The other stencil contains shapes that enable the developer to bind the elements of the application flow to messaging ports, scripts, or components. Dataflow and transaction behavior is specified on separate drawing pages. Once the definition of an Orchestration schedule is complete, it is compiled into XLANG, an XML-based workflow definition language that drives the Orchestration engine.

The Orchestration engine itself is a COM+ application. This is an important distinction from the messaging service. You will not find the Orchestration engine listed as a Windows 2000 service. (There is an XLANG Schedule Restart Service, but that is not the engine itself.) There is no way and no reason to explicitly start the engine. You can find limited XLANG engine configuration and control options on the XLANG property page of the XLANG scheduler package. (Go to the COM+ Applications branch of the Component Services MMC snap-in that is included with Windows 2000.)

So how are schedules started and administered? Chapters 8 and 11 explore the component nature of schedules and show that they are really not standalone entities; rather, they are building blocks that you can use from within applications or other schedules.

Overall, BizTalk shows more characteristics of a huge integration toolset for intercompany document messaging and application and service orchestration than a standalone server product that is instantly useful, such as Exchange Server. Therefore, and because of the required background knowledge for a whole range of functionality, BizTalk doesn't lend itself well for trial-and-error exploration. The learning curve is steep, but fortunately, short.

INSTALLING BIZTALK SERVER

Many of the explanations and most of the examples throughout this book assume that you have the Developer, Enterprise, or Evaluation Edition of BizTalk Server 2000 installed. All three editions are essentially identical. The limitations of the Standard Edition make it a (significantly) cheaper option for small deployments, but one of the "big" editions is certainly better to learn about the product. The BizTalk Evaluation Edition is available from Microsoft for a nominal charge as a CD copy (or as a free download from the BizTalk product web site) and will time out 120 days after installation. The Developer Edition ships through the Microsoft Developer Network subscription program and can also be separately purchased through the usual Microsoft distribution channels.

Installing a complete development and evaluation configuration for BizTalk Server 2000 is pleasantly easy. Much later in this book, in Chapters 19 and 20, we will look at more advanced installation and deployment options for production systems, but to get started, a full installation onto a local server machine is the best choice.

Preinstallation Tasks

For a development machine, you should have a minimum of 256MB of RAM on at least a single-processor Pentium II 400 machine. While developing and testing the samples for this book, this minimum configuration was found to be useable. BizTalk requires some 70MB of hard disk real estate, including the SQL Server databases, but you should leave ample room for the databases to grow.

BizTalk Server 2000 must be run on the Windows 2000 operating system with Service Pack 1 applied. Although BizTalk will run on Windows 2000 Professional, you are unlikely to use the desktop edition in a production environment; hence, it is advisable to install the product on one of the Windows server editions. The operating system must be installed onto an NT File System (NTFS) partition (to ensure proper file system security settings). Additional components for Windows 2000 that must be installed are Internet Information Services, including the WWW service and Microsoft Message Queue. For a standalone installation, you should not integrate the local message-queue service with a Windows 2000 domain; rather, configure it as a standalone server.

Once you have installed Windows 2000 and the service pack, you must install Microsoft SQL Server 7.0 or Microsoft SQL Server 2000 on the development machine. Microsoft SQL Server 2000 is the preferred choice, but both products will work. Although you can (and will later) use a remote SQL server for BizTalk, keeping the databases local will prevent you and your colleagues who share the same server from "accidentally" setting up a BizTalk Server cluster while evaluating the product or developing solutions for it.

Install SQL Server with binary sort order for the master database, and set the security settings for SQL Server to Mixed or SQL Server. Mixed means that the database server should allow both Windows 2000–integrated security and SQL Server security with direct authentication at the database. BizTalk services use only SQL Server authentication. You need not consider any other special options for the database beyond this.

The next prerequisite for a developer installation is Microsoft Visio 2000 SR-1. Visio is required for the BizTalk Orchestration Designer tool. If you do not install Visio before installing BizTalk, you can still install the server and use the entire messaging portion, but you will not be able to create or edit BizTalk Orchestration workflow drawings (schedules) until you add Visio 2000 SR-1 to the machine.

You may optionally install Microsoft Exchange Server 2000 if you want to test or develop for SMTP transports via Microsoft Exchange. However, if you want to coinstall Exchange onto the same machine, you should add another 128MB–256MB of RAM and a faster processor.

Installing the Server

Once you have installed all the prerequisites, the setup procedure for BizTalk typically requires you to simply accept the defaults of the setup wizard. Installation begins, of course, by invoking setup.exe from the BizTalk installation CD. To ensure successful installation, you must be logged on with an administrator account for the local machine. Once the installation process begins, you will be greeted by the BizTalk 2000 Setup Wizard's Welcome page (see Figure 5-1).

On the lower lefthand side of the page, click the View Installation Guide button, which provides the installation instructions for your BizTalk edition and discusses possible issues with your particular machine's installation or environment. Be sure to take the time to read through the instructions. The following procedure is basically just a summary of what you will learn there.

Now click the Next button (as you will do on all following pages as well). You must agree with the license terms for BizTalk Server (Figure 5-2) and enter your personal information and the BizTalk product key (Figure 5-3).

Depending on your BizTalk edition and distribution channel, the product key may be printed on the CD or on your license certificate, or it may be located in a file. Without a product key, you will not be able to install the product. Microsoft's product keys are printed with capital letters, but they are actually not case sensitive. The input cursor will also hop automatically between the five edit boxes, so you can just type through. Leave the Install This Application For option at the default setting Anyone Who Uses This Computer; otherwise, you may run into security and profile issues later.

Figure 5-1.   The BizTalk 2000 Server Setup Wizard Welcome page

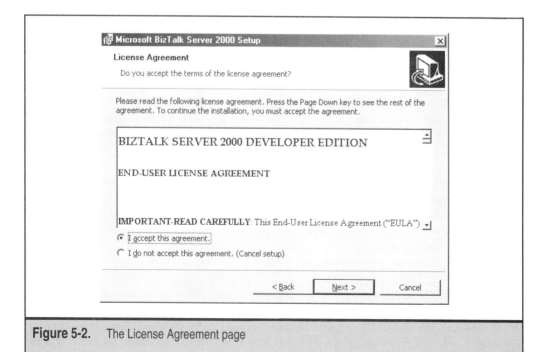

Figure 5-2.   The License Agreement page

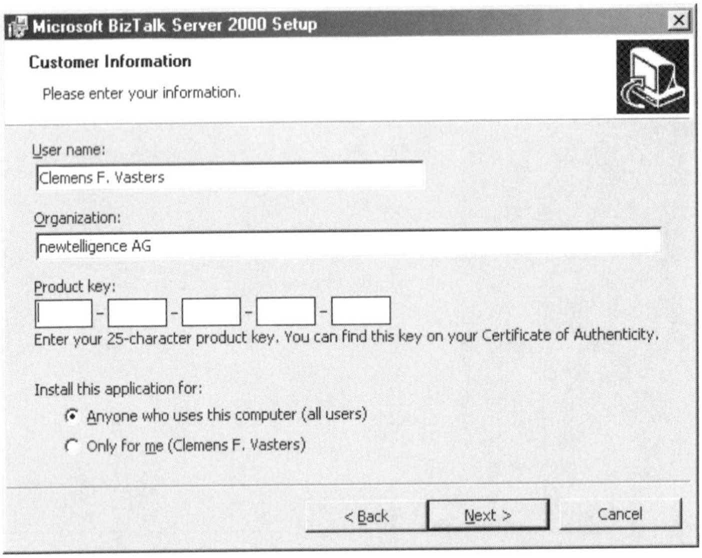

Figure 5-3. The Customer Information page

By default, BizTalk will be installed in the Program Files folder of your local Windows 2000 installation (see Figure 5-4). The folder must be on a local hard disk and must reside on an NTFS drive; otherwise, the installation won't be able to apply proper security settings.

On the next page, the wizard will prompt for the installation type, as shown in Figure 5-5. You can choose between a Complete install, a Tools install, which will not install the server components, or a Custom install, which will allow you to install the server without the development tools. (You would use this setting for a production system.) For a development installation, leave the setting at Complete and proceed.

The next page (shown in Figure 5-6) serves to create a new local group for BizTalk Server administrators to which the local administrators group and the user account of the configuring user will be added. You can leave this setting alone and proceed. (Or, of course, rename the group if you have certain naming rules in your organization.)

On the following page (shown in Figure 5-7), you configure the account under which the BizTalk Messaging Service will be installed. The default is Local System Account. This is indeed the best choice for a development installation. When you need to tighten security for a production deployment, you will probably want to create a special service account with fine-tuned access rights and its own Public Key Infrastructure (PKI) certificate store.

When you choose a custom installation, you will be able to select from the list of components on the Ready To Install the Program page. For the Complete or Tools installation

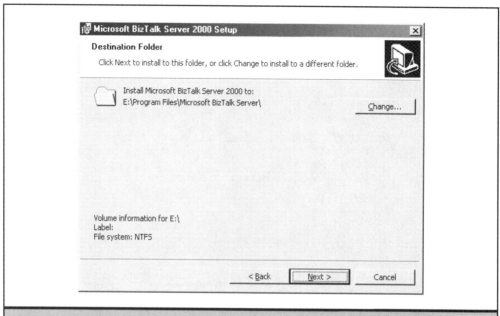

Figure 5-4. The Destination Folder page

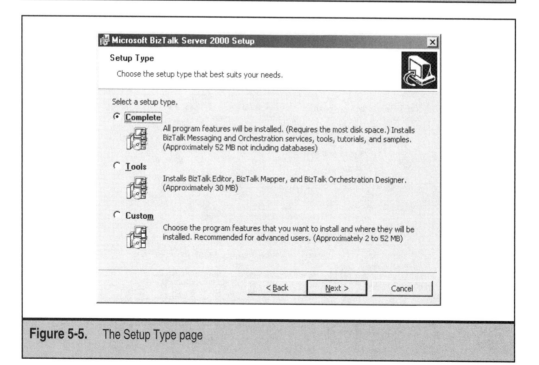

Figure 5-5. The Setup Type page

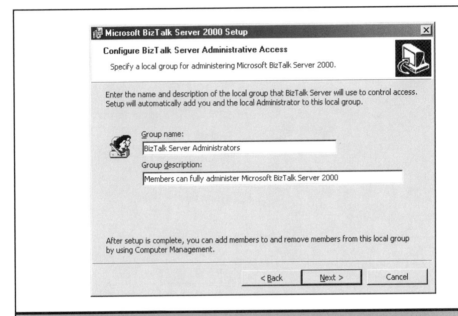

Figure 5-6. The Configure BizTalk Server Administrative Access page

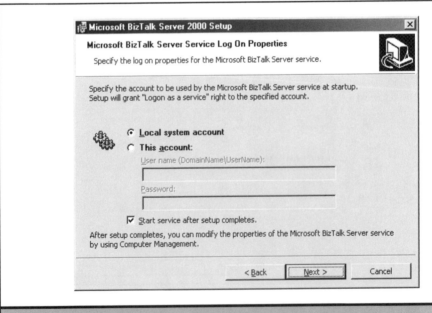

Figure 5-7. The Microsoft BizTalk Server Service Log On Properties page

options, the tree view will be dimmed, as shown in Figure 5-8. That's fine for now. Shut down all applications, including COM+ packages. Then click the Install button to start the installation (see Figure 5-9).

While BizTalk is installing, don't do anything else on the machine. The installer will not only install quite a few files, but it will also make considerable changes to the registry, the COM+ registration database, and the Windows Management Instrumentation (WMI) configuration. Especially when scripts are run against the WMI services, you do not want any collisions to happen because the installer cannot recover from them.

Once the installation of the BizTalk run-time components is complete, the Messaging Database Setup Wizard will appear. Here, you will create and configure the BizTalk management, document tracking, and shared queue databases. You will learn about all three databases in detail later in this book, in Chapter 11. Just accept the default settings here (see Figure 5-10).

A BizTalk server stores all configuration data in the management database. To avoid conflicts with configuration settings of other BizTalk installations that may exist within your local network, don't use an existing database at this point. Instead, choose to install a new database, as shown in Figure 5-11. If you have been running the BizTalk Server 2000 Beta release, and databases by the same name still exist on your system, you must remove them completely from SQL Server (using SQL Server Enterprise Manager) before you proceed. There is no upgrade path between the BizTalk Server Beta release and the production version.

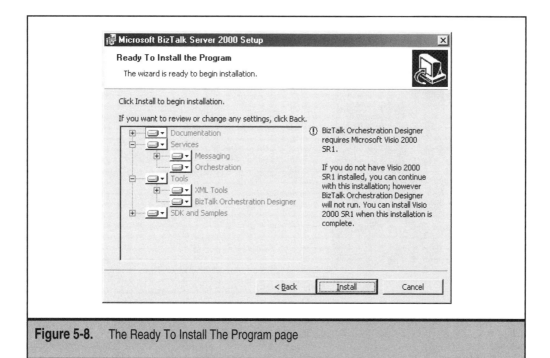

Figure 5-8.   The Ready To Install The Program page

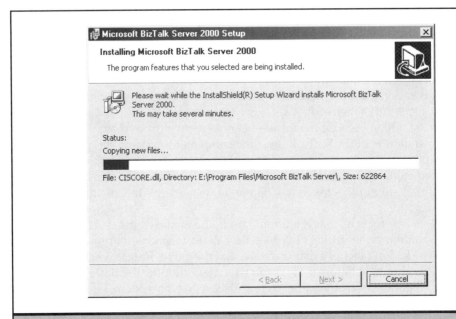

Figure 5-9. The Installing Microsoft BizTalk Server 2000 page

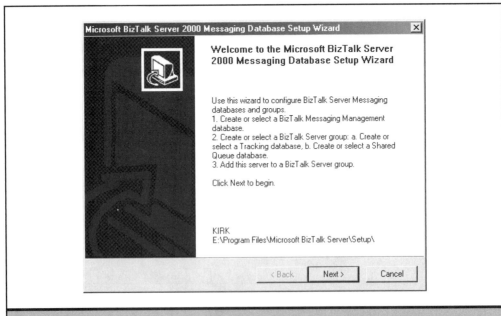

Figure 5-10. The BizTalk 2000 Messaging Database Setup Wizard Welcome page

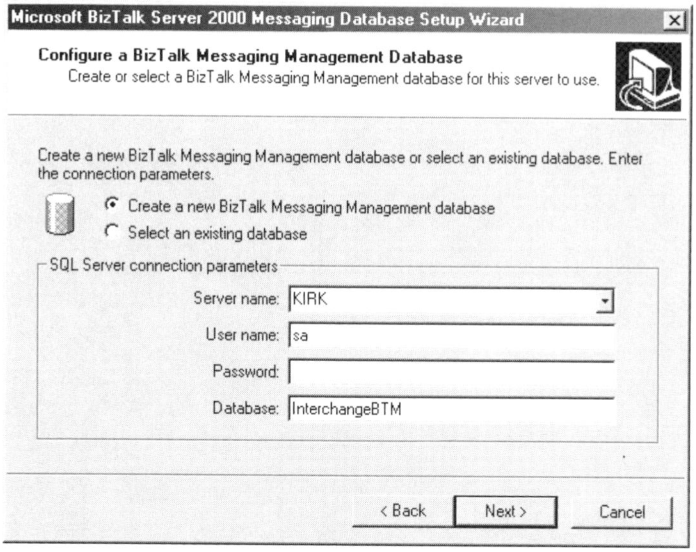

Figure 5-11.   The Configure A BizTalk Messaging Management Database page

On the next page (Figure 5-12), leave the default Create A New BizTalk Server Group. BizTalk Server groups are objects that reside in the management database and are not related to local groups or even Active Directory groups in Windows 2000. A server group is a clustered installation of BizTalk servers that concurrently and cooperatively work on the same data.

BizTalk records all incoming and outgoing traffic in the document tracking database. This database grows the most in a production BizTalk installation. Depending on how many documents are processed, you may easily and quickly stack up a couple of gigabytes in data in the document tracking database on high-volume systems. BizTalk is serious about logging every single detail of every single interchange. On a development system, the document tracking database will hardly ever exceed 50–100MB. Create a new document tracking database here and proceed (see Figure 5-13).

In the shared queue database, BizTalk Server stores all documents that wait to be processed, documents that wait for a processing retry, or those documents whose processing has been suspended due to errors. Again, you should create a new database as shown in Figure 5-14, and proceed.

The final two pages of this wizard let you review what you just have done and give you the opportunity to go back and make changes. Click Next on the Verify BizTalk Server Group page (see Figure 5-15); click Finish on the following page (Figure 5-16) to complete the messaging database configuration and enter the Orchestration Persistence Database Setup Wizard.

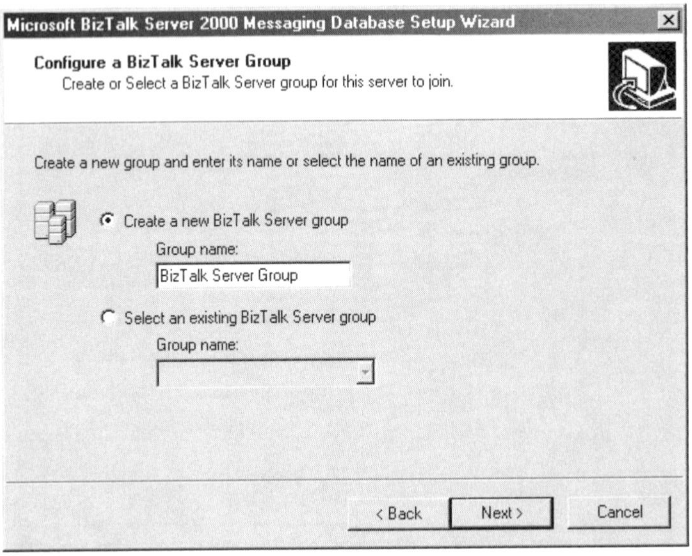

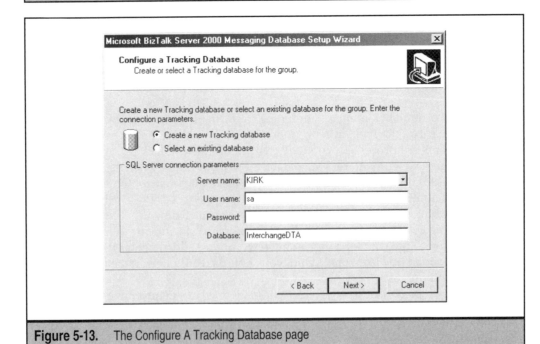

Figure 5-12.   The Configure A BizTalk Server Group page

Figure 5-13.   The Configure A Tracking Database page

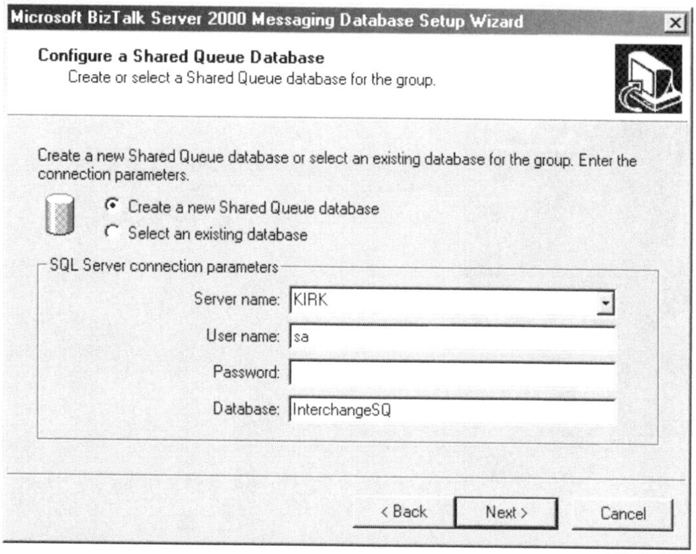

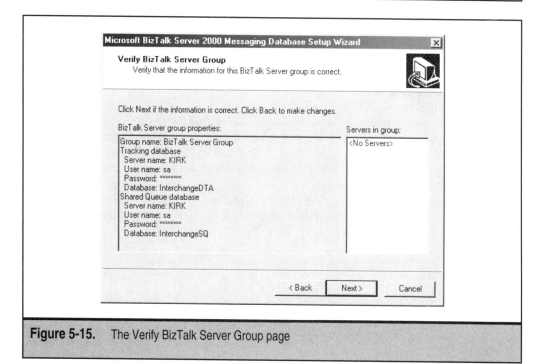

Figure 5-14.   The Configure A Shared Queue Database page

Figure 5-15.   The Verify BizTalk Server Group page

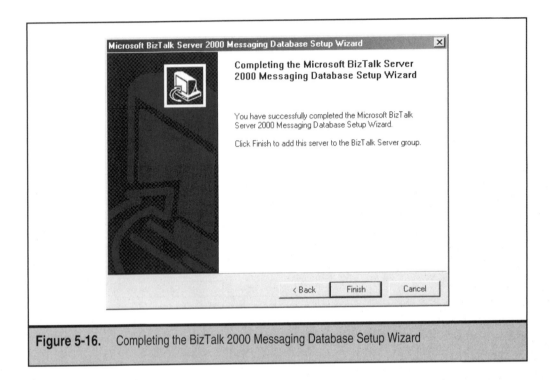

Figure 5-16. Completing the BizTalk 2000 Messaging Database Setup Wizard

The Orchestration Persistence Database Setup Wizard, of which Figure 5-17 shows the only important page of a three-page sequence, creates a new database where Orchestration schedules will store their runtime state. Later, we will explore what this means. For now, just accept the defaults.

Once you are done with this installation step, you will be returned to the main setup wizard. Click Finish to complete the installation of BizTalk Server.

All BizTalk tools will be in the Microsoft BizTalk Server 2000 program group on the Start menu. Although you may be tempted to start poking around in the product immediately, it would be better to continue reading the basics up through Chapter 12. If you want to work through the tutorial that ships with BizTalk, the background information provided in the following chapters will greatly enhance your understanding. The tutorial only guides you through the configuration steps keypress by keypress. It does not provide much of the background on the way.

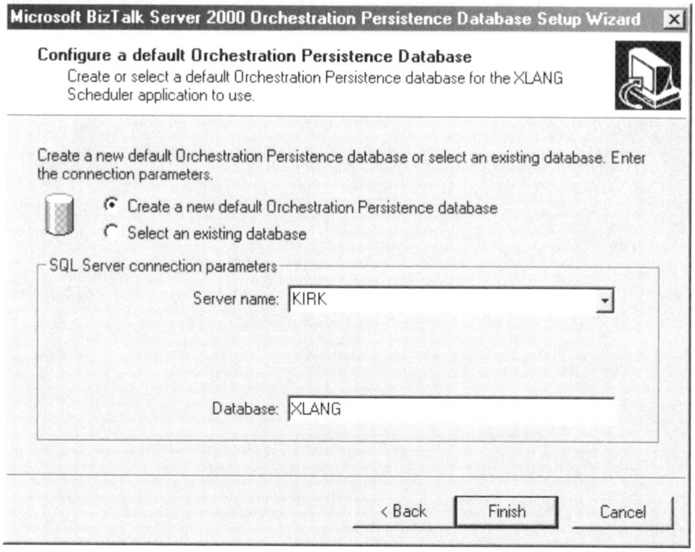

Figure 5-17.   The Configure A Default Orchestration Persistence Database page

CHAPTER 6

BizTalk Ideas and Concepts

This chapter introduces some fundamental BizTalk ideas and concepts, such as the BizTalk Framework and the BizTalk.org community.

Another important concept that this chapter covers is BizTalk's *document-driven* development model and run-time behavior. This paradigm is new for most developers. Business applications are typically interactive and react to user activities. However, BizTalk solutions will probably never interact with users directly; instead, users will receive documents from an application to be processed and forwarded to yet another application either within the same company or at another organization.

This chapter also discusses BizTalk Orchestration's potential to allow for rapid adaptation to changing business needs and short turnaround times when your solutions need to be adjusted to new processes. This allows BizTalk to create more efficient integration solutions. To leverage that power, you need to know how and where to draw the line between programming and Orchestration; you also need to know when to use your own code to import and parse formats down to the last bit and when to use the more generic BizTalk extensibility approach.

The BizTalk vision is indeed greater than the server product itself. More than a year before the product launch, Microsoft created the BizTalk.org community as a meeting point for developers to jointly create and exchange schema or to discuss BizTalk and schema-related issues. The BizTalk Framework, also presented in this chapter, is already in its second major revision.

NOTE: Whenever the BizTalk Framework is mentioned here or in later chapters, the discussed version release is always the BizTalk Framework Specification 2.0. The predecessor version 1.0 was published quite a while before the BizTalk product release and was only supported in early pre-release versions of BizTalk Server.

DOCUMENT-DRIVEN SYSTEMS

Electronic documents are used to eventually replace most formal and informal paper-based text communication, including faxes and even e-mail. The disadvantage these media share is that their content is either not machine-readable or, if it is, it's not formalized enough to allow automatic processing. But consider the impact on software design if business documents like invoices, orders, or bank transfers could be digitally exchanged between virtually all businesses and had the same legal status as their paper equivalents.

Consider the software systems you and your clients use. Most likely, the primary function of the user interface is to transfer information from paper or from some free-form document media into the system and to collect and assemble information to be ultimately output on paper. This means that systems are user-driven. Most software acts and reacts only to user input and interaction and otherwise plays dead. Even interactive e-commerce systems are the same in this respect; in this case, the clients do the work to enter data into your system. Just as your clients do that for you, you do it for other companies as well. It all balances out somehow.

Consequently, software development is generally user-interface centric. In that context, it does not matter whether you create desktop or client/server applications by using Visual Basic or web-server applications by using Active Server Pages (ASP), the all new Microsoft .NET implementation of ASP, called ASP.NET, or PHP.

Building BizTalk solutions is different. BizTalk Server acts in the background, receives electronic documents either from external sources or internal applications, scans them for information, and uses this information to route them to specific recipients or to select an appropriate business process to initiate. If businesses use BizTalk to exchange their formal documents by using EDI or XML, the efficiency gains are automatic—no paper, no manual input, and no transfer errors (typos!) in the process.

This is not restricted to business-to-business exchange, though. Take the e-commerce poster example of the Internet-enabled refrigerator. You decide that you always want to have a liter of milk (about two pints for the metric-challenged), and you tell the fridge. Using some smart mechanism that we won't go into here, the fridge knows how much milk you currently have and when you are close to using up your milk (or when the milk is about to go bad). Being a clever "iFridge," it talks to the "iShelf" and collects everything that needs to be replaced or refilled, creates an electronic order, and sends it off to your favorite e-grocery. There, the electronic order is picked up. A robot hunts through the high storage to get the ordered items and bundles everything for delivery after the purchase has been debited from your customer account. Of course, if an article hits its reorder threshold by that order, the supplier for that article receives an immediate purchase order to prevent it from going out of stock.

The first human being to see that order is the delivery boy; the second person is you. In this process—which actually somewhat mirrors corporate procurement processes on a smaller scale—interactive applications do not play any important role. The entire process is data-driven; more precisely, it is document-driven. The order that is automatically sent by your iFridge and signed on your behalf is just as much a formal purchase order document as one that is sent to order a two ton steel-cast machine part.

BizTalk Server's Messaging services enable you to tap into the optimization potential of electronic document exchange on the Internet and within the enterprise. With HTTP and SMTP, BizTalk's Messaging services support the most popular Internet transport protocols; with message queuing (potentially bridged to IBM's MQSeries through Host Integration Server 2000), the services open the door to the most common enterprise data channels.

BizTalk's native support of X12 and UN/EDIFACT formats enables you to integrate your processes with the largest international corporations, and you can also leverage these established international standards for your own organization. The XML support gives you the highest flexibility for your own document definitions and the future XML-based successors of those EDI formats.

RAPID ADAPTATION AND SHORT TURNAROUND TIMES

Orchestration, BizTalk's universal glue for business process integration, is based on a visual programming language. The language is simple, and it's designed to be understood by both business analysts and developers.

The goal is that business analysts and developers can together define business processes exactly as the organization requires, thereby closing the communication gap that typically exists between the technology and business camps. This is essential to achieving quick and efficient results; time is indeed money if processes need to be newly defined or adjusted.

Essentially, Orchestration is the rapid application development (RAD) tool for business process integration. Just like you can quickly build interactive Windows or web applications by using Visual Basic, Visual InterDev, or the new VisualStudio.NET, Orchestration enables you to implement the data flow for document-driven business processes visually and equally as fast.

However, Orchestration does not stand alone. Because the focus is on dataflow and integration, the logic behind the business processes will mostly be found elsewhere. The key flexibility that you gain through Orchestration is that you can tie all of your current information resources into a workflow, and you can easily integrate new and customized business logic into the processing chain.

To achieve the desired efficiency gains from Orchestration, you must draw a clear line between business logic components and applications, which are programmed for high performance and reuse, and Orchestration, which allows you to group and regroup these components and applications quickly to shape the dataflow as required. You must weigh the speed of delivering solutions against the overall performance and depth of functionality.

Orchestration is not designed as a universal programming language or solution framework, it is designed for dynamic change and easy deployment. The nature of Orchestration schedules is essentially different from business code, which implements fundamental, logical building blocks. Code is typically implemented by highly qualified personnel or external consultants who use efficient programming languages. The rules for creating invoices, handling corporate accounting, and calculating rebates on volume purchase orders are fundamental and subject to only infrequent, incremental changes.

However, the processes that coordinate the execution of special promotions or special bundling deals of a company's own products with products of cooperating business partners are highly volatile. They may allow for only a few days of preparation time, and they may last for only a few weeks. Orchestration enables businesses to arrange their systems' fundamental processing tools to suit their needs without having to resort to the complexity of traditional programming tools.

In addition, Orchestration is also an answer to the developer crisis. Information technology is one of the most vital building blocks for any business' success. Well-trained developers who master complex technology and who have a good grasp of the business cases at hand are a scarce resource with natural limitations. Organizations across all industries and branches have literally millions of open positions around the globe—many of these highly specialized positions will never be filled. Developers can pick and choose jobs at will. Most developers do not enjoy creating the 1,000[th] variant of a data import parser or export serializer, nor do they like recoding the sequence of when and how systems are tied together; thus, these tasks are not very attractive unless they come with extreme salaries.

A clear distinction is needed between development tasks that require masters of computer science to build reusable components and those that require people who can assemble such components into solutions for business. Orchestration is a step in this direction. The intentional programming paradigm that you will see in future Microsoft development products is another one. Intentional programming (currently in the product development stage and of which little is known publicly at this time), will allow you to develop applications visually and express what solution you need (stating intent) rather than writing code on a technical level as it is done today.

When you design BizTalk Orchestration solutions, you should make very conscious decisions about component use and reuse. Chapter 13 drills down a bit more on these analysis tasks and discusses how to make such decisions.

THE BIZTALK COMMUNITY—BIZTALK.ORG

Chapter 2 already discussed the significance of document standardization. Products like BizTalk that are built to exchange electronic documents are nearly useless if the shape and structure of the data to be exchanged between partners does not conform to accepted standards. BizTalk has great potential to rapidly integrate new partners and quickly react to changes in communication for established partner relationships; however, it can be leveraged to the maximum extent only if integration is not synonymous with the invention of new document definitions for all peers and any exchange task. While BizTalk is indeed flexible enough to manage such a multitude of formats and would still provide striking advantages over most other approaches in such a scenario, standards ultimately mean less work and, thus, faster solution implementation.

Therefore, standardization is clearly desirable for any type of formal business document exchange. The most common and most obvious documents such as purchase orders, invoices, or shipping advices are standardized in UN/EDIFACT and X12. The BizTalk Server repository includes ready-to-use templates for such documents. Most industries dominated by large corporations and heavily dependent on information exchange, such as health care, banking, or utility companies, also have a vast range of standardized EDI documents for their respective fields. However, all of these standards capture only the most common cases. If you want to exchange highly specialized information or provide services that are not covered by any of the major standards, you are likely caught in a gray zone of proprietary document formats.

This situation is even more complicated when every company that works in such a field considers themselves a pioneer and therefore claims to be the one and only candidate to set the standards for their domain. For example, financial collections is a very important but somewhat unpopular financial services area. If you need to submit or even sell a case of an unpaid, overdue invoice to a financial collections services bureau, you would need to provide a lot of information, such as the history of the customer's addresses. While thousands of such collection bureaus exist everywhere and they are an essential part of the economy (an average of 3–5 percent of all invoices are left unpaid, depending on the industry), no standard method exists to transfer this information between clients and providers.

As a result, IT providers start setting their own standards bound to their own solutions and try to use that as a means to stand above the competition. However, this doesn't really help the service bureaus or the clients. Service bureaus are interested in being able to instantly sign up clients to their services, without having to adopt the formats of their own IT suppliers. Likewise, clients are interested in choosing the service provider with the highest collection return and best collection fees, without having to worry about the technical ability to work with their selected best choice. Setting such data exchange standards should not be left to a single technology solution provider even if they have a dominant market position: it's a matter of industry consensus. Solution providers implement standards; they do not set them single-handedly. The IT industry, most prominently Microsoft, has learned that this rule applies to document standards just as much as it applies to technology standards.

But creating actual standards for an industry by consensus is difficult. Some fields do not have enough technology-minded associations that could help set such standards on an international scale. Or they are haggling over standards forever so that the standards are hopelessly outdated before they are even released. Meanwhile, their member companies are left out in the cold without a solution. Other companies are recognizing the power of XML and find the established EDI standards to be too limited to leverage its full potential.

BizTalk.org is a meeting place on the Web for companies that want to share or codevelop document definitions for their businesses. The site is not designed for hard-core developers who want to get into the details of BizTalk Server. The focus is to provide a forum that complements BizTalk Server in allowing companies to define a lingua franca for their fields. The document definitions exchanged in the BizTalk.org schema repository are also not necessarily bound to BizTalk Server.

THE BIZTALK FRAMEWORK

BizTalk.org is actually part of a larger initiative: the BizTalk Framework. The BizTalk Framework encompasses the BizTalk.org web site with its schema repository, the BizTalk Framework Specification discussed in this section, and the BizTalk Framework Toolkit, which provides a toolset to implement BizTalk Framework compliant (BFC) services.

As you may have noticed in the discussion about data formats in Chapter 3, XML is rich in its syntactic and structural rules, which are far beyond any of the EDI formats. On the other hand, X12, UN/EDIFACT, and SWIFT contain precise routing information for the contained payload. XML, however, is missing the equivalent standards constructs because it is designed as a general-purpose data format. All of the additional XML specifications are of the same generic nature. The agility of XML data and a standardized packaging mechanism that wraps XML for transport have been addressed only recently, with the publication of the joint Simple Object Access Protocol (SOAP) specification by UserLand Software, DevelopMentor, Microsoft, Lotus, IBM, and others. This protocol serves as the basis for the W3C XML Protocol workgroup, which aims to lift SOAP to a W3C-recommended standard.

SOAP is a simple transport wrapper expressed in XML. It defines an envelope that encloses one or more arbitrary XML documents. You can also specify an arbitrary number of optional or mandatory headers that narrow the purpose and transport rules for the message. As you would expect—and just like the other specifications from the XML technology set—SOAP is very generic. You can use compliant messages either for remote procedure calls (RPCs), like you do in the Microsoft .NET Framework, or for asynchronous messaging. With its fitness for messaging, SOAP is a base technology candidate for electronic document exchange, but it still lacks most fundamental rules such as routing, content description, and support for attachments, among others. The BizTalk Framework aims to provide this support.

The BizTalk Framework 2.0 is an application of SOAP. The Framework uses SOAP's extensibility mechanisms to define additional headers that contain all properties and routing information to enable electronic document exchange using XML. Therefore, BizTalk Framework complements the XML standards to create EDI-equivalent functionality. The relationship of the BizTalk Framework to XML is similar to the relationship of the X12 or UN/EDIFACT structural rules for interchanges and functional groups to X12 transaction sets or UN/EDIFACT messages and all their nested elements. In X12 terms, the BizTalk Framework defines what interchanges and functional groups are, while XML XDR Schema describes transaction sets and all elements nested within.

BizTalk Server 2000 is a BizTalk Framework compliant (BFC) server that implements the BizTalk Framework specification. Microsoft published version 2.0 of this specification on the day of BizTalk Server's release to manufacturing. Microsoft explicitly grants every interested party a "…perpetual, nonexclusive, royalty-free, worldwide right and license…to copy, publish and distribute the Specification. Microsoft further agrees to grant to users a royalty-free license…to implement and use the BizTalk Framework XML tags and schema guidelines included in the Specification for the purpose of creating computer programs that adhere to such guidelines…." In essence, Microsoft invites any interested party to implement BizTalk-compliant servers that can exist and actually compete alongside BizTalk Server.

The Simple Object Access Protocol

SOAP is a simple protocol that explains how XML messages are exchanged between endpoints. Simply put: If XML is a letter, SOAP is the envelope.

The SOAP message in Listing 6-1 shows all fundamental elements of a message. The namespace qualifier for the SOAP elements is "http://schemas.xmlsoap.org/soap/envelope". This qualifier unambiguously identifies SOAP messages that are compliant with the specification version 1.1. SOAP does not employ a traditional versioning scheme; if the namespace qualifier is different, the message is not compliant and may not be accepted by a SOAP 1.1 endpoint.

```
<SOAP:Envelope xmlns:SOAP="http://schemas.xmlsoap.org/soap/envelope">
   <SOAP:Header>
      <dsc:description xmlns:dsc="urn:schemas-newtelligence-com:schemas:dsc"
                     SOAP:mustUnderstand="0">
         <dsc:text>This is a sample SOAP message</dsc:text>
      </dsc:description>
   </SOAP:Header>
   <SOAP:Body encodingStyle="http://schemas.xmlsoap.org/soap/encoding">
      <m:CustomerSignup xmlns:m="urn:schemas-newtelligence-com:schemas:mymsg">
         <NewCustomer>
               <Name>Ben Grenfield</Name>
               <Street>8832 Westershire Rd.</Street>
               <City>London</City>
               <PostalCode>AD7KC</PostalCode>
               <Country>UK</Country>
         </NewCustomer>
      </m:CustomerSignup>
   </SOAP:Body>
</SOAP:Envelope>
```

Listing 6-1: A Sample SOAP message

Any SOAP message is rooted at the <Envelope> element, which contains, at most, two other immediate child elements: an optional <Header> element and the mandatory <Body> element.

The <Header> element can contain any number of user-defined headers, all of which must be uniquely namespace-qualified. The SOAP attribute *mustUnderstand* specifies whether such a header must be understood by the remote endpoint (value 1) or whether the header has to be only optionally recognized (value 0). Another attribute for headers, which is not shown in the example, is the *actor* attribute. Potential actors in SOAP terms are all intermediate message destinations along the route or the ultimate destination of the message. The *actor* attribute allows you to specify handling instructions for SOAP-aware firewalls or other preprocessors that need to inspect the message before it reaches its ultimate destination.

The required SOAP <Body> element contains the message payload. The payload should be (but does not have to be) namespace-qualified. (This is why all other elements must be namespace-qualified: to leave the default namespace to the body message.) Table 6-1 lists all SOAP elements.

Element	Parent	Contains	Order	Function
Envelope	None	Header, Body	1	Wraps the entire message and qualifies it as SOAP-compliant.
Header	Envelope	Custom header elements; must all be uniquely namespace-qualified. Headers may contain a *mustUnderstand* attribute. A value of 1 indicates that processing *must* fail if the header is not understood. Headers may contain an *actor* attribute with a URI value or the reserved value *next*, identifying the intermediate actor to process this header.	0 or 1	Wraps all custom headers that contain processing hints and description for the body content.

Table 6-1. SOAP Elements

Element	Parent	Contains	Order	Function
Body	Envelope	Message payload; optionally namespace-qualified. Elements immediately below may have the SOAP encoding attribute *root* that identifies them either as an independent (value 1) or dependent (value 0) entity, according to SOAP encoding rules. Elements at any level may contain the SOAP *encodingStyle* attribute identifying the data encoding used. If the message relays a fault, the Fault element is the only permitted content.	1	Wraps message content.
Fault	Body	faultcode, faultstring, faultactor and detail elements only.	0 or 1	Relays processing faults back to the sender.
faultcode	Fault	Machine-readable error code in text form. Prefixed with Client., Server., or MustUnderstand., depending on error source.	1	Describes the reason for the error using a machine-readable code. SOAP defines only categories, not specific error. Codes are therefore implementation-specific.
faultstring	Fault	Human-readable description for the error.	1	Describes the reason for the error in human-readable language.
faultactor	Fault	URI describing the actor that raised the error.	0 or 1	Identifies an intermediate actor that failed in processing this message.
detail	Fault	Custom XML data detailing the reason for the error.	0 or 1	Provides a container for relaying XML information regarding the error back to the caller.

Table 6-1. SOAP Elements *(continued)*

The body "payload" can be any arbitrary XML data stream. However, section 5 of the SOAP specification provides optional encoding rules for data and data types to ensure compatibility across SOAP implementations. Based on the data-type model of the W3C's XML Schema specification, it provides a range of simple types, and it defines how complex types like arrays and single- or multi-reference structures should be encoded. SOAP can support most data types used in today's programming languages and is therefore ideally suited to be used as a container for RPC messages. In fact, the SOAP 1.1 specification comes with an HTTP protocol binding for RPC purposes that allows it to use XML and HTTP as a technology and platform-agnostic means of executing direct program calls between applications across the Internet: web services.

The BizTalk message specification discussed in the next section implies that you could use SOAP encoding rules to eliminate redundancy when you send multiple business documents together within a single SOAP message. While this solution does make sense conceptually, it implies that such documents are separate entities based on a common schema that share an identical data-type model, which is rather unlikely in the real world. Therefore, we won't explore SOAP encoding here in any more depth (you can read more about the encoding rules in the SOAP specification at http://www.w3c.org/TR/SOAP). For the purpose of exchanging data electronically, the actual focus is therefore on creating and using a set of headers containing all necessary data and processing hints to route a message properly to its intended destination.

BizTalk Messages

The BizTalk Framework defines an infrastructure for electronic documents as an extension to SOAP 1.1. The message format basically mirrors the interchange and functional group definitions of X12 and UN/EDIFACT, but it also implements additional requirements such as arbitrary binary attachments. Before studying the syntactical elements of the format in detail, take a look at the key features:

▼ The message format is independent of the transport protocol used. It also makes no assumptions about the implementation platform. Transport bindings for the preferred Internet application protocols, HTTP and SMTP, are provided. BizTalk messages are always one way; the request/response rules as defined in the SOAP HTTP binding do not apply.

■ Origin and destination for a message are definable independent of any transport protocol. Instead, you can use business-related identifiers such as Dun & Bradstreet numbers to uniquely identify a destination organization.

■ You can group multiple documents into a single interchange to allow transmission of technically independent but—for the business case—related documents.

■ Each interchange has a unique identifier, allowing for an unambiguous retransmission in case of failures in transit.

■ Every interchange can have a well-defined lifetime after which it expires. This feature avoids conflicts and creates well-defined behavior for messages that become clogged up in message queues or are in some other way lost in transit.

■ You can attach binary, non-XML data to the messages. If a message is a car-insurance claim after an accident, for instance, you can attach photos of the damaged car.

■ Each interchange can carry a description that declares the contained documents with their related attachments.

■ The interchange or parts of the interchange can be digitally signed and/or encrypted.

■ You can request delivery and commitment receipts (the latter are approximately equivalent to read receipts for interactive messaging systems) and specify the location where such receipts must be sent and the timeframe in which the receipts must be returned. It is important to provide reliable messaging features with transports that do not reliably guarantee delivery, such as HTTP and SMTP.

▲ There is a standardized way of relaying the business process type and instance that produced the interchange so that it can be interpreted in the correct process context at the destination.

To provide the functionality outlined above, the BizTalk Framework 2.0 specification defines seven new SOAP headers, an enhanced HTTP binding for SOAP with support for attachments, and rules for how to sign and encrypt SOAP messages using the S/MIME (Secure Multipurpose Internet Mail Extensions) protocol, which you may know from secure e-mail.

Document Identification and Properties

All documents exchanged between peers must be uniquely identifiable. A unique identification tag serves several purposes. First, it can be used as a storage key in document repositories and archiving systems. Second, unique IDs for document instances ease the correlation of receipts with their original documents; they also guarantee only-once delivery rules by matching newly received document identifiers against those previously received and recorded. Because the identifier must be unique relative to the sender's and any potential receiver's domain, document identification tags must actually be universally unique.

If the unique identifier is to be used as tracking information in a database, a seemingly arbitrary binary number like a universally unique identifier (UUID) does provide a unique key, but that is not very descriptive in and of itself. The document identifier should therefore be grouped with an additional identifier qualifying the type and purpose of the document.

Just as important as a unique identification for each document is the creation date and the time when the document will expire and must no longer be processed. The expiration time is technically similar to the expiration time found on commercial offers. If you don't purchase the offered goods by a specified date, the offer is invalid. However, multiple concepts exist for expiration duration. If you send the commercial offer by mail, there is a certain timeout period, possibly set by the recipient, by which the offer must have arrived to be acknowledged. If you send it by certified mail with request for a return receipt (assume for a moment that this would make sense for an offer), there is a certain amount of time that you accept for the receipt to arrive before you start picking on your post office. The BizTalk message specification covers these types of expiration timeouts. This section looks at the first type: allowed transport duration.

In electronic document transfer, the transport duration is typically quite short. Latency of more than one hour, and sometimes even latency of less than a minute, often already indicate failure of some sort. By specifying expiration times, the document sender clearly indicates how much time he or she is willing to allocate for the message to be accepted at the destination. The expiration period should be reasonable enough to allow delivery even in an expected worst-case scenario. However, it should also be short enough so that even with unreliable transport protocols, the transmission can succeed within an acceptable timeframe by resending the information without colliding with previous attempts.

You must specify document identity and creation and expiration times for every BizTalk document by using the mandatory <properties> header (see Listing 6-2).

```
<prop:properties SOAP:mustUnderstand="1"
                 xmlns:prop="http://schemas.biztalk.org/btf-2-0/properties">
   <prop:identity>uuid:74b9f5d0-33fb-4a81-b02b-5b760641c1d6</prop:identity>
   <prop:sentAt>2000-05-14T03:00:00+08:00</prop:sentAt>
   <prop:expiresAt>2000-05-15T04:00:00+08:00</prop:expiresAt>
   <prop:topic>http://electrocommerce.org/purchase_order/</prop:topic>
</prop:properties>
```

Listing 6-2: The BizTalk <properties> header section sample

According to SOAP rules, the header is uniquely namespace-qualified with the URI "http://schemas.biztalk.org/btf-2-0/properties". (The uniqueness requirement explains why this and all other headers each have their own namespace and schema.) The elements of the <properties> header are further explained in the following table:

Tag Name	Cardinality	Required	Description
identity	1	yes	Unique document identifier. This is a URI specific to this document instance. This may actually be a path to a location, but it is much more likely a UUID or similarly unique number.

Tag Name	Cardinality	Required	Description
topic	1	yes	URI identifying the message topic. This is used in conjunction with the identity. The identity identifies and the topic classifies the document.
sentAt	1	yes	XML Schema (XSD) *timeInstant* type value, equivalent with ISO-8601–compliant date notation. Specifies the time when the document was sent. More specifically, it represents the exact time when the header was generated.
expiresAt	1	yes	XSD *timeInstant* representing the date and time when this document instance expires.

Document Source and Destination

Because every document has a sender and a receiver, BizTalk documents always have a mandatory header <endpoint> that declares the source and destination of the message. Considering that the message is sent through a physical channel that has some clearly identifiable endpoints like IP address and port, which are required for transmission to begin with, it seems odd to include such information in the business document while source and destination are already unambiguously stated in the transport layer.

Documents can be routed over multiple, intermediate routing servers, and the endpoints may indeed be located at a service provider's data center, which handles document traffic for many clients. In such a setting, an address scheme that uses any form of physical transport-dependent addressing is essentially useless. Any transport-dependent scheme also limits the usable endpoints to that specific protocol. But in fact, you may be able to use two or even more alternate data links between any two organizations, which use entirely different protocols and addressing schemes. You can use any of them interchangeably, based on availability or system load. Therefore, there must be a transport-*independent* means to identify both the sender and receiver.

Business logic frequently requires reliable and—under the best of all circumstances—constant identifiers for organizations. If your order-processing system must make exceptions for a certain customer based on specifically negotiated contractual conditions, you must be able to pinpoint that organization by name, Dun & Bradstreet number, or even by its International Air Transport Association (IATA) code—and not by something as obscure and volatile as an IP address or even an Internet Domain Name System (DNS) name that is, technically, only valid within the Internet space.

Consequently, the BizTalk headers to declare the endpoints for an interchange do not specify addresses in a technical sense. Instead, they define addresses strictly in a business sense either by using the clear-text name of the organization, or, much better, by using uniquely assigned numbers or identifiers given out by trade or industry associations, business registries, or even standardization institutions. Any of these numbers or tags is likely to be valid as long as the respective business and its trade organization exist—which should be sufficient to satisfy our requirement for such numbers being constant in a business process.

Listing 6-3 uses the German bank routing codes to identify source and destination.

```
<eps:endpoints SOAP:mustUnderstand="1"
         xmlns:xsi="http://www.w3.org/1999/XMLSchema-instance"
         xmlns:eps="http://schemas.biztalk.org/btf-2-0/endpoints"
         xmlns:blz="http://schemas.newtelligence.com/BLZ/">
    <eps:to>
       <eps:address xsi:type="blz:bankleitzahl">31260518</eps:address>
    </eps:to>
    <eps:from>
       <eps:address xsi:type=" blz:bankleitzahl">30050010</eps:address>
    </eps:from>
 </eps:endpoints>
```

Listing 6-3: The BizTalk <endpoints> header

The mandatory <endpoints> header—qualified by the URI "http://schemas.biztalk.org/btf-2-0/endpoints"—contains exactly two required elements with trivial semantics: <from> and <to>.

The <from> and <to> elements both contain exactly one child element, <address>, that contains the identifier for the source or destination entity, respectively. The <address> element's data is basically expressed as a simple string but employs a special construct, the mandatory *xsi:type* attribute, derived from the XML Schema (XSD) type system. This attribute must occur on each <address> element and specifies an XSD type that defines both the semantics of the element content and its permissible string format. The specification does not provide any standard type definitions for such identifiers so that the choice of address types is implementation-specific.

Document Catalog

Every BizTalk message can contain any number of related business documents with associated binary attachments that are communicated between two distinct endpoints. The document catalog, formulated in the <manifest> header, contains references to all parts of such a compound message. If a BizTalk message has attachments, the header must be present; otherwise, it is optional.

The <manifest> header is optional for most actual applications. (Attachments are great, but how often are they actually needed in application-to-application data exchange?) However, it may still make sense to use this header all the time. Besides providing a complete catalog for all contained documents and attachments, the manifest also allows for a textual description for each of the components sent in the interchange. A complete <manifest> header is therefore ideal to index interchanges for lookup and diagnostic purposes.

If the BizTalk message is just one of the parts of a multipart MIME message (much like an e-mail with a couple of attached files), the <manifest> header is essential because it identifies all parts of the MIME collection that belong to the BizTalk message.

The <manifest> header, of which an example is shown in Listing 6-4, can contain any number of child elements of type <reference>, each one referencing either one of the business documents that are immediate children of the message body (SOAP Body element) or one of the attachments within the same MIME multipart entity. "Any number" is not entirely accurate, of course. There cannot be more <reference> elements than documents and attachments combined.

```
<fst:manifest xmlns:fst="http://schemas.biztalk.org/btf-2-0/manifest"
          SOAP:mustUnderstand="1">
    <fst:reference>
        <fst:document href="#insurance_claim_document_id"/>
        <fst:description>Insurance Claim</fst:description>
    </fst:reference>
    <fst:reference>
        <fst:attachment href="CID:claim.tiff@claiming-it.com"/>
        <fst:description>
            Facsimile of Signed Claim Document
        </fst:description>
    </fst:reference>
    <fst:reference>
        <fst:attachment href="CID:car.jpeg@claiming-it.com"/>
        <fst:description>Photo of Damaged Car</fst:description>
    </fst:reference>
 </fst:manifest>
```

Listing 6-4: The BizTalk <manifest> header

Depending on whether a referenced entity is a business document or an attachment, the element <attachment> or <document> is used as a child element of <reference>. One or both must be used, and they are mutually exclusive. Both elements have empty content and require a single attribute *href*, which contains the reference to the declared entity.

In the case of the <document> element, the reference must be a relative URI reference to another element within the message body. For the <attachment> element, the *href* attribute contains a content-ID URI that references another component of the MIME multipart package in which the BizTalk message resides.

Requesting and Returning Receipts

If you send important documents by mail or via an express delivery service, you certainly want to know whether and when the document arrived. So when you drop off the envelope at your local post office or register it for delivery with FedEx, you request a delivery receipt that is returned to you once the documents have been accepted at the destination.

But with postal mail delivery, you cannot find out if and when the documents have actually been committed into the destination organization's internal processing. If the document cannot be committed due to a business-related exception (maybe the ordered items are out of stock) or for some other reason , you will certainly want to be able to correlate this information with the business case the document interchange is related to.

To enable BizTalk Framework compliant (BFC) servers to consistently implement both the essential functions of requesting and returning receipts, the BizTalk Framework defines two separate types of receipts: the delivery receipt and the commitment receipt. In BizTalk Server terms, receipts are used to implement the reliable messaging feature.

A source organization requests receipts by using the BizTalk <services> header, qualified by the namespace URI "http://schemas.biztalk.org/btf-2-0/services". The request for receipts is rather indirect. You advertise a drop-off location for either the delivery receipt or the commitment receipt and thereby indicate that you expect a receipt to be delivered to that location for the containing interchange. The optional <services> header may have either or both of the child elements <commitmentReceiptRequest> and <deliveryReceiptRequest>, each containing a mandatory <sendTo> element with an <address> child equivalent to those used in the previously discussed <endpoints> header. Both receipt requests are also required to contain a date/time value in the <sendBy> tag, which defines the time by which a receipt is requested. If either of the receipts is not received by the specified time, the BFC server at the source organization may consider the interchange as failed and initiate transaction recovery and retransmission.

The responses, the actual receipts, are sent to the specified destination either immediately by using a transport address relayed in the request, as shown in the commitment receipt request in Listing 6-5, or by correlating a business identifier sent in the header with a transport service already known to the destination organization.

```
<srv:services xmlns:srv="http://schemas.biztalk.org/btf-2-0/services"
              xmlns:SOAP="http://schemas.xmlsoap.org/soap/envelope/"
              xmlns:xsi="http://www.w3.org/1999/XMLSchema-instance"
              xmlns:xsd="http://www.w3.org/2000/08/XMLSchema"
              xmlns:agr="http://www.trading-agreements.org/types/"
              SOAP:mustUnderstand="1">
  <srv:deliveryReceiptRequest>
    <srv:sendTo>
       <srv:address xsi:type="agr:httpURL">
            http://www.we-love-books.org/receipts
       </srv:address>
    </srv:sendTo>
    <srv:sendBy>2000-05-14T08:00:00+08:00</srv:sendBy>
  </srv:deliveryReceiptRequest>
  <srv:commitmentReceiptRequest>
    <srv:sendTo>
       <srv:address xsi:type="agr:duns_number">11-111-1111</srv:address>
    </srv:sendTo>
    <srv:sendBy>2000-05-14T10:00:00+08:00</srv:sendBy>
```

```
  </srv:commitmentReceiptRequest>
</srv:services>
```

Listing 6-5: The BizTalk <services> header

The commitment and delivery receipts are sent as separate BizTalk documents with their own identity and expiration time, and they are each identified by a specific header structure. The delivery receipt uses the <deliveryReceipt> element; commitment receipts are relayed by using the <commitmentReceipt> header.

The delivery receipt must contain two child elements. The <receivedAt> element holds a time stamp indicating the time when the document was accepted by the destination. The <identity> element contains a copy of the identity value found in the <properties> header of the original document, and it allows the receiver to correlate the receipt with the original message. The delivery receipt must be immediately generated when the header is processed. It must be sent as soon as the incoming document has been safely stored for further processing and can therefore be assumed not to be lost by the destination organization due to system failure or some other loss of volatile system state. Listing 6-6 shows a sample delivery receipt for a BizTalk message.

```
<SOAP:Envelope
      xmlns:SOAP="http://schemas.xmlsoap.org/soap/envelope"
      xmlns:xsd="http://www.w3.org/2000/08/XMLSchema"
      xmlns:xsi="http://www.w3.org/1999/XMLSchema-instance">
  <SOAP:Header>
    <ept:endpoints SOAP:mustUnderstand="1"
              xmlns:ta="http://schemas.trading-agreements.com/"
              xmlns:ept="http://schemas.biztalk.org/btf-2-0/endpoints">
      <ept:to>
        <ept:address xsi:type="ta:httpURL">
              http://www.we-love-books.org/receipts
        </ept:address>
      </ept:to>
      <ept:from>
        <ept:address xsi:type="ta:department">Book Orders</ept:address>
      </ept:from>
    </ept:endpoints>
    <prp:properties SOAP:mustUnderstand="1"
              xmlns:prp="http://schemas.biztalk.org/btf-2-0/properties">
      <prp:identity>uuid:24d304a0-b6e1-493a-b456-4b86c684d6f3</prp:identity>
      <prp:sentAt>2000-05-13T10:34:00-08:00</prp:sentAt>
      <prp:expiresAt>2000-05-14T08:00:00+08:00</prp:expiresAt>
      <!-- expiration is at delivery deadline -->
      <prp:topic>http://electrocommerce.org/delivery_receipt/</prp:topic>
    </prp:properties>
    <dlr:deliveryReceipt xmlns:dlr="http://schemas.biztalk.org/btf-2-0/receipts"
                    SOAP:mustUnderstand="1">
      <dlr:receivedAt>2000-05-13T10:04:00-08:00</dlr:receivedAt>
      <dlr:identity>uuid:74b9f5d0-33fb-4a81-b02b-5b760641c1d6</dlr:identity>
```

```
          <!—-the above is the identity of the original message -->
       </dlr:deliveryReceipt>
    </SOAP:Header>
    <SOAP:Body/>
    <!-- the body is always empty in a delivery receipt -->
</SOAP:Envelope>
```

Listing 6-6: The BizTalk delivery receipt

Like the delivery receipt shown in Listing 6-6, the commitment receipt also contains a copy of the original document's identity reference. Because it acknowledges more than just the document reception, the commitment receipt is a bit more verbose than the delivery receipt. The commitment receipt relays a decision about accepting the message for business processing back from the system that is actually performing the business task requested by the message content. Whether such an action is performed depends on a decision made either by a human being or by some automated rule on behalf of the destination organization. The outcome of this decision and the related explanation must be communicated back to the sender of the original document.

To contain this information, the <commitment> header must contain the <decidedAt> and <decision> elements. The <decidedAt> element contains a time stamp value indicating the time when the decision was made. The outcome can be either absolutely "positive" or "negative", expressed as either of these string values carried in the <decision> element.

To provide the other organization with more information than a plain yeah or nay, two optional elements <commitmentCode> and <commitmentDetail> can contain any information the recipient of the original document deems useful to send back. The commitment code is an XSD-qualified name that serves as a machine-readable reason code, while the commitment detail can carry any arbitrary content. Listing 6-7 shows a sample commitment receipt (with a negative decision).

```
<SOAP:Envelope
    xmlns:SOAP="http://schemas.xmlsoap.org/soap/envelope"
    xmlns:xsd="http://www.w3.org/2000/08/XMLSchema"
    xmlns:xsi="http://www.w3.org/1999/XMLSchema-instance">
  <SOAP:Header>
    <ept:endpoints SOAP:mustUnderstand="1"
              xmlns:ept="http://schemas.biztalk.org/btf-2-0/endpoints"
              xmlns:ta="http://schemas.trading-agreements.com/">
      <ept:to>
        <ept:address xsi:type="ta:duns_number">11-111-1111</ept:address>
      </ept:to>
      <ept:from>
        <ept:address xsi:type="ta:department">Book Orders</ept:address>
      </ept:from>
    </ept:endpoints>
    <prp:properties SOAP:mustUnderstand="1"
              xmlns:prp="http://schemas.biztalk.org/btf-2-0/properties">
      <prp:identity>uuid:1d394ac1-cadf-47cf-9a1e-aaa40531b97d</prp:identity>
```

```
        <prp:sentAt>2000-05-13T10:55:00-08:00</prp:sentAt>
        <prp:expiresAt>2000-05-14T10:00:00+08:00</prp:expiresAt>
        <!-- expiration is at commitment deadline -->
        <prp:topic>http://electrocommerce.org/commitment_receipt/</prp:topic>
    </prp:properties>
    <cmr:commitmentReceipt
            xmlns:cmr="http://schemas.biztalk.org/btf-2-0/receipts"
            xmlns:cmt="http://schemas.electrocommerce.org/commitment/"
            SOAP:mustUnderstand="1">
        <cmr:decidedAt>2000-05-13T10:44:00-08:00</cmr:decidedAt>
        <cmr:decision>negative</cmr:decision>
        <cmr:identity>uuid:74b9f5d0-33fb-4a81-b02b-5b760641c1d6</cmr:identity>
        <!-- the above is the identity of the original message -->
        <cmr:commitmentCode>cmt:outOfStock</cmr:commitmentCode>
        <cmr:commitmentDetail>
            <cmt:restockExpectedOn>2000-06-15</cmt:restockExpectedOn>
        </cmr:commitmentDetail>
    </cmr:commitmentReceipt>
  </SOAP:Header>
  <SOAP:Body/>
</SOAP:Envelope>
```

Listing 6-7: The BizTalk commitment receipt

The body of both receipts must always be empty, which clearly indicates that the receipt has no business content but serves only as a control message. All related headers are flagged, with the SOAP attribute *mustUnderstand* set to 1. Therefore, receipts must be understood and properly handled by sender and receiver.

Business Process Correlation

The optional BizTalk Framework <process> header is specifically designed to support BizTalk Orchestration or equivalent business process management. While all of the previously explained headers should be sufficient to unambiguously identify purpose, origin, and destination of any BFC message, the <process> header enables you to relay additional, precise information about the business process context in which the message was generated at the originating organization and can be used to optimize handling at the receiving end.

The <process> header conceptually references an interchange schedule that defines rules and sequences of a series of related document interchanges implementing a business process. The schedule identifier is provided as a URI in the <type> element. The term "conceptually" is used here because the specification does not mandate any format for such a schedule. The <instance> element specifies the position of this interchange in the context of the schedule.

The <detail> element may contain any information useful to further detail the business process context. An example <process> header is shown in Listing 6-8:

```
<prc:process SOAP:mustUnderstand="1"
            xmlns:SOAP="http://schemas.xmlsoap.org/soap/envelope/"
            xmlns:xsi="http://www.w3.org/1999/XMLSchema-instance"
            xmlns:dtl="http://www.trading-agreements.org/process/detail/"
            xmlns:eps="http://schemas.biztalk.org/btf-2-0/endpoints"
            xmlns:prc="http://schemas.biztalk.org/btf-2-0/process">
    <prc:type>purchasing:Book_Purchase_Process</prc:type>
    <prc:instance>purchasing:Book_Purchase_Process#12345</prc:instance>
    <prc:detail>
        <dtl:targetPort>po_request</dtl:targetPort>
        <dtl:exceptionAddress>
           <eps:address xsi:type="dtl:escrow">
            common_escrow_provider
           </eps:address>
        </dtl:exceptionAddress>
    </prc:detail>
</prc:process>
```

Listing 6-8: The BizTalk <process> header

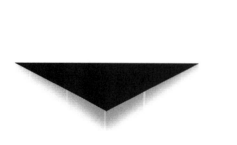

CHAPTER 7

BizTalk Server
Messaging Terminology

This chapter introduces BizTalk Server's core messaging terminology and explains how the various concepts interrelate. The terminology discussed in this chapter somewhat overlaps with the previous chapter, which introduced the BizTalk Framework. Of course, BizTalk Server 2000 is a BizTalk Framework compliant (BFC) server that implements the Framework in its RELIABLE messaging envelope format. However, the Framework is only one of the messaging envelope formats that BizTalk supports; don't assume you know everything about BizTalk receipts just because you read the discussion in Chapter 6.

ORGANIZATIONS AND APPLICATIONS

BizTalk serves to *connect* organizations and *integrate* applications. As you would expect, these terms are a significant part of the product's terminology. Their importance is reflected even in the licensing agreement that defines the difference between the BizTalk Server Standard and Enterprise editions. Besides clustering and multiprocessor support, the only other important difference between the two editions is that the Standard Edition server is limited to five external organizations and five internal applications. In almost every other respect, the editions are identical.

NOTE: The Developer Edition is equivalent to the Enterprise Edition.

Organizations represent trading partners, or—to use a more generic term—messaging destinations. Therefore, organizations can provide a transport- and technology-independent way of specifying the messaging source and target. In EDI and many cross-organization integration scenarios, messages are commonly carried over many intermediary hops that route information based on some abstract corporate identifier, which may even have to be handled by humans somewhere in the business process. For example, banks often expect *you* to know their bank routing codes when you wire money to another bank to pay bills. Technology-bound addressing schemes like IP numbers or Internet mail addresses are useless in such a case.

Organization Identifiers

Each BizTalk organization is identified by one or more categorized organization identifiers. When an organization definition is initially created, the organization is assigned a human-readable identifier—a plaintext name that must be unique for the category qualified as OrganizationName. The organization name identifier is required for every organization in BizTalk and cannot be removed.

As for organization names, uniqueness of identifiers is required across all other identifier categories as well. You can use telephone numbers, Dun & Bradstreet identifiers, International Air Transport Association (IATA) codes, and many other common, unambiguous business identifiers either by choosing a predefined organization identifier category or by specifying a new custom category. The identifier category is itself identified by a qualifier. For all predefined identifier categories, these qualifiers are based on the ISO 6523 standard and are derived from the UN/EDIFACT service directories. ISO 6523 defines a standard numbering scheme for organization identifiers that are used for electronic document interchange; the qualifiers identify the ISO-approved authorities that issue such identification numbers. Appendix B lists all of these authorities, along with their qualifiers and an explanation, including those not predefined in BizTalk. At the time of this writing, the ISO 6523 standard qualifiers range between 1 and 148. Expect more numbers to be added.

For X12 or UN/EDIFACT messaging, you will likely be using either these standard identifiers or a well-known custom identifier scheme. Identifier category qualifiers can be no longer than two characters for X12 and four characters for UN/EDIFACT. The qualifier can have an arbitrary length for XML messaging use.

The actual organization identifier is an alphanumeric value that must comply with the numbering scheme defined by the identifier category. The organization identifier has no particular limits in length for XML messaging, but it cannot exceed 15 characters for X12 and 35 characters for UN/EDIFACT.

NOTE: BizTalk will not verify identifiers against the numbering scheme's rules.

The Home Organization

The *Home Organization* is a special type of organization that is automatically created at installation and cannot be removed. The home organization obviously represents your own organization.

Just like every other organization, the home organization can have multiple identifiers. Here, the support for multiple identifiers actually makes the most sense. While you typically need only one standard identifier for any single trading partner, your home organization will likely need to use several identifiers when exchanging data with multiple partners, each in a different business context.

Unlike all other organizations, the home organization is not a valid direct messaging source or destination. Instead, it has an additional set of identifiers for internal applications that you designate as messaging origins or targets.

Application Identifiers

When messages are received at the home organization, they need to be processed. BizTalk can process messages by using XLANG Orchestration schedules or hand them over to any internal business application. Likewise, BizTalk can accept messages from internal applications and route them to external recipients or another internal application.

Each internal application that sends or receives messages through BizTalk is configured with its own unique identifier on the *Home Organization*. Like organization identifiers, application identifiers are an abstraction. In larger enterprises, you might have two or more separate instances of the same or subtly different software systems running in different departments; also, applications may be capable of using multiple alternative transports to receive and submit messages and documents.

However, application identifiers are not equivalent to organization identifiers relative to addressing. When documents are submitted to BizTalk, the destination identifier for the application is always that of the home organization. The reason for that should be obvious: if external partners send messages to you, they will (and probably should) not know which internal application is responsible for handling the respective message.

DOCUMENT DEFINITIONS

A document specification serves to validate inbound documents for proper data content and structure, and it is the basis for mapping data to other specifications. Document specifications also drive the parser and serializer components for X12, UN/EDIFACT, and custom formats by containing all necessary structural information that associates a non-XML data format with its respective internal BizTalk XML representation. In the BizTalk Messaging context, a *document definition* is a labeled storage location for a document specification expressed in BizTalk Schema with additional messaging-related properties.

Although the BizTalk documentation uses the term "reference" when you associate a document specification with a definition, specifications are actually physically imported into the BizTalk Messaging configuration database. This feature not only speeds up processing, but it also helps guarantee consistency in processing. If a specification changes, you must explicitly reimport it into BizTalk Messaging by using the Messaging Manager Channel Wizard. Otherwise, it would just be reimported randomly whenever you placed a new specification to a certain referenced file location while BizTalk actively processes documents. Keeping all configured document specifications in the management database also provides a simple version-control mechanism because you can keep multiple (deprecated) versions of the same specification side by side in the internal document definition repository and phase them out gracefully, instead of just replacing them from one second to the next. If a channel is actively using a document definition, you will not be able to change or remove it.

A document definition allows you to configure global tracking fields. This feature works exactly like the tracking fields that you can specify for channels, but it is global in that it is valid for all channels that use this document definition. If global tracking fields exist for a document definition, they are always tracked, regardless of whether the tracking fields feature is explicitly switched on for a specific channel.

Another important feature of the document definition is selection criteria. Recall the structure of X12 and UN/EDIFACT discussed in Chapter 3. The physical representation of both formats is really only a sequence of data segments, and the higher-level control structures are more a semantics concept than a property of the syntax. Both formats understand the concept of functional groups that may contain any number of documents.

The document type is not declared within the documents; rather, it is declared in the functional group header that envelops them.

Therefore, the document type cannot be derived immediately from the document itself, as is the case with XML. The selection criteria establish the relationship between the entries with the functional group header and a document definition through name-value pairs. When the functional header is parsed and evaluated for inbound X12 and EDIFACT documents, the selection criteria of all document definitions are matched against the header entries, and from this, the correct document definition is chosen. Outbound, the selection criteria serve to construct the functional group header.

PORTS

When BizTalk Messaging service actively talks to a messaging destination, and when XLANG Orchestration schedules communicate with queues, BizTalk Messaging, or components, they do so through ports. While BizTalk Orchestration and Messaging use the same term for their communication paths with the outside world, the concepts are entirely different.

XLANG schedules generally use the term "port" to refer to the binding of workflow activities to data sources or sinks or to external components and scripts. However, only when XLANG schedules bind to the BizTalk Messaging services is an XLANG port synonymous with a BizTalk Messaging port. In all other instances, XLANG port names have no relationship with the ones defined for BizTalk Messaging. To alleviate confusion and be more precise, the terms "messaging port" and "orchestration port" are used throughout the rest of this book. (Orchestration ports will be explained in more detail and in context in Chapter 9.)

Messaging Ports

Simply speaking, a *messaging port* is a transport-bound gateway through which BizTalk pushes information to an application or destination organization. Messaging ports are write-only; for the receiver side, a messaging port can have any number of associated receiving channels (as discussed in the following section). The general architecture of BizTalk Messaging ports is shown in Figure 7-1.

Each messaging port has a primary and an optional backup transport binding to communication endpoints that link to either a remote organization or to an internal application. Messaging ports provide the mapping between the abstract addressing scheme of organization identifiers and the physical, technology, and transport-dependent addresses. Consequently, many messaging ports can exist for a single destination organization or application. No set or suggested scheme exists to name messaging ports, but it would help to include both destination and purpose in the port name, for example, Purchase Orders to Sample Trading Inc.

Open destination ports are special cases. These ports have all of the properties described in the following sections except for destination identifiers and transports. You

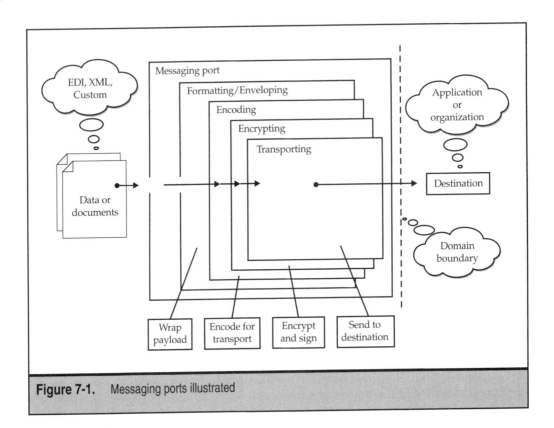

Figure 7-1.   Messaging ports illustrated

use open destination ports to take advantage of the full range of BizTalk's messaging features without having to preconfigure certain communication destinations. Communicating through open destination ports is essentially as easy and flexible as directly using the Windows Internet APIs (WinInet) or the Microsoft SOAP SDK, but with the added advantage that all BizTalk features are available between your code and the endpoint.

Transports

Primary and *backup transports* are push services that use a BizTalk-supported transport protocol to deliver messages to the destination address. Out of the box, BizTalk supports the web-like protocols HTTP and its secure variant HTTPS. Both HTTP variants are only supported using the POST verb. The following are also supported: the e-mail transport standard Simple Mail Transfer Protocol (SMTP), the Microsoft Message Queue (MSMQ), and simple flatfile output to a predefined directory. The special transport options are Application Integration Components (AIC) and the Loopback transport.

Application Integration Components allow messages and documents to be submitted directly to applications or to be carried over proprietary protocols. BizTalk Server includes a simple SAP R/3 AIC that you can use in conjunction with the SAP DCOM connector to drop SAP IDOC documents (a proprietary flatfile format) into an R/3 system. While SAP R/3 is the only external application that enjoys support from right within the BizTalk distribution, application integration components are not a limited or even made-for-SAP solution. AICs are actually easy to build and click right into BizTalk; they require only a single, simple COM interface to be implemented.

The Loopback transport does not send anything. Rather, it returns the document synchronously (immediately) to the application from which it was sent. The Loopback transport protocol is actually a powerful tool that allows you to leverage BizTalk's document transformation and validation capabilities from within applications. Because using the Loopback transport with organization destinations is pointless, it can be used only with messaging ports that talk to applications.

Any time BizTalk needs to send a document to the destination identified by the port, it uses the primary transport. It uses the backup transport only if a transport-level error occurs, which may be caused by an unreachable or crashed server. Therefore, primary and backup transports that use different application protocols targeted at the same remote IP address are not very useful. If messages absolutely must get there under all circumstances, primary and backup transports should point to different servers and take different routes.

Because the backup transport is really only a last resort option if there is panic on the Titanic, you can specify service windows only for the primary transport. A *service window* is a period during the day (with a granularity of one hour) when messages can be sent on this port. Using service windows is useful if your server or your destination server is only periodically available, or if sending messages by using the chosen transport or AIC is too expensive at certain times of the day (for instance, when using international long-distance, dial-up telephone lines).

Destination Identifier

The physical endpoint—whether it be the primary or backup transport's destination address—is not necessarily sufficient to get a document to its ultimate destination. If you use intermediate hops in your routing infrastructure (like intermediate BizTalk servers) or you are connected to a closed-network value-added network (VAN) that handles secure and reliable routing of documents as part of its services, a physical endpoint serves only as a sufficient address specification to the first hop. Not supplying a better address for the ultimate destination would be like going to the closest mailbox and dropping your letter off enclosed in a blank envelope.

Depending on whether the messaging port is targeted at an application or an organization, you can choose either from the defined identifiers for the configured organization or from the applications of the home organization. The destination identifier is the logical address for documents sent through a particular messaging port, and like letters you drop in a mailbox, the destination identifier is written on an envelope.

Envelopes

Besides the transport protocol's settings that tell BizTalk *where* data is to be sent, messaging ports have a few more optional properties that allow BizTalk to fine-tune *how* data is communicated with the endpoint.

The X12, UN/EDIFACT, and reliable (BFC) messaging formats require the use of envelopes. *Envelopes* are structures that wrap messages and business documents for transport. With X12 and UN/EDIFACT, the envelope consists of the Interchange and functional group headers; with BizTalk's reliable messaging format, the envelope is a SOAP envelope with all applicable BizTalk Framework headers. Envelopes are not restricted to these message formats, though. Many common flatfile formats used for business-to-business data exchange employ some form of headers or envelopes that contain the payload for transfer between endpoints.

Internally, BizTalk Messaging handles only the payload of electronic documents. In the BizTalk Editor, you (typically) define schemas only for the data portion of an exchange, and the BizTalk Mapper also only looks at the payload for creating transformation rules. Because envelopes are thus relevant only for transport, they are directly bound to messaging ports.

To ensure consistent formatting of outbound messages, binding an envelope format also ultimately defines the document standard to be used on a specific messaging port and indirectly selects a matching serializer. All documents, independent of whether they are conceptually using X12, UN/EDIFACT, or some custom flatfile format, are processed using XML inside BizTalk. Only immediately before it is prepared for transport and the outbound data stream needs to be produced is the XML data converted into the native format by the serializer component that handles the document standard of the configured envelope.

Encryption, Signature, and Encoding

Once messages are enveloped (or intentionally left unwrapped), the resulting package might need some further preprocessing for transport. The encoding property of the messaging port selects how data is being formatted at the transport level. BizTalk gives you the option of using either no special encoding (that is, data is being sent as written by the envelope serializer) or using Multipurpose Internet Mail Extensions (MIME) encoding.

MIME is an Internet standard that allows you to wrap multiple arbitrary binary or text data streams, flag each with its own identity and a media format identifier, and package the compound data stream nicely into a text-based format that the existing Internet Mail infrastructure understands. Obviously, the SMTP transport requires MIME encoding to be specified.

When you use the reliable BizTalk Messaging format or a custom XML format without an explicit envelope specification, selecting the MIME encoding option does nothing. BizTalk always sends XML as XML *unless* you use attachments as defined in the BizTalk Framework SOAP extension specification for messages with attachments. At least that's what the BizTalk documentation tells you; unfortunately, there is currently no way to submit attachments with documents in the BizTalk Server 2000 version, but that will change soon. Likewise, the documentation suggests support for custom encoding components, which is not documented elsewhere.

As soon as the payload has been enveloped and properly bundled with its additional baggage (attachments, plaintext messages, etc.), you might want to protect it from unauthorized access by encrypting it. Maybe you already use secure data channels with HTTPS or virtual private network (VPN) links, but consider that these privacy mechanisms are sufficiently secure only for peer-to-peer connections between fully trusted partners. Once messages are routed over intermediary hops that are beyond your immediate control, your data might travel entirely out in the open and over insecure channels part of the way if you rely only on transport-level encryption. Transport-level data encryption on a routed communicating path is only as good as the encryption quality on the weakest path segment.

Besides encrypting documents, you will also want to sign them for authenticity and consistency. (Chapter 2 already describes the fundamental concepts of the digital signature in detail, so we are not going to reiterate this here.)

A security solution is required that supports encryption and digital signatures, independent of the transport paths and transport protocols used. Such a solution, and the one BizTalk supports out of the box, is the security-enhanced version of MIME, Secure Multipurpose Internet Mail Extensions (S/MIME). S/MIME allows asynchronous encryption and digital signing for arbitrary data blocks using the standardized Public Key Infrastructure (PKI) as per ITU X.509. For other, less popular or proprietary transport-independent encryption mechanisms, BizTalk supports custom encryption components.

CHANNELS

If messaging ports serve to push information to destinations, where does the data come from? You need a mechanism to submit data into the BizTalk Messaging engine that can subsequently be routed to a physical destination through a predefined messaging port. In BizTalk terms, this mechanism is a channel.

A *channel* is a named entity that is used as a reception gateway for data from either a previously known originating organization or from an open messaging source. An *open messaging source* is a generic channel that is smart enough to figure out the message origin from the actual message content. We will get to this in more detail in the next chapter when we look at *document routing*.

Channels are always bound to a messaging port. In fact, a *messaging port*—that is, a single physical destination with all associated transport properties—can have any number of receiving channels. This mirrors practice: you will likely have a single internal order-processing application bound to a single messaging port that pushes purchase orders into that application's handling queue, but you will probably have hundreds of trading partners that are dying to buy your products; thus, orders will keep flowing into your system. In turn, the order-processing system and many other applications may need to channel their financial data into the central accounting system. Here again, the accounting system is bound to a single messaging port, with all other applications using several different channels bound to this port to provide their data.

What if data could be expected to arrive from your partners or applications in identical formats and it always contained all necessary information for onward routing? Then the channel concept would apply only to the transport paths into the system, and BizTalk could mostly ignore it because transport is the job of the surrounding infrastructure. In reality, though, each partner can send or expect a different data format, and data submitted for messaging cannot be expected to contain any BizTalk-compatible routing information.

To successfully route a message, BizTalk must be able to associate any data transfer with source and destination organizations. However, data submitted into BizTalk messages from anonymous sources, like message queues, may not be properly identified for BizTalk. Similarly, organizations that send documents to you in custom formats may not be using envelope or data formats that carry usable source qualifiers. To properly associate the message with a source identifier, the channel can explicitly define that relationship. If you have multiple, equally anonymous messaging sources, you need multiple channels for the same port. If the source identifier can be extracted from the data or can be specified at submission time, the channel can be configured as an open source.

The remote endpoint of a messaging port is a single physical destination bound to a distinct system that expects messages to arrive in certain formats. The messages are likely to be limited to exactly one format per message type. But in real life, the sender side stores a lot of data formats and message types, 99 percent of which may be perfectly incompatible with the system bound to the port. Channels are the gatekeepers: negotiators and translators in this babylonic data format confusion.

Only properly formatted and verifiable data should be sent through channels. To ensure that this is the case, each channel must define in which format it expects to receive messages (the inbound document definition) and how this data will subsequently be forwarded through the associated messaging port (the outbound document definition). Both the inbound and the outbound document definitions are references to document specifications expressed in BizTalk Schema format. When data is submitted, it is always verified against the inbound specification; if the document is not compliant with the BizTalk Schema for any reason, processing is rejected and the document is quarantined in the suspended BizTalk Messaging queue.

If the inbound document definition is not identical to the outbound document definition, you must also provide a mapping specification. For instance, if you use XML-formatted invoice documents internally, but the destination expects them in UN/EDIFACT D98B INVOIC format, the invoices must be transformed into the target format before they are sent. BizTalk solves this task with XSLT style sheets produced with the visual BizTalk Mapper tool. The style sheets are applied to the inbound document to produce a properly organized outbound document.

The data mapping capability of BizTalk's channels is undoubtedly the most powerful single feature of the messaging portion of the product, and it is a real time- and cost-saver. With data mapping, you can submit a document of any type that can be described with

BizTalk Schema into a BizTalk channel and produce a document of any other such type. Previously, such a task almost certainly required custom programming code to parse the document and retrieve the data, correlate it with the target structure, and then format it. Even if you needed only a handful of such mappings, thousands of lines of code had to be built, maintained, and paid for. The BizTalk Mapper tool not only allows you to create such mappings in a fraction of the time, but it is actually easy and intuitive to use and enables nonprogrammers to create these mappings. (Chapter 16 is entirely dedicated to the BizTalk Mapper.)

When you receive digitally signed and encrypted documents, you must be able to decrypt them, verify whether they have actually been sent from the assumed origin, and make sure they have not been tampered with. You perform these tasks by specifying two public X.509 PKI certificates, one for decryption and one for signature verification, that you can assign to a channel. The difference between the certificates that you use with messaging ports and these certificates is that the port certificates are your own. They contain your own private key; the channel certificates are the public certificates that your communication peers give you.

At this point, let's recap the relationship between ports, channels, and destinations (illustrated in Figure 7-2) to clarify how BizTalk Messaging works. Any message, independent of its origin, is always submitted to and through a channel to a port, which uses a configured transport to route the message to the destination. For BizTalk Messaging, every operation is always a send task. In fact, BizTalk has no immediate concept of receiving messages over any type of transport. This is why the expression "submit to BizTalk" is typically used. Any message that needs to be transported by using BizTalk Messaging must to be explicitly pushed into the system through the Interchange programming interface on the BizTalk Interchange service object. For message queues and files, BizTalk also has special receive functions, but internally, these also use that service object to submit received documents.

Therefore, if you need to receive data via SMTP or HTTP (or any other protocol), you will always have a script or plug-in for Internet Information Server (IIS), Exchange 2000, or some other server product that actually receives the data and then uses the Interchange object to submit it to BizTalk. (Basic scripts ship with BizTalk, of course.) The Interchange object always drops submitted data into a channel that is explicitly specified by the caller, determined from the message source and/or destination, or selected by channel filters that inspect message content to pick an appropriate channel.

Channel filters are defined on a channel using one or more XPath expressions that query into the document, and each XPath expression must evaluate to a Boolean expression (True or False). All expressions are combined by using a logical AND, meaning that all expressions must evaluate to True for the combined filter expression to be True. With filters, you can inspect any aspect of a document, like certain content, cardinality, or presence of elements, and can implement scenarios like the one that follows.

An insurance company receives new policies from their sales agencies and needs to assign them to the handling departments; departments are organized by the insurance clients' last names. Department 1 gets clients with last names from *A* through *F*, Depart-

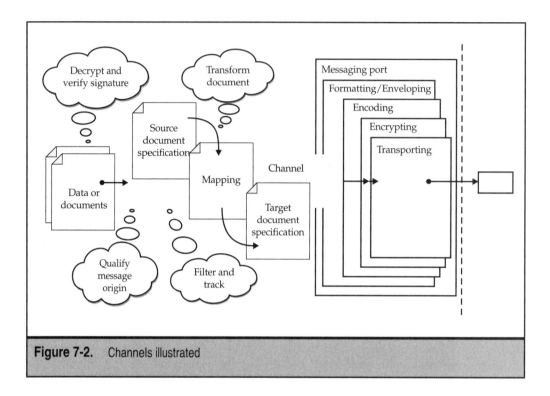

Figure 7-2. Channels illustrated

ment 2 gets *G* through *L,* and so on. By using channel filters, you can peek into the document and make that routing decision in the channel. Assuming there are five departments in the described scenario, you would have five channels (very possibly with each bound to a different port) that will all accept the insurance policy document type. Given that they are compatible with the source organization (or are open source), BizTalk Messaging tests all these channels to see whether they would accept the incoming data: that is, whether their XPath expressions evaluate to "true" for the presented data. The channel whose filter accepts the data gets the data.

Once data is accepted by a channel based on filter conditions, decryption, and signature verification, as well as validation of data against the inbound document definition, it is technically accepted for processing. If the document is accepted, any receipt request of the sender must be honored. While BizTalk's reliable messaging protocol automatically handles receipts for inbound data, sending any other type of receipt is performed through specially designated channels, so-called receipt channels. (This is also the case for reliable messaging but happens invisibly under the hood.)

In most respects, receipt channels are like normal channels. The major difference is that the inbound document definition is predefined and fixed to be the BizTalk canonical receipt, which is a document type containing all receipt information that BizTalk is able to provide.

If you communicate with a partner by using X12, the channel will use an outbound document definition that implements the functional acknowledgement transaction set 997, which is compliant with the respective standards release. If UN/EDIFACT is the data exchange format of choice, the respective acknowledgement is the message type CONTRL. As can be expected, the transformation to produce these outbound receipt formats (or any other receipt) uses a mapping specification.

To produce receipts, you assign a receipt channel to receiving channels. Whenever a document is accepted by a channel, the receipt channel is automatically provided with the canonical receipt and sends it through an associated messaging port to the receipt destination.

Any channel (except receipt channels) can also request receipts from their destination and specify a deadline for receipt delivery. If the requested receipt does not arrive within the specified time, BizTalk will automatically resend the document without further intervention. The number of retries and the time interval between retries is configurable.

Besides verifying, mapping, decrypting, validating, and acknowledging documents, channels also handle a task that is essential for any business document exchange: tracking and archiving. Every document that passes through a BizTalk channel is archived either in its native format (like X12 or UN/EDIFACT), in BizTalk's internal XML representation of that data, or in both versions. All documents are stored in the BizTalk document-tracking database in their entirety. Tracking is crucial for your business: because electronic documents do replace their paper equivalents, the document-tracking database equally replaces your paper file folders. The tracking database will therefore hold legally important data that may need to serve as proof in a courtroom.

To qualify your archive and make it searchable by certain document properties, you can define tracking fields based on the channel-assigned document definitions. When the document is archived, the tracking fields are located and their data is extracted and stored, in addition to the full document. For example, if you receive a purchase order through a channel, you may want to specify the customer ID and the customer's name and address as tracking fields. Then if there's a question about the purchase order later, you can search the document-tracking database by using those criteria. Tracking fields can also help you locate documents in record time when problems arise, so it is essential to define them correctly.

ENVELOPE DEFINITION

Envelopes wrap data for transport and select the destination. For the BizTalk-supplied EDI formats and reliable messaging, an *envelope definition* is nothing but a user-defined name for the data format. It is therefore possible to define three envelopes with the user-defined names RELIABLE, X12, and EDIFACT that are of the respective built-in types with the same names and use them as envelope formats wherever needed.

The need to configure envelopes arises when you use custom XML (not BFC) envelope formats or ones that are based on flatfiles or any other custom data format. In this case, BizTalk is not able to place routing information into the envelope header because it has no idea how that custom envelope format is laid out.

Therefore, you need to provide a document specification for custom formats much like you need to do it for document definitions. Envelope specifications are explicitly flagged as such. They contain a dictionary that associates the source and the destination address data elements with fields within the envelope format and identifies the location where the document data is inserted when data is serialized out for transfer.

DISTRIBUTION LISTS

Distribution lists could also be described as port multipliers. A *distribution list* is a group of ports that will simultaneously receive and forward data from a bound channel. They distribute information such as catalogues or notifications that should be submitted only once into the system and then automatically forward that information to many partners.

For an airport, this could be the current list of scheduled arrivals, departures, and possible related delays that must be relayed to many partners at least every five minutes. With BizTalk, you need to submit this information only once into a channel bound to the distribution list, and the data will subsequently be formatted and pushed on all associated ports, each using an individual transport protocol and endpoint.

From the user's perspective, channels that are bound to a single port or to a distribution list behave almost exactly alike. The only significant (and obvious) difference is that channels with distribution lists do not allow open destinations, that is, destinations that are defined by document content.

CHAPTER 8

BizTalk Messaging Concepts

The previous chapter explored BizTalk's core terminology and explained how messaging ports, channels, document definitions, envelopes, and all the other terms apply in the context of BizTalk. This chapter looks at the actual BizTalk Messaging service process and examines how it uses these concepts to handle documents. It will also provide an introductory discussion on BizTalk's internal queues and show how document routing works.

BIZTALK MESSAGING SERVICE

The BizTalk Messaging service is a Windows 2000–service process that continuously runs in the background on a BizTalk Server machine. The messaging service accepts messages through the transactional COM+ BizTalk Interchange component.

To guarantee transactional behavior and to allow multiple servers to collaborate in processing messages and distributing workload equally, all messages are persisted in the BizTalk work queue once the submitting transaction commits its work. From the work queue, the messaging service picks up the waiting messages on a first come, first served basis and processes them.

Processing involves associating a message with a channel, validating the message against the document definition, possibly transforming the document, and then enveloping, encrypting, and signing the document for delivery by the associated port. If the port has a configured service window, the message is queued in the scheduled queue and waits there until the service window's configured time.

A message that either failed to be delivered by the port or that is waiting to be acknowledged with a receipt sent by the receiver is placed into the retry queue. If a message does not process because of a failed transmission or because it exceeds the permitted number of retries, it is placed in the suspended queue. Once a message has been successfully sent, it is removed from its queue and archived as is in the BizTalk tracking database after the global and local tracking fields have been extracted and separately stored.

The transition of a message from one queue to another or from a queue to the tracking database is always transactional. When a processing thread picks up a message from the work queue, it flags the message as being processed (and therefore, locks it for other servers). Then the work queue places the message into the appropriate queue or into the tracking database—everything within the scope of a transaction. This behavior guarantees that messages will not be lost during processing and can be reliably delivered, even if the server (or an extension component) or the entire machine should crash.

BizTalk Queues in Detail

As you probably gathered from the previous overview, BizTalk uses four queues: the work queue, the scheduled queue, the retry queue, and the suspended queue. Figure 8-1 should help clarify the following discussion.

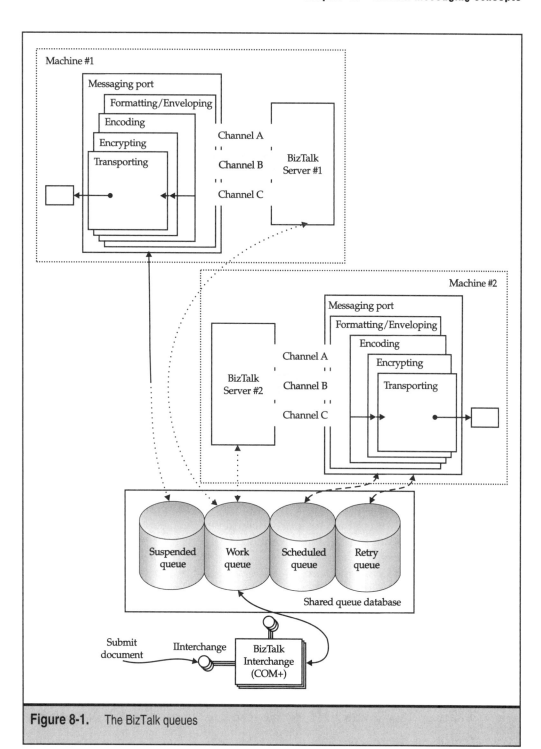

Figure 8-1.   The BizTalk queues

The *work queue* holds all messages that have been submitted into BizTalk for asynchronous processing but have not yet been picked up. The BizTalk Interchange component writes new documents directly into the work queue. If message processing is synchronous, the work queue is not used and the document is processed immediately. For synchronous messages, the messaging service and the interchange component are linked only indirectly. The messaging service will only be able to "see" messages that the transaction has committed into the queue. The Interchange component does not need to be enlisted into a transaction, though. This behavior is optional, not required.

Each BizTalk server polls the work queue in a configurable interval (two seconds, by default) to pick up the next document for processing. If you expect to receive only a few messages, you can set this to a much higher interval to reduce overall system load. If messages come in almost continuously, you can reduce the polling interval to one millisecond, indicating that BizTalk should pick up the next message immediately when the next processing thread has completed its previous job. The number of threads that concurrently process messages on each system CPU (one processor only for the Standard Edition) is also configurable and defaults to four. All queue settings can be adjusted with the BizTalk Administrator tool.

NOTE: Chapter 19 provides a complete explanation and walk-through of the tasks involved using the BizTalk Administrator tool. You will also learn more about how to balance the values just discussed to optimize performance.

When a message is being processed, BizTalk associates a channel and, indirectly, a messaging port with it. Messaging port definitions can specify certain *service windows*—timeslots defined as a time interval between two full hours; for example, between 08 and 11 (8 A.M. to 11 A.M.). The time interval is expressed in local time as set on the machine (in other words, this setting is not using GMT or UTC). If a messaging port defines a service window and the message is processed at a time outside the specified time period, the message is placed in *the scheduled queue.* Once the service window opens, that is, when the actual current server time is within the defined time period, the messaging service attempts to send the message through the previously determined port.

If the message fails to send due to communication errors or because the channel is configured to expect a receipt, the message is placed into the *retry queue.* If a receipt is expected, the message remains in the retry queue until that receipt has been received and successfully correlated with the message. If the receipt has not been received within the time frame specified in the channel, the message is treated like any other message in the retry queue and is automatically resent. For failed transmission attempts, the server tries to resend retry queue entries according to the frequency and number of retry attempts configured for the channel.

Configuring the number and frequency of retries in a channel makes sense because some communication links may be less reliable or less available than others; also, the tolerance you have for the number of retries may vary depending on the importance or urgency of the respective documents. Like the scheduled queue, the retry queue honors service windows. If an entry is placed into the retry queue, retransmission attempts are initiated only during the service window hours.

If everything fails, for example, when the number of permitted retries is exceeded for a message or if some fatal, unrecoverable processing error occurs, like if a document cannot be properly validated or mapped, the message is quarantined in the suspended queue. The *suspended queue* is BizTalk's message hospital. There, messages can be inspected and the error reports explaining why the message was placed into the suspended queue can be read. If the cause of the error is not a show-stopper like a parsing fault or some other nonrecoverable problem that is inherent to the submitted document, the document can also be resubmitted from the suspended queue.

All four BizTalk queues are held in the shared queue database running on Microsoft SQL Server 2000 or Microsoft SQL Server 7.0. The database is called *shared* because it is jointly used by multiple BizTalk servers in a collaborative Enterprise Edition setup. For the Standard Edition, this term does not make much sense—it does not support sharing the queue database among servers.

In a multiserver environment, the shared queue database is the central work-data repository for all servers. Shared queues allow optimal load balancing of larger BizTalk Server installations because new work items from all servers as well as scheduled and retry entries can be picked up and processed by any other server. Depending on your processing needs, you can also explicitly exclude specific servers from actively handling work queue entries while they can still access the other queues for dropping suspended, scheduled, or retry items. Excluding servers from processing work items can help you optimize their performance in conjunction with receiving functions for message queues that receive a lot of inbound data.

Receive Functions

Typically, data is submitted to BizTalk through the BizTalk Interchange COM+ component. The component is used either from within your own applications, Exchange Server scripts, Active Server Pages (ASP), or any other application that can either produce or receive documents.

The two most popular data receivers in enterprise systems are message queues and—mostly because nothing else even comes close in terms of simplicity—plain files dropped into a pickup directory in the file system. In both of these transport systems, no active server product is involved that could push data into BizTalk. Yes, message queues actively transfer data between endpoints, but once data has arrived at the destination queue, it just sits there and waits to be picked up by an application. The same is true for files: some type of transport or application drops files into a pickup directory, but then the files quietly wait (forever) and pile up until they are processed.

Rather than everyone writing their own version of a "pickup and submit" program for inbound files and message queues, BizTalk supports both of these transports directly through *receive functions*—the watchdogs that monitor either a certain message queue or a directory in a file-system directory. Once a message arrives in the queue or a file is placed in the directory, the receive function grabs the file and submits it directly into BizTalk for processing. For increased performance, you might want to dedicate one server of a multiserver environment to handle only receive functions; this is the example we touched on briefly at the end of the last section.

Each receive function must run on a specific, preassigned server machine. This eliminates competitive situations in which multiple machines may want to pick up the same file or queue entry simultaneously, thereby producing duplicate messages in the process. Within a server group (that is, a collaborating unit of BizTalk servers), each receive function must have a unique name that identifies it for administrative purposes.

File receive functions can watch a certain directory identified either on a logical drive or on a universal naming convention (UNC) file path. The directory can be located on the same machine, but it can also reside somewhere else on the network. If the file location is remote or if the BizTalk service account does not have read/write access to the specified local directory, the file receive function can be configured with a username and password to dynamically log on to the respective server. The function continuously monitors the directory for new files that have specified file extensions and subsequently submits them to BizTalk for processing.

The message queue receive function monitors any private or public queue and submits arriving items. The queues should be configured to support transactions, although BizTalk Messaging does not require them to be transactional.

The message queue receive function and the file receive function both allow you to select *custom preprocessors*: a COM component that you can provide to scan and transform file or message-queue data before BizTalk processes it. Custom preprocessors perform tasks ranging from code-page translations (for instance, translating from the EBCDIC mainframe character code-page to Unicode) to a full conversion of a proprietary data format into XML.

BIZTALK INTERCHANGE APPLICATION

You already know that documents are submitted into BizTalk through the Interchange component. When BizTalk is installed, this component is placed into a COM+ package called the BizTalk Server Interchange Application. The package is preconfigured as a server package, meaning that it always runs in its own process. The Interchange component is the only component that resides in this package.

The Interchange component is configured to support transactions. As a result, it adopts the transaction properties of the caller application. If the caller is a component residing within a transactional COM+ context, the component is transactional; otherwise, it is not.

You may not be aware of what COM+ does and how its transaction model works. To provide the groundwork for the discussion of configuration and performance issues later in this book, the following section provides a "COM+ in six paragraphs" crash-course.

COM+ in a Nutshell

COM+ evolved from the COM software development model and component technology and was introduced with the Windows 2000 operating system. The COM+ component management and the COM+ Transaction services are the next major release of the Microsoft Transaction Server (MTS) technology that had been introduced in 1997 with the Windows NT Option Pack for Windows NT 4.0 and Windows 95. MTS was a revolutionary product that introduced a transaction-handling model that has been adopted in virtually all other component-oriented transaction systems. CORBA's OTS object transaction services, Sun's Enterprise Java Beans, and many other application server systems implement transactions the COM+ way.

In COM+, each configured component runs within the scope of a *context*—a shared execution space for a number of components that share the same properties. Transactions are created automatically. Components are flagged for one of the following categories: *requires transactions*, *requires new transactions*, *supports transactions*, or *does not support transactions*. If transactions are required, the component will check the context of the component that created it. If that context is flagged to have a transaction, the component is created within that context; otherwise, a new transactional context is created and the new component is placed in that context. In case the component to be created has the *support transactions* flag (like the Interchange component), the transaction property of the creating component's context is inherited.

The context's transaction attribute controls how COM+ uses resource managers. Open Database Connectivity (ODBC), OLE Database (OLE DB) API database drivers, or the Microsoft Message Queue (MSMQ) can be resource managers. If any of these resource managers opens a connection to a resource (a database), any such connection is automatically enlisted into the context's transaction if the context is transactional. If you open a queue, a SQL Server database connection, and an Oracle connection from within a single context, all of these resources automatically participate in a coordinated transaction.

All operations that are performed on these resources are isolated from any other concurrent transaction and will either jointly succeed or jointly fail. If everything goes well on SQL Server but an error occurs on Oracle, all operations on both the Oracle database and the SQL Server database will be annulled and rolled back. The decision of whether the transaction succeeds or must be aborted is made either by one of the resource managers, in the case of an unrecoverable fault, or by one of the components residing in the context. The components may either flag the context as *transaction complete* or *abort* based on the outcome of their processing.

Because the Interchange component is flagged as *support transactions*, it inherits the transaction properties from its caller. Therefore, the transaction support for its database connection to the shared queue database also depends on that attribute. If the caller does not reside in a transactional context, that is, if it is not a COM+-configured component with transaction support, the Interchange application will not behave transactionally. In this case, any call to the *Submit()* method on the component's *IInterchange* interface will immediately write to the work queue.

If it is such a COM+ component, any calls to the *Submit()* method, even consecutive ones, are not committed to the work queue until the transaction completes. This allows you to implement correct transactional behavior for submitting BizTalk documents. This requirement is key for reliable document processing and application integration.

Therefore, the code calling the Interchange component should reside in a COM+-configured component that requires a transaction if the code retrieves data from a database or a queue to prepare the document to be submitted. While this type of configuration is optional, it will improve the reliability of your solution.

Submitting Documents

The Interchange component exposes a single interface: *IInterchange*. The interface is shown in the MIDL (Microsoft Interface Definition Language) code snippet shown in Listing 8-1. The interface methods can be categorized into two functional groups:

▼ Data submission to the work queue or for immediate synchronous processing
Submit() submits a document to the work queue.
SubmitSync() hands a document to BizTalk for immediate processing.

▲ Management of the suspended queue
CheckSuspendedQueue() allows searching the suspended queue for documents of a certain document type, source identifier, or destination identifier.
GetSuspendedQueueItemDetails() serves to retrieve details about one of the items returned by *CheckSuspendedQueue()*.
DeleteFromSuspendedQueue() deletes one or more of the suspended queue items.

```
[
  object,
  uuid(7D2A8C8A-645C-11D2-B605-00C04FC30E1A),
  dual,
  helpstring("IInterchange Interface"),
  pointer_default(unique)
]
interface IInterchange : IDispatch
{
  [helpstring("Submit documents")]
  HRESULT Submit(
    [in] BIZTALK_OPENNESS_TYPE  lOpenness,
    [in, defaultvalue(L"")] BSTR Document,
    [in, defaultvalue(L"")] BSTR DocName,
    [in, defaultvalue(L"")] BSTR SourceQualifier,
    [in, defaultvalue(L"")] BSTR SourceID,
    [in, defaultvalue(L"")] BSTR DestQualifier,
    [in, defaultvalue(L"")] BSTR DestID,
    [in, defaultvalue(L"")] BSTR ChannelName,
```

```
    [in, defaultvalue(L"")] BSTR FilePath,
    [in, defaultvalue(L"")] BSTR EnvelopeName,
    [in, defaultvalue(FALSE)] BOOL PassThrough,
    [out, retval]  BSTR* SubmissionHandle);

  [helpstring("Submit a document and get a response")]
  HRESULT SubmitSync(
    [in] BIZTALK_OPENNESS_TYPE  lOpenness,
    [in, defaultvalue(L"")] BSTR Document,
    [in, defaultvalue(L"")] BSTR DocName,
    [in, defaultvalue(L"")] BSTR SourceQualifier,
    [in, defaultvalue(L"")] BSTR SourceID,
    [in, defaultvalue(L"")] BSTR DestQualifier,
    [in, defaultvalue(L"")] BSTR DestID,
    [in, defaultvalue(L"")] BSTR ChannelName,
    [in, defaultvalue(L"")] BSTR FilePath,
    [in, defaultvalue(L"")] BSTR EnvelopeName,
    [in, defaultvalue(FALSE)] BOOL PassThrough,
    [in,out, optional] VARIANT* SubmissionHandle,
    [in,out, optional] VARIANT* ResponseDocument);

  [helpstring("Retrieve suspended document handles")]
  HRESULT CheckSuspendedQueue(
    [in, defaultvalue("")] BSTR DocName,
    [in, defaultvalue("")] BSTR SourceName,
    [in, defaultvalue("")] BSTR DestName,
    [out, retval]  VARIANT* DocumentHandleList);

  [helpstring("Retrieve details for a suspended document")]
  HRESULT GetSuspendedQueueItemDetails(
    [in]  BSTR ItemHandle,
    [in,out] VARIANT* SourceName,
    [in,out] VARIANT* DestName,
    [in,out] VARIANT* DocName,
    [in,out] VARIANT* ReasonCode,
    [in,out] VARIANT* ItemData);

  [helpstring("Delete suspended documents")]
  HRESULT DeleteFromSuspendedQueue([in] VARIANT* DocumentHandleList);
};
```

Listing 8-1: The IInterchange interface expressed in IDL

The two submission methods differ in their execution mode. Documents submitted by using the *Submit()* method are placed in the work queue, while those submitted by using

SubmitSync() are immediately and synchronously processed. *Synchronous processing* means that the document is immediately assigned to a channel and port and sent to the destination. In this case, service windows are not honored.

If the protocol used for the messaging port is also synchronous (HTTP, Application Integration Components), the method returns the document returned by the endpoint. Should the document submission match multiple channels, or if the channel is configured to expect receipts for reliable messaging, the synchronous call cannot be executed and the method will fail.

Most of the arguments for both *Submit()* and *SubmitSync()* and the matches-multiple-channels mystery will be explained in context with document routing in the following section.

The *PassThrough* flag that exists in both methods is quite interesting. A pass-through submission bypasses all validation, encoding, encryption, and signature stages defined on channels and ports, and it routes the submitted document to the destination as is. This allows applications to use BizTalk's routing and transport capabilities to directly exchange custom or binary data formats.

DOCUMENT ROUTING

The *core* feature of BizTalk's Messaging services is *document routing* (as opposed to the *killer* feature, which is document mapping—it is really hard to pick a favorite between the two).

BizTalk enables applications to have documents automatically routed independently of transport protocols and protocol endpoints. Applications need to know only unique source and destination identifiers, and BizTalk will handle all routing autonomously.

This is ideal for both EDI and EAI scenarios. If an application produces an invoice as an electronic document, it can easily tell who the receiver is. The identity of the destination organization ABC Trading Enterprises, Inc., is an important fact in the business process. How a document actually reaches its destination and which physical path the data takes is not the responsibility of the business logic; rather; it's the task of the communications infrastructure. BizTalk provides the bridge between the business logic's concept of a destination and the physical delivery.

Routing Fundamentals

Any BizTalk document is routed from a source to a destination. As trivial as that may sound, that is the most fundamental principle for routing. Both source and destination are qualified by an organization identifier. As you know from the previous chapter, those identifiers are one of the following: either a plain-text string for an application identifier of the home organization, or a combination of an organization identifier qualifier that declares the standard for the identifier numbering scheme (like 02 for Dun & Bradstreet IDs) and a value that is the organization's ID within that scheme.

Whenever a document is submitted through the interchange component or a receive function, source and destination identifiers can be specified either explicitly as an argument to either of those submission methods, or one or both identifiers can be extracted directly from the document. Documents that contain complete routing information with both the source and destination identifiers and qualifiers are called *self-routing* because they can be handled without additional hints from the submitting application.

Self-routing documents are ideal. BizTalk Framework compliant (BFC) documents as well as X12 and UN/EDIFACT interchanges and many custom formats carry all necessary routing information in their envelopes. However, the necessary information might just as well be contained in the document payload. The four data items containing the source and destination qualifier and identifiers required to support self-routing are specially flagged within the document specification. For this, the BizTalk Schema defines four special attributes whose value is an XPath expression pointing to documents compliant with that schema. Using this information, the parsers know where to find the identifiers. (This applies to all formats.)

If documents are not self-routing, source and destination must be specified at submission time. If the identifier qualifier is omitted, it defaults to OrganizationName; this means that the source identifier must be the configured plain-text identifier of the source or destination organization.

Channel Selection

Documents are routed through channels. Which channel actually receives a document depends on a multitude of selection criteria. This mechanism is at the heart of BizTalk's routing capabilities—and its complexity is proportional to its power.

To make routing as clear as possible anyhow, let's establish a couple of prerequisites that will work within the scenarios discussed in the following sections. We will discuss the entire scenario in theory first. Later, in Chapters 14 through 17, we will actually implement and test a very similar scenario.

▼   Three organizations exist: Organization Alpha, Organization Beta, and the Home Organization. The home organization has one internal application called Order System. All three organizations are identified only by their organization name, so the qualifier OrganizationName applies.

■   Two document types exist: XMLPO, a generic purchase order expressed in XML, and X12PO, based on the X12 transaction set 850, which is also a purchase order. In addition, two mappings exist: one from XMLPO to X12PO, and one from X12PO to XMLPO.

■   Four messaging ports exist. For this discussion, we will neglect the transport details and just focus on the envelope format and destination identifier.

     ■   Port A is configured to have a BizTalk Framework (RELIABLE) envelope, and its destination identifier points to Organization Alpha.

     ■   Port B has an X12 envelope and points to Organization Beta.

     ■   Port C has no envelope assigned and points to Organization Beta.

     ■   Port D has no envelope either, and points to the internal application.

▲   Six channels exist, each bound to the port with the same respective letter in the name. So Channel A binds to Port A, and Channel D2 binds to Port D.

■   Channel A is configured to originate from the application. The inbound and outbound document type is XMLPO.

■   Channel B is set like Channel A, but with the outbound document type of X12PO and the XMLPO-to-X12PO document mapping.

■   Channel C1 is configured to have an open source and an inbound and outbound document format of XMLPO.

■   Channel C2 originates from the internal application and has an inbound and outbound format of XMLPO.

■   Channel D1 has the source organization set to Organization Alpha with the inbound document type being X12PO and the outbound format being XMLPO, and it has the X12PO-to-XMLPO document mapping.

■   Channel D2 originates from Organization Beta with inbound and outbound types set to XMLPO.

Now we can start exploring how channel selection works by using the components just outlined. In the following scenarios, *submitting* refers to either a submission using a receive function or the Interchange component.

Scenario 1

A document of type XMLPO is submitted with the following arguments:

Argument	Value
Openness	Not open
Source qualifier	OrganizationName
Source identifier	Home Organization
Destination qualifier	OrganizationName
Destination identifier	Organization Alpha
Document name	XMLPO
Envelope name	-
Channel name	-

In this case, the source qualifier matches all channels that are explicitly configured for the Home Organization, that is, all channels that have been configured for an application. There is no way to immediately specify a source application. Because Channel A, Channel B, and Channel C2 are configured accordingly, these are the first three matches in the selection process.

Now we look at the associated ports. Port A points to Organization Alpha, which is also a match for our arguments. Port B has the destination set to Organization Beta and therefore does not qualify. Port C does not qualify because it has an open destination, and openness was specifically excluded in the arguments.

Finally, we inspect the document type configured on Channel A. The type is indeed compatibly defined as XMLPO. Before the document type is checked against the channel configuration, the document is first validated against the document definition. If the document is not compliant with the XMLPO schema, processing is rejected.

If the document name argument were not given, BizTalk would first attempt to infer the document type from the document itself. This is done by matching the document against all schemas available in the management database until a schema is found with which the current document complies.

In this case, and also if the document name argument were blank, we have a match in Channel A and the document is routed through Channel A and out of Port A.

Scenario 2

A document of type XMLPO is submitted with the following arguments:

Argument	Value
Openness	Open source
Source qualifier	OrganizationName
Source identifier	Home Organization
Destination qualifier	OrganizationName
Destination identifier	Organization Beta
Document name	-
Envelope name	-
Channel name	-

Looking at the source identifiers in this case, and with prior knowledge from scenario 1, channels A, B, and C2 are again candidates for the initial channel selection. However, none of them will actually qualify. The difference in this scenario is that we have specified *open source* for the openness argument. An *open-source channel* is one that relies on either the submission function or the data contained in a self-routing document to find the source qualifier and identifiers.

If *open source* is specified, only channels that are configured as having an open source are selected. That said, Channel C1 is actually the only channel that matches. Because Port C matches for Organization Beta and the document is equally compatible, this is the route BizTalk picks.

Scenario 3

A document of type XMLPO is submitted with the following arguments:

Argument	Value
Openness	Not open
Source qualifier	OrganizationName
Source identifier	Home Organization
Destination qualifier	OrganizationName
Destination identifier	Organization Beta
Document name	-
Envelope Name	-
Channel Name	-

In this scenario, the openness flag is again set to *not open*. As in scenario 1, the initial matches are the channels A, B, and C2. This time, the destination is Organization Beta, so that eliminates Channel A because its port points to Organization Alpha. Channel B and Channel C2 remain as choices with identical source identifiers and the same destination identifiers on their bound ports.

Because no further constraints are defined and the inbound document format XMLPO also matches both channels, the document is routed through *both* channels in this case. The document is actually sent twice.

To avoid this behavior (which is by design and actually useful in certain scenarios), you can either explicitly specify the envelope to constrain the port use (Port B uses X12, Port C uses no envelope) or address the channel directly by name.

Scenario 4

You submit an X12PO document with the following arguments:

Argument	Value
Openness	Not open
Source qualifier	-
Source identifier	-
Destination qualifier	-
Destination identifier	-
Document name	-
Envelope name	-
Channel name	-

In this case, the document is dropped into BizTalk without any additional hints. For inbound traffic, this case is actually the most common. BizTalk asks all registered *parsers* (components that translate the document into BizTalk's internal XML representation) whether they recognize the document format. The X12 parser replies to this question with a firm "yes" and is chosen as the parser for this document.

Next, the parser is asked to retrieve source and destination information from the document. So whenever you do not specify any of the arguments at submission time, you can assume that the documents are self-routing.

The extracted information is Organization Alpha for the source organization and Home Organization for the destination. A quick look at the channel list reveals that the match is Channel D2 because it also has the correct document type X12PO assigned to it.

Sent through Channel D2, the document is converted into XMLPO and pushed to the internal application.

Channel Filters

Channel filters are also part of the routing process; they allow a level of control over the channel selection that goes considerably beyond the standard criteria. A *channel filter* is a complex XPath query into the XML representation of any document that enters the channel, which ultimately yields a Boolean True or False value.

If the filter expression evaluates to "true," the document is accepted into the channel; otherwise, it is rejected. You can construct the channel filter expression by using a wizard in the channel definition of the BizTalk Messaging Manager.

Open Destination Routing

The previous scenarios covered open source routing but not open destination routing. The reason is that *open destination routing* is indeed quite different from the abstract routing mechanisms that those examples show. Channel selection is performed based on data filters and organization identifiers. This is indeed a high-level operation that does not regard the physical routing destination, but serves only to pick the correct port whose settings are then used to perform the physical transport.

Open destinations are actually inconsistent with this concept. To phrase it differently: the open destination for ports is *not* equivalent to what open source is for a channel.

Unlike open source channels, where the source organization is intentionally left undefined and can be supplied later at submission time, open destination ports do primarily omit the definition of the transport. The BizTalk design logic here is that if the transport cannot be specified, the destination identifier cannot be specified either. Therefore, an open destination port has neither an associated transport nor a destination identifier.

Open destination ports are therefore not about an undefined, open messaging destination identifier; rather, they are directly about physical destination locations. Consequently, when you submit documents to a channel that is bound to a messaging port with an open destination, the destination identifier is not an organization identifier but a transport address expressed in URL format. The destination qualifier does not play any role for open destinations.

With an open destination port configuration, you can use BizTalk's Messaging just as an API, similar to the Windows Internet API that allows you to send validated and transformed documents to any physical destination that your application sees fit.

The downside is that the design decision that was made here—namely to use the destination identifier to specify the transport destination address and to leave no room for an organization identifier to be specified alongside the transport address—prohibits the standards-compliant use of UN/EDIFACT and X12. Surprisingly, and if we go by the words and intent of the endpoint header specification, even the BizTalk Framework envelope format cannot be used with open destination ports.

Because BizTalk hands the destination identifier (which is now the transport address) all the way to the serializer, the envelope is written with the transport address as the destination identifier. No matter how you look at it, a URL-formatted transport address will never be compliant with any of the identifiers permissible for EDI, so you can't use open destination ports for EDI envelopes. And without an EDI envelope, there is no functional group and no interchange and, consequently, no standards-compliant EDI document. While this does not preclude the use of custom envelope formats, the standard formats cannot be used. The bottom line is this: open destination ports are only for XML, flatfiles, or custom data formats that do not use any of the standard formats.

CHAPTER 9

BizTalk Orchestration Concepts

Orchestration is about logic. BizTalk's Orchestration services aim to provide the universal glue between applications and communication endpoints. Orchestration encapsulates business and decision logic in an easy-to-understand language and provides services that can execute this logic in a scalable manner. In effect, Orchestration is actually a very high-level programming language.

Typically, developers distinguish between high-level and low-level programming languages. Low-level languages are extremely powerful and allow the developer to go "down to the iron," controlling all aspects of the machine and accessing every API of the operating system and run-time environment. Using low-level languages also yields maximum performance.

Assembly is the fastest but most rudimentary and most simplistic of these languages, and it is the native tongue of the underlying machine. However, assembly is not very popular because it lacks structure and is bound to certain machine architecture. The C language family represents an almost ideal balance between the control qualities of Assembly and the powerful structural elements and expressiveness of C. For developers who need to exploit all features of an operating system, C and its object-oriented derivative C++ are therefore the most popular choices for system-level development on virtually any operating system on the market. Because so many developers and especially those in lead positions speak C fluently, the C language family is also often chosen as the implementation tool for business code. However, the low-level nature of C that allows a lot of control also mandates that a lot of control actually is executed.

Microsoft's Visual Basic (VB) has become the most popular language for business logic. Visual Basic's recipe for success is its simplicity. From the start, the Basic language family was designed to provide a simple, high-level development environment that is easy to understand and learn and that allows you to solve common programming tasks quickly. Basic carries the "beginner" even in its name: Basic is the "beginner's all-purpose symbolic instruction code."

Visual Basic hides the grueling details of the machine and the operating system from the developers' view and allows them to focus on providing business solutions. They do not need to worry about machine details and can easily design user interfaces like windows and dialog boxes. Visual Basic also provides the flow of data between those user-interface elements by reading and manipulating their properties. VB does an equally good job of creating nonvisual business components while hiding almost all of the complexity of the COM development model. Another advantage of VB is that it fully supports the core data types needed for business applications as part of the language.

All traditional programming languages represent logic, which requires very good and very specific abstraction skills. The most important asset of developers is their capacity to transform real-life requirements into a concept that is an abstraction of these requirements and then to implement that concept in even more abstract form in programming code. When developers claim that it takes talent to create good programs, they mean the ability to deal with those abstractions and the equally required skill to absorb and quickly understand masses of information. Software development is a world in which everything is logic and where everything seems to be doable.

On the other side of the fence are the people who feed developers—the business.

A COMMON LANGUAGE FOR DEVELOPERS AND ANALYSTS

Programs for BizTalk Orchestration, called *schedules* in BizTalk terms, are defined by using a simple graphical flowchart language. The flowchart language consists of no more than nine simple shapes that can be used to describe a business process.

Simplicity is key here. There is a scientifically well-established understanding that on average, people are capable of juggling only between five and nine different concepts at a time. (Chapter 13 digs into this subject in a bit more detail.) Traditional programming languages typically have many more elements, which makes them difficult to understand.

However, once you are accustomed to the typical elements, switching from one programming language to the other is usually quite easy. Developers are driven by the desire to grasp and tackle the complexity of computer programs: mastering a language is like climbing a mountain or running a marathon. (This explains why some developers climb mountains and run marathons once they know the most important programming languages.)

Luckily, BizTalk is a language that both developers and business experts can understand; it allows them to identify and implement business processes up front.

Table 9-1 lists the elements of the flowchart language used in the BizTalk Orchestration Designer and describes their purpose. The properties that are available for these shapes are discussed when we build schedules in Chapter 14. Ideally, you should be able to use

Shape	Purpose
Begin	The Begin shape is the single starting point for any flowchart. The text of the Begin shape always reads *Begin*. The Begin shape must have exactly one shape connected to its bottom edge.
End	The End shape terminates a workflow. While there is always exactly one Begin shape, there can be numerous terminators. An End shape must terminate each branch in a flowchart that results from a decision or a parallelism started with a Fork shape or a While loop (discussed later in this table). The End shape always has exactly one predecessor and is logically the only shape without a mandatory successor.

Table 9-1. The Elements of the Flowchart Language Used in the BizTalk Orchestration Designer

Shape	Purpose
	The Action shape represents actions. It generally describes any activity within a business process. This can be an action as precisely defined as receiving or sending a certain document (as shown here for Receive PO); it can also represent a more complex task like writing an invoice or even something very general like purchasing supply parts, which is a very complex business process in itself. Any action always has exactly one predecessor and one successor.
	The Decision shape serves to select from one of two or more sequences of workflows based on rules. The Decision shape can have 64 associated rules. A rule can evaluate certain conditions of the state of the workflow or of workflow messages, as you will see in Chapter 14. The outcome of a rule is always "true" or "false." If the outcome is "true," the connected path is chosen and all other paths are ignored. The Else rule is predefined and cannot be removed. The path connected to the Else rules is chosen if none of the other rules is "true." For example, if you model a purchase order–processing workflow, possible rules after receiving the purchase order could be Client's Credit Rating Okay?, Volume Requires Management Approval?, or Ordered Items in Stock? Each rule has a description associated with it, which should explain the rule in plain text. The actual rule is defined as a relational or logical expression, such as OrderVolume < 50000. Each rule, including the Else rule, must have exactly one successor.
	The While shape represents repetitive actions. Like the Decision shape, it works with rules. Each While shape can have one rule assigned to it. As long as the rule evaluates to "true," the connected workflow branch is executed. The branch connected to the rule is always terminated with an End shape. Once the flow has reached the End shape of the branch, the rule is evaluated again and the branch is executed as long as the rule is "true." Once the rule becomes "false," the Continue branch is executed. Like the Else rule of the Decision shape, the Continue rule cannot be removed.
	The Fork shape serves to create parallelisms in a workflow. While this is a very real requirement for business processes, forks often create major headaches for developers. With the simple Fork shape, the Orchestration flowchart language actually has the edge over traditional programming languages in terms of simplicity. A fork has exactly one predecessor and two or more successors. All successor paths are executed concurrently. Use forks if two actions or sequences of actions should be executed concurrently and independently of each other. In a business process, that may be preparing and sending an invoice while you order shipment of the goods.

Table 9-1. The Elements of the Flowchart Language Used in the BizTalk Orchestration Designer *(continued)*

Shape	Purpose
	The Join shape serves to synchronize parallel workflows and to rejoin flows after a decision was made. To allow for both, the Join shape comes in two flavors, which can be switched in the shape's property settings. The AND join waits for any number (the technical limit is 64) of parallel branches to reach the Join shape until the workflow proceeds to the successive action. The AND join must be used only for branches produced by the Fork shape because only one of the branches produced by a Decision shape will actually execute; thus, two Decision branches can never fulfill the conditions for the AND join to proceed.
	The OR join waits for the first branch to reach the Join shape until the workflow proceeds. It is actually an error if another branch hits the Join shape once the workflow has gone past an OR join. Consequently, the OR join can be used only for branches produced by the Decision shape. Generally, the Join shape can have two or more predecessors and exactly one successor.
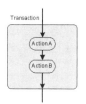	The Transaction shape serves to group multiple actions into a transaction. Generally speaking, a *transaction* is a group of actions that must jointly succeed or jointly fail.
	The traditional example for this is a bank money transfer. The first action debits one account and the second credits another account. If only the first action succeeds and the second fails, the money would simply vanish without a trace.
	Transactions group actions that are tightly related, as in this example, and ensure that either both of them work or both fail. If the first action has already been executed when the second fails, any result of the first action is annulled and ineffective.
	In business processes, annulling an action is more complex than in databases. If a letter has been printed and mailed, it is a whole different ballgame than deleting a row from a database. To implement compensation steps that rescue situations like these, the Transaction shape allows you to associate compensation transactions for any transaction in case of failure.
	The Transaction shape can have exactly one predecessor and one successor. Any number of actions can be inside the shape: the first action is bound to the top edge of the shape and the last to the bottom edge.
	You can use the Abort shape only within transactions. If the transaction cannot logically succeed and must be aborted, the shape terminates the flow within the transaction and cancels it. If a compensation transaction is defined, it is started by the Abort shape.

Table 9-1.   The Elements of the Flowchart Language Used in the BizTalk Orchestration Designer *(continued)*

this language without the Designer tool (with pencil and paper or on a flipchart). This is actually an excellent idea while you are in the analysis stages and need to actively discuss business process design with larger groups of people.

Now let's put all of these shapes into context with an example: a simple business workflow that we will incrementally refine to include all shapes.

Figure 9-1 shows a simple workflow that starts, waits to receive a purchase order, processes it, and terminates. The illustration is so obvious that everyone in a business who performs any type of trade transactions, from the CEO to the mail person, should easily understand it. That is exactly the purpose of the BizTalk flowchart language. In Chapter 14, we will explore how you can actually preserve that simplicity and large-scale overview even for very complex workflows by using cascaded schedules. For now, we are going to extend this example.

NOTE: Cascaded schedules is not an official BizTalk term; rather, it is a term invented for this book to describe subordinate schedules that are being launched by other schedules.

Figure 9-2 is a more detailed view of the same process.

Here we first check the inventory based on the ordered items and then decide how to proceed based on whether all items are in stock. If all items are in stock, we proceed to further handle the order. If not, we put the order in the backorder queue for later execution. That does not necessarily mean that we just let the order rest, but we may also want to notify the customer of the situation and let the inventory organization know that we have open orders for out-of-stock items. Figure 9-3 reflects this.

When we put items on backorder, we want to make sure that the order is placed in our own backorder queue, notify the customer of the delay, and notify our inventory department

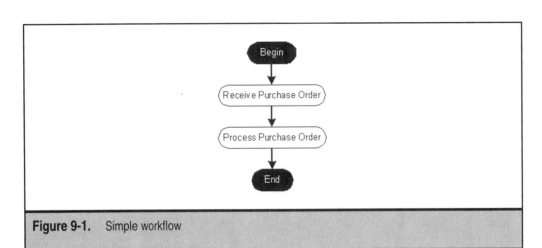

Figure 9-1.   Simple workflow

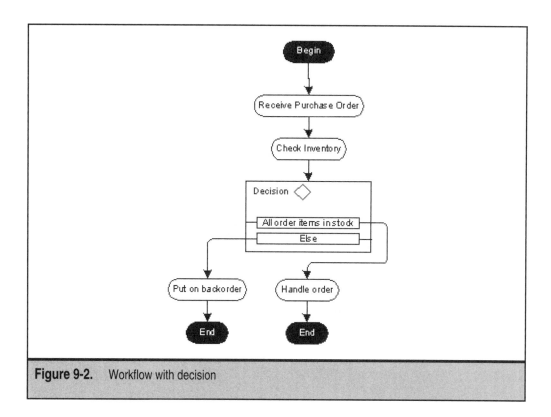

Figure 9-2. Workflow with decision

that they need to get the ordered items quickly. If we cannot properly place the order into the backorder queue or we cannot notify the inventory organization, we do not want to send a notification to the customer yet. First, we want to retry the entire sequence. In the drawing, we use a Transaction shape to express this.

Now we take care of handling orders (see Figure 9-4). When we do this, we can actually perform a few tasks at once. We let the shipper company know that we will have an order ready for pickup (which gives us a tracking ID and label to put on the package). At the same time, we advise our accounting department to write an invoice that we can later attach to the package and appropriately debit the internal customer account. While we do this, we tell our inventory to collect the items from the warehouse. Having done all of this, we hand invoice and shipper tracking information to the inventory to ready the package for shipment.

"A few tasks at once" is expressed by using the Fork shape here. The three actions that follow the fork are executed in parallel. This optimizes our process. None of the three actions depends on the other, so we can do them all at once and then resynchronize when all

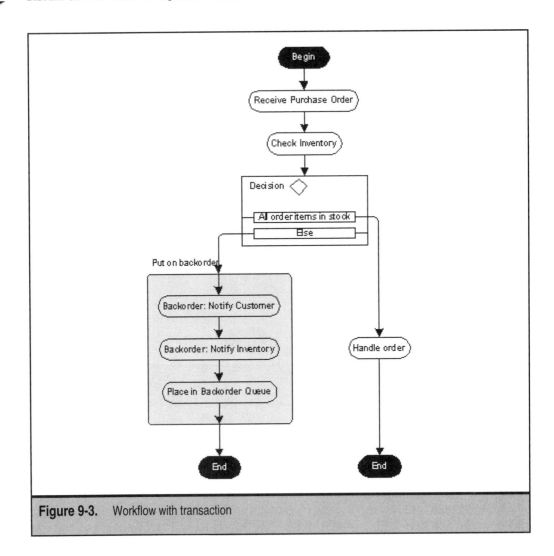

Figure 9-3. Workflow with transaction

have been executed. This gives the warehouse some lead time to get the ordered items out of the storage while we wait for the other two tasks to complete.

In Figure 9-5, we enhance the backorder process. After the order is placed into the backorder queue, the workflow enters a While loop. We want the loop to execute while the order is in the backorder queue. In the loop, the workflow first halts for two days and then rechecks the inventory. If all items are now in stock, the order is removed from the backorder queue and the branch ends. At this point, the while condition is evaluated anew, will fail to meet the condition, and proceeds into the regular order-handling process. Otherwise, we will send a polite apology e-mail to the customer explaining that we are working hard to get the order processed soon.

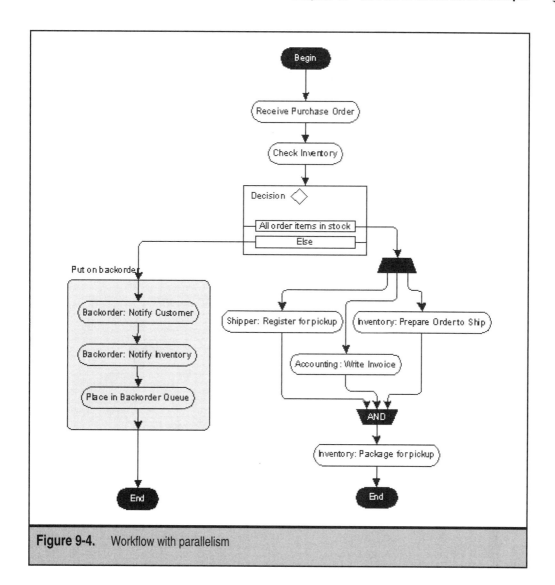

Figure 9-4.   Workflow with parallelism

To enable rejoining of the original handling process, an OR join has been placed right after the initial decision. Orders flow there either right after determining that the order can be executed immediately or after they have been in the backorder loop.

We have not yet considered that an item may be out of stock permanently because the supplier is not producing it anymore. In this case, shown in Figure 9-6, the transaction to place the order on backorder must be aborted explicitly, and in the compensating transaction the customer must be notified that the order cannot be executed as ordered.

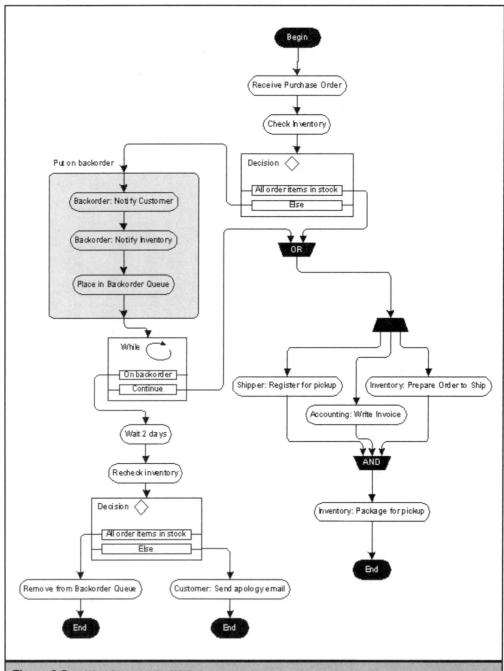

Figure 9-5. Workflow with the While loop

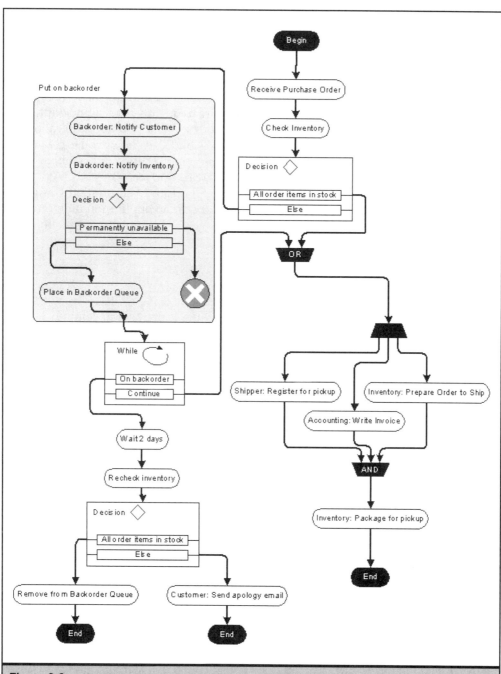

Figure 9-6.   Workflow with transaction abort

Assuming you are on the developer side of things, if you sit down with a customer or internal business analyst and develop the business processes incrementally, as in this example, both sides will understand exactly what is being talked about. Once you have found and mutually agreed on a solution that precisely fits the business needs, you can go implement it. Then the likelihood that the result will exactly match the requirements is very high. This is because the analysis language that was presented here is also the implementation language.

Flowchart drawings like the ones you just saw are frequently made with graphics applications that were designed for that task. One of the most popular applications for drawing structured business graphics is Microsoft Visio 2000. It allows you to create business workflow drawings by using a stencil with predefined shapes and symbols, which you can drag with your mouse and drop on the drawing surface.

Because Visio enjoys such great popularity, the BizTalk Orchestration Designer—BizTalk Server's XLANG schedule design tool—is a custom application built on top of Visio, and everyone who knows that drawing package will be immediately familiar with how to use it.

FROM DRAWINGS TO APPLICATIONS

What is most interesting about these flowchart drawings is that they are entirely technology-agnostic. If you define business workflows in the BizTalk Orchestration Designer language, you can implement them in any technology, including traditional paper-based processes and postal mail services. The same is true for the reverse case. If you already have predefined processes in your organizations, they may be expressed in a similar graphical flowchart language and translate easily, or they may be quickly formalized in the Orchestration language from plain-text documents, which was done in the previous examples. Whether they are actually implemented in software, purely manual processes, or a mix of both is not important at the design stage. What is important is that you get a clear picture of what your processes are and which steps are required to achieve certain business objectives.

So how do you create actual programs from these flowchart drawings?

If you look at the example flowcharts, you will find that seven of the nine elements that were presented are used to implement structure and flow control. The Begin, End, and Abort shapes mark beginning and endings of workflows. The Decision, While, Fork, and Join shapes serve to model application flow, and the Transaction shape groups tightly related activities. The only shape that is "active" in that it implements specific business tasks is the Action shape.

An *action* is the finest level of granularity available to Orchestration schedules. An action is typically a complex task in itself. Such a task may be receiving or sending a document, but also preparing invoices, submitting financial data to accounting, or executing other specialized business logic. None of these tasks is thought to be implemented in the Orchestration language itself; instead, they are provided by external logic created with

Visual Basic or other programming languages or by messaging services such as BizTalk's. Only if an action in a workflow is so generic that it represents a workflow by itself is it possible that it might be implemented as an Orchestration schedule. However, in the end, these subschedules must also call external code to perform any meaningful tasks.

This restriction is by design. Having looked at the simplicity of the graphical symbols, you probably did not expect Orchestration to be an all-purpose programming language. The rationale for Orchestration is reuse.

The most successful development paradigm of the past decade is *not* object orientation but component orientation. *Components* are reusable blocks of code that implement well-defined aspects of a user interface, a server infrastructure, or a business-logic model. Components are built as generic solutions and are typically designed for reuse. For example, an implementation of the calculation formula for monthly health-insurance fees based on insurance customer profiles is universally useful for the insurance company in any of their applications, no matter whether the application is used by traveling salespeople on a PocketPC device or in the back end of their Internet portal application. The reusability of the component is independent of whether the component is implemented using a sophisticated object-oriented language or assembly language, as long as it can be accessed via a component model like COM or an open access protocol like SOAP.

Because components allow business logic to be used and reused in many contexts, many line-of-business applications employ a three-tier or N-tier application model where the user interface (or generally any interface with the outside world) is clearly separated from the business logic, which by itself has a sharply defined boundary with the data access and storage layer. If a web site's user interface must get a major overhaul because the marketing department changed their minds on site design and navigation, the core (expensive) business logic can typically be fully reused while every single pixel of the user interface is moved around. With a proper three-tier design, even radical changes to the underlying data storage should not affect the business logic implementation because data access belongs to the bottommost layer.

Indeed, many companies already have a vast array of componentized business logic available as the back end of their Internet and intranet solutions. BizTalk Orchestration allows you to reuse these building blocks to implement partially or fully automated business processes and to regroup these components quickly to adjust for changes in the way your organization conducts business. This goes back to the document-driven systems discussion in the beginning of this book. As data integration between partners gets tighter and enabling technology and standards become more available, interactive applications, even on the Web, will decrease in significance, and data that has previously been entered interactively will increasingly be exchanged directly as electronic documents.

Interactive desktop and web applications provide the glue between business logic components based on the user interface layout and navigational structure. The combination of user interface and business logic is typically perceived to be a full application. For automated business processes, this model does not apply. For those we just have a process definition, components that execute logic within the scope of the process, and possibly no user interface at all. Consequently, such applications lack the entire layer that previously served to bind all those components and provided flow control. BizTalk Orchestration is the replacement.

So if you go back and look at the last example workflow drawing from this perspective, you may be able to easily imagine a fully interactive web application that implements the depicted process. In that imaginary web application, any "action" would be some business component or data sink/source that you would have to tap, and the flow control would likely be coded somewhere in your page's scripts. Orchestration is exactly like this model. Control flow is implemented using the visual Orchestration language, and actions are calls to external components or some kind of read or write access to external data sources.

Ports

The links between actions and components or communication channels are called *ports*. This use of the term "port" is entirely different than the one used in messaging. A port in Orchestration is simply a communications gateway from a scheduled action to some external communication or component that has properties reflecting the data that can flow in and out of that component.

Each port is associated with exactly one external component but may be linked to multiple actions. That said, looking at Figure 9-7 reveals that the inventory is being checked at two separate instances. This is a typical scenario where you would reuse one port for multiple actions.

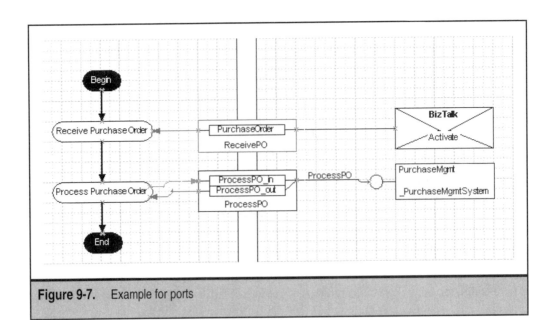

Figure 9-7.   Example for ports

In the Orchestration schedule drawing, ports are represented by squares sitting on a white bar, which serves to separate the business drawing and the implementation portion of the schedule. This visually reflects their gateway functionality.

A port is labeled with a unique name that must not contain any special characters or white space and may be at most 32 characters long. These restrictions result from the fact that schedules are being compiled into XML before they can be executed, and the port name is actually used as an identifier within that XML file. The XML format used to express Orchestration schedules is called XLANG. Before you can run a schedule, you must produce an XLANG file with the Orchestration Designer, and only these XLANG files can actually be executed by the XLANG Scheduler service.

Each port has a number of properties that reflect the data that can be submitted or received through that port. The port properties are an abstraction of the arguments of bound components or data received or submitted through bound communication services.

Orchestration supports four different kinds of components and communication elements that can be bound to ports, as shown in Table 9-2.

Shape	Purpose
	This shape represents COM components. You can bind almost any COM or COM+ component to a schedule. However, only components that expose dual and dispatch interfaces can be bound, which must be described by a type library.
	Ideally, all components that are being bound to schedules are fully stateless. This means that they do not keep any information in local variables across function calls that affect the component's behavior. This aids scalability and overall performance of schedules but is not required.
	If components hold state, they should implement the IPersistStream or IPersistStreamInit interfaces. When BizTalk suspends processing of a schedule while it waits for inbound messages for it, it "dehydrates" the schedule's state by writing it to disk and removes the schedule from memory. This includes saving all states that components hold. To let components save their state, BizTalk creates a stream and invokes the component's *IPersistStream.Save()* method. If a component does not support either of these two interfaces, the schedule cannot be dehydrated, which leads to higher resource consumption and an overall decrease of system performance.
	Ports to COM components are always synchronous. Therefore, they are bidirectional and always exhibit the inbound and outbound arguments of a COM method as attributes.

Table 9-2. Components and Communication Elements That Can Be Bound to Ports

Shape	Purpose
	This shape serves to bind windows script components (WSC) to a schedule. Windows script components are essentially COM components implemented with VBScript or JScript. Scripts are useful when prototyping BizTalk systems or in the very unlikely case that you want to build BizTalk solutions but do not have a COM-enabled development environment available. The BizTalk SDK examples use far more scripting components than Visual Basic or ATL COM components. It is probably best if you do not take this as a hint for best practices, because it is not. Because WSC use COM, these components are also synchronous and bidirectional.
	The message queue port connects an action to an inbound or outbound queue of the Microsoft Message Queue (MSMQ) service that is included with Windows 2000. Message queuing ports are always unidirectional. You either use the port to send a message or to receive a message. Target queues may be private local queues or public queues that are registered in a Windows 2000 network domain. If the port is inbound, the schedule is suspended and dehydrated until a message arrives in the specified queue. Once that happens, the schedule is rehydrated. The message is picked up and the schedule proceeds. If the port is outbound, the message is placed into the queue. If you plan to build larger Orchestration applications, this shape is going to be your best friend. You will love it so much that you will give it a nickname after a week and put a poster of it on your office wall. I promise!
	BizTalk Orchestration also directly supports BizTalk Messaging. This shape represents an outbound port to a BizTalk Messaging channel or an inbound messaging port. (Beware of the terminology differences!) Outbound BizTalk Messaging Orchestration ports are quite simple in that they are bound to a messaging channel and with this function, much like the submit function on the messaging Interchange component. Inbound BizTalk messaging ports are substantially more complicated. Therefore, they are explained in the following section.

Table 9-2. Components and Communication Elements That Can Be Bound to Ports *(continued)*

BizTalk Messaging Integration

The complexity of integrating Orchestration schedules with BizTalk's Messaging services proves that Orchestration and Messaging are indeed two different products bundled into one product. You would expect Messaging and Orchestration to be tightly and seamlessly integrated; unfortunately, that is not the case.

The Messaging Side

When you create a messaging port to an application, you have the choice of creating a port to a new XLANG Orchestration schedule. Such messaging ports function like any of their siblings, but their endpoint is a new instance of a certain schedule instead of a file or HTTP location. The schedule is specified using a simple path reference to an XLANG file and the Orchestration port name to which the message shall be delivered.

The XLANG schedule must contain a BizTalk messaging shape connected to a port with that name. Figure 9-8 illustrates that relationship.

Sending messages to new XLANG schedules is indeed just as easy as the reverse way of sending a message to a well-known channel from an outbound BizTalk port in a schedule.

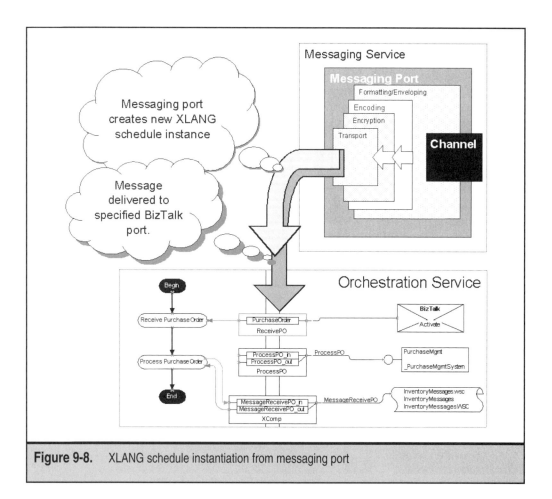

Figure 9-8.   XLANG schedule instantiation from messaging port

The whole topic gets very hairy when you want to receive BizTalk messages in running schedules. The core of that problem is that BizTalk Messaging is a service that always actively pushes messages to a destination. This is fundamentally different from COM or message queuing, where the service is passively waiting for the client (which would be the schedule in our case) to invoke a method or fetch the next message from the queue. Orchestration schedules implement flow control and execute actions. They require their associated communication and logic components to be passive and invoked whenever the schedule deems it is time to do so. Consequently, BizTalk Messaging and running BizTalk Orchestration schedules cannot be fully integrated, except for starting schedules from Messaging or submitting documents from Orchestration.

Because this problem is clearly not acceptable within what is supposed to be a single product, BizTalk works around it with what can only be described as a hack.

Active schedules can only receive messages from the BizTalk Messaging Service when they have previously sent a message to or through that service. This is because only the immediate creator of a schedule instance and the schedule instance itself know about its existence and identity. If a scheduled instance wants to receive a BizTalk message, it must therefore publish its identity to the sender before any inbound message can be correlated and routed to the scheduled instance.

To establish that link, the schedule sends a message through BizTalk's Messaging Service to the communicating party that contains a reference to a return port. A *return port* is a combination of an HTTP URL and a BizTalk Messaging channel name. From the base URL, the channel name, and a special message queue name—which is created on the fly and is unique to the schedule—a reply-to address is built when the message is sent to the destination system. The receiver on the other side can use this address to send a response document back.

Back at the sender system (where the schedule runs), this response is processed by what the documentation calls a *specially configured* ASP page located at the HTTP URL defined in the return port parameters. This page extracts the channel name and queue name from the URL. The response message is then posted to the channel, whose associated Messaging port must be configured as open destination because the message queue is used as the destination identifier.

Under the hood, the scheduler process listens on that message queue, picks up the message, and associates it with the matching Orchestration port in the active schedule.

Besides being so complicated that it takes a few hours to figure out the functional principles described in the previous four paragraphs, this model has several other flaws:

▼ **Problem #1**   The reply-to address must be communicated within the outbound document that is initially sent through a BizTalk channel to establish the link. The problem is that the reply-to address belongs in the protocol layer and not in the payload. The appropriate place would therefore be in the message envelope. The only way to achieve this is to populate an envelope format directly from within the schedule. Of course, this conflicts with BizTalk Messaging's automatic use of envelopes.

■ **Problem #2**   The other side must be aware of the configuration requirements. It must be capable of identifying the reply-to address from a field of an inbound document and use that address to send a message back.

■ **Problem #3**   HTTP is the only transport that is supported. This also requires the source and target system to have a direct connection with no intermediary messaging routing hops.

▲ **Problem #4**   The configuration effort is immense. Receiving a BizTalk message in a schedule requires setting up an ASP page as well as configuring two channels and two messaging ports.

The bottom line is, you should definitely use BizTalk Messaging to instantiate new XLANG schedules. You should also use the BizTalk Messaging shape to send documents to channels. You should stay as far away as you can from inbound (receiving) BizTalk Messaging Orchestration ports. They are simply not worth the hassle.

Because the scheduler itself relies on them, the most elegant solution is to use private message queues to exchange messages directly between BizTalk Messaging and active BizTalk Orchestration schedules. Chapter 14 addresses this subject in more detail.

CHAPTER 10

BizTalk Messaging Tools Overview

This final chapter of the overview portion of this book presents the tools that you will use to create BizTalk messaging solutions and to manage BizTalk services. Part IV looks at each tool and the related tasks in more detail. The tasks surrounding Orchestration and the BizTalk Orchestration Designer are presented in their entirety in Chapter 14. For now, here's the list of tools described in this chapter:

▼ **BizTalk Editor**   The document specification definition tool

■ **BizTalk Mapper**   The tool to interactively create mappings between document types

■ **BizTalk Messaging Manager**   The configuration tool for BizTalk Messaging

■ **BizTalk Administrator**   The administration tool for monitoring activities

▲ **BizTalk Document Tracking**   The interactive interface to the document tracking database

BIZTALK EDITOR

BizTalk Editor, shown in Figure 10-1, is the tool that you use to create or modify BizTalk document specifications. Although the Editor's native format is BizTalk Schema, which by itself is a superset of the XML Data Reduced (XDR) schema format, the Editor is not limited to creating specifications for XML. Because BizTalk's parser and serializer components are schema-driven, they use specifications created with the Editor to read and write UN/EDIFACT, X12, or flatfile documents. The design of the Editor and the BizTalk Schema language also allows for custom extensions that you can use as processing hints for your own custom components. BizTalk Editor is the one-stop solution to describe all data formats that pass through BizTalk.

The Editor tool has three different panes. The upper two panes define the document structure. The bottom pane displays warnings from specification and document validation tasks; it also provides you with sample output from XML document instances.

The upper-left pane contains a tree view that reflects the hierarchical structure of the document. While flatfiles and EDI formats are sequential physical formats, the hierarchical organization reflects their conceptual structure with nested segments, composites, and elements, which in turn may be repeated in loops. For XML, the tree is a 1:1 representation of the physical document hierarchy. The terminology used in the Editor is a bit different from XML, though. Elements that contain other elements or that have attributes (!) are called *records*, while attributes or elements that have text-only content are called *fields*. In X12 and UN/EDIFACT terms, the record is a composite, a single segment, or a predefined sequence of segments (loop). A field corresponds to a single element.

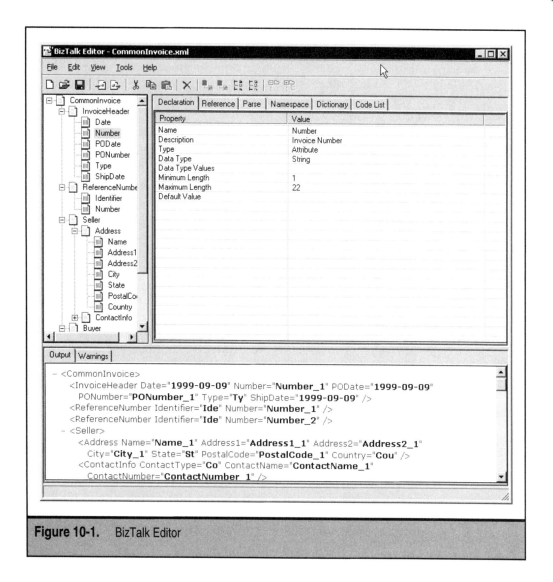

Figure 10-1. BizTalk Editor

The upper-right pane serves to review and define the details of each field and record. It is grouped into six different views that you can reach via tabs (or by using the View menu, if you prefer keyboard navigation).

▼ The Declaration view contains information about the field or record in the context of its specific data format. This includes the element name and a description, the element type (element or attribute), and the type of the contained data and applicable constraints.

- The Reference view serves to specify how often the element is referenced by its immediate parent. For the root element of a specification, this view contains information about the document type, the document standard (XML, UN/EDIFACT, X12, or others), and the respective standards version and revision. Envelopes and receipt specifications that play a special role in BizTalk are flagged in this view as well.

- The Parse view is used only for non-XML formats. When non-XML formats enter the BizTalk domain, they are always translated into an internal XML representation and are serialized back to the native format immediately before they are sent to the destination. In this view, you define the hints for the parsers and serializers to properly perform this task.

- The Namespace view serves to define namespaces for the schema. This is *not* the place to define namespaces that will appear in document instances. You cannot define mixed-namespace documents by using BizTalk Editor. Rather, namespace references allow you to specify custom namespaces to augment the produced BizTalk Schema with your own extensions. This is useful primarily if you write your own parsers or serializers and need extra hints and attributes in the schema to perform that work. Each BizTalk Schema references three standard namespaces: XDR (urn:schemas-microsoft-com:xml-data), XDR data types (urn:schemas-microsoft-com:datatypes), and BizTalk Schema (urn:schemas-microsoft-com:BizTalkServer). With additional namespace references, you can add custom properties to both the Declaration and Reference views, which you can evaluate in your custom serialization and parsing components. If you are OK with BizTalk's built-in data format support, you do not need to touch this view.

- The Dictionary view allows you to define a data dictionary for an XML document that consists of XPath references. This dictionary is used to unambiguously provide information for parsers or serializers for where they can find or should insert certain well-known information such as the source and destination identifiers. The most common entries are preset, but you can extend the dictionary list for your own purposes.

- ▲ The Code List view applies only to UN/EDIFACT and X12. Code lists are part of the semantics model of both standards and provide scores of predefined values that are applicable to a certain data element. For each standard field that has an associated code list, you can pick a range: all or none of the values provided in the code lists. If you select code list entries, you automatically create a constraint that allows only one of the selected values to be used for the current element.

BizTalk document specifications are XDR documents; as such, they can be saved as and loaded from files. BizTalk also supports storing and retrieving documents via the

Web Distributed Authoring and Versioning (WebDAV) protocol. WebDAV is a special HTTP-based protocol that enables file-system type access to so-called web-storage systems. BizTalk Editor allows you to access remote schema repositories directly, instead of having to download and upload documents manually through an intermediate tool like an FTP client or Internet Explorer. When BizTalk is installed, it automatically creates such a WebDAV storage system on the server machine by setting up a new virtual directory called BizTalkServerRepository on the default Internet Information Server (IIS) web site.

If you primarily use BizTalk Messaging, you should get in the habit of using the WebDAV system as the main storage location for your specifications because BizTalk Messaging Manager can import documents only from there and not from file locations.

Now here comes the surprise: if Orchestration is your focus, storing your specifications in the file system makes more sense because the Orchestration Designer can import only from there and does not support WebDAV. Just take that as another sign that BizTalk is really two different products in one box.

When you want to create a new BizTalk specification, there are essentially three ways to start. You can begin building specifications from scratch or based on a predefined template, or you can have BizTalk Editor derive a specification from an existing XML document instance, an XDR schema, or an XML DTD. The predefined templates include a trade-centric selection of full-scale interchange definitions from UN/EDIFACT versions D93A, D95A, D95B, D97B, D98A, and D98B, as well as from the X12 releases 2040, 3010, 3060, and 4010.

A couple of XML templates are also included, which are very useful for representing data internally. You may even be able to use one of these templates as an intercompany data exchange format. However, these XML templates are not based on any standard; rather, they reflect what Microsoft saw as the most common definition for the respective purpose. Hence, the names are CommonInvoice, CommonPO (Purchase Order), etc.

For new specifications that are built from scratch or based on a template, select File | New (or use the keyboard shortcut CTRL-N) or click the New toolbar button (looks like a blank sheet; see Figure 10-2). If you want an existing document on which to base that specification, select Tools | Import.

Most of the basic editing capabilities and tools are very easy to pick up indeed. For that reason—and assuming that you have at least a basic understanding of how to get around in Microsoft Windows even though you may have previously worked with another operating environment—we are not going to do a basic walk-through demonstrating how to move around in BizTalk Editor, but just point to the navigational elements by name.

The most important element for creating and modifying the structure of a document specification is the tree view. The tree view in BizTalk works much like it does in Windows Explorer in that you add, delete, and rename fields and records through the Edit menu or the context menu (the menu that appears when you right-click your mouse or the menu-key on a Windows-enhanced keyboard). Each node in the tree has an associated Properties dialog box that allows you to store documentary notes on the Notes tab.

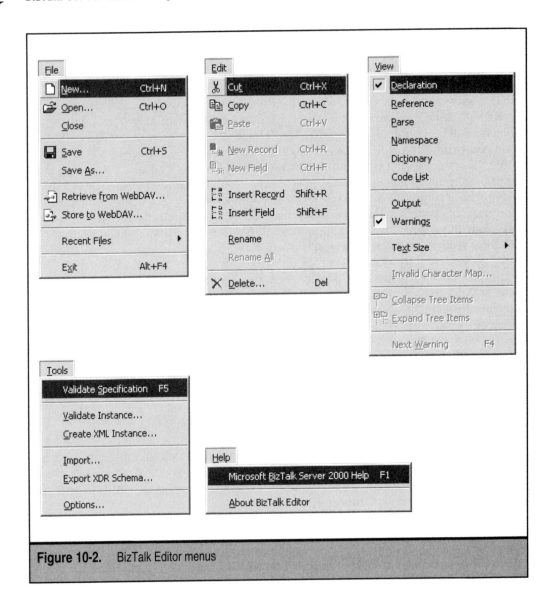

Figure 10-2. BizTalk Editor menus

For X12 and UN/EDIFACT formats, the Properties dialog box has an additional tab that contains a description of special syntax rules that are part of the specification but that cannot be directly reflected in BizTalk Schema. On this tab, you will typically find descriptions of intersegment dependencies. Because these dependencies are part of the standard, they are read-only.

> **NOTE:** BizTalk Editor will not always give you full control over all details of the specification shape and content. For example, BizTalk Editor does not allow you to implement X12 and UN/EDIFACT specifications that are of equivalent functionality as the BizTalk-supplied ones because it is hiding a few specialties of the BizTalk Schema format—building templates for itself is apparently not its purpose. The appendix contains an unofficial, partial, no-guarantee-for-accuracy decoding of the BizTalk Schema format, and you will learn how to work around this limitation to adopt transaction sets that do not ship with BizTalk.

The tasks that you perform in the tree view depend on the document standard you are working with. For XML, you will typically create entirely new specifications, adjust and extend one of the predefined document structures, or shape the structure to comply with a bilaterally or consortium-defined schema format. When you work with flatfile formats, you will model a specification narrowly on the format's syntax rules. For X12 and UN/EDIFACT, the default action is Delete.

As you will recall from the document format introduction in Chapter 3, both EDI standards define huge transaction sets that include the cross-product of any data that any business may ever want to exchange. In reality, a group of partners (or even an entire industry for that matter) will use only a fractional subset of any transaction set. So for the EDI formats, you use BizTalk Editor to cut out all definitions that are not part of your industry or partner agreement's subset definitions. (Chapter 15 provides more specifics on how to perform these tasks.)

BIZTALK MAPPER

Document standardization is good. The vision of UN/EDIFACT, X12, BizTalk.org, SWIFT, and all those other EDI standards bodies, communities, or consortia is to define a single global standard for electronic documents that every organization uses and understands.

Unfortunately, document standardization doesn't work on a global scale. Within the ISO- or UN-sanctioned megastandards, the sheer mass of definitions is too large to handle, and individual businesses do not produce the data for even half of what could be transported. Therefore, definitions based on those standards are designed to be cut down to a useful subset, leaving only bare-bones syntax rules and a basic mutual understanding of the document segments. The overall document structure is typically proprietary. For XML, such standards do not even exist (yet). Here you have virtually every company that wants to have their chunk of the trillion-dollar B2B market trying to set their own standards (including Microsoft, of course).

Fortunately, BizTalk Mapper, shown in Figure 10-3, is an amazing tool that allows you to map between all these different document formats.

A quick reminder to start with: internally, BizTalk routes all documents as XML data streams, independent of the external physical format. As such, documents can be transformed from one schema into another schema by using XML Stylesheet Language

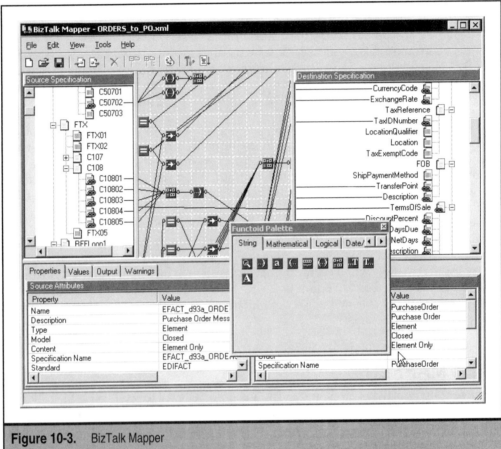

Figure 10-3. BizTalk Mapper

Transformations (XSLT). XSLT can be applied to map between XML schemas, from or to EDI, from or to XML, or equally well between any EDI formats.

BizTalk Mapper lets you create these XSLT documents visually, without having to write a single line of XSLT code yourself. The Mapper stores these "maps" in its own XML schema format, which contains the resulting XSLT, the source and destination schemas, and additional information that is required by the tool to recreate the exact same visual representation of your map every time you open it. This format is also understood by BizTalk Messaging Service.

However, the Mapper also allows you to export the XSLT map individually and thus enables you to use those maps with the Microsoft XML parser (MSXML, version 3.0), entirely independent of BizTalk. To do this, select File | Save Compiled Map As or use the keyboard shortcut CTRL-M.

Other XML parsers have difficulty understanding and processing BizTalk XSLT documents fully because MSXML already supports the scripting capabilities that are going to be part of only the next revision of the XSLT specification. To use the Mapper for non-BizTalk purposes, you must describe your XML documents in the BizTalk Schema language by creating them with or importing them through BizTalk Editor, of course.

The scripting support is required because the Mapper provides much more than simple field-to-field assignments and the XSLT function set. You can combine and group field values from the source specification in several ways to produce values for the destination, including using functoids. *Functoids* are small scripts that you implement either as XSLT expressions or by using Microsoft's VBScript scripting language. Out of the box, BizTalk Mapper comes with over 60 predefined functoids that cover string manipulation, basic and scientific mathematical calculations, logical operations, date and time functions, data-type conversions, cumulative operations, database lookups, operations that work on the document structure, and finally, script writing.

BizTalk Mapper has four separate visual areas.

On top is a tree view for the source specification pane (left side) and one for the destination specification pane (right side), which displays the document structures the same way as BizTalk Editor does. Between them is the *grid*: the area where you create the mappings between the two specifications.

To create a mapping between fields, you create a direct link between them by selecting an item either in the source or in the destination and then dragging that link to the matching node in the other specification. As you can probably tell, mapping is entirely mouse-driven. If you cannot or do not want to use a mouse, you must resort to the Windows 2000 MouseKeys accessibility feature.

If no one-to-one mapping exists for a field, you use a functoid, which you access from a special toolbox window. To open this window, select View | Functoid Palette or click the toolbar icon that looks like a painter's palette. The toolbox contains all available functoids, nicely grouped in categories. If you want to add up a range of numeric source specification fields and insert the calculated sum into the destination, click the Mathematical tab, drag the plus sign (+) functoid, and drop it into the grid. Then you connect all source fields that will be summed up to that icon and afterwards connect the target field of the destination specification. Connecting fields to functoids always starts at the field from where you drag the link onto the functoid. If you try it the other way around, you will only move the functoid in the grid.

On the bottom is the messages and warnings pane, which allows you to view the details of the individual elements, to specify test data for the source, and to view the results and warnings of testing the map while you are working on it. This pane contains the following four tabs:

▼ The Properties tab shows the definition details and the description for the selected tree-view element of the source specification (on the left) and the destination specification (on the right). This allows you to understand the purpose, cardinality, data type, and constraints of the individual elements and thus provides you with the necessary hints to select an appropriate mapping functoid.

- On the Values tab, you can enter a test value for every source element. When you test the map, this value will be run through the functoids and inserted at the respective place in the output document. For the destination document, this is the place to enter constant values for fields, which have no corresponding source value in the source document.

- On the Output tab, you can view the result from test runs of the specification (which is even more important than brushing your teeth and can be done by pressing CTRL-F5 or by selecting Tools | Test Map).

▲ The Warnings tab lists all the problems that the Mapper finds based on the document structure definitions. Here you will find warnings in case you have not connected a required destination field or have mappings that have other logical or technical errors. You should really consider every warning as a serious definition error and make sure that every map has no warnings before you start using it in BizTalk Messaging.

In Chapter 16, you will learn how to create document maps.

BIZTALK MESSAGING MANAGER

The tool you use to configure BizTalk's Messaging services is BizTalk Messaging Manager (see Figure 10-4), which provides the user interface to define messaging ports, channels, organizations and applications, envelopes, document definitions, and distributions lists.

Although Messaging Manager looks suspiciously like any other desktop application, it is actually a web application. It is implemented as an ASP-based (Active Server Pages) web service that runs from the virtual directory MessagingManager on the default IIS web site on the BizTalk Server machine. The Messaging Manager user-interface is merely a pretty wrapper around the web application. This is a good example that shows that web-based applications are not necessarily HTML based but may have rich user interfaces that communicate with their active backend via HTTP and XML.

The tool's visual interface is split into two panes. In the search pane, you select an item type like Messaging Ports or Channels by clicking one of the hyperlink-style options in the lower part of the search pane. Then you are presented with the applicable search criteria for the selected item type. Unless you have large numbers of definitions in your messaging configuration repository, just leave the search criteria blank and click the Search Now button.

The result of the search operation is then shown in the results pane on the right side of the window. You can then view and modify the definition for the found items either by double-clicking them, by selecting them with the keyboard and pressing the ENTER key, or by selecting Edit from the context menu.

After a fresh install of BizTalk, all lists will come up empty simply because you have not made any definitions. You can create new items either by right-clicking in the blank space of a search result, by selecting New from the context menu, or by selecting File | New. The only items that must be created from a certain context are channels.

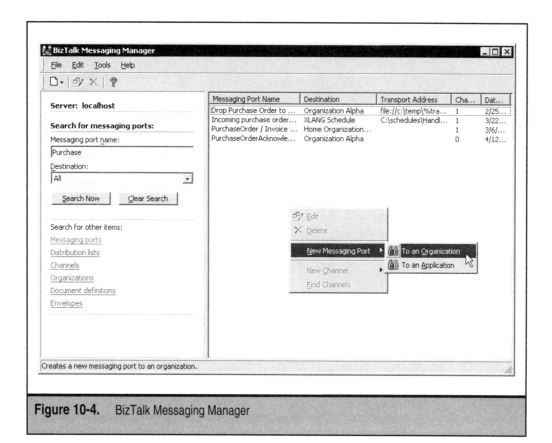

Figure 10-4.   BizTalk Messaging Manager

In Chapter 7, you learned that channels are bound to a specific messaging port. Hence, you must have a certain messaging port selected in the results pane to create a new channel. On the selected port, you can use the context menu or select File | New to start defining a new channel. Alternatively, you can choose to automatically start creating a new channel immediately after having completed a messaging port definition and therefore perform those connected tasks in sequence.

You will define the channel by using one of six different dialog boxes, which are covered in the following overview. You will recognize most of the terminology from Chapter 7. And Chapter 17 discusses all of these dialog boxes in more detail.

The Messaging Port Wizard (see Figure 10-5) serves to create new or modify existing messaging ports. Ports to applications (internal) and to organizations (external) are slightly different relative to how you configure the transport properties. Therefore, you create new messaging ports either to an organization (CTRL-R) or to an application (CTRL-SHIFT-R). You reach this choice by selecting File | New | Messaging Port or by clicking the toolbar icon that looks like a blank page.

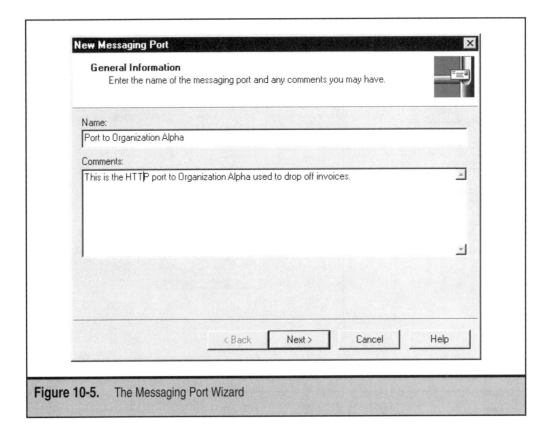

Figure 10-5. The Messaging Port Wizard

The difference between the two variants is that when you create a new port to an organization, you will be presented with the Destination Organization page, while for applications, it is no surprise that you will be presented with the Destination Application page. Both pages serve to define the transport to be used to transfer documents to the destination. For that, the Destination Application page shows only internal application identifiers and also allows XLANG schedules to be invoked, while the Destination Organization page displays only external organization identifiers and associates them with physical transport protocols that can be used with the outside world.

The Channel Wizard (see Figure 10-6) can be launched immediately from the Port Wizard when you have just created a new messaging port. In that case, the last page of the Messaging Port Wizard will allow you to create a channel either from an application or from an organization that will be bound to the port. So for channels, the user interface makes the same distinction as for messaging ports; however, in this case, it is the inbound direction.

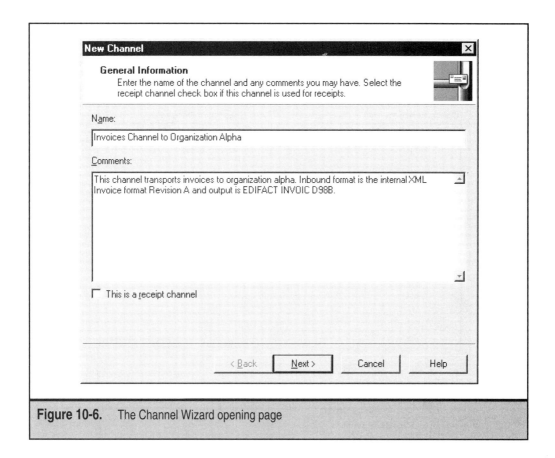

Figure 10-6.   The Channel Wizard opening page

Otherwise, you create new channels with a prior search result for messaging ports being present in the results pane. Then right-click one of the entries and select New | Channel | From. When you have selected an item, you can also select File | New or just press CTRL-L to create a new channel from an organization or press CTRL-SHIFT-L to create a channel from an application.

As with the port wizard, the wizard variants differ only on one page. The Source Application page allows you to select an internal application identifier, while the Source Organization page expects an organization identifier to be picked.

Distribution lists are used to group Messaging ports. So opening the New Distribution List dialog box (see Figure 10-7) makes sense only if you already have ports defined. (Press CTRL-T or select File | New | Distribution List to open this dialog box.) You will create distribution lists, which technically act like ports, if you want to send the same message to multiple destinations. The newest product catalog or other informational messages would be candidates for this.

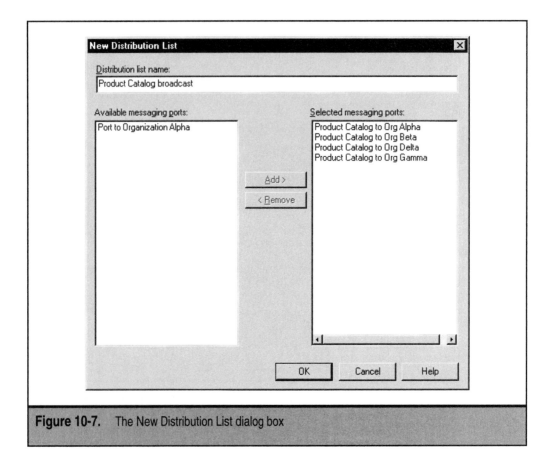

Figure 10-7. The New Distribution List dialog box

This dialog box has two list boxes. On the left is a list of all ports, and on the right is a list of all those ports that belong to the distribution list. You can change the assignment with the Add and Remove buttons between both lists. While all other user-interface components of Messaging Manager are designed for large volumes of definition data, the selection lists here just show every port available. Should you indeed have hundreds of messaging destinations, the design choice here may cause some problems.

You can define new organizations by using the Messaging Manager's menu, similar to all other items, or by pressing CTRL-G. In the Organization Properties dialog box (see Figure 10-8), you can name the organization and add additional organization identifiers. The *Home Organization* is always defined and is the only item that is preconfigured in the BizTalk Messaging configuration database. Only on the home organization item can you also define the internal application identifiers.

When adding additional organization identifiers, another dialog box will allow you to either pick one of the predefined qualifiers as per ISO 6523 or specify your own custom qualifiers for the identifier. You should define such qualifiers with great care so that you

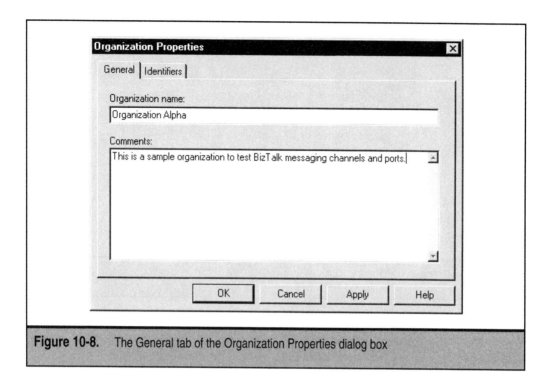

Figure 10-8.   The General tab of the Organization Properties dialog box

do not violate the standards. As a rule of thumb, stay away from custom qualifiers for any data exchange format narrowly defined by a standard like X12 or UN/EDIFACT. You can designate one of the organization identifiers for the organization as the default; this is then the identifier, which will be presented for all subsequent definitions.

Within each qualifier group, identifiers must be unique across all organizations.

To create new envelopes, press CTRL-E or select File | New. The New Envelope dialog box (see Figure 10-9) is certainly the simplest of all Messaging Manager dialogs. It will allow you to create definitions for all of the standard envelopes like X12, UN/EDIFACT, and RELIABLE, and also for custom envelope formats that must be backed by an envelope document specification. You will learn how to create such specifications in Chapter 15.

While you are looking at the dialog box here, you may want to open it and add three definitions right away because they should really be preset and present in all BizTalk installations:

Envelope Name	Envelope Format
ANSI X12	X12
UN/EDIFACT	UN/EDIFACT
BizTalk Framework 2.0	RELIABLE

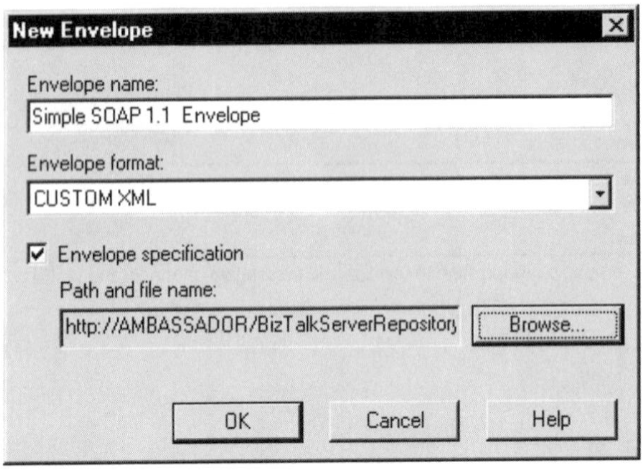

Figure 10-9. The New Envelope dialog box

All of these envelope formats are built in and do not allow or require any special configuration.

You insert new document definitions into the configuration database by using the Messaging Manager menu or by pressing CTRL-D. Note that when you create a document definition, any external document specification is actually loaded into the configuration database. The New Document Definition dialog box (see Figure 10-10) will let you name a document definition and will prompt you to provide a WebDAV reference for a specification. Once you click OK in this dialog box, the specification will be pulled from the WebDAV location and permanently stored in the configuration database. Therefore, if you make any changes to a document specification and want to use this updated version with messaging, you must actually know all messaging document definitions where the specification is used, open them for editing, and reimport them by simply clicking OK in the dialog box.

The New Document Definition dialog box also allows you to define global tracking fields that will be recorded in the document tracking database independently of the channel used to route the document. The Selection Criteria tab is used for the UN/EDIFACT and X12 formats. As you may recall, the Interchange component requires only a minimal set of arguments to be provided when a document is submitted. Because UN/EDIFACT and X12 documents do not have the same level of syntactic expressiveness as XML, the parsers therefore need to know whether a certain inbound stream is actually a document that conforms to a certain transaction set.

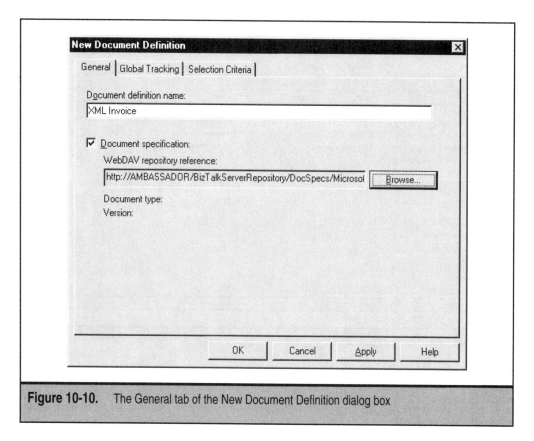

Figure 10-10.   The General tab of the New Document Definition dialog box

Furthermore, a single transaction set type may have been individually customized for many partners; and now, based on the inbound document, you need to decide which subvariant of that standard transaction set a certain instance actually complies with. For example, if the document definition is customer- or supplier-specific, you can create a filter based on a customer ID or supplier ID contained in the document instance.

The Configuration Assistant

BizTalk Configuration Assistant (see Figure 10-11) is Messaging Manager's little brother, and it implements some functionality that should really have been put into Messaging Manager itself. You can find Configuration Assistant in the software development kit (SDK) portion of the product installation. The path from the product installation directory is .\SDK\Messaging Samples\BTConfigAssistant\EXE\BTConfigAssistant.exe.

When you look at Messaging Manager from an administrator's point of view, you will have noticed that there is no mention of export or import for messaging definitions.

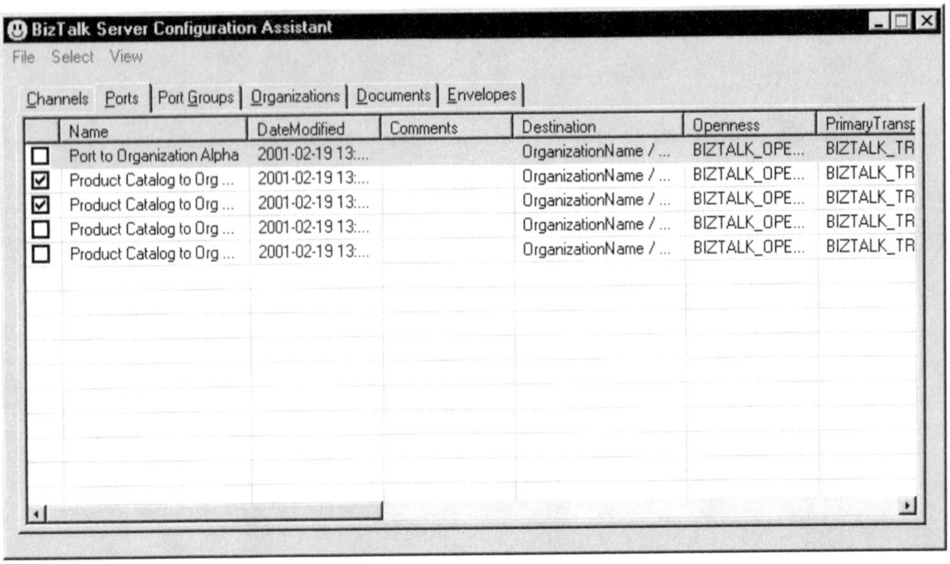

Figure 10-11. BizTalk Server Configuration Assistant

In fact, the standard BizTalk tools will not allow you to export definitions from a development environment to be imported into a production environment or to move or share definitions between servers that are not part of a cluster that looks at the same definition database.

For all of these tasks, BizTalk Configuration Assistant will be your friend. It looks at the *local* management database. (In contrast to the Messaging Manager client that can be executed remotely, this tool must be run directly on a BizTalk server machine.) And it presents all definitions existing in the database. From there, you can either selectively pick single items or just export the entire definition database. At export time, the tool creates a single XML document that contains all definitions and three subdirectories that hold the definition files for document, envelope, and mapping definitions, which were stored in the management database.

You can then move the export file and the three subdirectories to the target machine. (You may want to put them in a ZIP archive immediately to make sure everything is consistent.) Then you can import them by using Configuration Assistant there.

Administrators will therefore want to copy the application to a more obvious location and include it in the Start menu. You will appreciate two advantages of this tool: it ships with full Visual Basic source code (it is thus a complete how-to example for the BizTalk Configuration Object Model), and it is capable of automatically creating configuration scripts from your development environment that you can use to programmatically transfer definitions into a production environment. If you look at the scripting code that Configuration Assistant generates, you will notice that the scripts look suspiciously like the ones that all other messaging samples use to set up the run-time environment.

Unfortunately, Configuration Assistant is mentioned nowhere in the main BizTalk documentation, and its own documentation is somewhat brief. Its location in the SDK also tells you that it is an unsupported tool. One of the reasons is that the tool does not always produce accurate results and the generated VBScripts will not always work immediately and without changes. Chapter 20 looks a bit more closely at what you can do with Configuration Assistant.

The BizTalk Direct Integration Tool

When you create definitions, you may also want to test them out immediately. Again, Messaging Manager falls short of providing this functionality. And also in this case, there is a tool in the SDK that provides this functionality: the Direct Integration tool, shown in Figure 10-12. The name "Interactive Test Application" would have been more accurate. Anyway, the tool resides in the .SDK\Messaging Samples\DirectIntegration\EXE subdirectory, and just as with Configuration Assistant, you may want to move it to a more obvious place.

The Direct Integration tool provides you with a complete user interface to the BizTalk Integration component's *Submit* and *SubmitSync* methods and lets you interactively drop documents into BizTalk for processing. This tool is invaluable if you want to test complex setups in which you really exploit the flexibility of messaging. Because this tool also lacks documentation, it is one of the highlights of Chapter 18, in which testing and troubleshooting are discussed.

BIZTALK ADMINISTRATOR

BizTalk Administrator (see Figure 10-13) is the primary tool to control BizTalk in action. The Administrator is a snap-in for the Microsoft Management Console (MMC). The default configuration after a fresh BizTalk install is that the Administrator sits in its own MMC console window alongside the Windows 2000 Event Viewer snap-in. You can, of course, also add the BizTalk Administrator snap-in to any other composite MMC console window.

As any other MMC snap-in, the Administrator provides a hierarchical view. On the top level of the hierarchy, it displays the BizTalk (Messaging) run-time environment in a group view. Each group reflects a cluster of collaborating BizTalk servers that share the same shared queue database and document tracking database. Also common to the entire group is the host address used for outbound SMTP traffic and the reply-to address set in the From field of those messages. Just as common are the global document-tracking settings and the order in which parsers are invoked to probe incoming documents.

The BizTalk Messaging management database (where the configuration is stored) is common to all servers; thus, the respective connection settings for the SQL Server

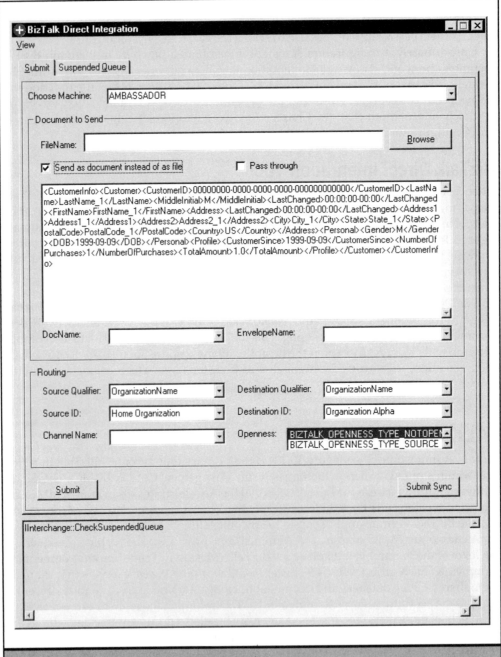

Figure 10-12. The BizTalk Direct Integration tool

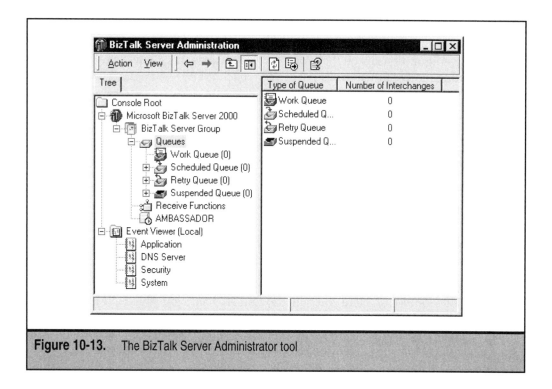

Figure 10-13.   The BizTalk Server Administrator tool

running that database can be reached and modified via the Administrator's root node properties. Unlike all other settings explained in the bullets that follow, the configuration on that node applies only to the local machine. All BizTalk Server machines that point to the same management database can be jointly configured, arranged in groups, and maintained.

The database selection on the root node and the group configuration provide you with two levels of creating BizTalk clusters. One is to create entirely separate clusters that do not share any information whatsoever, and the second is to use the same configuration repository but have separate document tracking databases and shared queues, creating multiple separate run-time environments.

Below each server group node are three or more additional subtrees.

▼   The Queues node contains the four messaging queues that are used by the server queue to process messages: Work Queue, Scheduled Queue, Retry Queue, and Suspended Queue. All four subnodes display a list of the current queue items in the right pane when selected. The queues are shared among the group cluster. In a typical environment, the Work Queue should be very short or even come up empty. The Scheduled Queue may show entries only if you have partners that accept data only in service windows, the Retry Queue may be fairly busy if you use receipts or the BizTalk Framework (BTF) reliable format, and, in an ideal case, the Suspended Queue should be empty.

■   The Receive Functions node lists all receive functions available for the group. Receive functions are always uniquely assigned to a single machine. The reason the configuration sits on the group level is because this allows you to move an existing receive function easily between machines.

▲   In addition, there is one node per machine existing in the group. On that node, you can configure each machine's processing capacity, including the number of active receive functions and processing worker-threads and the time that the machine idles between calls to the scheduler. The latter value is useful to balance between desired processing volume and load on the SQL Server database.

The Administrator allows you to perform a number of tasks. The most obvious tasks include creating new BizTalk Server groups, assigning existing servers to those groups, and tweaking server settings (all of which we will look in Chapters 18 through 22). However, the day-to-day purpose of BizTalk Administrator is troubleshooting. The two most important troubleshooting and diagnostics elements are the Retry Queue and the Suspended Queue.

The Retry Queue contains all documents that have failed transmission for some reason and are due for resend. Here you will also find all documents that have already been successfully sent, but for which a receipt has been requested but not yet received. If the receipt does not arrive within the required time, BizTalk Server will retry the transmission from the Retry Queue until the permitted number of send retries have been exceeded.

The Suspended Queue is the message hospital (or worse) and the place where all documents end up that either failed processing for some reason or exceeded their retry count when being sent. Only the latter can be resubmitted from the Suspended Queue. For all other documents, the most you can do is view a brief explanation of why the document failed processing and see the document instance itself. For most errors, the error description in the Suspended Queue will not be very helpful for troubleshooting, though. More interesting is the Interchange ID, which is a unique identifier for the messaging action.

For some odd reason, errors are logged not only in two separate places, the Suspended Queue and the Windows 2000 application event log, but even different portions of the error information are located in either place. To find the matching entry in the application event log, you need the Interchange ID, which is part of the matching entry's detail information. The application log entry will tell you more about what occurred during processing.

BIZTALK DOCUMENT TRACKING

The BizTalk document tracking database (see Figure 10-14) is where BizTalk stores the evidence about sent and received documents and the extra tracking fields that you have either defined globally for a document definition or individually on a certain channel. Whenever you need to know whether a certain document has arrived or has been sent, the document tracking database is the place to look for that information.

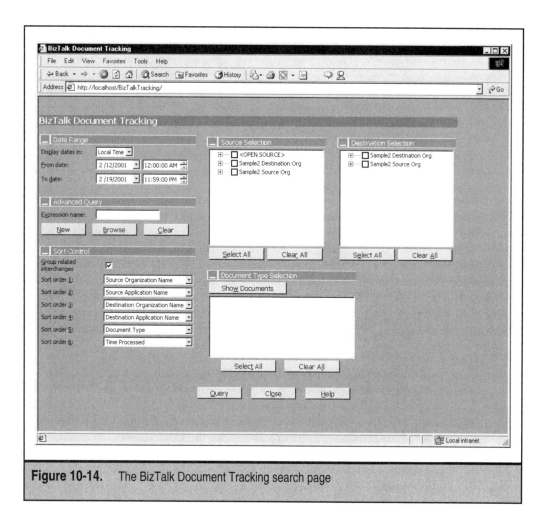

Figure 10-14.   The BizTalk Document Tracking search page

The BizTalk Document Tracking web site that is installed with any BizTalk Server by default is one interface to the document tracking database. If you write applications that submit documents directly into BizTalk, you can also access the document tracking database programmatically by using the BTSDocTracking component and its IBizTalkTrackData interface. Chapter 21 covers programmatic tracking in detail.

When you open the BizTalk Document Tracking page in Internet Explorer, you are presented with a fairly complex search page. This page allows you to narrowly specify which documents you want to find in the document tracking database that will grow rather quickly to contain many thousands of documents in a larger BizTalk deployment and thus justifies that page's complexity. The page is served out of the virtual IIS directory BizTalkTracking, pointing to the directory with the same name in the BizTalk installation directory.

NOTE: The BizTalk tracking application is not really a server-based application. Both the search page and the result pages are client-driven; most of the code is executed on the client-side by Internet Explorer with substantial help from the Microsoft Office Web Controls package. For the application to work, your default browser must be Internet Explorer 5.0 or later. The document tracking search results page is actually a Microsoft Access 2000 Data Access Page. From that, you should conclude that running the document tracking application requires those controls and with that, a local installation of Microsoft Office. Another side effect of using this controls package is that when you start the document tracking viewer the first time, you will likely receive a warning message: "This page accesses data on another domain. Do you want to allow this?" To fix this error, you must add the server to the trusted sites zone in the Internet Explorer Security settings.

When you open the document tracking application through the respective entry in the Microsoft BizTalk Server 2000 group on the Start menu, Internet Explorer opens a window with six different sections. Each section is a small, separate area on the page with its own title bar that is visible by default, but which you can hide by clicking the symbol to the left of the title. In each section, you can enter a set of specific search criteria to narrow your search. The query result that is presented in a separate window when you click the Query button at the bottom of the page is produced by combining all of the criteria of all search conditions.

▼ **Date Range** This section allows you to narrow a time period in which the documents to be found have been recorded in the document tracking database. You can specify both date and time and also can pick whether you want to use local time or Universal Time Coordinated (UTC), which is global time. Adopting UTC as a time scheme is especially useful if you have a lot of narrowly timed international data traffic—or, for countries like the United States, Canada, Australia, or Russia, coast-to-coast data traffic—and you want to avoid confusion about separate time zones.

■ **Advanced Query** In this section you can enter a special query on the tracking fields that you have either defined globally for the routed document definition or locally for the channel through which the document was routed. When you click the New button, a separate window opens that allows you to construct such a query, Browse allows you to select a predefined query, and Clear lets you reset the query condition. (More details follow in Chapter 21.)

■ **Sort Control** Because the number of documents returned by a query may be substantial, grouping and sorting the results helps to make sense out of them. Here you can set six sort orders that are processed with priority. That means that all results are first sorted by sort order #1, and within that order by sort order #2, and so on.

■ **Source Selection** In this section, you can check all source organizations for which you want to find documents. The source may be either an internal application (or all of them if you check the Home Organization directly) or an external partner organization. The source identifiers are displayed in a tree view in which applications are on the second level below the organizations. With what you already know about organization and application identifiers, it is clear that the tree will have data only for the Home Organization because applications can be defined only for your own system. The tree view is automatically produced from the contents of the document tracking database; that means that the database already contains data for all shown sources.

■ **Destination Selection**   This section is, of course, the counterpart of the source selection section for the destination identifier of the document and thus works similarly to narrow down the destination organization or application identifier.

▲ **Document Type Selection**   The list box for document types allows you to select one or multiple document types. The list is produced from all definitions that have already been recorded in the document tracking database.

Once you have defined all criteria (or just left everything as is for a test run), click the Query button at the bottom of the page.

The result window that will appear (see Figure 10-15) shows all recorded documents that match the specified criteria. By clicking the WordPad-style icon on a document row, you can see the original document that was routed, and the columns of the row will show you all information relevant for routing and information about the success of the interchange. Clicking the Plus sign (+) at the beginning of the row displays further details about the interchange, including all of the documents and the respective tracking fields.

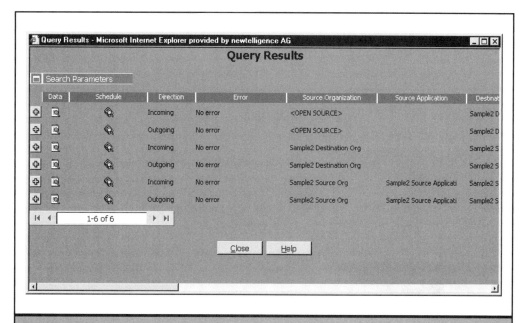

Figure 10-15.   The BizTalk Document Tracking result page

PART III

BizTalk Architecture and Components

CHAPTER 11

BizTalk Messaging Architecture

This chapter drills down into the architectural details of the BizTalk Server 2000 Messaging service. Especially when you deploy or administer BizTalk in larger installations or when you need to write custom extensions to BizTalk, you will want to know more about how the various components of the product actually "click" together. And maybe you are just curious about how things work.

The main topics presented in this chapter are

▼ The Architectural Big Picture

■ BizTalk Management Database

■ BizTalk Document Tracking Database

■ BizTalk Shared Queue Database

▲ Document Processing Pipeline Components

THE ARCHITECTURAL BIG PICTURE

In Chapter 8, you already learned quite a bit about BizTalk messaging concepts, how the four queues work, and what the BizTalk Interchange component does. This chapter takes a look behind the scenes to find out how BizTalk's innards work. This entire part of the book probably would not even exist in most other beginner's guides; in fact, BizTalk's internals are generally not even covered in the BizTalk documentation. But this chapter has its place in this book for a couple of reasons.

For one thing, from a novice's standpoint, BizTalk is huge. There is really no handle to grab and no one good place to begin. Therefore, this book started with some extensive and very general discussions about the BizTalk rationale and how it fits into the real world. You learned all the theoretical background before you even put your hands on the product, so now it makes sense to take a look at the internals. While BizTalk appears complicated at first, the core and the interdependencies at the system level are actually quite simple to grasp.

While the Messaging Manager user interface does a great job of defining and maintaining configuration information, it does not help you figure out what your configuration settings actually contain and how one setting affects the other settings. Knowing about BizTalk's architecture helps with this. Also, after studying BizTalk's internal structure, a couple of behaviors that appeared to be bugs before will suddenly make a lot of sense. For instance, XML documents are never referenced from the WebDAV repository like the user interface makes you believe, but they are actually physically imported whenever you complete the definition of a channel. The reason for this is simply performance.

NOTE: You will need some prior knowledge of COM and COM+ near the end of this chapter, when the details of the processing pipeline are discussed. This information is useful primarily for developers wanting to write BizTalk applications and a bit less useful for administrators.

To start, here's a brief summary of what you have already learned about the architectural elements of BizTalk messaging:

▼   Messages are submitted to BizTalk through the BizTalk Interchange COM+ application using the interface IInterchange.

■   Messages are matched against pairs of channels and ports either based on parameters provided when the methods of the IInterchange interface are being called or based on data that is contained in the submitted documents themselves (mostly source and destination identifiers in that case).

■   Information about ports, channels, and all the additional configuration data is held in the BizTalk management database.

■   Asynchronous messages are held in a queue prior to transmission and are moved either to the Retry Queue or to the Suspended Queue upon transmission failure. Messages that can be transmitted only at a certain time of the day (constrained by a service window on the partner's end) are held in the Scheduled Queue.

■   The queue is managed (polled) by one or multiple BizTalk Messaging services, each located on its own machine inside a clustered group of BizTalk servers. The Messaging service (MSCIS.EXE) is executed as a Windows 2000 service process.

■   When messages are being processed and have been assigned to one (or multiple) channels for processing, they run through a sequence of processing stages in which they are validated, possibly transformed, enveloped, encoded, signed, encrypted, serialized to an outbound stream, and finally, transmitted to the destination.

▲   Immediately after having been received and prior to forwarding documents, messages are tracked, possibly with additional custom fields in the document tracking database.

Putting all the pieces together, we can summarize the big picture of the BizTalk Server architecture as follows.

All messages are processed by selecting one or multiple channel/port pairs and pushing the document into the channel. On the system level, channels and ports are implemented as a chain of pipeline components that are dynamically grouped based on the channel and port configuration data. For the purpose of this discussion, the term "document-processing pipeline" refers to the whole process of submitting a document into the server until it is transmitted through one of the transports. The model of a pipeline makes sense not only from an explanation standpoint, but it is actually the "official" term that is used in the BizTalk architecture and programming model. The document-processing pipeline is managed and hosted inside the messaging service.

The messaging service is backed by the management database from which it retrieves all information about handling submitted documents. Unlike most other Microsoft Server products (except maybe SQL Server), BizTalk does not store any run time–relevant information in Active Directory or the Windows Registry. Almost the only run-time information that can be found in the Windows Registry is the information that BizTalk needs to connect to the correct database when it boots up.

NOTE: You can find the registry keys for the local BizTalk Server installation at the following location: HKEY_LOCAL_MACHINE\SOFTWARE\Microsoft\BizTalk Server.

At run time, the messaging service is fed by the queue database. As you already know, the BizTalk Interchange component places all incoming asynchronous submissions into the Work Queue, from which the messaging service picks them up for processing. This way, the submission and processing stages are only loosely coupled, yielding better scalability of system components (because you can distribute them across several machines) and, thus, ultimately improving overall system performance in enterprise deployments. The only exceptions are synchronous messages. These are immediately handled by the Interchange component and are not handed over to the messaging service. When you send a synchronous message, the messaging service is essentially not in the picture and all action occurs on the server that accepts the message.

Whenever a message passes through a document-processing pipeline, it is tracked—more precisely, it is tracked twice. When a document enters the processing pipeline, it is first parsed into XML format (if the native format is not XML). And, by choice of configuration parameters, either the original document, the XML translation, or both are recorded, along with all submission parameters. When the document has passed the pipeline and immediately after it has been serialized back into native format (which may or may not be XML), the document is again recorded in native and/or XML format.

This process guarantees that you have a complete evidence trail of what happens with the documents in the processing stage. Recording documents twice is essential to tracking down problems, and it may also be necessary for legal reasons. In that case, you must be able to recreate the original inbound documents along with digital signature information before the data is mapped into a document format that your internal applications support.

THE BIZTALK MANAGEMENT DATABASE

BizTalk Messaging's heart and soul is the management database. It is so important that the BizTalk development team honored it with two different programmatic access interfaces besides the obvious way of accessing it directly via SQL Server (which is actually prohibited). First, you can manipulate server configuration information, rearrange server groups, and manage the BizTalk queues programmatically through the Windows Management Instrumentation (WMI) interfaces or interactively through the BizTalk Administrator snap-in for the Microsoft Management Console (MMC) and you can manipulate Messaging definitions through the BizTalk Configuration Object Model.

The Windows Management Instrumentation subsystem is one of the lesser-known innovations in the Windows operating system family. It implements a common access layer to all application and system configuration data, independently of whether such information is stored in application-owned databases, which is the case with BizTalk, the Windows Registry, or any other storage location. BizTalk's design embraces WMI fully and uses it as its primary interface to establish the communication between the MMC snap-in and the configuration settings that are held in the management database. Because even BizTalk's own administration component takes the route through WMI to access all configuration data, it is the only "legal" way to access this information at all.

The second interface you can use to navigate through the BizTalk messaging configuration data for ports and channels is the COM-based BizTalk Configuration Object Model or interactively by using the Messaging Manager application that uses this object model. In both instances, the data is ultimately stored in the management database.

You should *not* manipulate the SQL Server database directly. However, we will still look at the database schema in great detail because it reveals how BizTalk Server is organized internally and also shows some places where BizTalk's extensibility is quite limited in the first release. In short, if you cannot do it in the management database, you cannot do it at all. The database has two functional table groups that are prefixed with adm_ for the administrative data that can be manipulated via WMI and with bts_ for all configuration data accessible through the Configuration Object Model.

Administration Object Tables

The following sections present the administration database tables as provided in the InterchangeBTM database (or whatever you called that database at installation time). The right-most column shows the corresponding WMI property that you should use to manipulate these elements. All WMI properties share the common prefix root\Microsoft BizTalkServer\. You can see the relationships of the tables illustrated in Figure 11-1.

NOTE: In the following tables, the column "P*" identifies the primary key for the table and the "I*" column identifies those database columns that are indexed.

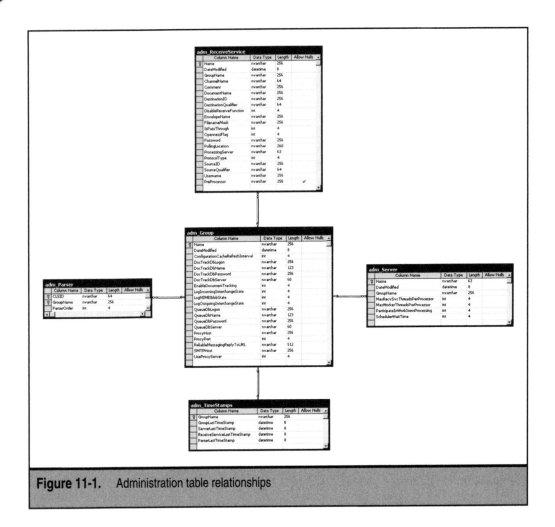

Figure 11-1.   Administration table relationships

adm_Group   This table lists all server groups within a BizTalk farm. Each server group has its own shared queue database and its own document tracking database but uses a common management database.

Column	Type	Size	P*	I*	Description	WMI Property
Name	nvarchar	256	X	-	Name of the server group	MicrosoftBizTalk Server_Group. Name (WMI datatype: string)
Date Modified	datetime	-	-	-	Date when the group settings were last modified	MicrosoftBizTalk Server_Group. DateModified (datetime)
Configur-ationCache Refresh Interval	int	-	-	-	Refresh interval (in seconds) when each BizTalk server must reread cached configuration information	MicrosoftBizTalk Server_Group. Configuration CacheRefresh Interval (uint32)
DocTrackDb Logon	nvarchar	256	-	-	Username to be used to log on to the document tracking database	MicrosoftBizTalk Server_Group. DocTrackDbLogon (string)
Doc TrackDb Password	nvarchar	256	-	-	Password to be used to log on to the document tracking database	MicrosoftBizTalk Server_Group. DocTrackDb Password (string)
DocTrackDb Name	nvarchar	123	-	-	Name of the document tracking database	MicrosoftBizTalk Server_Group. DocTrackDb Name (string)
DocTrackDb Server	nvarchar	60	-	-	Name of the SQL Server that hosts the document tracking database	MicrosoftBizTalk Server_Group. DocTrackDb Server (string)
Enable Document Tracking	int	-	-	-	Flag (0=false, -1=true) indicating whether document tracking is enabled	MicrosoftBizTalk Server_Group. EnableDocument Tracking (boolean)

Column	Type	Size	P*	I*	Description	WMI Property
Log Incoming Interchange State	int	-	-	-	Flag (0=false, -1=true) indicating whether incoming interchanges will be logged in native format independently of channel settings	MicrosoftBizTalk Server_Group. LoggingPoint State (uint32). If the database field is -1, the LoggingPoint State property's bit 0 (value 0x0001) is set.
LogMIME BlobState	int	-	-	-	Flag (0=false, -1=true) indicating whether incoming MIME attachments will be logged	MicrosoftBizTalk Server_Group. LoggingPoint State (uint32). If the database field is -1, the LoggingPoint State property's bit 1 (value 0x0002) is set.
LogOutgoing Interchange State	int	-	-	-	Flag (0=false, -1=true) indicating whether outgoing interchanges will be logged in native format	MicrosoftBizTalk Server_Group. LoggingPoint State (uint32)If the database field is -1, the LoggingPointState property's bit 2 (value 0x0004) is set.
QueueDb Logon	nvarchar	256	-	-	Username used to log on to the shared queue database	MicrosoftBizTalk Server_Group. QueueDbLogon (string)
QueueDb Name	nvarchar	123	-	-	Name of the shared queue database	MicrosoftBizTalk Server_Group. QueueDbName (string)
QueueDb Password	nvarchar	256	-	-	Password used to log on to the shared queue database	MicrosoftBizTalk Server_Group. QueueDb Password (string)

Column	Type	Size	P*	I*	Description	WMI Property
QueueDb Server	nvarchar	60	-	-	Name of the SQL Server hosting the shared queue database	MicrosoftBizTalk Server_Group. QueueDbServer (string)
ProxyHost	nvarchar	256	-	-	Name of the HTTP proxy through which HTTP transmissions will be routed	MicrosoftBizTalk Server_Group. ProxyHost (string)
ProxyPort	int	-	-	-	IP port number of the HTTP proxy	MicrosoftBizTalk Server_Group. ProxyPort (uint32)
Reliable Messaging ReplyToURL	nvarchar	256	-	-	HTTP URL to which receipts for BTF2.0 reliable transmissions will be sent by the receivers	MicrosoftBizTalk Server_Group. Reliable MessagingReply ToURL (string)
SMTPHost	nvarchar	256	-	-	SMTP server through which outbound SMTP messages will be relayed	MicrosoftBizTalk Server_Group. SMTPHost (string)
UseProxy Server	int	-	-	-	Flag (0=false, -1=true) indicating whether HTTP requests will be routed through a proxy	MicrosoftBizTalk Server_Group. UserProxyServer (uint32)

adm_Server   This table is for all servers that share this management database.

Column	Type	Size	P*	I*	Description	WMI Property
Name	nvarchar	63	X	-	Name of the server. This is typically the machine name.	MicrosoftBizTalk Server_Server. Name (WMI datatype: string)
DateModified	datetime	-	-	-	Date when the server settings were last modified.	MicrosoftBizTalk Server_Server. DateModified (datetime)

Column	Type	Size	P*	I*	Description	WMI Property
GroupName	nvarchar	256	-	X	Name for the group that this server is assigned to. This column has a foreign key relationship with adm_Group. Name.	MicrosoftBizTalk Server_Server. GroupName (string)
MaxRecvSvc ThreadsPer Processor	int	-	-	-	Maximum number of threads per processor that service receive functions.	MicrosoftBizTalk Server_Server. MaxRecvSvc ThreadsPer Processor (uint32)
MaxWorker ThreadsPer Processor	int	-	-	-	Maximum number of worker threads per processor. Worker threads actively process messages.	MicrosoftBizTalk Server_Server. MaxWorker ThreadsPer Processor (uint32)
ParticipateInWork ItemProcessing	int	-	-	-	Flag (0=false, -1=true) indicating whether this server participates in work item processing, that is, whether it polls the Work Queue.	MicrosoftBizTalk Server_Server. ParticipateInWork ItemProcessing (uint32)
Scheduler WaitTime	int	-	-	-	Number of milliseconds the server waits between calls to the Work Queue.	MicrosoftBizTalk Server_Server. SchedulerWait Time (uint32)

adm_Parser   This table contains the order in which parsers are invoked for processing for a particular server group.

Column	Type	Size	N*	P*	I*	Description	WMI Property
Group Name	nvarchar	256	-	X	-	Name of the server group to which this parser sequence belongs.	n/a
CLSID	nvarchar	64	-	X	-	COM class ID of the parser component.	MicrosoftBizTalk Server_Group. ParserOrder (string array). This WMI property contains the class IDs of the parsers arranged in the sequence as defined in this table.
Parser Order	int	-	-	-	-	Sequential order number of this parser within the server group. Order 1 has the highest priority.	n/a

adm_ReceiveService   This table provides all message queue and file receive functions that are configured for server groups. As you can assume from the table layout and the hard-coded ProtocolType flag, BizTalk Server will not allow you to implement custom receive functions for other protocols at this time.

Column	Type	Size	P*	I*	Description	WMI Property
Group Name	nvarchar	256	X	-	Name of the server group to which this receive function belongs.	MicrosoftBizTalk Server_Receive Function. GroupName (WMI datatype: string)
Name	nvarchar	63	X	-	Name of the receive function.	MicrosoftBizTalk Server_Receive Function. Name (WMI datatype: string)

Column	Type	Size	P*	I*	Description	WMI Property
Date Modified	datetime	-	-	-	Date when the server settings were last modified.	MicrosoftBizTalk Server_ ReceiveFunction. DateModified (datetime)
Channel Name	nvarchar	64	-	-	Name of the channel into which messages will be submitted. (Advanced property optional.)	MicrosoftBizTalk Server_ ReceiveFunction. ChannelName (string)
Comment	nvarchar	256	-	-	Additional user comment to describe the function.	MicrosoftBizTalk Server_ ReceiveFunction. Comment (string)
Document Name	nvarchar	256	-	-	Document type that is expected on this function. (Advanced property optional.)	MicrosoftBizTalk Server_ ReceiveFunction. DocumentName (string)
Destination ID	nvarchar	256	-	-	Destination Organization Identifier. (Advanced property optional.)	MicrosoftBizTalk Server_ ReceiveFunction. DestinationID (string)
Destination Qualifier	nvarchar	64	-	-	Destination Organization Qualifier. (Advanced property optional.)	MicrosoftBizTalk Server_ ReceiveFunction. Destination Qualifier (string)
Disable Receive Function	int		-	-	Flag (0=false, -1=true) indicating whether this function is disabled.	MicrosoftBizTalk Server_ ReceiveFunction. DisableReceive Function (boolean)

Column	Type	Size	P*	I*	Description	WMI Property
Envelope Name	nvarchar	256	-	-	Name of the envelope definition for receive documents. (Advanced property optional.)	MicrosoftBizTalk Server_ ReceiveFunction. EnvelopeName (string)
Filename Mask	nvarchar	256	-	-	For ProtocolType=1: filename mask with wildcards for files to be picked up (e.g., *.txt).	MicrosoftBizTalk Server_ ReceiveFunction. FilenameMask (string)
IsPass Through	int		-	-	Flag (0=false, -1=true) indicating whether submissions will be made in passthrough mode.	MicrosoftBizTalk Server_ ReceiveFunction. IsPassThrough (boolean)
Openness Flag	int		-	-	Indicates openness. (1=not open, 2=open source, 4=open destination.)	MicrosoftBizTalk Server_ ReceiveFunction. OpennessFlag (uint32)
Polling Location	nvarchar	260	-	-	For ProtocolType=1 this is a directory; for ProtoColType=2 this is a MessageQueue reference.	MicrosoftBizTalk Server_ ReceiveFunction. PollingLocation (string)
Username	nvarchar	256	-	-	Username for accessing the polling location.	MicrosoftBizTalk Server_ ReceiveFunction. Username (string)

Column	Type	Size	P*	I*	Description	WMI Property
Password	nvarchar	256	-	-	Password for accessing the polling location.	MicrosoftBizTalk Server_ ReceiveFunction. Password (string)
Processing Server	nvarchar	63	-	-	Name of the processing server. Only one server in a group will run this function.	MicrosoftBizTalk Server_ ReceiveFunction. ProcessingServer (string)
Protocol Type	int		-	-	For file receive functions, the protocol type is 1; for message queue functions, the protocol type is 2.	MicrosoftBizTalk Server_ ReceiveFunction. ProtocolType (uint32)
SourceID	nvarchar	256	-	-	Source Organization Identifier. (Advanced property optional.)	MicrosoftBizTalk Server_ ReceiveFunction. SourceID (string)
Source Qualifier	nvarchar	64	-	-	Source Organization Qualifier. (Advanced property optional.)	MicrosoftBizTalk Server_ ReceiveFunction. SourceQualifier (string)
Pre Processor	nvarchar	256	-	-	Name of the preprocessor component.	MicrosoftBizTalk Server_ ReceiveFunction. PreProcessor (string)

adm_TimeStamps   This table contains the time stamps of the objects that were last modified in a server group and is used to optimize refreshes of the server configuration caches.

Column	Type	Size	P*	I*	Description	WMI Property
GroupName	nvarchar	256	X	-	Name of the server group	n/a
GroupLast TimeStamp	datetime	-	-	-	Time of last update to the group entry	n/a

Column	Type	Size	P*	I*	Description	WMI Property
ServerLast TimeStamp	datetime	-	-	-	Time of last update to one of the group's server entries	n/a
Receive Service LastTime Stamp	datetime	-	-	-	Time of last update to one of the group's receive functions	n/a
ParserLast TimeStamp	datetime	-	-	-	Time of last update to one of the group's parser orders	n/a

Messaging Object Tables

The messaging object tables (that terminology does not officially exist in BizTalk, but it is used here to distinguish them from the administration tables) hold all the configuration data of the core BizTalk definitions such as organizations, ports, and channels (see Figure 11-2). This section provides the most interesting database analysis in this chapter because you will learn that some of the extensibility mechanisms that you assume would work in BizTalk actually do not work in this release.

For instance, while the documentation explicitly states that you can write custom encoders and encryption components, you will never be able to select them directly in the Port Configuration Wizard because there is simply no data field to back that up. However, and this should be of some relief, you can use your own components even if there is no "official" user interface to define this—a lesson you can learn here when you look at the bts_outputconfig table.

Throughout this section of the management database, a design pattern that is repeated is that virtually all tables have autoincrement primary keys of type int, and they have an additional unique identifier of type GUID, which is not used in any of the database relations. However, if you look at the BizTalk user interfaces that reference any of the definitions or if you track errors in the event log or Suspended Queue, you will always find those globally unique identifiers (GUIDs) instead of the integer numbers. The reason is that they are easier to pinpoint in large logs and independent of the storage medium. Integers, on the other hand, consume exactly a quarter of the space of GUIDs in the database and thus are better for cross-table references.

NOTE: In addition to the tables covered in the following sections, the database has two more tables that are not covered here because they do not seem to be actively used in BizTalk 2000: bts_appint and bts_certificate.

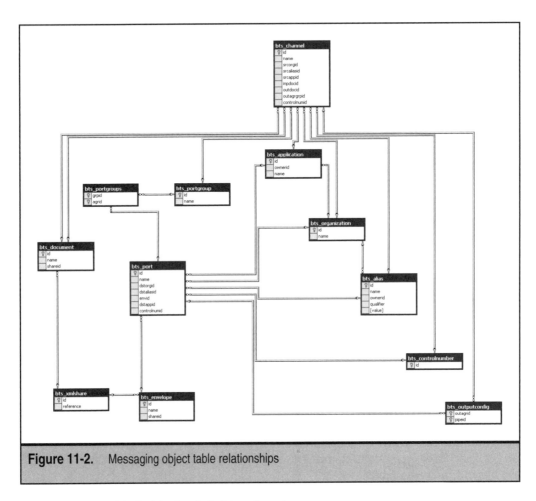

Figure 11-2. Messaging object table relationships

bts_port   This table holds the definition data for ports.

Column	Type	Size	P*	I*	Description	Configuration Object Model
Id	int	-	X	-	Primary key.	n/a
Name	nvarchar	64	-	-	Name of this port. The name must be defined in XML-compatible format without special characters.	IBizTalkPort.Name

Column	Type	Size	P*	I*	Description	Configuration Object Model
guid	uniqueid entifier	-	-	-	Additional unique identifier for this port that is being used for references that require a GUID.	n/a
date modified	datetime	-	-	-	Date when the port definition was last modified.	IBizTalkPort.Date Modified
dstorgid	int	-	-	-	Reference to the destination organization object (table bts_ organization).	IBizTalkPort. Destination Endpoint
dstaliasid	int	-	-	-	Reference to the destination identifier and qualifier pair to be used (table bts_alias).	IBizTalkPort. Destination Endpoint
envid	int	-	-	-	Reference to the envelope (table bts_ envelope).	IBizTalkPort. Destination Endpoint
dstappid	int	-	-	-	Destination application identifier— if applicable (table bts_ application).	IBizTalkPort. Destination Endpoint

Column	Type	Size	P*	I*	Description	Configuration Object Model
control numid	int	-	-	-	Reference to helper table for maintaining the interchange control number for X12 or UN/EDIFACT (table bts_ control number).	IBizTalkPort. Control NumberValue
Openness	int	-	-	-	Openness flag. (1=not open, 4=open destination, 16=to XLANG.)	IBizTalkPort. Destination Endpoint
service window	int	-	-	-	Flag (0=false, -1=true) indicating whether a service window applies for the port.	IBizTalkPort.Service WindowInfo
service window from	datetime	-	-	-	Begin time (date part is not relevant) for the service window.	IBizTalkPort.Service WindowInfo
service windowto	datetime	-	-	-	End time (date part is not relevant) for the service window.	IBizTalkPort.Service WindowInfo

Column	Type	Size	P*	I*	Description	Configuration Object Model
primary transport	int	-	-	-	Flag for the primary transport protocol. (8192=X LANG, 4096=Loop back, 2048=Reliable Response, 1024=HTTPS, 256=File, 128=MSMQ, 32=AIC, 8=SMTP, 4=HTTP.)	IBizTalkPort. PrimaryTransport
primary address	nvarchar	256	-	-	Address information for the primary protocol.	IBizTalkPort. PrimaryTransport
primary parm	nvarchar	256	-	-	Additional protocol parameters for the primary protocol.	IBizTalkPort. PrimaryTransport
secondary transport	int	-	-	-	Flag for the backup transport protocol. (See primary transport.)	IBizTalkPort. SecondaryTransport
secondary address	nvarchar	256	-	-	Address information for the backup protocol.	IBizTalkPort. SecondaryTransport
secondary parm	nvarchar	256	-	-	Additional protocol parameters for the backup protocol.	IBizTalkPort. SecondaryTransport

Column	Type	Size	P*	I*	Description	Configuration Object Model
Encodtype	int	-	-	-	Type of encoder to be used. (1=none, 2=MIME.)	IBizTalkPort. EncodingType
Encryptype	int	-	-	-	Type of encryption to be used. (1=none, 4=S/MIME.)	IBizTalkPort. EncryptionType
Signattype	int	-	-	-	Type of signature to be used. (1=none, 4=S/MIME.)	IBizTalkPort. SignatureType
encrypcert name	nvarchar	256	-	-	Name of the encryption certificate.	IBizTalkPort. Encryption CertificateInfo
encrypcert ref	ntext	-	-	-	Store reference to the encryption certificate.	IBizTalkPort. Encryption CertificateInfo
encrypcert store	int	-	-	-	Source certificate store. (1=Computer Store, 2=BizTalk Store.)	IBizTalkPort. Encryption CertificateInfo
encrypcert usage	int	-	-	-	Usage parameters for the certificate. (1=Encryption, 2=Signature, 4=Both.)	IBizTalkPort. Encryption CertificateInfo
Comments	nvarchar	256	-	-	User comments for the port.	IBizTalkPort. Comments

Column	Type	Size	P*	I*	Description	Configuration Object Model
Delimiters	image	-	-	-	Binary field containing the delimiter definitions for EDI documents.	IBizTalkPort. Delimiters

bts_alias   The bts_alias table holds the various organization identifiers and qualifiers that you can define for a single organization.

Column	Type	Size	P*	I*	Description	Configuration Object Model
Id	int	-	X	-	Primary key.	n/a
Name	nvarchar	64	-	X	Name of the organization qualifier category. (Clear text name for the actual qualifier.)	IBizTalk Organization. Aliases.Name
Guid	unique identifier	-	-	-	GUID.	n/a
Ownerid	int	-	-	-	Foreign key pointing at bts_organization .id.	
Default flag	int	-	-	-	Flag (0=false, -1=true) indicating whether this is the default identifier for a particular organization.	IBizTalk Organization. Aliases.Boolean
Qualifier	nvarchar	64	-	-	Qualifier.	IBizTalk Organization. Aliases.Qualifier
Value	nvarchar	256	-	-	Identifier within qualifier scope. (Probably a numbering scheme like DUNS.)	IBizTalk Organization. Aliases.Value

bts_application   The internal application identifiers (names) are held in this table. The column ownerid points to the home organization in bts_organization.

Column	Type	Size	N*	P*	I*	Description	Configuration Object Model
id	int	-	-	X	-	Primary key	n/a
ownerid	int	-	-	-	-	Reference to the home organization in bts_ organization	n/a
name	nvarchar	64	-	-	-	Name of the application	IBizTalk Organization. Applications

bts_channel   BizTalk's channel information is stored in this table.

Column	Type	Size	P*	I*	Description	Configuration Object Model
id	int	-	X	-	Primary key.	
name	nvarchar	64	-	-	Name of the channel.	IBizTalkChannel. Name
guid	unique identifier	-	-	-	GUID for the channel.	
date modified	datetime	-	-	-	Date when the entry was last modified.	IBizTalkChannel. DateModified
srcorgid	int	-	-	-	Source organization. Foreign key (FK) of bts_organization .id.	IBizTalkChannel. SourceEndpoint
srcaliasid	int	-	-	-	Alias (Identifier) for the source organization. FK of bts_alias.id.	IBizTalkChannel. SourceEndpoint
srcappid	int	-	-	-	Source application id. FK of bts_application.id.	IBizTalkChannel. SourceEndpoint
inpdocid	int	-	-	-	Input document definition. FK of bts_document.id.	IBizTalkChannel. InputDocument

Column	Type	Size	P*	I*	Description	Configuration Object Model
outdocid	int	-	-	-	Output document definition. FK of bts_document.id.	IBizTalkChannel. OutputDocument
outagr grpid	int	-	-	-	Output configuration reference. FK of bts_output config.id.	IBizTalkChannel. GetConfigData()
control numid	int	-	-	-	Reference to the bts_control number.id.	IBizTalkChannel. ControlNumber Value
mapref	nvarchar	256	-	-	WebDAV reference for the document map. Must be defined if inpdocid different from outdocid.	IBizTalkChannel. MapReference
map content	ntext	-	-	-	Content of the document map.	IBizTalkChannel. MapContent
lognative inp	int	-	-	-	Flag (0=false, -1=true) indicating whether the input document will be tracked in native format.	IBizTalkChannel. LoggingInfo
logxmlinp	int	-	-	-	Flag (0=false, -1=true) indicating whether the input document will be tracked in XML format.	IBizTalkChannel. LoggingInfo
lognative out	int	-	-	-	Flag (0=false, -1=true) indicating whether the output document will be tracked in native format.	IBizTalkChannel. LoggingInfo

Column	Type	Size	P*	I*	Description	Configuration Object Model
logxmlout	int	-	-	-	Flag (0=false, -1=true) indicating whether the output document will be tracked in XML format.	IBizTalkChannel. LoggingInfo
expression	nvarchar	1024	-	-	Channel filtering expression.	IBizTalkChannel. Expression
comments	nvarchar	256	-	-	User comments.	IBizTalkChannel. Comments
trackfields	image	-	-	-	Channel-defined tracking fields in some BizTalk internal format.	IBizTalkChannel. TrackFields
signatcert name	nvarchar	256	-	-	Digital signature certificate name.	IBizTalkChannel. Signature CertificateInfo
signatcert ref	ntext	-	-	-	Digital signature certificate reference.	IBizTalkChannel. Signature CertificateInfo
signatcert store	int	-	-	-	Digital signature store reference.	IBizTalkChannel. Signature CertificateInfo
signatcert usage	int	-	-	-	Digital signature usage flag.	IBizTalkChannel. Signature CertificateInfo
verifysign atcertname	nvarchar	256	-	-	Digital signature (inbound) certificate name.	IBizTalkChannel. VerifySignature CertificateInfo
verifysign atcertref	ntext	-	-	-	Digital signature (inbound) certificate reference.	IBizTalkChannel. VerifySignature CertificateInfo
verifysign atcertstore	int	-	-	-	Digital signature (inbound) certificate store reference.	IBizTalkChannel. VerifySignature CertificateInfo
verifysign atcertusage	int	-	-	-	Digital signature (inbound) certificate usage flag.	IBizTalkChannel. VerifySignature CertificateInfo

Column	Type	Size	P*	I*	Description	Configuration Object Model
verify encrypcert name	nvarchar	256	-	-	Encryption (inbound) certificate name.	IBizTalkChannel. Decryption CertificateInfo
verify encrypcert ref	ntext	-	-	-	Encryption (inbound) certificate reference.	IBizTalkChannel. Decryption CertificateInfo
verify encrypcert store	int	-	-	-	Encryption (inbound) certificate store reference.	IBizTalkChannel. Decryption CertificateInfo
verify encrypcert usage	int	-	-	-	Encryption (inbound) certificate usage flag.	IBizTalkChannel. Decryption CertificateInfo
openness	int	-	-	-	Openness flag.	IBizTalkChannel. SourceEndpoint
receipt TimeOut	int	-	-	-	Timeout in minutes until a receipt must be received.	IBizTalkChannel. ExpectReceipt Timeout
receipt ChannelID	int	-	-	-	Identifier of the related receipt channel.	IBizTalkChannel. ReceiptChannel
IsReceipt Channel	int	-	-	-	Flag (0=false, -1=true) indicating whether this channel is a receipt channel.	IBizTalkChannel. IsReceiptChannel
retry Count	int	-	-	-	Threshold value for how often a transmission may be retried until it is considered a failure.	IBizTalkChannel. RetryCount
retry Interval	int	-	-	-	Time period (in minutes) between retries.	IBizTalkChannel. RetryInterval

bts_controlnumber By definition, X12 and UN/EDIFACT interchanges must have a unique identifier for each transmission through a channel. This table holds the current counter for each port and is referenced by the field bts_port.controlnumid.

Column	Type	Size	P*	I*	Description	Configuration Object Model
id	int	-	X	-	Primary key.	n/a
date modified	datetime	-	-	-	Date when the record was last updated.	n/a
value	decimal	14,0	-	-	Current control number for the port.	n/a

bts_document This table holds the document definitions. A document definition is composed of a reference into the XML share table (bts_xmlshare) and additional properties (the selection criteria for EDI document) and a definition for the global tracking fields.

Column	Type	Size	P*	I*	Description	Configuration Object Model
id	int	-	-	-	Primary key.	n/a
name	nvarchar	64	-	-	Name of the document definition.	IBizTalk Document. Name
guid	unique identifier	-	-	-	GUID.	n/a
date modified	datetime	-	-	-	Date when the entry was last modified.	IBizTalk Document. DateModified
propset	nvarchar	450	-	-	Selection criteria.	IBizTalk Document. PropertySet
shareid	int	-	-	-	Reference to the XML share table.	n/a
trackfields	image	-	-	-	Tracking fields.	IBizTalk Document. TrackFields

bts_envelope   Envelope definitions are stored in this table.

Column	Type	Size	P*	I*	Description	Configuration Object Model
id	int	-	-	-	Primary key.	n/a
name	nvarchar	64	-	-	Name of the envelope definition.	IBizTalk Envelope.Name
guid	unique identifier	-	-	-	GUID.	n/a
date modified	datetime	-	-	-	Date when the entry was last modified.	IBizTalk Envelope. DateModified
format	nvarchar	-	-	-	Envelope format: X12, EDIFACT, RELIABLE, CUSTOM, or CUSTOM XML.	IBizTalk Envelope. Format
shareid	int	-	-	-	Reference to the XML share table.	n/a

bts_organization   Organizations are held in this table.

Column	Type	Size	P*	I*	Description	Configuration Object Model
id	int	-	-	-	Primary key.	n/a
name	nvarchar	-	-	-	Default name of the organization. Mirrors the Organization Name qualifier entry in bts_alias.	IBizTalk Organization. Name
guid	unique identifier	-	-	-	GUID.	n/a
date modified	datetime	-	-	-	Date when the entry was last modified.	IBizTalk Organization. DateModified
comments	nvarchar	-	-	-	User comments.	IBizTalk Organization. Comments

Column	Type	Size	P*	I*	Description	Configuration Object Model
defaultflag	int	-	-	-	Flag (0=false, -1=true) indicating whether this is the home organization.	IBizTalk Organization. IsDefault

bts_outputconfig   This table is the most interesting from the configuration database because its existence is not immediately apparent through any of the user interfaces. The output configuration permanently links a port and a channel and provides a consolidated view of the information required to transmit data to a destination. The term "view" may not actually be accurate to use here. When the port and channel definitions are complete, all information is replicated to this table. So, whenever BizTalk sends information through a document-processing pipeline, it will use the definitions from this table and mostly ignore the original entries from bts_port and bts_channel. The entries in those tables are relevant only once you reconfigure a port or a channel through Messaging Manager (or the Configuration Object Model) and, with that, rebuild and override the entries in this table.

Column	Type	Size	P*	I*	Description	Configuration Object Model
outagrid	int	-	-	-	Primary key.	n/a
pipeid	int	-	-	-		n/a
openness	int	-	-	-	Openness flag (See bts_port.)	n/a
service window	int	-	-	-	Flag (0=false, -1=true) indicating whether a service window applies for the port.	n/a
service window from	datetime	-	-	-	Begin time (date part is not relevant) for the service window.	n/a
service windowto	datetime	-	-	-	End time (date part is not relevant) for the service window.	n/a

Column	Type	Size	P*	I*	Description	Configuration Object Model
serializerclsid	unique identifier	-	-	-	COM class ID of the serializer component.	IBizTalkChannel .SetConfig Component()
pritranstype	int	-	-	-	Flag for the primary transport protocol.	n/a
pritransclsid	unique identifier	-	-	-	COM class ID of the transport component.	IBizTalkChannel .SetConfig Component()
sectranstype	int	-	-	-	Flag for the backup transport protocol.	n/a
sectransclsid	unique identifier	-	-	-	COM class ID for the backup transport component.	IBizTalkChannel .SetConfig Component()
encodtype	int	-	-	-	Type of encoder to be used (flag field).	n/a
encodclsid	unique identifier	-	-	-	COM class ID of the encoder component.	IBizTalkChannel .SetConfig Component()
encryptype	int	-	-	-	Type of encryption to be used (flag field).	n/a
encrypclsid	unique identifier	-	-	-	COM class ID of the encryption component.	IBizTalkChannel .SetConfig Component()
signattype	int	-	-	-	Type of signature to be used.	n/a
signatclsid	unique identifier	-	-	-	COM class ID of the signature component.	IBizTalkChannel .SetConfig Component()
pritransconf data	image	-	-	-	Primary transport configuration data.	IBizTalkChannel .SetConfigData()

Column	Type	Size	P*	I*	Description	Configuration Object Model
sectransconf data	image	-	-	-	Backup transport configuration data.	IBizTalkChannel .SetConfigData()
encodconf data	image	-	-	-	Encoder configuration data.	IBizTalkChannel .SetConfigData()
signatconf data	image	-	-	-	Signature configuration data.	IBizTalkChannel .SetConfigData()
encrypconf data	image	-	-	-	Encryption configuration data.	IBizTalkChannel .SetConfigData()
serializerconf data	image	-	-	-	Serializer configuration data.	IBizTalkChannel .SetConfigData()
overrideflags	int	-	-	-	The mysterious override flags.	n/a

bts_portgroup   A *port group* is what was previously explained as a distribution list. This table defines a port group. The ports are referenced through the bts_portgroups auxiliary table.

Column	Type	Size	P*	I*	Description	Configuration Object Model
int	id	-	-	-	Primary key.	n/a
name	nvarchar	64	-	-	Name of the port group.	IBizTalkPort Group.Name
guid	unique identifier	-	-	-	Additional GUID for this element.	n/a
date modified	datetime	-	-	-	Date when the entry was last modified.	IBizTalkPort Group.Modified

bts_portgroups   This table serves to resolve the m:n relationship between bts_portgroup and bts_port.

Column	Type	Size	N*	P*	I*	Description	Configuration Object Model
grpid	int			X		Port group identifier from bts_portgroup (id).	n/a

Column	Type	Size	N*	P*	I*	Description	Configuration Object Model
agrid	int			X		Port identifier from bts_port (id).	n/a

bts_xmlshare This table is the management database's XML storage location. All document specifications and document maps are stored in this table; there is no active link maintained between these documents and those located in the WebDAV repository. Therefore, if you change document specifications or document maps, you must run through the Channel Wizard once more to allow BizTalk to update this table.

Column	Type	Size	P*	I*	Description	Configuration Object Model
id	int	-	-	-	Primary key.	n/a
reference	nvarchar	256	-	-	The HTTP reference into the WebDAV repository to locate the original document for update purposes.	n/a
name space	nvarchar	256	-	-	The XML default namespace identifier for this document type.	n/a
type	nvarchar	32	-	-	Identifies the document type for non-XML documents (e.g., UN/EDIFACT "INVOIC").	n/a
version	nvarchar	32	-	-	A version of the document standard specification. Relates to the type field.	n/a
content	ntext	-	-	-	XML document.	n/a

THE SHARED QUEUE DATABASE

The shared queue database holds the four queues that you already learned about: the Work Queue, Scheduled Queue, Retry Queue, and Suspended Queue. You can access and test the queues through the BizTalk WMI provider, and you should therefore not use the shared queue database directly.

The shared queue database tables are not nearly as revealing or interesting as the management database tables and really hold only the status of a given interchange in transit, so we will not investigate the details. The tables in the InterchangeSQ database and their functions are listed here for completeness:

Table	Function
cs_SuspendedQ	Suspended Queue main table
cs_SuspendedQErrorStrings	Error strings for suspended queue entries
cs_WorkQ	Work Queue table
cs_RetryQ	Retry Queue table
cs_ScheduledQ	Scheduled Queue table
cs_DupRem	Duplicates record for Retry Queue

THE BIZTALK DOCUMENT TRACKING DATABASE

Of the three messaging-related databases, the BizTalk document tracking database is the only one that is fully documented in the BizTalk Server 2000 help system because the interface is truly simple. The IBizTalkTrackData interface has three methods that individually return ActiveX Data Objects (ADO) Recordsets, which let you inspect input and output documents and details about the entire interchange for a single submission handle (which you receive when you send a message through the Interchange component). The IBizTalkTrackData interface is absolutely sufficient to track documents from within the scope of a single transaction, but if you want to create larger status reports or need statistics about the traffic, you will need to access the document tracking database directly. Therefore, Chapter 21 is devoted to the BizTalk document tracking database and document tracking.

DOCUMENT-PROCESSING PIPELINE COMPONENTS

Now it's time to put on the hard hat. Understanding the document-processing pipeline's internal structure is essential if you want to write or use custom components for BizTalk Server. This section explores the internal structure and interdependencies of the many components that make up the active BizTalk messaging architecture. Figure 11-3 provides a functional overview on how the document processing pipeline "clicks" together.

BizTalk Server 2000 shares some of its architecture and indeed some of its programming interfaces with its sibling, Commerce Server 2000, which was developed at the same

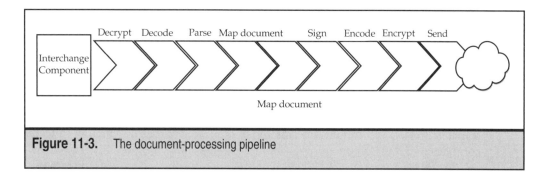

Figure 11-3.   The document-processing pipeline

time. Therefore, you will find Commerce Server–related files in the software development kit (SDK) portion of your BizTalk installation. Both servers share the concept of a processing pipeline that is dynamically assembled at run time on a per-incident basis from COM components implementing a certain set of interfaces and being specially marked in the Registry. As the term "pipeline" suggests, all components are invoked in a well-defined sequence so that each operates on the results of the previously called component.

In BizTalk Server, the processing pipeline consists of the following components that are executed in sequence:

▼   **Decryption component**   If the document that is being submitted into BizTalk is encrypted, it must of course be decrypted before it can be parsed and processed. To enable decryption, you must specify a verification certificate in the channel configuration. If such a certificate is present, BizTalk will first pass the documents to the matching decryption component. In the first release of the product, the only supported decryption component is the built-in Secure Multipurpose Internet Mail Extensions (S/MIME) component.

■   **Decoder component**   Especially with Simple Mail Transfer Protocol (SMTP) transports, documents may not simply arrive as plain text but may be MIME-encoded. Multipurpose Internet Mail Extensions (MIME) provides a way to place multiple entities (text documents, images, etc.) into a single stream for transmission via Internet e-mail. If BizTalk receives a MIME-encoded message, it passes the message on to the decoder component, which extracts the raw document data. MIME encoding is the only supported encoding for the first release of the product.

■   **Parser component**   A parser "probes" the encrypted incoming data stream for document format and type and then decides whether it will be able to parse the stream into an XML format. To allow all registered parsers to see the data stream for this task, the stream is handed to all of them in the sequence defined for the server group in which the processing server is located. The first parser that positively acknowledges the data stream for processing in the sequence gets the job of translating the inbound document into XML in compliance with the document specification that has been defined for inbound documents on the channel the parser is working on. Thus, it cannot later fail with unrecognized format class errors. Once it accepts the format for parsing, the component must be absolutely sure that it can handle the document. BizTalk supplies parsers for UN/EDIFACT, X12, flatfiles, and XML. If your solution requires other document formats, you can write your own custom parser components and plug them into BizTalk.

- **Validation and transformation**   Once the document has been parsed and translated into XML format, BizTalk must validate whether the document fully complies with the document specification. BizTalk must also possibly transform the document from one specification format into another specification format by using an XML Stylesheet Language Transformations (XSLT) transformation that you have built with BizTalk Mapper and associate it with the channel. Document validation and transformation is directly performed by the messaging service itself and, as such, is nonextensible.

- **Serializer component**   When the document has been validated, transformed, and revalidated so that it actually conforms to the outbound document specification, it can be prepared for transfer. At this time, the document that BizTalk is using internally is still into XML representation, even if the outbound document format is UN/EDIFACT, some flatfile format, or X12. The serializer component takes that XML stream and converts it to the desired outbound format. Although you might expect the serializer to be picked by the format definition that is contained in the outbound document specification, it is the envelope definition that actually causes a certain serializer to be instantiated. If you do not specify an envelope format on a messaging port, all output will be rendered in XML regardless of what the document definition's format information specifies. The serializer usually creates the outbound stream by using the annotations contained in the document specification schema. For instance, if you define a document specification for UN/EDIFACT by using BizTalk Editor, the tool will create special hints such as the names for the segments, which may differ from XML tag names. The serializer component reads these names and matches them against the XML document instance to produce outbound streams.

- **Encoder component**   You can configure your channel to pass the document to the appropriate encoding component if the endpoint requires MIME encoding, for instance. You can actually use custom encoder components, although the BizTalk documentation does not provide detail about how to do it. However, because there appears to be no way to use custom decoder components in this release of BizTalk, you would therefore produce messages that cannot be understood by other servers or your own BizTalk server.

- **Encryption component**   Typically, business documents contain information that is nobody's business but you and your partner's. Especially if you are sending documents over the Internet, you will want to use encryption on all exchanged information. To enable encryption, select S/MIME Encryption on your channel and specify an encryption certificate. If the configuration information is present, the S/MIME encryption pipeline component is handed the document and encrypts it by using the private key on the given certificate. Because S/MIME is really an extension to the MIME standard, the resulting data stream is automatically MIME-encoded even if you have not explicitly chosen MIME encoding. The extensibility issue is the same as with encoding components. Although it is possible to create your own encryption components, other BizTalk servers and your own BizTalk servers will not be able to understand it because they cannot configure custom decryption components.

- ■ **Signature component**   To apply digital signatures to documents, you can specify a signature certificate on the channel. If such a certificate is present on the channel, the document pipeline will invoke the signature component. At present, digital signatures are always applied in S/MIME format and by the S/MIME encryption component.

- ▲ **Transport component**   After being processed to all the components of the pipeline, the outbound stream is ready for transfer. The destination may be an internal application or a remote location that can be reached via SMTP, HTTP, file protocol, or any other transport means. If the destination is an internal application, the transport is handled by an Application Integration Component (AIC). Otherwise, the outbound stream is handed to a transport component. Out of the box, BizTalk supports HTTP, Hypertext Transfer Protocol/Secure (HTTPS), SMTP, the Microsoft Message Queue (MSMQ), and writing files to output directories. If you need support of other transports, you have multiple options. You can write an application integration component that will take care of carrying the documents to the destination location, or you could write your own transport component. However, just as with encryption and encoding components, plugging in your own transports is currently not officially supported by BizTalk, although it is technically possible.

Pipeline Components Under the Hood

All components in the pipeline except serializers and parsers, which use special interfaces that are discussed a bit later, are implemented as Commerce Server–compatible pipeline components. The pipeline component model was introduced with Microsoft Site Server 3.0 Commerce Edition and is now shared by Microsoft BizTalk Server 2000 and Microsoft Commerce Server 2000. For the purpose of this discussion, let's assume that you want to implement pipeline components, serializers, and parsers yourself.

When the server wants to send data through the pipeline, it creates a dictionary that contains the data to be handled by the pipeline components. For Commerce Server, the dictionary contains a so-called order form; in BizTalk, it contains what is called a transport dictionary. A *dictionary* is essentially a list of key-value pairs that contain data that the pipeline components will modify or that the components need to execute the desired operations and in which each data item is indexed by a string. The BizTalk transport dictionary always contains these seven entries:

▼ **Src_ID_Type** The identifier qualifier used for the source organization

■ **Src_ID_Value** The value of the source organization identifier

■ **Dest_ID_Type** The identifier qualifier used for the destination organization

■ **Dest_ID_Value** The value of the destination organization identifier

■ **Document_Name** The name of the input document definition

■ **Tracking_ID** A key value that is based on the GUID and used for tracking

▲ **working_data** The current state of the outbound stream

This dictionary is passed to each pipeline component through the *Execute()* method of its IPipelineComponent interface. The *Execute()* method has three inbound arguments and one outbound argument:

```
HRESULT IPipelineComponent::Execute(
                IDispatch* pDispTransportDictionary,
                IDispatch* pDispContext,
                long lFlags,
                long* plErrorLevel);
```

The *Execute()* method is called by BizTalk Server. The first argument receives the transport dictionary. The second argument, the context dictionary, applies only to commerce Server 2000 and is not used by BizTalk, just like the other two arguments.

To implement the transport dictionary, you use the IDictionary interface that is defined in the "commerce.h" header (for C++ programmers) and in the MSCSCore.dll type library. This library is located in the program files folder Common Files\Microsoft Shared\Enterprise Servers\Commerce\ if your tools support importing type libraries such as Visual Basic 6.0 or Microsoft Visual Studio.NET.

The only other method on the IPipelineComponent interface—*EnableDesign()*—can be safely ignored when you are implementing BizTalk pipeline components. The method serves only to distinguish between designer mode and production mode in Commerce Server, which does not apply to BizTalk.

When a pipeline component is invoked, it generally inspects the working_data field of the dictionary, which contains the current status of the outbound document. For instance, an encoder component would find the serialized outbound stream in working_data that will render in encoded format. Once it has completed this task, it writes the results back to the working_data field.

Of course the encoder needs some instructions on how to perform the encoding. The component can therefore implement the IPipelineComponentAdmin interface, which allows it to publish its supported configuration parameters through the *GetConfigData()* method and lets the pipeline host set the parameters through the *SetConfigData()* method at run time. The call sequence for every pipeline component is therefore that the infrastructure calls *IPipelineComponentAdmin.SetConfigData()* first to set the configuration data and then *IPipelineComponent.Execute().* To optimize reading and writing configuration settings, pipeline components can also implement the IPersistStream interface, which allows the host of the pipeline to have the component save its state to a flat stream.

If you want to know where BizTalk stores this configuration data, you just need to look at the bts_outputconfig table in the configuration database, specifically at the columns pritransconfdata, sectransconfdata, encodconfdata, signatconfdata, and encrypconfdata. When you modify the advanced settings on the Channel Wizard's last page and specify, for instance, a certain username and password for the HTTP transport component that is used at run time to authenticate BizTalk Server against a remote HTTP site, these configuration settings are stored in either the pritransconfdata or sectransconfdata columns (depending on whether HTTP is your primary or your backup transport). And at run time, the settings are passed to the pipeline component through the *SetConfigData()* method before the *Execute()* method is called.

Another optional interface to implement for pipeline components is IPipelineComponent Description. This interface has three simple methods—*ValuesWritten(), ValuesRead,* and *ContextValuesRead()*—that each return an array of VARIANT objects containing the names of the dictionary entries that they either read from or write to the transport dictionary or read from the context dictionary. (The latter applies only to Commerce Server.)

Even though BizTalk serializers and parsers are not real pipeline components in that they do not implement the IPipelineComponent interface, their native IBizTalkSerializerComponent and IBizTalkParserComponent interfaces also expect a transport dictionary to be passed.

How the Pipeline Works

Before we take a closer look at those interfaces, let's look at a sample pipeline sequence. Assume that we are receiving an S/MIME-encoded, encrypted, and signed XML interchange that we want to map to a different document format and then again encrypt, sign, and send to an HTTP destination within our own organization. The receiving process, which may be a Microsoft Exchange SMTP service, an Internet Information Server ASP page, or some other application, will submit the inbound stream into BizTalk through the Interchange component.

Once the entry is picked up from the Work Queue, the stream is passed to the S/MIME decoder pipeline component in the transport dictionary's "working_data" element. The decoder will then inspect the data stream and check whether it's actually an S/MIME-encoded entity. If so, it will attempt to decrypt the data stream using one of the certificates found in the local certificate store and will also try to identify the signature certificate if one is present. The decrypted data stream is then placed into the working_data element of the transport dictionary, and the identifier of the encryption certificate and the signature certificate are also placed into the transport dictionary with the keys encryption_cert and signature_cert.

When control returns to BizTalk from the decoder component, BizTalk Server will then match these identifiers against those configured in the channel settings as signature verification certificates and encryption verification certificates, respectively. The channel is selected only if both of the certificates match. Otherwise, BizTalk will report that no matching channel can be found, even if all other parameters would justify them to match.

If the data stream is not S/MIME-encoded, the components will not touch the working_data entry and will not insert these keys, but it will not fail; it will just quietly return.

Whether the S/MIME decoder could make sense of the stream's contents or not, the stream is passed on to the MIME decoder. If the S/MIME decoder had already picked up and decoded the stream, it will no longer be MIME format; thus, the decoder will ignore it. Otherwise, and if the data stream is actually MIME-encoded for some reason other than encryption, possibly because it was routed through SMTP, the MIME decoder will turn the stream into its native format. Some possible MIME encodings are base64, uuencode, 7bit plain text, or 8bit plain text; the MIME decoder supports all of these.

After this stage, the document is in its native format and the parsers come into play. According to the sequence configured for the BizTalk server group, the parser components are now sequentially invoked to probe the inbound streams. For this, BizTalk passes the data stream to each parser's *ProbeInterchangeFormat()* method that must be implemented on the IBizTalkParserComponent interface.

```
HRESULT IBizTalkParserComponent::ProbeInterchangeFormat(
    IStream* pData,
    BOOL FromFile,
    BSTR EnvName,
    IStream* pReceiptData,
    BSTR* Format
);
```

Each parser component will now inspect the data stream and determine whether the format is known and it can process the stream. To make implementation a bit easier if you want to write custom parsers, you can require callers to the Interchange components to always pass the envelope name when the documents are being submitted. This will at least allow you to tell whether the inbound document format is one of the EDI formats, some custom XML format, or another custom format.

However, if the envelope name is not given at submission time, the EnvName parameter passed to this method will be equally blank. In this case, it is your parser's responsibility to determine the correct envelope format. BizTalk's built-in XML parser, for instance, will derive the document's default namespace from the root of the XML document either by looking for an xmlns attribute or simply by taking the tag name of the root element and matching this against the namespace information contained in the configuration database's bts_xmlshare table for all those entries that have a matching entry in the bts_envelope table. While it is not clear whether BizTalk's internal parsers really do this, your parsers should in any event go through the BizTalk configuration object model to obtain such information because, as previously stressed, the internal database tables are officially undocumented and, thus, subject to change.

Once one of the parsers in the sequence has signaled that it can process the document, it will hold on to the stream pointer or cache the entire stream internally for processing. Once the parser tells the messaging service that it is able to process the document, it essentially makes a point-of-no-return decision. Even if a parser that follows in the sequence could parse the documents successfully, it would never be invoked because control is handed over immediately to this parser after it returns successfully from IBizTalkParserComponent *ProbeInterchangeFormat()*.

The parser's first job is to retrieve the Interchange details—specifically the source and the destination organization identifiers—from the envelope or wherever else they may be located in the document. For this, BizTalk calls the IBizTalkParserComponent *GetInterchangeDetails()* method on the interface. The only argument to this method is the transport dictionary, which may already contain some of the information if such was set in the call to the Interchange component. If the parser can find that information in the Interchange, it sets the dictionary entries src_id_type, src_id_value, dest_id_type, and dest_id_value.

The next method that is called is IBizTalkParserComponent *GroupsExist()*. You will certainly remember from the EDI discussion in Chapter 3 that X12 and UN/EDIFACT can carry more than one document in one Interchange. Even more, UN/EDIFACT and X12 interchanges are capable of carrying multiple functional groups, which, in turn, may contain multiple documents. If this method returns True, the messaging service assumes that the current Interchange contains multiple documents.

Parsers typically will not base the method return value on a decision, but the behavior is predefined by the parsed format; for instance, because UN/EDIFACT always has functional groups, it will always return True regardless of whether the Interchange contains one or many documents. If the document has groups, the messaging service calls the method IBizTalkParserComponent *GetGroupDetails()* to retrieve information about the group that is being inserted into the document tracking database. After this call and also if no groups are present, it calls the method IBizTalkParserComponent *GetNextDocument()*.

```
HRESULT IBizTalkParserComponent::GetNextDocument(
    IDictionary* Dict,
    BSTR DocSpecName,
    BOOL* DocIsValid,
    BOOL* LastDocument,
    GeneratedReceiptLevel ReceiptGenerated,
    BOOL* DocIsReceipt,
    BSTR* CorrelationCompProgID
);
```

The *GetNextDocument()* method has two inbound arguments: transport dictionary and the name of the document specification. Just as with the *ProbeInterchangeFormat()* method call, the latter argument is optional and is provided only if it has been specified in the call to the Interchange component. You can either require your callers to supply this information at submission time, or you can use this argument to verify the document name against the data that you actually find in the Interchange and fail if they don't match.

However, in most cases, you should not expect to receive this information and should be able to derive the document type from the data itself. To enable this type of "smart probing" and BizTalk's internal parsers to actually do this themselves, you can match the data that you find in the document against the property sets that are saved, along with the document definitions in the management database. You can find this information on the PropertySet property of the IBizTalkDocument interface. The BizTalk user interface calls these *selection criteria,* and that is exactly what you do here: select the document definition based on the property sets and match this against the data you find.

Once you have determined the document type, you can access the document specification by using the Contents property of the IBizTalkDocument interface. The document specification will help you to parse the document. If you actually want to write your own parsers, you may want to look at BizTalk's own parser use augmentations to the BizTalk Schema to drive the parsing effort. Chapter 22 looks at this topic in more detail, when we implement a simple custom parser.

If you were able to parse the document successfully—which always means that the document is transformed into an XML document that is an instance of the respective document specification—and the structure matches the document specification, you set the DocIsValid outbound parameter to "true". If an error occurred when parsing the document or if the document was not compliant with the specification, set this parameter to "false". However, unless the parser cannot recover from the error, you should not return failure result code from this method. If you have completed parsing the document and this is the last document in this group or the last document in this data stream, you should set the LastDocument argument to "true" as well. (The last three parameters will be ignored here. They are also covered in Chapter 22).

TIP: Regardless of whether the document successfully parsed or not, you should place the results into the working_data field of the transport dictionary so that they can later be analyzed by the system administrator in case of failure. After all, a failed parsing attempt may not be the fault of the parser to begin with.

To be able to isolate the native document data for the purpose of writing that data into the document tracking database, the messaging service will subsequently call the *GetNativeDocumentOffsets()* method, which must return the start position of the most recently parsed document relative to the beginning of the data stream and the size of the document. Based on this information, the messaging service will cut the native data out of the original data stream and submit it to the document tracking database. If the output argument LastDocument of the *GetNextDocument()* method indicated that this is the last document of the group or the stream and the parser had previously detected a group, the messaging service will then call the *GetGroupSize()* method. This method is very similar to *GetNativeDocumentOffsets(),* but it returns the size of the entire group, not just that of the document. This method's job is also to determine whether this is the last group of the Interchange.

If an interchange actually contains multiple documents, the transport dictionary is cloned every time before the *GetNextDocument()* method is called. Consequentially, all of the following actions happen in parallel: multiple documents in an interchange essentially fork to the processing pipeline and are handled as if each document were submitted individually.

At this point, the messaging service has all the information it needs to continue processing the documents. The documents are an XML format, the document types are known, and the source and destination organization identifiers have been isolated and placed into the transport dictionary. Based on this information, the messaging service can now identify the matching channels and, if multiple channels apply, it will evaluate the channel filters to find the appropriate channel. On synchronous submissions (IInterchange::SubmitSync), the messaging service will fail if multiple channels match in the end. Asynchronous submissions will succeed and deliver the document into all matching channels.

The next step is transformation. If the inbound and outbound document format are not identical, the documents must be mapped. Because all documents inside BizTalk are XML documents, all transformations can be and are done using XSLT. Document maps are created by using BizTalk Mapper and are stored in the Messaging management database. BizTalk Mapper uses a special XML format to save the document maps that includes both the source and the target schema and the XSLT transformation style sheet. The style sheet is saved as an immediate child of the document root element inside the tag <CompiledXSL>.

You can indeed bypass BizTalk Mapper and write custom XSLT style sheets to perform document mapping as long as you save them in the same way. At run time, the source and destination schemas are not needed. The actual transformation process is performed by the Microsoft XML parser's XSLT engine. The resulting document is immediately validated against the target schema. If validation fails, pipeline processing is suspended and the current document is placed into the Suspended Queue.

Now the entire process starts in reverse. Once the document has been successfully mapped to the outbound format and it has been validated that the document complies with the respective document specification, the document is passed on to the serializer. The choice of the serializer, as mentioned before, depends on the outbound envelope format. If no outbound envelope format is specified, the outbound format is assumed to be XML. If you want to use your own serializer or if you want to format documents in UN/EDIFACT or any other non-XML format, you need to choose an envelope format that is associated with the desired basic format type that is linked with a certain serializer. If you want to hook in your own serializers, you must either choose an envelope format of CUSTOM or CUSTOM XML type. The advanced property settings of the last page of the Channel Wizard allow you to choose your own serializer component.

```
HRESULT IBizTalkSerializerComponent::Init(
    BSTR srcQual,
    BSTR srcID,
    BSTR destQual,
    BSTR destID,
    long EnvID,
    IDictionary* pDelimiters,
    IStream* OutputStream,
    long NumDocs
);
```

The way serializer components work is quite similar to the functioning of the parsing components, just the other way around. The *Init()* method receives source and destination information, a reference to the envelope specification, a dictionary of delimiters, and a pointer to an output stream. If multiple documents are to be serialized, this is communicated through the NumDocs argument, which is otherwise set to 1.

After this initial call, the messaging service submits all documents that belong to the Interchange in calls to the *AddDocument()* method. The method gets as arguments a special document ID handle, the transport dictionary with the well-known working_data field, as well as the newly created tracking ID and the channel ID. When the method is called, the serializer transforms the inbound document into the native format.

The serializer is also responsible for creating the envelope. To do this, it obtains the appropriate IBizTalkEnvelope object from the Configuration Object Model using the envelope identifier, loads the envelope document specification (if required), and encloses the outbound stream into the envelope. Because the number of documents is known beforehand, you can write the envelope header when the first document is added, and you can write the envelope footer when the last document is added.

If the port that is associated with the channel specifies MIME encoding, the MIME encoder component is now invoked, receives the documents in the working_data field of the transport dictionary, and encodes the data appropriately. The MIME encoder is more powerful than what you can configure through Messaging Manager or even through the Configuration Object Model or the database. The pipeline component supports two special configuration parameters that can be set through *SetConfigData()*: ContentType and XferEncoding. The content type is the MIME type that should be used to flag the document type in the MIME headers, and the transfer encoding indicates how the document is prepared for transmission, which may be 7bit or 8bit plain text, base64 encoding, or uuencode.

If the port configuration specifies encryption, the S/MIME component is invoked with the document in the working_data field. Although Messaging Manager will allow this, you should not specify MIME and S/MIME encoding at the same time. Because all components are executed in sequence, the MIME encoder component will encode the document and then the S/MIME component will take that result and encrypt it. While this works flawlessly for the outbound stream, double MIME encoding will cause great trouble at the receiving end.

The S/MIME component can either encrypt, sign, or do both at once. For encryption, it will use the certificate that has been specified in the port configuration, and for the signature, it will use the certificate that has been given in the channel configuration. The output of the operation is placed into the working_data field of the transport dictionary, as expected.

After the encryption, encoding, and signature stages, which are all optional, the output stream can finally be sent to the destination. The easiest transport components to use for getting data to the destination are AICs (pipeline components just like the ones we have discussed here). An alternative way to implement integration components is to expose the IBTSAppIntegration interface, which is probably as easy as it could ever get. The interface has a single method, *ProcessMessage()*, which receives a document as its inbound parameter and has a single output parameter that allows you to return a response document.

If you do not want to push the documents into internal applications directly but you want to send them to external partners or via a message queue or other transports to internal applications, you must use a transport component. The BizTalk transfer components are pipeline components. As such, they receive the outbound stream through the working_data entry of the transport dictionary, and before the *Execute()* method is called, the transmission parameters are provided through *SetConfigData()*.

If the transfer component returns from the *Execute()* method without reporting errors, the messaging service assumes that sending was completed successfully and logs the interchange as being sent.

CHAPTER 12

BizTalk Orchestration Architecture

Τ his chapter presents the architecture and internals of the BizTalk Orchestration services. You will learn about Orchestration schedules and XLANG and see how to run schedules. You will look at the component nature of schedules and see how this affects system design. You will also learn about properties, constants, and the nonexistence of variables. Finally, you will study hydration and dehydration—the scalability concepts of Orchestration.

ORCHESTRATION SCHEDULES AND XLANG

In the previous chapter on the Messaging services architecture, we poked around under the hood quite a bit. In contrast, this chapter does *not* drill down into the Orchestration architecture in detail for a few reasons: First, creating Orchestration schedules is considerably easier than creating a working Messaging configuration. Second, Orchestration is designed to pull resources together, but it will not allow you to extend the basic internal mechanisms. Inspecting the internals in detail may be interesting, but it would serve no real purpose. Therefore, this chapter focuses only on the level of detail you need to create Orchestration schedules that perform and behave well and to optimize the system configuration for running schedules.

But beware. The fact that we are not going to descend into the depths of the internal BizTalk Orchestration architecture does not mean that this chapter is an easy read for everyone. Although designing Orchestration schedules is easy, monitoring them and getting them to run in the first place requires some prior knowledge about COM and specifically COM monikers. If you do not know much about the latter, this chapter is for you.

Before we begin, take a look at this brief recap of Orchestration schedules:

▼ You create Orchestration schedules by using a graphical language in Orchestration Designer. The language is designed to be so easy that business analysts with no prior programming experience can understand it, but at the same time, it is expressive enough to implement entire programmatic workflows.

■ All action elements of Orchestration schedule drawings are connected to ports in the visual designer. Each port is associated with a single COM component, a message queue, a Windows script, or a BizTalk Messaging channel.

■ Each port has a number of properties, which represent the inbound and outbound arguments for a synchronous method call or the data being transmitted for an asynchronous message transmission. (What you don't know yet is that you can actually pull out single fields from XML documents through an XPath expression and associate them with properties on the ports.)

■ When an Orchestration schedule is completely defined in Orchestration Designer, it is compiled into an XLANG schedule. XLANG schedules are an XML representation of the Orchestration drawing. They contain the entire control flow information, port assignments, and port configuration. The XLANG Scheduler engine uses the XML documents to shape its internal processes and execute the action in the desired sequence and with the defined conditions.

- ■ When a schedule is executed, execution starts at the Begin shape of the program flow and follows the rules that are expressed in the drawing. At every Action shape, a schedule either waits for an inbound message from a port, sends an available data item through the port, or executes a bidirectional method.

- ▲ Conditions in Decision shapes and While loops are based on the current state of the schedule. The current state of the schedule is defined by its constants, the port properties, and any state information of stateful COM components bound to these ports.

All of this information is pretty much what you can see on the surface. You design Orchestration schedules, save them to XLANG schedules (these are the *.skx files), and run them. Run them?

When the basic Orchestration principles were introduced in Chapter 9, we did not look at how Orchestration schedules are actually run. The reason for this is that schedules are not really standalone applications; rather, they are components that are designed to be embedded into the larger context of an application. Thus, hosting and launching Orchestration schedules is actually a programming task and just as much part of the system architecture design decisions.

At run time, Orchestration schedules look, feel, and behave very much like any other COM+ component. When a schedule is started (by means that are discussed in the following section), the XLANG Scheduler engine uses the XLANG description to create a virtual component that is hosted within an XLANG COM+ application. BizTalk extends COM+ in such a way that you can flag any COM+ package as an XLANG schedule host through the Component Services Manager as shown in Figure 12-1. Every application that is configured this way is called an XLANG Group Manager. In the standard XLANG Scheduler package, you cannot make any changes to the XLANG settings, but when you create new COM+ packages, you can configure the settings (and the XLANG persistency database) individually for this new group manager.

If you flag your schedule in Orchestration Designer to require a transaction, the virtual component that is hosted by the group manager will have the same transaction behavior as any regular transactional COM+ component. You can access the dialog box shown in Figure 12-2 by opening the Properties dialog box of the Begin shape in BizTalk Orchestration Designer. If you make a schedule COM+-transacted in this dialog, the entire schedule and all its resources will be rolled into a single transaction. Of course, this has strong implications on the resource behavior and on database locks, for instance. You should use COM+ transaction behavior only for schedules that execute within very short periods of time.

We call these components *virtual* because they exist only in the running state and are dynamically created by the schedule engine. In BizTalk Orchestration terms, such a component

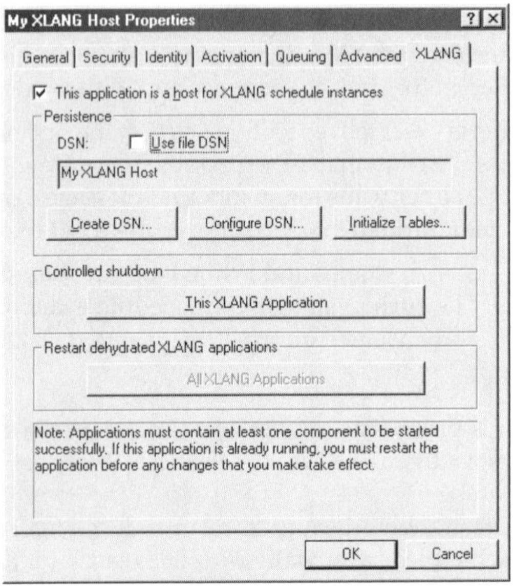

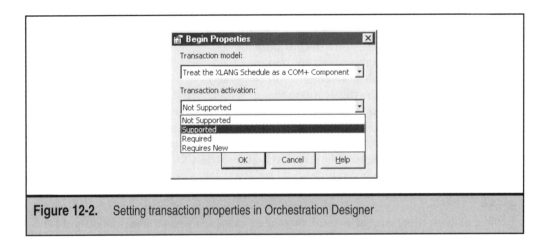

Figure 12-1. XLANG configuration in Component Services

is called a workflow instance object. *Workflow instance objects* expose the primary COM interface IWFWorkflowInstance, which allows external users to learn about the status of the workflow and, in a special case, helps to get the workflow started.

Figure 12-2. Setting transaction properties in Orchestration Designer

HOW TO RUN SCHEDULES

One of the most undervalued and coolest features of COM are *monikers*: objects that are able to transform a line of text into an object reference. (Moniker also means name or nickname.) The most obvious example is the file moniker, which has been part of COM since its initial release. When the file moniker is asked to bind to a file-system location—for instance, a filename with path and drive letter—it navigates to the file, starts the application that is associated with the file type, asks the application to load that file, and returns an object reference to the loaded document object within that application. (This is a bit simplified, but it is essentially what happens.)

Microsoft Internet Explorer and the entire Windows shell use monikers extensively. When you select Run from the Start menu and enter a filename or an Internet URL, the shell uses monikers to figure out the correct handler application and launch it. Internet Explorer leaves the entire resolution process for URL to so-called URL monikers. Every time Internet Explorer sees a hyperlink, it creates a URL moniker, hands the link information to the moniker, and asks it to bind to a data stream that contains the data to which the URL points. The Internet Explorer application that you can see does not even have any idea what HTTP is—all the work is done by the URL moniker infrastructure.

So how does this discussion relate to the BizTalk Orchestration context? BizTalk Orchestration schedules are launched through monikers. And indeed, using monikers is the only way to launch Orchestration schedules.

A Brief Moniker Lesson

Because BizTalk Orchestration Designer expects you to create moniker expressions to start Orchestration schedules, you should know how monikers work. Because this is not a COM book, you don't need the API-level details, though. The following discussion merely provides a high-level overview.

Let's start with an HTTP URL for simplicity: http://www.microsoft.com/default. asp#bk. When you enter this string into the Run box of the Windows Start menu, the following happens: The string is passed to an internal function that preanalyzes the string. The function specifically scans for known prefixes—http is one of those. These prefixes are not hard-coded into the function, but registered in the Windows Registry.

If you want to see how that is wired into the Windows Registry and you happen to be near a Windows computer with Internet Explorer version 3.0 or later, perform the following steps:

1. Select Start | Run and click OK to start regedit.exe, the Windows Registry Editor—no fear, we are just going to take a look.

2. Expand the HKEY_CLASSES_ROOT entry in the tree view by double-clicking it.

3. Quickly type **http**.

The Registry entry that you will see is named *http* and has two very interesting values. The first can be found in the shell/open/command subkey. It simply holds the command line of Internet Explorer. When the shell sees a command line that contains a colon (:), it checks to see whether the string to the left of the colon is a registered prefix. If it is, the shell runs the application that is registered under the shell/open/command subkey and hands the entire string to the application. The second, even more interesting (named) value is URL Protocol, whose actual value is blank.

Once Internet Explorer receives the string, it passes it to an internal COM function, which again goes hunting for prefixes. It will find that the prefix *http* is associated with the URL Protocol and will, in this special case, take a shortcut to create a URL moniker object that is able to resolve the HTTP URL into a file stream.

The moniker will "eat" the URL until it has found a completely bindable entity. In our case, it would be the entire string excluding the pound (#) character of the following two characters ("bk") of the above example URL. It then delegates the call to the Windows Internet API to asynchronously request the data stream from that location. Immediately thereafter, control returns to the Internet Explorer application, which memorizes the remainder of the URL that is #bk. Once the data stream—which is likely to be an HTML page—has been loaded and all dependent objects such as images have been loaded in much the same way, Internet Explorer assembles a page for display. Then it will use that remaining portion of the URL to locate a bookmark on the page and scroll to that position.

BizTalk Orchestration schedule monikers look suspiciously similar to and are, indeed, URL monikers. Here is one: sked://localhost!GrpMgr/c:\skeds\simple.skx/port1. You can verify this by looking up the prefix in the Registry. (You will also find that the entry is marked *obsolete*. However, the BizTalk product group changed their minds after the product shipped.)

You will find that there is no associated command; therefore, you cannot start schedules from the Run box. But there is a CLSID entry, which refers to the schedule moniker implementation (unlike the HTTP moniker, which does not have this entry because HTTP support is intrinsic to the URL moniker).

Otherwise, the binding mechanism is very much the same as it is with URL monikers. The string is passed to a COM function that isolates the prefix, locates it in the Registry, creates the matching moniker component instance, and hands it the string for resolution. This function is called *CoGetObject()*. It expects a string as an input argument and returns an interface reference to the object that the binding process resulted in.

What happens in the resolution process for schedule monikers is described as follows.

The moniker first evaluates the segment following the initial two slashes. This segment contains the machine name and the name of the group manager application, separated by an exclamation mark (!). If the name of the group manager is not given, it defaults to XLANG Scheduler, which is the default host for XLANG schedules. If the machine name is omitted, it defaults to localhost, and therefore, to the local machine.

The moniker then proceeds to evaluate the segment following the next slash (/) character. This segment contains the full pathname of an XLANG schedule, which must be expressed in universal naming convention (UNC) notation, or it contains a local path as seen from the target system. The path expression must not contain forward slashes (/) as separators between directory names.

Once the target system, the group manager, and the schedule filename are known, the moniker binds the schedule. *Binding* means that a new schedule instance is created on the target machine and in the defined group manager COM+ application that is based on the schedule information contained in the given file. If the schedule does not require any additional outside input, it is immediately started.

However, because you typically want to pass some arguments when you invoke a function in programming, you will likely want to do the same with XLANG schedules to parameterize them. Here, the BizTalk Orchestration approach is ingenious, but at the same time, a little bit weird. Get this:

When you want to pass parameters to a schedule, you do so by using a COM component. However, unlike you might think, this component is nowhere to be found in BizTalk: you provide it. To pass arguments to a schedule, you must create or at least use a component whose primary IDispatch interface has a method that expects the arguments that you want to pass to the schedule as input parameters or returns them as output parameters. This component is then bound to the first port in the schedule.

Now the moniker comes back into play. If we assume that the port to which the component is bound is called port1, and we look again at our sample schedule moniker sked://localhost!GrpMgr/c:\skeds\simple.skx/port1, it should be simple to infer that the moniker proceeds to bind to that component.

Because the binding process is completed once the schedule has been started and the moniker has bound to port1, the *CoGetObject()* function will return, handing you an interface. The returned interface is indeed the primary interface of the component bound to the port. To be a little more precise, it is a proxy to that interface because the scheduler engine is sitting in the middle, waiting and listening for what comes next.

Binding to ports and passing parameters is not supported when you start a schedule via BizTalk Messaging ports. Here is an example of passing arguments to a COM component bound to an Orchestration port.

```
Dim MySkedPort As Object
Set MySkedPort = GetObject("sked://localhost!GrpMgr/c:\skeds\simple.skx/port1")
MySkedPort.MethodToCall "Argument"
'at this point, the schedule has been kicked off
```

In your code, and in a similar way as shown in the previous code snippet, you will then simply call the respective function on the interface passing the arguments that you actually want to pass to the XLANG schedule. The method on the COM interface is called as expected. (This is not always the case, but this detail is covered later, in Chapter 14.) Then the COM component will do what it was designed for: set its output parameters and return.

Figure 12-3 illustrates how all the magic happens. Because the scheduler engine is sitting in the middle between your application and component, it intercepts and memorizes the input parameters, and it also intercepts the output parameters. So when the call returns, it sets the port properties of port 1 (in our example) to the values of the input in the output parameters. Then it kicks off the schedule immediately before the call returns to your application. By now, the schedule is an independent thread and runs in parallel to your program.

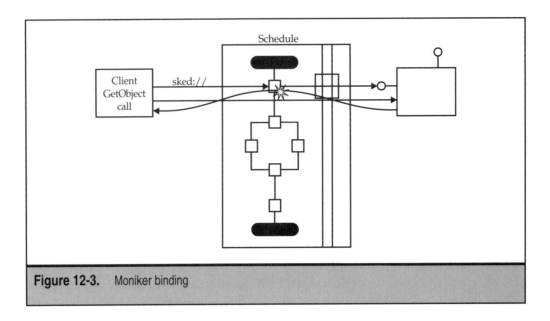

Figure 12-3. Moniker binding

In other words, you use a moniker to bind to a COM component reaching "through" a schedule, call a method, and when that call returns, the message arguments parameterize the schedule and allow it to start.

SCHEDULES AS COMPONENTS

At run time, schedules behave a lot like (and essentially are) COM+ components. You instantiate them either by simply binding them to a COM moniker if they don't expect any arguments, or by directly binding them to schedule ports and passing arguments through a "borrowed" interface. If you really accept XLANG schedules as components, BizTalk Orchestration becomes nothing less than another powerful way of implementing COM+ components.

However, accepting schedules to be components and making it part of the design consideration when creating enterprise applications creates a whole new challenge for the application architect. Architects and developers are accustomed to solving problems in code. You have a certain set of requirements, find a solution approach, break this solution into multiple components, and implement all these components by using your development tools of choice, whether it's Visual Basic, Visual C++, or another tool.

BizTalk Orchestration represents an approach in which the general circumstances for a business process environment are known; however, the business processes themselves may not be known when the hosting application is being created. Or business processes may not be known when they change so rapidly that you really cannot plan for anything except for the data that you can make available to them. The architectural challenge here is known as *whitespace*.

If you want to leverage the power of BizTalk Orchestration, you must accept that you have to leave large functional blocks of your application "blank" in the initial design. For instance, if you are writing a sales-support and order-handling system, you must create the user interfaces for the various parts of the application where you evaluate data or where data is entered by your users. You must also provide all the components that make up your essential business logic. However, when it's time to wire all these elements together, you should simply assume the place where you plug in the schedule as an undefined white area on your architectural blueprint. The only known interface into the order-handling process is that you have some kind of purchase order information that you will pass to a certain component with a certain interface: you will not really look at how the process works or is implemented.

In your planning, you need to provide and consider all the building blocks that are required to execute orders—calculating rebates, shipping, and taxes, requesting tracking numbers, requesting pickup times for shipping, and all of the other essential tasks. Even here, you should be cautious not to overdevelop your components that are designed to be embedded into the workflows. For example, requesting pickup times for shipping may be a field that you can solve dynamically by using Orchestration in conjunction with BizTalk Messaging, without requiring an additional line of code.

Even if it seems to be against your will and experience at first, you should design for Orchestration and leave significant blank space for schedules to implement their own thing within the hard-coded frame of your enterprise solutions. If you cage them into a very confined environment that basically preempts the functionality of schedules, then you should just ignore this BizTalk feature, because it will provide no benefit to you.

ABOUT PROPERTIES, CONSTANTS, AND THE NONEXISTENCE OF VARIABLES

Each port in an Orchestration schedule has a number of properties. In general, each of these properties represents a single data value that has been passed through the port in either direction. For method calls that are made into scripts or COM components, the properties are equivalent to the input and output arguments. For the message queuing and BizTalk messaging ports, which are always unidirectional, the port property *Document* reflects the entire document that has either been received or sent through the port.

Because Orchestration "knows" that documents are being passed in XML format, it allows you to extract any number of XML attribute or element values by using XPath expressions and to add them to the list of properties of the port. When the document is received through the port, the values will be extracted and assigned to the port properties.

The port properties concept is similar to that of variables in regular programs. The core difference is that you cannot declare variables locally for a schedule; you must rely on the port properties if you want to hold any local state. There's nothing that you can declare in the schedule directly that will hold any variable data independent of a port. For instance, if you wanted to use a local variable as the continuation condition for a While loop, pass it to a COM component method that would somehow modify the value, return it, and then use its value in the condition of the loop, you couldn't do it.

The trick is to have a dedicated COM component or script that will hold the variable state for the schedule and make those pseudo-variables available through method output parameters. This is possible because there is no one-to-one correspondence between actions and ports. A single port can indeed be called multiple times from within the same schedule. Each time the port is called, the port properties are updated with both the input and output arguments. The properties therefore always reflect the condition after the last call that was made through the port. So if you have a special variable container component, you can call it from multiple places within the schedule and update the values to reflect progress.

Just as important as defining the control flow is, of course, defining the data flow. Orchestration Designer therefore allows you to interconnect the port properties on a special data page, as shown in Figure 12-4. Imagine you have an action *A* that is bound to a port Alpha, which has a property *a* reflecting an output parameter. You also have an action *B* that is bound to a port Beta, which has a property *b* reflecting an input parameter. The actions are somehow executed in the sequence A—>B within the schedule. In this scenario, you can simply connect the properties *a* and *b*, and the respective data item that was returned through the Alpha port will be passed into the Beta port.

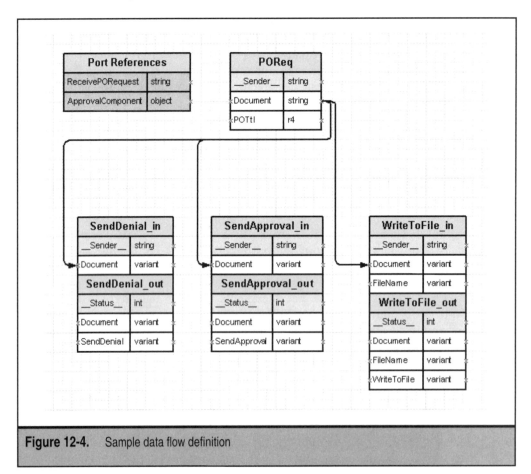

Figure 12-4.   Sample data flow definition

Constants are special but very simple cases of properties. Orchestration Designer allows you to define up to 64 named constant values, which you can also bind to ports. However, and as the term *constants* indicates, they are set once at design time and cannot be changed at run time.

HYDRATION AND DEHYDRATION

Although running schedules are indeed COM+ components, as you just learned, they are very different from typical COM+ components in one very important respect: execution time.

Orchestration schedules represent business processes and therefore operate in business real time. A typical business process that is represented by an Orchestration schedule takes anywhere from multiple hours to multiple weeks to complete. Indeed, this length of time is very different from typical COM+ backend components, where you start hunting for a good profiling toolkit when the execution time of a single method goes into the 100-milliseconds range.

Imagine an e-commerce storefront that receives somewhere around 2,000 orders per day. Each order is orchestrated by a main schedule with five subordinate schedules (a schedule that is used as a COM component in another schedule). Each of the subordinate schedules takes care of the more detailed issues. The average delivery time is 10 days, and the overall processing time is 40 days (including the essential 30-day money-back-guarantee handling schedule). Your system may have to juggle 2000×6×10 + 2000×30 = 180,000 schedules at any given time, likely more. Of course, each of these schedules will be idle some 99.99 percent (or more) of the time. When some external events triggers the schedule to proceed, the traversal from one step to the next step should take no longer than a few seconds, at most.

Therefore, keeping all these schedules in memory would unnecessarily clog up server resources. Keeping operations data in memory for too long is not smart because you'll risk losing that information if the machine goes down. Do not think "software failure;" think "six-hour power outage." Administrators from many parts of the world (including those that work for my publisher in energy-deficient California) can easily relate to these kinds of system failures.

These are the reasons why BizTalk hydrates and dehydrates XLANG schedules. The principle is easy: when the schedule becomes idle for a long time (this value is actually configurable), the schedule or engine dehydrates it. The sci-fi term *cryostasis* (when astronauts are frozen for space travel and are woken up once they reach the destination) is a more fitting way to describe this process.

When a schedule is *dehydrated,* its entire state is saved to disk and the schedule is removed from memory. Just before it goes to sleep, it tells the XLANG schedule restart service which event it is waiting on. The schedule restart service runs permanently as a Windows 2000 service. Once the event arrives, the schedule is *hydrated* (reinstantiated) by the service and continues running, which may result in another wait event and hydration/dehydration cycle.

Dehydration and hydration are possible only if external services can actually wait for the event. Therefore, they are not supported in the bidirectional orchestration ports for COM components and Windows scripts. Once the call into the component is initiated, it is impossible to put the schedule to rest and have the service pick up the return result from the method call. Therefore, methods of components that are used in conjunction with orchestration should return within a very short time; otherwise, scalability is adversely affected if both the schedule and COM components have to remain in memory too long because of the large number of active schedules in the typical orchestration usage scenario.

If you still need to bind to a component or an out-of-process service where a method call takes a significant time to complete, you should consider talking to that service asynchronously through a message queue.

Message queuing and BizTalk integration are the two Orchestration port types that support hydration and dehydration of schedules. As you will see later in Chapter 14, you can control the dehydration behavior of schedules on a per-port basis. If you define for a port that you expect a message to arrive from the particular data source in less than 180 seconds, the schedule will never be dehydrated while waiting at this port. If the estimated time of arrival is more than 180 seconds, the schedule will be dehydrated immediately when reaching the action.

To achieve maximum scalability within schedules but also in general with server-side applications, components should be stateless. A *stateless* component does not hold any variable information that would affect its run-time behavior across method calls. Stateless components are the exact opposite of the typical ActiveX control that you use with Visual Basic, in which you first set a couple of properties before you execute a method to get the desired behavior. Even if a stateless component supported such properties, setting a property must never affect the run-time behavior of any of the component's methods. In effect, stateless components do not "remember" anything about any method call; thus, they can be pooled in memory and recycled for any client who wants to have a particular action performed—or, as is the case with XLANG schedules, they can just be unloaded at will. "At will" is exactly that time when the schedule is dehydrated.

However, as you already know, stateful components can simulate variables for schedules. If you have such components that hold information on behalf of the schedule in memory, doesn't that completely rule out dehydration? Not if the components support persistency. All components that implement either the IPersistStream or IPersistStreamInit interfaces are automatically saved to a stream when the schedule is dehydrated, and they are restored from the stream when the schedule is hydrated. So if you implement COM components in schedules that hold state, you should always implement either of these interfaces to enable schedule dehydration. Of course, this is never true for scripting components because they will not allow you to inherit and implement interfaces.

PART IV

Architecting, Designing, and Configuring BizTalk Server 2000 Solutions

CHAPTER 13

Finding and Defining the Solution Architecture

Creating BizTalk solutions, regardless of whether you need to integrate systems or communicate with partners, is typically very complex. Because you will use BizTalk as either a central communications gateway or as the data-exchange hub between the core line-of-business applications, BizTalk solutions are not only mission-critical, but they also require solid planning.

Many specialized software solutions that are designed to solve specific department tasks within larger organizations are data islands—they are not integrated with other systems; rather, they import and export data from and to their own proprietary databases through files and data streams. It is unrealistic to assume that a single software solution could provide the functionality to cover the requirements of day-to-day operations in all areas of business. Therefore, software integration is a persistent and central task of corporate IT departments. Data must be routed, synchronized, and translated between systems and across platforms, and business processes must be automated across the entire software applications "zoo."

Organizations might consider using BizTalk Server in a lot of different scenarios. It enables these integration and automation tasks, but to create a working architecture, you must be aware of the functionality and requirements of each application to integrate. Software architects who create BizTalk solutions must therefore not only know about their core integration tools and related technologies, but must also act as information brokers and negotiators between departments and external software suppliers.

If you need to create integration solutions that involve external trading partners, the challenges may be even greater. For example, you might experience the following situations: your trading partners cannot readily supply certain data that is required for internal business processes; data formats and even the way standardized formats are used differ vastly; or systems are simply unable to exchange information due to incompatible protocols and transports. The rapidly expanding use of XML formats for business data interchange and the resulting battles on the market for the "right" way of communicating XML information often cause more problems than they solve.

NOTE: All major software vendors, including Microsoft, are clearly committed to XML. However, the means by which XML is enveloped and transported and the way XML formats are described are still disputed for a couple reasons: the more advanced XML protocols lack finalized specifications, and some vendors still ignore the standardization processes.

This chapter introduces a simplistic and practical approach to managing complexity and performing short-track requirements analysis for BizTalk Messaging and Orchestration, which is based on the 7±2 rule (explained in the next section) and simple language heuristics.

MANAGING COMPLEXITY

Enterprise integration solutions are complex. Although neither BizTalk Orchestration nor BizTalk Messaging are object-oriented development systems like the Microsoft .NET Framework, using object-oriented analysis and design principles will help you manage the vast amount of information and tasks that must be organized and executed to create integration solutions.

The greatest advantage of object-oriented programming is not that you can group code and data into a single unit or that you can use inheritance to reuse and enhance existing code. The greatest advantage is that it allows you to program the way as you think.

Even when you are just quietly standing at a bus stop or in line to buy metro tokens, your brain sends thousands of commands per second throughout your body to manage your body's balance and to simply keep you on your feet. At the same time, your nervous system controls the beat of your heart and all the other organs that make your body work with many thousands of other commands. Compared to the concurrency that your nervous system can handle, the capabilities of your conscious thinking seem very restricted. Typically, your attention is limited to one or, at most, two different events at once. You can drive a car while listening to the news and manage not to run into the car ahead of you, but as soon as you do something additional, like reaching for a soda, you become immediately distracted either from driving, or you miss a couple of sentences from the news.

But even when you're focusing on a single issue, things easily get out of hand if you need to deal with more than nine aspects of the issue at the same time. Even when we are very familiar with an issue, humans are typically limited to considering 7 ± 2 aspects of the same topic at the same time. Being aware of this limitation leads to a very natural structuring of complex issues.

When you sit down to analyze and structure a certain technical or business problem, it is very likely that you will find only 7 ± 2 main topics to analyze, and within those main topics, you will again find 7 ± 2 subtopics—with the pattern repeating into the deeper nesting levels. The maximum nesting depth when analyzing very complex issues will likewise hover around 7 ± 2.

You can even make this a rule. Consider a certain issue, write down whatever comes to mind when brainstorming about it, and then begin to structure the information. You will find only 7 ± 2 independent items. Each of the other items on the paper will somehow depend on one of the main items. Try it.

Short-Track Analysis Principles

Many academic approaches exist to object-oriented analysis and design. This section presents a very simple, practical approach to object-oriented analysis (OOA) that is based on some of the terminology of classic OOA, but which is not necessarily a complete process in the academic sense.

The short track analysis process is driven by the 7±2 rule and some very simple heuristics. The described techniques generally apply to business process analysis and prestructuring software solutions. We will assume that the analysis process starts with one or a combination of the following: already-written business process documentation, a discussion of the business process and integration requirements with business specialists in a group, or one-on-one interviews.

Discussing systems integration tasks at a technical level is a popular approach, but it rarely makes sense. Integration that occurs only at a technical level lets systems talk to each other, but it totally ignores the business effects and requirements. If systems integration is not aimed at business process optimization and streamlining of the process organization, it is entirely pointless.

When you begin discussing business process integration requirements in an enterprise scenario, assembling specialists from many areas of the business, you will learn many of the same issues as seen from different perspectives. The way people who are responsible for certain tasks talk about the requirements may seem to be diametrically opposed to the way others who rely on those services talk about the same requirements. You may wonder whether they are talking about the same issues. If you have worked for a large corporation, you have probably attended a meeting in which some of the positions were so contradictory that you wondered how the business survived! In most cases, the main problem is a subtly different interpretation of the same terminology and consequently, just misunderstanding instead of disagreement.

For example, if you analyze the business processes for a trading company and discuss the global requirements with the responsible managers from all departments, you will find that the sales department and the purchasing departments have radically different ideas about what a purchase order is. The sales department accepts purchase orders from external trading partners, of course, while the purchasers issue them to other partners. While they are indeed using the same term, they are really talking about two very separate issues. Therefore, whenever a discussion hits a dead end, it is smart to verify that everybody agrees on the same interpretation of the terminology.

Therefore, the first step in the analysis process is to agree on a very basic dictionary of terms. Look at the following high-level view of how the imaginary business for this chapter operates. The description is simple—many business specialists will rightfully complain that the description is oversimplified—but the goal is really to reach some basic consensus and to isolate the core terminology. Once we have done this, we will look at the separate tasks in a bit more detail, and we will formulate a couple of questions for the use case and requirements analysis process. The following is a verbal description that a business specialist formulated in an imaginary meeting:

> Customers receive catalogs or sales offers (either by request or through marketing or sales personnel activities) on which they make their purchasing decisions. When they have decided which merchandise to buy from us, they send us an order. We first check the customer's credit-worthiness for the total order amount and possibly request prepayment or a letter of credit to execute the order. Then (or at the same time as doing the credit check), we check

whether we have the ordered merchandise in stock. If we are out of stock on one or all of the requested merchandise, we either wait for all merchandise to be restocked and put the order on hold until we can execute it fully, or we split the order into multiple shipments if one or more of the items cannot be replenished within a week. If we delay an order in full or in part, we notify the client.

If we run out of stock for a certain item or the inventory falls below a certain limit, we issue an order to our regular supplier for the particular item or to that supplier who can currently offer the best price and/or best quality, depending on what the primary purchasing criteria are for the merchandise. When the supplier accepts the order, we expect to receive estimated delivery dates and expect to be notified as soon as the goods have been shipped to us. Based on these dates, we notify our customers about the estimated delivery dates of when their order can be fulfilled. As long as the merchandise is not shipped, we allow our clients to fully or partially cancel an order. For any order item whose value exceeds $5000 and which we typically sell up to only five times a year, we request firm orders, however.

To allow us some flexibility when selecting the shipping methods, we charge our clients a flat shipping rate on a per-item basis, which is typically already contained in the offer and which depends on various factors like weight and dimension of the merchandise and the number of items. Once a complete or partial order is ready for shipping, we select the appropriate shipping method depending on the destination, requested time of delivery, and the total number of packages that we need to ship. Once we have selected a shipper, may it be UPS, FedEx, the Postal Service, or a more specialized cargo firm, we send them a shipping order. Once they have accepted the order, confirmed the arranged pickup time, and estimated the time of delivery, we notify our client that the order is due for shipping and give them the shipper's tracking numbers for the merchandise so they can track the delivery via the Web.

If we have no established relationship with the client, shipping will not be arranged until either the credit check has been positively acknowledged or we have received prepayment. If the item requires a firm order based on the conditions stated previously, even prepayment must be confirmed before we order the items from our suppliers.

Otherwise, we write an invoice for the portion of the order that we have prepared for shipping and send it to the customer as soon as the shipper has picked up the packages. The amount is debited from their internal customer account. If they have credit on their customer account, we debit the account first and make only the remaining portion payable, of course. Typically, if our customers pay the invoice within five business days, they will receive a 3 percent discount on the total order amount, and the due date for the invoice is 21 days. After that, we send them the first reminder. The reminder includes all other overdue invoices that have been debited from the customer account.

All of our clients get a flat 30-day money-back guarantee. Within that time, they can return the merchandise at their expense for a full refund. If the customers take advantage of that, we waive the shipping charges as well. However, this is not applicable to the goods that require firm orders. In that case, we accept returns only for warranty claims that we can forward to our suppliers. If a customer sends back the merchandise within 30 days and has not paid the invoice, we need to annul the invoice internally. If the customer did pay, we credit this to their customer account. We only credit them directly to their credit card, using a bank wire transfer or a check if they request this explicitly.

This is a typical unstructured description of a very large process. If you start drilling into the details of every single statement, you will find that there are a lot of open questions contained in this description. But before we start doing that, we must extract the core terminology and establish consensus about the meaning of those terms. (Later, in the "Collecting Requirements" section, we will use the term *top-level objects* to refer to the terminology.)

The easiest way to find these terms is to isolate the most used nouns from the description. Without really counting, we can assume that the result will contain "customer," "client," "merchandise," "goods," "stock," "order," "shipper," "account," "invoice," "supplier," and "return." The next step is to eliminate synonyms like "customer" and "client," agree on a single term, and find other synonyms in the description that match the isolated terms. In the same step, we will also check whether all of the found terms are always used in the same context or whether we need to further qualify them. A possible raw result from this process is the following basic dictionary:

- ▼ *Customer*   Used synonymously with "client." Organization or person who orders, receives, and pays sales items from us (not simply "purchases items" because that would hide the process).

- ■ *Sales items*   Used synonymously with "merchandise," "goods," and "items." What we acquire from our suppliers to sell to our customers. The chosen term is not used in the text but is considered more precise.

- ■ *Inventory*   Used synonymously with "stock," but "inventory" is considered to be the clearer term. Sales items are held in the inventory.

- ■ *Shipper*   Companies that ship the sales items to our customers.

- ■ *Account*   Every customer has an internal account from which purchases are debited and to which returns are credited.

- ■ *Invoice*   The payment request sent to customers.

- ■ *Supplier*   Companies from which merchandise is bought.

- ■ *Sales order*   Order received from a customer.

- ■ *Supply order*   Order sent to a supplier.

- ■ *Shipping order*   Order sent to a shipper.

- ■ *Sales shipping notice*   Notice about shipment sent to customers.

- ▲ *Supply shipping notice*   Notice received from our suppliers about shipments due.

We have not even considered discounts, returns, and other such important terms, but we already have 12 different terms to consider. Because this breaks the 7±2 rule, we must stop here and think about how we can reorganize the terminology so that we stay within this limit. Remember, there can be only five to nine main topics.

By considering that the invoice is really part of the account management, that sales items are managed through the inventory, and that the orders, order acknowledgments, and notifications on either side of the process can be grouped into the more general term "order process," the final main categories that we get as a result are the following:

- ▼ *Customer relations*   Customer relationship management, including marketing and sales offers. Customers include potential customers that do not have active accounts or orders pending.

- ■ *Inventory management*   Inventory management, shipment packaging, and cataloging.

- ■ *Supply management*   Supply management, supplier selection, and supply order management.

- ■ *Accounting*   Customer account tracking, invoicing, and financial collections.

- ■ *Shipping and distribution*   Management of shipping logistics.

- ▲ *Order processing*   Handling of incoming purchase orders, order notifications, and handling returns.

If this list looks suspiciously like the first level of a trading company's organizational diagram, this is not accidental or artificially constructed for this discussion. It is just the way things fall into place naturally because of the 7±2 rule.

The result from this first high-level analysis step is that we have made a sharp distinction between supply orders and customer purchase orders and will look at them separately. If the supply management department speaks about an "order," we will not confuse this with the customer order that the sales department is speaking of. The most important goal of the first analysis steps is to get everyone involved in the analysis and definition process to agree on this basic understanding of the terminology and the division of responsibilities.

You may think that it is too trivial to waste so much time on this task, but defining and documenting the obvious terms is one of the most important fundamental tasks when you create software architectures. This is especially true if you need to create solutions for scenarios that are not as commonly known as the described purchasing process. Handling corporate loan applications at banks or booking travel arrangements with flight, hotel, and rental car are complex processes that require highly specialized knowledge and special terminology. The result from the analysis process must be that everyone—software architects, developers, and business specialists—can speak the same language and about the same issues.

Collecting Requirements

Now that we have a basic agreement on the terminology, we will try to isolate and classify use cases. A *use case* is a usage scenario for our solution that we need to implement. To find use cases, we will look at the previous process description again, but now we will seek verbs instead of nouns. The business process description is written from the business perspective. So whenever one of the subjects in the process (for example, the customer) receives some message, our system must have previously sent it. If it is the other way around—one of the subjects sends us a message—the system needs to be able to process it.

The first sentence of the business process description is "Customers receive catalogs or sales offers (either by request or through marketing or sales personnel activities) on which they make their purchasing decisions." This sentence implies two use cases. The first use case is that the customer relations subsystem needs to be capable of sending catalog information. The second use case is that the sales department must be able to send custom sales offers.

NOTE: The information customers use to make their decisions (based on the catalog information or sales offers sent to them) is outside the scope of the system we are planning and therefore irrelevant for us.

The second sentence "When they have decided which merchandise to buy from us, they send us an order" implies that the customer may or may not issue an order for an offer. Because the customer may order from the catalog, may order based on the sales offer, or may order spontaneously, there's not necessarily always a link between an incoming order and any of the customer relationship activities like marketing or sales. Accepting and processing the order is obviously the job of the order-processing system.

Let's look at one more sentence: "We first check the customer's credit-worthiness for the total order amount and possibly request prepayment or a letter of credit to execute the order." From this, we can derive two use cases for two different objects. The credit check is certainly customer-dependent and must therefore exist in the customer relations subsystem. The request for prepayments depends on the transaction and must therefore be realized by the order-processing application. As we learn later in the description, shipping—and in certain circumstances, even ordering the merchandise at our own suppliers—requires the prepayments be confirmed, if there was no previous relationship with the customer.

However, although the order-processing application uses it, the proper place for implementation of this use case is the accounting subsystem. So if we got an order and decided that we require prepayment, we must be able to request an invoice to be written by the accounting subsystem and halt any further processing in the order-processing system until payment on the invoice is confirmed. This analysis results in the use cases "write invoice" (which we can reuse further down in the process) and "monitor payment and notify."

You can either go through the text from top to bottom or focus on one of the top-level objects looking for use cases. Both ways work equally well.

In the process of collecting the use cases for a larger system, you will find that the top-level objects will quickly have more than nine use cases, which exceeds our "magic" boundary. As soon as this happens, you should start categorizing the use cases by creating subobjects for each top-level object and assign all use cases to those subobjects.

From this process of "qualified reading," we will gather a first outline for the use cases that we need to look at. These use cases are candidates for our system implementation, but they may not make it through the analysis process or later through product and/or project planning. The great luxury of the analysis process is that it is (and must be) entirely disconnected from time and budget constraints for the later project phases. A perfectly valid result of the analysis process is that the project cannot be done within the limits of a preallocated budget or that it is too complex to handle with the available development staff.

Requirements Analysis

Once you have a structured collection of use cases, you need to drill down into each of them to find out which data and activities are required for their implementation. We will take the "write invoice" use case of the top-level accounting object as an example here.

Which information is contained in the description about invoices, and which information is additionally needed to write them and send them to customers?

The business case description states that our exemplary business will either require prepayment from first-time customers or will bill existing customers once the order ships. While this information describes when the invoices are written within the process, it does not give us any specifics about the use case itself. The position of this action within the process is indeed not relevant for its proper execution because the pricing and shipping charges are identical in either case. It is important to clearly distinguish between the requirements for the use case itself and the conditions under which the use case becomes executed.

Let's go through the description and pick out the other statements related to invoices. We will use "invoice" and terms related to payments as signal words to isolate the requirements from the text. However, we will intentionally leave out all requirements for when the invoice has been written and sent. These requirements are to be met by the accounts receivable management in accounting.

▼ "We charge our clients a flat shipping charge on a per-item basis" that "depends on various factors like weight and dimensions of the merchandise and the number of items."

■ "We write an invoice for the portion of the order that we have prepared for shipping and send it to the customer."

- ■ "If they have credit on their customer account, we debit the account first and make only the remaining portion payable, of course."
- ▲ "If our customers pay the invoice within five business days, they will receive a 3 percent discount on the total order amount, and the due date for the invoice is 21 days."

Now we want to isolate single requirements from these statements and make these requirements as simple as possible. Each requirement should be expressed in one or two sentences at most. Some of these requirements are really obvious:

- ▼ Invoices are written for complete or partial orders.
- ■ Invoices can have multiple order items.
- ■ Shipping charges are calculated per item.
- ■ Customers have accounts.
- ■ The account is debited before an invoice is written.
- ■ A 3 percent discount is granted if payment is received within five business days.
- ▲ The due date for the invoice is 21 days.

After this step, it's time to be really curious because there are quite a few unclear points here: What are the exact criteria for the shipping calculations? How do you split orders? What happens when the invoice is overdue? Such questions must be answered before the requirements analysis phase is completed.

The problem at this point is that the business case description does not provide enough information to answer these questions. This is an absolutely expected and "by design" result of this analysis process. In addition to finding the main objects and use-cases, identifying these open questions is essential to achieve a complete analysis result and to avoid implementing immature solutions that do not address key business aspects. Business users tend to take for granted a lot of the facts that are so much part of their daily work; thus these facts go unstated. By running this type of analysis, you will sooner or later get to these issues and will be able to create a catalogue of questions for your business users to answer. Doing this in a recurring manner will continue to refine your analysis results and you will achieve objective completeness once no questions remain open.

CHAPTER 14

Creating Orchestration Schedules

Orchestration schedules document and define the "big picture" of business processes and are executable components at the same time. This chapter introduces Orchestration Designer in detail by implementing a sample order-handling workflow.

INTRODUCING ORCHESTRATION DESIGNER

The BizTalk Orchestration Designer application is an extension for Microsoft Visio 2000 Service Release 1 (SR-1). This explains the quite unusual software-prerequisites list for a server product. You need to install Visio only if you want to create schedules on that particular BizTalk machine, though, and this is typically true only for development and testing machines. At run time, the XLANG Scheduler will not require any Visio component to be present.

When you open Orchestration Designer, it starts with a blank drawing page and a Visio "stencil" loaded on each side of the drawing page, as shown in Figure 14-1. The left stencil contains the Orchestration language shapes that you already learned about in Chapter 9, and the right stencil provides the shapes for creating the implementation ports, which were also discussed in Chapter 9. The drawing page is split into two separate areas that have different functions. The left side is the flowchart drawing, where the business process is modeled, and on the right side, developers place the Orchestration port components to integrate data sources and applications.

Because Visio has been such a popular application for business graphics and technical drawings for quite a while now, you may have already used it. If you have no experience using Visio at all, you will be surprised by how easy it is to create Visio drawings (and therefore, Orchestration schedule drawings).

Visio for Beginners

Visio is a very mouse-centric, drag-and-drop application.

You can select one of the shapes from the Flowchart stencil, drag the element onto the left portion of the drawing surface, and drop it there, as shown here:

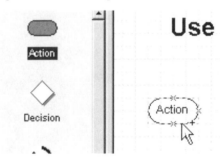

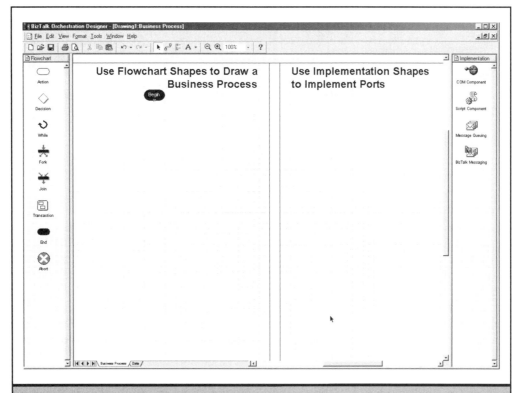

Figure 14-1. BizTalk Orchestration Designer

Likewise, you can select one of the shapes from the Implementation stencil and drop it onto the right "implementation" side of the drawing.

Once you have dropped a few shapes into the drawing surface, you will have to connect them to define the application flow. You do this by connecting the elements in the same order in which they will be executed. Each of the predefined shapes has connection points that appear in green whenever you select an element by clicking on it with the mouse pointer. To create a connection from an element to another element (which means that the flow of control executes in that direction), you simply drag the connection shape to one of the connectors (small blue cross symbols) of the target element.

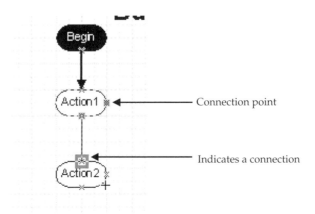

As soon as the connection "sticks" to the connector, you will see a square (red), as shown in the illustration. If you release the mouse button once the connector sticks, the connection will be established. If you want to reroute a connection, you can either pick up the connecting line from the connector, or delete it (select the line and press the DEL key) and drag a new line from the source connector.

When you right-click one of the shapes, a context menu will appear for the shape. The Help and Properties menu entries are common to most of the BizTalk Orchestration shapes. With the Properties command (or a simple double-click on a shape), you be will able to access and change the XLANG "magic" of the respective shape.

This concludes our general Visio lesson. It's really that easy.

DEFINING THE BUSINESS FLOW

Figure 14-2 shows the sample business workflow that we want to implement in this chapter. The workflow is a simplified model of the process that was analyzed in the previous chapter. As you have learned, even a seemingly simple business process gains considerable depth if you look at all aspects in a structured way. We will therefore consider only the core purchase-order-handling process and even then, leave out a few details for this example. In the following chapters, we will create the required document specification and document maps and configure ports and channels for BizTalk Messaging to create a full-scale, executable implementation of this example process.

As you will soon find out, there are indeed circular references (albeit very few) between this and the following three chapters. The document specifications that we require here are defined in Chapter 15, and the Messaging configuration that we will refer to is explained in Chapter 17. For some of the functionality shown here, you will indeed need actual copies of these files on your machine. To make things easy, you can download them from the book's web site, use them here, and worry about the details later.

Now let's begin to create the workflow. Create a blank Orchestration drawing by either starting a fresh instance of Orchestration Designer or by selecting File | New (CTRL-N).

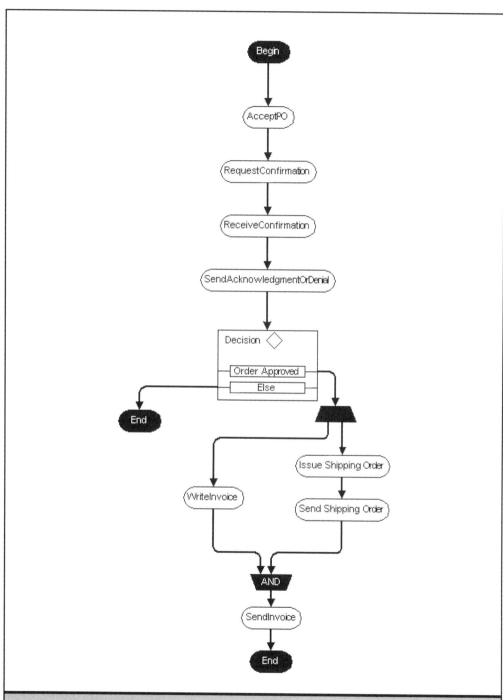

Figure 14-2.   Sample business workflow

First, you will draw the Action shapes. Drag and drop the eight Action shapes that are shown in Figure 14-2 to the approximate places in your own schedule drawing and name them as shown:

- ▼ **AcceptPO**   Accepts an inbound purchase
- ◼ **RequestConfirmation**   Invokes a subordinate schedule that handles the order-approval process and produces the purchase-order-acknowledgment document
- ◼ **ReceiveConfirmation**   Receives the purchase-order acknowledgment from the subordinate schedule
- ◼ **SendAcknowledgmentOrDenial**   Sends the acknowledgment to the buyer
- ◼ **IssueShippingOrder**   Issues the shipping order to the shipping company
- ◼ **SendShippingOrder**   Sends the shipping order to the destination
- ◼ **WriteInvoice**   Writes the invoice for the order
- ▲ **SendInvoice**   Sends the invoice to the buyer

NOTE: This schedule contains several simplifications as compared to a real-life trading process. For instance, there is no handling of the shipping-order response. The shipping company may deny the order or accept it with a target shipping date that we cannot accept ourselves and will therefore require a cancellation. Also, no provision exists for returns or cancellations, and the workflow obviously assumes that the shipping company also handles the storage of our inventory, because no separate messages are sent. (This case is actually common for trading firms.)

Now connect the Begin shape and the four Action shapes below it, and place a new Decision shape under the SendAcknowledgmentOrDenial shape and connect it, as shown in Figure 14-2.

The Decision shape "decides" something only if you add rules to it. The rule definitions are shared among all Decision and While-loop shapes, and the same rule can be used wherever applicable. To create a new rule, you select the Add Rule command from the shape's context menu.

The Add Rule dialog box (see Figure 14-3) that displays when you select this command allows you to pick one of the shared rules or create a new rule. This dialog box will be skipped if no rules are defined in the drawing. That the dialog box is not shown for the second and subsequent rules when you define multiple rules on the same shape at once and the first rule on the shape was the overall first in the schedule (complicated condition…) is a bug.

Another way to add rules to a Decision shape is by clicking the Add button in the Decision Properties dialog box of the Decision shape. In this dialog box (shown in Figure 14-4), you can also add or remove existing rules and, most importantly, reorder them. All rules are

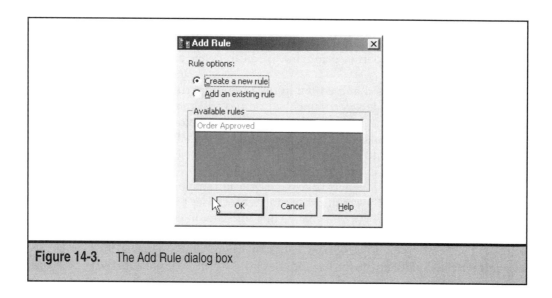

Figure 14-3.   The Add Rule dialog box

executed from top to bottom as shown in the dialog box and in the Orchestration schedule drawings. If you add a new rule and want to assign it a higher priority in evaluation, you can move it with the up and down arrows on the lower-right side of the dialog box.

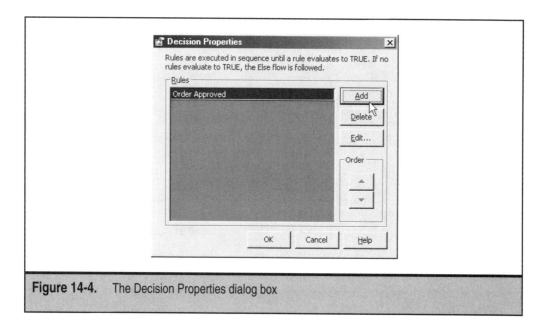

Figure 14-4.   The Decision Properties dialog box

In Orchestration schedule drawings, you can edit individual rules by double-clicking the respective rule bar within the Decision shape or by opening the context menu of the rule and selecting the Properties command. You can delete any rule by selecting it and pressing the DEL key.

Each rule can be defined and edited in the Rule Properties dialog box. This dialog box, shown in Figure 14-5, lets you name the rule and add an additional description that explains the purpose of the rule. The Script Expression field expects a rule expression that evaluates to True or False, much like the condition in a VBScript If … Then … End If expression. Because the rule is expressed in VBScript, you can also use all language-intrinsic VBScript functions in the expression.

For now, you should add a new rule to the Decision shape, name it **Order Approved**, and simply enter **True** as the script expression. This causes the path associated with the rule to always be executed. We will change this rule later in this chapter.

Next, place the two End shapes and the Fork shape into the drawing, as shown in Figure 14-2. The Decision shape's rule bars have connection points on both sides. Connect the Else rule with the End shape to the left and the Order Approved rule with the Fork shape.

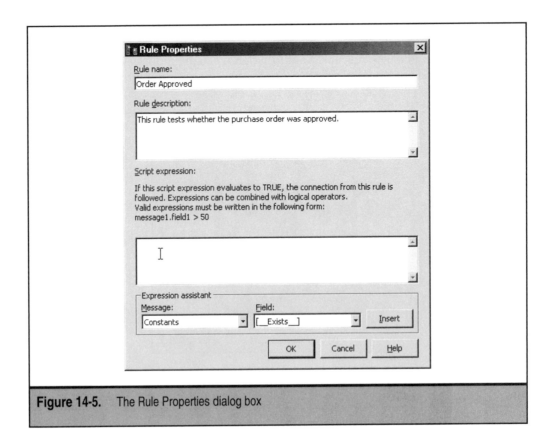

Figure 14-5. The Rule Properties dialog box

Fork shapes have a single visible connection point that creates a new connection each time you drag it to another shape's connector. This differs from all other shapes' behavior, which will reroute the existing connection to the new shape. Every connection that you make from a Fork shape causes a new parallel execution path (thread) to be spawned at run time. Connect the Fork shape with both the WriteInvoice and the IssueShipping Order actions.

To complete the example flow, you need to add the Join shape. After you have dropped the shape into position, you can finish connecting all elements. The Join shape has two different modes: AND and OR. If the mode is AND (which is the default), the schedule will wait at this point until all execution paths have arrived. If the mode is OR, the schedule will proceed immediately when the first path reaches the join. You can switch between both modes by using the Properties dialog box of the Join shape, which lets you choose between those two modes.

NOTE: There are several restrictions to using joins. The most important one is that you cannot join paths from different Decision shapes (even if they are nested) to a single Join shape. Every Decision shape (and every Fork shape) can also have only a single associated join.

A good idea is to use the comment fields available for the Decision and While-loop rules, and for additional documentation, also add Visio Text shapes to the drawing (the only other shape type allowed except for the Orchestration shapes). You can add text by using the A icon on the Orchestration Designer toolbar.

DEFINING PORTS

Up until now, all we have is a pretty drawing of an exemplary business process. To turn the drawing into a valid XLANG schedule, we must implement the Orchestration ports. When we are done with these tasks, the port configuration in the drawing should look they do in Figure 14-6.

The first port to configure is going to be connected to the AcceptPO Action shape. This action will accept a purchase order that has been received via BizTalk Messaging as a UN/EDIFACT ORDERS document and has been converted into an internal XML document format. Whenever such a purchase order arrives via BizTalk Messaging, a new instance of this schedule will be started.

Implementing BizTalk Messaging Ports

To implement the port, drop a BizTalk Messaging shape onto the implementation half of the drawing page. Port shapes should be dropped at the same vertical height as the port it is implementing. The horizontal alignment of new Port shapes is automatic. Even if you tried to place them somewhere else, they will always be placed on the very right of the drawing page.

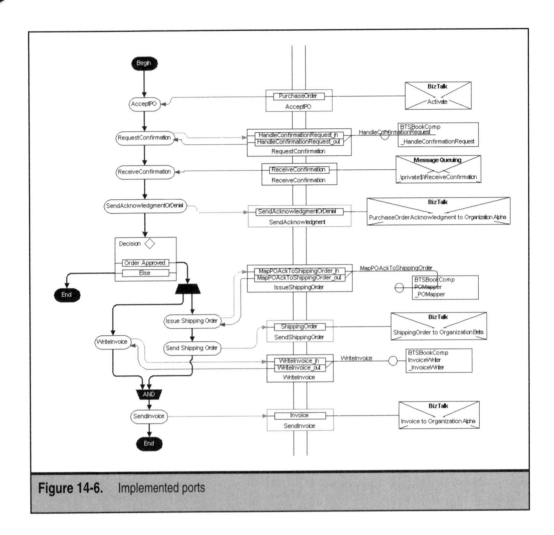

Figure 14-6. Implemented ports

As soon as you drop the Messaging shape onto the drawing surface, the BizTalk Messaging Binding Wizard opens. (See Figure 14-7). On the welcome page, you must name the new port. The names for Orchestration ports have the same restrictions as XML tokens because they will be expressed in XML when the schedule is later saved as an XLANG schedule file. Among the restrictions are a maximum length of 32 characters, and names can neither start with an underscore (_) character nor contain colons (:). Name the first port AcceptPO.

The next page of the wizard sets the communication direction. (See Figure 14-8.) In this case, we want to receive an incoming message and thus, we select the Receive option. This page also contains this note: "This wizard only enables receive through http URLs." For All Other URLs, Use A Message Queue In Between BizTalk Messaging And The Schedule.

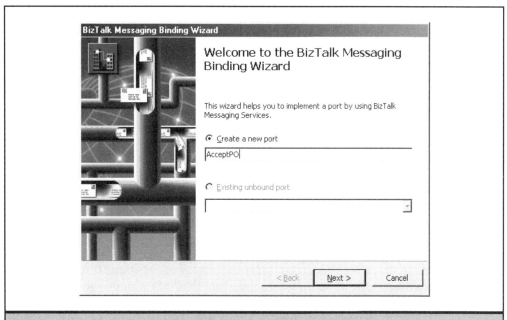

Figure 14-7. The BizTalk Messaging Binding Wizard welcome page

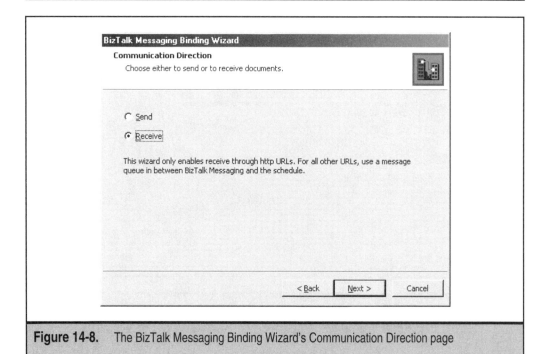

Figure 14-8. The BizTalk Messaging Binding Wizard's Communication Direction page

This note is vague and factually incorrect. The wizard does enable receiving from non-http sources if they start a new schedule. For active schedules, the restriction relates not only to the HTTP transport as the message implies, but to reliable XML messaging in conjunction with HTTP. By using this wizard and the BizTalk Messaging shape, you can receive messages received through HTTP only by using the reliable messaging envelope format. The additional restriction is that you can receive anything through such a port only if you have previously sent a message to the remote destination.

The following page (see Figure 14-9) is a good example of how two radio buttons and a simple static text field can cause a lot of confusion. The basic question to be answered here is whether the port will activate a new schedule if a message is received through BizTalk Messaging. If you choose to activate a new schedule as the transport option for a BizTalk Messaging port, setting this option to Yes is correct (as it is in our case); otherwise, it must be set to No. Regarding the comment below the Yes option, ignore it—it is obviously supposed to help but falls short.

When you click Finish, the Port shape and an associated Message shape sitting on the middle white bar will be shown on the drawing surface, as you can see in Figure 14-6. When you connect the AcceptPO Action shape to the Message shape by dragging its right connection point onto the Port shape's connector, the XML Communication Wizard opens. (See Figure 14-10.)

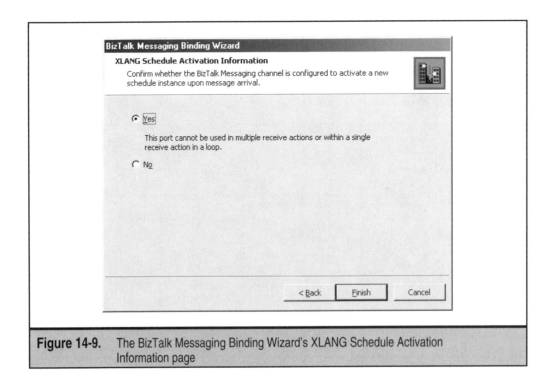

Figure 14-9. The BizTalk Messaging Binding Wizard's XLANG Schedule Activation Information page

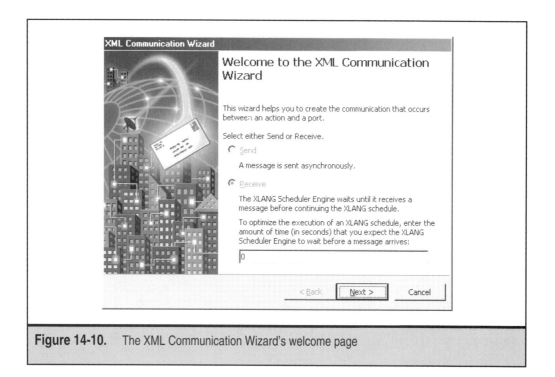

Figure 14-10.   The XML Communication Wizard's welcome page

The XML Communication Wizard serves to define and configure the message that is received through the port. The message direction on the welcome page is automatically set based on the directionality of the port to which the message is bound. Here we have a reception port; therefore, the preset option is Receive. The edit control at the bottom of the page allows you to enter the time when you expect a message to arrive on this port. Because this port is an activation port, this setting does not apply here. The value here serves to control the hydration and dehydration behavior that was already discussed in Chapter 12.

On the next page (see Figure 14-11), you can decide whether you want to create a new message or reuse a message type that already exists in the schedule. Reusing messages is always an option when you need to pass the same XML document through different ports. In this case, you need to configure the message settings only once, and you can use them for multiple port bindings.

In our case, we want to create a new message that we will call PurchaseOrder.

Messages that are passed around within XLANG schedules must be expressed by using XML. The XML Translation Information page (see Figure 14-12) serves to define whether the incoming message is already XML by default, or whether it needs to be enclosed in an XML wrapper. The XLANG engine's standard wrapper is <StringData>data</StringData>.

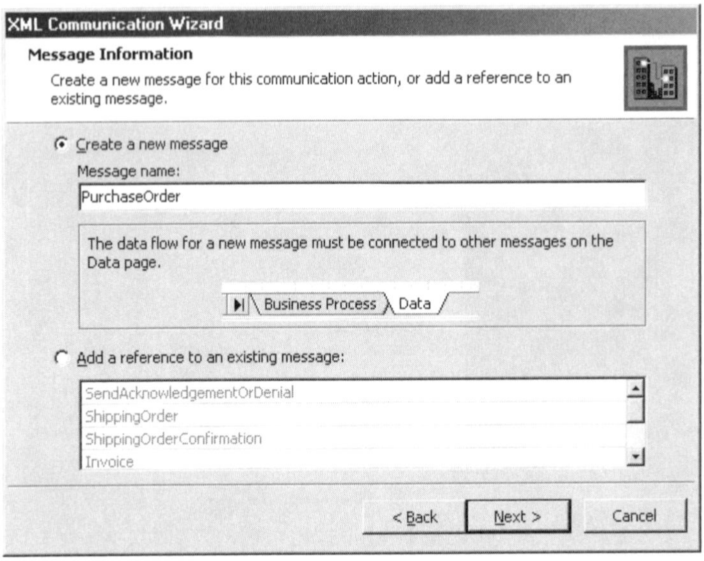

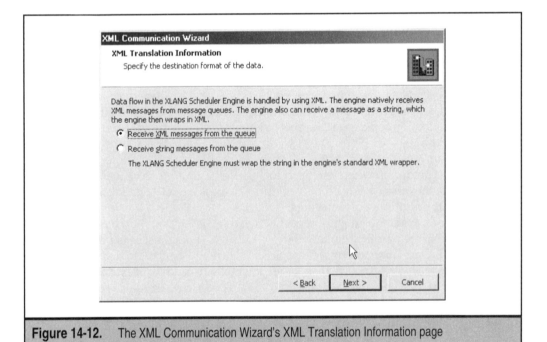

Figure 14-11. The XML Communication Wizard's Message Information page

Figure 14-12. The XML Communication Wizard's XML Translation Information page

For this example, we receive the purchase order expressed in XML and therefore select the first option, Receive XML Messages From The Queue, before we proceed to the next page. (See Figure 14-13.)

The message type is either the message label found in the message queue (if the wizard is used for a message queue binding) or must equal the root element of the expected XML document. Unfortunately, XLANG cannot detect XML documents based on their default namespace, so you must know the exact tag name of the root element. If the incoming message cannot be matched against this expression, the message will be ignored.

The last page of the XML Communication Wizard requires a little time warp. (See Figure 14-14.) Here, we need to assume that you have already defined the purchase order XML specification, but you will not learn how to do this until Chapter 15. Let us just assume you already have the file.

The XML Communication Wizard understands (only) BizTalk Schema and must indeed use the same definitions as you will later use for configuring the Messaging portion of the sample. However, it is not able to access the WebDAV repository, where you will typically store your document specifications. This somewhat spoils the idea of having a central repository for document specifications because Orchestration cannot access it. You cannot even use the built-in Windows 2000 support for WebDAV network places, because the permanent and reliable file-system location is required for the file. References that you make here must exist wherever the schedule is executed, if you choose to have the scheduler engine validate the document against the specification.

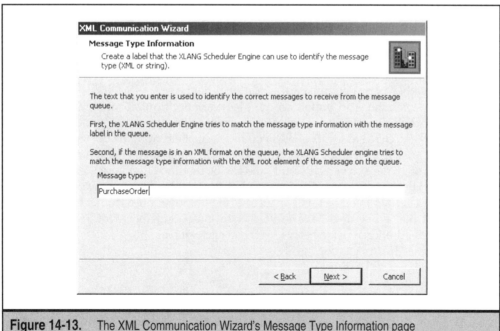

Figure 14-13.   The XML Communication Wizard's Message Type Information page

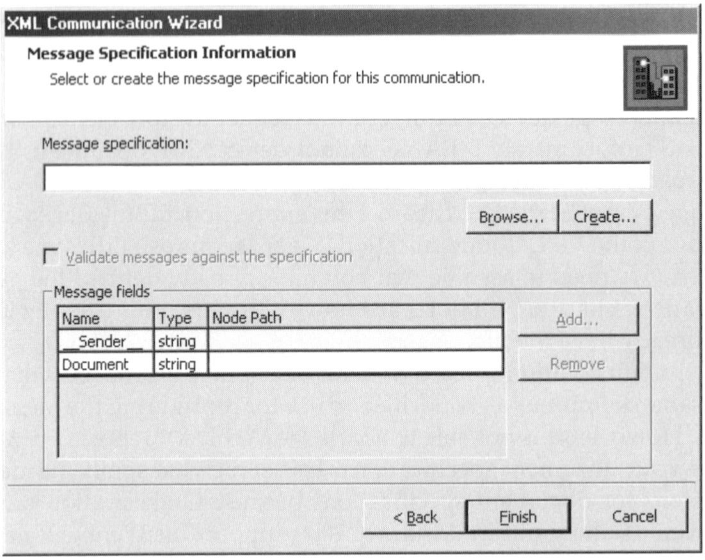

Figure 14-14. The XML Communication Wizard's Message Specification Information page

The message fields for any XML document are the __Sender__ field, which contains the security identity of the sender if that could be determined, and the Document field, which contains the entire document as is. If you need to control the application flow based on document content or want to pass any of the document fields to a COM or Script method on another port, you must add additional fields.

When you click the Add button on the Message Specification Information page, the Field Selection dialog box will open if the document specification can be located and is valid. (See Figure 14-15.) This dialog box allows you to select a field from the document specification whose value will be extracted by using XPath. The XPath expression that is created by navigating through the tree view is simple and can be modified if required. When the document is passed through the port, all of these additional fields will be extracted by using the XPath expressions. XPath extraction is available only for inbound documents. When documents are sent, the field settings have no effect on the outbound document. For our example, we do not need additional fields here, so you can click Finish.

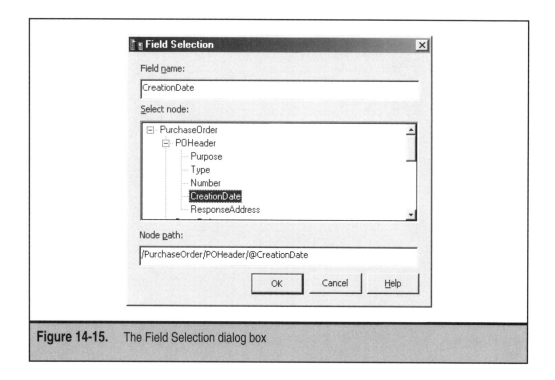

Figure 14-15.   The Field Selection dialog box

Launching Other XLANG Schedules

The next action we want to implement is RequestConfirmation. This action processes the purchase order and creates a positive or negative purchase-order acknowledgment. This decision process is implemented in a subordinate schedule. This example demonstrates how you can split a complex workflow into multiple schedules and invoke schedules from other schedules.

Figure 14-16 shows the schedule that implements the confirmation process. The schedule is easy and does not contain much logic, as you can see. Here, you would typically invoke components that do catalog lookups to verify the order information, store the order in you local order-processing system, and run credit checks on the customer. To keep things simple, we are leaving this part of the process out and will only convert the purchase order into a purchase-order acknowledgment. To do this, we will invoke a loopback channel in BizTalk Messaging that will map the purchase order to a purchase-order acknowledgment and return it immediately.

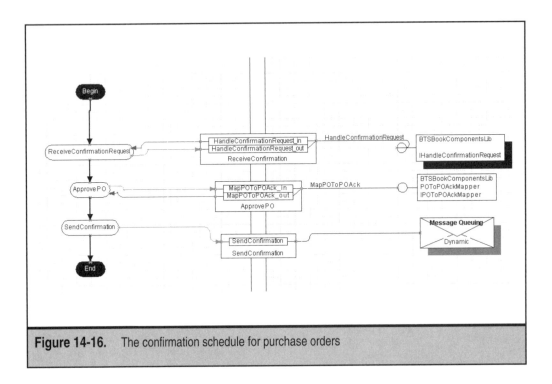

Figure 14-16. The confirmation schedule for purchase orders

But first, we have to take care of starting the subordinate schedule. If you compare the RequestConfirmation port in Figure 14-6 with the ReceiveConfirmation port in Figure 14-16, you will find that they both bind to the same COM component. You will also find out in a second that, in fact, the main schedule does not bind to a local component, but it actually binds directly to the ReceiveRequest port in the subordinate schedule.

You pass arguments to and between schedules by using COM components. More precisely, it is sufficient to have a COM type library that contains an interface with a method definition, whose invocation signature allows you to pass all needed arguments. (We discussed this mechanism in detail in Chapter 9.)

Here, we will see the schedule moniker in action. However, before we can begin implementing this port, we need a COM component. For simplicity, we will create the component in Microsoft Visual Basic, although Visual C++ would give us more control for type-library creation.

To begin, open Microsoft Visual Basic 6.0 (assuming that you have VB available) and select ActiveX DLL from the New Project Wizard. (See Figure 14-17.)

When the project has been created, change the name of the new project from Project1 to BTSBookComp and rename the Class1 class to HandleConfirmationRequest. You perform

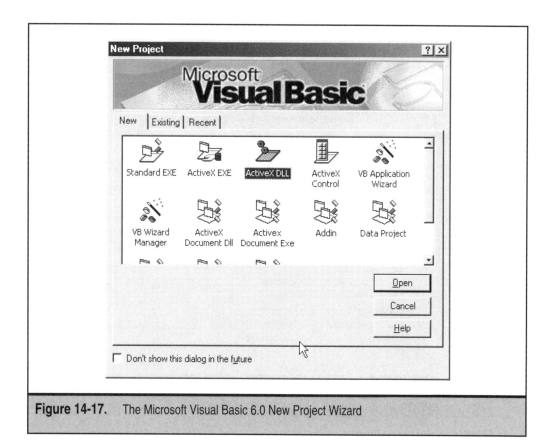

Figure 14-17.   The Microsoft Visual Basic 6.0 New Project Wizard

both of these actions by selecting the respective node in the project tree view and renaming the element in the Properties window, as shown in Figure 14-18.

The arguments that we want to pass to the confirmation schedule are the original purchase-order document and a reference to a per-instance message queue that the confirmation schedule will use to pass the produced acknowledgment document back to the parent schedule.

The required Visual Basic code is very simple:

```
Sub HandleConfirmationRequest( Request As String, ReplyQueue As String )
End Sub
```

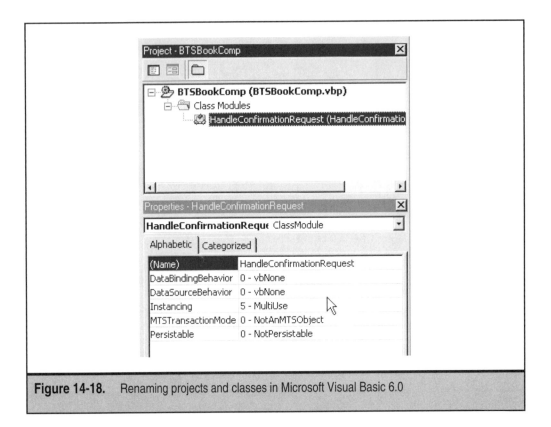

Figure 14-18. Renaming projects and classes in Microsoft Visual Basic 6.0

As you can see, the method does nothing. Its only purpose is to provide the call signature. Write this code into the code window and save the project and the class file. When you have saved the two files (by selecting File | Save Project), you should build the component DLL. You do this by selecting the Make BTSBookComp.DLL command on the File menu. When you invoke this command, Visual Basic will prompt you for a filename to be used for the new DLL. By default, the file will be saved into the project directory, which is fine. The result from this stunt is that we now have a COM component and associated type library that we can use.

The next action in the schedule is to drop a COM Component shape onto the drawing at the same height as the RequestConfirmation action. Once you drop the shape, the COM Component Binding Wizard opens. Name the new port RequestConfirmation by entering it on the welcome page, as shown in Figure 14-19.

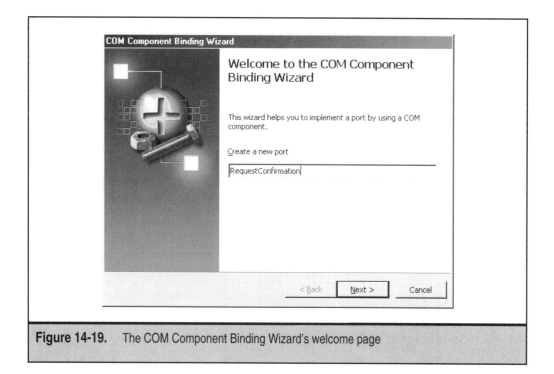

Figure 14-19.   The COM Component Binding Wizard's welcome page

On the Static Or Dynamic Communication page (see Figure 14-20), you can select how the component is created. You have the following choices:

▼   **Static**   When you select this option, the component will be created by the XLANG scheduler like any other application would create a COM component.

■   **Dynamic**   This option allows you to pass COM interface pointers into the schedule and have the schedule later bind dynamically to those components. Interesting, but not for the faint of heart.

▲   **No Instantiation**   In this case, XLANG will use the type library only to pass arguments, but will not actually create a component.

Now our example is getting a tiny little bit twisted. We indeed want to create a new instance of a component, although we will talk to a component that is never instantiated. The component that we are going to create in this schedule is the secondary XLANG schedule. In that schedule, we will configure a port that is similar to this port and that we will set to No Instantiation. Therefore, and in the current context, you should select the Static option.

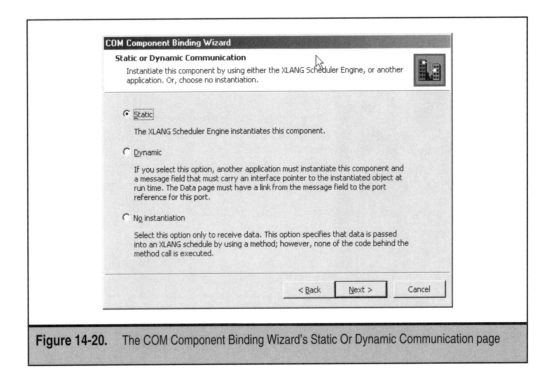

Figure 14-20. The COM Component Binding Wizard's Static Or Dynamic Communication page

On the Class Information page (see Figure 14-21), you select the COM class to instantiate by using a tree view that lists all registered COM classes available on the local system. However, we do not want to invoke a component directly, but rather, launch a schedule. Therefore, you should select the From A Moniker option and enter a moniker expression for the subordinate schedule. We will assume for a second that you already have the compiled schedule available on your machine and have placed it into the c:\schedules\directory as ConfirmPO.skx. The correct moniker would therefore be sked:///c:\schedules\ConfirmPO.skx/ReceiveRequest, because we want to "bind through" to the ReceiveRequest port.

On the next page (see Figure 14-22), you need to select the appropriate interface to use. Here, you must navigate in the tree view to find the COM component library that we have just created by using Visual Basic. The library will appear as BTSBookComp. If you open the tree branch, you will find a _HandleConfirmationRequest interface, which you should select. Because the interface contains only a single method, it will be automatically selected and imported for creating the message information (what you will do in the next step).

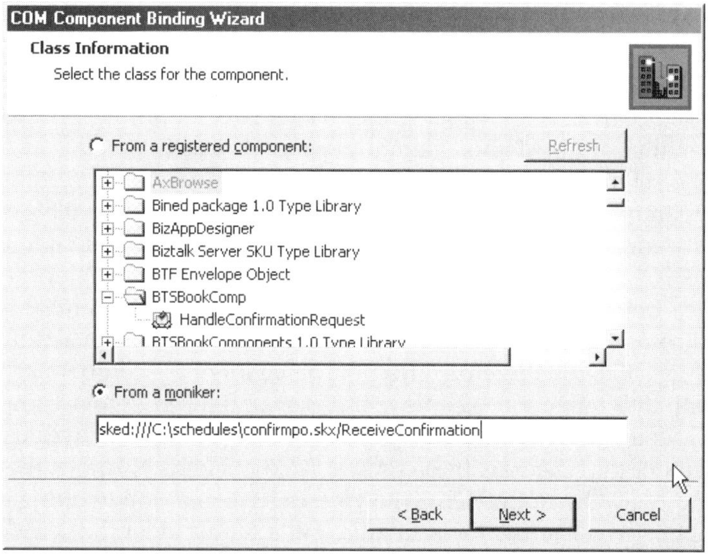

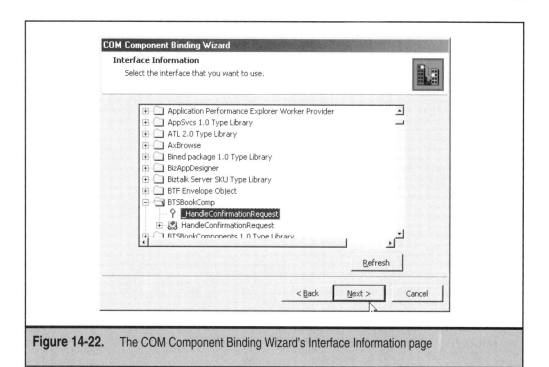

Figure 14-21. The COM Component Binding Wizard's Class Information page

Figure 14-22. The COM Component Binding Wizard's Interface Information page

Should multiple methods exist on an interface, the page shown in Figure 14-23 will be displayed. (Because there is only one method on the _HandleConfirmationRequest interface, it will not show up in our case here.) You can select one, multiple, or all methods to be included in the port binding. This will allow you to call multiple methods on the same component instance from within a schedule. We will get to this in a bit when we discuss the message settings of the Method Communication Wizard.

The Advanced Port Properties page (see Figure 14-24) serves to fine tune the behavior of the invoked component. For our example, we will leave everything at the default values.

The security and transaction properties on this page are equivalent to those that you can find in the COM+ Component Configuration dialog boxes in Windows 2000. When XLANG creates a new COM component, it creates a new COM+ context into which the newly created components are placed. The security and transaction settings are applied to the new context and will therefore affect the behavior of the component. They must be compatible with the component's settings if it is a configured COM+ component.

The State Management Support option serves to optimize the hydration and dehydration behavior of the schedule. If the setting is left at Holds No State, the schedule will automatically discard the component when it is dehydrated. If the setting is Holds State, And Does Support Persistence, the schedule will attempt to let the component save its state to a stream via the IPersistStream interface before the schedule is mapped out of memory. If the option is set to Holds State, But Doesn't Support Persistence, the schedule will never be dehydrated.

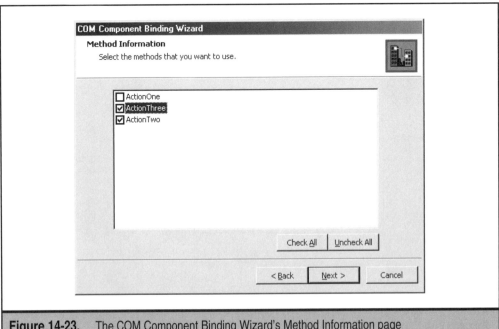

Figure 14-23. The COM Component Binding Wizard's Method Information page

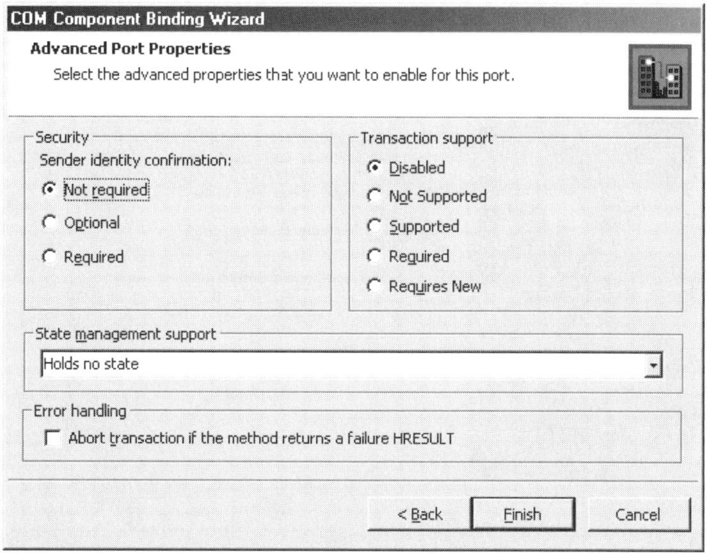

Figure 14-24.   The COM Component Binding Wizard's Advanced Port Properties page

Finally, the Error Handling option allows you to control XLANG transaction behavior if a called component returns an error. Typically, you will want to select this option if you use COM components from within XLANG transactions (which is not the case here).

To complete the port configuration, click Finish. Now we need to configure the message. The two messaging ports use the XML Communication Wizard. However, the COM and scripting port types, which allow a bidirectional message flow due to their synchronous nature, have their own message definition tool: the Method Communication Wizard. (See Figure 14-25.) This wizard opens automatically as soon as you connect the RequestConfirmation Action shape with the newly created Port shape.

Method calls have two vastly different modes. The XLANG schedule can either wait for some external caller to invoke the method by "reaching through" a schedule moniker, or it can initiate the call itself. If it waits for a call, the schedule instance will continue processing only if an external caller references it through a moniker and invokes the method. While this technique is commonly done only to pass arguments to schedules (and this is the case with the confirmation schedule that we are going to look at in more detail a bit later in this chapter), such ports can exist anywhere in the schedule as long as an external client is capable of obtaining a reference to the running instance. This is possible by querying the FullyQualifiedName property of the schedule when the schedule is started and connecting to the schedule instance later using this name, which is a specialized form of

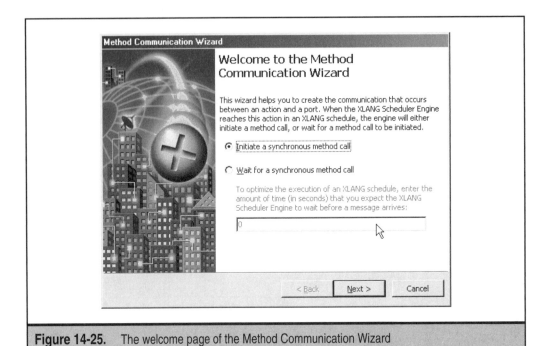

Figure 14-25. The welcome page of the Method Communication Wizard

the schedule moniker. This principle is illustrated in the following VB pseudocode, which assumes to be using the XLANG Scheduler Runtime Library type library:

```
Set schedule = GetObject("sked:///c:\schedules\SampleSchedule.skx")
sScheduleRef = schedule.FullyQualifiedName() ' get the runtime moniker
Set schedule = Nothing ' discard the COM reference to the schedule
' execute other actions
Set schedule = GetObject(sScheduleRef) 'reestablish the connection
Set port = schedule.Port("ActionFour") 'get the port
port.ActionFour() ' execute the waited action
```

Generally, external calls will block until the schedule reaches the execution point at which the call is expected. Therefore, if you call ports out of order from a single thread, the application will become deadlocked. However, it is possible to "talk" to the schedule from multiple threads (or applications) at once, have all threads call "their" assigned ports that they need to talk to, and then the calls will be released and will return to their respective caller in the order in which they are processed in the schedule.

The "time until the message arrives" text box on the wizard welcome page has the same function as the respective field in the XML Communication Wizard in that it controls the dehydration behavior (as discussed in Chapter 12). If the value is greater than 180 seconds, the schedule will be dehydrated immediately when it enters the wait state for this message. If the value is less than 180, the schedule will not be dehydrated.

Before we get carried away, we should get back to the example flow, select the Initiate A Synchronous Method Call option, and proceed.

The Message Information page (Figure 14-26) is similar to its equivalent page in the XML Communication Wizard. You will either be able to choose to create a new message or select a previously configured method's message. However, unlike messaging messages, which are global to the schedule, method messages are always scoped to the component to which the port is bound. You will therefore be able to select from the list in the lower part of the page only if multiple method messages are configured for the same component.

The final page of the wizard (Figure 14-27) is merely informative in our case because we cannot really change anything here. However, if the target interface of the port has multiple methods and more than one method has been selected on the Method Information page of the COM Component Binding Wizard shown in Figure 14-23, the combo box will list all available methods and allow you to select the appropriate binding. When you click Finish, the message and the bidirectional port binding are completed.

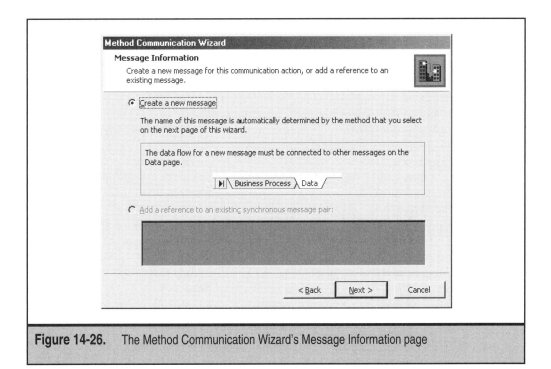

Figure 14-26. The Method Communication Wizard's Message Information page

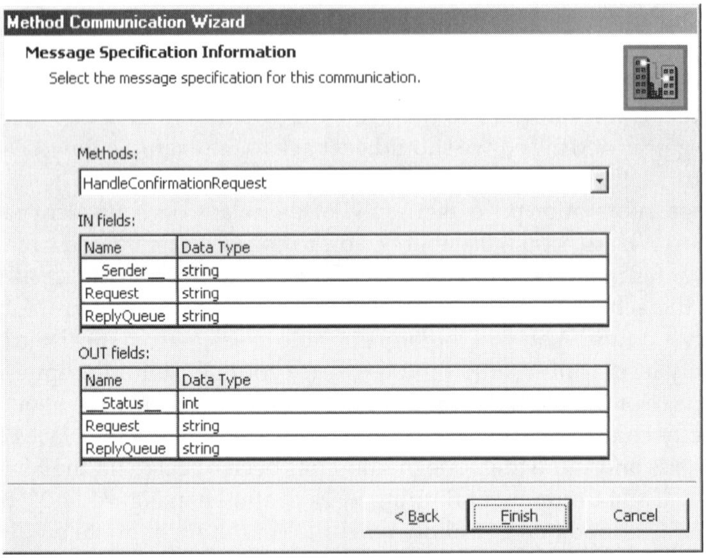

Figure 14-27.   The Method Communication Wizard's Message Specification Information page

Receiving Data from Message Queues

Now we will use a message queue to implement the port that we will use to receive the response from the subordinate schedule. Using the message queue is the preferred and almost only way to receive asynchronous events from external components or schedules and, fortunately, it is pleasantly easy.

To start, drop a new Message Queuing shape onto the drawing surface.

The Message Queuing Binding Wizard (Figure 14-28) serves to configure message queue ports. As with the other three wizards that we have already seen, you will need to name the port on the welcome page. For this port, set the name to ReceiveConfirmation.

The difference between static and dynamic queues is that the name (address) of a dynamic queue is known only at run time and must be provided with a port reference link, while the name or at least a prefix for the name can be provided at design time for static queues. We will use the dynamic queue option for the subordinate schedule a little later. For now, we want to define a well-known per-instance queue, which XLANG will dynamically create, but which is statically assigned to the schedule instance as long as it

BizTalk 2000
Blueprints

Table of Contents

The BizTalk Configuration Object Model (Relationships)...2

The BizTalk Document Processing Pipeline...4

BizTalk Server 2000 Conceptual Enterprise Setup for Internet Document Exchange...........6

Schematic Use of Select UN/EDIFACT and X12 Messages...7

Subordinate Schedules...8

1

The BizTalk Configuration Object Model (Relationships)

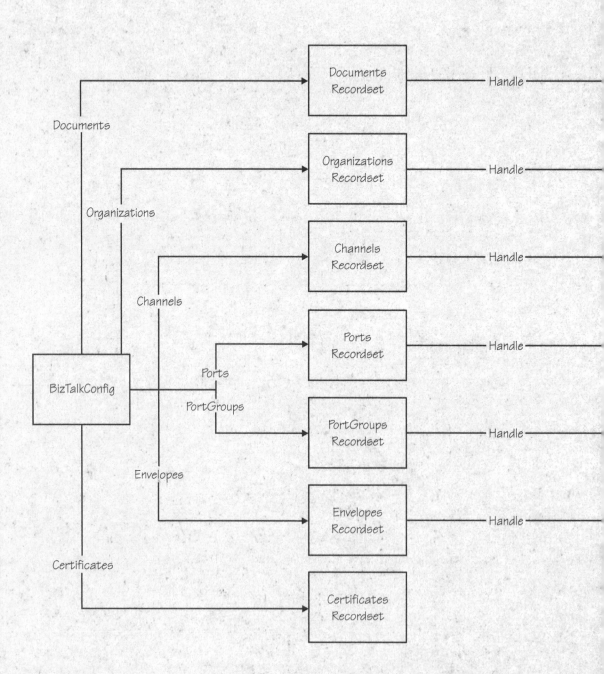

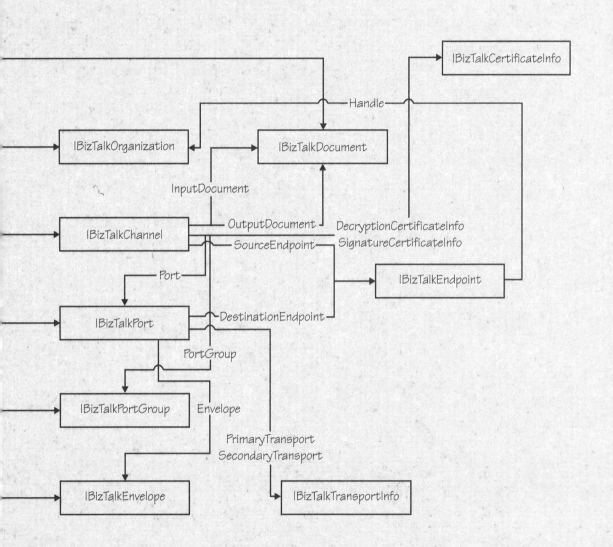

IBizTalkCertificateInfo

IBizTalkOrganization

Handle

IBizTalkDocument

InputDocument

IBizTalkChannel

OutputDocument

DecryptionCertificateInfo

SourceEndpoint

SignatureCertificateInfo

Port

IBizTalkEndpoint

IBizTalkPort

DestinationEndpoint

PortGroup

IBizTalkPortGroup

Envelope

PrimaryTransport

SecondaryTransport

IBizTalkEnvelope

IBizTalkTransportInfo

3

The BizTalk Document
Processing Pipeline

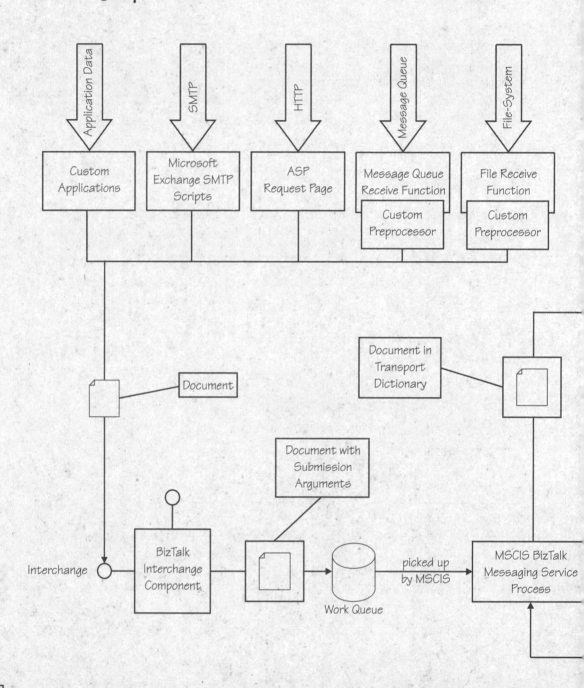

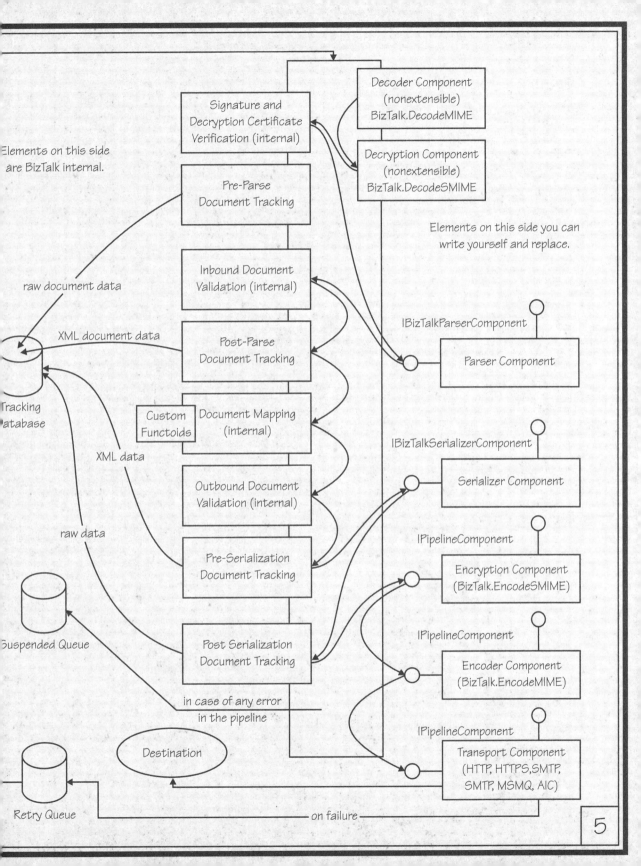

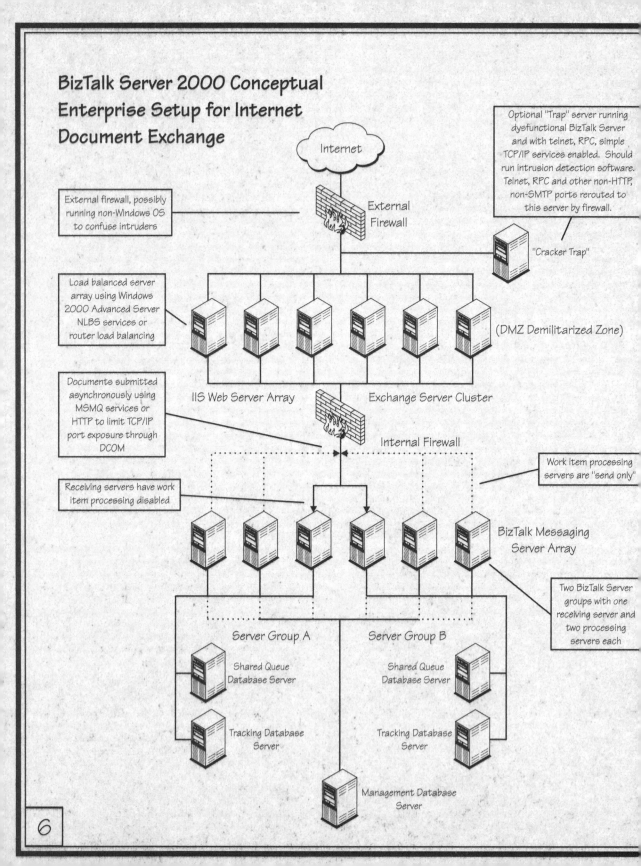

BizTalk Server 2000 Conceptual Enterprise Setup for Internet Document Exchange

Internet

External Firewall

Optional "Trap" server running dysfunctional BizTalk Server and with telnet, RPC, simple TCP/IP services enabled. Should run intrusion detection software. Telnet, RPC and other non-HTTP, non-SMTP ports rerouted to this server by firewall.

External firewall, possibly running non-Windows OS to confuse intruders

"Cracker Trap"

Load balanced server array using Windows 2000 Advanced Server NLBS services or router load balancing

(DMZ Demilitarized Zone)

IIS Web Server Array

Exchange Server Cluster

Documents submitted asynchronously using MSMQ services or HTTP to limit TCP/IP port exposure through DCOM

Internal Firewall

Work item processing servers are "send only"

Receiving servers have work item processing disabled

BizTalk Messaging Server Array

Two BizTalk Server groups with one receiving server and two processing servers each

Server Group A

Server Group B

Shared Queue Database Server

Shared Queue Database Server

Tracking Database Server

Tracking Database Server

Management Database Server

6

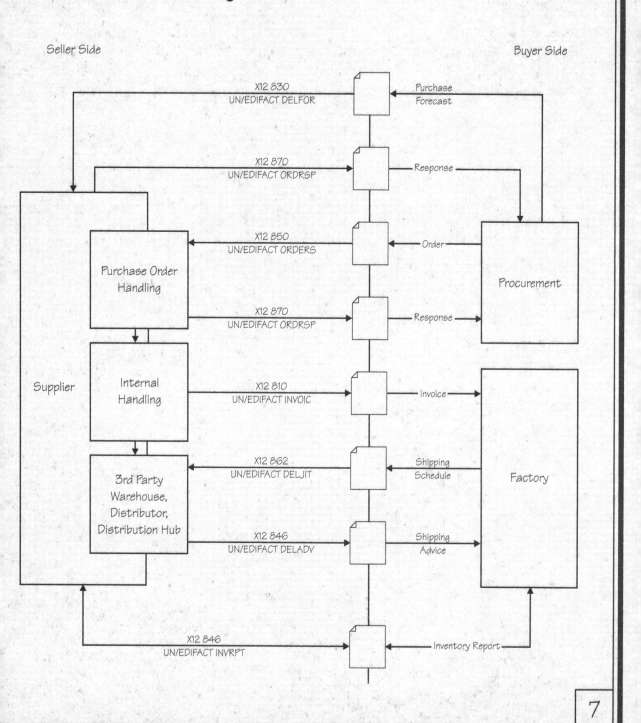

Seller Side

Buyer Side

X12 830
UN/EDIFACT DELFOR

Purchase
Forecast

X12 870
UN/EDIFACT ORDRSP

Response

X12 850
UN/EDIFACT ORDERS

Order

Purchase Order
Handling

Procurement

X12 870
UN/EDIFACT ORDRSP

Response

Supplier

Internal
Handling

X12 810
UN/EDIFACT INVOIC

Invoice

X12 862
UN/EDIFACT DELJIT

Shipping
Schedule

Factory

3rd Party
Warehouse,
Distributor,
Distribution Hub

X12 846
UN/EDIFACT DELADV

Shipping
Advice

X12 846
UN/EDIFACT INVRPT

Inventory Report

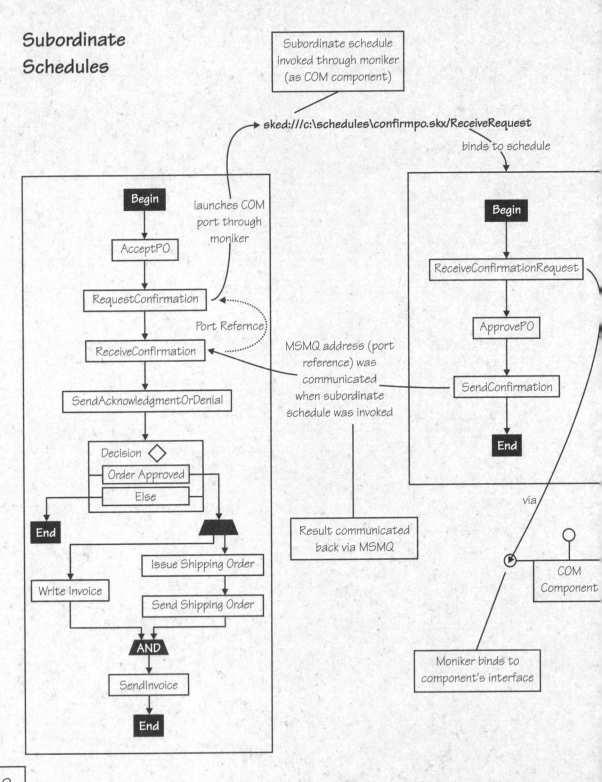

Subordinate Schedules

Subordinate schedule invoked through moniker (as COM component)

sked:///c:\schedules\confirmpo.skx/ReceiveRequest

binds to schedule

Begin

launches COM port through moniker

AcceptPO

RequestConfirmation

Port Refernce

ReceiveConfirmation

SendAcknowledgmentOrDenial

Decision
Order Approved
Else

End

Write Invoice

Issue Shipping Order

Send Shipping Order

AND

SendInvoice

End

Begin

ReceiveConfirmationRequest

ApprovePO

SendConfirmation

End

MSMQ address (port reference) was communicated when subordinate schedule was invoked

Result communicated back via MSMQ

via

COM Component

Moniker binds to component's interface

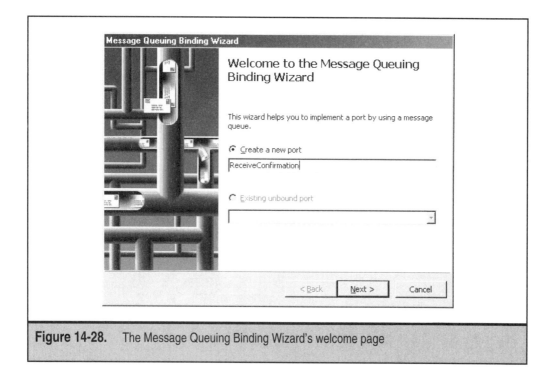

Figure 14-28.   The Message Queuing Binding Wizard's welcome page

runs. Therefore, you should leave this option at Static Queue (Figure 14-29) and proceed to the next wizard page.

The schedule that we are currently designing is run for each incoming purchase order. This means that there could be hundreds or thousands of instances of this schedule running concurrently. Whenever we invoke a subordinate schedule, we must therefore guarantee that the response from that schedule will reach only the caller. To enable this, XLANG supports creating per-instance message queues. A reference to the queue can then be passed as an argument to an invoked schedule, application, or component, and this will allow the callee to respond to the calling schedule. Such a queue reference string is used, for instance, for the ReplyQueue argument that we have put into the signature of our Visual Basic component. However, let us complete the port configuration first.

On the Queue Information page (Figure 14-30), you can define whether you want to create a new queue for every instance or whether you want to use a single well-known queue for all schedule instances. As per the previous explanation, we want to create a new queue per schedule instance, so you should select the Create A New Queue For

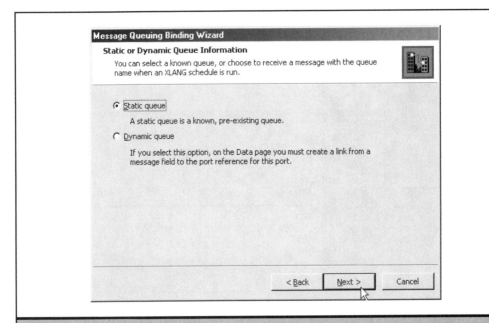

Figure 14-29. The Static Or Dynamic Queue Information page of the Message Queuing Binding Wizard

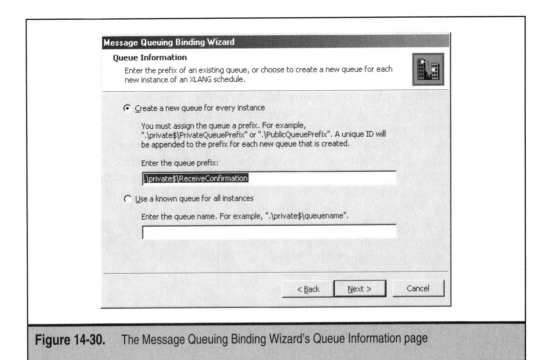

Figure 14-30. The Message Queuing Binding Wizard's Queue Information page

Every Instance option. The wizard will provide a recommendation for a private queue name prefix based on the port name, which you should accept if you do not have any conflicting port names in other schedules. (Even then, name collisions would not occur, but it is cleaner to have a unique prefix per port across all schedules.)

The advanced port properties for message queuing ports (Figure 14-31) are similar to the COM port options. Besides the security options, which we will skip here, you can select whether you want to use transactions with this queue. XLANG-created queues are always transactional, and to enable guaranteed delivery and consistency, it is always a good idea to make queues transactional. You can now click Finish to complete the configuration of the queue binding.

When you connect the ReceiveConfirmation Action shape with the ReceiveConfirmation Port shape, you will once again have to work with the XML Communication Wizard. The settings for this message are, of course, slightly different. On the welcome page (Figure 14-10), you will need to set the message direction to Receive, and because we expect that our subordinate schedule will complete its work rather quickly, we will leave the wait time at zero. On the Message Information page (Figure 14-11), you need to create a new message named ReceiveConfirmation. Because we will receive XML purchase-order acknowledgments through this queue, select the XML option from the XML Translation Information page (Figure 14-12) and enter **PurchaseOrderAcknowledgment** as the message type on the following page (Figure 14-13).

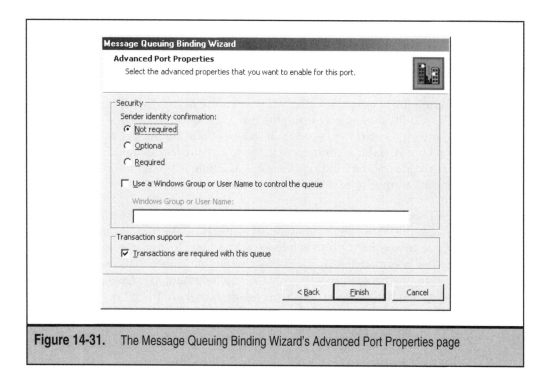

Figure 14-31.   The Message Queuing Binding Wizard's Advanced Port Properties page

The message type name follows the root tag name of the PurchaseOrderAcknowledgment.xml document specification—which, again, we will assume to have already defined, although we will not actually define it until the next chapter. This document specification file must also be referenced on the Message Specification Information page (Figure 14-14). This time, we also need the Field Selection dialog box shown in Figure 14-15. We will assume at this point that the specification contains a POHeader element below the root element, which has a *Type* attribute. If the Type field contains the value *AK,* the message is an acknowledgment message; if the value is *DN,* the purchase order is completely declined.

The condition /PurchaseOrderAcknowledgment/POHeader/@Type = 'AK' is therefore the rule condition that needs to be met to execute the schedule on the Decision shape. However, to make the value available for the decision, we need to extract it from the XML document first. When you open the Field Selection dialog box with this document specification referenced on the wizard page, you will be able to select the Type field from the tree view and assign a name to it. The dialog box will automatically preset the name Type when you navigate to the field in the tree view, which is perfectly acceptable for this case. You would have to provide a special name only if you had to select two different elements or attributes that have the same name in the specification. When you commit the Field Selection dialog box, you will find an additional field in the Message Fields list.

When you commit the wizard by clicking Finish, you can now go back to the Decision shape in the business-drawing portion and update the rule that checks whether the order was approved. To do this, double-click the Order Approved rule bar and enter the following rule expression:

```
ReceiveConfirmation.Type <> "DN"
```

Sending Messages to and Through BizTalk Messaging

The last port that we are going to cover in this walk-through fashion is the implementation port for sending the purchase-order acknowledgment (or denial) back to the customer. We will send the message by using the BizTalk Messaging service and through a well-known channel. To start, you need to drop a new BizTalk Messaging shape on the drawing area, whose Port shape connects to the SendAcknowledgmentOrDenial action.

On the BizTalk Messaging Binding Wizard's welcome page (shown in Figure 14-7), enter a new name for the port: **SendAcknowledgment**. On the next page, select the Send option this time.

The following page (see Figure 14-32) lets you choose between dynamic and static channels. A *dynamic channel* is a channel whose name is not known at design time and which is provided by setting the port reference at run time. In this case, we assume that we will (later) have a static messaging channel that we can submit this message to. The channel has the lengthy name PurchaseOrderAcknowledgment/S93A ORDRSP to Organization Alpha. When you click the Finish button on the wizard page, the port definition is complete and we can take care of the message definition.

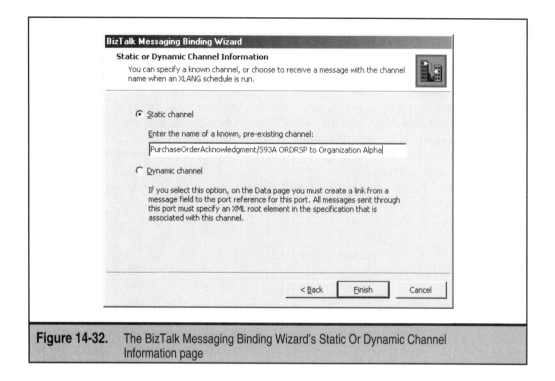

Figure 14-32.   The BizTalk Messaging Binding Wizard's Static Or Dynamic Channel
Information page

The message definition (connect the Action shape to the port to start) is fairly similar to what you did when defining the AcceptPO port. This time, you will create a new message called SendAcknowledgmentOrDenial, choose to send XML messages, make the message type PurchaseOrderAcknowledgment, and reference the PurchaseOrderAcknowledgment.xml specification.

Using BizTalk Messaging Loopback Channels for Document Conversion

Of course, we do not have a complete enterprise system available that could provide the actual business logic. Therefore, we will replace the tasks that the business logic would perform, like creating a shipping order from the acknowledged portion of the purchase order by using BizTalk Messaging's document mapping capabilities. We will implement the IssueShipping Order action by using this technique.

However, while XLANG schedules can both receive messages from and send messages to BizTalk Messaging, mapping documents require a COM component. When you use BizTalk Messaging's document-mapping capabilities in the context of a single application, you will typically configure the messaging port with the loopback transport. The loopback transport allows you to submit a document synchronously to Messaging and retrieve the mapped response document immediately as the call result. This task does, however, require that the document is submitted by using the Interchange component's synchronous *SubmitSync* method. The XLANG scheduling engine will submit documents only by using the asynchronous *Submit* method and will therefore not be able to pick up the response. In addition, BizTalk Messaging ports are always unidirectional.

We will therefore add an additional class POMapper to our Visual Basic component that has a method, which will call the *SubmitSync* method for us. Making another forward reference into Chapter 17, we will assume that we have a configured channel in BizTalk Messaging, which is bound to a loopback port, and which will perform the mapping from the purchase-order acknowledgment to the shipping order. The name of this channel is PurchaseOrder / PurchaseOrderAcknowledgment Loopback. The required Visual Basic code is shown in this snippet:

```
Function MapPOAckToShippingOrder(PurchaseOrder As String) As String
    Dim Interchange As New BTSInterchangeLib.Interchange
    Dim ResponseDocument As Variant
    Dim SubmissionHandle As Variant

    Interchange.SubmitSync BIZTALK_OPENNESS_TYPE_NOTOPEN, _
                           PurchaseOrder, Null, Null, Null, Null, Null, _
                           "PurchaseOrder / PurchaseOrderAcknowledgment Loopback", _
                           Null, Null, False, SubmissionHandle, ResponseDocument
    MapPOAckToShippingOrder = ResponseDocument
    Set Interchange = Nothing
End Function
```

To make this code work and compile, you need to add a reference from the Microsoft BizTalk Server Interchange 1.0 Type Library to the Visual Basic project, which you do by selecting Project | References and selecting this type library in the References dialog box. The code simply submits the purchase order to a well-known channel and picks up the result through the ResponseDocument by-reference argument. This document is then returned as the function result.

When you have saved the new class and have recompiled the component, you can start configuring the Orchestration port. Later, when you actively work with BizTalk Orchestration and need to create or alter auxiliary Visual Basic code interactively, you may experience situations where currently running schedules will hold locks on the COM component and will cause the compilation to fail. Therefore, BizTalk Orchestration Designer has a special command that you can reach on the Tools menu: Shutdown All Running XLANG Schedule Instances. Choosing this command causes all running schedules to be terminated and associated resources to be freed.

Also, if you change Visual Basic COM components and rebuild them, you will need to recompile the XLANG schedule as well, unless you have configured the Visual Basic project for binary compatibility. (See the Visual Basic documentation for details.) The reason for this extra step is that while BizTalk Orchestration Designer shows the programmatic identifiers (prog-id) only of the COM components, the XLANG files will contain the binary class identifiers of the components. Whenever Visual Basic rebuilds an ActiveX DLL project and makes changes, it will create new class identifiers and therefore cause the existing compiled XLANG schedule to be incompatible with the new DLL. The binary compatibility mode will fix this.

Equipped with the updated COM component, you can now proceed to configure the port. Of course, this is now trivial. Drop a new COM Component shape onto the implementation part of the drawing surface and configure the new port IssueShippingOrder to bind to the new class. When you connect the Action shape to the Port shape, you will need to confirm only the default settings of the Method Communication Wizard and will already be done with the port configuration.

For the same reasons explained before (we do not have a specific processing backend for this example), we will also use such a simple mapping to convert the purchase order into an invoice for the WriteInvoice action. You should therefore add a new InvoiceWriter class to the Visual Basic project and add the following method:

```
Function WriteInvoice(PurchaseOrder As String) As String
    Dim Interchange As New BTSInterchangeLib.Interchange
    Dim ResponseDocument As Variant
    Dim SubmissionHandle As Variant

    Interchange.SubmitSync BIZTALK_OPENNESS_TYPE_NOTOPEN, _
                        PurchaseOrder, Null, Null, Null, Null, _
                        "Map PurchaseOrder to Invoice", Null, Null, False, _
                        SubmissionHandle, ResponseDocument
    WriteInvoice = ResponseDocument
    Set Interchange = Nothing
End Function
```

The implementation is only subtly different from the Visual Basic method that we've seen before. The only real difference is that we are giving a different channel name in this case. You should not need any more help in configuring this port now.

The remaining two actions, SendShippingOrder and SendInvoice, send messages through well-known BizTalk Messaging channels and are therefore similar to the SendAcknowledgment port in terms of configuration. The message type name for the shipping order is ShippingOrder, and the document specification name is ShippingOrder.xml. Using the definitions that you will learn in Chapter 17, you can then (after reading Chapter 17) complete the schedule definition by associating this Orchestration port with the BizTalk Messaging Channel "ShippingOrder to Organization Beta".

The message type name for the invoice is Invoice, and the document specification name is Invoice.xml. (As usual, you should get the files from the web site.) The BizTalk Messaging Channel name, as defined later in Chapter 17, is "Invoice/S93A INVOIC to Organization Alpha".

Shaping the Data Flow

At this point, we have defined the workflow and the port bindings, but it is still unclear how the data flows between the different ports. This is what we are going to take care of now.

When you look at the bottom of your Orchestration drawing page in BizTalk Orchestration Designer, notice that it has two pages, the Business Process page that you have been working on up until now and a Data page. When you click the Data label, Orchestration Designer switches to that page. All port messages that have been configured in the business drawing are automatically placed on the Data page. In addition, you will find two predefined shapes for constants and port references. On the Constants shape, you can add constants values, which can be used as arguments to method calls. The Port References shape contains one entry for each port. A *port reference* is the transport address or interface pointer to which the port is bound.

The data flow of the Orchestration schedule is defined by connecting the message fields. This is best explained by looking at the example shown in Figure 14-33.

Luckily, the mappings between most of the elements (shown in Table 14-1) are trivial and do not need much further explanation—with one exception: the connection from the ReceiveConfirmation field of the Port References shape may not be immediately clear. To understand the rationale for why this connection needs to be made, let's take a look at the subordinate schedule that this port connects to through a schedule moniker.

Source	Target	Comments
PurchaseOrder. Document	HandleConfirmationRequest_in. Request	Routes the purchase order to the confirmation schedule
PortReferences. ReceiveConfirmation	HandleConfirmationRequest_in. ReplyQueue	Passes the address of the reply queue as an argument to the HandleConfimationRequest component call (see discussion immediately following)
ReceiveConfirmation. Document	WriteInvoice_in. PurchaseOrderAck	Routes the purchase order acknowledgment to the WriteInvoice COM component to produce invoice
WriteInvoice_out. WriteInvoice	Invoice. Document	Routes the output of the WriteInvoice component to the Invoice port
ReceiveConfirmation. Document	SendAcknowledgmentOrDenial. Document	Routes the acknowledgment document from the receive queue to the outbound messaging port

Table 14-1. Data Flow Mappings

Source	Target	Comments
SendAcknowledgment OrDenial. Document	MapPOAckToShippingOrder_in. PurchaseOrder	Routes the acknowledgment document from the receive queue to the shipping order mapping component
MapPOAckToShipping Order_out. MapPOAckToShipping Order	ShippingOrder. Document	Routes the output of the shipping order mapping component to the shipping order outbound port

Table 14-1.   Data Flow Mappings *(continued)*

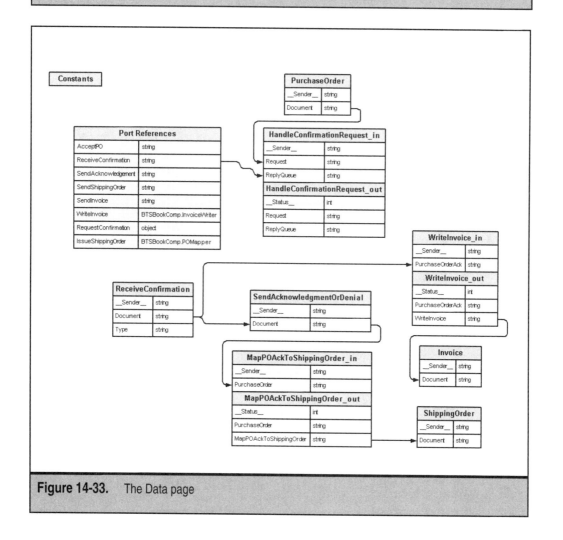

Figure 14-33.   The Data page

The confirmation schedule that is used in this example (see Figure 14-34) does nothing more than send the purchase order to a BizTalk loopback port that will transform the order into a purchase-order acknowledgment. The document map for this transformation simply marks the purchase order as accepted. Like the RequestConfirmation port in the main schedule, the ReceiveRequest port in the confirmation schedule is bound to the _HandleConfirmationRequest interface, which is configured as No Instantiation. This means that while the port will indeed be bound to the HandleConfirmationRequest component, it will never create an actual instance of component but will intercept the call immediately.

The ApprovePO port is bound to an additional method on the POMapper Visual Basic component, called *MapPOToPOAcknowledgment*, which differs from its sibling only in that it forwards the document to the channel PurchaseOrder / PurchaseOrderAcknowledgment Loopback.

What you can also see in the confirmation schedule is that the last action is bound to a dynamic message queuing port. As you know from the previous discussion, a dynamic port's destination transport address is unknown at design time. This means that the destination must be assigned to the port somehow at run time.

When you look at the confirmation schedule's data flow (see Figure 14-35), it will become apparent how the destination transport address is assigned to the dynamic port. The ReplyQueue argument of the *HandleConfirmationRequest* method, which is used to

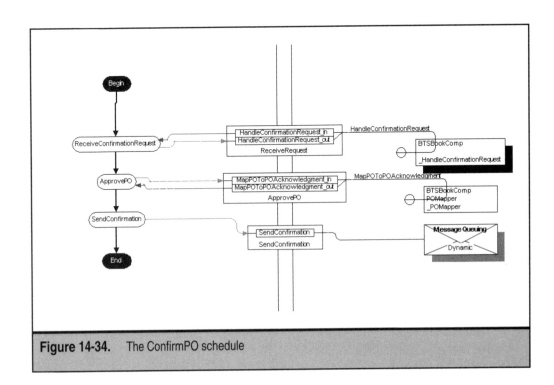

Figure 14-34. The ConfirmPO schedule

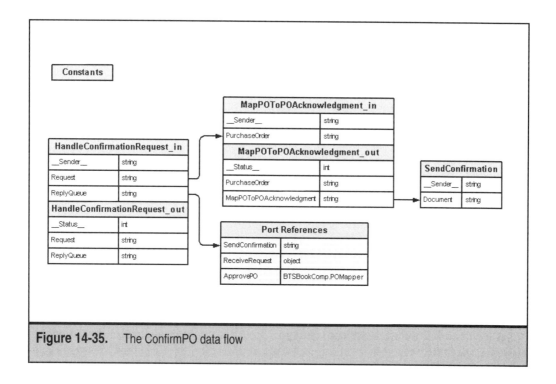

Figure 14-35.   The ConfirmPO data flow

launch to the schedule, must contain a valid transport address that is then assigned to the port reference for the SendConfirmation port.

The design pattern that we use in the main schedule is that we send a document and the reply queue address to a newly created subordinate schedule. Then we will wait for the response in a following action using an inbound message queue port, which has a per-instance queue configuration. The correct argument to be passed to the subordinate schedule as the ReplyQueue argument is therefore the name of the inbound queue that has been created for the current instance.

You should memorize this plan as a general design pattern. Using reply queues is useful not only when you create and launch subordinate schedules, but it is also a very scalable solution when you use schedules as part of a larger solution architecture. Code that invokes schedules can create private message queues through the standard Microsoft Message Queue (MSMQ) APIs, hand a reference to such a queue to the newly created schedule, and pick up the result at its convenience. This enables decoupled, highly scalable solutions.

A Generic Component for Loopback Channels

If you followed all the instructions so far, you now have the Visual Basic project, which consists of three components with a total of five methods. Of those five methods, three are basically identical; they differ only in which channel the message is submitted to. Common programming practice is to find a more generic solution in such cases, and the goal must be to write (and maintain!) this code only once.

Performing this task is obviously very easy. Create a new class called Interchange in the Visual Basic project and add this method:

```
Function SubmitSyncToChannel(Document As String, ChannelName As String) As String
    Dim Interchange As New BTSInterchangeLib.Interchange
    Dim ResponseDocument As Variant
    Dim SubmissionHandle As Variant

    Interchange.SubmitSync BIZTALK_OPENNESS_TYPE_NOTOPEN, _
                        PurchaseOrder, Null, Null, Null, Null, Null, _
                        ChannelName, _
                        Null, Null, False, SubmissionHandle, ResponseDocument
    SubmitSyncToChannel = ResponseDocument
    Set Interchange = Nothing
End Function
```

Now we have a fabulous one-for-all solution for the three places where we use BizTalk Messaging for mapping documents. Great, but how do we pass the channel argument? Constants!

You can add any number of constants to schedules by double-clicking the Constants shape on the Data page of any schedule. When you do that, the Constant Message Properties dialog box opens, in which you can add, edit, and remove arbitrary constant values to the schedule. As shown in Figure 14-36, you can then use these constants as arguments for components or connect them to any other message field.

LONG-RUNNING TRANSACTIONS

In addition to making integration of existing components and external resources very easy, BizTalk Orchestration is indeed a complete infrastructure to implement long-running transactions. You may consider using it even if the ease of definition and the feature set for implementing business process logic don't appeal to you. In today's transaction systems, excellent support exists for short-lived transactions that execute in a matter of seconds and milliseconds and that provide transaction coordination for atomic consistent isolated durable (ACID)–style transactions. ACID mandates that a transaction can be executed as a block and will either succeed with all parts of the transaction succeeding or that all of the transaction's parts will jointly fail.

Such transactions must also be isolated so that their intermediate results cannot be seen by other transactions while data is still being manipulated. To achieve this goal, ACID requires hard locks on all resources that are rolled into the transaction. If you store the underlying data in a database, all affected rows will be locked by the transaction so that no other transaction can access them while the transaction is running. This will effectively stall any concurrent transaction that has these rolls in query result sets, even if they are read-only.

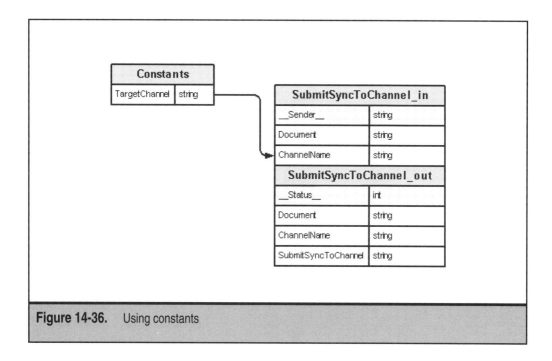

Figure 14-36.   Using constants

Obviously, this "traditional" style of handling transactions is not applicable for business processes that span days, weeks, or even months. To get around this problem, you use compensation transactions that are carefully designed to roll back the results of a long-running transaction step by step, based on errors that may occur. These actions really depend on the respective workflow, and some of them may be really tricky to do. (For example, when you have sent a letter out to a customer and you want to annul this action.) Therefore, no simple solution exists to implement compensation transactions on a technical level, which is the case with ACID transaction managers like Microsoft's Distributed Transaction Coordinator (MSDTC)—the underlying transaction technology for Microsoft Transaction Server and COM+ Transactions.

In fact, no support has existed at all for long-running transaction implementation on the Windows platform up until this point. BizTalk Orchestration's transaction features fill this void. Besides supporting ACID transactions through COM+ on the schedule level and using explicit Transaction shapes, Orchestration also contains support for long-running transactions with compensation and for transactions that are timed and must complete within a specific period of time.

Figure 14-37 shows the result of including a transaction to the scenario that we developed in the previous discussion. (Note that the following chapters on Messaging configuration assume that you are using the nontransacted version of the schedule.) To add a transaction, you have to drop it onto the drawing surface and connect the Transaction shape to the previous and following action. Then you must place the transaction actions into the Transaction shape, drag the connector handle on the top edge of the Transaction

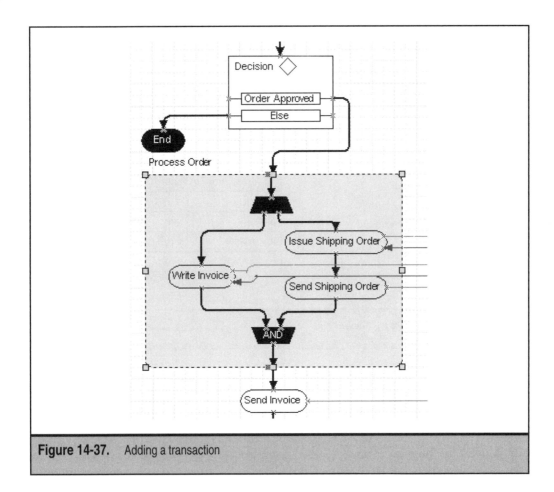

Figure 14-37.   Adding a transaction

shape to the first action, and connect the last transaction action to the connection point at the lower edge of the shape.

To configure the transaction behavior, double-click the Transaction shape. The Transaction Properties dialog box opens, as shown in Figure 14-38. To make the transaction long running, which we want to do here for the purpose of our discussion, select Long-Running from the Type option group. This works only if the transaction type of the schedule is set to Include Transactions Within XLANG Schedule, which you can configure on the schedule's Begin shape.

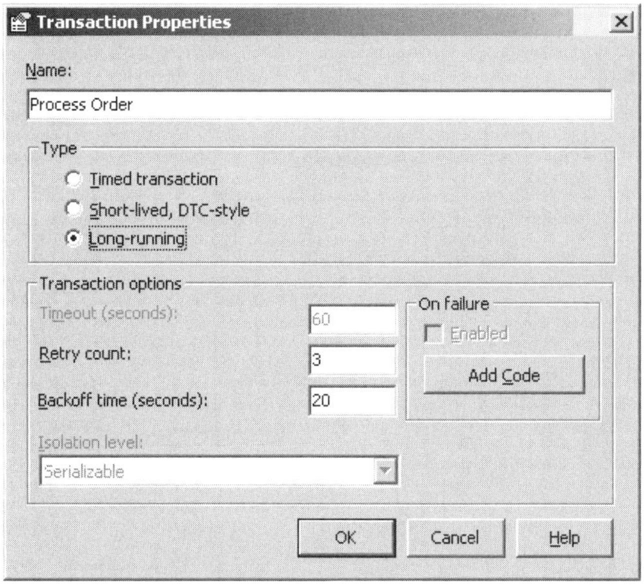

Figure 14-38. Transaction properties

To handle failures for long-running transactions, you will then have to add the failure schedule for the transaction. When you click the Add Code button in the dialog box and click OK, the schedule drawing will be extended with another page, whose name is always On Failure of *Transaction Name*. The new page can be found at the very bottom of the drawing area, just next to the Data page.

The compensation transaction for our scenario is quite simple. Because automatic processing apparently fails, we will place the original purchase order into a queue and send that off for manual review and handling. To do this, we add a new MSMQ Orchestration port named ProcessManually that sends messages of the already-existing message type PurchaseOrder to a private or public queue, from which the application that handles such manual review cases will pick them up. This is illustrated in Figure 14-39. Then the message will be sent to manual review whenever any of the actions within the transaction fails.

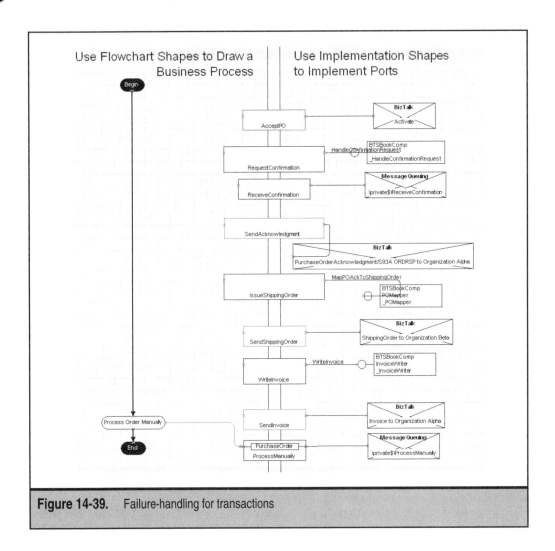

Figure 14-39. Failure-handling for transactions

If the branch that contains the shipping port succeeds but the branch that writes the invoice fails, we would, however, have to cancel shipping before we could hand the order off to manual processing. To perform this task, you can add a nested transaction (see Figure 14-40) that groups the two shipping actions and a compensation schedule that effectively annuls the result of that transaction, although it technically succeeded. To configure compensation, you must add a compensation schedule much in the same way as you added the failure-handling schedule before. The Properties dialog box of the inner

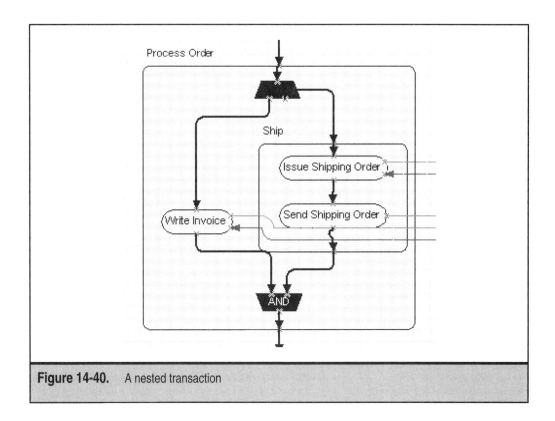

Figure 14-40. A nested transaction

Transaction shape will show an Add Handler button for Compensation in that case. The compensation schedule always runs whenever the nested schedule technically succeeds, but the outer schedule fails and needs to be rolled back.

The appropriate actions to implement here are to convert the shipping order into a cancellation message and send that cancellation to the warehouse.

With schedules to manually handle failures and with support for compensation transactions for nested transactions, BizTalk Orchestration provides a unique infrastructure for long-running transactions. In essence, Orchestration keeps track of all nested transactions and their completion status for you, until all nested transactions that are part of a larger transaction are successfully completed and the outer transaction successfully commits. Should any actions within the outer transaction or within one of the inner transactions fail without being caught and handled, Orchestration will fire all respective compensation schedules. This allows you to take reasonable steps to annul the result of these transactions, which may indeed include tasks like sending letters to customers.

CHAPTER 15

Creating Document Specifications

To begin, this chapter recaps document definition concepts, which you should already know by now. And because Chapter 10 already presented the basics of BizTalk Editor, this chapter provides only a brief overview of the tool. Then you will learn how to build XML document specifications, create specs for EDI, and create flatfile document specifications.

REVIEW

First, we're going to briefly summarize what document specifications and definitions are used for in BizTalk Server 2000 and take another look at the core features of BizTalk Editor. If you feel familiar enough with the concepts and the tool already you may just want to skip ahead to the "Defining XML Documents" section—the following is essentially a reminder.

Document Definition Concepts

The following reminders will help you when you start creating document specifications:

▼ All BizTalk document specifications, regardless of whether they represent X12, UN/EDIFACT, flatfile, or XML documents, are expressed in terms of XML. This means they are hierarchical representations of data.

■ The EDI and flatfile parsers and serializers are driven by document specifications. Each document specification for those formats contains special augmentations that help the serializer to output the correct data stream into native format. Likewise, the parser uses this information to scan the data stream and transform it into the correct XML representation of the native format.

■ The XML data format is syntax-centric and has strong abstract concepts of semantics; in contrast, the EDI format is semantics-centric, comes with a completely defined nonabstract semantics model, and has a very limited syntax concept. In an XML document type, a certain element name is used in exactly one context and meaning. In an EDI document, elements with the same name can appear multiple times and in entirely different contexts because the semantics are defined outside the syntax rules and typically in accompanying documentation.

▲ BizTalk document specifications are expressed in BizTalk Schema, which is a superset of XML Data Reduced (XDR) Schema.

BizTalk Editor

The Editor, shown in Figure 15-1, is the BizTalk tool you use to create document specifications. Because all document formats are described using the hierarchical XML-based BizTalk Schema, the Editor employs a tree view to reflect the structure of the document. Each element that may contain other elements is called a *record,* and each element that contains data is called a *field.* For the EDI format, a record is equivalent to a segment and a record that contains records is equivalent to a loop.

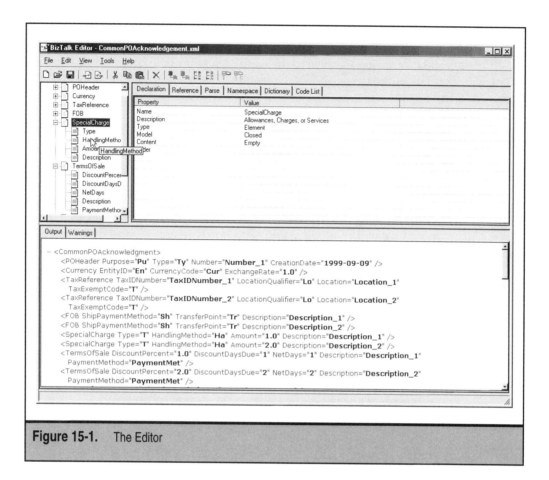

Figure 15-1. The Editor

Every field record has a number of special properties that can be configured in one of six different views in the Editor:

▼ The Declaration view contains the information about the field or record in the context of its specific data format.

■ The Reference view serves to specify when and how often its immediate parent references the element.

■ The Parse view contains hints for non-XML parsers and serializers.

■ The Namespace view serves to define auxiliary namespaces for the Schema.

■ The Dictionary view allows you to define a data dictionary for well-known values.

▲ The Code List view allows you to create constraints based on predefined code lists that are part of the EDI standard.

To assist you in creating consistent and correct specifications, the Editor helps validate the specifications by using a special command (Tools | Validate Specification). The results of the validation process appear in the warnings pane at the bottom of the BizTalk Editor window. The output pane shows the results from creating sample data (Tools | Create XML Instance).

DEFINING XML DOCUMENTS

Because XML is BizTalk's native data format and its syntax and structure is much stricter and clearer than those of the EDI formats, creating document specifications in this language requires the least effort. We will begin by creating a simple XML specification from scratch, and we will use this example to explore most of the features of BizTalk Editor. The specification that we will create here will serve to share and synchronize customer contact and sales information between divisions within an organization.

When you want to create a new specification, either select File | New, press CTRL-N, or click the respective icon on the toolbar. BizTalk Editor will open the New Document Specification dialog box (see Figure 15-2), which lets you pick one of the predefined templates for UN/EDIFACT, X12, or XML, or lets you begin with a blank specification. In this case, click the Blank Specification icon and click OK.

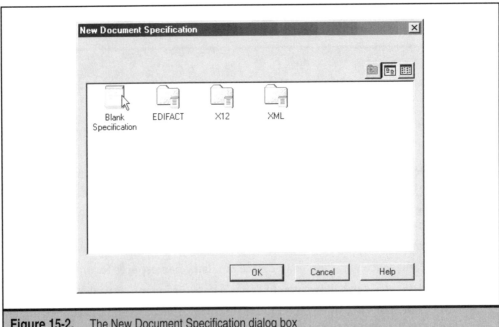

Figure 15-2.   The New Document Specification dialog box

The Editor will create a new XML document specification that has a single root element called BlankSpecification. Click the root node in the tree view and hold the mouse button down for about a second. You will then be able to rename the node. Alternatively, you can also right-click the node and select Rename from the context menu. Rename the node CustomerInfo. You can use the same process to rename the Name property on the Declaration tab with the root node selected in the tree view.

Root Elements: The Reference Tab

When you click the Reference tab (see Figure 15-3) in the properties pane (with the root node selected), notice that the name of the root element is mirrored in the Specification Name property. The value of this property is used as the name attribute for the XDR Schema root element. Therefore, it must be identical to the tag name of the root element in the tree view and is automatically set to CustomerInfo. In BizTalk's first public version, the

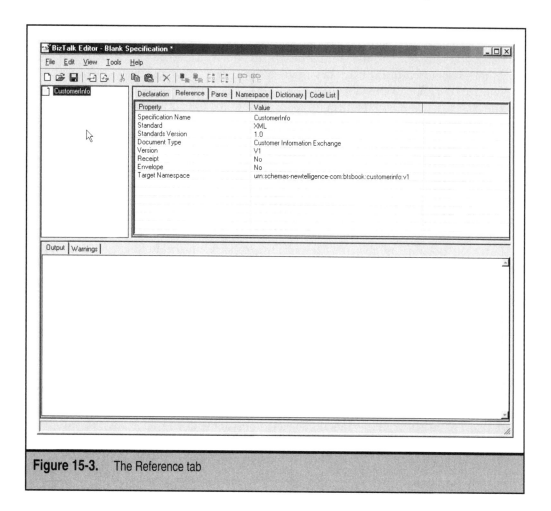

Figure 15-3.   The Reference tab

Editor does not synchronize the values once you begin editing the Specification Name property, so you may want to double-check to see whether the two values are equal before you save and use the specification.

The other properties on the Reference tab are accessible only by selecting the root node. The Standard property declares the document format standard for which this specification is created. After you select the property line, when you double-click the value or press the ENTER key, you can select one of these predefined choices: XML, UN/EDIFACT, X12, or CUSTOM. Changing the Standard property causes the Editor to switch between the different standards and make other properties sets available as needed. The EDI standards require many more hints for the parsers and serializers than XML documents. The additional properties that allow you to specify those hints will become visible only if you select the respective standard in this field.

The Standards Version property is relevant only to the EDI formats because the syntax-centric XML standard is quite stable, while the semantics-centric EDI standards change quite frequently. For completeness, you may want to set this property to 1.0, however.

The Document Type property references the standard for this particular document. Just like the Standards Version property, this property exists for documentation purposes, so you may want to use it for a descriptive reference to an XML document standard that exists for your industry or organization. The Version property documents the implemented version of this document standard.

The Receipt and Envelope properties designate the specification as either a receipt specification or as an envelope specification if the respective value is set to Yes. If the properties remain undefined, they default to No. A receipt specification defines a document type that is used as a technical acknowledgment of a document transmission. Envelope specifications define document types used as wrappers around documents and carry mostly technical transport information instead of business content. Such specifications are used with the CUSTOM XML envelope types or custom serializers and parsers. Because we are defining neither of them here, you should leave the Receipt and Envelope properties undefined or set them to No.

For XML documents, the most important property on the Reference tab is Target Namespace. The target namespace identifier serves to disambiguate the tags of a particular document type from other namespaces if they are merged into a compound XML document. This is especially the case when you wrap the document in an XML envelope. The target namespace qualifier is also a unique identifier for the document semantics. Because two versions of the same document specification are semantically different, even if these differences are minor, the target namespace identifier should be unique for each version.

To comply with XML standards, the target namespace identifier should be a Uniform Resource Identifier (URI). This URI can be a transport-bound URL, for instance, an HTTP location, where—ideally—the document specification can be found. If you use a URL, you should make sure that the host name is unique across the document's distribution space. Host names of your intranet will be used only if the documents based on the specification will never leave it. Otherwise, you should use fully qualified Internet host names.

If you do not want to make the specification available at a transport address, you should use a Universal Resource Name (URN) instead. A *Universal Resource Name* is a special type of URI that always begins with "urn:" and is followed by a unique identifier that may be a text-formatted Universally Unique Identifier (UUID) or a unique name that is qualified by your own Internet domain namespace. Possible examples are urn: 2EA109EA-036C-4183-B13B-39ABEB60901E or urn:schemas-newtelligence-com:btsbook: customerinfo:v1.

For the current sample specification, you can just leave everything on the Reference tab alone except for the Target Namespace property, which you should set to the value just described.

The Declaration Tab

You should now switch to the Declaration tab (see Figure 15-4). The Declaration tab contains all the XML characteristics that apply to the element selected in the tree view. For the root element, you should now see the "Name" property to be equal to the name of the

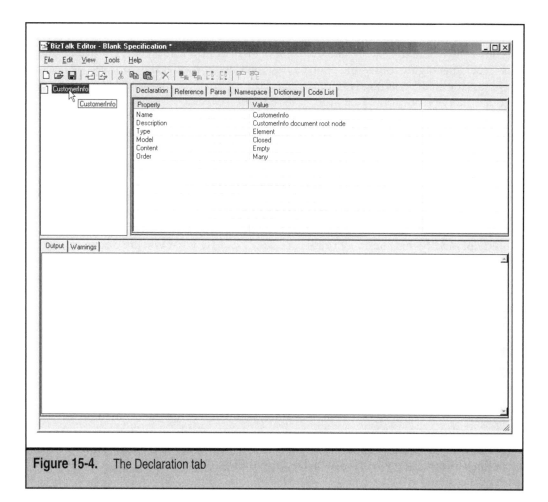

Figure 15-4. The Declaration tab

node, and the "Description" property being empty. The latter property can be individually set for each record or field and you should take it very seriously to provide precise and meaningful explanations for the purpose of the field or record. So even if it is very obvious, you should set this field to "CustomerInfo document root node" for our example.

The Type property for the root node is always set to the value Element and cannot be changed. The Model property defines whether the document's content model is closed or open. If the content model is closed, documents that are based on this specification can contain the exact elements and attributes only in the exact order as they are defined in the specification. Open content models allow for dynamic extensions. As long as document instances comply with the basic rules the specification sets forth, they can contain additional user-defined elements or attributes within the scope of the document namespace that carry extra information that was not specified in the Schema.

The open content model is quite attractive when you must merge XML documents from several specifications into one XML data stream, when you do not have XML namespace support, and when you have specialized evaluation code that can extract and handle the extra information. However, for business documents—or, in general, XML data streams where the exchange between partners or applications uses BizTalk (or any other XML messaging tool)—the open content model is typically not appropriate because the other side is rather unlikely to understand the extra information, and processing only becomes more error prone. Keep the content model closed.

The Contents property defines the content constraints for records. The value can be Element Only, Text Only, or Empty. A record with an Element Only constraint can only contain other records. The Text Only constraint only allows text contents (and with that, you would essentially turn the record into a field, which you should not do). And the Empty constraint indicates that the record cannot contain subordinate records. The Empty constraint does not mean the absence of fields. If all fields on the record are defined as XML attributes, the XML element that represents the BizTalk Editor record is technically empty, and an Empty constraint would be correct. The Editor manages the Content property automatically: you should not modify this manually unless you know exactly what you are doing.

The Order property reflects the equally named XDR "order" attribute on the element declaration. If the order is Sequential, all children must occur in the order in which they are declared. If it is One, at least one of the declared children must be present, even if they are all optional. Many allows the children to be in any order.

Creating Records

To proceed with our example, now you should right-click the CustomerInfo node and select New Record from the context menu (or press CTRL-R). Rename the new record *Customer*. The Customer record's properties on the Declaration tab are the same as for the root node. When you select the root node now, you will see that the Content property has automatically and appropriately changed from Empty to Element Only. Go back to the new Customer record by selecting it in the tree and add some meaningful description like Customer Information Record on the Declaration tab.

Because the customer information document will be designed to carry information on many customers, the cardinality for the Customer record must reflect this. At least one Customer record will be required, though. To define the cardinality constraints for a record, go to the Reference tab, which looks quite a bit different for a record than it does for the root node. The two properties that are available for records on this tab are Minimum Occurrences and Maximum Occurrences, and they let you define just that. However, the fine-tuning capabilities are somewhat limited. For the lower boundary, you can either set 0 or 1, and for the upper boundary, the options are 1 or *, where the asterisk (*) means unlimited. Figure 15-5 illustrates how you can access and change these settings.

Set Minimum Occurrences to 1 and Maximum Occurrences to *. Then right-click the entry in the tree, select New field (or press CTRL-F), and add a CustomerID field. Repeat this to add four more fields for FirstName, LastName, MiddleInitial, and LastChanged.

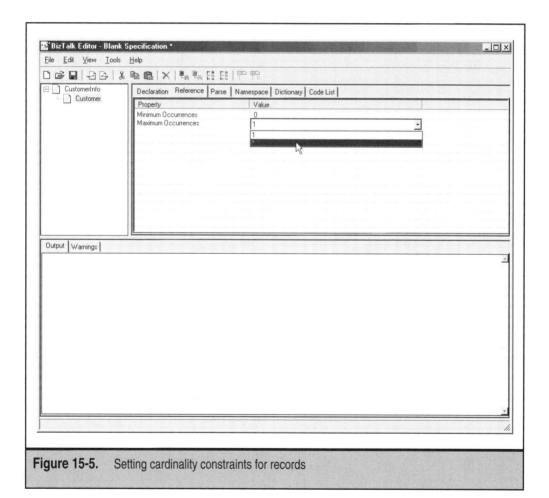

Figure 15-5. Setting cardinality constraints for records

Finally, and while you are at it, add three more child records to Customer named Address, Personal, and Profile. You can insert siblings of the currently selected tree node by pressing SHIFT-F for fields and SHIFT-R for records.

Your specification tree will now look like the one shown in Figure 15-6.

Defining Fields

Now let's fully define the five fields that you just added. The first candidate is the CustomerID field. The content of this field uniquely associates the customer with an identifier that can safely be used in separate distributed databases. This suits our needs perfectly because we want to use this document to synchronize exchange customer data among remote locations.

Select the "CustomerID" field in the tree view and click the Declaration tab. Notice that the choice of properties is a bit different from those available in the record field. The Type property lets you select between Attribute and Element for its value. By default, BizTalk Editor creates all fields as XML attributes that exist on the element representing the record. If you want the data to be contained in elements instead of attributes, you can change the Type property accordingly.

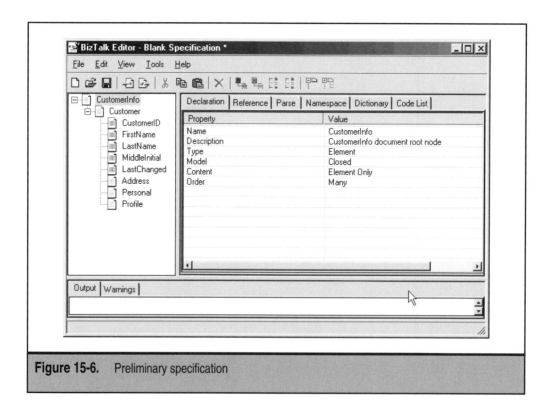

Figure 15-6.　Preliminary specification

Choosing which attributes and elements you want to contain simple data items is often treated as a matter of taste in the XML community, as long as you have a proper schema or Document Type Definition (DTD) to define and describe your preference. However, placing each data item into its own element should be your preferred choice. This allows you to augment the data with attributes from other namespaces, which you cannot do with attribute-bound values. Also, the advanced XML specifications have quite a few very powerful features, like the dynamic type facility of XSD Schema, which you can't use with attributes.

It would be quite annoying if you had to change the type from Attribute to Element for each newly created field because of the BizTalk Editor default setting. Therefore, you can (and for this example, you should) change this behavior by using the Options dialog box, which you access from the Tools menu. This is the only option you can configure at all. If you switch between the Attribute and Element types, BizTalk Editor will warn you that definitions may be lost. (The definitions the Editor is referring to are the Model and Content properties that you already know from the record definition.)

When you switch from Attribute to Element, the properties will merely be added (so the warning is actually meaningless), but if you change these settings when in Element mode and switch back to Attribute, these two property settings will be removed. The golden rule when defining fields as elements is this: do not touch the Content and Model properties. They default to TextOnly and Closed, which is exactly what you want in 99.9 percent of all cases; the 0.1 percent of cases will quite likely apply only to people other than you.

For now, change the type to Element for all five fields. The data type for the CustomerID guarantees uniqueness across databases that are not subject to central coordination and the only data type that will achieve this is the UUID. You can assign data types to fields by using the Data Types property. The assignable values are contained in a drop-down list that opens when you begin to edit the Data Type field. The available types are listed in Table 15-1.

Data Type	Description
Character	Contains a string, one character long.
String	Contains any text.
Number	Contains a number of digits and can have a leading sign, fractional digits, and an exponent. This follows English punctuation, for example, 15, 3.14, $-123.456E+10$.
Integer (int)	Contains a number and can include an optional sign. It cannot contain a fraction or exponent, for example, 1, 58502, -13.

Table 15-1.   Available Field Data Types

Data Type	Description
Float	Contains a number, with no limit on digits; it can potentially have a leading sign, fractional digits, or an exponent.
Fixed Point (14.4)	The same as Number, but can contain no more than 14 digits to the left of the decimal point and no more than 4 to the right, for example, 12.0044. This data type can be used for currency values.
Boolean	Contains an expression that is evaluated as either True (1) or False (0).
Date	Contains a date in a subset ISO 8601 format, with no time information, for example, 1988-04-07.
Date Time	Contains a date in a subset of ISO 8601 format, with optional time and no optional zone information. Fractional seconds can be as precise as nanoseconds, for example, 1988-04-07T18:39:09.
Date Time.tz	Contains a date in a subset ISO 8601 format, with optional time and optional zone information. Fractional seconds can be as precise as nanoseconds, for example, 1988-04-07T18:39:09-08:00.
Time	Contains a time in a subset ISO 8601 format, with no date and no time-zone information, for example, 08:15:27.
Time.tz	Contains a time in a subset ISO 8601 format, with no date information but with optional time-zone information, for example, 08:15:27-05:00.
Byte (i1)	Contains a number and can contain an optional sign, such as a minus (–) sign. It cannot contain a fraction or an exponent; the maximum range is –128 to 127.
Word (i2)	Contains a number and can contain an optional sign, such as a minus (–) sign. It cannot contain a fraction or an exponent; the maximum range is –32768 to 32767.

Table 15-1.   Available Field Data Types *(continued)*

Data Type	Description
Integer (i4)	Contains a number and can contain an optional sign, such as a minus (–) sign. It cannot contain a fraction or an exponent, for example, 1, 703, –32768, 148343, –1000000000.
Double Integer (i8)	Contains a number and can contain an optional sign, such as a minus (–) sign. It cannot contain a fraction or an exponent, for example, 1, 703, –32768, 148343, –1000000000.
Unsigned Byte (ui1)	Contains a number. It cannot contain a sign, fraction, or exponent; for example, the maximum range is 0 to 255.
Unsigned Word (ui2)	Contains a number. It cannot contain a sign, fraction, or exponent; the maximum range is 0 to 65535.
Unsigned Integer (ui4)	Contains a number. It cannot contain a sign, fraction, or exponent, for example, 1, 703, 3000000000.
Unsigned Double Integer (ui8)	Contains a number. It cannot contain a sign, fraction, or exponent, for example, 1, 703, 3000000000.
Real (r4)	Contains a number that has a minimum value of $1.17549435E-38F$ and a maximum value of $3.40282347E+38F$, for example, $3.14285718E+2$.
Double Real (r8)	Contains a number that has a minimum value of $2.2250738585072014E308$ and a maximum value of $1.7976931348623157E+308$, for example, $.314159265358979E+1$.
Universally Unique Identifier (UUID)	Contains hexadecimal digits representing a 128-bit-long, universally unique number, for example, 333C7BC4-460F-11D0-BC04-0080C7055A83.
Uniform Resource Identifier (URI)	Contains a Uniform Resource Identifier (URI).

Table 15-1. Available Field Data Types *(continued)*

Data Type	Description
Binary (base64)	Contains binary encoding of binary text into characters.
Binary (hex)	Contains a binary hexadecimal digit that represents octets, for example, 0x0ffaa.
ID	Specifies the field as the ID.
IDREF	Specifies that a field is referenced to another field that has a matching ID value.
IDREFS	Specifies that the field holds a list of IDs, each separated by a space.
Enumeration	Specifies one value from a predefined set of values.

Table 15-1.   Available Field Data Types *(continued)*

Pick the UUID for the CustomerID field and do not forget to add a good description. With the UUID choice, you mandate a special formatting for the field, which is xxxxxxxx-xxxx-xxxx-xxxx-xxxxxxxxxxxx: five groups of hexadecimal digits with the first group having 4 bytes (8 digits) followed by three groups with 2 bytes (4 digits) and a final group with 6 bytes (12 digits). The groups are separated by hyphens. This is 16 bytes, or 128 bits total. A special algorithm calculates this number, which has as a component a derivative of a computer's unique MAC (network-card identifier) address or highly variable machine state. It generates a semirandom number that also takes the system time into account as another component. The resulting number is very likely unique worldwide. By the definition and logic of the algorithm, the likelihood of two identical UUIDs being generated by two developers is miniscule.

Because CustomerID is a required data element for each Customer record that is exchanged, you should make this a hard constraint in the document specification. Go to the Reference tab and set the Required property for the field to Yes (which is No for all fields by default).

The next field we need to define is the LastName field, which holds the surname of the customer. The natural choice for the data type is String, of course. Because you can assume that the databases between which the data is being swapped have some field-length constraints, you should also apply these constraints to the field definition. The properties to define these constraints are on the Declaration tab, and they are called Minimum Length and Maximum Length. Both properties expect numbers as input. You can set those values only if you have previously set the Data Type property to String. Other data types that allow you to specify size constraints are Number and Binary.

For this example, set Minimum Length to 1 and Maximum Length to 80. This constraint does not implicitly cause the LastName field to be required, though. A minimum length of 1 enforces that the field content is at least one character only if the field is present. Because the last name is essential information, you should also set the Required property on the Reference tab to Yes.

The next field is MiddleInitial, for which we want to allow only a single character. The data-type choices are either Character (which allows exactly one character) or String, with a minimum and maximum size of 1. For extensibility and interoperability reasons, you may want to opt for the second alternative here. Because not everyone has a middle initial in his/her name, just leave the Required property at the default setting of No.

The first name should also be provided. In business you do not always know the first name, although in the United States, communicating by first name is indeed very common. In countries like Germany, however, business communication rarely uses first names. Therefore, you should set the FirstName field so that it is not required, use the String data type, and set the minimum length constraint to 1 and the maximum length constraint to 80.

The last field we need to define for the Customer record is LastChanged. This field holds a date/time value showing when the record was last changed in the source system. The LastChanged field also keeps track of replication. The content will be accepted and updated by the destination only if the timestamp of a customer record in the destination system is older than the time stamp that is communicated here. Of course this is only a simple replication mechanism, but it is sufficient for our example. The data type that you should select for this field is Date Time. In XML, all date fields must contain ISO-compliant dates. The string formats for the field values that correspond to the data types are shown in Table 15-2.

All time expressions require 24-hour format because it is used in most countries (except the United States—but that's the same story as with liters and meters). The tz formats

Data Type	Format	Example
Date	YYYY-MM-DD	2001-02-16
Date Time	YYYY-MM-DD"T"HH:MM:SS	2000-02-16T13:42:27
Date Time.tz	YYYY-MM-DD"T"HH:MM:SS"{+ | -}"HH:MM	2000-02-16T13:42:27+01:00
Time	HH:MM:SS	13:42:27
Time.tz	HH:MM:SS"{+ | -}"HH:MM	13:42:27+01:00

Table 15-2. Data Types and Formats

also need some extra explanation. The appended values +01:00 or –05:00 are the offset from Universal Time Coordinated (UTC) that applies to the time expression. The time expression 16:35:00-05:00 is equivalent to 4:35 P.M. EST, 18:45:00-00:00 is a quarter to seven in the evening in London, and 09:15:00+01:00 is a quarter past nine in the morning in Mönchengladbach, Germany.

Completing and Testing the Sample

We still have a bit to do to complete the specification. First, we will complete the Address record. Because we want to be able to capture multiple addresses for each customer (private home, P.O. box, business), the cardinality for the record will be at least one, so you should set Minimum Occurrences to 1 and Maximum Occurrences to *. The Address record will have the fields listed in Table 15-3.

Name	Type	Min Length	Max Length	Required	Description
AddressID	Integer	-	-	Yes	Identifier for the Address record scoped to CustomerID.
LastChanged	DateTime	-	-	Yes	Date when the record was last changed.
Address Type	Enumeration	-	-	Yes	The Address record type is a qualifier for the address information: BU business address HO home address PO P.O. box ST ship-to address BT bill-to address

Table 15-3. Fields of the Sample Address Record

Name	Type	Min Length	Max Length	Required	Description
Address1	String	1	80	Yes	First part of the address.
Address2	String	1	80	No	Second part of the address. (optional)
City	String	1	60	Yes	City
State	String	1	30	No	The state or the region. This is not marked as required because many countries do not have states or regions.
PostalCode	String	1	10	Yes	The postal code is equivalent to the U.S. ZIP code, and because the majority of countries have postal codes, we mark this as required and mandate escape dummy data ("XXXXXXXX XX") for other locations.
Country	Enumeration	-	-	Yes	The country code is equivalent to the ISO country code and the Internet top-level domain model for countries.

Table 15-3.   Fields of the Sample Address Record *(continued)*

The AddressID field is an integer-type identifier that is scoped to the Customer record; thus, it is unique among only a single customer's address records. The fields with the Integer data type can hold integer values of any size. If you need to constrain the size to a certain limit, you should select one of the size-bound integer data types.

When you add the LastChanged field, you will immediately notice something: the data type will have already been set! This is because your document specification already has a field by the same name. XML rules dictate that each element appearing anywhere with a certain tag name always has the same type, constraints, and semantics—because the type definition is indeed contained only once in the Schema and then referenced from multiple locations. (You may want to flip back to the "XDR" section in Chapter 3 for a quick memory refresher.)

The Editor does this automatic referencing of already existing types not only for fields, but also for entire records. If you add a record for which the type is already defined (through the existence of a record with the same name), the Editor will automatically insert a new instance of the entire type including all subfields and subrecords. The behavior is not applicable to fields that are implemented as XML attributes. If you are not creating fields as elements, you will not experience this effect.

The AddressType and Country fields are of type Enumeration. This type lets you define a constraint that is based on a list of values. If the field value is not equal to one of the values set in the Data Type Values property, document validation will fail. Therefore, when you define the Country field, you should simply enter all 200+ ISO country codes as a list separated by spaces. If you want to keep it short, enter **US UK FR DE JP CA IT RU**. (This selection is based on the G8 countries and therefore not arbitrary.) If your country is missing in the list, you should add the respective code, of course. For the AddressType field, you enter the values listed in Table 15-3.

You can also add custom hints and annotations to the Schema so that the additional information pertaining to it is not located in some separate plain-text document that subsequently gets lost (which happens to all program documentation that is not welded to the program code). The PostalCode field in the table defines a special rule for how to create dummy information that will be generated if postal codes are not applicable to the destination country. Because we do not want to abuse the Description field for this, there is really no good place to put this information.

Now the Namespaces tab comes into play. It allows you to define additional XML namespaces for BizTalk Schema with which you can qualify custom attributes. Add a namespace declaration with the prefix *doc-hint* and the value urn:schemas-newtelligence-com:btsbook:doc-hint. Now go back to the Declaration tab for the PostalCode property and double-click in the first column on the blank line immediately below Maximum Length. Enter **doc-hint:SpecialRule** into the field. Now you have extended BizTalk Schema with your own property that you can use to store the additional hints that you want to remember.

Set the new property's value to the explanatory string "Fill up with character X if not applicable for country". Alternatively, and if you use custom serializers or parsers, you could also use such fields to store machine-readable instructions.

Such hints can also be stored in the field notes. The field notes are available by right-clicking the element in the tree view and selecting Properties from the context menu. One difference between properties as you have just defined them and the notes is that the property is related to the type and the notes are related to the type instance. For example, in the LastChanged field, notice that adding a property to the LastChanged properties will be reflected in both locations, but writing a note will apply only to the place where you put it.

Now we complete the document specification by adding and defining the fields for the additional records.

The Personal record is an optional, nested structure of the Customer record. Therefore, its cardinality is at most once (0 to 1). Table 15-4 lists the fields that we want to be contained in the structure.

The Profile record holds a customer profile that we want to exchange. For simplicity, we will just track a few data elements as listed in Table 15-5. The record is required for each customer and must appear exactly once. The cardinality is therefore 1 to 1.

NOTE: The decimal point in XML is the simple dot (.) independent of the system locale, which is also the case for the C family of programming languages. Unfortunately, the scripting languages available on the Windows platform are user-friendly: they respect the regional settings of a system and will accept other decimal separators for actual calculations (instead of just output and input formatting). This will also indirectly affect BizTalk. If you want to avoid such problems from the start—and this is independent of whether you have a localized German or Italian version of BizTalk—you should run your system with a dot (.) as the decimal separator. Change this in the Regional Settings program of the Control Panel.

Now you have a complete document specification for a very simple customer data synchronization mechanism. The next step is to validate the specification. Every specification should be validated before it is saved (and BizTalk Editor actually enforces this). To validate the specification, select Tools | Validate Specification (or press F5). The validation result will appear in the warnings pane at the bottom of the Editor window. Validation will likely be OK because it is difficult to provoke errors even with XML specifications made with the Editor. (This is not true for EDI specs, as you may find out in "Defining EDI Documents," later in this chapter.)

Name	Type	Min Length	Max Length	Required	Description
Gender	Enumeration	-	-	No	(M)ale, (F)emale
DOB	Date	-	-	No	Date of birth

Table 15-4. Fields of the Sample Personal Record

Name	Type	Min Length	Max Length	Required	Description
CustomerSince	Date	-	-	Yes	Date when the record was created
NumberOf Purchases	Integer	-	-	Yes	Number of purchases
TotalAmount	Fixed Point (14.4)	-	-	Yes	Total amount of purchases expressed in US Dollars

Table 15-5.   Fields of the Sample Profile Record

If the validation is OK, you should save the specification. You can save the spec to the file system by selecting File | Save like in any other application. However, the preferred place to save is to the BizTalk WebDAV repository because BizTalk Messaging's configuration tools will use only the WebDAV repository to reference specifications. (BizTalk Orchestration, on the other hand, can retrieve specifications only from the file system.)

Therefore, save the example specification by selecting File | Store to WebDAV. A dialog box will appear similar to the one you use to save or load files from the file system, but it actually accesses a (potentially remote) WebDAV server location. WebDAV repositories look much like local directories but are accessed through the HTTP Internet protocol. For the example specification, you should create a new directory named BTSBook in the WebDAV repository (by using the New Folder button—the second button from the left in the upper-right corner of the dialog box), and save the specification to the new directory as CustomerInfo.xml.

Now you have a great schema, but if you actually want to run tests with it, you need sample documents. To simplify this task, BizTalk Editor allows you to create a sample document based on the structure, data types, and constraints of the schema. When you select Tools | Create XML Instance, you will be prompted to save an automatically generated sample instance to a local file-system directory. Once the instance has been written to the file, it will also appear in the output pane. Because BizTalk Editor has no concept of the intended business content of your document, it will generate the sample data solely based on the constraints information you have provided, and the produced document will indeed pass validation. However, from a business perspective, the document will definitely contain a lot of nonsense and will require manual editing.

Once you have modified the sample file to contain real data or if you want to validate another instance of the same specification, you can load the external file by selecting

Tools | Validate Instance and have BizTalk Editor check whether the structure and data complies with the schema rules and will list validation errors in the warnings pane. We will also use this feature in Chapter 18 for troubleshooting.

> **NOTE:** The Editor will always create XML documents, independently of the native format your are describing. You can therefore not create native EDI documents with BizTalk Editor; thus, you also cannot validate the produced output. Validation always requires a native document instance.

Creating Specifications from Templates

BizTalk Editor not only lets you create documents from scratch, but you can also create new specifications based on templates. BizTalk Editor's built-in templates are stored in the XML Tools\Templates subdirectory of the product's installation directory. A template is no different from any other BizTalk document specification. When you create generic specifications of which derivatives will be created, you can place them into the appropriate location in this directory tree.

For our example, we want to adjust the CommonPO, CommonPOAcknowledgment, and CommonInvoice XML templates to remove some information that we will never use and to add some fields that we require.

Let's begin with the CommonPO template, which represents a purchase order. To start, select File | New (or click the respective icon on the toolbar) and select the CommonPO.xml template from the XML folder in the New Document Specification dialog box. The dialog box is shown in Figure 15-7. Click OK. A new document will open with the structure cloned from the template specification.

The CommonPO template is one of several XML templates that ships with BizTalk. It reflects some common business scenarios. These template documents are typically very useful to get you started, but you should be aware that they are not based on any standard. They are BizTalk-specific and contain definitions that are commonly used for the respective purposes.

The first step is to make the specification unique and make it clearly identifiable. To do this, you need to rename the root node to become unique and also assign a target namespace identifier. For our example, simply rename the root node to PurchaseOrder and set the namespace URI to urn:schemas-newtelligence-com:btsbook:purchaseorder:v1. If you are handling different types of XML purchase orders within the scope of your organization that are based on different schemas, each one of them should have a unique root element name and target namespace identifier.

Now you should strip unwanted elements. Select the SpecialCharge node in the tree view, press the DEL key, and confirm deletion—because we do not need that record for our scenario. Next, add the following three records below the document root, which each have one field:

▼ A BuyerReference record with the BuyerNumber field as string type, 1 to 25 characters long. The field contains the buyer's ID as it is known to the seller.

This may also be referred to as customer ID on the seller's end. Field and record are optional.

■ A SellerReference record with the SellerNumber field as string type, 1 to 25 characters long. This field contains the seller's ID as it is known to the buyer. This may also be called supplier ID on the buyer side. Record and field are optional.

▲ A ContractReference record with the ContractNumber field with identical constraints. This field refers to a global purchasing agreement under which this order is executed.

All three nodes should appear in the listed order as siblings immediately under the POHeader node. To set this up, select the POHeader node and insert the new nodes by pressing SHIFT-R. Alternatively, you can also insert them by pressing CTRL-R on the root node and then drag and drop them to the desired position. (Dragging and dropping records and fields within the document tree is somewhat tricky, but once you get a feeling for it, it is actually quite comfortable.) When you are done with these changes, store the specification as PurchaseOrder.xml in your WebDAV location BTSBook.

NOTE: You should shape the XML document templates to your needs. The templates exist exactly for this purpose. Delete and add data as needed and if you do not understand some terminology, it may not even apply to your business or industry, so you can erase it.

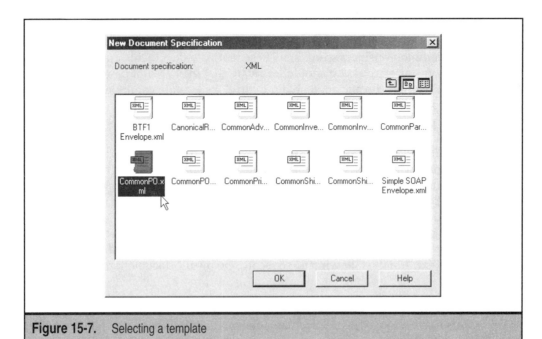

Figure 15-7. Selecting a template

The changes that you should make to the CommonPOAcknowledgment specification template are almost identical to the changes you just made to the CommonPO template. The acknowledgment differs from CommonPO only in the item detail section, where it has additional records that allow the seller to confirm or deny the acceptance of the purchase order on a per-item basis. For the acknowledgment message, you should also remove the SpecialCharge record and add the three records that were listed previously for the purchase order. Rename the root node of the acknowledgment to PurchaseOrderAcknowledgment and set the target namespace URI to urn:schemas-newtelligence-com:btsbook: purchaseorderacknowledgment:v1.

The next specification to adjust is CommonInvoice. Leave the current instance of BizTalk Editor running as is (with the purchase order acknowledgment loaded), start a second copy of BizTalk Editor, and load the template into the new instance. Why? Because we developers are lazy people and the clipboard is our friend.

The CommonInvoice specification that ships with BizTalk lacks some of the informational items that we can communicate in the purchase order, but it also contains some extraneous information items that we do not need. Because the invoice is produced based on the acknowledged purchase-order information, we therefore need to copy a few items from the purchase-order acknowledgment to the invoice specification so that we do not lose any information when the data travels through the system.

First, rename the root node of the invoice to InternalInvoice and set the target namespace URI to urn:schemas-newtelligence-com:btsbook:internalinvoice:v1.

The records that we are going to "steal" from the purchaser-order acknowledgment are ContractReference, BuyerReference, SellerReference, Currency, TaxReference (all following the InvoiceHeader node), and ShipTo (following the Buyer node). To do this, simply switch to the other BizTalk Editor instance, select the respective record in the tree, and copy it to the clipboard by pressing CTRL-C (or select the respective entry on the Edit menu). Once you have switched back to the Editor that holds the invoice, select the root node and press CTRL-V. Then drag and drop the records to the appropriate location. When you are done, save the document specification as Invoice.xml into the WebDAV repository.

Inferring Schema from Documents

If your information infrastructure is already XML-aware, you will already have several XML Schemas or DTDs that you use. Although the BizTalk Schema format is based on XDR, it is not immediately XDR-compatible. Thus, you cannot simply open XDR Schema by selecting File | Open.

You can, however, import an XDR Schema by using a special option on the Tools menu (Import) and then converting it to BizTalk Schema by selecting the appropriate import module, as shown in Figure 15-8. If your document specifications are not expressed in XDR (which would not be surprising given the plethora of schema formats that still exist and that are luckily starting to converge toward XSD), you may be able to create DTD by using the Schema tool that you used to create your existing schemas. As part of the core specification, DTD is the least common denominator for expressing XML document structure. The import option can also read DTD.

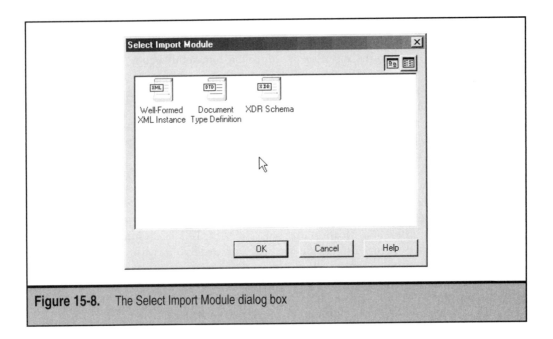

Figure 15-8.   The Select Import Module dialog box

It is not hard to predict that the Editor's ability to infer schema from plain XML documents will be very popular. If you choose the Import option, BizTalk Editor will read any XML document and derive a raw BizTalk Schema from the structure.

However, you should be very careful when relying on the XML import module. It cannot detect precise data types and only makes guesses on the cardinalities. To achieve good results, you should therefore use a maximum example of the XML document, which contains each field, alternates required and nonrequired elements, and has multiple occurrences for each record that may occur multiple times. Even so, you should still inspect the entire imported specification for completeness and correctness.

DEFINING EDI DOCUMENTS

Creating document specifications for UN/EDIFACT or X12 is difficult regardless of the tool you use. The following discussion uses UN/EDIFACT as an example, but it applies to X12 in the same way. The reason UN/EDIFACT is used here is simply because it is a global standard, while X12 is a U.S.-only standard (although deployed worldwide).

It is more difficult to create EDI document specifications than it is to create XML document specifications for a few reasons. First, the syntactic structure of the EDI formats is nowhere near self-explanatory. An XML document like the one you just specified is quite self-descriptive just by looking at the tag names. In contrast, EDI documents based on either standard are long sequences of multipurpose segments with numeric or cryptic identifiers, whose meaning in a particular context is defined by an external agreement document and narrowed by purpose codes that are contained in the instance data. Second, the EDI standards cover anything and everything that could occur in some form of international data exchange in trade and other commercial fields spanning virtually all major industries. Therefore, the standard transaction sets are huge, and they are composed from sequences of several hundred segments, which are cut down to a manageable set in partner agreements.

There are really two basic scenarios that you will encounter when you create EDI document specifications with BizTalk Editor: "heaven" and "hell."

"Heaven" is when the base transaction set that a particular partner agreement is implementing is indeed delivered as a template with the BizTalk product, or it is available from some third party. In this case, the definition of a specification that is equivalent and compliant with the partner agreement may ideally take only a few minutes. "Hell" is when such a template is not available for a larger interchange. Then you are in for some very serious definition work.

UN/EDIFACT Heaven

We start with the best case. The information in Table 15-6 is based on the ORDERS message of UN/EDIFACT version S93A. It shows the segment order of a sample partner agreement for a purchase order from buyer to supplier. (The ORDERS message is included as a template with BizTalk Server.)

Pos.	ID	Name	Usage	Level	Attr.	Req'd	Max. Segment Repeat	Max. Group Repeat
002	UNB	Inter-change Header		0	M	Yes	1	
005	UNH	Message Header		0	M	Yes	1	
010	BGM	Begin-ning of Message	Header infor-mation	0	M	Yes	1	
015	DTM	Date/Time/Period	Order date	0	M	Yes	1	

Table 15-6. Sample Partner Agreement for the ORDERS Message

Pos.	ID	Name	Usage	Level	Attr.	Req'd	Max. Segment Repeat	Max. Group Repeat
035	FTX	Free Text	Order information	1	C		5	
		Segment Group 1: RFF			C			2
040	RFF	Reference	Contract number and customer reference	1	M	Yes	1	
		Segment Group 2: NAD-SG3			C			1
050	NAD	Name and Address	Seller address	1	M	Yes	1	
		Segment Group 3: CTA			C			1
085	CTA	Contact Information	Seller contact	2	M	Yes	1	
		Segment Group 2: NAD			C			1
090	NAD	Name and Address	Bill-to address	1	M	Yes	1	
		Segment Group 2: NAD-SG3			C			1

Table 15-6. Sample Partner Agreement for the ORDERS Message *(continued)*

Pos.	ID	Name	Usage	Level	Attr.	Req'd	Max. Segment Repeat	Max. Group Repeat
092	NAD	Name and Address	Buyer address	1	M	Yes	1	
		Segment Group 3: CTA			M	Yes		1
092	CTA	Contact Information	Buyer contact	2	M	Yes	1	
		Segment Group 2: NAD			C			1
093	NAD	Name and Address	Ship-to address	1	M	Yes	1	
		Segment Group 4: TAX			C			1
095	TAX	Duty/ Tax/Fee Details	Purchaser tax identifier	1	M	Yes	1	
		Segment Group 5: CUX			C			1
110	CUX	Currencies	Reference currency for order amounts	1	M	Yes	1	
		Segment Group 6: PAT-PCD			C			1

Table 15-6. Sample Partner Agreement for the ORDERS Message *(continued)*

Pos.	ID	Name	Usage	Level	Attr.	Req'd	Max. Segment Repeat	Max. Group Repeat
125	PAT	Payment Terms Basis	Basic payment terms	1	M	Yes	1	
130	PAT	Payment Terms Basis	Discount payment terms	2	C		1	
135	PCD	Percentage Details	Discount percentage	2	C		1	
		Segment Group 7: TDT-SG8			C			1
145	TDT	Details of Transport	Primary transport carrier	1	M	Yes	1	
		Segment Group 8: LOC			C			1
150	LOC	Place/ Location Identification	Place where ownership is transferred	2	M	Yes	1	
		Segment Group 9: TOD			C			1
160	TOD	Terms of Delivery	Payment terms on delivery	1	M	Yes	1	

Table 15-6. Sample Partner Agreement for the ORDERS Message *(continued)*

Pos.	ID	Name	Usage	Level	Attr.	Req'd	Max. Segment Repeat	Max. Group Repeat
		Segment Group 10: LIN-PIA-IMD-QTY-DTM-FTX-SG11-SG12			C			>1
345	LIN	Line Item	Purchase item and order part number	1	M	Yes	1	
350	PIA	Additional Product ID	Vendor part identifier	2	C	No	1	
355	IMD	Item Description	Item free text description	2	C	No	1	
365	QTY	Quantity	Item quantity	2	C	No	1	
380	DTM	Date/Time/Period	Date when item delivery is requested	2	C	No	1	
415	FTX	Free Text	Additional free text comments	2	C	No	5	
		Segment Group 11: PRI			C			1

Table 15-6.   Sample Partner Agreement for the ORDERS Message *(continued)*

Pos.	ID	Name	Usage	Level	Attr.	Req'd	Max. Segment Repeat	Max. Group Repeat
440	PRI	Price Details	Item price	2	M	Yes	1	
		Segment Group 12: TAX-MOA			C			1
540	TAX	Duty/Tax/Fee Details	Tax rate		M	Yes	1	
545	MOA	Monetary Amount	Tax amount		C		1	
750	UNS	Section Control		0	M	Yes	1	
780	UNT	Message Trailer			M	Yes	1	
790	UNZ	Inter-change Trailer			M	Yes	1	

Table 15-6.   Sample Partner Agreement for the ORDERS Message *(continued)*

Two expressions—S93A and D93A—relate to the UN/EDIFACT documents in this discussion. They are used in BizTalk and in partner agreements that you will encounter. The expression S93A refers to the standards release, and D93A refers to the associated message directories, which are only one part of the standards release. For our purposes, D93A and S93A are basically synonymous.

The sample agreement in the table appears in the UN/EDIFACT ORDERS message that Compaq Computer Corporation uses for purchase orders sent to its suppliers. The web site for this book (www.osborne.com) provides the complete segment dictionaries for the UN/EDIFACT INVOIC, ORDERS, and ORDRSP S93A messages as Compaq Computer Corporation uses them with its suppliers. We will focus on how to create a specification only for the ORDERS message here. After this initial walkthrough, you should be able to easily create the additional document specifications for the purchase-order acknowledgment (ORDRSP—order response) and the INVOIC message for invoices.

NOTE: Typically, the segment overview shown in Table 15-6 is followed by a segment-by-segment list of the fields and how they are used in the data exchange between the partners; however, we will skip this detailed information now. You can look it up on this book's web site at www.osborne.com.

This agreement is also the basis for the sample UN/EDIFACT stream in Chapter 1. Like all other code snippets and documents in this book, the web site for this book (www.osborne.com) provides that data stream as a file. You can experiment with it if your primary focus has not been EDI until now and you do not have samples at hand. If you have been actively implementing EDI, after this initial walkthrough, you should start using your actual interchanges for further experiments instead of the sample given here.

To start creating the document specification, you need to create a new specification based on the ORDERSSchema.xml template. This template in available in the New Document Specification dialog box. Navigate to the EDIFACT folder and its D93A subfolder and access the template.

A specification will begin loading that reflects a full-scale implementation of the respective UN standard based on the original UN/CEFACT documents. (UN/CEFACT is the UN committee overseeing the standard.) Therefore, the specification needs a serious haircut to fit our needs.

The tree view shows a root element named EFACT_d93a_ORDERS with a number of subordinate records beginning at BGM and ending at ALCLoop3. If you compare this to the partner agreement, you will not be able to find the interchange and message headers (UNB, UNH) and trailers (UNT, UNZ). The reason for their absence is that from a BizTalk perspective, they belong to the envelope. These two headers and two trailers are therefore always implicitly defined and automatically written by the UN/EDIFACT serializer and parsed by the UN/EDIFACT parser. The headers are constructed by using the information that travels along with the message in the transport dictionary of the document-processing pipeline, like source and destination identifier; additional information is taken from the channel configuration data, like the interchange control number. BizTalk specifications for UN/EDIFACT cover only the segments between the interchange, group, and message headers and respective footers, and they typically start with the BGM segment.

Your task in the definition process is now to compare the document specification in the Editor against the partner agreement and simply get them to match. Table 15-7 lists the changes that you must make to the template specification loaded into BizTalk Editor to make it compliant with the agreement. The segments are listed in the order in which they appear in the Editor and the agreement. The references to the specification elements in Table 15-7 are expressed in XPath, rooted at EFACT_d93a_ORDERS.

ORDERSSchema.xml	Partner Agreement	Action
BGM	010:BGM	Leave
DTM	015:DTM	Leave
PAI	-	Delete
ALI	-	Delete
IMD	-	Delete
FTX	035:FTX	Leave
RFFLoop1/RFF	040:RFF	Leave
RFFLoop1/DTM_2	-	Delete
NADLoop1/NAD	050:NAD 090:NAD 092:NAD 093:NAD	Leave
NADLoop1/LOC	-	Delete
NADLoop1/FII	-	Delete
NADLoop1/RFFLoop2	-	Delete
NADLoop1/DOCLoop2	-	Delete
NADLoop1/CTALoop1/CTA	085:CTA 092:CTA	Leave
NADLoop1/CTALoop1/COM	-	Delete
TAXLoop1/TAX	095:TAX	Leave
TAXLoop1/MOA	-	Delete
TAXLoop1/LOC_2	-	Delete
slmult1CUXLoop1/CUX	110:CUX	Leave
CUXLoop1/PCD	-	Delete
CUXLoop1/DTM_5	-	Delete
PATLoop1/PAT	125:PAT 130:PAT	Leave
PATLoop1/DTM_6	-	Delete
PATLoop1/PCD	135:PCD	Leave
PATLoop1/MOA_2	-	Delete

Table 15-7. Mapping Between ORDERSchema.xml and the Partner Agreement

ORDERSSchema.xml	Partner Agreement	Action
TDTLoop1/TDT	145:TDT	Leave
TDTLoop1/LOCLoop1/LOC	150:LOC	Leave
TDTLoop1/LOCLoop/DTM_7	-	Delete
TODLoop1/TOD	160:TOD	Leave
TDTLoop1/LOC_4	-	Delete
PACLoop1	-	Delete
EQDLoop1	-	Delete
SCCLoop1	-	Delete
APILoop1	-	Delete
ALCLoop1	-	Delete
RCSLoop1	-	Delete
LINLoop1/LIN	345:LIN	Leave
LINLoop1/PIA	350:PIA	Leave
LINLoop1/IMD_2	355:IMD	Leave
LINLoop1/MEA_3	-	Delete
LINLoop1/QTY_3	365:QTY	Leave
LINLoop1/ALI_3	-	Delete
LINLoop1/DTM_13	380:DTM	Leave
LINLoop1/MOA_5	-	Delete
LINLoop1/GIN_2	-	Delete
LINLoop1/GIR	-	Delete
LINLoop1/QVA	-	Delete
ght LINLoop1/DOC_2	-	Delete
LINLoop1/PAI_2	-	Delete
LINLoop1/FTX_5	415:FTX	Leave
LINLoop1/PATLoop2	-	Delete
LINLoop1/PRILoop1/PRI	440:PRI	Leave
LINLoop1/PRILoop1/<others>	-	Delete
LINLoop1/RFFLoop3	-	Delete

Table 15-7.   Mapping Between ORDERSchema.xml and the Partner Agreement *(continued)*

ORDERSSchema.xml	Partner Agreement	Action
LINLoop1/PACLoop2	-	Delete
LINLoop1/LOCLoop2	-	Delete
LINLoop1/TAXLoop3/TAX	540:TAX	Leave
LINLoop1/TAXLoop3/MOA	545:MOA	Leave
LINLoop1/TAXLoop3/LOC	-	Delete
LINLoop1/NADLoop2	-	Delete
LINLoop1/ALCLoop2	-	Delete
LINLoop1/TDTLoop2	-	Delete
LINLoop1/TODLoop2	-	Delete
LINLoop1/EQDLoop2	-	Delete
LINLoop1/SCCLoop2	-	Delete
LINLoop1/RCSLoop2	-	Delete
UNS	750:UNS	Leave
MOA_10	-	Delete
CNT	-	Delete
ALCLoop3	-	Delete

Table 15-7.   Mapping Between ORDERSchema.xml and the Partner Agreement *(continued)*

Don't be irritated by the segment names as they appear in the Editor. Because BizTalk Editor produces a Schema for an XML representation of the format, it needs to disambiguate the elements. In XML, each element (*record* in the Editor's terms) has unique semantics, while records are multipurpose and multisemantics in EDI. Each time an EDI segment occurs in a different context, it consequently needs to be mapped to a distinct XML record that represents this contextual relationship.

Therefore, a segment named DTM_2 is disambiguating the second occurrence of a segment named DTM. The original segment name is retained for serialization and parsing in the Source Tag Identifier property.

EDI documents also feature *loops,* which are predefined sequences of segments that may immediately repeat multiple times in the same order. Notice that in Table 15-6, the name-and-address segment NAD and its dependent contact-address segment CTA are repeated exactly four times.

When you have made these changes, you will have a sample UN/EDIFACT specification for the agreement that will work to both parse and serialize compliant interchanges.

However, to leverage the validation features, you must do some additional definition work on the document specification based on the details of the partner agreement. We will look at the required additional tasks by example on the first DTM record.

The UN/EDIFACT DTM segment is a multipurpose segment to represent dates in many different contexts. If you fully expand the subtree below the DTM record, you will find three fields: C50701, C50702, and C50703. The C50701 field is the Date/time/period qualifier and declares the semantic context of the date value. At this position within the purchase order, the meaning of the DTM segment's content is time and date of the order. This exact meaning is encoded with a certain number code (4) in the UN/EDIFACT standard. Although you cannot define constant values in a Schema, you can set a constraint that enforces this exact number code to be defined at this position and have BizTalk consider the message invalid if the constraint is violated.

To make it more bearable to deal with the huge code lists that are part of the EDI standards, BizTalk Editor knows them. If you select the C50701 field in the tree view and click the Code List tab, you will see a list of over 340 different semantics (!) for what a DTM segment can express within the UN/EDIFACT S93A standard. In UN/EDIFACT S98A, the codes even grow to over 460 variants.

To create the desired constraint, click the box next to the value 4 on the Code List tab of the C50701 field and then switch back to the Declaration tab. There you will find your selection reflected in the Data Type Values property, and the Data Type property has been changed to Enumeration accordingly.

The third field of the group—C50703—serves to describe the date formatting for the second field, C50702 (which makes generic mapping of the DTM field into XML infinitely complicated, as we will see in the following chapter). The date format is also specified here as a selection from a code list. As per our agreement, the code that fits is 102. This code identifies the date format CCYYMMDD, which you should select in the code list to make it a constraint. Store the ORDERS specification in the WebDAV store and name it S93A_ORDERS_default.xml.

Even though working through the code lists and setting constraints is still quite a bit of work, creating EDI specifications based on templates is infinitely easier than building them up from scratch, as you are about to find out.

UN/EDIFACT Hell

Your job is much harder if you need to implement UN/EDIFACT or X12 specifications from scratch. BizTalk ships with only a limited number of specifications, and you will likely need to build up your own UN/EDIFACT specification at some point. Because walking you through that process is beyond the scope of this book, the ORDERS schema that you just created will serve as an example to point out the properties you need to build new segments.

All of the specific properties for records and fields are on the Parse tab. When you go back to the C50702 field of the first DTM segment in the Schema and click that tab, you will find the properties (listed in Table 15-8) that are applicable to fields.

Property	Value
Custom Data Type	The following UN/EDIFACT- and X12-specific data types are available:
	String (AN) Alphanumeric fields.
	Binary hexadecimal (B) Binary fields.
	Date (CY) Four-digit date fields.
	Number (D0-D4) Decimal fields. The single-digit number represents the number of digits to the right of the decimal.
	Date (DT) Date fields.
	String (ID) Identification fields.
	Number (N) Integer fields.
	Number (N0-9) Implied decimal fields. (The decimal character does not appear in the data.) The single-digit number represents the number of digits to the right of the decimal.
	Number (R) Real number fields.
	Number (R0-R9) Real number fields. The single-digit number represents the number of digits to the right of the decimal.
	Time (TM) Time fields.
Custom Date/Time Format	If you set Date (DT), Date (CY), or Time (TM) as the Custom Data Type property, you must choose the appropriate format from the list that is shown for this property.
Justification	Left justification is the default for EDI formats because they are delimited. Essentially applicable only to positional flatfile formats.
Pad Character	Applicable only to positional formats.
Wrap Character	Applicable only to flatfile formats.
Minimum Length with Pad Character	Applicable only to flatfile formats.

Table 15-8.   Parse Properties for EDI Format Fields

For records and the root node there is a different set of parse properties, as shown in Table 15-9.

Property	Value
Structure	This value is always Delimited for X12 and UN/EDIFACT.
Source Tag Identifier	This value is the name of the source tag identifier. This is the segment name as it appears in the UN/EDIFACT or X12 stream and that is used to match the record with the data. The Source Tag Identifier property is case sensitive.
Field Order	This value is Infix for EDI compound values and Prefix for EDI segments. The Field Order property describes the relationship between fields and their delimiters. If the delimiter is the plus sign (+), the prefix order is +a+b+c, the infix order is a+b+c, and the suffix order is a+b+c+. For segment records, the field order is always prefix because the segment identifier (source tag identifier) is not considered part of the physical record; hence, the first field follows a delimiter.
Delimiter Type	The options that you can select here allow you to specify the relationship between a record and its child records. If you create a loop, the segments on the following level are delimited by the default record delimiter; if the child element is a group of fields, the delimiter is the default field delimiter. When you have a compound type as child, the delimiter is the default subfield delimiter.
Escape Type	Not applicable for EDI.
Append New Line	Yes. Indicates that when the serializer reaches the record delimiter, the serializer automatically appends a new line (LF,0x0A). No. Indicates that when the serializer reaches the record delimiter, the serializer continues on the same line for the following record. (default)
Skip Carriage Return	Yes. Tells the parser to skip the carriage return (CR) value after a delimiter. (default) No. Tells the parser not to skip the CR value after a delimiter.

Table 15-9.   Parse Properties for EDI Format Records

Property	Value
Skip Line Feed	Yes. Tells the parser to skip the linefeed (LF) value after a delimiter. (default) No. Tells the parser not to skip the LF value after a delimiter.
Ignore Record Count	Yes. Tells the parser or the serializer not to count this record when counting the total number of records in the specification. No. Tells the parser or the serializer to count this record when counting the total number of records in the specification. (default)

Table 15-9.   Parse Properties for EDI Format Records *(continued)*

To make the task a bit more bearable when you have to create UN/EDIFACT specifications from scratch, you should look at the existing templates and pick the one that is closest to what you need. The tree view allows for drag-and-drop rearrangement of records and fields, which may make your life quite a bit easier. In this case, the clipboard is also your best friend. While BizTalk does indeed ship with only less than a tenth of the messages available for each UN/EDIFACT standards release, you may be able to copy and paste the segments from the existing ones to implement another message. In this respect, UN/EDIFACT is great because, for instance, the name-and-address (NAD) segment will be identical wherever it occurs.

As a rule-of-thumb, you should aim to copy and adopt as many segment specifications as you can and define new segments only if you really need to. Another important rule is, of course, not to mix between standards releases. If the message that you need exists in the S98A release but not in S95A, and you need the message of S95A, the newer standards release is taboo. When you need to create new segment definitions, create a master document specification to which you copy all segments and that you can later use as a clipboard repository.

Unfortunately, BizTalk Editor will not let you associate the UN/EDIFACT code lists with your own segment declarations. If you want to create segments with code-list support, you need to be brave and manipulate your specification with Notepad or another text editor. If you open the BizTalk Schema file with a text editor, you will find a <b:FieldInfo ... /> element for each field. If you want to associate a code list with the field, you need to manually insert an attribute like codelist="2379" into this element. The number of the code-list reference is equivalent to the number found in the UN/EDIFACT segment or compound value directories.

The code-list content is stored in an Access 2000 database, which is located in the XML Tools\Databases\CodeLists subdirectory and is called CodeListsX12a.mdb. Do not let the name fool you; it also contains the UN/EDIFACT code lists. BizTalk Editor selects the code-list values from the table named <standard>_<version>. If the document has the Standard property set to UN/EDIFACT and the Standards Version is set to d98a, the code lists will be loaded from the EDIFACT_d98a table. The codelist attribute value from the FieldInfo is used as a filter on the table to find out the correct value/description pairs.

So if you need to add code lists or make changes to the lists, this database is where you should look—solely at your own risk because these attributes are undocumented and therefore, probably subject to change in a future revision of BizTalk.

DEFINING FLATFILE DOCUMENTS

BizTalk also includes a serializer and a formatter for flatfiles. BizTalk's concept of flatfiles is that they are plain-text data streams with delimiters separating records and fields or that they are positional with fixed field lengths. In principle, flatfiles that can be handled by the parsers must conform to some minimum structural requirements for how records and fields must be laid out; very simple text streams that have one record per line with the fields separated by commas (comma separated values) are not immediately supported by the flatfile parser.

Listing 15-1 shows a sample delimited data stream that is supported by the flatfile parser. The format and data are entirely arbitrary and serve only for the purpose of this demonstration.

```
HDR,10,Data1,56,2001-01-01,29
DAT,Data2,Data3,This is some explanatory text
TXT,"This is text, which has a comma"
TXT,"This is some other text"
```

Listing 15-1: Delimited flatfile stream

The same expression in a purely positional format can take on the form shown in Listing 15-2.

```
HDR0010Data1         00562001010129
DATData2        Data3   This is some explanatory text
TXTThis is text, which has a comma
TXTThis is some other text
```

Listing 15-2: Positional flatfile stream

The complexity of creating a working specification for a flatfile data stream depends entirely on the cleanliness of the syntax definition. When you attempt to parse files like a SWIFT data stream, which is basically positional but sometimes also delimited, you will be busy for a while until you find that you just cannot do it with the flatfile parser at all.

If you have clean data streams like the two shown in Listings 15-1 and 15-2, the definition process is really straightforward.

Defining Delimited Flatfile Streams

First we are going to create a specification for the stream shown in Listing 15-1. You begin creating document specifications for delimited flatfile streams by selecting the blank specification template. The root element of the specification can be arbitrarily renamed, but just as you have seen with the UN/EDIFACT specifications, the root element name should be some meaningful representation of the document type. For our example, we will simply rename the root node to delimited_sample.

Much more important than the tag name of the root element are its properties. The first task is to switch BizTalk Editor into the appropriate mode for flatfiles. To do this, set the Standard property to CUSTOM on the Reference tab. When you switch between standards, a box appears with this message: "Changing the standard property might cause some properties to be cleared. Are you sure you want to continue?" You are; click Yes.

Switching the document standard to CUSTOM causes a set of properties to be displayed on the Reference and Parse tabs that closely resemble those available for UN/EDIFACT and X12 at first, but they are still a bit different.

On the Reference tab of the root node, you first need to specify the delimiter characters that documents that are compliant with the specification use by default. If different delimiters are used for a certain record or field, these can be overridden in the record or field's definition.

If you look at Listing 15-1, you will find that the delimiter should be set as follows:

Default Record Delimiter	Carriage Return (CR) 0x0d
Default Field Delimiter	Comma (",") 0x2c
Default Subfield Delimiter	N/A, set to Colon (":") 0x3a
Default Escape Character	N/A, set to Backslash ("\") 0x5c

The next setting is the Code Page property. For this example, assume that the data stream is using the Western European character set, code 1252. You should therefore choose the appropriate option from the code pages list.

Now switch to the Parse tab. Here you will define the basic settings that allow the parser to recognize the data stream correctly and split it into records. In our example, the records are separated by a CR-LF character sequence (hard line break). On the record level, we have a delimited format. Therefore, you should set the Structure property to Delimited. The last line of every file must also be terminated with a CR-LF sequence; thus, you should set the Field Order property to Postfix.

The delimiters that you define in the parse properties of the root node are those that separate the individual records in the file. Because we have already set the defaults appropriately, we want the Delimiter Type to be the Default Record Delimiter and the Escape Type to be the Default Escape Character. If you choose the defaults, the Delimiter Value and Escape

Character cannot be set. If you choose the Character delimiter type for either of the two options, you could override the default settings by entering a special character here.

Because the default delimiter character for records is a simple carriage return (CR), the serializer needs to be forced to emit a linefeed character (LF) after each record. You achieve this by setting the Append Newline property to Yes. When the file is being parsed, this extra linefeed must be ignored. Thus, set the Skip Line Feed property to Yes, and the parser will do so. Because the carriage return is significant in our case, the Skip Carriage Return property must be set to No.

Defining Records

As you can easily tell from the sample stream, you need to add three records to the root node: HDR, DAT, and TXT. Set the cardinality of the HDR and DAT records to exactly once (minimum occurrences 1, maximum occurrences 1) and the TXT record to at least once (1,*).

The parser configuration of all records is the same, so we will configure only the HDR record as an example. The structure of the records—that is, how the fields are separated—is delimited, of course ; thus, you set the Structure property to reflect this.

The Source Tag Identifier property is the expression by which the parser identifies the record type within the stream. For the format that we have at hand, this is the record name, and thus, HDR. Because the first value is separated from the record name by a comma, but the Source Tag Identifier property is not considered part of the record, the parser views the first field as having a leading comma; thus, you must set the Field Order property to Prefix.

Because we defined the Delimiter Type property in the global settings, it is the default field delimiter. You should leave the Escape Type property at the default setting. All other properties should also be left at their defaults except Skip Carriage Return and Skip Line Feed, which must both be set to No at the record level for this particular format because CR/LF handling is done at the file level.

Defining Fields

Because we have a very generic sample without any deeper meaning, we will keep the field names simple. The HDR record has five fields—Number1, Data1, Number2, Date1, and Number3—which need to be defined in this exact order.

The data types can be derived from the field names. They are Number for the NumberX fields, String for the Data1 field, and Date for the Date1 field. On the Parse tab, set the Custom Data Type property choices accordingly. A special case is the Date1 field, where you also need to select a Custom Date/Time Format. Set this value to YYYY-MM-DD.

The fields for the DAT record should be easy to set; only the single data field of the TXT record needs extra configuration. For this field, you set the Wrap Character value to double quotes (") because this character surrounds a single line, and it would otherwise be split in two by the comma embedded in the string.

When you have specified all settings as described, the data stream should validate correctly.

Defining Positional Flatfile Streams

The second flatfile stream that is shown in Listing 15-2 is a positional stream. More precisely, it is a mix between a delimited and positional stream because the line breaks still act as delimiters between records in this case, and only the individual records are positional. Therefore, the root and record level for both formats are essentially identical, and you must set the Structure property on the root element to Delimited.

The record level is different. When you set the record structure to Positional, each field will have two special properties on its Reference tab where you can enter the start and end position relative to the beginning of the record (including the source tag identifier). Counting begins at 1. If a field is exactly one character long, the start and end positions are identical.

The Pad Character is used to fill up unused space when data is serialized and is eliminated from the data when parsing. The Justification property tells where padding will be used and how the data is aligned within the allocated space. If Justification is set to Right, the data is aligned on the right side of the space between the start and end positions and padding fills up the space from the left.

In Listing 15-2, the data content of the positional data stream is identical to the delimited example; now you should be able to create a matching specification all by yourself.

CHAPTER 16

Mapping Documents

This chapter explores basic mapping tasks and includes a few brief examples of how to write custom functoid scripts. You will learn how to use BizTalk Mapper to perform mapping tasks. Specifically, you will create a mapping between the UN/EDIFACT ORDERS S93A specification and the PurchaseOrder XML specification, which were both defined by using BizTalk Editor in the previous chapter. Furthermore, we will discuss a few special problems when mapping from the InternalInvoice XML specification to the INVOIC UN/EDIFACT message, as well as when mapping from the PurchaseOrderAcknowledgment specification to the ORDRSP message.

BIZTALK MAPPER

Not all schemas are created equal. When you exchange data with many partners and you are not in a position to dictate all document standards and schemas to use, you will often have to create and understand documents based on many different schemas for a single business transaction type. For instance, if your company is a trading house that acquires goods from many large companies, your purchase orders must be sent in many different formats. Conversely, if you are a supplier to multiple large corporations, you will have to accept purchase orders in various formats, most likely one specific format per customer.

In your own organization, purchase orders are likely to be represented in one generic format that is understood by your internal applications. The task of BizTalk Mapper (see Figure 16-1) is to generate maps that produce the individually formatted data streams for each partner from this generic document type, or to map inbound data streams accordingly.

The "maps" that the Mapper produces are XSLT transformation style sheets. When BizTalk's Messaging services perform document transformations, they run a channel's inbound document through the style sheet to produce the outbound document. This is possible because inside the document-processing pipeline, all documents, regardless of their native format, are represented as XML.

BizTalk Mapper is unique because it hides the complexity of the XSLT language behind an intuitive user interface that employs the drag-and-drop paradigm. However, because complex tasks always require complex solutions, handling a few of the advanced tasks is tricky at first. But once you get the hang of it, the Mapper is a great tool whose vision and implementation deserve a lot of respect.

NOTE: Although you can actually cheat around the Mapper by implementing your own style sheets and masquerading them as if they were created by BizTalk Mapper (as mentioned in Chapter 11), there is little reason to do so. The Mapper can implement almost any style sheet.

MAPPING FUNDAMENTALS

Document maps are created on the basis of BizTalk Schema. Therefore, both the source and the destination document structure must be entirely defined (and be definable) in that format.

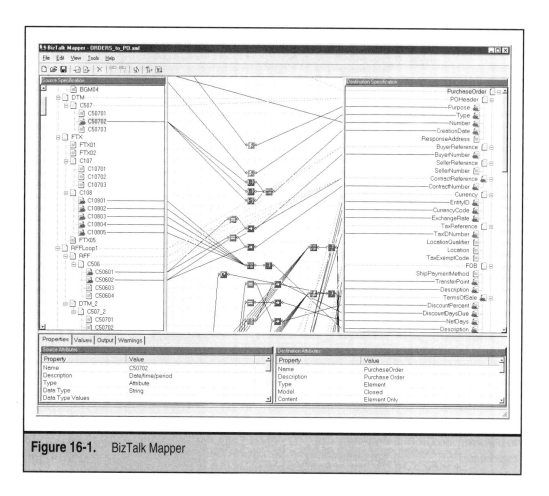

Figure 16-1.   BizTalk Mapper

This requirement practically excludes one of the popular uses of XSLT, which is mapping XML data to HTML documents or other text-based presentation formats. Even if you really wanted to describe an HTML document in Schema, doing so would at least require the use of XHTML, a reformulation of HTML in XML that is still unsupported by most browsers. For this reason, BizTalk document maps are really limited to clean, raw data mappings between specifications. If you want to produce XSLT style sheets that perform such conversions, you need to use another tool.

To begin creating a new document map, select File | New. A sequence of four dialog boxes follows.

In the Select Source Specification Type dialog box shown in Figure 16-2, you choose from which location you want to retrieve the source specification BizTalk Schema. The options are to pick a file from the local files system, to choose one of the predefined BizTalk templates, or to retrieve the specification from a WebDAV repository.

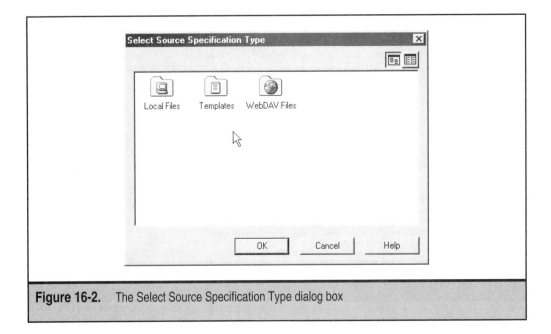

Figure 16-2. The Select Source Specification Type dialog box

When you select Local Files, the current dialog box closes and the Select Source Specification window opens, as shown in Figure 16-3, in which you can seek and select a BizTalk document specification from the local (or network) file system.

Selecting Templates in the Select Source Specification Type dialog box opens the Select Source Specification dialog box, as shown in Figure 16-4—the same dialog box that opens when you select File | New in BizTalk Editor, except that the Blank Specification selection is unavailable here.

Finally, when you select WebDAV Files in the Select Source Specification Type dialog box, the Retrieve Source Specification dialog box opens, which you also use with BizTalk Editor to retrieve a specification from the WebDAV repository. (See Figure 16-5.)

Once you select a source specification by using one of these dialog boxes, you will be asked to open the destination specification, for which the same dialog boxes will be presented. The only difference is the titles (Select Destination Specification). If you click Cancel any time in the sequence of the four dialog boxes, the entire command is cancelled.

For the source specification, you should find and load the ORDERS specification that you created in the last chapter. (And if you have not done so, this is a really good time to do it.) The destination specification should be the PurchaseOrder.xml specification that you have created (or at least can create) by using the instructions in the "Defining XML Documents" portion in Chapter 15.

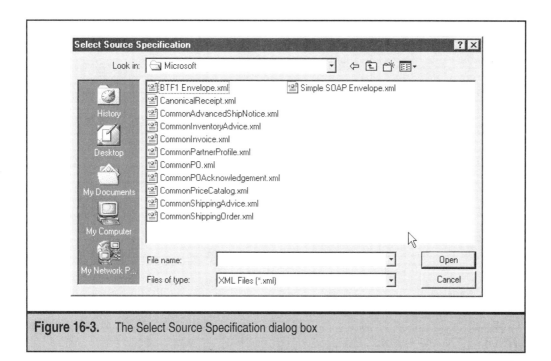

Figure 16-3. The Select Source Specification dialog box

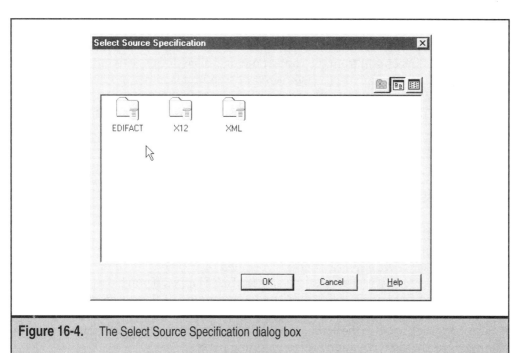

Figure 16-4. The Select Source Specification dialog box

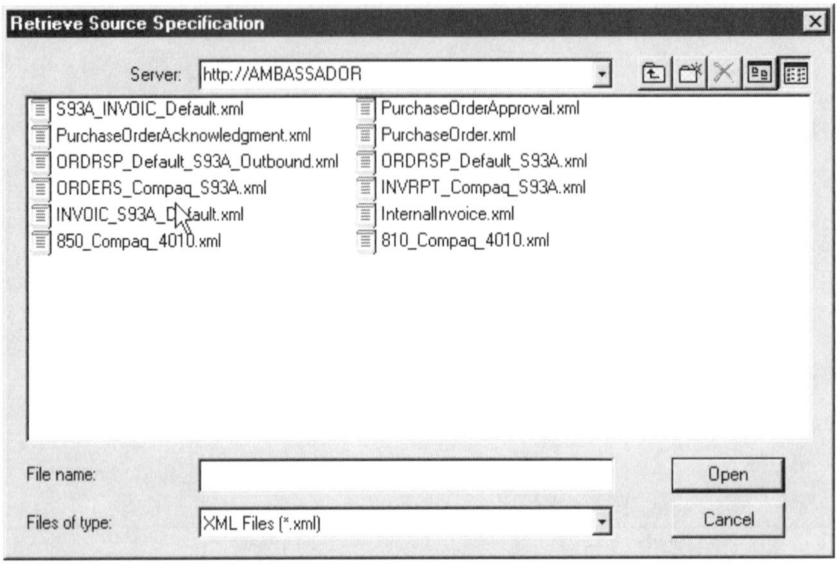

Figure 16-5. The Retrieve Source Specification dialog box

Once both specifications are loaded, right-click each one's root node and select the Expand Tree Items option from the context menu. This will fully expand the document hierarchy for both documents. (For some reason and under some circumstances—call it a bug—you may have to select Collapse Tree Items first before Expand Tree Items works as described.) What you see on your screen should be identical to the window shown in Figure 16-6.

Before we proceed, though, you must understand a few basic principles of how mapping works.

Mapping Fields

If you have a clear one-to-one correspondence between a field in the source specification and a field in the destination specification, you can simply connect them by dragging a link from either field to the respective other field, just like you would move a directory between two Windows Explorer folders. Document mapping is mouse-centric. You will collect quite a few extra mouse miles by using BizTalk Mapper. If you have problems using the mouse, your only other option is to use the Windows 2000 MouseKeys accessibility option, which you can enable by using the Accessibility Options program in Control Panel (on the Mouse tab in the Settings dialog box), because the Mapper itself provides no alternative keyboard navigation for the mapping process.

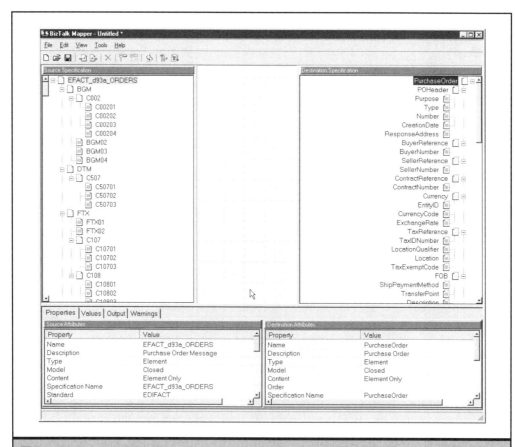

Figure 16-6.   A BizTalk Mapper window—the start view of mapping ORDERS to PurchaseOrders

NOTE: It is nearly impossible to memorize all the details of fairly complex document specifications. Therefore, at the bottom of the BizTalk Mapper window, on the Properties tab, you will always see a consolidated view of all specification properties for the selected entries in either specification's tree view.

When you are about to start the mapping process, you may think that direct one-to-one matches between records and fields in two different specifications that deal with the same topic—two purchase-order specifications in this case—should be easy to find, and that there should actually be plenty of fields that correspond directly. In reality, and this is an experience that you will have virtually every time you create document maps, two fields that are identical both in terms of data definition and semantics are quite rare, especially when you map between different document standards. The more common cases are fields that have identical semantics but differ slightly in their data definition and constraints. The typical differences are variations of the minimum and maximum field lengths and discrepancies in data-type use.

Unless you want to create some sophisticated data-type checks and conversions by using the provided functoids or custom scripts for each field, creating direct links between fields of different lengths is always a gamble. Doing so depends on the actual interchange data that is transformed by using the document map. For instance, if the UN/EDIFACT standard allows one to three characters for the country code in the address portion of the name-and-address NAD segment, but only two-letter country codes are used in practice—and this agreement is unanimous with your partners—you can quite safely map the field to the /BillTo/Address/@Country field of the PurchaseOrder XML specification, although this mandates a maximum of two characters.

Another concern is the use of incompatible data types. While the restricted type system of the UN/EDIFACT and X12 standards essentially limits numeric expressions to one or two types (integer and decimal types), your options in XML are very broad. XML provides the full range of data types available in common programming languages, which is very convenient and powerful for producing documents from and reading them into applications. The important issue to be aware of in this context is that all XSLT mapping occurs only through text representations of data. On the XML text level, there is no visible difference between a double-precision IEEE floating-point number and a high-precision currency (or decimal) type that could adversely affect mapping, unless the IEEE Double type field in the source document used exponential notation for its text representation (1.2662E+15). This is rather unlikely in business documents.

The risks are similar to those of incompatible text field lengths. When you map a Number type field from an X12 specification to a Byte type field in XML, the chances of running into range overflow exceptions in the validation stage of the XML document are very real. However, even this depends entirely on the purpose and usage profile of the source field. Mapping any arbitrary data type to a string is always safe, given that the maximum length of the target field can hold the complete string representation of the value.

By default, the Mapper opens a warning message box that informs you of such incompatibilities when you create a potentially problematic link, if such links may result in problems at run time. If both fields are of type String, the length constraints for the source field are 1 to 60, and the length constraints for the destination field are 1 to 80, there will be no data loss; thus, there is no need for a warning. If the field configuration is the other way around, the Mapper will show a message box telling you that the mapping may result in a loss of data.

If the minimum size of the source is less than that of the destination, the Mapper will display an additional warning that telling you that documents produced by this mapping may result in validation errors of the destination document, while the validation of the inbound document will pass correctly. And, of course, incompatible data types will also trigger a warning message box.

If you are getting annoyed by the warning message boxes, you can switch them off by clearing the check mark from the Warnings For Simple Linking Errors check box in the Options dialog box (Figure 16-7). To open this dialog box, select Tools | Options. However,

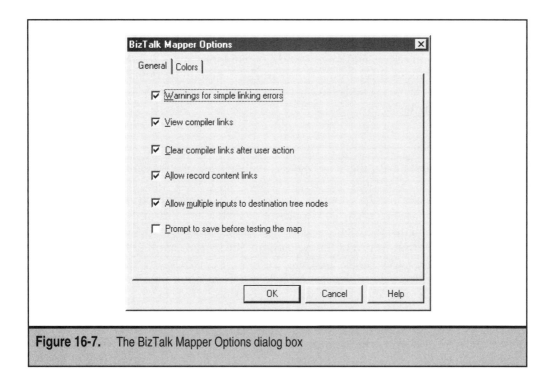

Figure 16-7. The BizTalk Mapper Options dialog box

even if you have a long series of fields that you need to map and you really become annoyed by acknowledging the warnings, you should still leave this check box checked because sometimes, you simply expect types to be compatible. The extra yellow flag that the Mapper throws on the field will be a useful reminder to compare the field properties and make a conscious decision about what you are doing.

The other options available in this dialog box are the following:

▼ **View Compiler Links**   Displays compiler-generated (read: tool-generated) links between records if selected.

■ **Clear Compiler Links After User Action**   Causes the compiler links to be hidden whenever a new manual link is created (this is an "avoiding confusion" option).

■ **Allow Record Content Links**   Allows links to and from record nodes.

■ **Allow Multiple Inputs To Destination Tree Nodes**   Allows multiple input links from the source tree. This is required for mapping from more complex to less complex structures.

▲ **Prompt To Save Before Testing The Map**   Asks you to save the map to a file before testing it.

To implement the solution explained in the following discussion, and essentially for every other complex document map as well, you should access the BizTalk Mapper Options dialog box again and select the Allow Record Content Links and Allow Multiple Inputs To Destination Tree Nodes check boxes, which are switched off by default. This will allow you to create links to record nodes in the target specification, which is required for some advanced mapping tasks.

Mapping Records

When you create field mappings, the Mapper will make a qualified guess about the relationship of the fields' container records and create implicit compiler links whenever the map is compiled (select Tools | Compile Map). These links are shown as thin, dotted lines that connect the related records. The existence of such a link indicates that if a record is found in a document instance of the source type, the document map will always produce a corresponding output record of the type pointed to by the compiler link, regardless of whether any of the subordinate field mappings will produce any results. Because all these links are created behind the scenes, deleting them is not possible. These compiler links are visible only if the View Compiler Links check box is selected in the BizTalk Mapper Options dialog box.

There are two basic problems with the implicitly created compiler links, which by default assume a flat one-to-one correspondence between source and destination records.

If the complexity of the source specification is higher and has more levels of nested records than the destination specification, or vice versa, the automatic compiler links may not produce the results you want. The predefined behavior for each explicit, user-defined link is to flatten links. The effect of this is shown in Figure 16-8. If fields are mapped from a more complex to a less complex structure, the default causes the source structure to be flattened (nested records look like a single, combined record) and mapped to the immediate container of the target field.

You can control how the Mapper creates the compiler links by providing certain hints on the field-mapping level. Each hard link that you create by directly connecting two fields has a set of properties that you can access by selecting the link (click the line), right-clicking it to bring up the context menu, and selecting Properties from the menu. The Compiler tab in the Link Properties dialog box gives you these options: Flatten Links, Match Links Top-Down, or Match Links Bottom-Up.

Generally speaking, the effect of all of these settings is that for each occurrence of a record in a source document, an instance of the target record pointed to by the compiler link is produced. If multiple compiler links point to the same destination record, the number of records produced is a logical AND product of the source records: one record is produced for each occurrence of all records.

When the structure is flattened, the compiler creates a single destination record for each container node tree of a source field. In the example shown in Figure 16-8, the link that connects the fields is contained in a nested hierarchy of records. Flattening results in the entire tree above the source field being treated as if it were indeed a single record.

When links are matched bottom up as shown in Figure 16-9, the record matches are cascaded above the source field. This means that the immediate parent record of the source field is matched against the parent of the target record, their respective parents are matched, and so on. So the parent records of the fields are matched bottom-to-top.

Matching links top down as shown in Figure 16-10 is the exact opposite. In this case, the entire parent hierarchy of the parent records is traversed from the root, and records are matched level by level until one of the container nodes is reached.

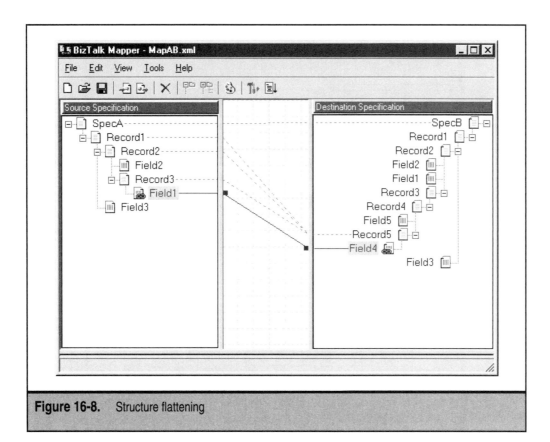

Figure 16-8. Structure flattening

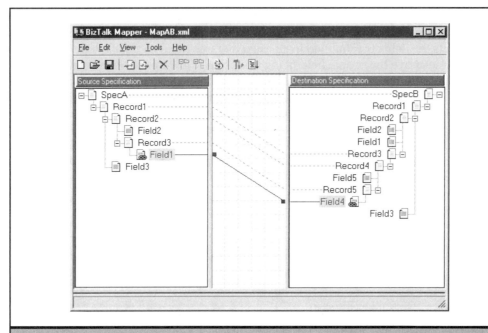

Figure 16-9. Matching links bottom up

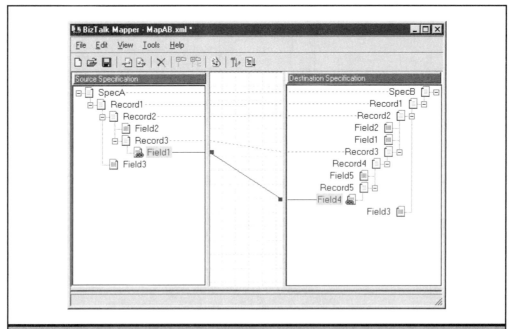

Figure 16-10. Matching links top down

The effects of the three different options will hopefully become clearer when you look at the three XSL style sheets that are produced when the same map is compiled with different settings. The style sheet for structure-flattening looks as follows:

```
<xsl:stylesheet xmlns:xsl='http://www.w3.org/1999/XSL/Transform'
                xmlns:msxsl='urn:schemas-microsoft-com:xslt' xmlns:var='urn:var'
                xmlns:user='urn:user' exclude-result-prefixes='msxsl var user'
                version='1.0'>
<xsl:output method='xml' omit-xml-declaration='yes' />
<xsl:template match='/'>
   <xsl:apply-templates select='SpecA'/>
</xsl:template>
<xsl:template match='SpecA'>
<SpecB>
   <Record1>
      <Record2>
         <Record3>
            <Record4>
               <xsl:for-each select='Record1'>
                  <xsl:for-each select='Record2'>
                     <xsl:for-each select='Record3'>
                        <Record5>
                           <!-- Connection from source node "Field1" to
                                destination node "Field4" -->
                           <Field4><xsl:value-of select='Field1/text()'/></Field4>
                        </Record5>
                     </xsl:for-each>
                  </xsl:for-each>
               </xsl:for-each>
            </Record4>
         </Record3>
      </Record2>
   </Record1>
</SpecB>
</xsl:template>
</xsl:stylesheet>
```

The Flatten option always generates the Record1, Record2, Record3, and Record4 element in the output, and only the output of Record5 and its contained field will be conditional. The top-down mapping produces the following output:

```
<xsl:stylesheet xmlns:xsl='http://www.w3.org/1999/XSL/Transform'
                xmlns:msxsl='urn:schemas-microsoft-com:xslt' xmlns:var='urn:var'
                xmlns:user='urn:user' exclude-result-prefixes='msxsl var user'
                version='1.0'>
<xsl:output method='xml' omit-xml-declaration='yes' />
<xsl:template match='/'>
   <xsl:apply-templates select='SpecA'/>
</xsl:template>
<xsl:template match='SpecA'>
```

```
<SpecB>
   <xsl:for-each select='Record1'>
      <Record1>
         <xsl:for-each select='Record2'>
            <Record2>
               <xsl:for-each select='Record3'>
                  <Record3>
                     <Record4>
                        <Record5>
                           <!-- Connection from source node "Field1" to
                                destination node "Field4" -->
                           <Field4><xsl:value-of select='Field1/text()'/></Field4>
                        </Record5>
                     </Record4>
                  </Record3>
               </xsl:for-each>
            </Record2>
         </xsl:for-each>
      </Record1>
   </xsl:for-each>
</SpecB>
</xsl:template>
</xsl:stylesheet>
```

Top-down mapping matches record by record from the top. Record1 in the target is produced only if a Record1 exists in the target. The whole structure is essentially matched from the topmost (outermost) element down. By now, you may be able to guess what the result from bottom-up mapping looks like:

```
<xsl:stylesheet xmlns:xsl='http://www.w3.org/1999/XSL/Transform'
                xmlns:msxsl='urn:schemas-microsoft-com:xslt' xmlns:var='urn:var'
                xmlns:user='urn:user' exclude-result-prefixes='msxsl var user'
                version='1.0'>
<xsl:output method='xml' omit-xml-declaration='yes' />
<xsl:template match='/'>
   <xsl:apply-templates select='SpecA'/>
</xsl:template>
<xsl:template match='SpecA'>
<SpecB>
   <Record1>
      <Record2>
         <xsl:for-each select='Record1'>
            <Record3>
               <xsl:for-each select='Record2'>
                  <Record4>
                     <xsl:for-each select='Record3'>
                        <Record5>
                           <!-- Connection from source node "Field1" to
                                destination node "Field4" -->
                           <Field4><xsl:value-of select='Field1/text()'/></Field4>
```

```
                    </Record5>
                 </xsl:for-each>
               </Record4>
             </xsl:for-each>
           </Record3>
         </xsl:for-each>
       </Record2>
     </Record1>
  </SpecB>
  </xsl:template>
  </xsl:stylesheet>
```

In this case, the structure is matched beginning at the innermost element of the mapping operation (the field), and the structure is matched level by level from the bottom up. By doing this, each Record3 of the input specification yields an output Record5, each input Record2 yields an output Record4, and Record1 from the input maps to Record3. Because the input specification is less complex than the output specification, the outermost target records Record1 and Record2 are always produced for any input document.

If the shape of certain sections of the two document specifications is very different, the automatic compiler links, even in conjunction with the compiler hints, still may not produce the desired results, though. In this case, you can explicitly control how the output records are produced by associating the target record node with a "true" or "false" Boolean value. (This requires enabling the Allow Record Content Links check box in the BizTalk Mapper Options dialog box.) If the value is "false," the record is created; otherwise, the record and all subordinate mappings are entirely ignored.

From where do you get this "true" or "false" value? From functoids!

Understanding Functoids

A lot of the data that you need to map is not compatible. The document specifications and the document structure may differ so vastly that field mapping and tweaking the compiler behavior—even when being very tolerant about potential conversion and validation errors—does not solve the problem. For all of these cases, the BizTalk Mapper provides functoids.

Functoids are little functions that are either written in VBScript or are custom XSLT expressions. You can place functoids on the mapping grid by dragging them from the Functoid Palette window, which you open by selecting View | Functoid Palette.

A functoid takes one or more nodes from the source specification as input arguments, and the result can be mapped to one of the destination nodes. It is also possible—and for some functoids, even the only meaningful use—to connect functoids to functoids. Some of the advanced functoids, for instance, need to be fed with Boolean expressions that are produced by one of the logical functoids. Functoid arguments can also be constant values, which you can set on the General tab in the Functoid Properties dialog box, as shown in Figure 16-11.

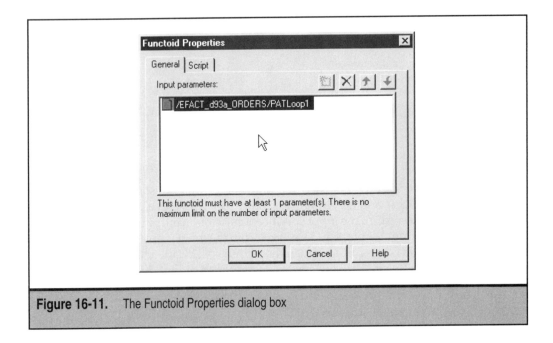

Figure 16-11. The Functoid Properties dialog box

So if the source specification had two nodes A and B, and the destination had node C, you could connect A and B to an Addition functoid and connect the functoid to the destination node. When the transformation is done, C would then receive the result of the numerical addition of the values of A and B, as shown in Figure 16-12.

BizTalk comes with over 60 canned functoids, which are listed in the following tables. If these functoids do not provide what you need, you can write your own scripts and even bundle them into a custom functoid library, which you can then plug into BizTalk Mapper.

You should not expect all of the functoids to be useful for your purposes. In fact, quite a few functoids apparently exist more for completeness than for any meaningful function. The trigonometric math functions, for example, can be assumed to appear only rarely in real-life document maps, and even then, only in technical or scientific contexts.

The string functoids, listed in Table 16-1, are very important when you need to map between string fields with differing field constraints and you want to avoid validation errors in the destination document—for instance, if the input data exceeds the maximum field length of the destination field. By default, mapping produces a verbatim value copy from source to destination. To make sure that the document mapping succeeds in any event, you may want to truncate the input string from the left, being well aware, of course, that you may lose data in the process.

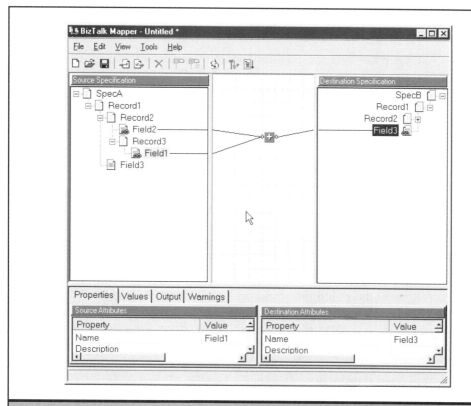

Figure 16-12. A simple functoid mapping

Symbol	Functoid	Arguments
	String Find Returns the position in a string at which a substring begins	First linked item or constant: String to be searched Second linked item or constant: Find pattern Result: Position of the first occurrence of the find pattern in the string to be searched Zero if not found

Table 16-1. String Functoid

Symbol	Functoid	Arguments
	Uppercase Converts a text item to uppercase characters	Linked item or constant: String to be converted Result: Input string converted to uppercase
	Lowercase Converts a text item to lowercase characters	Linked item or constant: String to be converted Result: Input string converted to lowercase
	String Left Returns the leftmost portion of a string, up to a given number of characters long	First linked item or constant: Input string Second linked item or constant: Number of characters Result: Left part of the string with at most the given number of characters
	String Right Returns the rightmost portion of a string, up to a given number of characters long	First linked item or constant: Input string Second linked item or constant: Number of characters Result: Right part of the string with at most the given number of characters
	String Length Returns the size of the input string	First linked item or constant: Input string Result: Length
	String Extract Extracts a string specified by the start and end positions of the input string	First linked item or constant: Input string Second linked item or constant: Start position Third linked item or constant: End position Result: Extracted string
	Concatenate Concatenates a series of input strings	May have an arbitrary number of input arguments and input constants Result: Concatenation of all input strings
	String Left Trim Removes leading spaces from a string	First linked item or constant: Input string Result: Trimmed string
	String Right Trim Removes trailing spaces from a string	First linked item or constant: Input string Result: Trimmed string

Table 16-1.   String Functoid *(continued)*

Some output formats, especially some older flatfile data formats, allow only capital letters to be used for string data; thus, you will have to use the Uppercase functoid to properly convert the data before it is placed into the destination stream. We will use the string functoids to convert a UN/EDIFACT date expression into the appropriate ISO8601 format for XML in Chapter 24.

Obviously, the mathematical functoids, listed in Table 16-2, are useful for consolidating or splitting numeric expressions in the transformation process. In the European Euro zone, in the current transition process between the local currencies and the common single Euro currency, currency values in the input document may be expressed in a local

Symbol	Functoid	Parameters
	Absolute Value Returns the absolute value of a number	First linked item or constant: Input value Result: f(-4) = 4; f(4) = 4
	Integer Returns the integer portion of a number	First linked item or constant: Input value Result: f(10.127) = 10; f(6) = 6
	Maximum Value Returns the maximum value from a series of numeric values	Arbitrary number of linked items or constants: Input values Result: f(1,2,3,4,5) = 5
	Minimum Value Returns the minimum value from a series of numeric values	Arbitrary number of linked items or constants: Input values Result: f(1,2,3,4,5) = 1
	Modulo Returns the remainder after the number is divided by an integer	First linked item or constant: Dividend Second linked item or constant: Divisor Result: f(8,3) = 2; f(9,2) = 1
	Round Rounds a number to a specified number of decimal places or to a whole number if no decimal places are specified	First linked item or constant: Input value Second linked item or constant: Number of decimal places Result: f(10.127,2) = 10.12; f(10.127,0) = 10

Table 16-2.   Mathematical Functoids

Symbol	Functoid	Parameters
	Square Root Returns the square root of a number	First linked item or constant: Input value Result: f(9)=3; f(2)=1.4142…
	Addition Calculates the sum of a series of numbers	Arbitrary number of linked items or constants: Input values Result: f(1,2,3,4,5) = 15
	Subtraction Subtracts a series of numbers from a base number	First linked item or constant: Input base value Additional, arbitrary number of linked items or constants: Subtraction values b f(1,2,3,4,5) = –13
	Multiplication Creates the product of a series of input numbers	Arbitrary number of linked items or constants: Input values Result: f(1,2,3,4,5) = 120
	Division Divides one number by another number	First linked item or constant: Dividend Second linked item or constant: Divisor Result: f(8,3) = 2.666… ; f(9,2) = 4.5

Table 16-2.   Mathematical Functoids *(continued)*

currency (like Deutsche Mark DEM), while the output fields will be expressed in Euro. The Multiplication functoid can therefore perform the fixed-rate conversion of DEM*1.95583. Outside the Euro zone where varying exchange rates apply, you will have to use the database functoids or custom scripts to achieve this.

If you provide invalid input values, causing division-by-zero errors, or if you try to calculate the square root of a negative number, the map will fail from a scripting error.

CAUTION: Generally, you should not move too much logic into your functoids because this may blur the boundaries between your application logic and scattered logic, which becomes buried somewhere in the document maps. Keep the expressions in the document maps as simple as possible.

All of the logical functoids (see Table 16-3) produce Boolean values as output. The most common uses for them are to make decisions about whether a destination record will be produced as indicated in the previous "Mapping Records" section. You can, for instance, compare a field value against a constant and assign that result to an output record node. If the comparison evaluates to "false," the output record is never produced (including any field mappings that it may have). The output of certain field values may also be controlled by such decisions. (This is done by using the Value Mapping functoid listed in Table 16-9.)

Symbol	Functoid	Parameters
	Greater Than Returns True if the first parameter is greater than the second parameter	First (#1) linked item or constant: Left argument Second (#2) linked item or constant: Right argument Result: True if (#1) > (#2)
	Greater Than or Equal To Returns True if the first parameter is greater than or equal to the second parameter	First (#1) linked item or constant: Left argument Second (#2) linked item or constant: Right argument Result: True if (#1) >= (#2)
	Less Than Returns True if the first parameter is less than the second parameter	First (#1) linked item or constant: Left argument Second (#2) linked item or constant: Right argument Result: True if (#1) < (#2)
	Less Than or Equal To Returns True if the first parameter is less than or equal to the second parameter	First (#1) linked item or constant: Left argument Second (#2) linked item or constant: Right argument Result: True if (#1) <= (#2)
	Equal Returns True if the first parameter is equal to the second parameter	First (#1) linked item or constant: Left argument Second (#2) linked item or constant: Right argument Result: True if (#1) = (#2)

Table 16-3.   Logical Functoids

Symbol	Functoid	Parameters
	Not Equal Returns True if the first parameter is not equal to the second parameter	First (#1) linked item or constant: Left argument Second (#2) linked item or constant: Right argument Result: True if (#1) <> (#2)
	Logical String Returns True if the parameter is a string value	First linked item or constant: Argument to be tested for string type
	Logical Date Returns True if the parameter is a date value	First linked item or constant: Argument to be tested for date type
	Logical Numeric Returns True if the parameter is a numeric value	First linked item or constant: Argument to be tested for numeric type
	Logical OR Returns the logical OR of parameters	Arbitrary number of linked items or constants: Input Boolean values Result: f(true,true,false) = True
	Logical AND Returns the logical AND of parameters	Arbitrary number of linked items or constants: Input Boolean values Result: f(true,true,false) = False

Table 16-3. Logical Functoids *(continued)*

The date functoids, listed in Table 16-4, give you access to the current date and time in the mapping process to produce time stamps and similar values in the output document or to allow comparisons of inbound data against *now*. The Add Days functoid allows a limited manipulation of data values by allowing you to add (and subtract) days from a given date value. Unfortunately, the built-in date functoids are ISO8601-only and understand and produce only the YYYY-MM-DD['T'HH:MM:SS] data format. This creates quite a few complications with the EDI formats, in which simple, positional formatting like YYYYMMDD is commonplace (or in fact the default, as with X12). Therefore, you cannot use the date functoids in conjunction with UN/EDIFACT and X12 unless you do some prior conversions of the date expression by using string functoids.

Symbol	Functoid	Parameters
	Add Days Adds a specified number of days to a date	First linked item or constant: Base date Second linked item or constant: Number of days to be added to the base date Result: Result date
	Date Returns the current date	Result: The current date expressed in ISO date format YYYY-MM-DD
	Time Returns the current time	Result: The current time expressed in ISO time format (24h) HH:MM:SS
	Date and Time Returns the date and time	Result: The current date and time expressed in ISO date/time format YYYY-MM-DD'T'HH:MM:SS

Table 16-4. Date Functoids

The conversion functoids (Table 16-5) could be a good place to search for the date conversion functoids and for the functoids that convert between the different data types.

Symbol	Functoid	Parameters
	ASCII from Character Returns an ASCII value when given a character	First linked item or constant: Single character value Result: The ASCII code (numeric value) that corresponds to the character (The term "ASCII" is entirely misplaced here, but it's the product terminology. Correct terminology would be "numeric character code.")
	Character from ASCII Returns a character when given an ASCII value	First linked item or constant: Numeric character code Result: The character that corresponds to the code in the character set

Table 16-5. Conversion Functoids

Symbol	Functoid	Parameters
	Hexadecimal Returns a hexadecimal value when given a decimal number	First linked item or constant: Numeric value Result: The input value converted into hexadecimal format
	Octal Returns an octal value when given a decimal number	First linked item or constant: Numeric value Result: The input value converted into octal format

Table 16-5. Conversion Functoids *(continued)*

However, the conversion functoids available here are quite limited. Still, when you use BizTalk for EAI, being able to produce hexadecimal numbers could prove to be very useful. Being able to convert them back would be, too, but that functionality is not available.

The scientific functoids, shown in Table 16-6, provide higher-math functions like trigonometry and logarithms. If you deal with technical documents, you may find a good use for some of these. For the typical business document, however, you can likely ignore them.

Symbol	Functoid	Parameters
	Arc Tangent Returns the arc tangent of a number	First linked item or constant: Numeric value (in radians) Result: The arc tangent of the input argument
	Cosine Returns the cosine of a number	First linked item or constant: Numeric value (in radians) Result: The cosine of the input argument
	Sine Returns the sine of a number	First linked item or constant: Numeric value (in radians) Result: The sine of the input argument
	Tangent Returns the tangent of a number	First linked item or constant: Numeric value (in radians) Result: The tangent of the input argument

Table 16-6. Scientific Functoids

Symbol	Functoid	Parameters
	Natural Exponential Function Returns e raised to a specified power	First linked item or constant: Numeric value (x) Result: e^x
	Natural Logarithm Returns the logarithm (base e) of a value	First linked item or constant: Numeric value (x) Result: ln(x)
	10^X Returns 10 raised to a specified power	First linked item or constant: Numeric value (x) Result: 10^x.
	Common Logarithm Returns the logarithm (base 10) of a value	First linked item or constant: Numeric value (x) Result: log x
	X^Y Returns a value raised to a specified power	First linked item or constant: Numeric value (x) First linked item or constant: Numeric value (y) Result: x^y
	Base-Specified Logarithm Returns the logarithm (base-specified) of a value	First linked item or constant: Numeric value (x) First linked item or constant: Numeric value (y) Result: logx y

Table 16-6. Scientific Functoids *(continued)*

The cumulative functoids, listed in Table 16-7, are very interesting when you need to consolidate verbose data into some brief structure. The most commonly used is the Cumulative Sum functoid, which can sum up values over a sequence of records.

The database functoids, shown in Table 16-8, allow you to perform database lookups in the transformation process. This feature is infinitely powerful and lures you into implementing huge data-bound document maps. You can even tap databases whenever the source document does not provide the data you need.

Symbol	Functoid	Parameters
	Cumulative Sum Sums all values for the connected field by iterating over its parent record	Linked item: Numeric Value Result: Sum of all occurrences of this particular field in the source document
	Cumulative Average Calculates the average of all values for the connected field by iterating over its parent record	Linked item: Numeric value Result: Average value of all occurrences of this particular field in the source document
	Cumulative Minimum Returns the minimum of input spanning over the parent record	Linked item: Numeric value Result: Smallest value in all occurrences of this particular field in the source document
	Cumulative Maximum Returns the maximum of input spanning over the parent record	Linked item: Numeric value Result: Largest value in all occurrences of this particular field in the source document
	Cumulative String Returns the concatenated string of the string values for the connected field by iterating over its parent record	Linked item: String value Result: combined string produced from all occurrences of this particular field in the source document

Table 16-7.   Cumulative Functoids

If the source document lacks information that you can retrieve at the time of document transformation, this could happen for one of two reasons:

▼   Your internal application does not provide enough data.

▲   The document comes from an external partner.

In the first case, it would be smart to tackle the problem at the source and modify your internal application so that the data supply is sufficient. In the second case, the data mapping serves to produce a document that you can submit to an internal application,

Symbol	Functoid	Parameters
	Database Lookup Compares a column in a database table against an input value and returns the matching row as an ADO Recordset	First linked item or constant: Value to compare Second argument: ADO connection string Third argument: Table name Fourth argument: Column name Result: ADO recordset Must be evaluated by using the Value Extractor functoid
	Value Extractor Extracts a value from a specific column of the first row of an ADO recordset that has been retrieved by the Database Lookup functoid	First argument: Link from Database Lookup functoid Second argument: Column name Result: Value of the column
	Error Return Returns the error string, if any, returned by ADO when using the Database Lookup functoid	First argument: Link from Database Lookup functoid Result: Error string

Table 16-8.   Database Functoids

and in that case, the application should be responsible for gathering the additional information. If a document map can do it, your line of business application can certainly do it, too. However, there are still some good reasons to use database lookups, and this is what you should focus on: mapping between code lists.

If you need to map between several document standards, you will also have to deal with a multitude of different code lists and key codes. For example, in telecommunications, some industries identify countries by their country code, other industries use three-letter codes, and yet other industries (including the Internet domain) use two-letter codes. When you have to deal with many standards, you can create auxiliary databases with tables that contain all these corresponding codes in a row for each country (or whatever other data element is described) and with which you can use a database functoid to correctly map between all these codes. You can also use the same technique to perform mappings between numerically encoded semantics, as they often exist in UN/EDIFACT, and their cleartext equivalents exist in your custom XML documents.

The Advanced Functoids tab in the Functoid Palette window should really be named "Important" functoids. These functoids, listed in Table 16-9, are the most essential when mapping between different structures.

Symbol	Functoid	Parameters
	Scripting Custom Visual Basic script	The number of input parameters for this functoid is configurable, based on a custom script.
	Record Count Returns a total count of the records found in the instance	This functoid must have one input parameter.
	Index Returns the value of a record or a field at a specified index	This functoid must have at least two input parameters. The maximum number of input parameters is limited by the number of levels in the specification hierarchy.
	Iteration Returns the iteration number (in a loop) of the source record	This functoid must have one input parameter.
	Value Mapping Returns the value of the second parameter if the value of the first parameter is "true"	This functoid must have two input parameters.
	Value Mapping (Flattening) Returns the value of the second parameter if the value of the first parameter is "true" and flattens the source document hierarchy	This functoid must have two input parameters.

Table 16-9. Advanced Functoids

Symbol	Functoid	Parameters
	Looping Creates multiple output records by grouping many input records into an iteration sequence and then producing one record for each item of the sequence	This functoid must have at least one input parameter. There is no maximum limit on the number of input parameters.

Table 16-9.   Advanced Functoids *(continued)*

The most versatile advanced functoid is the Scripting functoid. It lets you write your own little VBScript functions, which can do everything that VBScript can do anywhere else, but now it's in the context of a document map. This includes calls to external COM components. The database functoids are simply VBScripts that use ADO through COM.

But the Swiss army knife of the mapping functoids is the Looping functoid: it solves the majority of the most difficult problems that you face when you need to map between radically different schemas. The Looping functoid's functionality is quite simple: it produces one instance of the target record for each occurrence of a source record. This functionality lets you solve two basic scenarios.

First, it lets you reduce the complexity from the source to the target by grouping an entire subtree of a document hierarchy so that one target record will be produced for the entire group. If, for instance, two sibling records are mapped to a single destination record, the default behavior is that two instances of the destination record are created—one for every source record. However, if you connect the common parent record of the siblings to a Looping functoid and create a connection from the functoid to the target record, the Looping functoid produces only as many target records as there are parent records. This allows you to effectively flatten a complex source into a single record. Use this with caution, though. If one or both of the sibling records (or any of their children) inside the flattened group occurs more than once, the second and all additional occurrences will be ignored.

The second use is to map between differently shaped schemas with similar complexity (without losing data). If you have three sibling records A, B, and C in the source, which need to be mapped to a single destination record D, you can connect all three input records to a single Looping functoid. This causes a D record to be produced for each occurrence of either A, B, or C. Without the Looping functoid, the Mapper is not able to produce a correct result because you will have multiple source loops for a single input record, which results in unwanted interdependencies in the map. The Mapper has no other choice but to create a logical AND product of the three input records.

Therefore, a record is guaranteed to be produced only when all siblings appear together. Because the AND product is a result of hierarchical nesting, the output depends on the order in which records are connected, and may yield seemingly arbitrary results. The BizTalk documentation therefore states that multiple source loops are unsupported, and the Mapper will emit a warning message. The Looping functoid creates an entirely separate iteration loop for each bound input record, thereby eliminating these interdependencies.

MAPPING DOCUMENTS

TIP: All the document specifications, data streams, and also the maps from this book are available at http://www.osborne.com. Before continuing this section, it's a good idea to download at least the document specifications, because they will help you to understand the following discussion.

To proceed, you should be sitting at your computer, and the BizTalk Mapper application should look like it does in Figure 16-6; the UN/EDIFACT ORDERS specification is loaded as the source, and the XML PurchaseOrder specification is loaded as the destination for the document map.

The mapping task that we have before us is not trivial (unlike the typical examples); rather, it is quite realistic. The goal is to map an inbound purchase order that was sent to us in UN/EDIFACT format to the internal XML PurchaseOrder format without losing any (significant) information. To keep the explanation brief, all fields and records are referenced in the text with a simplified XPath notation.

The expression /PurchaseOrder/POHeader/@Purpose therefore refers to the *Purpose* attribute within the POHeader record of the PurchaseOrder specification.

The following explanation does not go from easy to difficult, but rather, from top to bottom, as the elements are encountered in the source specification. In the process, we will skip some of the input fields. Whenever we skip them, it's because the source value is typically technical and not relevant for the destination or simply not transmitted by the partner agreement.

/EFACT_d93a_ORDERS/BGM/C002/@C00201 to /PurchaseOrder/POHeader/@Purpose

The first field that we need to map is the "Document message name coded" field of the begin of message (BGM) segment. This field holds one of the values of the UN/EDIFACT 1001 data element code list, and—per our sample Compaq partner agreement, (see this book's web site at www.osborne.com)—is further restricted in use to codes 105 (purchase order) and 221 (blanket order).

The target specification field Purpose accepts two letter codes, and we assume here that some fictitious documentation defines the code for the purchase order as PO. And for a blanket order (a bulk allocation order with some details submitted separately), the code is BO.

You can perform such a mapping between two different code lists in two ways. You can use database functoids for this task, as previously discussed. But because the scope is really restricted to only a two-to-two mapping here, we will create a little custom script that will do the job instead. Select the Scripting functoid, drop it on the grid, and connect the two fields to the functoid. Then write the following code into the script field on the Script tab:

```
Function MapPOCode( strC00201 )
  Select Case strC00201
      Case "105"
          MapPOCode = "PO"
      Case "221"
          MapPOCode = "BO"
    Case Else
        MapPOCode = "XX"
    End Select
End Function
```

This little script will do what was just described, and if the input value is not what was expected (105 or 221), the output will be set to XX. When you have closed the dialog box, you should immediately proceed to test what you have just done. Testing such a function requires data. For testing purposes, you can therefore enter a source test value for the source node on the Values tab of the Mapper window. Enter either 105 or 221.

Now you can compile and test the map for the first time. The Mapper will complain quite a bit because you have not provided a whole lot of mappings for mandatory fields in the destination specification. Try it anyway. Select Tools | Test Map or press CTRL-T and accept all the following warnings. In the process, the Mapper will also prompt you to save the specification. If this annoys you (and it will!), you can switch this off in the BizTalk Mapper Options dialog box. The respective setting is Prompt To Save Before Testing The Map. Clear this check box.

After all this, you will be rewarded with your first mapping result, which is automatically shown in the output pane. Depending on whether you entered 105 or 221 as your test value, the result will either be BO or PO in the Purpose field. Any other values will produce the output XX, which is what we want.

/EFACT_d93a_ORDERS/BGM/@BGM02 to /PurchaseOrder/POHeader/@Number

The field BGM02 in the input specification has the generic meaning "Document/message number" in UN/EDIFACT, but the content of the field that was just mapped narrows this down to what it really contains—the Purchase Order Number as it was assigned by the sender. Therefore, we want to map this to the Number field in the POHeader of the destination specification. While the BGM02 field can hold up to 35 characters, the target field can contain only 22 characters. So do we want to take the risk of blindly truncating the data, or should we make a verbatim copy with which we will cause the destination document to fail validation if the length of the inbound field exceeds 22 characters?

Although the PO numbers are unlikely to exceed 22 characters, losing data for this special element could make it nearly impossible to track the problem back to the source in the partner's system; thus, we will decide to have the specification fail validation if the input field is too long. This way, the document will be quarantined in the Suspended Queue during processing, and we can give the partner a reference number to find the suspect data in their system.

Therefore, the mapping action is to just connect the two fields. The warning message box about data truncation is actually inaccurate. The data will be fully mapped, and truncation will not occur. When the data exceeds the permitted length after having been mapped to the destination, validation will fail, which is what we want to achieve.

/EFACT_d93a_ORDERS/BGM/@BGM03 to /PurchaseOrder/POHeader/@Type

BGM03 contains the message function taken from the UN/EDIFACT code table 1225. The codes of interest for our use are (1) Cancellation, (5) Replacement, (6) Confirmation, and (9) Original.

This scenario is almost identical to the C00201 element because we need to map these codes to the equivalents that are valid for our internal XML document: (CL) Cancellation, (RP) Replacement, (CF) Confirmation, and (OR) Original.

What to do? Insert a Scripting functoid, enter the code that follows, and connect the two fields. Voilá!

```
Function MapMsgCode( strBGM03 )
  Select Case strBGM03
      Case "1"
          MapMsgCode = "CL"
      Case "5"
          MapMsgCode = "RP"
      Case "6"
          MapMsgCode = "CF"
      Case "9"
          MapMsgCode = "OR"
      Case Else
          MapMsgCode = "XX"
  End Select
End Function
```

/EFACT_d93a_ORDERS/DTM/@C50702 to /PurchaseOrder/POHeader/@CreationDate

The next segment is the most ubiquitous UN/EDIFACT segment: date/time (DTM). Instead of creating an intrinsic data type, the UN/CEFACT committee overseeing the standard created a separate segment type that is used for every date and time expression in UN/EDIFACT interchanges. It should be obvious that segments are not necessarily a complete semantic unit, but that a single semantic unit (like the purchase order header information) is indeed split over multiple segments. The complete header of the UN/EDIFACT PO that we have here is therefore really composed of the following segments: begin of message (BGM), date/time (DTM), free text (FTX), and references (RFF).

The interesting point about the DTM segment is that it expresses format, data, and the precise meaning of the date value in a single compound value. This is in sharp contrast to common programming practice, where single data values receive their semantics only from their context, like compound data structures. This concept may appear odd at first, but this self-contained inner context model makes just as much sense as the outer context model once you allow yourself to look at the data from this different perspective. You could even view this treatment of simple data values as an extreme form of object orientation because each single date/time expression becomes a self-explanatory object. (This paragraph does not promote the inner context model—it merely points out the rationale for the design.)

Unfortunately, the inner context model also poses a great problem when mapping date values. Mapping is typically performed based on the specification structure and the semantics that are expressed by this structure, but the DTM segment carries the semantics and even the data format information in the data. Therefore, it is nearly impossible to create a generic, direct mapping between a DTM segment (and many more UN/EDIFACT segments) and any target field: the inner context model is not compatible with the XML spirit, wherein semantics are defined solely by the document structure and context.

The only way to handle the complexity is to take a look at the partner agreement. In our case, it defines that the "Date/time/period qualifier" (C50701) must have the value 4, which means "Date when an order was issued" (as per code list 2005). And the "Date/time/period qualifier" (C50703) must have the value 102, which is the format CCYYMMDD (as per code list 2379). For a reliable mapping, the date and the format qualifier must be assumed to be constant, and both must therefore be protected by a constraint that assures that the DTM segment at this position will always have those values. If this is guaranteed, the contextual meaning of the DTM segment is restored; therefore, mapping can be safely performed. To make sure that only these values are accepted, the ORDERS specification should restrict the use by allowing only these values on the fields by checking the appropriate entries on BizTalk Editor's Code List tab.

Under these preconditions and with the inbound document validation enforcing C50701 and C50703 to have the exact values as defined, we can ignore them in the mapping process and proceed with only field C50702 in focus. As per definition, the inbound date format is now CCYYMMDD (C is for century); hence, is incompatible with the ISO format that XML expects. Although it would be fairly easy to solve this problem with yet another custom script, we will solve this with a small group of four prebuilt functoids instead.

We need three String Extract functoids and one Concatenate functoid from the string functoid set, arranged as shown in Figure 16-13. The String Extract functoids isolate the Year, Month, and Day portions from the input data, and the Concatenate functoid reassembles them into ISO format. The purpose of the entire construct is simply to insert hyphens between the three portions of the date expression. To do this, you first need to connect the C50702 field to all three String Extract functoids and connect those to the Concatenate functoid. The connection order is significant here: always connect the topmost functoid first. The Concatenate functoid is then connected to the CreationDate field.

The configuration also goes from top to bottom. First, we extract the date portions from the input data. Configure the functoids by double-clicking them. In the Functoid

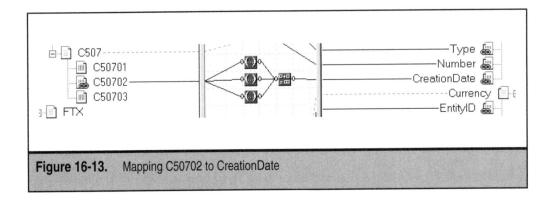

Figure 16-13. Mapping C50702 to CreationDate

Properties dialog box shown in Figure 16-14, you insert a new constant argument (of which we need two) by clicking the button that the mouse is pointing to in the figure. The topmost functoid extracts the date portion; therefore, we set the arguments to 1 (start position in the string) and 4 (end position in the string). You extract the month with the functoid just below it (looking at Figure 16-14) by setting the start position to 5 and the end position to 6. The value pair for the day-value is 7, 8. Now the three functoids will parse out the date portions at run time.

To reassemble them, we must configure the Concatenate functoid as shown in Figure 16-15. When you open the Functoid Properties dialog box, three of the arguments will already be configured. These are the inbound links from the three extraction functoids.

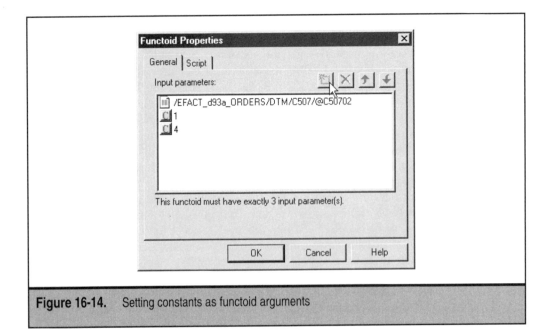

Figure 16-14. Setting constants as functoid arguments

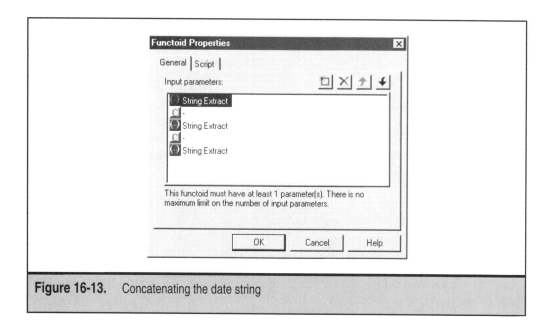

Figure 16-13. Concatenating the date string

You need to add two constants containing a simple hyphen each, which you can shift to the desired position with the up and down arrows in the dialog box.

The document map will now properly convert between the date formats. (Because this task is common, you will learn how to write a canned functoid DLL for this in Chapter 24).

/EFACT_d93a_ORDERS/FTX/FTX/C108/* to /PurchaseOrder/TermsOfSale/@Description

The FTX segment contains free text, and according to our partner agreement, it contains textual remarks pertaining to the purchase order that will be read and understood on the seller side before the order is executed. As such, the remarks fit best into the Description field for the TermsOfSale record of our destination specification. The text data is contained in the compound element C108. Because this compound element essentially mimics a multiline text field, we are going to concatenate all subfields of C108 into a single string and map the result to the target element after truncating it past the eightieth character to avoid validation errors.

Doing this is pretty simple. Place a Concatenate functoid on the grid and a String Left functoid to the right of it. Then connect all subfields of C108 to the Concatenate functoid and the functoid to the String Left functoid. Because the target field can hold only 80 characters, you should truncate the string at that position; hence, you should set this boundary as the constant argument for this functoid. Last, connect the functoid to the target field.

TIP: By now, your grid may be a little crowded. The mapping grid is a lot bigger than the section that you see between the tree views. If you bring the cursor near the edge of the grid, the cursor shape will switch into a larger arrow shape. Clicking the mouse will cause the grid to scroll.

/EFACT_d93a_ORDERS/RFFLoop1/RFF/@C50602 to / PurchaseOrder /BuyerReference /@Buyer Number
/EFACT_d93a_ORDERS/RFFLoop1/RFF/@C50602 to / PurchaseOrder/ ContractReference/@ContractNumber

Now we get to the more difficult tasks. The RFF loop—which occurs twice in the source documents according to the partner agreement—carries the buyer's (customer's) reference number for the purchase order and the contract number of the global purchasing agreement under which the purchase order is executed. The complicated issue here is that the RFF loop is an iterating record, which maps two different records in the target specification. If the field value RFF/C506/@50601 is equal to CR, the data in RFF/C506/@50602 is a customer reference that needs to be mapped to BuyerReference/@BuyerNumber. If the value is equal to CT, the source data field contains a contract reference that must be mapped to ContractReference/@ContractNumber.

This description also explains how to express the record mapping in BizTalk Mapper. Drop an Equal logical functoid on the grid, as shown in Figure 16-16, and connect the RFF/C506/@50601 field. Then add a constant value CR to the functoid and connect the Equal functoid to a new Value Mapping functoid. The Value Mapping functoid produces output only if the condition pointing to it is Boolean "true." The value to be mapped in this case is connected as the second argument of the Value Mapping functoid. In this case, you will connect the RFF/C506/@50602 field to the functoid and connect the BuyerReference/@BuyerNumber from there. Then build the same group of functoids with the test condition CT and connect the ContractReference/@ContractNumber destination field.

/EFACT_d93a_ORDERS/NADLoop1/NAD/@NAD01 to /PurchaseOrder/BillTo
/EFACT_d93a_ORDERS/NADLoop1/NAD/@NAD01 to /PurchaseOrder/ShipTo

The NAD segment is a generic container for names and addresses. If you flip back a couple of pages and look at Table 15-6 (or look at the entire agreement on this book's web site at www.osborne.com), you will see that there are indeed four NAD segments in the agreed input stream. The precise semantics of these segments are listed in Table 16-10.

One complication in mapping the NAD segments to the destination specification is that the destination specification has the capacity to accept only two of these addresses

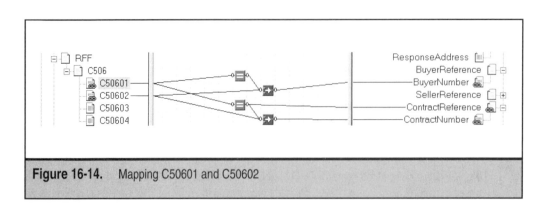

Figure 16-14. Mapping C50601 and C50602

Position	ID	Name	NAD01	Meaning
050	NAD	Name and Address	SE	Seller: Selling party
090	NAD	Name and Address	BT	Bill To: Party to be billed
092	NAD	Name and Address	BY	Buyer: Party to which the goods are sold
093	NAD	Name and Address	ST	Ship To: Party to which the goods will be shipped

Table 16-10. NAD Segments in Source Specification

(BillTo and ShipTo). But of even more concern is that the target records are actually different types of records, while all NAD records appear within a single loop (NADLoop1) and are therefore just four instances of the same record.

For the first issue, we will assume that the shipping and billing addresses are sufficient for our purposes, so we can ignore the other two records. The latter problem is similar to the scenario that we just solved for the RFF loop, but this time, we are mapping the condition to the record level, and we are controlling the production of the output by connecting the target records directly from the Equal functoid.

The solution is similar to that for the RFF mapping: drop an Equal functoid on the grid and connect the NAD01 field as shown in Figure 16-17. Then add a constant value BT to the functoid and connect the functoid to the BillTo record node. (If this does not work, you must select Allow Record Content Links in the BizTalk Mapper Options dialog box.) Then you repeat this action with another Equal functoid for the value ST connected to the ShipTo node. Now the mappings for the individual fields should be pretty straightforward.

The subfields of C058 contain the data for the first address line. Hence, you want to consolidate (concatenate) fields C05801 through C05805 into a single string value, truncate it at a maximum of 80 characters (from the left), and map it to the Address1 fields in both ShipTo/Address and BillTo/Address. This procedure is exactly the same as what you did with field FTX/C108 previously.

It is important that you create the links to the corresponding output fields in both the ShipTo and BillTo destination records. If the decision logic just described yields a ShipTo output record, the data will flow along the link to the ShipTo/Address/@Address1 field; if it yields a BillTo record, the value will map to the respective BillTo field.

The subfields of C080 map to the Address/@Name field, and those of C059 map to Address/@Address2 in the same way. Even easier are the mappings for the fields NAD06 (to Address/@City), NAD07 (to Address/@State), NAD08 (to Address/@PostalCode), and

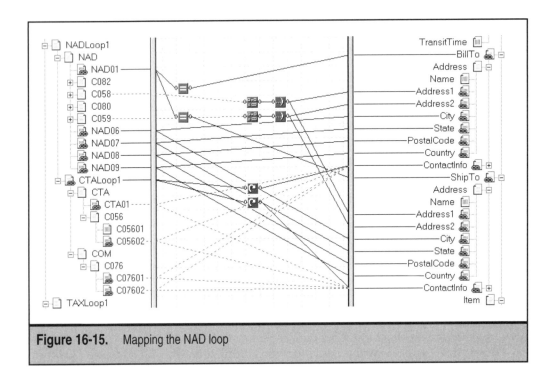

Figure 16-15. Mapping the NAD loop

NAD09 (to Address/@Country). These are all direct links that point to the respective fields in both ShipTo and BillTo. You can safely ignore the warning messages that appear when you create the links because the data to be expected in the incoming data is assumed to be compatible.

Equally direct links are those from the subordinate CTALoop1 (Contact Information). The field CTA/@CTA01 maps to ContactInfo/@ContactType, and CTA/C056/@C05602 maps to ContactInfo/@ContactName. The telephone number of the described contract is also information we would like to keep; therefore, we will also map COM/C076/@C07601 (Communication Number) to ContactInfo/@ContactNumber and COM/C076/ @C07602 to ContactInfo/@NumberType. The latter case produces a warning that you should ignore. The number type should be a two-letter code by mutual convention.

/EFACT_d93a_ORDERS/TAXLoop1/TAX/@TAX07 to /PurchaseOrder/TaxReference/@TaxIDNumber
The TAX07 field of the TAX segment contains the ordering party's tax identifier. This field corresponds exactly to the TAXIDNumber field in the TaxReference record in the target specification (a rare case where data type and constraints match); thus, you can link the fields directly.

/EFACT_d93a_ORDERS/CUXLoop1/CUX/C504/@C50402 to /PurchaseOrder/Currency/@CurrencyCode
The CUX loop defines the currency in which all monetary amounts in this interchange are expressed. The fields in the standard source loop can provide information on two currencies (the buyer and seller currencies), along with the exchange rate at the date of the order. In our

case, we will transfer the currency code for the order only in subfield C504/@C50402, which maps directly to the CurrencyCode field located in the Currency record of the destination specification. By convention (and according to international standards for currency codes), the source document always contains codes with exactly three character currency codes, so you can ignore the warning about incompatible constraints.

/EFACT_d93a_ORDERS/PATLoop1 to /PurchaseOrder/TermsOfSale

The mapping process does not continue to be as easy as for the last two fields. The payment and terms (PAT) loop is another puzzle.

The PAT segment is repeated twice, once with the PAT01 field being set to 1, indicating that the data in subfield C11204 represents the number of net days for payment. In the second instance, the payment terms type qualifier in PAT01 is set to 22, showing that the subfield contains the number of discount days due. The second instance of the PAT segment is also accompanied by a subsequent percentage details (PCD) segment, whose second subfield (C50102) contains the applicable discount percentage.

Net days for payment, discount days due, and the discount percentage all fit perfectly into the TermsOfSale record of the destination specification that contains a field for each of these values. However, the problem is that the source document carries this data in two separate, independent records, whereas the data of the same single field contained in two records of the source specification must be mapped into two different fields in a single record of the destination specification.

This task somewhat resembles mapping the data of the NAD loop and conditionally distributing it to the ShipTo and BillTo destination records, but this time on the field level rather than on the record level.

To map the base terms (net days), drop an Equal functoid on the grid, connect this from PAT01, just as shown in Figure 16-18, and enter the constant **1**. The next functoid we need is the advanced functoid Value Mapping (Flattening), which is linked with the

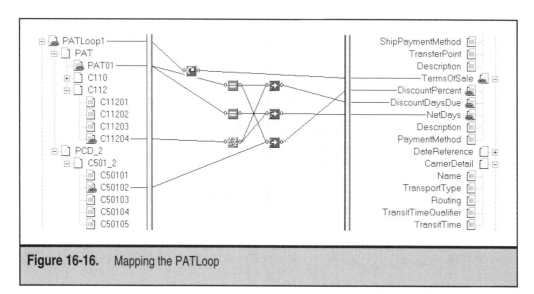

Figure 16-16. Mapping the PATLoop

result from the Equality functoid as the first argument. The side effect of this functoid is that the input structure is flattened into a single record. The second argument linked to this functoid is the field PAT/@C11204, and the functoid itself is linked to the destination field TermsOfSale/@NetDays.

With this combination for the mapping between C11204 and TermsOfSale/ @NetDays, we express that the mapping takes place only if the PAT01 field equals 1, which is what we want. The mapping between C11204 and TermsOfSale/ @DiscountDueDays is much the same, but with a different additional equality condition for which you must add additional Equal and Value Mapping (Flattening) functoids to the grid. In this case, the PAT01 field must equal 22.

The Equal functoid for the second mapping is also used to map PCD_2/ C501_2/@C50102 to TermsOfSale/DiscountPercent, which is equally dependent on this condition and thus also mapped through a new Value Mapping (Flattening) functoid.

However, if we left the mapping like this, the result would be two TermsOfSale records in the output XML data stream that will look approximately like this:

```
<TermsOfSale NetDays="30" />
<TermsOfSale DiscountDaysDue="14" DiscountPercent="5.0" />
```

What we want, though, is this:

```
<TermsOfSale NetDays="30" DiscountDaysDue="14" DiscountPercent="5.0" />
```

The tool to achieve this is the mighty Looping functoid, which produces a single output row by consuming the input loop. While the mappings of the source record are indeed executed for each iteration, all mappings from all iterations produce only a single, common output record. The Looping functoid is connected from the PATLoop1 field and connects to the TermsOfSale record.

/EFACT_d93a_ORDERS/TDTLoop1/LOCLoop1 to /PurchaseOrder/FOB
/EFACT_d93a_ORDERS/TDTLoop1/LOCLoop1 to /PurchaseOrder/CarrierDetail

The transportation terms (TDT) loop's information is easy to map.

The TDT/@TDT01 maps immediately to field /PurchaseOrder/CarrierDetail/@ TransportType, and TDT/C040/@C04004 maps to /PurchaseOrder/CarrierDetail/@Name.

The location information (LOC) loop corresponds fairly directly with the target "free on board" (FOB) shipment terms record. The fields to map are TDTLoop1/LOCLoop1/ LOC/@LOC01 to /PurchaseOrder/FOB/@TransferPoint and TDTLoop1/LOCLoop1/ LOC/C517_3/@C51704 to /PurchaseOrder/FOB/@Description.

/EFACT_d93a_ORDERS/LINLoop1 to /PurchaseOrder/Item

Now we get to the whole purpose of the order—the order items. The information is contained in the line items (LIN) loop and is mapped to the Item record and subrecords of the target specification.

The fields to be mapped between the records are mostly direct links. The LINLoop1/ LIN/@LIN01 field contains the line number and, as such, maps directly to the ItemHeader/

@LineNumber field. The quantity of the particular item is contained in the LINLoop1/
QTY_3 (quantity) segment's subfield C18602 and maps to Item/ItemHeader/@Quantity.
The mapping is illustrated in Figure 16-19.

The LINLoop1/DTM_13 segment provides the date by which the buyer requests delivery for the particular item. The mapping for this segment is done in the same way as
the topmost DTM segment that we handled in the very beginning and is mapped to the
Item/DateReference/@Date field. For the description of this date (Item/DateReference/
@Description) in the output document, you should enter the constant value **Requested by**
on the Values tab.

The description of the item is carried in the following LINLoop1/FTX_5 segment's
subfield C10801. (And we assume that all other siblings of that field remain empty.) We
map this directly to ItemDescription/@Description.

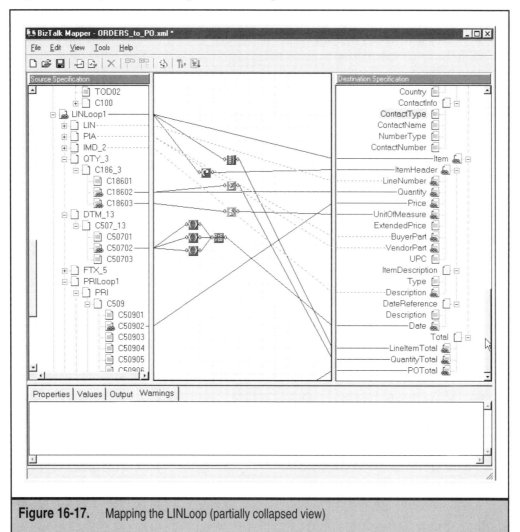

Figure 16-17.   Mapping the LINLoop (partially collapsed view)

Finally, we need to map the price information to the Item/ItemHeader/Price field, which we get from the LINLoop1/PRILoop1/PRI (price) segment's C50902 subfield that will map directly to the destination.

Because the destination ItemHeader now receives inbound items from two separate loops—the outer LIN loop and the inner QTY loop—the Mapper will complain that it is unable to resolve this situation. Multiple, independent source loops that map to a single record in the target specification simply cannot be properly mapped without additional hints. Therefore, we need to flatten the LIN loop (each occurrence of the block) for proper mapping to the ItemHeader record. What we want to achieve is that only a single output record is produced no matter how many subordinate loops appear. Because the QTY record is a loop, the default behavior is that the compiled map will want to produce one mapping to ItemHeader/@Quantity for each occurrence of this subordinate loop; obviously, this is not what the target specification describes. You should therefore drop another Looping functoid on the grid and connect from the LINLoop1 node and to the ItemHeader node.

The effect here is slightly different than when we previously used the Looping functoid. Because we map from the loop to a subordinate record here, the result is that the structure of the entire source loop is flattened only in respect to the target record—once per iteration.

/EFACT_d93a_ORDERS/LINLoop1 to /PurchaseOrder/Total/LineItemTotal

We are almost there. The last destination record that we need to complete is the Total record, which sums up the purchase order items. The first value required is the total number of line items, which we can simply determine by counting the LIN loop iterations using a new Record Count functoid that should be connected by the LINLoop1 record and should point to the Total/@LineItemTotal field.

/EFACT_d93a_ORDERS/LINLoop1/QTY_3/C186_3/C18602 to /PurchaseOrder/Total/@QuantityTotal

The destination specification also asks for a grand total of the ordered quantities. Therefore, we connect the quantity source field that we have already mapped to the line items to a Sum functoid (from the cumulative set) and from there, to the QuantityTotal target field.

/EFACT_d93a_ORDERS/MOA_10/C516_10/C51602 to /PurchaseOrder/Total/POTotal

Finally, we have arrived at the last field. Connect MOA_10/C516_10/C51602 to Total/POTotal for the total monetary sum of the overall order. If you have followed each step correctly, the map should now test without warnings. If it does not, recheck the map contents against this walk-through and verify that you followed all steps.

Once the map is complete, you store it in the WebDAV repository as S93AORDERS_ to_PurchaseOrder.xml. Because document maps always map between two specific document types, the name should precisely reflect the name of both specifications.

MORE MAPPING EXAMPLES

To complete the example solution, we need at least four additional document maps. Of course, walking through all those additional maps just would not be educational anymore, so we will focus on some of the trickier issues in these maps. (You can obtain all completed document maps from the book's web site.)

You must complete the following maps:

▼ XML purchase order to the XML purchase order acknowledgment

■ XML purchase order acknowledgment to the XML invoice

■ XML purchase order to the UN/EDIFACT ORDRSP message

▲ XML invoice to the UN/EDIFACT INVOIC message

The first map is really easy to do. It literally creates a one-to-one mapping between the records and fields of the XML purchase order to the XML purchase order acknowledgment, because the latter is a real superset of the purchase order. The second map is slightly more complex, but you should still be able to do it. And, based on the previous discussion, you should even be able to tackle the third one.

The fourth map, however, is a beast. Mapping most of the fields of the internal XML invoice document to the UN/EDIFACT INVOIC message is rather simple. However, mapping the distinct Seller, Buyer, and ShipTo records of the XML document into the INVOIC message's NAD loop is really tricky.

The basic goal is to produce three NAD segments, one for each input record. The NAD01 field for the Seller record should be set to SE, the field for the Buyer record should be set to BY, and the field for the ShipTo record should be set to ST. Otherwise, and because the structure of the three input records is mostly identical, all field links are equivalent between all records.

We can achieve the first requirement, producing the three output records, by using our Swiss army knife—the Looping functoid. When you place this functoid on the grid and connect all three input records to the functoid, connecting NADLoop1 from the functoid results in the desired three entries.

Now comes the puzzle. In the source data, there is no hint of any of the three source records that would identify the role. Therefore, there is no source field to map from for assigning a value to the NAD01 field. The seller, buyer, or ship-to role is defined solely by the semantics that are defined in the XML structure. At the same time, the NAD01 field must contain the individual role identifier for each record when mapping is complete.

The solution to the puzzle comes as three tiny, innocent scripting functoids, which differ only in their VBScript function name (arbitrarily named, just different). They look like this:

```
Function GetSellerCode( Arg1 )
  GetSellerCode = "SE"
End Function
```

The argument of the scripting functoid is linked from the source record node (either Seller, Buyer, or ShipTo), and the target field for all functoids is the NAD01 field.

The argument does nothing but establish the relationship between the source record and the value. When the Looping functoid emits the three output records, the correct scripting functoid is executed for each NAD01 field only due to the existence of the input link.

BizTalk Mapper is a powerful tool. However, figuring out how to map between two arbitrary schemas can become mind-bogglingly complex—and that may be an understatement. At the same time, solving the puzzles can really be fun, too.

CHAPTER 17

Configuring the Application

W ith the document specifications that we created in Chapter 15 and the document map from Chapter 16, we now have enough material to configure the first messaging document-processing pipelines by using the BizTalk Messaging Manager application. In this chapter, we will also integrate the results from Chapter 14, where we created the handling logic for incoming purchase orders by using an XLANG schedule. Whenever a new purchase order arrives, a new instance of this schedule will be instantiated and receives the XML purchase order through its first Orchestration port. At the end of this chapter, we will also set up a special port configuration that will let you test the document maps from Chapter 16 independently.

BIZTALK MESSAGING MANAGER

BizTalk Messaging Manager is the primary tool for configuring BizTalk messaging services. As you already know, the BizTalk Messaging Manager application is indeed a front end to an Active Server Pages (ASP) application. Messaging Manager resides in the MessagingManager virtual directory of a BizTalk Server machine's default web site. All data that you can see in Messaging Manager and all actions that are performed are communicated between the Messaging Manager application and the web application by using an (undocumented) XML format.

In the Messaging Manager Options dialog box, which is shown in Figure 17-1, you can configure the server machine that BizTalk Messaging Manager communicates with. The configuration assumes that the MessagingManager application is available on the default HTTP port (80) of the target machine. However, if you append the port number the same way you do HTTP URLs (like myserver:8080), you can also use a nonstandard configuration and move the ASP application to a different web site that uses a nonstandard port. The server timeout value determines how long the application waits for a response

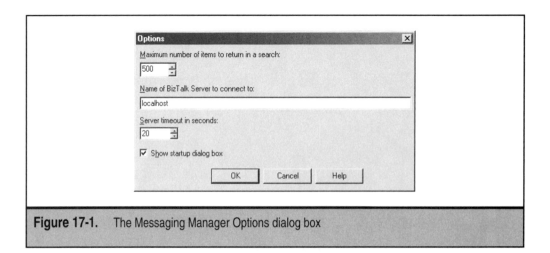

Figure 17-1. The Messaging Manager Options dialog box

from the server until it will display an error message. If you know that the server is running and accessible and you get these error messages frequently, you may want to increase the timeout value. The data that is displayed in Messaging Manager is always retrieved from the management database that the target server is configured to use.

In general, you should never change configuration data if any of the servers in any of the BizTalk server groups that use this management database are actively processing documents. If you change configuration information that is being actively used, you risk data loss and inconsistencies. Even adding new configurations to a running BizTalk server farm could result in run-time problems. Imagine a case where the document could not be sent due to some problems in an initial transmission attempt, and it has been placed into the Retry Queue where it is now waiting for retransmission. If you change the configuration in this situation, the message in the Retry Queue could be invalid in the context of the new configuration data, even though it has already passed all validation stages.

You should therefore strictly differentiate between production environments and development environments.

The development environment (which is being described here) should be strictly isolated from the production environment, but it should be a fairly realistic mirror of the production scenario. If your production environment runs multiple servers, you should likewise use at least two machines in your development setup. Ideally, you should never use Messaging Manager on a production system; instead, all configurations that you build with it in the development environment should be transferred to the production system using scripts or replication of the management database contents. Chapter 20 discusses how you can create and run those scripts, describes how you can set up the server farm redundantly to transition safely between different versions of the configuration data, and explains the advantages of versioning and using a release-cycle system.

Chapter 10 already explained the Messaging Manager user interface, so we will skip any further introduction and get right to work.

DEFINING APPLICATIONS AND ORGANIZATIONS

We begin to configure the messaging application by defining its contents.

The first item of interest is the Home Organization. This organization identifier is the only item in a fresh management database that is already preconfigured and cannot be removed. The Home Organization organization identifier represents your own organization. The name is qualified by the OrganizationName qualifier, which BizTalk uses for the cleartext, human-readable descriptions of organizations. You can use organization identifiers of this qualifier group like any other organization identifier, but you should favor using more official identifiers assigned by recognized authorities. If you plan to use X12 or UN/EDIFACT, you must use official identifiers if you want to receive documents with fixed (not self-routing) channel assignments. (You will very likely need them.)

Therefore, we will first edit the Home Organization identifier to configure it appropriately. Locate this identifier by clicking the Organizations link in Messaging Manager's search pane. Then click the Search Now button. The results window on the right displays a single entry: Home Organization. (This will be the case only if you have just done a fresh install of BizTalk Server—otherwise you will of course get all other organizations that already exist.)

When you double-click the entry, the Organization Properties dialog box will open. On the General tab, you can appropriately name your own organization and add some further comments. If you change the organization name here, this will be reflected in the OrganizationName identifier.

Switching to the Identifiers tab, as shown in Figure 17-2, you will find that the home organization has two predefined organization identifiers. The first is the one that we already know and that you may have just renamed, and the other has the qualifier SMTP. Its value is your BizTalk system's SMTP e-mail address. This identifier is used as a reply-to address for receipts if reliable messaging is used over SMTP. If you plan to use SMTP in conjunction with BizTalk, you should always set this identifier.

Providing an SMTP reply-to address has a few implications, of course. Because BizTalk cannot receive SMTP messages by itself, the reply-to address that you specify here must be properly configured in your mail system, and it must be bound to a script that can forward incoming messages to the BizTalk Interchange component. The related tasks depend on the SMTP e-mail package you are using and can therefore not be described within the scope of this book. Sample scripts for Microsoft Exchange 5.5 and Microsoft Exchange 2000 are located in the MessagingSamples\ReceiveScripts subdirectory of the SDK portion of the BizTalk installation.

So that you will have at least one identifier that is technically correct for any document type, you should now add an identifier that is unique and that every business should have: the telephone number. To do this, click the Add button on the Identifiers tab to open the New Identifier dialog box, which is shown in Figure 17-3.

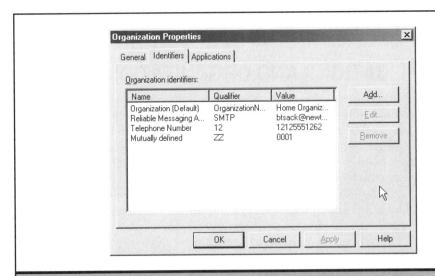

Figure 17-2. The Identifiers tab of the Organization Properties dialog box

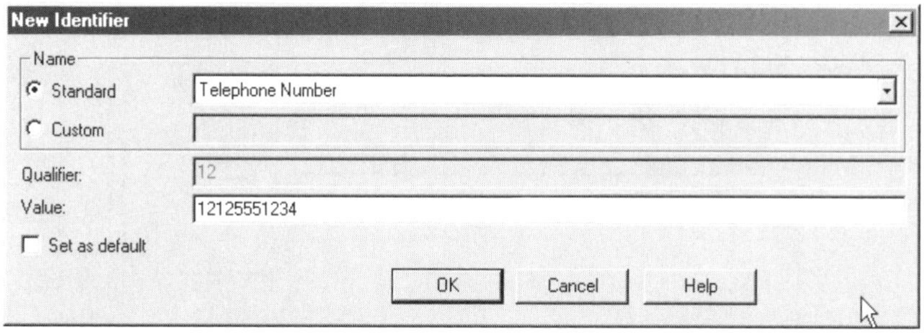

Figure 17-3. The New Identifier dialog box

In the dialog box, select the Standard option and select the Telephone Number entry from the combo box. Now enter your own business's main telephone number or the telephone number of your own department into the Value box. The main concern here is that the telephone number is unique and is assigned to your business. Prefix the telephone number with the international dialing code of your country, for instance, 1 for the United States, or 49 for Germany. Click OK to confirm and save the new entry. If you plan to use BizTalk as your primary gateway for EDI documents, you should scan the list of standard identifiers and provide any number in these namespaces that your business has been assigned. A more thorough explanation of this list can be found in Appendix B.

To have some valid identifiers for the purpose of this discussion, let's create a special namespace for this book. Add a new identifier, 0001, to your organization and select Mutually Defined from the Standard list, which will cause the qualifier value to be set to ZZ.

The task is to configure the internal applications for the home organization. The application identifiers are plaintext strings that you define on the Applications tab of the Organization Properties dialog box. (See Figure 17-4.) The only internal application that we want to configure at this point is Order Processing. Click the Add button and enter the identifier in the dialog box that appears. Then click OK or Apply in the Organization Properties dialog box. The new organization identifiers will be entered into the management database.

Now add four more organizations to the database and name them Organization Alpha, Organization Beta, Organization Gamma, and Organization Delta. Each of these organizations also gets a Mutually defined identifier: 0011 for Organization Alpha, 0012 for Organization Beta, 0013 for Organization Gamma, and 0014 for Organization Delta. To create new organization identifiers, press CTRL-G or choose File | New | Organization.

CREATING PORTS

The first messaging port to be configured will forward an accepted purchase order to a new instance of the handling XLANG schedule. To begin, select File | New | Messaging

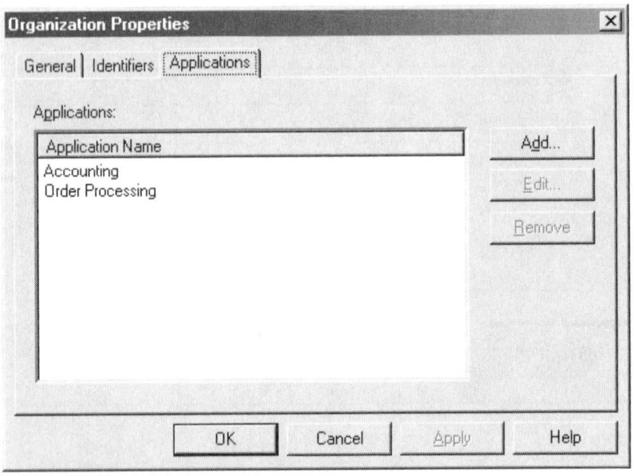

Figure 17-4.　The Applications tab of the Organization Properties dialog box

Port | To An Application or press CTRL-SHIFT-R. The New Messaging Port Wizard will open to the General Information page, as shown in Figure 17-5.

First, you must enter each port's name and some explanatory comments on its use. Choose the name and comments carefully so that you can derive the port use from the name and so that the comments will help you later to sort the port definition into the bigger picture. In a realistic BizTalk scenario, you will have quite a few port definitions, and introducing a proper naming scheme in the beginning helps keep it organized.

The port name that you set here is shown in the Messaging Manager port list. For this example, select "Incoming Purchase Orders To XLANG" on the General Information page.

When you move to the next page of the New Messaging Port Wizard, you can select the destination application. (See Figure 17-6.) Because we want to start a new XLANG schedule whenever a new document arrives, select the New XLANG Schedule option and click the Browse button to find the location where you stored the ConfirmPO.skx file that we created in Chapter 14.

The location of the destination XLANG schedule file should be permanent so that it can be accessed at run time. It should also reside on a local drive of the BizTalk Server machine to eliminate problems with network access due to the identity of the XLANG Scheduler application. This constraint somewhat limits the usefulness of the Browse button and subsequent dialog box: Messaging Manager will not import the XLANG schedule file and place it into the management database as it does with document specification and document maps. Indeed, if you run BizTalk Server in a clustered environment, this seemingly simple task is quite a bit more complex than you would expect. This is because the

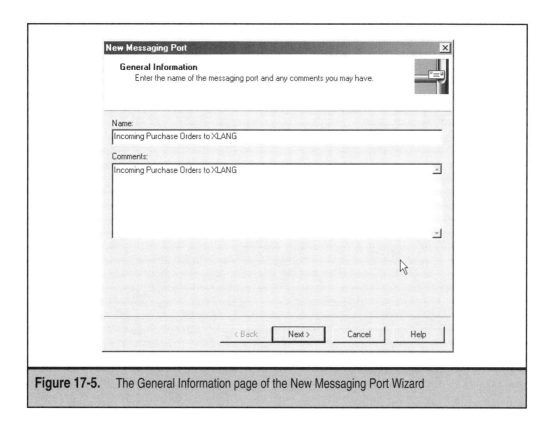

Figure 17-5. The General Information page of the New Messaging Port Wizard

XLANG file must reside in the same local drive location on every cluster server that will process messages routed through this messaging port. If you create such a definition for a BizTalk cluster, you must therefore assure proper distribution and synchronization of the respective schedule files.

The user interface also suggests by its design (as shown in Figure 17-6) that the Schedule Moniker field expects the portion of the schedule moniker immediately following the sked:// portion, as if you could indeed and optionally enter the target machine and group name here as well. That is unfortunately not the case. You can enter only a filename in this box, and when the port is processed, the schedule will thus always be launched on the processing BizTalk Server machine and in the default schedule host (XLANG Scheduler).

In the Port Name field, you must enter the name of the Orchestration port to which the BizTalk Messaging shape accepting the purchase order is bound. In Chapter 14, we named this port AcceptPO, and this is the same name that goes here. If you forget to enter the port name for an XLANG schedule and try to go to the next page in the wizard, a message box will appear that prompts you to enter a valid messaging port name—don't let the message confuse you. The wanted entry is an Orchestration port, not a messaging port: this is a bug.

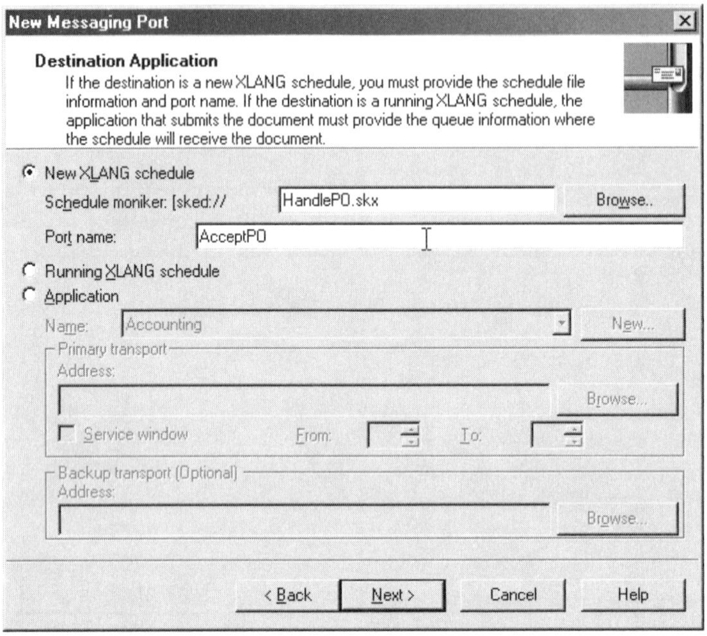

Figure 17-6. The Destination Application page of the New Messaging Port Wizard

Click Next and go to the next page (Envelope Information) of the New Messaging Port Wizard, as shown in Figure 17-7. Here, you select an envelope that is used to wrap the data and, as you know from previous discussions about envelopes, also determine which serializer is chosen for data formats other than XML. We want to pass the data into the schedule in XML format without a wrapping envelope; therefore, leave the envelope set to None and proceed to the next page in the wizard.

On the Security Information page, as shown in Figure 17-8, you can set the encoding type and select the signature type. Because we are forwarding the message to an XLANG schedule, we will leave these settings at None because the XLANG Scheduler cannot decode MIME and also cannot verify the signature or decrypt data. Both options would be useful only in conjunction with XLANG, if you wanted to route the document as unparsed strings through a schedule.

If Messaging Manager is in new messaging port mode (in contrast to editing mode), the Create A Channel For This Messaging Port check box at the bottom of the page will be checked and you can select the channel type to create. When you leave this checked, pressing the Finish button on this page causes the New Channel Wizard to launch and create a channel configuration for the port. When you open the port for editing later, this check box will be unavailable.

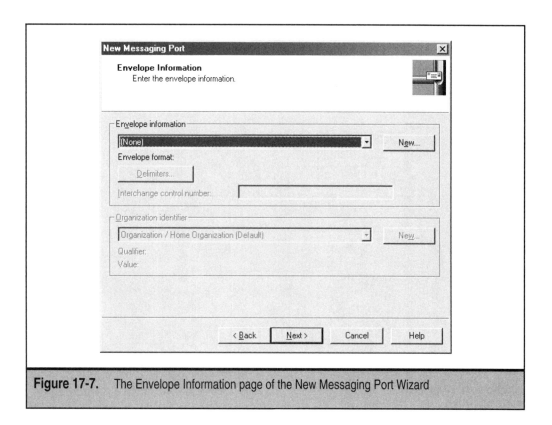

Figure 17-7.   The Envelope Information page of the New Messaging Port Wizard

Set the channel type to From An Organization and click Finish.

CREATING CHANNELS

Channels are always dependent on specific ports. You can begin creating channels immediately in the process of defining a new port (as you have done just now). Or you can select a port list entry from the resulting list of a search for ports in Messaging Manager,
right-click it, and select New Channel | From An Organization, or New Channel | From
An Application from the context menu in Messaging Manager. (See Figure 17-9.). Any of
these commands will launch the New Channel Wizard.

The channel defines the type and handling options for the documents that are sent
through the associated port. There can be any number of channels bound to a single delivery destination (which the port ultimately represents). For our current example, we
want to accept a UN/EDIFACT S93A ORDERS document, map it to our internal purchase order XML document, and hand it to the port for creating a new XLANG schedule.

Channels are either *open source,* meaning that the source organization must be extracted
from the document data, or they are exclusively defined for a specific source organization.
For simplicity, we will begin by using the latter option and tightly bind the channel to one

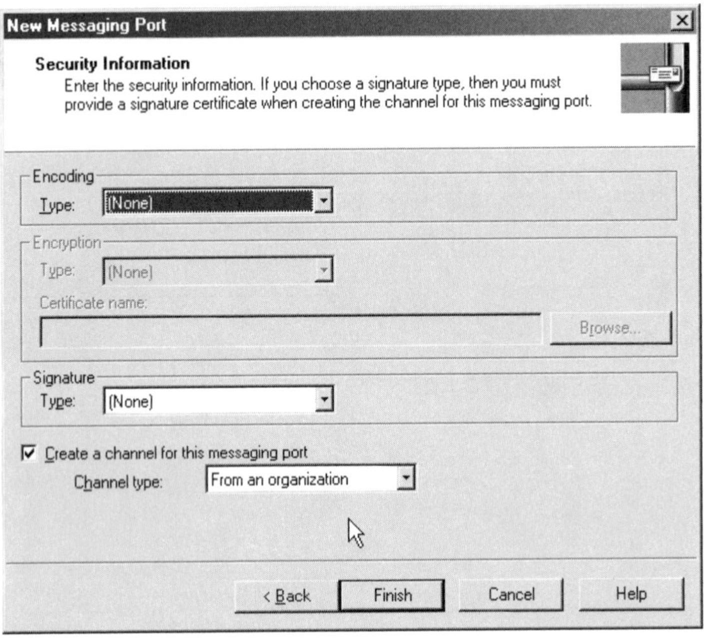

Figure 17-8. The Security Information page of the New Messaging Port Wizard

of our sample organizations, Organization Alpha. In a second step, and after you have tested the channel, you may want to replace this configuration with an open-source channel because UN/EDIFACT documents are typically enveloped and are self-routing.

Like you do with ports, you should give the channel an expressive name like S93A ORDERS/PurchaseOrder from Organization Alpha to XLANG, which describes the full route for the channel as shown in Figure 17-10. Then proceed to the Source Organization page of the wizard, as shown in Figure 17-11.

As just stated, we are going to bind the channel to a source organization first. Therefore, select the Organization option and click the Browse button, which will open a dialog box listing all defined organizations. Select Organization Alpha and click OK.

The New Channel Wizard now lets you select one of the organization identifiers that you have defined for that organization. Because we have created a special mutually defined identifier, you should select that one from the list. The entry should read Mutually Defined / 0011.

TIP: If you want to create the organization identifiers or organizations as you go, you could also click the respective New buttons and create new organizations and identifiers from within the New Channel Wizard, which will probably become your favorite way to do this.

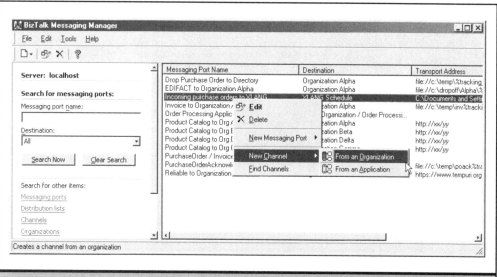

Figure 17-9. Creating a new channel from Messaging Manager

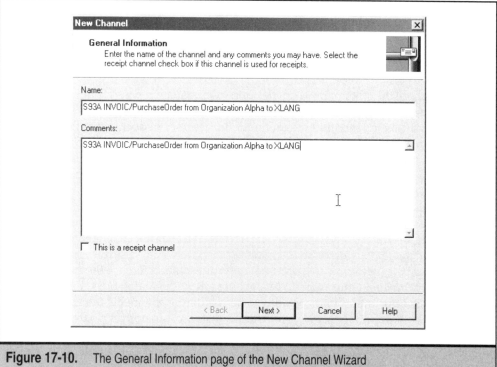

Figure 17-10. The General Information page of the New Channel Wizard

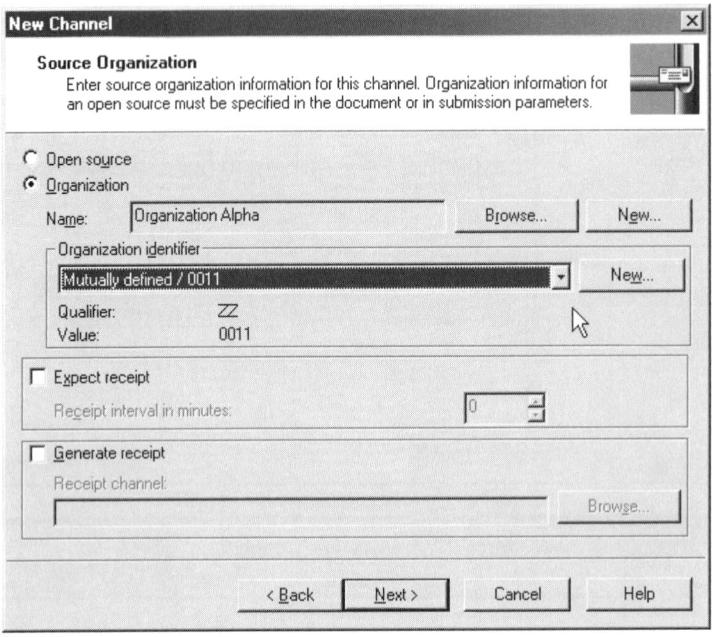

Figure 17-11. The Source Organization page of the New Channel Wizard

We will ignore the other options on the Source Organization page for now and proceed to the next page: Inbound Document. (See Figure 17-12.)

Now we will set the inbound document definition for the documents that we expect to arrive on this channel. Because we have not created any document definitions in the management database, click the New button to the right of the Inbound Document Definition Name field. The Document Definition Properties dialog box will appear, as shown in Figure 17-13, where you will define the document definitions.

In this dialog box, you will create a named association with the document specifications that you have created with BizTalk Editor. When you create such a document definition, the specification will be physically imported into the BizTalk management database. Whenever you make changes to the specification and you want to use the updated version, you need to edit and resubmit all document definitions that reference the specification to refresh the documents (which you do by clicking OK in the dialog box).

The inbound document that we want to define on the channel is the UN/EDIFACT ORDERS specification; hence, you should choose an appropriate name like UN/EDIFACT S93A ORDERS default, which expresses the following: the document is based on the S93A UN/EDIFACT standards release (which is still a quite popular one,

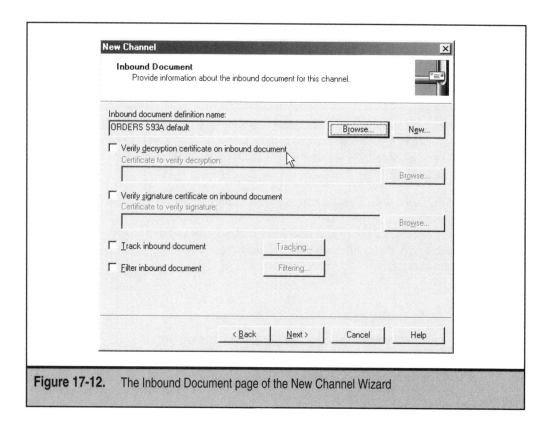

Figure 17-12.   The Inbound Document page of the New Channel Wizard

despite frequent updates by UN/CEFACT); it is an implementation of the ORDERS message; and this is the default implementation that we use for all partners unless there is a different agreement.

Next, set a reference to the WebDAV storage location for the document specification that you created in Chapter 15. Click the Browse button, which will open a dialog box that lets you browse the WebDAV repository to find the specification. When you have selected a specification (select S93A_ORDERS_default.xml for our example), the document type and the standards version will be parsed from the document and shown below the link information. Then you can verify whether you have selected the correct file.

For UN/EDIFACT documents, you must now define the selection criteria, which are absolutely required for the UN/EDIFACT parser to work. (See Figure 17-14.) The parser will match these values against the information found in the message header (UNH segment) and identify the matching document definition solely based on these values, because UN/EDIFACT does not provide syntactical hints as XML does.

Add the following name-value pairs:

▼ functional_identifier is the name of the message definition; hence, ORDERS is the value.

- standards_version_type is the type of the UN/EDIFACT standards release that the document complies with. In our case, it is the standards prefix *S.*

▲   standards_version_value is the version number of the standard; the applicable value is 93A for our document.

NOTE: You can find out about the applicable values for the X12 and UN/EDIFACT documents by clicking the Help button in this dialog box, so in the beginning, you may want to look them up every time you define selection criteria. These values have to be right or you will have problems that may be quite difficult to track.

When you are done with these settings, click OK and return to the New Channel Wizard, which now shows the document definition name in the respective field. The other options on this page do not apply to the task at hand, so proceed to the next page, which is shown in Figure 17-15. (We will get back to those other options at the end of this chapter when we cover security.)

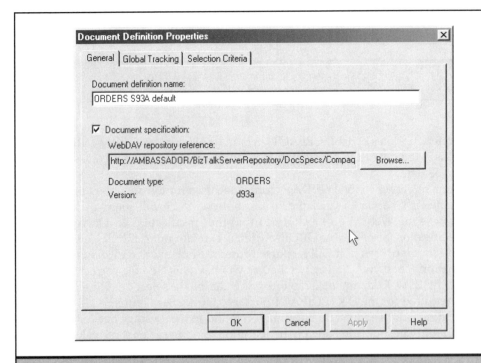

Figure 17-13.   The General tab of the Document Definition Properties dialog box

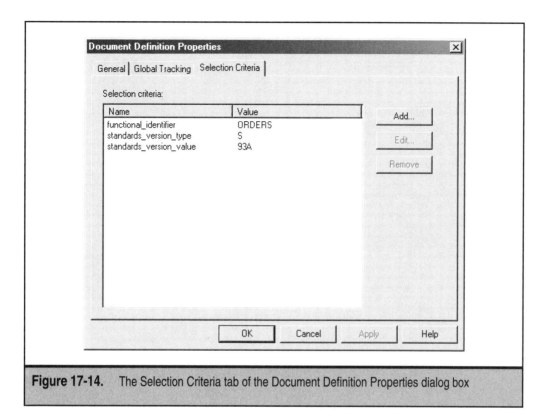

Figure 17-14.   The Selection Criteria tab of the Document Definition Properties dialog box

This wizard page serves to associate the outbound document format with the channel. The format that will be submitted into the XLANG schedule is defined in the PurchaseOrder.xml specification that was defined in Chapter 15. The first step is similar to that of the previous wizard page: create a new document definition for the purchase-order document and import the specification file into the management database. Name the new document definition PurchaseOrder XML default.

NOTE: These steps for the selection criteria do not apply for XML documents because BizTalk detects the document type of an XML document by looking at the name of the root element and/or the target namespace.

Once you have created the new document definition, you will be returned to the New Channel Wizard. Because the source and target document definitions are now different for this channel, the Map Inbound Document To Outbound Document check box will be selected by default. The next step is therefore to import the appropriate document map, which you have already defined in Chapter 16 and stored in the WebDAV repository as S93AORDERS_to_PurchaseOrder.xml.

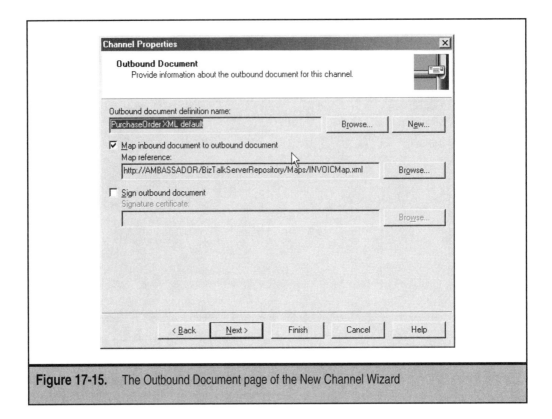

Figure 17-15.   The Outbound Document page of the New Channel Wizard

On the following New Channel Wizard page (Figure 17-16), you specify the document logging options to define how the inbound and outbound documents are being tracked in the document tracking database. Because we perform document mapping here and the inbound document is a non-XML format, you may want to select the In Native Format check box and the In XML Format check box so that the inbound document is able to see the original UN/EDIFACT interchange and its XML representation. For the outbound document, you can select either check box because the native output format is XML.

The Advanced Configuration page (see Figure 17-17) does not need any special settings in this case because our output format is XML and the transport option for the port is to send the document into an XLANG schedule, which does not require any special advanced settings. Click Finish to complete the channel definition and the port configuration.

Now click the Messaging Ports link or the Channels link in the search pane of the Messaging Manager application and click the Search Now button. The new port and the new channel should show up in the respective lists.

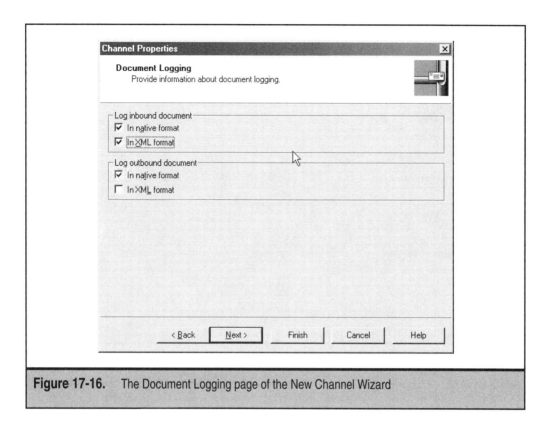

Figure 17-16. The Document Logging page of the New Channel Wizard

CREATING LOOPBACK PORTS

Theoretically, you should now be able to test this channel, but in fact, we still have quite a long way to go to complete the solution and to get the XLANG schedule to work without errors. To make the wait a bit more bearable, we are going to create an exact clone of the previous port and channel configurations that you can use immediately: a loopback port.

You define a loopback port just like any other port and the channel definition is very similar. The main differences are that loopback ports use the Loopback transport protocol and can be executed only synchronously (by using the *SubmitSync()* method of the Interchange component).

To create the loopback port, create a new port to an application and name it S93A ORDERS/PurchaseOrder Loopback. Set the primary transport on the Destination Application page (Figure 17-6) to Loopback. All other settings are identical to the port you have already defined. Give the channel the same name as the port (for simplicity), and leave the other settings the same as the channel you have already defined.

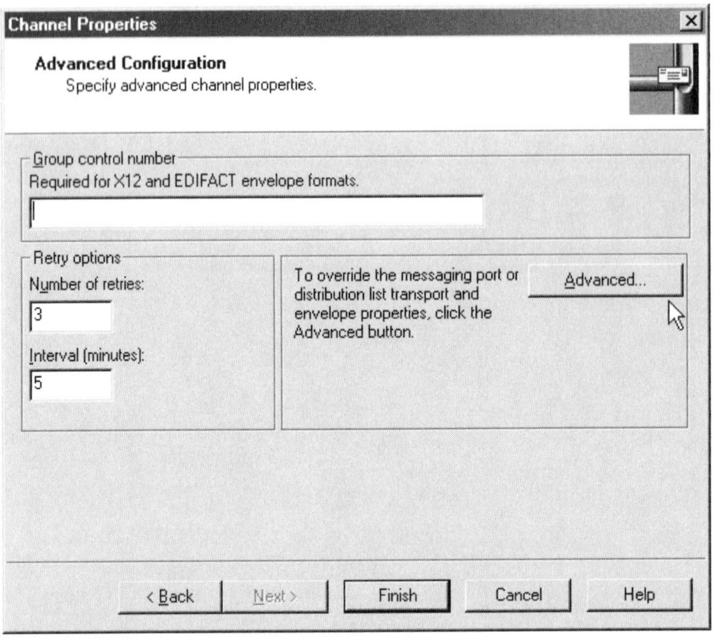

Figure 17-17. The Advanced Configuration page of the New Channel Wizard

Once you are done with the loopback port definition, you can test it. This is the moment for the DirectIntegration SDK sample to step into the limelight. From here on, consider this tool as one of your best friends when it comes to configuring BizTalk Messaging. The compiled version of the sample is located in the ./SDK/Messaging Samples/ DirectIntegration/EXE subdirectory of the BizTalk program files directory. The best idea is to immediately create a shortcut to the tool's executable on the Start menu or on the Windows Explorer launch bar.

The loopback port lets you test a couple of things at once. You can verify whether both document specifications are correct and also whether the document maps work as desired. Therefore, it is generally advisable to create loopback ports every time you want to test a new document definition or document map in a realistic environment.

Once you have launched the tool (see Figure 10-12), select the Send As Document Instead Of As File check box and enter the raw UN/EDIFACT interchange from Chapter 10 exactly as printed. (Alternatively, you may want to download the interchange from the book's web site and paste it). Then select the S93A ORDERS/PurchaseOrder Loopback entry from the Channel Name combo box to make sure that the interchange is submitted to the desired channel. By default, the Openness box should have the BIZTALK_ OPENNESS_NOTOPEN selected.

Drum roll.

Thunder.

Lightning.

Click Submit Sync.

(This is the moment where the author should grin, duck, and run! The likelihood of this action succeeding after you merely followed the walk-through in this book is improbable enough to power Douglas Adams's mighty Infinite Improbability Drive.)

If the SubmitSync button opens a window that contains an XML purchase order compliant to the PurchaseOrder XML default document definition, the action succeeded in its entirety, confirming that you have indeed implemented the UN/EDIFACT ORDERS message, the PurchaseOrder XML message, and the document map correctly. If it fails and displays an error message, do one of the following: go back and read Chapters 15 and 16 again; leave it as is and read how to fix the problems in Chapter 18 which covers troubleshooting; go to the web site, get the specifications from there, and compare them against what you have defined.

If it did work, you will see how the transformed document looks after a complete pass through the document-processing pipeline. This is one of the most valuable techniques for verifying definitions and debugging both specifications and document maps.

COMPLETING THE SAMPLE CONFIGURATION

The next port to configure is another loopback port. This port is used by the OrderApproval COM component that is bound to the sample schedule's Orchestration port by the same name. Because the PurchaseOrder and PurchaseOrderAcknowledgement schemas are mostly identical, it is indeed easier to create a document map and use BizTalk's Messaging services to map between the schemas than traversing the XML Document Object Model (DOM) in the component. It is also much safer than executing the XSLT transformation directly from within the component by using the XML parser because using the loopback port also validates both the inbound and outbound documents.

Table 17-1 lists the configuration options for this port. You create the port with the Port To An Application option.

Page	Configuration Property	Setting
General Information	Name	Order Processing Application Loopback.
	Comment	Order Processing Application Loopback port.
Destination Application	Application	Select the Application option and select Order Processing.
	Primary Transport Address	Click Browse and select Loopback transport.
Envelope Information	Envelope Information	Leave the None option selected.
	Organization Identifier	Leave the default (home organization's OrganizationName identifier).
Security Information	Encoding type	Leave the None option selected.
	Encryption type	Leave the default setting.
	Signature type	Leave the default setting.

Table 17-1. The Port Configuration for Order Processing Application Loopback

The channel that you create for this port should be from an application and the settings should be set as listed in Table 17-2.

Because this is a loopback channel, you may now want to test the port with the DirectIntegration tool. If you do not have an XML purchase-order document handy, you could open BizTalk Editor and create a sample document by selecting Tools | Create Instance. Of course, you could also use a loopback-bound variant of the S93A ORDERS/ PurchaseOrder from Organization Alpha to XLANG channel in conjunction with the DirectIntegration tool to convert the UN/EDIFACT stream into an XML purchase order and generate your sample data this way.

Page	Configuration Property	Setting
General Information	Name	PurchaseOrder / PurchaseOrderAcknowledgment Loopback.
	Comment	PurchaseOrder / PurchaseOrderAcknowledgment Loopback.
Source Organization	Application and Name	Select the Application option and select Order Processing for the application name.
Inbound Document	Inbound Document Definition Name	Click Browse and select PurchaseOrder XML default.
Outbound Document	Outbound Document Definition Name	Click New and create the PurchaseOrderAcknowledgment XML default document definition with a WebDAV reference to the PurchaseOrderAcknowledgment .xml specification.
	Map Inbound Document To Outbound Document	Automatically checked.
	Map Reference	Click Browse and select the PurchaseOrder_ to_PurchaseOrder Acknowledgment.xml document map.
Document Logging	Log Inbound Document	Clear both check boxes. (We do not want to log this internal conversion.)
	Log Outbound Document	Clear both check boxes. (We do not want to log this internal conversion.)
Advanced Configuration		Leave the defaults.

Table 17-2. Channel Configuration for PurchaseOrder/PurchaseOrderAcknowledgment Loopback

The next port will be used to send UN/EDIFACT messages to Organization Alpha. For simplicity and to enable you to view the serialization results, we will drop the files into a file-system directory and therefore use the file transport. The assumed drop-off location is c:\dropoff\Alpha. Unless you have already done so, you will also need to create a UN/EDIFACT envelope definition in the process.

The port to an organization should be created and should have the settings listed in Table 17-3.

For this port, we will define two channels. The first channel (the properties are listed in Table 17-4) routes the purchase order acknowledgement to Organization Alpha, and

Page	Configuration Property	Setting
General Information	Name	EDIFACT to Organization Alpha.
	Comment	EDIFACT port to Organization Alpha.
Destination Organization	Organization	Select Organization, click Browse, and select Organization Alpha from the dialog box.
	Primary Transport Address	Click Browse and select File Transport as the transport type. Set the transport address to file://c:\dropoff\Alpha\ %tracking_id%.edifact so that a new file is created with the document tracking ID embedded in the filename each time a document is sent through the channel.
Envelope Information	Envelope Information	Select UN/EDIFACT. If the envelope is not defined, click the New button. Specify UN/EDIFACT as the envelope name and select EDIFACT as the envelope format in the dialog box.
	Delimiters	Click the Delimiters button and enter the following values in the dialog box: Component element separator character: plus sign (+) Element separator character: colon (:) Release indicator character: question mark (?) Segment terminator character: single quote (') (Hex 27)
	Interchange Control Number	Set to 1. This is the seed for the UN/EDIFACT interchange control numbers for this channel.
	Organization Identifier	Select Mutually Defined / 0011.

Table 17-3.   Port Configuration for EDIFACT to Organization Alpha

Page	Configuration Property	Setting
Security Information	Encoding Type	Leave the default.
	Encryption Type	Leave the default.
	Signature Type	Leave the default.

Table 17-3.   Port Configuration for EDIFACT to Organization Alpha *(continued)*

the second one relays the invoice a bit later in the handling process. Create both channels from an application.

Page	Configuration Property	Setting
General Information	Name	PurchaseOrderAcknowledgment/S93A ORDRSP to Organization Alpha.
	Comment	PurchaseOrderAcknowledgment/S93A ORDRSP to Organization Alpha.
Source Application	Application and Name	Select the Application option and select Order processing. This setting is indeed correct, although we send the message directly from an XLANG schedule. The XLANG option applies only if you need to route the response address defined in the XLANG schedule through to the destination as the source identifier for BizTalk Messaging integration in conjunction with reliable XML messaging. This is not the case here, and it is incompatible with UN/EDIFACT and X12 envelope formats (and flatfiles, depending on the envelope), regardless.
	Organization Identifier	Select Mutually Defined / 0001 for the organization identifier.
Inbound Document	Inbound Document Definition Name	Click Browse and select PurchaseOrderAcknowledgment XML default.

Table 17-4.   The Channel Configuration for PurchaseOrderAcknowledgment/S93A ORDRSP to Organization Alpha

Page	Configuration Property	Setting
Outbound Document	Outbound Document Definition Name	Click New and create an ORDRSP XML default document definition with a WebDAV reference to the S93A_ORDRSP_default.xml specification. The selection criteria should be set as follows: functional_identifier: ORDRSP standards_version_type: S standards_version_value: 93A
	Map Inbound Document To Outbound Document	Automatically checked.
	Map Reference	Click Browse and select the PurchaseOrderAcknowledgment_to_ S93AORDRSP.xml document map.
Document Logging	Log Inbound Document	Select In XML Format.
	Log Outbound Document	Select both check boxes.
Advanced Configuration	Group Control Number	Set to 1. This is the automatically updated sequentially counted identifier seed for the functional groups that contain the emitted ORDRSP messages.
	Advanced	Click Advanced, select the Envelope tab, and click its Advanced button. As per the UNB segment description of the ORDRSP message (see this book's web site at www.osborne. com), the following advanced UN/EDIFACT serializer settings should be modified/verified: Syntax identifier: UNOB UNA control: Send UNA Only When Required

Table 17-4. The Channel Configuration for PurchaseOrderAcknowledgment/S93A ORDRSP to Organization Alpha *(continued)*

The second channel to define on the EDIFACT port to Organization Alpha port maps and routes the invoice to the trading partner. Table 17-5 lists the properties you need to configure.

Page	Configuration Property	Setting
General Information	Name	Invoice/S93A INVOIC to Organization Alpha.
	Comment	Invoice/S93A INVOIC to Organization Alpha.
Source Application	Application and Name	Select the Application option and select Order Processing. (Same rationale as for the previous channel.)
	Organization Identifier	Select Mutually Defined / 0001 for the organization identifier.
Inbound Document	Inbound Document Definition Name	Click New and create a new Invoice XML default document definition based on the Invoice.xml specification that is stored in the WebDAV repository.
Outbound Document	Outbound Document Definition Name	Click New and create an INVOIC S93A default document definition with a WebDAV reference to the S93A_I NVOIC_default.xml specification. Selection criteria: functional_identifier: INVOIC standards_version_type: S standards_version_value: 93A
	Map Inbound Document To Outbound Document	Automatically checked.
	Map Reference	Click Browse and select the Invoice_to_S93AINVOIC.xml document map.
Document Logging	Log Inbound Document	Select In XML Format.
	Log Outbound Document	Select both check boxes.
Advanced Configuration	Group Control Number	Set to 1.

Table 17-5.   Channel settings for Invoice/S93A INVOIC to Organization Alpha

Page	Configuration Property	Setting
	Advanced	Click Advanced, select the Envelope tab, and click the Advanced button. As per the UNB segment description of the ORDRSP message (see this book's web site at www.osborne.com), the following advanced UN/EDIFACT serializer settings should be verified: Syntax identifier: UNOA UNA control: Send UNA Only When Required

Table 17-5. Channel settings for Invoice/S93A INVOIC to Organization Alpha *(continued)*

The internal XML invoice is produced by the InvoiceWriter component. This component employs the same technique as the OrderApproval component: it uses the Order Processing Application Loopback port to map from the purchase order acknowledgment document to an invoice document, and it adds the additional information to the invoice document after the mapping has been successfully performed. You should therefore create another channel from an application on that port that has the settings listed in Table 17-6.

Page	Configuration Property	Setting
General Information	Name	PurchaseOrderAcknowledgment / Invoice Loopback.
	Comment	PurchaseOrderAcknowledgment / Invoice Loopback.
Source Application	Application and Name	Select the Application option and select Order Processing for the application name.

Table 17-6. Channel Settings for PurchaseOrderAcknowledgment/Invoice Loopback

Page	Configuration Property	Setting
Inbound Document	Inbound Document Definition Name	Click Browse and select PurchaseOrderAcknowledgment XML default.
Outbound Document	Outbound Document Definition Name	Click Browse and select the Invoice XML default document definition.
	Map Inbound Document To Outbound Document	Automatically checked.
	Map Reference	Click Browse and select the PurchaseOrderAcknowledgment_ to_Invoice.xml document map.
Document Logging	Log Inbound Document	Clear both check boxes. (We do not want to log this internal conversion.)
	Log Outbound Document	Clear both check boxes. (We do not want to log this internal conversion.)
Advanced Configuration		Leave the defaults.

Table 17-6. Channel Settings for PurchaseOrderAcknowledgment/Invoice Loopback *(continued)*

The third channel configured on the loopback port is used to map the purchase order acknowledgment to the shipping order document. It is used by the ShippingOrder component in much the same way as the other two channels. The channel settings are shown in Table 17-7.

IMPLEMENTING ADVANCED FEATURES

The shipping order is sent to another partner, of course. Organization Beta will represent the company that handles shipping for our organization. Organization Beta receives the shipping orders in XML format, using our (assumed to be mutually agreed) ShippingOrder document specification. The data is exchanged using the BizTalk reliable document transport.

Page	Configuration Property	Setting
General Information	Name	PurchaseOrderAcknowledgment / ShippingOrder Loopback.
	Comment	PurchaseOrderAcknowledgment / ShippingOrder Loopback.
Source Application	Application and Name	Select the Application option and select Order Processing for the application name.
Inbound Document	Inbound Document Definition Name	Click Browse and select PurchaseOrderAcknowledgment XML default.
Outbound Document	Outbound Document Definition Name	Click New and create the ShippingOrder XML default document definition with a WebDAV reference to the ShippingOrder.xml specification.
	Map Inbound Document To Outbound Document	Automatically checked.
	Map Reference	Click Browse button and select the PurchaseOrderAcknowledgment_ to_ShippingOrder.xml document map.
Document Logging	Log Inbound Document	Clear both check boxes. (We do not want to log this internal conversion.)
	Log Outbound Document	Clear both check boxes. (We do not want to log this internal conversion.)
Advanced Configuration		Leave the defaults.

Table 17-7.   The Channel Settings for PurchaseOrderAcknowledgment / ShippingOrder Loopback

This port configuration is quite a bit more complex than what we've done thus far because it shows how to implement a fully featured reliable messaging channel including encryption and signature support, receipt requests, and client certificate-based authentication.

Certificates for Signatures, Encryption, and HTTPS

Because Secure Sockets Layer (SSL) client authentication for HTTP/Secure (HTTPS), Secure Multipurpose Internet Mail Extensions (S/MIME) encryption, and signatures require certificates, we need to look at BizTalk's support for certificates a bit more closely.

The Microsoft Windows 2000 operating system has built-in support for the Public Key Infrastructure (PKI), which is the basis for the S/MIME e-mail encryption protocol and also for HTTPS certificate-based authentication. It supports the issuing of new certificates by using Certificate Services, an optional component that ships with the server editions of the Windows 2000 operating system.

NOTE: To learn how to set up and configure Certificate Services, refer to the Windows product documentation or see the detailed certificates discussion in *Windows 2000: A Beginner's Guide* (Osborne/McGraw-Hill, 2000).

Generally, Microsoft BizTalk Server 2000 uses two different certificate stores, which are both scoped to the local machine: The machine's Personal store and the BizTalk store. You can manage the certificate stores of the local machine by opening a new Microsoft Management Console (MMC) window (Select Start | Run, and type **mmc.exe**) and adding the Certificates snap-in for the local computer. To use certificates from the local computer's store, the BizTalk Messaging service must run under the local system account or an account that belongs to the local Administrators group in Windows 2000. To configure certificates, the user account from which Messaging Manager is run must also belong to the Administrators group.

The PKI knows a lot of certificate types that may be issued for different usage scenarios. Certificates that are used for BizTalk's S/MIME encryption and signature require secure e-mail capabilities; those used for certificate-based client authentication with HTTPS require client authentication capabilities.

Whenever you want to encrypt or sign outbound documents, you must use your own certificate(s) that hold(s) your private encryption key. The remote site will receive an exported copy of your certificate that contains only the public key. The document content is then encrypted by using your private key and decrypted by using the public key. Whenever your BizTalk server is a remote site for a partner, you must therefore import you partner's public key certificates into the local certificate stores so you can decrypt their data and to validate their digital signatures.

For outbound signatures, BizTalk requires the desired digital signature certificate (which must have a private key) to be stored in the local machine's Personal certificate store. Outbound encryption requires (a potentially different) certificate that is taken from the BizTalk store. This certificate must have a private key and encryption authorization.

Inbound documents that are S/MIME-encrypted and/or signed also require certificates to be installed on BizTalk Server. These are the certificates that you receive from (or assign to) your trading partners and that contain only public keys. The S/MIME decoder component in the document-processing pipeline will automatically locate and use the matching public key certificates from the certificate stores. The certificates that you can configure on the Inbound Document configuration page of the New Channel Wizard are used only to check the detected certificate against the certificate that is expected.

The public certificates for inbound signatures must be stored in the local machine's Personal store, and the decryption certificates must be stored in the BizTalk store. The same certificates are commonly used for both signature and decryption because this is the typical feature combination of secure e-mail certificates. In this case, the certificate must be imported into both certificate stores.

SSL client authentication requires your own private key certificate to be installed in the local computer's Personal store; the exported public key certificate must, of course, be installed on the remote server.

Implementing the Sender of a Secure Connection

Unlike all other channels and ports that we have discussed in this chapter, we will look at both the receiver and sender side of the secure connection. Only the sender side belongs to our solution, though. As you can probably already tell from the previous discussion about certificates, setting up these ports and channels requires quite a lot more preparation work than any of the others.

Therefore, this section of the chapter is an optional part of our example. A realistic setup of this scenario is possible only with at least two physically separate BizTalk Server machines anyway. The previous chapters also did not include a detailed walk-through for the document specification used in this example for the same reason: all of them are available for download.

The sender-side port is, of course, configured as To An Organization and has the properties listed in Table 17-8.

The channel to the imaginary shipping company is sent by the XLANG schedule and should therefore be created as From An Application. The sample configuration should be set as shown in Table 17-9.

Now you have a channel and port combination that has the maximum security and reliability that BizTalk can provide. The content is signed and encrypted end-to-end using S/MIME, and it is encrypted on the transport level using SSL; the connection is authenticated using client and server identity certificates, and it is delivered using the BizTalk Framework RELIABLE envelope.

Page	Configuration Property	Setting
General Information	Name	Secure, Reliable to Organization Beta.
	Comment	Secure, Reliable to Organization Beta.
Destination Organization	Organization	Select Organization, click the Browse button, and select Organization Beta in the dialog box.
	Primary Transport Address	Click Browse and select HTTPS transport as the transport type. The transport address should be set to a target server that is configured for HTTPS.
Envelope Information	Envelope Information	Click the New button and specify BizTalk Framework 2.0 Compliant as the envelope name. Select RELIABLE as the envelope format in the dialog box.
	Organization Identifier	Select Mutually Defined / 0011.
Security Information	Encoding Type	Select MIME.
	Encryption Type	Select S/MIME.
	Certificate Name	Click the Browse button and select your organization's private key encryption certificate from the BizTalk certificate store. (Of course, this requires that you put it there, first!)
	Signature Type	Select S/MIME. (The signature certificate is configured on the individual channels.)

Table 17-8. The Port Configuration for Secure, Reliable to Organization Beta

Page	Configuration Property	Setting
General Information	Name	ShippingOrder to Organization Beta.
	Comment	ShippingOrder to Organization Beta.
Source Application	Application and Name	Select Application and select Order Processing for the application name.
	Expect Receipt	Select Value and leave the receipt interval at 120 minutes. Within this time, a receipt must be received.
Inbound Document	Inbound Document Definition Name	Click Browse and select ShippingOrder XML default.
Outbound Document	Outbound Document Definition Name	Click Browse and select ShippingOrder XML default.
	Map Inbound Document To Outbound Document	Not checked.
	Sign Outbound Documents	Select Option, click the Browse button, and choose a valid signature certificate of your own organization.
Document Logging	Log Inbound Document	Clear both check boxes. (We do not do any conversion, so logging the outbound document will suffice.)
	Log Outbound Document	Select the XML Format check boxes.
Advanced Configuration	Advanced	Click the Advanced button and click the Properties button on the Primary Transport tab. In the Advanced Configuration dialog box for the HTTP transport, you can then select the client certificate to use for authenticating BizTalk against a remote server.

Table 17-9. The Channel Settings for ShippingOrder to Organization Beta

Setting up HTTP Receive Capabilities

Receiving HTTP messages requires that you set up a Microsoft Internet Information Server site or a (virtual) subdirectory of an existing site and place the receive scripts ReceiveResponse.asp and ReceiveStandard.asp from the .\SDK\Messaging Samples\ReceiveScripts product subdirectory into the new location. If we assumed that you place them immediately into the root of the site, the submission URL for inbound documents would be http://hostname/ReceiveStandard.asp. The correct URL for inbound receipts, for instance, receipts for the reliable channel that you have just configured, will be directed to http://hostname/ReceiveResponse.asp by your external partner's system.

The two ASP files are located in the Messaging Samples directory for good reason, though. You can merge this code into other ASP code and even enable your main web-site based URL to accept BizTalk submissions.

If we assume the setup just described, you need to make the response URL known to BizTalk Messaging because the receipt request in the BizTalk Framework envelope must contain a valid response address.

On the General tab of the BizTalk Server Group Properties dialog box, as shown in Figure 17-18, you must configure the response URL that is valid for an entire BizTalk Server group. Otherwise, attempts to send messages with the reliable protocol will fail.

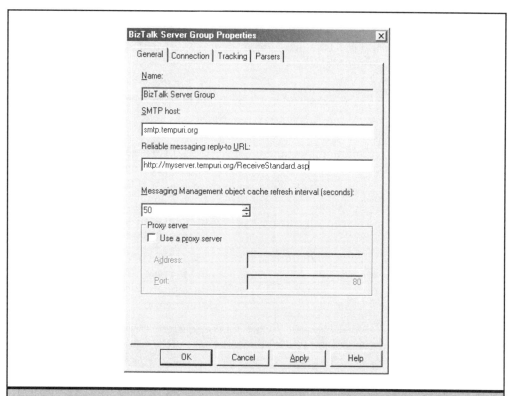

Figure 17-18.   The General tab of the BizTalk Server Group Properties dialog box

Implementing the Receiver Side of a Secure Connection

Because we will not make any assumptions about where the receiving application will route the shipping order we are sending, we will look at the channel configuration only on the receiving system. We also assume that our public key certificates are properly installed on the target system. The channel is created as From An Organization: in this case, our own organization. Table 17-10 lists the properties of interest only for security.

Notice that there are no special configuration settings for the receipt request. This is a very convenient feature of the RELIABLE messaging envelope format. If BizTalk receives a RELIABLE messaging envelope, it will inspect the header, generate the receipt, and send it to the origin server automatically.

SENDING FUNCTIONAL ACKNOWLEDGMENTS AND RECEIPTS

We have not yet covered how to send receipts for envelope formats other than the reliable XML format. The good news is that this is pretty straightforward to set up. If we were using the UN/EDIFACT S98A standards release for our UN/EDIFACT interchanges, you could create a ready-to-use CONTRL functional acknowledgment message by selecting the matching template in BizTalk Editor and saving the new document to the WebDAV repository without changes. The same is true for the X12 functional acknowledgment with the transaction set number 997.

Page	Configuration Property	Setting
Inbound Document	Inbound Document Definition Name	Click Browse and select ShippingOrder XML default.
	Verify Decryption Certificate…	Select the check box, click the Browse button, and select the decryption certificate of the organization.
	Verify Signature …	Select the check box, click the Browse button, and select the signature certificate of the organization.

Table 17-10. The Remote Channel Security Settings

The next step is to create a document definition for the CanonicalReceipt.xml XML specification, which is located in the Microsoft subdirectory of the WebDAV repository. The document definition should have a self-explanatory name, but it cannot be BizTalk Canonical Receipt because that name is reserved by BizTalk. This receipt name is reserved for the automatic receipt type that BizTalk uses internally.

Next, create a map between the CanonicalReceipt.xml file and the target receipt specification. You can find two sample implementations in the Microsoft subdirectory of the WebDAV document map store.

On the receiver side (the system that sent the original messages), receipts are always handled automatically; no special configuration steps are required. The correlation receipt—which matches the receipt with a previously sent interchange—is handled by the parser components in conjunction with receipt correlators.

The setup of the receipt sender (the receiver of the message to be acknowledged) is fairly easy from here. Assume that you have an existing port to the receipt destination because UN/EDIFACT is typically conversational: if two parties communicate by using UN/EDIFACT, they do it both ways. On this port, you create a new channel From An Application and select This Is A Receipt Channel on the first page of the Channel Wizard (Figure 17-10).

From there, the rest of the procedure is just like creating any other channel except that quite a few options will be unavailable. Usually, you will need to configure only the inbound document definition and set it to the document definition for the canonical receipt XML message. When you get to the Inbound Document Definition wizard page, the inbound definition will already look as if it is properly configured. It is not. You must assign the document definition that was previously mentioned; otherwise, the option to choose a different outbound document definition will not be available.

For a proper UN/EDIFACT response, you must set the outbound document definition to the UN/EDIFACT CONTRL message, which you still need to configure properly with WebDAV reference-and-selection criteria, of course. Finally, you set the document map. On the last wizard page, you must set the seed for the group control number for X12 and UN/EDIFACT.

The receipt channel is triggered by the channel that receives the inbound document. Figure 17-11 shows the Source Organization page where you can select the Generate Receipt check box and then select the newly created receipt channel. Whenever a new document arrives, BizTalk automatically constructs the canonical receipt and pushes it through the appropriate receipt channel back to the message source.

CHAPTER 18

Testing and Troubleshooting BizTalk Messaging

When you are working with BizTalk Mapper and you need to map complex specifications, creating document maps is always a little like solving a puzzle (which is not the Mapper's fault). In general, though, creating document specifications and configuring BizTalk messaging is easy once you have a little routine. However, if the definitions and configurations are not exactly correct or if the submitted documents are faulty, troubleshooting will remain difficult. This chapter helps you pinpoint such problems at the development stage. At times, this chapter paints a pretty grim picture about what could happen and what you need to check to avoid such problems. Don't let this scare you: planning for and thinking about the worst case is a good habit to get into.

The chapter starts with techniques to avoid messaging problems at the configuration stage and also explains how you can effectively test document definitions and maps in an isolated environment. Following that you will learn how to track down errors at run time by gathering error information from the Suspended Queue and the Windows 2000 event log.

AVOIDING MESSAGING PROBLEMS BEFORE THEY HAPPEN

Working with BizTalk Messaging is somewhat like learning to walk. Once you have crawled your way through the BizTalk documentation and tutorial (or this book), you will begin making baby steps to create your document specifications, definitions, ports, and channels. It is realistic to expect that in the beginning, things just won't work. You must have a little experience with a product to get a complete messaging configuration with all the required components to work seamlessly in a short amount of time. So in the beginning, you will stumble and fall. Just accept this as part of the game.

The main problem with troubleshooting BizTalk Messaging is that BizTalk's diagnostic tools are somewhat underdeveloped. In all honesty, this chapter tells a sad story about an otherwise exciting product. When you submit a document to a channel and it gets moved to the Suspended Queue because of some processing error, finding the exact cause is difficult. When errors occur in document parsing, validation, or in the mapping stage, the problems will be recorded in the application event log. However, the Interchange (the enveloped document or documents) causing the problems will be quarantined in the Suspended Queue, and this is also the place where the error will become initially obvious.

Therefore, you will need to find the exact event log entries that correspond to the respective Suspended Queue entry. This task is tedious and is almost impossible to handle in a production environment where hundreds of documents may fail within a short time due to a faulty specification or configuration mishaps. We will look at how you can correlate the Suspended Queue entries with the event log entries in "Finding and Isolating Messaging Errors," later in the chapter, but first, we will look at the best approach for troubleshooting: prevention.

Run-time errors that occur in BizTalk Messaging fall into six categories:

▼   **Document specification errors**   Although BizTalk Editor is really specialized
for creating BizTalk specifications, it will not guarantee that specifications are
completely correct. If it let you save only complete and correct specifications, you
simply would not be able to save work at the end of the day. Common problems
include missing or invalid properties for records and fields, incorrect definitions
for cardinalities and required fields, wrong or missing parser hints for non-
XML formats, and, of course, forgetting to reimport changed document
specifications into the management database. The Validate Specification
command on the BizTalk Editor Tools menu will catch most of the common
problems, though.

■   **Document map errors**   Because BizTalk document maps can employ VBScript
for custom functoids, the potential for document-mapping errors is just as high
as with any other programming language if you use such custom scripts: it's huge.
Other problems include mapping incompatible data types, mapping incompatible
field lengths, improperly mapping records structures with differing complexity,
and, most importantly, losing significant data due to missing or incomplete
mappings. A huge potential for errors is the fact that the Mapper embeds the
source and target specifications into the document maps. Should the specification
change, you must manually replace them; otherwise, your setup becomes out-
of-sync. Of course, you must reimport any changes to maps into the management
database as well.

■   **Configuration errors**   Even though messaging configuration is wizard-based
and hides a lot of the definition complexity by guiding you through the definition
tasks, even the Messaging Manager user interface will not catch all configuration
problems. For EDI documents, it is common to "forget" the selection criteria
settings on the document definition. Messaging Manager will also not look into
the document specifications and the document maps you specify; therefore, it
allows you to configure completely incompatible specifications for a channel.
Also, it allows you to use organization identifiers that are incompatible with
the EDI envelope formats.

■   **Installation and transport errors**   BizTalk Messaging uses the Microsoft XML
parser version 3.0. This component has a pretty wild history and has seen
frequent updates over the past two years. Because the XML parser provides a
fairly complete implementation of the core XML standards—of which some
have been finalized only recently—the parser had to be updated with every
major milestone of one of the related specifications. Because this also caused
some significant changes in the programming interfaces, a different version
of the Microsoft XML parser might be present on a system and, depending
on the order of installation, this can cause headaches for BizTalk. If you're
using HTTP through proxy servers or firewalls and did not specify those in
the configuration, you may also experience problems that are difficult to track.

■ **Incorrect inbound documents**   The most common reasons that interchanges end up in the Suspended Queue is because they are incomplete, contain invalid data, or are incorrectly formatted. In some cases, finding out whether an error is caused by an incorrect interchange or whether the document specification is not correct is like walking a thin line. Let's say you are implementing document specifications for the flatfile parser for documents that have been successfully exchanged between partners in that particular format since the 1970s. In this case, suspecting incorrect formatting of an inbound document from such a system may be a somewhat bold claim. The flatfile parser is especially unforgiving about trailing linefeeds or carriage returns past the data, and that can cause additional problems. However, in most cases where messages get quarantined in the Suspended Queue, the inbound document is at fault.

▲ **Server run-time errors**   Of course, BizTalk itself is also just another piece of software and indeed a very complex one. For instance, it depends heavily on SQL Server, and if one of the core databases becomes corrupted or the connection between BizTalk and SQL Server breaks for some reason, BizTalk will just stop working. Other problems involve custom application integration components, serializers, and parsers. If you create such components and your code crashes, they may take down the entire BizTalk Server process.

The best time to concentrate on avoiding these problems is in the development stage. Because of the complexity of BizTalk configurations, the number of components involved, and the high volume of documents that BizTalk typically handles, solving problems and doing rigid quality assurance before you deploy your solutions is key. If you deploy an incorrect setup when EDI is one of the lifelines of your client's businesses, it can seriously affect the business' bottom line, which you want to avoid.

NOTE: This is true for every software solution regardless of the product involved. Do not see this statement as a suggestion that BizTalk may not qualify for business-critical usage scenarios.

No matter what the problems are, troubleshooting is always expensive because it eats up valuable time. When the individual components of a messaging configuration seem okay when you verify them only superficially but then the composed setup fails, you may end up having to seek a needle in a haystack. If such problems occur in production, the cost factor can explode into infinity.

The most elementary components for BizTalk Messaging are document specifications. As a result, you should make them bulletproof at definition time and do intensive quality assurance from the start to avoid much of the trouble. Based on the preceding list of error categories, you can see that it would be helpful to be 100 percent sure that a document specification is correct and is normative for the documents to be exchanged, so that you can seek and encircle occurring problems elsewhere. Creating accurate document specifications from the beginning is the most efficient way to achieve solid results.

Although this approach is pessimistic, you should not blindly trust document specifications that you obtain from third parties (unless the supplier explicitly guarantees correctness) or public repositories like BizTalk.org. Also, the document templates that ship with BizTalk Server are supplied to help you get results more quickly, but to be sure that they express your exact intent, you will need to verify them step by step against the mutual agreement you have with your partners. The BizTalk documentation explicitly encourages you to do this especially for the EDI templates, and for good reason.

Validating Standards-Based Document Specifications

To verify document specifications, the merely technical validation that the BizTalk Editor performs is not sufficient. You must consider two basic scenarios when you want to create solid document specifications: specifications that describe standardized documents and EDI messages, and specifications that you create yourself.

When you create a BizTalk document specification for standardized document formats that are as precisely defined as the UN/EDIFACT or X12 standards, and they have equally precise partner agreements, verifying the document specifications at the definition stage is pretty simple. It is really only a field-by-field walk through all segments, fields, and subfields while checking them against the records and fields of the BizTalk specification. For typical partner agreements like the Compaq UN/EDIFACT specifications available on this book's web site (http://www.osborne.com) and the ones that we defined in Chapter 15, doing a thorough crosscheck should be a matter of less than an hour. You should consider this a good investment of time.

This is not true only for EDI documents, of course. When you define XML documents that are based on standards or that you receive from other partners for implementation on your end, you may not get them in a verified BizTalk Schema format; rather, they may be expressed as XML Document Type Definitions (DTD) or XSD Schema.

While BizTalk Editor supports you by being able to import DTDs, the DTD format is limited—it requires additional work and additional, external communication and documentation. For instance, DTDs entirely disregard data types. Data types are important for proper document mapping and application integration, though. Therefore, importing DTDs is always only a first step. To create a solid specification, you must precisely define the constraints for each field.

The XSD Schema format is a recently finalized World Wide Web Consortium (W3C) recommendation, and it is bound to become the lingua franca for expressing the shape of and constraints for XML documents. Many schemas are therefore expected to be expressed in XSD in the near future. The pity is that BizTalk was released before XSD was finalized and therefore does not immediately support this schema format. (Microsoft has publicly committed itself to deliver XSD schema support for its products through regular updates and service packs once the specification is finalized.) The XSD format has also grown to become so much more powerful than BizTalk's XDR schema foundation that a conversion from XSD back to its "parent" format XDR would potentially result in so much loss of information that it would be impractical. However, upgrading from XDR to

XSD is very practical, and the BizTalk SDK even contains an XSL style sheet that provides this functionality if you need to publish your XDR documents to your partners in XSD.

Sometimes you need to implement document specifications that are expressed in XSD, or, even worse, another vendor's pre-XSD proprietary schema format. (XDR is only one of a dozen rather popular pre-XSD schema formats.) In that case, you will probably need to rebuild the document specification from scratch and model it after the specification of the other schema. Until BizTalk Server fully supports XSD, certain essential elements, constraints, or schema attributes of such a schema specification may not be able to be expressed entirely in BizTalk Schema. This limitation does not preclude you from using BizTalk with your partner; however, it will require both parties to look beyond what the schema defines and examine the document instances to isolate the potential problems. Again, doing such research in the early development stages will save you time and money in the long run.

Implementing Strict Validation

When documents are moved to Messaging's Suspended Queue, positive or negative consequences can result. Positive results occur when BizTalk Messaging detects that an inbound document is invalid and is not entirely conformant to a document specification. To eliminate more difficult-to-trace problems further down the processing stages, it is essential that you perform a thorough and unforgiving validation of inbound documents as soon as they arrive from an external partner or an application. Consider tightening the constraints for document specifications in the areas described in the following sections.

Assign Precise Data Types   If you expect numeric information in a field, the document specification should express this explicitly. By default, all fields are treated as plain strings and will therefore positively validate any incoming data. However, if you create specifications for EDI, use the data-type definitions with care because the date and time formats are incompatible with the XML formats. What you can do, regardless, is mandate a fixed field length if an EDI date field is precisely defined to have only a CCYYMMDD format when exchanged between you and your partners. In that case, you may want to mandate a minimum and maximum field length of 8 to ensure that the correct number of digits is contained in the field. (Do not make the field numeric, though: a date expression is not a number, and the specification correctness will never be traded for better validation qualities.)

TIP: For non-XML formats, you should always define the correct native data type in the parser properties of the document specification in BizTalk Editor. This strategy will help the parser perform proper numeric data-type conversions for formats that do not have the same numeric formatting as XML and that must perform format conversions when transforming the inbound streams into XML.

A great BizTalk Editor feature is the code-list support available for UN/EDIFACT and X12: use it. If only a certain set of values is permitted in an interchange between partners, you should change the field type to Enumeration and define the precise set as the permissible data values. This is true not only for UN/EDIFACT and X12, but for any other data format, including XML.

Verify Record Cardinalities and Required Fields   If a certain XML element or EDI segment is essential for executing a certain business task or for locating or storing certain information, the specification should reflect this, and you should make it a required field or a record with a minimum occurrence of 1. If a certain record or segment is expected no more than once at a certain place based on a partner agreement, set the maximum occurrences to 1.

Even if the document standard on which the specification is based allows a higher cardinality for a certain segment/element or flags a field as optional, you should always make such alterations based on your exact requirements and override the standard rules. Be aware that tightening the rules of a standard is typically acceptable, because you essentially create a definition superset, which is in full compliance with the basic rules. If you relaxed the rules, you would begin violating the base standards by creating rule subsets, which you should never do.

An additional source of problems at design time—and a limitation of the product—is that BizTalk provides only limited support for required fields inside optional records. BizTalk Editor allows you to define them, and quite a few examples exist in the templates that ship with the product. But when you create document mappings to such specifications and decide not to emit an optional record that has a required field, BizTalk Mapper will complain that the mapping is incomplete.

Verify Type and Parser Settings for non-XML Formats   In Chapter 3, you learned that the UN/EDIFACT and X12 syntax rules are rather weak. For many custom flatfile formats, syntax rules have not even been given much thought. If you consider the inconsistencies that were pointed out for the SWIFT formats (which serve as the "negative example" standard), you will certainly understand this point well.

You must therefore check the parser rules for such formats thoroughly and verify them against the written documentation (which often lacks precision, although that's luckily not the case for broadly distributed standards like SWIFT). You must also verify them against a collection of live data streams. Such a collection should contain maximum and minimum data-volume examples and a randomly picked selection of real-life interchanges.

Especially when you integrate aging legacy systems that import and export data in such streams, the documentation may not be up to date with the data streams. Extra fields or extra records or transport elements might be used for purposes other than the documented purposes. When such changes occurred in a much smaller setting with only a few systems involved in the data exchange, you were able to easily tweak peer-to-peer systems. They guaranteed fairly rapid reactions to the business demands and did no harm. But they may harm you now, so take a closer look.

Inconsistent end-of-document formatting will definitely cause problems. To the BizTalk flatfile parser, it makes a huge difference if an input stream ends with the last character of the last record's last field or if there is a trailing linebreak. In many flatfile format descriptions, that seemingly minor detail often goes unnoticed. However, remember that the BizTalk parsers are designed to dissect enveloped, multidocument interchanges; therefore, a parser must know exactly where it should stop looking for more data for a particular document, and it must also give up and return an error if data is left unparsed—even if it is a single carriage-return character.

Eliminate Unnecessary Definitions   On of the simpler programming rules is "deleted code doesn't crash." This rule is just as true for document specifications. Unless a standard mandates the presence of certain elements that you do not use in a document, get rid of them. Scaling down document specifications not only reduces the complexity and sources for unexpected problems, but it also yields higher performance.

However, even when you delete elements from specifications, you need to be careful. You must not compromise the integrity of standard composites or segments when you are dealing with the EDI formats. Even a predefined message segment has some 60 elements and composites, and you use only three of them. You must leave the segment intact because the parser must be able to count the field and composite positions based on these settings.

Implementing Tolerant Validation

Obviously, this topic is the exact opposite of the previous discussion about implementing strict validation. In certain scenarios, you do indeed want to have minimum validation rules. When it became clear that XML would become the next great wave for getting data from here to there, many companies jumped on the train before it had even left the station: they started to wildly implement XML data exchange without proper schemas or even DTDs. And they relied on the extensibility and traversing the XML Document Object Model (DOM) to produce and read XML, ignored data that they did not understand, and performed no validation at all.

If you are an XML "veteran," you can probably relate to this scenario. Most XML veterans originally worked in HTML. In the HTML philosophy of "validation," browsers are designed to ignore anything they don't recognize and to "do their best" with everything else. In other words, HTML browsers are designed to be as forgiving as possible, and some of that philosophy often carried over into the XML world when the technology was new.

Hence, such forgiving implementations still exist and you will have to adapt to their lack of definition-precision if you happen to have them in your software portfolio. To adapt, you must make the respective BizTalk document specifications fairly tolerant to avoid validation errors and to leverage BizTalk's document-routing and mapping capabilities.

The core issue is that you cannot disable document validation with BizTalk. To send a document without validating it, the only option is to push it straight through to the transport component to send it to the destination.

So if you have such a system, you must create a BizTalk Schema for the maximum extent of the XML data stream. Although with BizTalk Editor, you can use the open content model for XML elements (which means that an element can carry arbitrary, unspecified XML content), the BizTalk document-processing pipeline will not be able to handle such arbitrary content. You will need to know what the precise structure is. If your implementation is too "flexible" (used synonymously with "random"), you will have to adjust it.

All of the described techniques are just ways to enable BizTalk to understand immature XML implementations. Avoid using BizTalk document maps to transform such loosely de-fined XML data streams into narrowly defined document specifications because you will merely move the potential problems a step further down the processing pipeline.

Validating Custom Document Specifications

The other scenario for document specifications that must be verified and validated are those that you create yourself. The specifications are not those that you model after some existing standard (like implementing UN/EDIFACT messages for which no templates are supplied with BizTalk), but rather, those XML documents that you define from the ground up for use within your organization or with external partners.

Although you have full control over the definition process—and your specifications will always be normative in this case—you must give some issues special consideration, especially if you work in an international environment. This section focuses on how to keep documents from getting stuck in the Suspended Queue such that processing is denied due to limitations of the specification that you may have set for a good reasons, but for which the precondition may not always be true.

When you open your business for direct document interchange and invite the world to exchange data with you, you must plan for the possibility that the world will actually accept your invitation. Consequently, you must plan the size constraints and data types with an eye on what is customary in other countries.

For example, if you live in the United States, you might assume that phone numbers are organized in three groups with an optional two-to-four digit extension that is typi-cally not dialed through except when the PBX system has picked up. If you make this a rule and split up the phone number into area code (three digits), phone number (seven digits), and extension (four digits), and you model your XML specification accordingly, the field will be nicely structured but incompatible with most countries outside the United States.

In the same vein, consider the following points from a European perspective:

▼   Postal codes (or ZIP codes) appear in virtually any shape or form throughout the world. Some countries use only digits (with varying lengths), some use a mix of letters and digits (like the United Kingdom), and some do not use any.

■   Many countries are not organized into states (consider Vatican City or San Marino, both of which would fit into a few New York City street blocks). Or if they do have subdivisions, they are relevant only politically, but they are not used anywhere in business-to-business data exchange. For instance, in Germany, it doesn't make sense to specify your state as a mandatory part of a postal address.

■   The associated ISO standards for measurements, weights, and time are based on the metric system and a 24-hour day—like it or not. For instance, a company in France could not make use of electronic quotations or inquiries involving an American (English) pound or ton.

▲   BizTalk documents are internally Unicode—and for good reason. International partners will generally use the spelling and diacritic marks as they are used in their own language. You should therefore not assume that all characters are between *A* and *Z* or *a* and *z*. This applies most to document mapping, but you should not make this a documented restriction in your specification either.

When you create business-to-business documents, you should generally not derive constraints and data types only from the rules that are common in your own country, even if that isn't an immediate business requirement. Take a much broader approach and consider the rules that apply elsewhere. Creating international definitions right once and in the beginning is cheap; if you have to correct them later, when you actually need international data exchange, the cost of change will be immense.

Testing Document Specifications and Document Maps

BizTalk Editor helps you define correct specifications by letting you validate existing document instances against a specification. It even employs the native document parsers to do so and simulates the parsing process on the document level. However, this may not be sufficient. When your real setup uses envelopes, you should always test document specifications together with those envelopes. If you expect to receive interchanges with multiple documents at a time (BizTalk cannot produce them but can handle them inbound), you should test them in a more realistic environment.

In the previous chapter, we defined a loopback channel for testing purposes, and we used the DirectIntegration tool from the SDK to submit documents into this channel. Make this a habit for testing both document specifications and document maps before you release them. If you want to test a document specification, define a channel (on a generic loopback port) that uses the same document definition as the inbound and outbound document, and import the specification with the document definition. If you want to test a map, you should have already tested the used document specifications thoroughly, and then you should use different inbound and outbound definitions to test the mapping.

If you want to use the produced documents as files or you want to use the asynchronous submission mode, use the file transport and store files to a temporary work directory.

In any event, you should use actual data to test your document specifications. The sample instances that you can create with BizTalk Editor can help you find out what the documents will look like and make some simple validation tests. However, you must use "the real thing" to verify whether all constraints will work as desired and whether the specification will work when used in conjunction with an envelope. The instances generated by the Editor are guaranteed to work because they are precisely modeled after the instance constraints. For serious testing, using the Editor generated specifications is just as useful as not testing at all.

To run some more realistic tests for schemas that you create yourself, you may even want to simulate a client site that does not run BizTalk Server and cannot readily use the

BizTalk Schema formats. Take some other XML editor tool or even the famous Microsoft Visual Notepad, create a few instances from scratch based on actual business cases, and try to follow the rules of the Schema manually. Better yet, ask someone else on your team to do it. Clearly, this type of testing is easier said than done, but it will be far more realistic than just using onboard BizTalk tools.

When you use EDI, testing is not an option—it is a necessity. You should always test complete inbound interchanges that represent the maximum extent of data that you can expect from your partners. You must also do a field-by-field walk through the output format and check that output against the partner agreement.

Setting up the document definitions in the process will also eliminate the configuration problems related to EDI selection criteria. These problems will emerge immediately in a testing environment. If you forget to set up the selection criteria for non-XML documents, neither the parsers nor the serializers will be able to locate the proper schemas; thus, they will not produce the desired results. This issue becomes even more critical with non-XML envelopes because BizTalk will "fail to XML" in this case. It will succeed technically, but it will produce incorrect results. Beware of the selection criteria.

The bottom line is, never use a document specification or document map in a production setup that you have not thoroughly tested by using the same configuration with realistic production data. This goes for updating specs and maps as well. You should thoroughly test any changes in the test environment before rolling into production. There is a tendency to say "it's a small change, I don't need to go through all of that again." To state it bluntly: go through the testing, or go through the help-wanted ads.

Simulating Routing

What if a specially discounted sales offer for one of your key accounts ends up in some other customer's inbox? Or what if sensitive human resources information is routinely dropped into some other system's Suspended Queue? Both of these scenarios could have devastating consequences.

To avoid such situations, your test environment should emulate the real world as closely as possible. You need at least two physical machines with separate setups to do testing that is anywhere near close to reality. The reason for this is that the home organization from which all internal traffic will originate in a production setup can exist only once on a BizTalk cluster. If you want to test routing and proper behavior when getting receipts from the destination, you will have to simulate your home system and the destination system.

Testing with reality in mind means that you should also use the same transports that you would use in the production deployment. If you plan to send documents by using HTTP and expect to receive receipts via an Internet Information Server ASP page, you need to simulate that just as much as if you were using SMTP as a transport.

Your test environment should therefore be reasonably isolated from your internal LAN and the Internet, and it should employ a simulation of the outside Domain Name

Service (DNS) setup. If your own company is samplesource.org and the destination is sampledest.org, both domains should be registered in your test environment's DNS service and be assigned to the respective machines that take on the home and destination organization's roles. If you use SMTP, you should also simulate a remote destination using Microsoft Exchange Server or any other mail server. Fortunately, and unlike BizTalk Server, which can manage only a single home organization per cluster, Exchange can host multiple domains; therefore, a single Exchange Server with the proper setup is sufficient to create the required environment.

The BizTalk Server that plays the remote destination can, however, take on the role of a document router—something that hasn't been explicitly mentioned throughout this book and that may be interesting to ASPs.

To set up a document router configuration with BizTalk Server, you should simply forget about the existence of the home organization and treat all sources and destinations as remote. To avoid confusion in the following discussion, the originating BizTalk Server on which you deploy your test scenario is called Home Server, and the server that you use to simulate remote destinations is called Remote Server. For the purpose of this discussion, we will also recycle the organization identifiers that were created in the previous chapter.

Assume you want to send an XML document with a reliable format from a home organization with the organization qualifier/identifier pair ZZ/0001 to Organization Alpha with the qualifier/identifier pair ZZ/0011. This is the configuration of the Home Server.

On the Remote Server, you would have to set up both organizations as external and configure a channel that accepts the interchange from ZZ/0001 as the source organization (the channel is therefore "From an Organization") and routes it through to a port bound to ZZ/0011 ("To An Organization"). The transport protocol for the port should preferably be the FILE transport and should drop the documents to a local directory, because that is the easiest way to investigate the data. If you want to test documents headed from the Remote Server to the Home Server, the channel and port setup for the organization identifiers simply needs to be reversed, and you will need to bind the port to the correct endpoint on the Home Server.

Testing in Realistic Deployments

This heading sounds pretty important, as if there were a complicated background, but the message behind it is surprisingly simple. Still, it is very important: test on clean systems.

Your BizTalk production machine is unlikely to have Microsoft Office, Microsoft Visio (!), or Microsoft Visual Studio 6.0 installed (let alone the new .NET release). It is also unlikely to have a release or even prerelease version of Microsoft Windows XP installed. BizTalk Server 2000 is designed for Windows 2000, and it should run on Windows 2000.

The message is, if your production machine does not have certain components installed, do not install them on your test machine. Hard disk drives are so cheap today that it should be easy to run multiple installations on separate partitions, even with a limited hardware budget.

FINDING AND ISOLATING MESSAGING ERRORS

When a document cannot be parsed or positively validated, or mapping errors or other problems occur somewhere in the document-processing pipeline, the BizTalk Messaging service will move the interchange into the Suspended Queue and will record one or several errors in the event log.

As previously mentioned, correlating entries in the Suspended Queue with their respective error messages from the event log is very tedious. It is really not clear why BizTalk Server does not provide a consolidated view for this information. Every event log entry that is caused by some problem in the document-processing pipeline is recorded with a Suspended Queue identifier, which you can also find in the Suspended Queue window.

Although that identifier is therefore the primary means to correlate both entries, unfortunately, BizTalk Administrator's default setting does not help much. The column containing these values in the Suspended Queue view is preset to be the rightmost column; it will likely be hidden when you look at the queue entries, as shown in Figure 18-1.

To move the entry into view, you can select View | Choose Columns from the Suspended Queue node's context menu and move the Interchange ID column further up in the column order. (You can also drag and drop columns in the view.) Unfortunately, BizTalk Administrator will not save the adjustments to the view settings, though. The Suspended Queue identifier column contains a unique identifier (UUID) for every interchange as you can see from Figure 18-2.

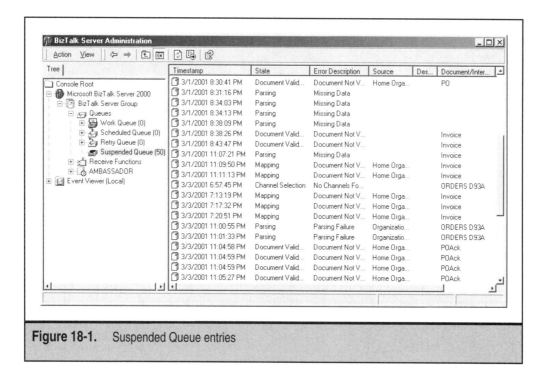

Figure 18-1.   Suspended Queue entries

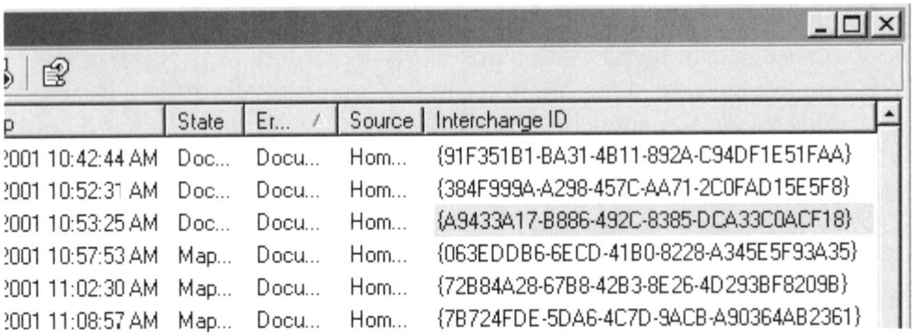

Figure 18-2. The Suspended Queue Identifier column

To find out what went wrong for a given Suspended Queue entry, you need access to the interchange identifier (or Suspended Queue ID), the document that caused the error, and the error messages.

We have the identifier, and now we will get the document. When you want to track down errors effectively, you should always have your favorite text editor handy. You will want to save the document to investigate it later in more detail. You can obtain the document from the Suspended Queue by selecting an entry and accessing its context menu.

When you select View Document Command from the context menu, the document that caused the problem will appear in the Document Content dialog box. If the error occurred before or in the parsing stage for non-XML formats, the document will be displayed as shown in Figure 18-3(a); otherwise, the XML representation of the document will be displayed in a simple edit control as shown in Figure 18-3(b). Regardless of the display mode, the dialog box is certainly too small, and the flat text display of the XML data stream does not help you gain much insight. To paste the contents into a text editor so that you can either inspect them manually or validate them with BizTalk Editor or other tools, place the cursor in the content box and press CTRL-A to select the contents. Then press CTRL-C to move the contents to the clipboard and paste them into a text editor for saving the contents to a file and to either inspect them manually or save them to a file to validate them with BizTalk Editor or other tools.

Next, you want to find out what happened. You can find the first hint in the associated event log entry. The BizTalk Administrator Microsoft Management Console (MMC) setup includes the snap-in for the local event log for that reason. Finding the matching entry unfortunately requires some manual searching.

You can assume that the entry into the Suspended Queue and the matching event log entry occurred in the same second or at least within a few seconds of each other. The BizTalk Server event log entries can be found in the Application log and are identified

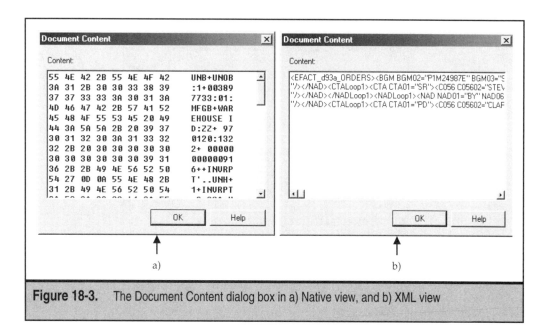

Figure 18-3. The Document Content dialog box in a) Native view, and b) XML view

with the BizTalk Server. If you seek the associated event log entry, you will need to know both the exact time and the Interchange ID of the Suspended Queue entry.

For the entry highlighted in Figure 18-2, the corresponding event log entry occurred one second before the Suspended Queue entry. The details of the event log entry are contained in the Suspended Queue ID, as shown in Figure 18-4.

The complete error description that could be found for this particular entry on the test machine was the following:

```
An error occurred in BizTalk Server.
  Details:
 -----------------------------
 The XML document has failed validation for the following reason:
Length is greater than the maximum length.

 Suspended Queue ID: "{A9433A17-B886-492C-8385-DCA33C0ACF18}"
```

So the level of error information you get is basically an XML document and this message. This is certainly not much to go on.

State, the second column in the Suspended Queue view, tells you the processing stage in which the error occurred. In this case, the particular error occurred in the document validation stage. The following sections describe typical errors in the various stages and explain how you can track them down. BizTalk Messaging provides 23 different global

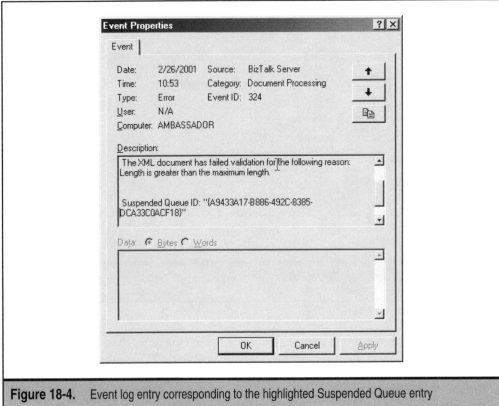

Figure 18-4. Event log entry corresponding to the highlighted Suspended Queue entry

codes that help explain why documents are placed into the Suspended Queue. We will address only the most common here. You can find the complete list of codes in the BizTalk documentation by searching for CISReasonToQueue.

Parsing Stage Errors

Errors that occur in the parsing stage typically imply incorrect input data. If you use UN/EDIFACT, X12, or any other custom data format that allows multiple documents within a single interchange, and if your partner agreements allow multiple inbound documents, Suspended Queue entries with the state Parsing should ring alarm bells. By BizTalk's current design, parsers that encounter errors while processing an interchange must stop and return an error. If this occurs while a multiple document interchange is being parsed, all documents that follow the document in the interchange (this is not limited to functional groups) will be ignored.

In this case, you may find the hex display of the original interchange to be somewhat informative but of little help. If you want to track down the problem to rescue and resubmit the interchange, you will have to retrieve the original from the document tracking database. (See Chapter 21 for procedures.) You should therefore configure the document-tracking settings for each channel that either accepts or writes non-XML data formats to track the native document format.

Finding problems in complex multidocument interchanges may indeed prove to be very difficult if they do not jump out at you when you are looking at the document. While BizTalk Editor lets you validate documents, it does not understand any of the surrounding envelope information. Figure 18-5 shows a UN/EDIFACT sample data stream for an ORDER message that contains a minor bug and will therefore fail processing (hint: the TDT segment has no segment terminator character). To find this error, you first need to open BizTalk Editor and load the document specification that is supposed to match the interchange.

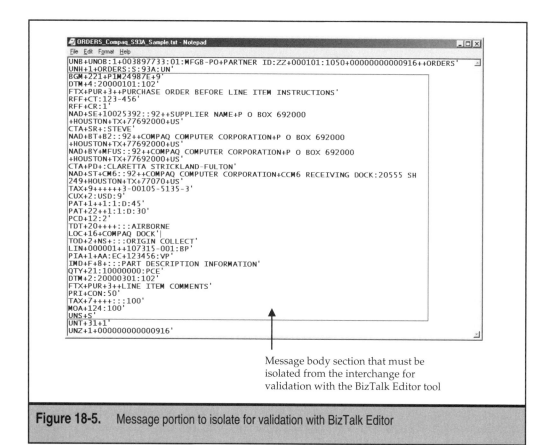

Message body section that must be
isolated from the interchange for
validation with the BizTalk Editor tool

Figure 18-5. Message portion to isolate for validation with BizTalk Editor

Figure 18-5 shows which portion of the interchange needs to be isolated from the data stream. In the UN/EDIFACT and X12 cases, the message is framed by the interchange headers and footers or by functional group headers and footers. Once you have saved the isolated message of the interchange to a file, you can select Tools | Validate Instance in BizTalk Editor and load the file for validation. (To load non-XML files, you will have to switch the file-type combo box to All Files in the Open File dialog box.) When you load files for X12 or UN/EDIFACT formats, the Editor will immediately prompt you for the delimiter characters to use. Set them as required by your partner agreement, as defined by the standard, or as you find them in the UN/EDIFACT UNA header segment. In this case, the delimiters are a single quote (') for the record delimiter, a plus sign (+) for the field delimiter, a colon (:) for the subfield delimiter, and a question mark (?) as escape character.

The result of the validation process will then appear on the Warnings tab of BizTalk Editor's bottom pane. In our case, the message will be as follows:

```
The data contains a field value ("COMPAQ DOCK") that doesn't meet
maximum length requirement for tag "C40101" (maximum length is 3).
The parser failed to convert the document due to processing errors.
See the following messages for details.
```

First, the "following messages" that BizTalk Editor promises will never appear. There is no more information than this. Also, the error in this interchange is definitely that the segment terminator for the TDT segment is missing and there is no field-length mismatch. Let's zoom in on the problem to understand what is going wrong:

```
TDT+20++++:::AIRBORNE
LOC+16+COMPAQ DOCK'
```

Because the segment terminator is missing, the UN/EDIFACT parser will proceed to treat the following line as data of the TDT segment. The COMPAQ DOCK value would therefore end up mapping to the first subfield of the seventh element of the TDT segment, which is the compound element for Excess transport information. Because the subfield "Excess transport information, coded" will allow only three characters, the validation fails at this point.

This reveals one critical problem with such formats: if the value that triggered the error were within this limit and the following LOC segment were optional (which it is), parsing would succeed, and the LOC segment would be incorrectly mapped into fields of the TDT segment.

Before you panic, keep in mind that this example is rather unlikely to happen in the real world. It was chosen to represent one of the many problems that could potentially occur in the parsing stages, and it is easy to construct from the material you have. The systems you will talk to using UN/EDIFACT will not likely forget something as fundamental as a segment terminator, and BizTalk's UN/EDIFACT serializer will not do that either.

However, let's continue to assume that this case really happened on a production system. Besides picking up the phone and calling your partner to notify them of the problem, you may want to fix the problem this one time and resubmit it.

Although the Suspended Queue entry's context menu will allow you to resubmit documents into processing, this function is really useful only for those documents that have exceeded the transport retry counts or that have repeatedly not been acknowledged by the remote site. Resubmitting through this mechanism will not allow any changes to the documents; thus, the interchange that we are currently looking at would just make a loop and end up in the same place.

This is another good use for the DirectIntegration SDK tool. When you have corrected the interchange (including headers), you should paste the document into the tool and set the submission parameters to the respective values that you see in the columns of the Suspended Queue entry. If a column is blank, you should leave the argument blank as well.

CAUTION: The ease with which you can submit documents using the DirectIntegration tool should worry you when considering security. Therefore, you should tighten network security around your BizTalk Server systems as much as possible, and use signatures and strong authentication with your transports (client-side certificates, as discussed in Chapter 17). Otherwise, smuggling false documents into the processing flow would be incredibly easy. This is not a BizTalk issue; rather, it is a network-access security issue to be aware of. This cannot be stressed enough.

Channel Selection Stage Errors

When interchange has been parsed and the source and destination identifiers have (possibly) been extracted from the transport envelope, the Messaging service will try to match the available criteria of each document contained in the interchange against the channel definitions and also evaluate the channel filter expressions against the XML representation of the document.

If the document has been submitted synchronously, documents that do not match exactly one channel will cause an error that is immediately relayed to the client, which will not be posted to the Suspended Queue. Asynchronous submissions will land in the Suspended Queue if the document cannot be matched against any channel.

Channel selection errors can occur for two reasons:

▼   **Configuration errors**   Your channel filters may be too tight or you may receive correct interchanges from partners or applications that have not been properly configured. A common problem would be selecting organization qualifier/identifier pairs that are different from those found in the actual interchange headers.

▲   **Incorrect input documents**   Just as much as you can make configuration errors, the sender side of the communication may do that as well. Again, the common reason for these problems is incorrect identifiers.

There is no better way of avoiding such errors than reviewing your channel filters and configuration settings, picking up the phone, or writing an e-mail to notify your partner of the problem.

If you encounter these problems in this or any of the following stages, resubmitting the multidocument interchanges as explained in the previous section may be fatal. When the parsing stage fails, nothing will have happened with the interchange at all. If it fails parsing, it will not produce any documents. However, if you have multiple documents that have been successfully parsed and isolated, some may actually make it successfully through the document-processing pipeline, and just one of them may be quarantined in the Suspended Queue. If this happens, you should address the problem locally and communicate with your partner to resubmit the request.

Document Validation and Mapping Stage Errors

The bulk of nonrecoverable messages that end up in the Suspended Queue will likely contain document validation errors. These may occur either when the document is first accepted or immediately after a document mapping has been performed and the document is validated against the target specification. Documents that "only" failed transmission may appear in bursts when a network connection goes down for a long time, but document validation failures are the most common unrecoverable errors.

As stated in the discussion about tightening document constraints, finding Suspended Queue entries that failed validation is not necessarily a bad sign. If document content is invalid and you catch the problems before they enter business processing, you will avert more expensive errors. Still, you must be able to tell what the problem is and try to address it at the source by using the error information to correct either the originating internal or external application.

Luckily, you already know all the required steps. Unfortunately, it takes a lot of steps. You need to get the document from the Suspended Queue, copy it to a text editor, and save it. Then you need to open BizTalk Editor, load the document specification, and validate the instance. For the document validation just described, the Editor displays the following warning message:

```
The XML document has failed validation for the following reason:
Length is greater than the maximum length.
Line:2, Position:363
" City="HOUSTON" State="TX" PostalCode="77692000" Country="US"/>
```

The information that we have gained from the event log entry is indeed only the exact position in the XML document that caused the error to occur. The XML snippet that will be displayed below the position is only the line that *caused* the error. Do not take that as a hint about *where* the error occurred. In our case, it is 363 columns into the displayed line. If you want to find that position in the original document, you need an editor that counts column numbers or you need to count them out yourself.

In this case, the position is at the closing angle bracket (>) of the following element:

```
<ItemDescription Type="00" Description="LINE ITEM COMMENTS"/>
```

What do we garner from this information? Only that something is wrong somewhere within this element. A quick look at the document specification then reveals that the maximum length for the Type attribute is one character. Strike.

This is indeed very cumbersome! Let's hope that the procedures described in this chapter become obsolete with a BizTalk Server service pack.

PART V

Administering BizTalk Server 2000

CHAPTER 19

Installing BizTalk in a Production Environment

T his chapter and the following two chapters explain how to install and configure BizTalk Server. This chapter focuses on the architecture and deployment planning that you must perform to set up the run-time components of BizTalk Server 2000. The following chapters examine how you manage and monitor BizTalk Server installations programmatically through the BizTalk Configuration Object Model or the Windows Management Instrumentation (WMI) interfaces.

NOTE: In Chapter 5, you learned how to perform a minimal installation of BizTalk Server 2000 for evaluation and development purposes, but this type of installation will probably be very different from an actual production deployment.

This chapter intentionally excludes a step-by-step setup because, as you will see, the number of possible configuration combinations is endless and such a walk-through may not be right for your needs. Therefore, we will not go into the details of exactly how you attach an existing database during setup and install a machine into a server group (take a peek at the figures of the installer in Chapter 5 to help you with this) or how you install Visio 2000 and the BizTalk Orchestration Designer on a production server.

CONSIDERATIONS FOR PLANNING DEPLOYMENTS

Once you get comfortable with the terminology and have created a couple of ports, channels, document specifications, and document maps, the procedures for creating BizTalk solutions described in this book so far should be fairly easy to handle if you are a developer. Deploying those solutions to run with maximum efficiency is a whole different ballgame, however, and you will probably need to rely on team members with very specialized expertise to create and optimize large BizTalk Server deployments.

It would indeed go far beyond the scope of a single individual (and would probably require a multiple-volume set of books) to examine all the tuning and deployment options for BizTalk Server 2000 installations. The topics to cover range from hardware issues like picking disk controllers, storage arrays, multiprocessor boards, and high-bandwidth memory, to networking issues like setting up high-performance network server backbones, to clustering topics like creating shared-disk clusters with Windows 2000 Advanced Server and using network and component load balancing with Microsoft Application Center 2000. On top of that, squeezing the most out of BizTalk Server 2000 requires top-gun, low-level tuning skills for Microsoft SQL Server 2000.

Because not all BizTalk Server deployments require large server farms, we will look at some of the most common tasks that you can perform to get the most out of BizTalk Server for small- and medium-sized deployments, and we will examine some strategies to make your systems scale up later as your requirements grow. But before we go into the details of how to install the product in production environments and how to distribute the BizTalk components and the databases, we will first look at some basic considerations for planning BizTalk Server deployments.

Performance Considerations

BizTalk Server is a platform for high data volume and high frequency systems integration and electronic document exchange. If an organization had to exchange only a handful of documents between applications or between partners daily, there would certainly not be enough optimization potential to justify introducing a product of the complexity and power—and honestly, the price tag—of BizTalk Server 2000.

However, once your incoming or outgoing data traffic hits a certain threshold of volume as well as data format and transport option diversity, BizTalk Server 2000 is one of the best price/performance options that exists on the market today. Where that threshold is depends entirely on your business and your integration scenarios. You will ultimately have to compare your current costs for maintaining your existing integration and messaging solutions against the long-term cost-saving effects that BizTalk's XML-based messaging and Orchestration integration tools can provide.

If you have no such solutions in place but want to start electronic document exchange using BizTalk Server, you must determine how much manual work you can eliminate that currently goes into producing, reading, and transferring printed information relayed by postal mail, fax, or informal e-mail. You must also weigh the cost of human error that these manual or semiautomatic media transfers cause against the machine-to-machine data exchange that is possible with XML and BizTalk's support for multiple electronic document formats. If you conclude that using BizTalk Server 2000 makes sense for EAI and/or EDI in your organization, this decision will have a broad scope and reach within a relatively short time.

If your organization (or your client's) is a trading firm and you decide to accept purchase orders electronically, it is only consequent to confirm these orders back to the messaging-enabled sender electronically. Soon enough, you will also send shipping advices, full or partial invoices, and catalogues to your customers and will also encourage your suppliers to take advantage of your electronic document exchange infrastructure. Using electronic documents is somewhat like being pregnant—you really are or you really are not. Businesses that become "infected" with BizTalk and begin to feel the cost-saving effects will want to formalize as much document traffic as possible and move it from fax and mail to the BizTalk platform.

Why is all this mentioned under the performance topic? Because unless you have some precisely measurable and plannable enterprise integration scenario in which using BizTalk provides a benefit over other solutions, beginning with a small subset of your business processes in electronic document exchange scenarios may soon result in a more extensive solution than you initially planned for. And by then, planning for optimum performance becomes an issue.

The problem with discussing how to plan for optimum performance is that it really depends on your situation. We could look at very few hard numbers without looking at specific scenarios. Trying to do that would be like giving you a medicine handbook and telling you not to go to the doctor anymore. However, we can discuss the performance issues to look out for.

Memory Usage and Processor Performance

Most operations within BizTalk involve using XML. XML is great because it is a platform-agnostic text format that is self-describing and that comes with great additional technologies like XPath, XSLT, and XML Schema, which elevate it from a mere data format to a complete solution platform. However, and like most technologies that make other technologies simpler, this universality comes at a price: XML is hungry for processing power and memory. In fact, even with the resources of the typical mid 1990s, such as personal computers, PC-based servers, and text-based verbose data technology like XML, most software architects and developers would have never thought of them as the universal glue between applications or even between a single application's layers. For many, these performance concerns are still the reason why they remain skeptical about the merits of XML.

Let us assume for a moment that you only exchange XML documents only by using BizTalk Server and you use document maps to convert between different schemas. In this scenario, BizTalk will have to load (and parse) any document into memory along with the associated schema (which is an XML document and also has to be parsed) and then validate the document instance against the schema by comparing the structure against the definition. Then it will need to load the document map, find and isolate the XSLT transformation style sheet from the map, parse the style sheet, and then run the source document through the style sheet to produce the outbound document. While doing that, it must execute all database lookups, external component calls, and calculations defined through the map's functoids.

When the output document has been produced, BizTalk needs to load the associated schema document for validation and match the result against the ruleset of the schema. This means that for a single pass through a transforming channel, XML documents, style sheets, and schemas have to be loaded and parsed at least five times, and each of the documents has to be traversed (multiple times) in the process. Of course, the highly optimized Microsoft XML parser does most of this work, but even it cannot eliminate these steps.

If you are using one of the EDI formats or other formats through custom parser or serializer components, the processing load even grows, because the additional parsing code has to parse and walk the schema at least one additional time to produce the internal XML data or output native data formats.

Microsoft isn't kidding when they recommend "as fast as possible" symmetric multiprocessing (SMP) Pentium III Xeon systems with one or two megabytes on processor level 2 caches and four to eight processors for high-volume installations. The more parser code and data that fits into the processor cache, the faster all these activities that feed on clock cycles will be handled because the processor cache eliminates the comparatively expensive access to the onboard cache or even into the main memory banks.

Using Secure Multipurpose Internet Mail Extensions (S/MIME) encoding with digital signatures or encryption or using transport-level HTTPS with encryption or client authentication through the Secure Sockets Layer (SSL) rather dramatically affects processor use and the overall processing performance. This is because the asymmetric RSA encryption algorithm and symmetric DES algorithm typically used are a heavy drain on CPU resources. That's the price for security and, therefore, a feature set that you will not want to give up too easily.

If transport-level privacy and authentication is sufficient (for which you would typically use HTTPS), you can reduce the adverse effects on the machine's processor load by routing traffic through a virtual private network with dedicated router hardware that takes care of encrypting the traffic. Or you can reduce the adverse affects by using local bridgehead servers that accept documents from BizTalk Server by using plain HTTP and forward the data to the destination by using HTTPS, which acts as a proxy for client authentication at the same time.

Another option to deal with increased processor use through encryption is to use dedicated encryption hardware boards that support the Win32 CryptoAPI and replace its software layer by circuit-printed algorithms (read: fast!). The *CryptoAPI* is the encryption support layer that is built into the Windows operating system platform and is used by most Microsoft Internet software, including BizTalk.

XML is also the reason why BizTalk is pretty memory hungry. From the start, you should not even consider setting up a BizTalk server machine with less than 256MB of RAM per processor. Anything upwards from 1GB of RAM is where it starts to become more than just acceptable in high-volume systems that typically have to crunch documents of more than 100 to 200KB.

Let's do a little math to get a feeling for the memory requirements of BizTalk Messaging alone: A typical XML schema specification has between 50KB to 100KB when expressed in Unicode UTF-8 (8-bit) character encoding. If we use 75KB as an average—and considering that when expanded into the XML DOM, XML documents grow easily by a factor of 5–6—the minimum in-memory size is about 400KB. Now assume that the inbound document is 256KB when expressed in UTF-8, doubling to 512KB when expressed as a regular Unicode string, and, thus, at least 2.5MB when fully folded up into the internal format. In addition, the same document, also Unicode, sits in the transport dictionary, so that it is another 512KB in memory cost.

More complex document maps are easily somewhere around 120KB (and bigger), so that we get at least 600KB when loaded. When the source document is being processed and the target is being produced, the source document's data will likely be mostly replicated, so that we get another 2.5MB for the target document (and another 400KB for the schema). In addition, we have to take into account that the documents will likely need to be copied to local buffers when they are pushed into the document tracking database. Let's assume that this costs another source-document size unit.

If we add this all up, it results in more than 8MB of memory being used at the same time or at least within a very short time, and that is only the static net data for a single document conversion without even looking at the auxiliary structures and buffers. And in fact, these internal buffers are the most costly. Depending on what you do in the document conversion, your memory requirements may be easily tenfold that of the static data if the XSLT processor needs to create larger subset fragments of the source or target documents. So even for relatively small documents (256KB is not really big), you are easily hitting 80MB of memory being used for processing.

If you have four worker threads per processor (which depends on the type of transport), this adds up to 320MB of memory use for the XML portion of channel processing alone. Of course, that is not the only task that BizTalk Server needs to perform for Messaging. When you add encoding and decoding, encryption and decryption, and all the other tasks, you will again need ample space for processing buffers. In addition, you will have to consider caches for configuration data, disk caches, and the memory needed for additional middleware like Microsoft Internet Information Server (IIS). In sum, 256MB per processor for BizTalk Server Messaging alone (not counting the operating system requirements) seems like the absolute minimum figure.

BizTalk Orchestration's appetite for RAM is up there with BizTalk Messaging, although this is difficult to derive as clearly as for the messaging system. If you plan to use BizTalk Orchestration, you should simply double the previous estimate. The bottom line is, the absolute minimum per-processor memory requirement for a single BizTalk Server that handles both Orchestration and Messaging is between 384 and 512MB of RAM.

Disk Performance

Unless you use file receive functions or the outbound file system drop-off transport option extensively, BizTalk Server's core Messaging service itself makes only a few direct accesses to the local disks. Instead, the heavy users of local disks are Microsoft SQL Server and the Message Queuing services (for Orchestration integration and the Microsoft Message Queue (MSMQ) transport).

As you have learned, BizTalk Server uses four different databases: the messaging management database, which contains all configuration data; the shared queue database, which holds the messaging work items; the document tracking database, where messaging documents are logged; and the XLANG persistence database, which holds the state and dehydration information for BizTalk Orchestration services. Of the three messaging databases, the messaging management database receives the least traffic, although it holds all configuration data. This is because BizTalk Server caches all configuration data and refreshes this data only periodically instead of rereading settings for each single request. (You can manage this interval from the group properties in BizTalk Administrator.) The shared queue database and the document tracking database, however, receive very heavy traffic, especially in high-volume environments.

The shared queue database holds all work items that are either due for processing, are queued for sending retries, are scheduled to be processed later, or have been quarantined in the Suspended Queue because of processing errors. In any event, each single work item will be placed into the shared queue database at least once. This means that the entire interchange will be moved into the database by the Interchange component and that it will be pulled from there by the internal scheduling service. Both actions occur in a transactional manner and through COM+ Transactions and the Microsoft Distributed Transaction Coordinator (MSDTC), which requires logging in the MSDTC log, causing additional disk traffic.

If document tracking is important to your business solution (which is very likely at least for EDI), the BizTalk document tracking database will receive by far the most traffic of all three messaging-related databases. For EDI formats, you can log as many as four complete copies of the documents of an interchange into the document tracking database, along with quite a bit of related information about the interchange, like source and destination and the time when the interchange was received and forwarded.

Because BizTalk relies heavily on SQL Server and because SQL Server requires both sufficient processing and memory resources, the minimum production setup should therefore consist of at least two machines, with SQL Server and the three messaging databases located on one machine and BizTalk Server on the other machine. If you use the BizTalk document tracking database intensively, you should move to a three-machine setup with the document tracking database on a separate machine.

For the database machine(s), you should follow the general guidelines for achieving maximum scalability with Microsoft SQL Server. These guidelines, which you can find in the SQL Server documentation and which are also repeated in the BizTalk installation guidelines, state that you should use separate physical disks and, depending on the actual load, even separate drive controllers for the data file, the transaction log, the MSDTC log, and the Windows 2000 page file.

Network Performance and Bandwidth

The positive effects on the overall system performance of locating BizTalk Server and the databases on separate machines will vanish if you do not provide an adequate network link between the machines. Generally, and when we are considering only a single BizTalk Server machine, the connections between the BizTalk machine and (each of) the database machine(s) hosting the management, queue, and document tracking databases should have a dedicated network link of at least 100MBps that is not shared with the rest of the network.

Taking care of sufficient bandwidth and low-latency links between BizTalk and its supporting databases is certainly not the only issue to consider for network performance. The most optimized BizTalk Server setup will not be able to do its job if the links to the outside world or to the internal systems that need to be integrated are inadequate for the expected traffic.

In most scenarios, the frequency and volume of traffic in and out of BizTalk Server should be predictable. Depending on the number and size of your trading partners and the patterns that you can statistically derive from past data exchanges, you will be able to calculate the average bandwidth requirements and reserve enough additional bandwidth for unexpected traffic bursts. However, those should occur much less frequently than with, say, interactive web sites, where you sometimes cannot tell why the number of interactive users suddenly doubles.

When you estimate your bandwidth requirements for external data traffic, you should also take into account that incoming data is typically not leveled out over the day or week. In certain trade scenarios, orders may come in extreme bursts at certain times of the day or on certain days, while at other times, you may see very little traffic or even no traffic at all. Data exchange is driven by the way businesses work. Knowing this is essential for accurate bandwidth planning.

Scaling BizTalk Systems

Until now, we have mostly considered the basic system requirements like CPU power, memory use, disk speed, and network bandwidth. However, at some point, the number of documents to process may become so high that scaling up by adding more processors or adding more RAM may no longer be an option because it would simply exceed the box capacity. If it doesn't, you may still find that a serious highend server with more than four processors is insanely expensive when you compare it to an equivalent number of separate servers with dual or single processors. BizTalk supports both the scale-up and the scale-out models.

Scaling Up

In the scale-up model, you simply keep adding more firepower to a single server machine and exchange and upgrade components that deliver maximum throughput and speed. When scaling up, you will see linear increases in system throughput until the machine becomes either physically full or the internal management and coordination overhead between the components of a single systems start affecting system performance. By then, the linear increase in system performance will flatten.

The scale-up model is best used when you need massive processing power. If BizTalk needs to crunch relatively few but very large documents so that there is not much load to distribute on an item-by-item basis, the scale-up model is the answer. If you prefer processing speed and low latency (for instance, when bridging between enterprise systems) over the ability to chew large numbers of smaller documents, the scale-up model will probably be the better choice. In fact, in most cases, scaling out and distributing the workload over many machines is the preferred solution. It is less costly because many smaller machines are usually far cheaper to run than one huge box with the equivalent firepower of all the smaller machines combined.

Scaling Out

In the scale-out model, you can theoretically add any number of servers and devices to a server farm and see linear increase in overall system performance. For typical web or application server farms, you achieve this goal by setting up multiple, identically configured machines that access the same backend data storage and that are coordinated through some sort of load-balancing solution like Windows 2000 Advanced Server's network load balancing service (NLBS). The scale-out model also eliminates many single-point-of-failure scenarios. Users of a properly configured scale-out cluster typically will not notice if a machine suddenly fails due to an unexpected system crash because other machines can seamlessly jump in and take over that machine's workload. Public demonstrations of Windows 2000 Advanced Server routinely include pulling the power plug of running servers under load—and you can even do this at home.

BizTalk Server can take advantage of this network load-balancing model, which distributes workload based on incoming external network traffic when data is accepted through Active Server Pages (ASP) hosted on IIS. A similar load-balancing model is component load balancing (CLB), which is available through Microsoft Application Center 2000. CLB does not act on incoming network traffic, but on the number of requests made to COM+ components. The BizTalk Interchange component—which is used to submit any type of data into BizTalk unless you are using file or Message Queue receive functions—is a COM+ component and can therefore be balanced by using CLB. However, both NLBS and CLB will only balance out submissions to the Work Queue that are somehow made through the Interchange component.

For incoming traffic that is relayed through the receive functions and all data that is picked up from the Work Queue, BizTalk server farms work a bit differently and with a much more controlled approach than distributing traffic with the garden hose as NLBS does—and, to some degree, CLB. Scaling out is the default case for BizTalk Server by design, and running single-machine configuration is indeed a rather special setup.

BizTalk Server is designed to process huge volumes of data in collaborating server groups, which can all share the same configuration data. A BizTalk Server group can consist of any number of servers that share the same shared queue and document tracking databases. The messaging management database can be shared among any number of BizTalk groups—theoretically, at least. In reality, there are some practical limits to sharing the messaging management database in terms of database traffic; there may even be some good reasons to intentionally split up the databases in systems that see massive volume or that require rather frequent maintenance.

By using the BizTalk Administrator tool at installation time and afterwards, you can install servers to join existing groups or you can create entirely new BizTalk Server groups. Creating groups requires setting up new shared queue and document tracking databases and subsequently configuring one or multiple BizTalk Servers to join this group. By sharing a single queue database (hence the name), multiple BizTalk Servers can pull work items for the Work Queue in a transactional and coordinated manner. Actually, each of the worker threads polls the work in configurable intervals as soon as it has finished processing the previous item. This ensures that all threads of all servers receive the maximum workload that they can process, and it also guarantees that all items are properly handled even under high load, because all processing occurs asynchronously by default.

You will want to set up separate groups if the database load or the network traffic to the queue and/or document tracking databases exceeds the database machine's or network's capacity. Because all configuration data is shared through the management database, each group is capable of talking to the same partners and implements the same rules. However, because the shared configuration of the management database does not cover the receiving transport bindings through either receive functions or external server processes like Exchange or IIS, each of the groups may process data from an entirely different set of senders.

Alternatively, two or more groups can be configured identically and accept data from the same sources. For the proper distribution of inbound data to both groups, you can use NLBS, CLB, or some other load-balancing scheme that is configured to work across all servers of all groups. Such a scenario makes sense if you need to process high volumes of large documents on high-speed networks and you need to perform verbose tracking for technical or even legal reasons. In that case, a single shared document tracking database and/or shared queue database may become a bottleneck. To eliminate the bottleneck, you would group equally sized groups of servers that each manage their own item processing and tracking. For the shared queue database, this process is similar to the aforementioned web-farm model. In fact, you could set up a separate group for each BizTalk Server and run them in a purely network-balanced fashion.

Because the setup for the document tracking database and shared queue database is separate and can be allocated to different database servers, you can even mix and match databases between groups. You could, for instance, keep the queue databases separate for each group, but share the document tracking databases. If you decide to run multiple document tracking databases because of the data volume and you need the tracking data as legal proof, you will have to subsequently and periodically either replicate the data into a single database or create consolidated views running distributed queries (more on this in Chapter 21).

Security Considerations

Computing could be so easy if it weren't for the bad and the nosey. Especially on the Internet, a lot of people are curious about what other people send and receive, while other people have fun cracking systems and stealing data—or they are even well paid for it. If someone were seeking a really great place to get as much information as possible in a short time that reveals a lot of corporate internals, intercepting BizTalk traffic and eavesdropping on the document tracking database would indeed be an excellent starting point. It would also be great fun to intercept incoming or outgoing orders (or any other documents) and alter them to add or drop a couple of items or change the ship-to address to some obscure location without anyone noticing. The message is this: if you run BizTalk Server on the Internet without properly managing security, you may be serving a lot of the internals of your business on a silver platter.

The following discussion makes a clear distinction between inbound and outbound traffic. As you already know, BizTalk Server is capable of immediately sending data to destinations, but—and with the exception of receive functions—it does rely on other intermediate servers like IIS to receive data. Securing BizTalk Server installations therefore also means securing these intermediate servers and choosing technologies for authentication, authorization, and encryption that are appropriate for interbusiness document exchange.

Authentication and Authorization

When you accept business documents from partners such as orders or invoices, you must make sure that these documents are authentic and that the sender is authorized to submit this information into your system. Conversely, your systems must also be authenticated whenever data is sent from your end.

The term *authentication* means that the sender of a message can be positively identified and matched against some kind of security account on the receiving system. The receiving system may check the provided proof of identity either against a password database, against a digital certificate store, or against some other type of evidence, depending on the authentication method used. If the sender can be positively identified and this identity can be verified against the evidence, the sender is said to be authenticated. In password-protected systems, users who sign up provide a username and a password. The username provides the identity and the password provides the proof of identity. The receiving server has a local copy of this user's password (or some type of value immediately derived from that password) and uses a match between the password that has been provided by the user and the stored password as evidence that the remote user is actually who he or she claims to be.

Once the identity has been determined and verified, the next step is to *authorize* the user or prevent the user (or the remote system) from performing the requested actions.

Such actions include accessing certain resources like files or printers, running a certain program, or making a call to a component. Authorizations are typically granted on a per-object basis or through certain roles. On web sites, directories and files are usually protected by adding certain users or user groups to an access control list. If the user is on that list (directly or indirectly), access is granted; if not, access is denied.

In applications, authorizations may be indirectly assigned through roles, where a set of users may have permission to perform a specific action, for instance, submitting a document in BizTalk when they are in the role of a "Trading Partner". Roles are more flexible than user groups because they add an additional level of indirection, and they allow fine-tuned authorization management without having to go through the hassle of building a network-wide user group for each individual securable feature of a specific application.

NOTE: Because authorization obviously works only with previous authentication (because any system will need to know who to authorize), the following sections focus only on authorization unless authentication is explicitly mentioned.

Inbound Transport-Level Sender Authentication and Authorization   BizTalk accepts documents through a single interface: the BizTalk Interchange component. Whether data arrives through an ASP page running on Internet Information Server, comes in via SMTP and is forwarded to BizTalk by Microsoft Exchange Server 2000, or is picked up by a receive function, the documents are always passed into the BizTalk Interchange component.

Enforcing authorization on the BizTalk Interchange application therefore covers all possible inbound transport options at the same time and establishes a common level of access security for all document submissions, regardless of which application is submitting them. In fact, securing the COM+ application is your last line of defense in terms of transport-level security; therefore, you should take security very seriously here.

Securing the Interchange application is also important because the installation default settings (insecured) allow anyone who can access the server machine through the network to submit documents into BizTalk. This issue may not seem to be immediate for an intended deployment. You might think that nobody from within your own network would want to sneak false documents into BizTalk and that the internal users wouldn't be able to figure out how to do it anyway. However, even if that assumption were true, securing the Interchange application is actually a very critical issue: You just can't tell what software people are running. For example, a malicious Trojan horse application that comes to an unsuspecting employee in the disguise of a funny animation e-mail may be enough to compromise your security and sneak "random" documents into BizTalk Server (or do other damage that the employee may cause without even knowing it).

On the level above the Interchange application, you must secure the software components or servers that provide the receive capabilities. The following discussion looks at the two protocols—HTTP and SMTP—that you will most likely use where security matters most: on the Internet.

If you receive documents via e-mail through SMTP, you must include in the list of authorized senders for the Interchange application the service account of the mail server application that receives the documents. SMTP servers are typically not able to impersonate the mail's sender because SMTP is a decoupled, asynchronous protocol that is designed to work with many intermediate hops. In fact, SMTP security is terribly weak. While you can limit access to an SMTP server by enforcing password-based authentication for servers that drop mail into your system, this is not a common setup and will severely limit interoperability with the existing Internet e-mail infrastructure.

In addition, the standard SMTP authentication protocol is inherently insecure because it transmits cleartext passwords. So, while you are able to secure the connection between your mail server and the BizTalk Interchange application, it is still possible to sneak random data into BizTalk Server if you are running your SMTP server on the Internet. Of course, you also will not be able to trust the e-mail's sender address. As you know, you can enter any sender address into any e-mail application and successfully send mail acting as someone else. If you wanted to send mail as mickey.mouse@disney.com, for instance, you would only have to set up an account in, say, Outlook Express with that mail address, and you would probably be able to successfully send that mail through your ISP's SMTP server. This example should tell you that transport-level security in SMTP is essentially absent.

The problem is, security is only as good as its weakest point. If transport-level security is not an option with SMTP and there is virtually no trust in the entire infrastructure, securing the Interchange application via COM+ is really pointless because anyone is able to send anything into BizTalk via SMTP. That means that if you are planning to use SMTP on the Internet, you are essentially forced to use the S/MIME features of BizTalk to establish security on the document level, as discussed in Chapter 17. If you use SMTP on the Internet to exchange business documents without also using S/MIME, you are asking for trouble.

HTTP is a synchronous protocol that is not designed for anonymous routing like SMTP, but rather, works point to point. Therefore, authentication is quite a bit easier and hence, much more advanced than with SMTP. First, the Internet standard RFC 2617, issued by the Internet Engineering Taskforce (IETF), provides a mechanism called *digest authentication* to authenticate users who use a password-based authentication scheme in which the passwords are never sent over the network. Instead, both sides work with a shared secret (the password) from which they generate a hash value (checksum) that is transmitted instead.

Second and more importantly, HTTP can be implemented on top of the Secure Sockets Layer that implements client authentication using digital certificates. HTTP on top of SSL is commonly referred to as HTTPS, the widely deployed standard protocol for secure connections on the Web. Although RFC 2617 is good for password-based authentication, it comes with all the weaknesses of password-based authentication schemes. If you are using HTTP with BizTalk by implementing an inbound gateway with an ASP script, you should seriously consider using HTTPS with client authentication through digital certificates.

Outbound Transport-Level Authentication   Outbound transport-level security matters when you need to configure BizTalk Server to communicate with external systems that require authentication. Just as you require external clients to properly identify themselves for authentication, servers that your systems talk to will likely require the same.

BizTalk's built-in transport options like HTTP, HTTPS, and MSMQ, allow you to configure how BizTalk Server can identify itself to a remote system for authentication. The level of support for authentication directly reflects the capabilities of the respective transport. HTTPS and MSMQ allow you to use certificate-based authentication, while the file transport and the HTTP transport support only simple password authentication schemes.

Once you have configured a transport for a port and have created a channel, you can configure the authentication settings in the Transport Properties dialog box, which you can open by clicking the Advanced button on the Advanced Configuration options page of the Channel Wizard (yes, the Channel Wizard, not the Port Wizard).

Encryption

The requirement for encryption of data sent between BizTalk systems is so obvious that it is almost superfluous to mention it. Virtually all data that you exchange with external partners should be seen by nobody except the receiver. You already learned how to configure a secure port and channel by using certificates in Chapter 17, so we don't need to cover it again.

Intrusion Detection and Defense

In general, crackers want to exploit leaks in security either to achieve some monetary advantage or just to prove that they can. Cracking or bringing down Internet-enabled commerce systems that process high volumes of sensitive business data and that are essentially one of the lifelines of a business is a challenge for crackers. Today's operating systems and server products, including Windows 2000 and Microsoft BizTalk Server 2000, are complex and difficult to lock down (harden) in terms of access security without additional, specialized software or hardware solutions. (The same applies to Sun Solaris, Linux, etc.)

To make your systems reasonably secure against such external attacks, you should therefore use firewall software or hardware to shield BizTalk Server 2000. If you plan to run your business or your client's on the Internet, firewalls are not an option—they are a necessity.

However, firewalls are not some kind of medicine that you apply and then the problems simply go away. Just like any other piece of software, even firewall products may have security leaks that hackers can find and exploit. In addition, there are some attack patterns that a firewall may not even be able to detect because they come from inside your network.

Let's look at two of the more serious attack types here to illustrate the problem:

The ultimate goal of crackers is to take control of your system to either steal data, to install monitoring (spy) software that routinely collects data and sends it to some location on the Internet, or to completely erase your system. To do this, crackers must sneak in some sort of code that executes these tasks programmatically.

One of the more advanced but very successful techniques is to exploit buffer overflows. A *buffer overflow* occurs in an application when the application reserves a certain memory block for an operation and the data that is being placed into that block is larger than the reserved size. This is a common programming error and is typically hard to trace down even for the developer who has written the application. Crackers search for such buffers and try to find ways to produce overflows by sending data from the outside. If they find such a place in the operating system, your server software, or the firewall product, you may be in trouble.

The trick is that while a buffer overflow typically causes programs to crash, placing the "right" sequence of bytes in the overflow portion may intentionally—and as a side effect—cause your application to do the exact things the cracker wants it to do instead of crashing. Depending on how well the cracking code is written, such attacks may even go largely unnoticed and have no visible, adverse effects on the stability of the system.

Using the cracking code, the cracker may then direct your system to download a certain application from a web location, install it into the system and, maybe only four weeks later, cause it to activate itself. If that hostile application is in some way capable of gaining administrative rights, your entire network may be defenseless against data theft. Gaining these rights is not difficult if the attacked software has administrative rights as well. Therefore, you should lock down any application's set of rights to the absolute minimum it needs to function properly.

The second scenario is hostile attacks from an employee's computer. Impossible? No. The easiest way to compromise network security is to e-mail one of those cute little animations that shows something funny to an unsuspecting non-IT worker in your company who isn't aware of all these issues and hide hostile code in that application. Suddenly, you have an intruder application inside your network that has effectively passed by your firewalls. The only effective way to shield against these types of attacks is to enforce a rigorous security policy even inside your local networks and take measures against malicious code sent through e-mail. (Some good filtering solutions will catch quite a few of these problems—but not all of them.)

Your defense will probably never be perfect all the time, but you can definitely fight to give crackers a hard time by following these guidelines:

▼ **Use multiple firewalls** Place your Internet Information Servers or mail servers behind a firewall to create a so-called demilitarized zone (DMZ) that has no direct access to your internal network except through well-defined ports on separate network adapters. The internal network (where your BizTalk Server(s) sits) is shielded against the DMZ with another firewall.

■ **Use multiple firewall products** As mentioned already, firewalls are not universal cures against network security problems. If a bug in a firewall becomes known, your network may be as insecure as it is without having a firewall. However, the same problem is unlikely to exist in two firewall products from different vendors. It is therefore a good idea—although costly in terms of maintenance—to run multiple different firewall products. If you are really paranoid about security, running a hardware firewall in combination with a software firewall for your first line of defense (the outermost firewall) creates a very tough nut for crackers to crack.

■ **Use multiple operating systems** Using Linux, BSD, or Solaris can help shield Windows 2000 networks. These operating systems are not necessarily better or generally more secure, but they let attackers make wrong assumptions. If you expose your network through a Linux system that does nothing but just function as a router, the signatures of your TCP/IP packets will tell crackers that they need to unpack the Linux toolbox, and they will realize that they're on the wrong track only once they get through that first barrier.

▲ **Waste a cracker's time** Crackers test the easiest ways to get into your systems first. If you place "bait" in your system configuration that they can "bite on" and that allows you to detect intrusions, you or a specialized security firm may be able to track down the attack path while they are trying to figure out what's going on in your system. To do this, you could set up a server system that is configured to look like the real thing to the outside (maybe a Windows 2000 Server with BizTalk Server 2000 installed), but which actually has nothing to do with your internal systems and is just a trap. On the outer firewall, you can then redirect typical attack paths to that machine like remote procedure call (RPC), NetBIOS, and other protocol ports that are not used by your internal systems and that weaken security such that a cracker may be able to get in and explore (with some effort). So, while the cracker thinks he's in, you have him cornered.

Securing the Run-Time Environment for BizTalk Messaging The minimal security measure that you should implement is to grant BizTalk Server 2000 only those permissions that it requires to execute properly and not to run it using the local system account. Using the local system account is quite convenient for maintenance, but it essentially grants BizTalk Server full access to any part of your system. In case someone could somehow crack BizTalk Server through a faulty parser component, for instance, and smuggle in malicious code, the only way to limit the damage is to restrict that code's run-time permissions.

Therefore, you should assign a specific user account (service account) to the BizTalk Server Messaging Service to enable you to appropriately restrict file and network access as well as access to other services. The service account must be granted to act as part of the operating system, which enables it to run in the background and without an interactively logged on user. Otherwise, the account should be a member only of the default Users group, which enables you to restrict access to those parts of the system that the core messaging service requires. This includes the BizTalk product directory, the common components in the Common Files folder of your Program Files directory, and, of course, read access to the Windows 2000 system directories.

Because you can configure individual credentials for file receive functions and the file drop-off transport (taking that as an example), you can limit to the bare minimum access to storage locations for the core service and enable access to file locations only through these transport-level extra credentials and specific access accounts. This will essentially shield your outbound and inbound data against unwanted access in case someone manages to successfully intrude into your system by sending you documents that cause BizTalk to crash.

You should also restrict access to the COM+ Interchange application. By default, the Interchange application is configured to run as the interactive user, which makes sense for development and debugging, but which requires you to have a logged on user at all times when running BizTalk Server.

To configure a noninteractive account for the Interchange application, you must open the Component Services management application from the Administrative Tools menu. You can open this menu either from the Windows 2000 Start menu or from Control Panel. Locate the BizTalk Server Interchange Application (as shown in Figure 19-1) and open the Properties dialog box through its context menu.

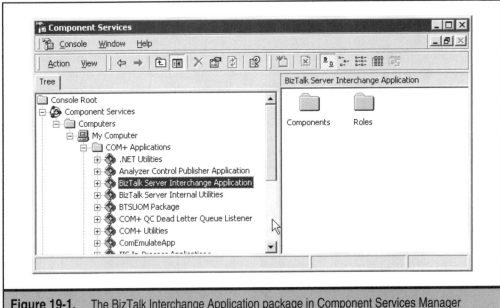

Figure 19-1. The BizTalk Interchange Application package in Component Services Manager

To allow changes to any of the settings (everything will be dimmed when you access the properties the first time), you first have to go to the Advanced tab, clear the Disable Changes check box (see Figure 19-2), and close the dialog box by clicking OK. At this point—and for all other changes you will make—Component Services Manager will warn you that the application was installed by an external product and alert you of whether the changes you are making are indeed supported. Because changing the identity is supported, you can click Yes.

The COM+ package can and should run with the same identity as the BizTalk Messaging Service. As you can see in Figure 19-3, you should therefore reopen the dialog box, select the This User check box on the Identity tab, and enter the BizTalk Server service account and password that you have configured for the Messaging service.

Finally, you should make sure that the Enforce Access Checks For This Application check box on the Security tab is enabled, as shown in Figure 19-4. This option allows you to configure which users and services have access to the Interchange application. This is essential to restrict access to the document-processing pipeline only to trusted sources. Once you have made these changes, click OK.

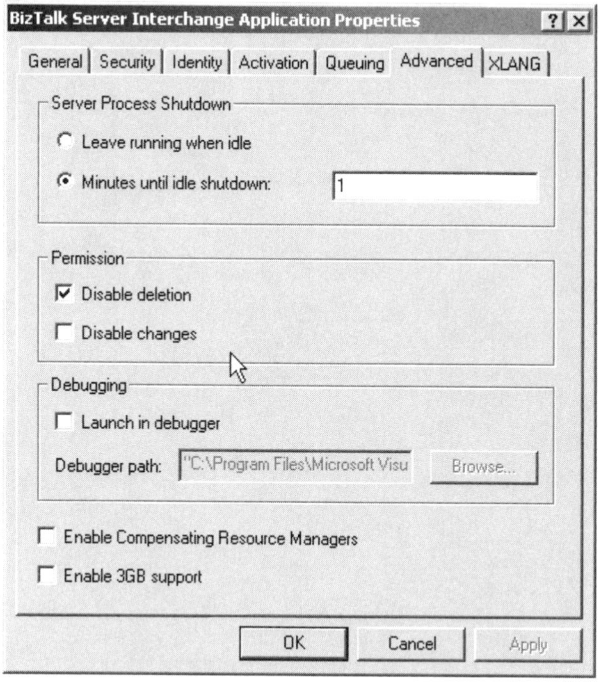

Figure 19-2. Enabling changes in the Properties dialog box

The Component Services management application allows you to create roles for applications that let you configure access restrictions. To do this, you simply go to the Roles node below the Interchange Application node in the tree view, as shown in Figure 19-5, and select New | Role from the context menu. Once you do that, a simple dialog box opens that asks you for the name of the new role. Once you have entered a meaningful name, click OK, and the role is created.

Once a role has been defined, go to the BizTalk.Interchange.1 component beneath the Components node, open its Properties dialog box, select the Enforce Component Level Access Checks check box on the Security tab (see Figure 19-6), and select all those roles that should have access to the component.

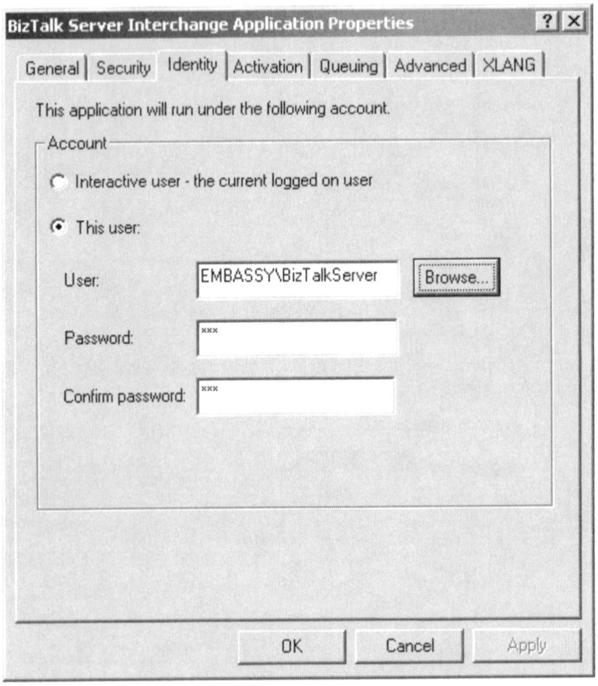

Figure 19-3. Setting the service account

To allow users to "wear the hat" of a "Trading Partner" (notice the role icons in Component Services Manager), as in the example shown in the figures here, go to the Users node below the newly configured role and add users to the role by using the context menu and selecting New | User.

Securing the Run-Time Environment for XLANG Schedules The procedures just described also apply to the XLANG services and the XLANG Scheduler application. You can reuse the service account to configure the XLANG Restart Service (through the Services administration tool in the Computer Management administration console of Windows 2000) and the XLANG Scheduler COM+ application, which you configure in much the same way as the Interchange component.

However, the XLANG Scheduler application has a slightly different model for using the COM+ roles. Instead of using the external access control model that we used previously, the XLANG application checks a set of preconfigured roles internally and grants access to

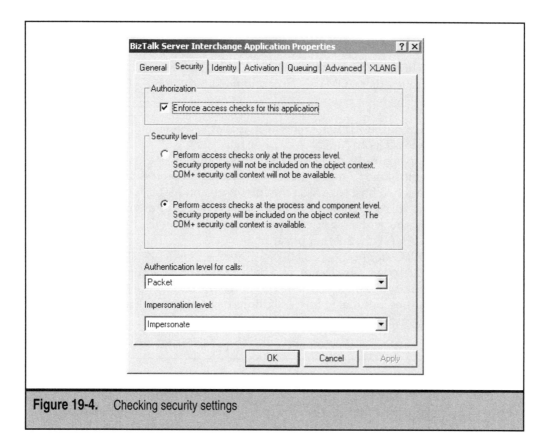

Figure 19-4.   Checking security settings

certain functionality by group membership. So, instead of creating a new role, you will simply have to add users to the respective roles, as described in the following list:

▼ **XLANG Schedule Creator**   This role allows specified users to create XLANG schedule instances. This means that all user and service accounts that create schedules directly by using the schedule moniker or by using BizTalk Messaging must be members of this role. By default, this role is assigned to the Everyone group. If you want to restrict access here, you must be sure to include at least the BizTalk Messaging service identity.

■ **XLANG Schedule User**   This role allows specified users to interact with XLANG schedule instances. "Interacting" means API-level access through the moniker and the Workflow interfaces (prefixed with "IWF", see product documentation for details) once the schedule has been created.

■ **XLANG Scheduler Administrator**   This role allows you to indicate who has administrative rights to configure XLANG applications, including shutting them down forcefully or configuring the advanced COM+ settings for XLANG applications.

▲ **XLANG Scheduler Application**   This role is used by the XLANG Scheduler to interact with other COM+ services and must include the XLANG Scheduler application's own identity.

A special advantage of the XLANG Scheduler is that it extends COM+ to allow any COM+ application to act as an XLANG schedule host.

As you can see in Figure 19-7, the XLANG tab is available for any new COM+ application that you create in the Component Services manager. On this tab, you can enable any COM+ application to host XLANG schedules with an unique runtime identity and application-specific role assignments. However, if you enable an application to host XLANG schedules, you will have to configure the roles manually, essentially copying the setup of the XLANG Scheduler application.

For arbitrary COM+ applications to host schedules, you will furthermore have to create a persistency database for hydration and dehydration of schedules. Connecting to a database and initializing the database tables (building the database schema) can be done directly from this Properties dialog box. In addition, you must have at least one COM+ component residing in the application to make it functional.

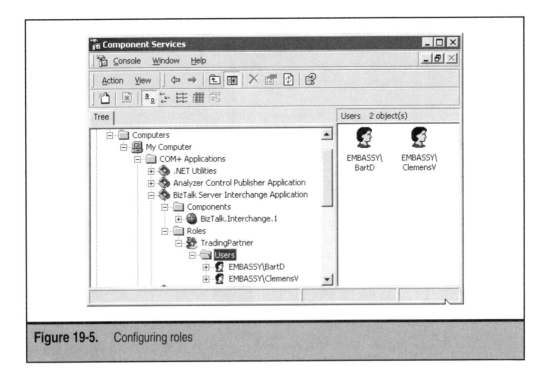

Figure 19-5.   Configuring roles

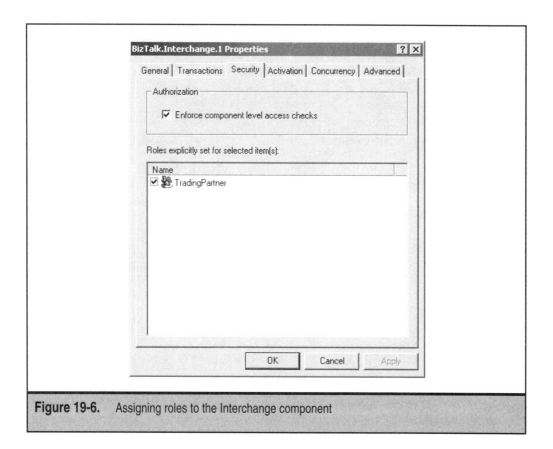

Figure 19-6. Assigning roles to the Interchange component

AUTOMATED DEPLOYMENT

Automated deployment, or simply taking a staged configuration from one server into a production environment, is the sore spot in BizTalk Server 2000. In the official toolset that is installed on the Start menu, you will not find import or export functionality for Messaging configuration settings.

The BTConfigAssistant is the only tool that allows for automated deployment (apart from swapping the physical management database between staging and production systems by using SQL Server Enterprise Manager). It is located in the SDK section of the product under Messaging Samples. Be advised that you must understand the following chapter on programmatic configuration to actually use the configuration scripts produced by the Configuration Assistant. If you don't, you may risk losing configuration data in the process.

In brief, the BizTalk Configuration Assistant allows you to select configuration settings from your local BizTalk Server and create XML descriptions of these settings. Using a set of XSLT style sheets that are located within the application's directory, it will then turn those XML files into VBScript code that you can run against another BizTalk Server.

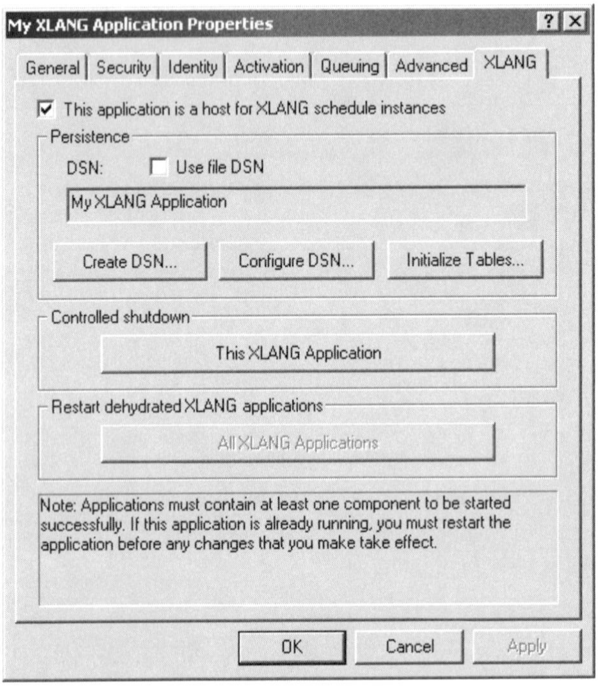

Figure 19-7. The XLANG tab on the COM+ application Properties dialog box

When you look at Figure 19-8, it should become quite obvious how to select and group your settings. Configuration Assistant has six tabs for each configurable BizTalk object class (Channels, Ports, Port Groups, Organizations, Documents, and Envelopes). Each tab includes a selectable list that allows you to choose those elements for which you want to create configuration scripts or XML documents.

Once you have selected the element you want to export, you can obtain script code for configuration (don't use it until you understand what it does based on the information in the next chapter). Or you can export an XML configuration file to a directory, which also extracts and exports all document specifications and document maps from the current database and places those files into subdirectories of the generated XML file.

To create the export package, you select File | Export | Selected Items and specify a blank directory for exporting the configuration. Once you have exported the configuration, you will find a newly created XML file along with three subdirectories in the export

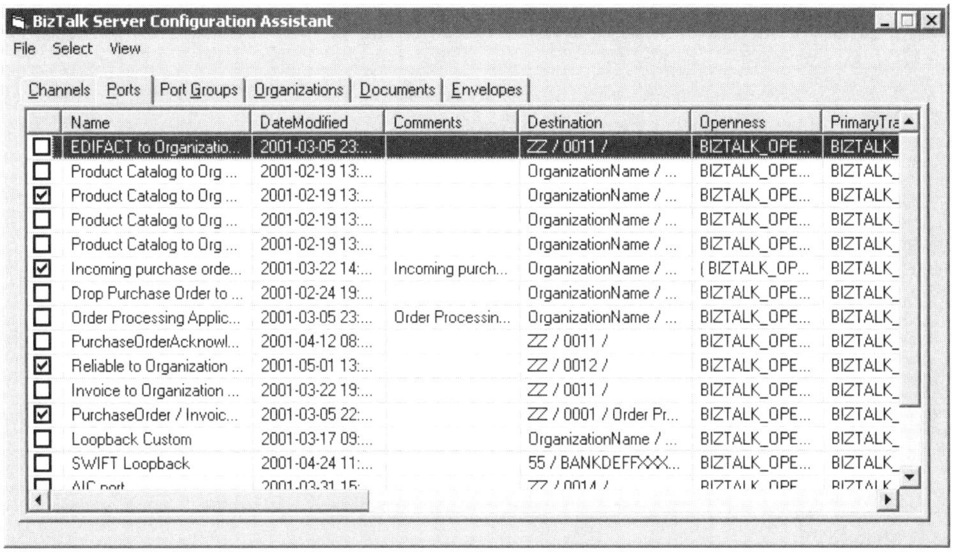

Figure 19-8.   Configuration Assistant

location. The subdirectories contain all document maps, specifications, and auxiliary components needed to recreate the configuration on another machine.

On that other machine, you can point Configuration Assistant to the export directory and import the data by using the Import Configuration command on the File menu. Here's where it gets a little disturbing: The configuration scripts fire "blindfolded." Should any of the settings already exist or should names clash with existing settings, the scripts will simply fail and your management database may become inconsistent. So an initial deployment is always possible, but to make updates, you will essentially have to wipe out the settings first and rebuild them from scratch to be on the safe side.

What actually happens when you run the scripts can be seen when you select View | Selected Items. The dialog box that opens has two tabs. The first tab shows the XML document that is produced from the configuration settings, and the second tab shows the VBScript that is created by running the accompanying XSLT scripts against the file. An example of this is shown in Figure 19-9. You should always inspect the scripts thoroughly and test them before you run them against a production server. To understand what these scripts do, read the next chapter.

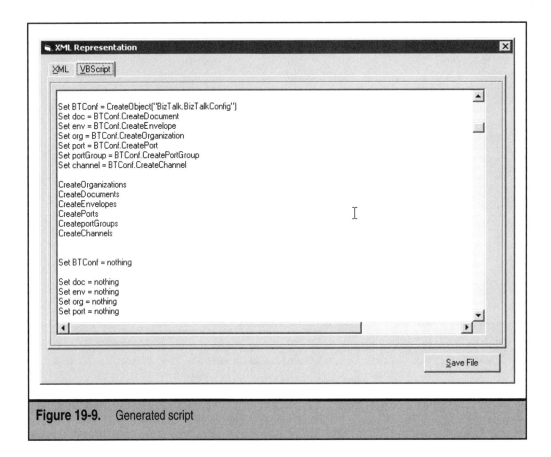

Figure 19-9. Generated script

CHAPTER 20

Programmatic Application Deployment and Configuration

As your BizTalk Server solutions grow, you may find that the interactive configuration tools like BizTalk Messaging Manager or BizTalk Administrator are no longer sufficient to manage all connections to external partners or to coordinate your BizTalk server farms. If BizTalk Server powers large data hubs with hundreds or even thousands of destinations and you need to add, change, and remove destinations frequently, more integrated solutions that tie BizTalk management right into your Customer Relationship Management (CRM) system or other systems may become a very attractive option.

This chapter explains the BizTalk Configuration Object Model, which lets you configure BizTalk Server 2000 programmatically, and which provides access to almost all BizTalk configuration data for extension components like serializers, parsers, and Application Integration Components (AICs). The BizTalk Configuration Object Model covers "almost all" configuration data because the most fundamental configuration data that defines how servers are grouped and which databases they connect to is accessible only through the Windows Management Instrumentation (WMI) interfaces. At the end of this chapter, you will learn how to use WMI for managing this low-level configuration and how to use WMI to peek into the BizTalk queues.

THE BIZTALK CONFIGURATION OBJECT MODEL

Imagine that you run a business with thousands of independent resellers, which you want to enable to exchange XML or EDI documents with your business. Let's take Microsoft's worldwide retail partner network as an example. In that case, you may get a couple dozen or even hundreds of applications a day from potential new partners and see many partners' information change frequently. In such a scenario, you may want to tightly integrate your call centers and web sites with a (very controlled) management interface to your BizTalk information hub instead of having to manually transfer all partner information into BizTalk Messaging Manager.

Let's make this scenario a bit more tangible. Assume that each of your retailers must submit electronic orders and other documents through a single drop-off point at the HTTPS address https://www.tempuri.org/business/edi/dropoff. Because you want every partner to be properly authenticated, you need to issue client authentication and digital signature certificates to them and configure these certificates for Internet Information Server (IIS) and the BizTalk channels that process inbound documents from that particular client.

Also, you may want to give your retail partners a choice between using the X12 transaction set 850, the UN/EDIFACT message ORDERS, or a custom XML document schema to submit their orders. Because BizTalk gives you that flexibility, offering multiple alternate formats may turn out to be a competitive advantage over your business rivals. All responses are sent either to a client-specified HTTP(S) address or to an SMTP address, depending on what the partners prefer. For authenticating your system against the client's systems, your partners need to be provided with the proper public-key certificates, and for validating your digital signatures, they may need to get a different (set of) certificate(s).

Wouldn't it be great if you could manage all this through an automated web-based signup procedure that lets your partners configure their profiles—including data formats to exchange and destination addresses to be used—and through which they can also acquire their certificates? Well, you can. The BizTalk Configuration Object Model is designed to fully automate all BizTalk Messaging administration tasks. And, as you will find out, it actually gives you more control over BizTalk's functionality than the interactive management interface.

Throw your customer database, the BizTalk Configuration Object Model, the Certificate Enrollment Control from the Windows Platform SDK (that's the one used with the Windows 2000 Certificate Server), the Active Directory interfaces, and Active Server Pages in a bowl. Stir well. As a result, you can actually create a fully automated solution for the previous scenario.

In practice, you may want to implement a partner signup form that is submitted by prospective retailers to apply for trading partner status. Once they have completed the signup form successfully, and after running some automated plausibility checks on the provided data (credit-card verification, address verification, etc.), the application gets forwarded to your sales staff for additional review if required. Once the sales staff has positively reviewed the applications, your new partners are notified that their application has been accepted (and this notification should *not* be sent using unsecured e-mail), along with a signup username and password.

Using that information, the partners sign up to your secure configuration site, where they can obtain their own certificates for S/MIME and HTTPS client authentication, download your public-key certificates, and select their options for exchanging electronic documents. Once these settings are confirmed, you grant them access to a test-and-trial BizTalk Server endpoint, let's say, https://www.tempuri.org/business/edi/test, where they can submit test documents until possible incompatibilities are ironed out and their documents pass without error.

Of course, you will be able to create the entire configuration for this testing area automatically because you know the exact document formats they will need to use and have queried all additional information from them through the web site. Hence, you can use the BizTalk Configuration Object Model to create the appropriate organization settings, ports, and channels for testing purposes.

Before your partners are admitted to the production system, you require that they send in a set of test documents, probably purchase orders, for a predefined set of goods so that you can technically verify the incoming data against a template. Using WMI and the document tracking database, your system can determine whether all required test documents have been submitted, and whether they ended up in the Suspended Queue or were successfully processed.

Once the required test suite has been passed, you notify your partners, configure the settings in the production environment, and grant them access to the "live" submission endpoint (and remove the testing configuration). All these tests are on a technical level, and BizTalk tracks all incoming data for verification. Therefore, the configuration process and testing and admitting them for the live system can indeed be fully automated once your sales staff has decided that the partners are accepted from the business end. In essence, the BizTalk Configuration Object Model enables you to develop "hands-off" administration applications for BizTalk Server that are driven by your business solutions.

But also on a much smaller scale, the BizTalk Configuration Object Model is very useful—no, it's even absolutely essential. As you learned in the previous chapter, the BizTalk Server 2000 1.0 release (before any service packs) has no officially supported way to export or import configuration data. BizTalk Configuration Assistant that can be found in the SDK's Messaging Samples hints at how such a tool could look, but it doesn't really work all that well out of the box, as you have seen. However, even though the usefulness of the ConfigAssistant is somewhat limited in version 1.0 and didn't initially make it into the product directory, it is still a great example of how to use the BizTalk Configuration Object Model to configure applications and to redistribute configuration settings.

The following sections provide examples of how to use the Configuration Object Model instead of providing a complete reference guide. The Component Object Model is fully documented in the BizTalk product help. Merely replicating that documentation here would be of little use.

The Configuration Object Model's Configuration Object

All aspects of the Configuration Object Model (there is no official acronym) are always accessed through the central BizTalkConfig class. This class is implemented in an in-process COM component that resides in the BizTalkObjectModel.dll in the product directory. The BizTalkConfig class implements the interface IBizTalkConfig, whose methods we are going to inspect one by one in the following discussion.

In general, the implementation of the object model shows that it is somewhat of a compromise solution between a database access API to the management database and the more abstract object models as they are exposed by other applications. Whenever you request object collections like all ports through the Ports property or all configured documents through the Documents property, the Configuration Object Model uses ActiveX Data Objects (ADO) recordsets instead of returning strongly typed, programmable collections. The use of recordsets sometimes makes the object model somewhat awkward to use.

Anyway, to do anything with the BizTalk Component Object Model, you need to acquire a reference to a BizTalkConfig instance. The data on which that the BizTalkConfig object operates is always scoped to the BizTalk machine on which the object is created; the returned data depends immediately on the BizTalk management database connection settings of the local machine. Therefore, the Configuration Object Model works locally only on a BizTalk Server machine. If you want to be able to access the object model remotely from a client that does not have a local BizTalk Server installation, you will have to import the BizTalkConfig class into a COM+ package, configure it to run as a server application, and export a proxy package for the client.

Because the BizTalkConfig object is so essential, a variety of ways are presented to create an instance of this object from Visual C++, Visual Basic, and Visual C#.

Using classic COM from C++, you create an instance of the BizTalkConfig object and access it by including the biztalkobjectmodel.h header—which is located in the Include directory of the BizTalk SDK in your application—and use the following code:

```
IBizTalkConfig * configObject;
if ( SUCCEEDED( hRes = CoCreateInstance(CLSID_BizTalkConfig,
                                        NULL,
                                        CLSCTX_SERVER,
                                        IID_IBizTalkConfig,
                                        (void**)&configObject)))
{
    // ... work with the configuration
    configObject->Release();
}
```

If you use the Active Template Library (ATL), the code gets somewhat more compact because ATL takes care of the details under the hood.

```
CComPtr<IBizTalkConfig> configObject;
if ( SUCCEEDED( configObject.CoCreateInstance(__uuidof(BizTalkConfig)) ) )
{
    // ... work with the configuration
}
```

For both of these variants, you will have to include the adoint.h header file as well; otherwise, you will not be able to access the ADO recordset-based collections. This header file is updated through the Visual Studio Service Packs and the Platform SDK.

Very similar is the option of using the native COM support technology in Microsoft Visual C++, which allows you to import type information directly instead of going through header files. For simplicity, we're showing both the BizTalk and the ADO Include option, although the ADO record is not yet used here. If you haven't used ADO from C++ before, don't be confused. The import statement in the following code imports the most recent release and not version 1.5, like the DLL name may indicate.

For the import statements to work, you need to include the BizTalk program files directory and the ADO system directory (x:\program files\common files\system\ado) in the include path for your project. Using native COM support is the preferred method because it is definitely the easiest way of using chatty APIs like the BizTalk Configuration Object Model or ADO with C++. The following code instantiates the configuration object:

```
#import <BizTalkObjectModel.dll> no_namespace
#import <msado15.dll> no_namespace rename("EOF","eof")

// ... other stuff

IBizTalkConfigPtr configObject;
configObject.CreateInstance(__uuidof(BizTalkConfig));
```

Using Visual Basic, you can access the configuration object in two ways. The following one-liner is the classic late-bound way, which also works with Visual Basic Scripting Edition and, hence, also with Active Server Pages and with the Windows Scripting host:

```
Set configObject = CreateObject("BizTalk.BizTalkConfig.1")
```

The more sophisticated VB way is to add references to your project to the "Microsoft BizTalk Server Configuration Objects 1.0 Type Library," the "Microsoft ActiveX Data Object 2.6 Library," and the "Microsoft Commerce 2000 Core Components Type Library" and use the following line to construct the configuration object:

```
Dim configObject As New BizTalkConfig
```

Don't let the use of a Microsoft Commerce Server type library confuse you—it is merely proof that Commerce Server and BizTalk Server share some of their architecture. This type library is installed with BizTalk Server and does not require Commerce Server to be present.

If you want to create your management code as managed C# code on the new .NET platform, you will have to add COM references to the same type libraries to your Visual Studio.NET project and use the following expression:

```
BTSObjectModelLib.BizTalkConfig configObject
    = new BTSObjectModelLib.BizTalkConfig();
```

From here, this chapter uses Visual Basic 6.0 syntax for all code illustrations, and it should be rather easy to translate them into your language of choice by using the configObject as a starting point.

Managing Ports

The IBizTalkConfig interface of the BizTalkConfig object exposes two items related to ports. The Ports property returns an ADO recordset that contains all ports that exist in the management database. The returned recordset has the following somewhat disappointingly terse set of columns:

Column	Type	Description
id	Long	Handle for the port object that is used to reference ports elsewhere in the object model.
name	String	Name of the port as configured by the user.
datemodified	Variant	Date when the port was last modified.

To work with messaging ports, you need to create a port object by using the *CreatePort()* method on the configuration object, as shown here:

```
Dim portObject As BizTalkPort

Set portObject = configObject.CreatePort()
```

The name of this method is somewhat misleading, though. With this method, you are not creating a new port object in the messaging configuration; rather, you are creating a new empty "shell" for port configuration data that you can use to actually create a new configuration, but which you can likewise use to access existing data. This shell is the BizTalkPort object (implementing the IBizTalkPort interface).

Most of the subordinate configuration interfaces like IBizTalkPort and IBizTalkChannel are derived from a common interface, IBizTalkBase. This interface provides a common API to load, create, and save configuration data. The methods and properties exposed by IBizTalkBase are listed in the following two tables.

Property	Type	Description
Handle	Long	Handle for the object that is used to reference that object elsewhere in the object model.
Name	String	Name of the object as configured by the user.
DateModified	String	Date when the object was last modified. The date is expressed as an ISO string using UTC.

Method	Description
Sub Load(lBiztalkObjectHandle As Long)	Loads an object from the management database based on a handle value. This may come from the id column of one of the recordsets returned by the BizTalkConfig object.
Sub LoadByName(strName As String)	Loads an object from the management database by its exact name.
Sub Clear()	Erases all data from the in-memory object (has no immediate effect on the underlying configuration data).
Sub Create()	Creates a new object for the management database. This method requires that all data on the object is already valid and will immediately store the object.
Sub Remove()	Removes the previously loaded object from the management database.
Sub Save()	Saves all changes to the object to the management database.

So, if we want to modify an existing port, we can either load it by its handle or by its name. If we assume that a port with the name Port to Organization Alpha exists in the messaging database, the code to access that object would look like this:

```
Dim configObject As New BizTalkConfig
Dim portObject As BizTalkPort

Set portObject = configObject.CreatePort()
portObject.LoadByName "Port to Organization Alpha"
```

If you want to enumerate all ports from a recordset returned by the BizTalkConfig object's Ports property, you would use the *Load()* method, using the handles from the recordset rows as follows:

```
Dim configObject As New BizTalkConfig
Dim recordsetPorts As Recordset
Dim portObject As BizTalkPort

'get the recordset
Set recordsetPorts = configObject.Ports

'make sure its on the first record
recordsetPorts.MoveFirst

'loop until all rows have been traversed
Do While Not recordsetPorts.EOF

  'create a new port object
  Set portObject = configObject.CreatePort()

  'load it based on the current cid column's value
  portObject.Load (recordsetPorts("id"))
  '
  ' work with or manipulate the port object
  '
  Set portObject = Nothing
  'advance the recordset pointer
  recordsetPorts.MoveNext
Loop
```

This technique works identically for the BizTalkPort, BizTalkChannel, BizTalk Document, BizTalkEnvelope, BizTalkOrganization, and BizTalkPortGroup objects. For each of these objects, you will also find corresponding Channels, Documents, etc. properties and related Create*XXX* methods on the BizTalkConfig object.

In addition to modifying existing ports, you will also want to create new ones. Just like with the interactive configuration using Messaging Manager, creating ports requires that you at least assign a destination organization and primary transport—unless you want to create the port as an open destination port, where this information is supplied at run time. Therefore, we will have to look at how to create or load organizations before we can continue creating ports.

Loading and Creating Organizations

The basic management for organizations is similar to that of ports and all other objects. Creating new organizations is fairly straightforward:

```
Dim destinationOrganization As BizTalkOrganization

Set destinationOrganization = configObject.CreateOrganization()
destinationOrganization.Name = "XYZ Corporation"
destinationOrganization.CreateAlias "Mutually Defined", False, "ZZ", "99999"
destinationOrganization.Create
```

Assuming that we are creating a new port object in a similar way, we can use the organization's handle to configure the port's BizTalkEndpoint object right after calling to *destinationOrganization.Create()*. BizTalkEndpoint objects precisely define which organization identifier should be used for the destination of a port or the source of a channel and which alias of the organization identifier applies. The endpoint object always exists on the port and therefore cannot be explicitly created. Each endpoint object has four properties: the Openness property defines whether the port is an open destination port or not open; the Organization property receives the handle to the organization; the Application property is set to the handle of the destination application (if the organization is the home organization); and the Alias property selects the alias identifier to use.

```
Dim portObject As BizTalkPort
Dim endpointObject As BizTalkEndpoint

Set portObject = configObject.CreatePort()
portObject.Name = "Sample Port"
portObject.Comments = "New sample port"
Set endpointObject = portObject.DestinationEndpoint
endpointObject.Openness = BIZTALK_OPENNESS_TYPE_EX_NOTOPEN
endpointObject.Organization = destinationOrganization.Handle
```

In the previous snippet, the endpoint isn't fully defined yet because we haven't assigned an alias to use. If you look at the example where we created the destinationOrganization object, you will notice that we created a new alias with the qualifier ZZ and the value 99999, which is the one that we want to assign here. Unfortunately, there is no direct method that allows us to search for the alias object by using the qualifier or the value, so we will have to iterate over all aliases defined for destinationOrganization to obtain the alias handle:

```
Dim aliasId As Long

aliasId = -1
Set Aliases = destinationOrganization.Aliases
Do While Not Aliases.EOF
   If Aliases("qualifier") = "ZZ" Then
      aliasId = Aliases("id")
      Exit Do
   End If
   Aliases.MoveNext
Loop
If aliasId <> -1 Then
   endpointObject.Alias = aliasId
Else
   'raise an error condition or alert the user
End If
```

If you want to find the home organization and don't want to rely on the string "Home Organization" (which the user can change) or seek for an existing organization by a quali-fier-value pair, you must iterate over all organizations to find it. To find the home organization, use the following snippet that tests for the defaultflag Boolean property on the Organizations recordset:

```
Dim homeOrgId As Long

Set organizations = configObject.Organizations
Do While Not organizations.EOF
   If organizations("defaultflag") <> 0 Then
      homeOrgId = organizations("id")
      Exit Do
   End If
   organizations.MoveNext
Loop
```

The Organizations recordset has the following structure:

Column	Type	Description
id	Long	Handle for the organization object that is used to reference organizations elsewhere in the object model.

Column	Type	Description
name	String	Name of the organization as configured by the user. This is equivalent to the value of the alias with the OrganizationName qualifier.
datemodified	Variant	Date when the organization was last modified.
defaultflag	Boolean	Set to True if this is the home organization; otherwise, it's False.

If you want to seek for an unknown organization just by its qualifier-value pair, you have to create a nested loop:

```
Dim destOrgId As Long
Dim aliasId As Long
Dim org As BizTalkOrganization

destOrgId = -1
aliasId = -1
Set org = configObject.CreateOrganization()
Set organizations = configObject.Organizations
Do While Not organizations.EOF
   org.Load (organizations("id"))
   Set aliases = org.Aliases
   Do While Not Aliases.EOF
     If aliases("qualifier") = "ZZ" And aliases("value") = "99999" Then
        destOrgId = org.Handle
        aliasId = aliases("id")
        organizations.MoveLast 'this terminates the outer loop
        Exit Do
     End If
     aliases.MoveNext
   Loop
   organizations.MoveNext
Loop
Set org = Nothing
```

If the source or destination endpoint is an application (assuming that the endpoint is the home organization), you have to assign an application handle as well. Figuring out the appropriate handle works pretty much the same way as with aliases, given an application name:

```
Dim accountingAppId As Long

accountingAppid = -1
```

```
Set applications = destinationOrganization.Applications
Do While Not applications.EOF
  If applications("name") = "Accounting" Then
    accountingAppId = applications("id")
    Exit Do
  End If
  applications.MoveNext
Loop
```

Configuring Transports

The port object has two properties, PrimaryTransport and SecondaryTransport, which reflect the primary and backup transport protocols defined for the port. These two properties, which are of the type BizTalkTransportInfo, are always present on the port object, so you don't need to explicitly create them. However, they are initially empty, and at least the PrimaryTransport object must be properly configured before the port can be created.

If the port will be bound to an HTTP address, the configuration could look like this:

```
Dim primaryTransport As BizTalkTransportInfo

Set primaryTransport = portObject.primaryTransport
primaryTransport.Type = BIZTALK_TRANSPORT_TYPE_HTTP
primaryTransport.Address = "http://tempuri.org/edi/dropoff/"
```

If the transport type is BIZTALK_TRANSPORT_TYPE_SMTP, an additional property Parameter has to be set, which contains the response e-mail address. If you want to configure an open destination port, you will have to specify this as a transport type:

```
primaryTransport.Type = BIZTALK_TRANSPORT_TYPE_OPENDESTINATION
```

Once at least the primary transport option is property configured, you can create the port in the management database by simply calling Create:

```
portObject.Create
```

Managing Channels

Now that you can create ports, we can take care of the channels. There are quite a few surprises here: BizTalk can do some tricks that you won't be able to configure without using the Configuration Object Model. However, let's get through the basics first. In the following snippet, we assume that we have a portObject that represents a valid port, and that we have a sourceOrganization, along with an application identifier and an alias, created and/or loaded:

```
Dim channelObject As BizTalkChannel
Dim endpointObject As BizTalkEndpoint
Set channelObject = configObject.CreateChannel()
```

```
channelObject.Port = portObject.Handle
channelObject.Name = "Sample Channel"

Set endpointObject = channelObject.SourceEndpoint
endpointObject.Openness = BIZTALK_OPENNESS_TYPE_EX_NOTOPEN
endpointObject.Organization = sourceOrganization.Handle
endpointObject.Application = accountingAppId
endpointObject.Alias = aliasId
```

Creating channel objects is very similar to creating any other object and therefore nothing spectacular. Assigning SourceEndpoint is equivalent to the port's DestinationEndpoint; thus, this is nothing new either. The association between the channel and a port is created by assigning the handle of an existing port to the Port property of the channel. Because channels cannot exist independently from ports, this association must exist for the channel to be created.

Creating and Loading Documents

Before you can create a channel, you need to have configured document definitions in the management database. This works just like it does in Messaging Manager. First, you must create a document specification with BizTalk Editor and store it in a WebDAV repository. Then you must create a document definition in the messaging database and provide a reference to the WebDAV location. This is exactly what the following code does:

```
Dim doc As BizTalkDocument

Set doc = configObject.CreateDocument()
doc.Name = "My Spec"
doc.Reference ="http://myserver/BizTalkServerRepository/DocSpecs/spec.xml"
doc.Create
```

When you execute the previous code and inspect the doc object just after the Reference property has been set, you will notice that the BizTalkDocument class immediately resolves the reference and loads the document into the Content property. The BizTalkEnvelope object that is used to create envelope specifications that can be assigned to the Envelope property of the BizTalkPort object works similarly.

This is, of course, only the simplest case. If you need to specify selection criteria, you will have to create a CDictionary object (that's the reason you need the Commerce Server type library) and fill this with your selection criteria. Note that this is different from all other objects: here you have to actively create a dictionary object by using New instead of going through a create method on the configuration object. When the dictionary is configured, you assign it to the PropertySet property of the document object. The following code snippet illustrates this:

```
Dim selectionCriteria As New CDictionary

Set doc = configObject.CreateDocument()
```

```
doc.Name = "EDIFACT ORDERS S98B"
doc.Reference ="http://myserver/BizTalkServerRepository/DocSpecs/orders.xml"
selectionCriteria("functional_identifier") = "ORDERS"
selectionCriteria("standards_version_type") = "S"
selectionCriteria("standards_version_value") = "98B"
Set doc.PropertySet = selectionCriteria
doc.Create
```

In Chapter 22, you will see how selection criteria are used in custom serializers and parsers. Schema-driven components like these will use such property sets to correlate document specification hints contained in the native document formats with the document definitions located in the management database. In other words, they are used to find the correct document definition based on data contained in a document.

Now that we have a document definition, we can proceed to define the channel:

```
Set ordersDocument = configObject.CreateDocument()
ordersDocument.LoadByName ("EDIFACT ORDERS S98B")
channelObject.InputDocument = ordersDocument.Handle
channelObject.OutputDocument = ordersDocument.Handle
```

In this case, both document definitions are equal; therefore, you do not need to specify a document map to perform document transformation. However, if you want to perform operations on the document, you can, of course, provide a map even if you are using the same document definition for input and output documents. If you had two different document definitions, creating or saving the channel would fail unless you provided a valid map reference:

```
Set ordersEDIDocument = configObject.CreateDocument()
Set ordersXMLDocument = configObject.CreateDocument()
ordersEDIDocument.LoadByName ("EDIFACT ORDERS S98B")
ordersXMLDocument.LoadByName ("XML Purchase Order")
channelObject.InputDocument = ordersEDIDocument.Handle
channelObject.OutputDocument = ordersXMLDocument.Handle
channelObject.MapReference = _
    "http://myserver/BizTalkServerRepository/Maps/ordermap.xml"
```

When you have configured the inbound and outbound documents of the channel properly and the source organization is likewise properly defined, you can create the channel with the following code:

```
channelObject.Create
```

Opening the Treasure Chamber: Advanced Configuration Options

When you enable MIME encoding on ports by using Messaging Manager or through the Configuration Object Model, the effect on the output stream is minimal. The MIME encoder prepends the output document with a MIME header with the content type text/xml, regardless of the rendered output stream, and leaves the output document unencoded as is. Enabling MIME encoding on the port object works like this:

```
portObject.EncodingType = BIZTALK_ENCODING_TYPE_MIME
```

If that limited functionality were the only task the MIME encoder could perform, it would be really embarrassing, but it can actually perform a couple more tasks. The only problem is that Messaging Manager will not let you use that functionality, and it is entirely undocumented in the first BizTalk Server release (prior to any service packs). In fact, the MIME encoder supports encoding the output stream in the standard formats base64, uuencode, quoted-printable, and 8bit, covering the most common Internet data encodings. These encodings are essential if you want to transmit arbitrary custom data formats that are not XML, but rather, may be binary data streams. If you just consider text streams that are encoded in 16-bit Unicode or EBCDIC code pages, the default MIME encoding that essentially doesn't do any encoding at all may cause more problems than it solves.

Also, it is of course completely wrong to mark a UN/EDIFACT or X12 document with a text/xml content type. The correct MIME type for UN/EDIFACT is application/EDIFACT, and for X12, it's application/EDI-X12.

Configuring all these details on a channel is pleasantly easy and is done by using the configuration dictionary of each component that you can obtain with *GetConfigData()* set with *SetConfigData()*. For the MIME encoder, the two configurable properties are XferEncoding for the MIME transfer encoding and ContentType for the content type. The following code enables base64 encoding for UN/EDIFACT on a specific port, which allows you to target specific ports for channels bound to a port group (hence the explicit use of the port handle).

```
Set configData = _
  channelObject.GetConfigData(BIZTALK_CONFIGDATA_TYPE_ENCODING, _
                              portObject.Handle, Null)
configData("XferEncoding") = "base64"
configData("ContentType") = "application/EDIFACT"
channelObject.SetConfigData BIZTALK_CONFIGDATA_TYPE_ENCODING, _
                            portObject.Handle, configData
```

But you can even go a step further and actually *replace* the built-in encoder and supply your own. Writing custom encoders works exactly like writing pipeline application integration components, of which you will see an example in Chapter 23. The only difference is that the component works on the data in the working_data field in the transport dictionary and writes the result back to the dictionary when it has finished processing. With that, the data is handed to the next component in the pipeline. If you want to replace the encoder, you can use the following code, assuming that the shown GUID is the CLSID of your component. (It's not! Don't use it.)

```
channelObject.SetConfigComponent BIZTALK_CONFIGDATA_TYPE_ENCODING,
                                  portObject.Handle,
                                  "{7181B246-E898-484f-B731-9DB4DBCA5010}"
```

You can replace the encoder, encrypter, serializer, parser, signature, and both transport components by using this mechanism—in short, you can replace the entire document-processing pipeline except for the document validation and mapping stage if you wish. Well, officially you're not supposed to, since the BizTalk documentation does not really mention or even hint at this technique—this here is really the socket wrench.

The built-in encryption component and the transport components have their own little secrets that can be additionally configured. However, due to the lack of documentation, only trial-and-error results could really be documented here. To help you figure out undocumented features of BizTalk and Commerce Server's pipeline components, this book's web site includes a little utility called BTSPipeCompSpy that automatically lists all configurable properties for all pipeline components found on your system.

USING WINDOWS MANAGEMENT INSTRUMENTATION

You already learned a little bit about Windows Management Instrumentation (WMI) in Chapter 4, and it has also been mentioned many times in other chapters. WMI is one of the core innovations of the Windows 2000 platform. It makes systems administration in enterprise environments more manageable by providing network-wide inventory and configuration services. WMI, which is an implementation of the multicompany standard Web-Based Enterprise management (WBEM), puts a unified API on top of the diverse data sources and APIs that you would typically use to manage configuration settings for hardware, operating systems, and application software.

With WMI, read access to most machine and software configuration settings can be performed through the WMI API and the WBEM Query Language (WQL), which is a subset of the well-known database query language SQL. Applications can support WMI explicitly by providing WMI interfaces for their configuration data. The Windows 2000 operating system is fully instrumented for providing this information (hence the name), and most .NET Enterprise Servers including Microsoft BizTalk Server 2000 also fully support WMI.

In fact, as already pointed out earlier, WMI is BizTalk's native API for quite a few management tasks. Testimony for this is that the BizTalk Administrator Microsoft Management Console (MMC) implementation sits entirely on top of the WMI provider for BizTalk. It is hard to draw the line between WMI and the BizTalk Configuration Object

Model that was described earlier in this chapter. As a rule of thumb, you could say that WMI is used to configure the per-machine and per-server group settings like database connections to get the run-time environment going, and it lets you monitor the Scheduled Queues; in contrast, the Configuration Object Model serves to set up all shared messaging settings that are used when the system is actively processing data. Because receive functions are configured to run on a specific machine, they are also configured by using WMI.

The WMI API in Brief

The WMI API is somewhat of a hybrid between a generic object-oriented API and a database API like Open Database Connectivity (ODBC). It provides a strictly navigational programming model that follows relationships as well as a WQL query-driven programming model that treats any WMI class as if it were a table in a database. As you may already expect, the topic of WMI is too big to cover fully in the context of this book, so we will just scratch the surface, which should be sufficient to enable you to access BizTalk's low-level configuration data programmatically.

To work with WMI using Visual Basic, VBScript, or JScript, you must use the Microsoft WMI Scripting V1.x Library contained in the wbemdisp.tlb type library, which is well hidden in the wbem subdirectory below your Windows 2000 system32 system directory. For Visual Basic, you should add a reference to your project to this type library. The scripting library is a rather thin layer on top of the original WMI call-level interface (CLI), which you can mostly use only from C/C++ through the wbemcli.h header file. However, we will look only at the scripting language's syntax, focusing on Visual Basic:

```
Dim Services As SWbemServices
Dim Groups As SWbemObjectSet

Set Services = GetObject("winmgmts:root\MicrosoftBizTalkServer")
Set Groups = Services.ExecQuery("select * from MicrosoftBizTalkServer_Group",, _
                         wbemFlagForwardOnly Or _
                         wbemFlagReturnImmediately)
```

Whenever you want to access BizTalk Server through WMI, you must access the BizTalk Server WMI provider by using the GetObject() command and moniker shown in the previous code. There are some alternative ways to do this as well, but we'll skip those for brevity.

Once you have acquired a reference to the service object, you can run queries against it that will return the SwbemObjectSet class. This class is a data container that may contain any number of SWbemObject elements and is enumerable. So if we were to enumerate the name of all BizTalk Server groups of a certain installation into a list box Lbx1, the previous code would best be continued like this:

```
Dim Group As SWbemObject

For Each Group In Groups
    Lbx1.AddItem Group.Name
```

```
        'alternatively: Lbx1.AddItem Group.Properties_("Name")
Next
```

What is really cool about the WbemObject class is that it is a navigable object with a range of powerful methods *and* a proxy object at the same time—at least for Visual Basic and any other late-bound language. This means that you can always use the explicit core WMI API along with the more implicit API that is defined by the BizTalk WMI provider. If you look at the previous example and verify that against the type library manually, you will find that the SWbemObject class does not define a Name property; using low-level C++, you would probably have to use the expression that is commented out in the previous example and explicitly refer to the Name property through the *Properties_* method (mind the trailing underscore!) on the base interface.

WMI even lets providers publish and consumers access methods, which can also be called either explicitly through the ExecMethod_ API or in the same proxied fashion just by invoking it by name. If you were to refresh the list of parser components from the Registry, you could consequently make the following two calls in Visual Basic, which would both be equally legal:

```
Group.ExecMethod_ "RefreshParserListFromRegistry"
Group.RefreshParserListFromRegistry
```

The WBEM Query Language (WQL) syntax that you use to acquire objects is really simple even if you aren't a SQL specialist. If you were to select all Suspended Queue entries for the BizTalk server group TradeHub that were produced due to problems with the document definition S93A INVOIC, you would issue the following query:

```
Dim Entries As Object
Set Entries = Services.ExecQuery( _
        "select * from MicrosoftBizTalkServer_SuspendedQueue " & _
        "where Group='TradeHub' and Document='S93A INVOIC'",, _
        wbemFlagForwardOnly Or _
        wbemFlagReturnImmediately)
```

BizTalk WMI Classes

The BizTalk WMI object model, which is unfortunately not fully covered by the BizTalk documentation, consists of the classes that are listed in the following sections. Working with these objects is quite easy if you understand the few code snippets just discussed; they are therefore presented in tabular form as an easy reference.

Class: MicrosoftBizTalkServer_MgmtDB

This class represents a machine's settings for establishing a connection to the BizTalk management database. All properties are writeable, so that you can either move servers between management databases or, for instance, manage passwords using this WMI object.

Name	Type	Description
LocalServer	string	Machine for which this object was requested and on which these settings exist.
MgmtDbLogon	string	Logon name for the management database.
MgmtDbName	string	Name of the database to connect to.
MgmtDbPassword	string	Password to use for logging on to the database.
MgmtDbServer	string	Name of the database server.

Class: MicrosoftBizTalkServer_Group

This WMI class provides access to all shared configuration data of a BizTalk Server group.

Name	Type	Description
ConfigurationCache RefreshInterval	uint32	Number of seconds to keep configuration information from the management database cached in BizTalk Messaging until data is reread from the database.
ConnectToDbStatus	uint32	Current connection status with the database.
DateModified	datetime	Date when this entry was last updated.
DocTrackDbLogon	string	Logon name for the document tracking database.
DocuTrackDbName	string	Name of the document tracking database to connect to.
DocTrackDb Password	string	Password to use for logging on to the document tracking database.
DocTrackDbServer	string	Name of the document tracking database server.
EnableDocument Tracking	Boolean	Set to True to enable document tracking in the group or to False to disable it for all group servers.
LoggingPointState	uint32	Flag field indicating at which processing stages the document shall be logged to the document tracking database.
Name	string	Name of the server group.
ParserOrder	string[]	Order in which parsers are invoked. This property is an array of strings containing the COM class IDs of the parser components.
ProxyHost	string	Hostname of the proxy server to use (when UseProxyServer is True).
ProxyPort	uint32	IP Port to use on the proxy server.

Name	Type	Description
QueueDbLogon	string	Logon name for the shared queue database.
QueueDbName	string	Name of the shared queue database to connect to.
QueueDbPassword	string	Password to use for logging on to the shared queue database.
QueueDbServer	string	Name of the shared queue database server.
ReliableMessaging ReplyToURL	string	URL to use as the reply-to address for BizTalk Framework (RELIABLE)–compliant messages. The address is used by the receiver to drop off receipts.
RetryQueueCount	uint32 (ro)	Number of entries currently contained in the Retry Queue.
ScheduleQueue Count	uint32	Number of entries currently contained in the Scheduled Queue.
UseProxyServer	Boolean	Indicates whether or not to use an Internet proxy server.
WorkQueueCount	uint32	Number of entries currently contained in the Work Queue.
PurgeSuspended Queue()		Call this method to remove all entries from the Suspended Queue.
RefreshParserList FromRegistry()		Call this method to update the internal parser list from the Registry. This is useful when installing parsers in a "live" system (which you shouldn't do).

Class: MicrosoftBizTalkServer_Server

This class represents a single BizTalk server machine within a BizTalk server group.

Name	Type	Description
DateModified	datetime	Date when this entry was last modified.
GroupName	string	Name of the server group this machine belongs to.
MaxRecvSvcThreads PerProcessor	uint32	Maximum number of threads to use for receive functions per CPU.
MaxWorkerThreads PerProcessor	uint32	Maximum number of messaging worker threads to use per CPU.
Name	string	Name of the server.

Name	Type	Description
ParticipateInWork ItemProcessing	Boolean	Signals whether this server participates in work-item processing, meaning whether it picks up and processes elements from the Work Queue.
SchedulerWaitTime	uint32	Time, expressed in milliseconds, that the machine will wait between attempts to pick up new items from the Work Queue.
ServiceState	uint32	Current state of the service (started/stopped).
FreeInterchanges()		Commands the server to free interchanges that are currently associated with it, so that other servers in the group can process the interchanges. This is typically done when the server is taken offline.
StartServer()		Starts the messaging services.
StopServer()		Stops the messaging services.

Class: MicrosoftBizTalkServer_ReceiveFunction

This class serves to configure and administer file or message queuing receive functions.

Name	Type	Description
ChannelName	string	Name of the channel to submit data to.
Comment	string	Comment for the receive function.
DateModified	datetime	Date when this entry was last modified.
DestinationID	string	Destination organization identifier.
Destination Qualifier	string	Destination organization identifier qualifier.
DisableReceive Function	Boolean	Indicates whether this receive function is disabled.
DocumentName	string	Name of the document definition applicable for the channel.
EnvelopeName	string	Name of the envelope to use.
FilenameMask	string	Filename mask for file receive functions. This is a comma-separated list of wildcard expressions like "*.txt".
GroupName	string	Name of the server group the receive function is defined for.

Name	Type	Description
IsPassThrough	Boolean	Indicates whether the data should be submitted in passthrough mode.
Name	string	Name of the receive function.
OpennessFlag	uint32	Openness flags to be used with the Interchange component when submitting the data.
Password	string	Password to use for authentication when picking up data from the Message Queue or file location.
PollingLocation	string	Location where data will be picked up. This is a directory for the file transport and a queue name for the Microsoft Message Queue (MSMQ).
PreProcessor	string	Class ID of the custom preprocessor to use.
ProcessingServer	string	Server that will run this function. (Only one server at a time can execute such functions.)
ProtocolType	uint32	Type of protocol (File or MSMQ).
SourceID	string	Source organization identifier.
SourceQualifier	string	Source organization identifier qualifier.
Username	string	Username to use for authentication when picking up data from the Message Queue or file location.

Class: MicrosoftBizTalkServer_Queue

This is the base class for all queue classes described in the following sections. WMI supports class inheritance, which means that all subclasses of this class (like MicrosoftBizTalkServer_ SuspendedQueue) will automatically have the same properties as the base class. The queue class objects describe a single queue entry, not the queue itself.

Name	Type	Description
Destination	string	Text description of the destination organization where this queue entry is supposed to be sent.
Group	string	Server group that the queue is associated with.
QID	uint32	Unique identifier of the entry within the queue.
Source	string	Text description of the source organization from where this queue entry was submitted.
Timestamp	datetime	Time stamp of when this entry was placed into the queue.

Class: MicrosoftBizTalkServer_RetryQueue

Base Class: MicrosoftBizTalkServer_Queue

This class describes objects that are contained in the Retry Queue. Objects of this class have all the properties of the MicrosoftBizTalkServer_Queue class plus the following:

Name	Type	Description
LastRetryTime	datetime	Last time a retry was attempted for the queue entry.
ProcessingServer	string	Name of the server that is responsible for processing this entry.
RemainingRetry Count	uint32	Number of retries until this item is moved into the Suspended Queue.
RetryInterval	uint32	Interval, in seconds, between retries.
ServiceWindow FromTime	datetime	Start time of the service window.
ServiceWindow ToTime	datetime	End time of the services window.
MoveToSuspended Queue()		With this method, you can move this queue entry into the Suspended Queue immediately.

Class: MicrosoftBizTalkServer_ScheduledQueue

Base Class: MicrosoftBizTalkServer_Queue

This class describes objects that are contained in the Retry Queue. Objects of this class have all the properties of the MicrosoftBizTalkServer_Queue class plus the following:

Name	Type	Description
ProcessingServer	string	Name of the server that is responsible for processing this entry.
ServiceWindow FromTime	datetime	Start time of the service window.
ServiceWindow ToTime	datetime	End time of the services window.
MoveToSuspended Queue()		With this method, you can move this queue entry into the Suspended Queue immediately.

Class: MicrosoftBizTalkServer_SuspendedQueue

Base Class: MicrosoftBizTalkServer_Queue

This class describes objects that are contained in the Retry Queue. Objects of this class have all the properties of the MicrosoftBizTalkServer_Queue class plus the following:

Name	Type	Description
DocName	string	Name of the document definition.
ErrorDescription	string	Description of the error that caused the object being suspended.
QGUID	string	Unique identifier (interchange id) for the document. This is a text-form GUID.
State	string	Processing state in which the object has been suspended.
Resubmit()		Allows you to resubmit the document into the Work Queue.
ViewDocument()	string	Retrieves the document that causes the error.
ViewError Description()	string	Call this method to retrieve a more elaborate error description for the document.
ViewInterchange()	string	This method returns the complete interchange of the suspended document.

Class: MicrosoftBizTalkServer_WorkQueue

Base Class: MicrosoftBizTalkServer_Queue

This class describes objects that are contained in the Work Queue. Objects of this class have all the properties of the MicrosoftBizTalkServer_Queue class plus the following:

Name	Type	Description
DocName	string	Document name.
EngineState	uint32	State of the processing engine.
ProcessingServer	string	Server processing this document.

CHAPTER 21

Tracking Documents

When you create and send business documents in a traditional way—by printing them on paper, putting them in an envelope, and sending them via postal mail—you will most certainly retain a copy and store it in a binder. The same is true for incoming mail. Keeping track of and storing business documents is indeed essential for business; not only is it necessary for reasonable organization, but it also serves as proof in legal disputes.

When businesses replace paper-based processes with electronic document exchange, these key organizational and legal qualities must be retained. If you were to accept purchase orders through BizTalk Server, everything was nicely processed, but the original order just faded into binary nirvana, a customer could easily claim to have never placed the order, and you would not be able to prove otherwise. You could argue that it should be sufficient to accept the order and pass that on to your order-management system so that the order could be safely reproduced from there. However, you would lose the only evidence that a certain order was indeed sent by a certain customer—and that's the digital signature. Digital signatures are applied to the exact appearance of digital documents and can no longer be linked up with the data once the exact binary data stream is not kept. This prevents the sender from tampering with the signed data and gives the receiver reliable proof that a certain document has been produced by a certain well-known source.

For this reason and, of course, other more technical reasons like debugging, BizTalk Server maintains a document tracking database. By using configuration settings on your BizTalk channels, you can enable document tracking for each unparsed incoming document, the intermediate XML documents, and the final output. When document tracking is enabled, the entire document is stored in the document tracking database as is, and you have the additional option of defining tracking fields that will make it easier for you to search for specific documents.

In this chapter, you will learn about the structure of the document tracking database and the document tracking tool that provides a basic user interface for retrieving information from the document tracking database. You will also learn how to use the document tracking database programmatically from within your own applications that submit data into Microsoft BizTalk Server 2000.

THE DOCUMENT TRACKING DATABASE

To enable document tracking, go to the Tracking tab in the BizTalk Server Group Properties dialog box within BizTalk Administrator. (See Figure 21-1.) By default, BizTalk logs to the document tracking database all documents that pass the document-processing pipelines of all servers that belong to the server group. However, you can override that behavior by clearing the tracking option for an individual channel, as you may have seen while experimenting with channel configurations in Chapter 17.

Based on the traffic your systems receive and on the detail of tracking information you require, the document tracking database may quickly grow to contain large amounts of data. Therefore, it is essential that you understand the structure of the document tracking

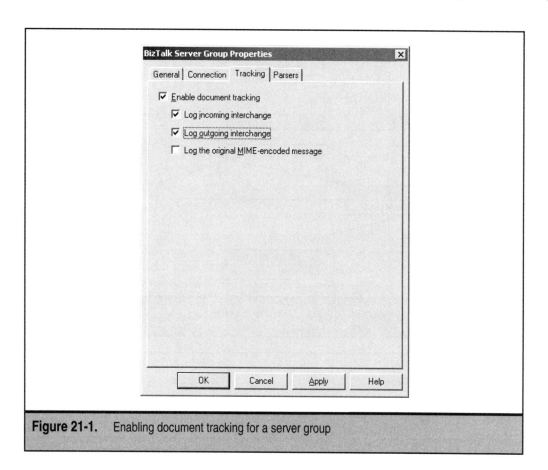

Figure 21-1. Enabling document tracking for a server group

database so that you can replicate data out of the database into offline archive databases and/or to delete data from the database.

Figure 21-2 shows the relationship between the core tables that hold the bulk of the data. Whenever you want to move data out of the document tracking database or delete data altogether, you must make sure to delete the information from all of these connected tables.

The document tracking database's central data table is dta_interchange_detail (see Table 21-1). As you already know, the initial BizTalk version has at least partial support for multidocument interchanges. While BizTalk cannot produce batched output sending multiple documents within an interchange, it can at least handle them inbound. However, when looking at the structure of the document tracking database, you can safely assume that this support will be substantially extended over time. In essence, all tracking information in the document tracking database is kept under the assumption that data is relayed through BizTalk in the form of interchanges that can contain multiple groups of documents. The primary-key (PK) column of dta_interchange_detail is nInterchangeKey.

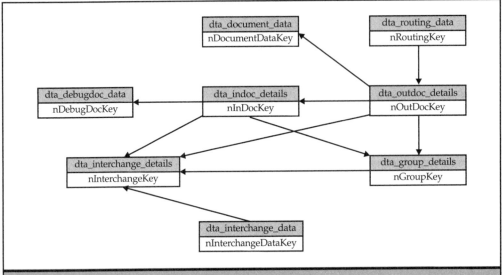

Figure 21-2. Document tracking database structural overview

Column	Type	PK	FK	Description
nInterchange Key	int	X		Primary key (PK).
nInterchange DataKey	int		dta_inter change_ data	Foreign key (FK) to dta_interchange_data.
nResponse DocDataKey	int		dta_ document_ data	Foreign key to a dta_document_data record containing binary data for the response document (receipt) returned by the recipient of an outbound transport.
uidInter changeGUID	unique identifier			Globally unique identifier (GUID) for the interchange. This corresponds to the entries in the shared queue databases (retry queue, scheduled queue, suspended queue) for this interchange.

Table 21-1. The dta_interchange_detail Table

Column	Type	PK	FK	Description
uidSubmission GUID	unique identifier			GUID for the submission. This corresponds to the submission handle returned by the *Submit()* and *SubmitSync()* methods of the Interchange component. The submission GUID is propagated into all interchanges produced by a single submission, including documents that are produced by XLANG schedules based on a single submission.
dtProcessed TimeStamp	datetime			Time the record was created.
nvcSyntax	nvarchar			Text code for document syntax (XML, X12, EDIFACT, etc.). This is the value that is returned by a parser component when it has positively identified the data. In the case of unrecognized syntax due to parsing failure or passthrough submission, this field has a value of "UNKNOWN."
nvcVersion	nvarchar			Version of the syntax.
nvcControlID	nvarchar			Unique control number for electronic data interchange (EDI) interchanges or an identifier for BizTalk Reliable Messages (BTF 2.0–compliant).
nDirection	int		dta_ direction_ values	Flag indicating whether the interchange is incoming or outgoing. Possible values are 0 (outbound) or 1 (inbound). This is a foreign key to dta_direction_values, the table that contains text expressions for the direction values and that can be used to produce human-readable reports.

Table 21-1.   The dta_interchange_detail Table *(continued)*

Column	Type	PK	FK	Description
dtTimeSent	datetime			Time stamp for when the interchange was successfully sent.
nError	int		dta_ error_ message	Code that indicates the occurrence of an error. This is a foreign key to dta_error_message, which contains human-readable error message descriptions.
nTestMode	int			Test or production indicator. This field is reserved and is not used.
nvcSrcAlias Qualifer	nvarchar			Sender organization identifier qualifier value extracted from the submitted or transmitted interchange.
nvcSrcAliasId	nvarchar			Sender organization identifier value extracted from the submitted or transmitted interchange.
nvcSrcApp Name	nvarchar			Interchange-level identifier for the source application extracted from the submitted or transmitted interchange.
nvcDestAlias Qualifier	nvarchar			Destination organization qualifier extracted from the submitted or transmitted interchange.
nvcDestAliasID	nvarchar			Destination organization identifier value extracted from the submitted or transmitted interchange.
nvcDestApp Name	nvarchar			Interchange-level identifier for the destination application extracted from the submitted or transmitted interchange.
nAckStatus	int		dta_ack_ status_ values	Code for the status of the receipt for this interchange, if it was sent using the Reliable messaging transport (BTF), EDIFACT, or X12 requiring a receipt. The dta_ack_status_ values table contains the human-readable status descriptions for reports.

Table 21-1. The dta_interchange_detail Table *(continued)*

Column	Type	PK	FK	Description
nvcSMTP MessageID	nvarchar			SMTP transport message identifier (to be used later for SMTP-based EDIINT). This field is currently reserved and is not used.
nDocuments Accepted	int			Number of documents accepted in the interchange.
nDocuments Rejected	int			Number of documents rejected in the interchange.
nTransport Type	int		dta_ transport_ type_ values	Transport protocol indicator code, mapping to text descriptions in dta_transport_type_values.
nvcTransport Address	int			Target address for the transport protocol.
nvcServer Name	nvarchar			Server that processed the interchange.
nNumberOf Bytes	int			Size of the interchange in bytes. This field represents what is tracked in the related dta_interchange_data record and can be different than what is actually transmitted. This is the number of bytes as reported from the respective parser component.
nNumOf Transmit Attempts	int			Transmission attempt counter.

Table 21-1.   The dta_interchange_detail Table *(continued)*

The original data of the entire interchange as BizTalk Server received it is contained in the dta_interchange_data table (see Table 21-2), whose primary key (PK) is nInterchangeDataKey and is referenced by a foreign-key (FK) column by the same name from dta_interchange_detail.

The dta_interchange_data table contains the global routing information about the entire interchange, such as the source and destination identifiers, the document syntax type and version, and also the transport type reference, along with the handling server. If you wanted to obtain the raw interchange data based on a certain source identifier, you could therefore express it the following way in SQL:

```
SELECT data.imgInterchangeData
FROM dta_interchange_data data INNER JOIN dta_interchange_details details
    ON data.nInterchangeDatakey = details.nInterchangeDataKey
WHERE
   details.nvcSrcAliasQualifier='ZZ' AND
   details.nvcSrcAliasId='0011'
```

Column	Type	PK	FK	Description
nInterchange DataKey	int	X		Primary key unique record identifier.
nCodePage	int		dta_ui_ codepage_ charset	System code page for the character-encoded stored data. This has a value of –1 if BizTalk Server does not have any code-page information about the data, or if the data is tracked as a result of a passthrough submission. In this case, the value of the nBLOBType field might provide information about how to interpret the data.
nlsFile	int			Flag indicating file-based data submission. Possible values are 0 (nonfile-based) or 1 (file-based).
nvcOriginalFile Name	nvarchar			Universal naming convention (UNC) path to the originally submitted file, if the nlsFile field has a value of 1. This is an informational value. The complete interchange is stored in the imgInterchangeData field regardless.

Table 21-2.   The dta_interchange_data Table

Column	Type	PK	FK	Description
nBLOBType	int		dta_blobtype_values	Flag that indicates the type of data stored in the imgDocument Data field. Possible values are 0 (Unknown) or 1 (XMLDOM Loadable). XMLDOM Loadable indicates that BizTalk has determined that the data can be successfully loaded into and manipulated by the MSXML DOMDocument object.
imgInterchange Data	image			Storage location for the original interchange as binary large object.

Table 21-2. The dta_interchange_data Table *(continued)*

Depending on the document syntax, inbound and outbound document data may be transported in groups. A group, or more explicitly, a functional group, serves to envelope multiple documents that need to be routed to the same destination within an organization. Groups are created and maintained within the document tracking database only if the inbound document formats support them and if incoming data was actually transmitted using groups. Otherwise, the dta_group_details table, whose details are listed in Table 21-3, will not be filled.

Column	Type	PK	FK	Description
nGroupKey	int	X		Primary key unique record identifier.
nInter changeKey	int		dta_interchange_details	Reference to the interchange containing this group.
dtProcessed TimeStamp	datetime			Time the record was created.

Table 21-3. The dta_group_details Table

Column	Type	PK	FK	Description
nvcSyntax	nvarchar			Text code for document syntax (XML, X12, EDIFACT, etc.). This is the value that is returned by a parser component when it has positively identified the data. In the case of unrecognized syntax due to parsing failure or passthrough submission, this field has a value of "UNKNOWN."
nvcVersion	nvarchar			Version of the syntax.
nvcRelease	nvarchar			Release of the version.
nvcFunctional GroupID	nvarchar			Functional group identifier relative to the interchange document.
nvcControlID	nvarchar			Unique control number for EDI interchanges or an identifier for BizTalk Reliable Messages (BTF 2.0– compliant).
nvcSrcApp Name	nvarchar			Group-level identifier for the source application.
nvcDestApp Name	nvarchar			Group-level identifier for the destination application.
nAckStatus	int		dta_ack_ status_values	Code for the status of the receipt for this interchange if it was sent using the reliable messaging transport (BTF), EDIFACT, or X12 requiring a receipt. The dta_ack_status_ values table contains the human-readable status descriptions for reports.
nDirection	int		dta_direction_ values	Flag that indicates whether the group was incoming or outgoing. Possible values are 0 (outbound) or 1 (inbound).
nDocuments Accepted	int			Transactions accepted in the group.

Table 21-3.   The dta_group_details Table *(continued)*

Column	Type	PK	FK	Description
nDocuments Rejected	int			Transactions rejected in the group.
nNumberOf Bytes	int			Size of the interchange in bytes.

Table 21-3.   The dta_group_details Table *(continued)*

For instance, if an interchange contains groups, you could get the name of the source and/or destination applications interchanges sent by a certain partner by using the following query:

```
SELECT grp.nvcSrcAppName, grp.nvcDestAppName
FROM dta_group_details grp INNER JOIN dta_interchange_details details
    ON grp.nInterchangeKey = details.nInterchangeKey
WHERE
    details.nvcSrcAliasQualifier='ZZ' AND
    details.nvcSrcAliasId='0011'
```

All inbound documents (consequently, that's the raw data that is contained within interchanges and/or groups) are referenced in the dta_indoc_details table, and their raw data is held in the dta_document_data table (see Table 21-4). Both tables are linked by the

Column	Type	PK	FK	Description
nDocumentDataKey	int	X		Primary key unique record identifier.
nCodePage	int		dta_ui_code page_charset	System code page for the character-encoded stored data. This has a value of -1 if BizTalk Server does not have any code-page information about the data, or if the data is tracked as a result of a passthrough submission. In this case, the value of the nBLOBType field might provide information about how to interpret the data.

Table 21-4.   The dta_document_data Table

Column	Type	PK	FK	Description
nBLOBType	int		dta_blobtype_values	Flag that indicates the type of data stored in the imgDocumentData field. Possible values are 0 (Unknown) or 1 (XMLDOM Loadable). XMLDOM Loadable indicates that BizTalk has determined that the data can be successfully loaded into and manipulated by the MSXML DOMDocument object.
imgDocument Data	image			Storage of a document, as a binary large object.
nNumberOf Bytes	int			Size of the document, in bytes, as returned by the parser component.
nNumberOf Records	int			Records or segments comprised in the document.

Table 21-4. The dta_document_data Table *(continued)*

nDocumentDataKey column, which is the primary key for the dta_document_data table and hence, a foreign key in the dta_indoc_details table (see Table 21-5).

Column	Type	PK	FK	Description
nInDocKey	int	X		Primary key unique record identifier.
nDocument DataKey	int		dta_document_data	Foreign key to dta_document_data, referencing the storage for the raw data.
nDebugDoc DataKey	int		dta_debugDoc_data	Foreign key to dta_debugDoc_data that holds the XML form of the received document, regardless of what the native format is.
nGroupKey	int		dta_group_details	Foreign key to dta_group_details if the document was submitted in a group.

Table 21-5. The dta_indoc_details Table

Column	Type	PK	FK	Description
nInterchange Key	int		dta_inter change_details	Foreign key to dta_interchange_details that holds the data of the parent interchange.
uidTracking GUID	unique identifier			Tracking key value for this document.
dtProcessed TimeStamp	datetime			Time the record was created.
nvcSyntax	nvarchar			Text code for document syntax (XML, X12, EDIFACT, etc.). This is the value that is returned by a parser component when it has positively identified the data. In the case of unrecognized syntax due to parsing failure or passthrough submission, this field has a value of "UNKNOWN."
nvcVersion	nvarchar			Version of the syntax.
nvcRelease	nvarchar			Release of the version.
nvcDocType	nvarchar			Document type or transaction set identifier.
nvcControlID	nvarchar			Unique control number for EDI documents and functional groups.
nlsValid	int		dta_validity_ values	Code that indicates validation results. Possible values are 0 (invalid), 1 (valid), or 2 (passthrough).
nError	int		dta_error_ message	Code that indicates the occurrence of an error. This is the foreign key to dta_error_message, the table that contains the descriptions of the error messages.

Table 21-5.   The dta_indoc_details Table *(continued)*

Getting to the raw data works as shown in the following snippet, given that you had an nInDocKey value to look up, which is the primary key of the dta_indoc_details table, and which is simply set to 1 in this case:

```
SELECT doc.imgDocumentData
FROM dta_document_data doc INNER JOIN dta_indoc_details indoc
```

```
    ON doc.nDocumentDataKey = indoc.nDocumentDataKey
WHERE
  indoc.nInDocKey = 1
```

Outbound documents are referenced through the dta_outdoc_details table (see Table 21-6). The raw data of these documents is linked just like that of the dta_indoc_tables, so the previous SQL expression applies in much the same way. Because output documents in BizTalk would not exist without having a previous input document, these two tables are linked through the nInDocKey column that also exists in the dta_outdoc_details table as a foreign key.

The dta_outdoc_details table also has some other noteworthy specialties.

The values of the tracking fields that you can define for a document definition in Messaging Manager are stored in eight typed fields, with two for each of the data types string, integer, real, and date time (nIntValue1, nIntValue2, nStrValue1, nStrValue2, nDateValue1, nDateValue2, nRealValue1, and nRealValue2). The name of the tracking fields is centrally managed through the dta_custom_field_name table. For this reason,

Column	Type	PK	FK	Description
nOutDocKey	int	X		Primary key unique record identifier.
nInDocKey	int		dta_indoc_details	Reference to the input document from which this output document was created.
nDocumentDataKey	int		dta_document_data	Reference to the raw data for this document.
nDebugDocDataKey	int		dta_debugDoc_data	Foreign key to dta_debugDoc_data that holds the XML form of the received document, regardless of what the native format is.
nGroupKey	int		dta_group_details	Foreign key to the dta_group_details table.
nInterchangeKey	int		dta_interchange_details	Foreign key to the dta_interchange_details table.
uidTrackingGUID	unique identifier			Master tracking key value based on a GUID.
dtProcessedTimeStamp	datetime			Time the record was created.

Table 21-6. The dta_outdoc_details Table

Column	Type	PK	FK	Description
nvcSyntax	nvarchar			Text code for document syntax (XML, X12, EDIFACT, etc.). This is the value that is returned by a parser component when it has positively identified the data. In the case of unrecognized syntax due to parsing failure or passthrough submission, this field has a value of "UNKNOWN."
nvcVersion	nvarchar			Version of the syntax.
nvcRelease	nvarchar			Release of the version.
nvcDocType	nvarchar			Document type or transaction set identifier.
nvcControlID	nvarchar			Unique control number for EDI interchanges or an identifier for BizTalk Reliable Messages (BTF 2.0–compliant)
nlsValid	int		dta_validity_values	Code that indicates validation results. Possible values are 0 (invalid), 1 (valid), or 2 (passthrough).
nError	int		dta_error_message	Code that indicates the occurrence of an error. This is a foreign key to dta_error_message, the table that contains the error message descriptions.
nAckStatus	int		dta_ack_status_values	Code for the status of the receipt. This is a foreign key to dta_ack_status_values, the table that contains the receipt status descriptions.
nRoutingKey	int		dta_routing_details	Foreign key to dta_routing_details.
nReceiptFlag	int			Flag that indicates to which table a receipt is associated. Possible values are 1 (Interchange), 2 (Group), 4 (indoc), and 8 (outdoc).

Table 21-6.   The dta_outdoc_details Table *(continued)*

Column	Type	PK	FK	Description
nReceiptKey	int			Unique number that identifies the receipt.
ntReceipt DueBy	timestamp			Receipt deadline time stamp, computed to be the processing time stamp.
nRealName1	int		dta_custom_ field_names	Reference to name and type for this custom tracking field.
rlRealValue1	float			Real capture field 1. This field must be an 8-byte real value.
nRealName2	int		dta_custom_ field_names	Reference to name and type for this custom tracking field.
rlRealValue2	float			Real capture field 2. This field must be an 8-byte real value.
nIntName1	int		dta_custom_ field_names	Reference to name and type for this custom tracking field.
nIntValue1	int			Integer capture field 1.
nIntName2	int		dta_custom_ field_names	Reference to name and type for this custom tracking field.
nIntValue2	int			Integer capture field 2.
nDateName1	int		dta_custom_ field_names	Reference to name and type for this custom tracking field.
dtDateValue1	datetime			Date capture field 1.
nDateName2	int		dta_custom_ field_names	Reference to name and type for this custom tracking field.
dtDateValue2	datetime			Date capture field 2.
nStrName1	int		dta_custom_ field_names	Reference to name and type for this custom tracking field.
nvcStrValue1	nvarchar			String capture field 1.
nStrName2	int		dta_custom_ field_names	Reference to name and type for this custom tracking field.
nvcStrValue2	nvarchar			String capture field 2.
nvcCustom Search	nvarchar			Binary large object for concatenated string capture as XML.

Table 21-6. The dta_outdoc_details Table *(continued)*

there are fields like nStrName1 numeric and there are references to the dta_custom_field_name table.

Another important aspect is that the routing information about the source and destination organizations is not stored in the dta_outdoc_details table. Instead, it is stored externally in the dta_routing_details table (see Table 21-7), which allows tracking of the same document that is being sent to multiple destinations through port groups.

All tables with the name suffix values are statically filled when the document tracking database is created and will typically not change. The table dta_ack_status_values contains, for instance, the text equivalents of the status codes for the nAckStatus acknowledgment

Column	Type	PK	FK	Description
nRoutingKey	int	X		Primary key unique record identifier.
nvcSrcOrgName	nvarchar			Source organization name, as specified on the sending channel object.
nvcSrcAppName	nvarchar			Source application name, as specified on the sending channel object.
nvcDestOrgName	nvarchar			Destination organization name, as specified on the sending messaging port object.
nvcDestAppName	nvarchar			Destination application name, as specified on the sending port object.
nvcDistributionName	nvarchar			Name of the port group/distribution list.
uidChannelGUID	uniqueidentifier			Unique key for the parent channel based on a GUID. This is used as a channel correlation key into the BizTalk Messaging management database.
uidPortGUID	uniqueidentifier			Unique key for the parent port based on a GUID. This is a port correlation key into the BizTalk Messaging management database.

Table 21-7. The dta_routing_details Table

status fields in the dta_indoc_details and dta_outdoc_details tables, and the dta_blobtype_values table contains the text descriptions for the dta_document_data Binary Large OBjects (BLOBs). For replication and cleanup, you can therefore ignore the values tables because they are fairly static.

THE DOCUMENT TRACKING TOOL

The BizTalk Document Tracking web page that is installed with any BizTalk Server by default is the interactive interface to the document tracking database. This application is helpful to run ad hoc queries against the document tracking database. However, to do sophisticated data reporting or queries, you may actually prefer directly accessing the document tracking database for more flexibility and to supply an end-user safe user interface.

As already explained in Chapter 10, you open the search page through the "BizTalk Document Tracking" entry in the Microsoft BizTalk Server 2000 group on the Start menu. Most of the options on the page are really easy to use and do not require much explanation beyond what is already explained in Chapter 10. The only feature that we will look into more closely here is Advanced Query Builder (see Figure 21-3), which is the most powerful part of this application.

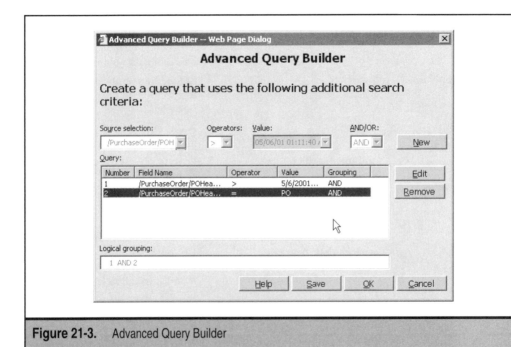

Figure 21-3. Advanced Query Builder

Advanced Query Builder allows you to create query expressions using global or channel-specific tracking fields that you can define through Messaging Manager. This allows you to find result sets for queries like "all purchase orders from organization Alpha since September 2000," given that you have the tracking fields defined that would filter this data from the original documents and make it accessible in the document tracking database.

To create a new advanced query, click the New button on the BizTalk Document Tracking page's Advanced Query page-nugget. This opens Advanced Query Builder.

Using Advanced Query Builder is quite easy. The Source Selection combo box contains all document-definition global or channel-level tracking fields that have entries in the tracking database. This may or may not correspond with your messaging configuration settings. When you select one of the tracking types, Advanced Query Builder will recognize its data type, suggest compatible operators in the Operators combo box, and properly format the Value argument against which the tracking field value will be tested.

When you are done defining a query condition, click the Done button. The button will then turn into a New button, which allows you to add an additional condition to the query expression. To use the expression, click OK, and this expression will be used for this exact tracking query. Or you can click the Save button, which allows you to save this query by assigning a name so that you can reuse it later.

Figure 21-4 shows the list of advanced queries that you can open from the main tracking page when you click the Browse button. This box allows you to edit, delete, and create new advanced queries.

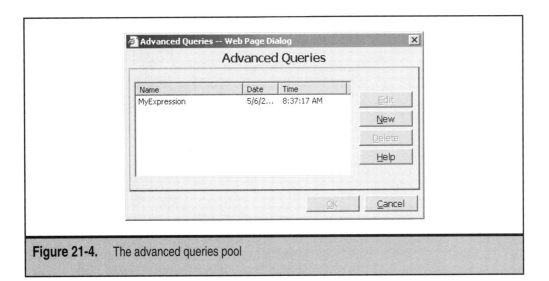

Figure 21-4.   The advanced queries pool

Using Document Tracking from Applications

For programmatic access to the document tracking database, BizTalk offers two levels of support: little and none. The Microsoft BizTalk Server Doc Tracking 1.0 type library and component provide only limited convenience access to the document tracking data. However, the component is very handy in a couple cases: when you want to externally track specific documents that you have submitted through the Interchange component from within the scope of your applications, and when you want to report back to the user or your internal system whether and when a document could be successfully delivered.

The IBizTalkTrackData interface provides access to tracking data based on the submission identifier returned by *IInterchange.Submit()* and *IInterchange.SubmitSync()*.

The methods *GetInDocDetails(), GetOutDocDetails()*, and *GetInterchangeDetails()* each return a recordset containing the respective rows (from dta_indoc_details, dta_outdoc_details, and dta:interchange_details) from the document tracking database that were produced based on this submission.

For any other access to the document tracking database, you have to use direct database access and SQL queries, for instance, via ADO.

PART VI

Extending BizTalk Server 2000: The Basics

CHAPTER 22

Custom Parsers and Serializers

izTalk's support for the most commonly used EDI formats, flatfiles, and XML will cover most organizations' needs. However, many data-exchange formats are not based on any of the supported standards and are either too complex or too irregular to be parsed and serialized with BizTalk's flatfile support. If you need to deal with such formats, you must build custom serializer and parser components. This chapter teaches you how to implement such components, using a subset of the SWIFT standard as an example.

In contrast to earlier chapters, this chapter and the following two assume that you are fluent in C++ (specifically Microsoft Visual C++ 6.0) and have already created components with the Active Template Library (ATL) for COM. If you have no ATL experience, there is still hope, though. If you have a solid C++ background, ATL is not rocket science. You may just want to grab one of the many excellent books on COM and ATL or learn it by accessing the grand portfolio of articles about ATL at MSDN Online (http://msdn.microsoft.com).

If you know ATL, you will have noticed that its code mixes ATL and the Visual C++ native COM support; thus, we deal with two different VARIANT classes (CComVariant and _variant_t) and also two different BSTR classes (CComBSTR and _bstr_t). While this leads to some inconsistencies in the code's appearance, it is perfectly OK to mix both models. Using the native COM support's #import directive to create smart pointers and property wrappers makes dealing with the Microsoft XML parser classes a lot more bearable than using the somewhat clumsy raw COM interfaces.

The code samples in this chapter use BizTalk Schema–specific attributes extensively, which are unfortunately not documented in BizTalk Server. Appendix A contains a BizTalk Schema reference for this reason.

IMPLEMENTING A CUSTOM PARSER

If you have worked on projects involving systems integration, you may have already written some kind of data import parser. Writing such parsers is not only tedious, but the result is typically so custom tailored for a specific data stream that it requires (often substantial) code changes if the data format is updated. Good alternatives to such hard-coded parsers are table-driven parsers, but they typically require that you write your own tools to maintain and manage the table definitions, which is often beyond the scope (and budget) of your current project.

A great advantage of BizTalk Server is that it already comes with such tools (BizTalk Editor, WebDAV support). Furthermore, BizTalk Schema is a very expressive definition format to describe virtually any data format that you would want to read with a custom parser. We will therefore implement a complete schema-driven parser for the example in this chapter, whose implementation techniques you can adopt for your own formats.

In this chapter, the parser and the serializer implement a subset of the SWIFT data formats and have been tested only with a couple of samples for the most common SWIFT message that you may see in nonbanks: the account statement message MT940 that banks commonly forward to their large clients. (This is true at least in Europe.) For completeness, we will also add support for the SWIFT headers, although these are typically used only within the SWIFT network and are stripped from the message when the data is forwarded to nonbanks.

The parser supports incoming data streams in ASCII (actually, the ASCII superset code page ISO 1252), in 16-bit Unicode encoding, and in the IBM mainframe character code page EBCDIC (code page 1026).

Keep in mind that this code serves solely to demonstrate how you can implement parsers. It is neither validated against the standards nor does is provide a complete implementation even for the MT940 format. As you already know from Chapter 3, the SWIFT data format is sometimes a bit warped and tends to have many inconsistencies. While most of these consistency exceptions can be expressed by using BizTalk Schema (or any other definition table format), some rules in the message definitions may indeed require very specialized handling, which could be implemented as pluggable components in a production SWIFT parser.

Field 86 in the MT940 message is such a case. The SWIFT standard defines 86 as a multipurpose field that contains a maximum of 6 lines with 65 characters of free text describing a transaction to the customer; in reality, it is mostly used to carry (bank-proprietary) formatted information that is not covered anywhere else in the message standard, and therefore often requires customized parsing to extract all essential data on the customer end.

How BizTalk Parsers Plug into BizTalk

Before we drill down into the sample code, we are first going to take a look at how BizTalk uses its parser components.

To be usable with BizTalk, each parser must implement the IBizTalkParserComponent interface and must be registered in the COM category with the identifier CATID_BIZTALK_ PARSER. The category settings allow BizTalk to dynamically find all parsers that exist on a system. Also, although BizTalk Server will always call the parser from within a single thread and will never do any concurrent calls, the component must also be registered as free threaded or be registered to support both COM threading models (free threaded and apartment threaded). If you register the component only for apartment threading, the parser will not work correctly because the transport dictionary does not support marshaling between threads. (If you do not fully understand the threading issues, don't worry; just do it right).

These threading-model requirements are the primary reason that BizTalk parsers and serializers cannot be implemented in Visual Basic: VB only supports creating single- and apartment-threaded components.

BizTalk Server determines the installed parsers at startup time and whenever you explicitly refresh the parser list from the registry in the BizTalk Server Group properties dialog box in BizTalk Administrator. When a new parser is detected, it is automatically placed at the lowest priority position in each BizTalk Server group. If you have multiple parsers for similar formats, you may want to change that order in the properties dialog box. The order defines which parser's *IBizTalkParserComponent::ProbeInterchangeFormat()* message is called first. The call sequence for when a parser acknowledges the format was already explained in Chapter 11, but the essentials will be pointed out again when we look at the code now.

The Job

The sample parser must translate the following (mostly) SWIFT-compliant document into an XML document. SWIFT experts will notice that the trailer block is missing (because our parser will ignore it) and that the headers may not really make sense for an MT940 message, since it is actually a bank-to-customer message. However, because it only serves for technical demonstration purposes, the message should work quite well. German readers will understand the sample data a lot better than anyone else (because the sample is a German account statement):

```
{1:F01BANKBEBBAXXX2222123456}{2:I940BANKDEFFXXXXU3003}{4:
:20:951110
:25:45050050/76198810
:28C:27/01
:60F:C951016DEM84349,74
:61:951017D6800,NCHK16703074
:86:999PN5477SCHECK-NR. 0000016703074
:61:951017D620,3NSTON
:86:999PN0911DAUERAUFTR.NR. 14
:61:951017C18500,NCLRN
:86:999PN2406SCHECK
:61:951015D14220,NBOEN
:86:999PN0920WECHSEL
:61:951017D1507,NTRFN
:86:999PN0920SCHNELLUEB
:61:951024C4200,NMSCN
:86:999PN2506AUSSENH. NR. 1
:61:951017D19900,NTRFN
:86:999PN0907UEBERTRAG
:61:951017D400,NTRFN
:86:999PN0891BTX
:61:951018C3656,74NMSCN
:86:999PN0850EINZAHLG.N
:61:951019C23040,NMSCN
:86:999PN0812LT.ANLAGE
:61:951027D5862,14NCHKN
:86:999PN5329AUSLSCHECK
:62F:C951017DEM84437,04
- }
```

The desired target document (that was produced by the previous implementation) must look like the following XML document. The document is cut short so that it doesn't take up too much space here:

```
<MT940 xmlns="urn:schemas-newtelligence-com:swift:mt940">
  <x20>
    <F20_1>951110</F20_1>
  </x20>
  <x25>
    <F25_1>45050050/76198810</F25_1>
  </x25>
  <x28C>
    <F28C_1>27/01</F28C_1>
  </x28C>
  <x60F>
    <F60F_1>C</F60F_1>
    <F60F_2>1995-10-16</F60F_2>
    <F60F_3>DEM</F60F_3>
    <F60F_4>84349.74</F60F_4>
  </x60F>
  <x61Loop1>
    <x61>
      <F61_1>1995-10-17</F61_1>
      <F61_2>D680</F61_2>
      <F61_3>0,</F61_3>
      <F61_4>N</F61_4>
      <F61_5>CHK16703074</F61_5>
    </x61>
    <x86>
      <F86_1>999PN5477SCHECK-NR. 0000016703074</F86_1>
    </x86>
  </x61Loop1>
  <x61Loop1>
     ... additional data omitted ...
  </x61Loop1>
  <x62F>
    <F62F_1>C</F62F_1>
    <F62F_2>951017</F62F_2>
    <F62F_3>DEM</F62F_3>
    <F62F_4>84437,04</F62F_4>
  </x62F>
</MT940>
```

Finally—and this code may help you understand the sample code for the parser and the serializer a bit better as you browse through it—the following is the schema for the MT940 document that we will use and that will help to convert the SWIFT stream into the XML stream shown in the previous code. Of course, this assumes that you can understand XDR Schema and BizTalk Schema extensions. They should be straightforward to interpret from this example even without looking them up in Appendix A. (Never mind the fact that the Schema becomes somewhat boring toward the end. Simple BizTalk Schemas like this are not a particularly entertaining read.)

```xml
<?xml version="1.0"?>
<!-- Generated by using BizTalk Editor on Tue, Mar 20 2001 04:27:56 PM -->
<!-- Microsoft Corporation (c) 2000 (http://www.microsoft.com) -->
<Schema name="MT940" b:BizTalkServerEditorTool_Version="1.0" b:root_reference="MT940"
b:schema_type="MT940"
                b:version="1996" b:def_record_delim="0xd" b:def_field_delim="0x3a"
b:def_subfield_delim="0x2f"
                b:def_escape_char="0x9" b:codepage="0x4e4" b:is_receipt="no"
b:is_envelope="no"
                b:standard="CUSTOM" b:standards_version="S"
                b:target_namespace="urn:schemas-newtelligence-
com:swift:mt940"
                xmlns="urn:schemas-microsoft-com:xml-data"
                xmlns:b="urn:schemas-microsoft-com:BizTalkServer"
                xmlns:d="urn:schemas-microsoft-com:datatypes"
                xmlns:swift="urn:schemas-newtelligence-com:swiftparser">
  <b:SelectionFields/>
  <ElementType name="x86" content="eltOnly" model="closed">
     <b:RecordInfo tag_name="86" tag_position="1" structure="positional"/>
     <element type="F86_1" maxOccurs="1" minOccurs="0" b:posStart="5" b:posEnd="100"/>
  </ElementType>
  <ElementType name="x65" content="eltOnly" model="closed">
     <b:RecordInfo tag_name="65" tag_position="1" structure="positional"/>
     <element type="F65_1" maxOccurs="1" minOccurs="0" b:posStart="5" b:posEnd="5"/>
     <element type="F65_2" maxOccurs="1" minOccurs="0" b:posStart="6" b:posEnd="11"/>
     <element type="F65_3" maxOccurs="1" minOccurs="0" b:posStart="12" b:posEnd="14"/>
     <element type="F65_4" maxOccurs="1" minOccurs="0" b:posStart="15" b:posEnd="29"/>
  </ElementType>
  <ElementType name="x64" content="eltOnly" model="closed">
     <b:RecordInfo tag_name="64" tag_position="1" structure="positional"/>
     <element type="F64_1" maxOccurs="1" minOccurs="0" b:posStart="5" b:posEnd="5"/>
     <element type="F64_2" maxOccurs="1" minOccurs="0" b:posStart="6" b:posEnd="11"/>
     <element type="F64_3" maxOccurs="1" minOccurs="0" b:posStart="12" b:posEnd="14"/>
     <element type="F64_4" maxOccurs="1" minOccurs="0" b:posStart="15" b:posEnd="29"/>
  </ElementType>
  <ElementType name="x62M" content="eltOnly" model="closed">
     <b:RecordInfo tag_name="62M" tag_position="1" structure="positional"/>
     <element type="F62M_1" maxOccurs="1" minOccurs="0" b:posStart="5" b:posEnd="5"/>
     <element type="F62M_2" maxOccurs="1" minOccurs="0" b:posStart="6" b:posEnd="11"/>
     <element type="F62M_3" maxOccurs="1" minOccurs="0" b:posStart="12" b:posEnd="14"/>
     <element type="F62M_4" maxOccurs="1" minOccurs="0" b:posStart="15" b:posEnd="29"/>
  </ElementType>
  <ElementType name="x62F" content="eltOnly" model="closed">
     <b:RecordInfo tag_name="62F" tag_position="1" structure="positional"/>
     <element type="F62F_1" maxOccurs="1" minOccurs="0" b:posStart="5" b:posEnd="5"/>
```

```xml
      <element type="F62F_2" maxOccurs="1" minOccurs="0" b:posStart="6" b:posEnd="11"/>
      <element type="F62F_3" maxOccurs="1" minOccurs="0" b:posStart="12" b:posEnd="14"/>
      <element type="F62F_4" maxOccurs="1" minOccurs="0" b:posStart="15" b:posEnd="29"/>
</ElementType>
<ElementType name="x61Loop1" content="eltOnly" model="closed">
      <b:RecordInfo delimiter_type="inherit_record" skip_CR="no"/>
      <element type="x61" maxOccurs="1" minOccurs="0"/>
      <element type="x86" maxOccurs="1" minOccurs="0"/>
</ElementType>
<ElementType name="x61" content="eltOnly" model="closed">
      <b:RecordInfo tag_name="61" tag_position="1" structure="positional"/>
      <element type="F61_1" maxOccurs="1" minOccurs="0" b:posStart="5" b:posEnd="10"/>
      <element type="F61_2" maxOccurs="1" minOccurs="0" b:posStart="11" b:posEnd="14"/>
      <element type="F61_3" maxOccurs="1" minOccurs="0" b:posStart="15" b:posEnd="16"/>
      <element type="F61_4" maxOccurs="1" minOccurs="0" b:posStart="17" b:posEnd="17"/>
      <element type="F61_5" maxOccurs="1" minOccurs="0" b:posStart="18" b:posEnd="32"/>
      <element type="F61_6" maxOccurs="1" minOccurs="0" b:posStart="33" b:posEnd="36"/>
      <element type="F61_7" maxOccurs="1" minOccurs="0" b:posStart="37" b:posEnd="52"/>
      <element type="F61_8" maxOccurs="1" minOccurs="0" b:posStart="53" b:posEnd="54"/>
      <element type="F61_9" maxOccurs="1" minOccurs="0" b:posStart="55" b:posEnd="70"/>
      <element type="F61_10" maxOccurs="1" minOccurs="0" b:posStart="71" b:posEnd="72"/>
      <element type="F61_11" maxOccurs="1" minOccurs="0" b:posStart="73" b:posEnd="106"/>
</ElementType>
<ElementType name="x60M" content="eltOnly" model="closed">
      <b:RecordInfo tag_name="60M" tag_position="1" structure="positional"/>
      <element type="F60M_1" maxOccurs="1" minOccurs="0" b:posStart="4" b:posEnd="4"/>
      <element type="F60M_2" maxOccurs="1" minOccurs="0" b:posStart="5" b:posEnd="10"/>
      <element type="F60M_3" maxOccurs="1" minOccurs="0" b:posStart="11" b:posEnd="13"/>
      <element type="F60M_4" maxOccurs="1" minOccurs="0" b:posStart="14" b:posEnd="28"/>
</ElementType>
<ElementType name="x60F" content="eltOnly" model="closed">
      <b:RecordInfo tag_name="60F" tag_position="1" structure="positional"/>
      <element type="F60F_1" maxOccurs="1" minOccurs="0" b:posStart="4" b:posEnd="4"/>
      <element type="F60F_2" maxOccurs="1" minOccurs="0" b:posStart="5" b:posEnd="10"/>
      <element type="F60F_3" maxOccurs="1" minOccurs="0" b:posStart="11" b:posEnd="13"/>
      <element type="F60F_4" maxOccurs="1" minOccurs="0" b:posStart="14" b:posEnd="28"/>
</ElementType>
<ElementType name="x28C" content="eltOnly" model="closed">
      <b:RecordInfo tag_name="28C" tag_position="1" structure="positional"/>
      <element type="F28C_1" maxOccurs="1" minOccurs="0" b:posStart="5" b:posEnd="13"/>
</ElementType>
<ElementType name="x25" content="eltOnly" model="closed">
      <b:RecordInfo tag_name="25" tag_position="1" structure="positional"/>
      <element type="F25_1" maxOccurs="1" minOccurs="0" b:posStart="5" b:posEnd="39"/>
</ElementType>
<ElementType name="x21" content="eltOnly" model="closed">
      <b:RecordInfo tag_name="21" tag_position="1" structure="positional"/>
      <element type="F21_1" maxOccurs="1" minOccurs="0" b:posStart="5" b:posEnd="20"/>
</ElementType>
```

```
<ElementType name="x20" content="eltOnly" model="closed">
   <b:RecordInfo tag_name="20" tag_position="2" structure="positional"
append_newline="no"/>
   <element type="F20_1" maxOccurs="1" minOccurs="0" b:posStart="5" b:posEnd="20"/>
</ElementType>
<ElementType name="MT940" content="eltOnly" model="closed">
   <b:RecordInfo structure="delimited" delimiter_type="inherit_record"
field_order="postfix"
                escape_type="inherit_escape" skip_CR="no"/>
   <element type="x20" maxOccurs="1" minOccurs="0"/>
   <element type="x21" maxOccurs="1" minOccurs="0"/>
   <element type="x25" maxOccurs="1" minOccurs="0"/>
   <element type="x28C" maxOccurs="1" minOccurs="0"/>
   <element type="x60F" maxOccurs="1" minOccurs="0"/>
   <element type="x60M" maxOccurs="1" minOccurs="0"/>
   <element type="x61Loop1" maxOccurs="*" minOccurs="0"/>
   <element type="x62F" maxOccurs="1" minOccurs="0"/>
   <element type="x62M" maxOccurs="1" minOccurs="0"/>
   <element type="x64" maxOccurs="1" minOccurs="0"/>
   <element type="x65" maxOccurs="1" minOccurs="0"/>
</ElementType>
<ElementType name="F86_1" content="textOnly" model="closed">
   <b:FieldInfo/>
</ElementType>
<ElementType name="F65_4" content="textOnly" model="closed">
   <b:FieldInfo/>
</ElementType>
<ElementType name="F65_3" content="textOnly" model="closed">
   <b:FieldInfo/>
</ElementType>
<ElementType name="F65_2" content="textOnly" model="closed">
   <b:FieldInfo/>
</ElementType>
<ElementType name="F65_1" content="textOnly" model="closed">
   <b:FieldInfo/>
</ElementType>
<ElementType name="F64_4" content="textOnly" model="closed">
   <b:FieldInfo/>
</ElementType>
<ElementType name="F64_3" content="textOnly" model="closed">
   <b:FieldInfo/>
</ElementType>
<ElementType name="F64_2" content="textOnly" model="closed">
   <b:FieldInfo/>
</ElementType>
<ElementType name="F64_1" content="textOnly" model="closed">
   <b:FieldInfo/>
</ElementType>
<ElementType name="F62M_4" content="textOnly" model="closed">
```

```
      <b:FieldInfo/>
</ElementType>
<ElementType name="F62M_3" content="textOnly" model="closed">
      <b:FieldInfo/>
</ElementType>
<ElementType name="F62M_2" content="textOnly" model="closed" d:type="date">
      <b:FieldInfo edi_datatype="DT" format="YYMMDD"/>
</ElementType>
<ElementType name="F62M_1" content="textOnly" model="closed">
      <b:FieldInfo/>
</ElementType>
<ElementType name="F62F_4" content="textOnly" model="closed">
      <b:FieldInfo/>
</ElementType>
<ElementType name="F62F_3" content="textOnly" model="closed">
      <b:FieldInfo/>
</ElementType>
<ElementType name="F62F_2" content="textOnly" model="closed" d:type="date">
      <b:FieldInfo edi_datatype="DT" format="YYMMDD"/>
</ElementType>
<ElementType name="F62F_1" content="textOnly" model="closed">
      <b:FieldInfo/>
</ElementType>
<ElementType name="F61_9" content="textOnly" model="closed">
      <b:FieldInfo/>
</ElementType>
<ElementType name="F61_8" content="textOnly" model="closed">
      <b:FieldInfo/>
</ElementType>
<ElementType name="F61_7" content="textOnly" model="closed">
      <b:FieldInfo/>
</ElementType>
<ElementType name="F61_6" content="textOnly" model="closed">
      <b:FieldInfo/>
</ElementType>
<ElementType name="F61_5" content="textOnly" model="closed">
      <b:FieldInfo/>
</ElementType>
<ElementType name="F61_4" content="textOnly" model="closed">
      <b:FieldInfo/>
</ElementType>
<ElementType name="F61_3" content="textOnly" model="closed">
      <b:FieldInfo/>
</ElementType>
<ElementType name="F61_2" content="textOnly" model="closed">
      <b:FieldInfo/>
</ElementType>
<ElementType name="F61_11" content="textOnly" model="closed">
      <b:FieldInfo/>
```

```
   </ElementType>
   <ElementType name="F61_10" content="textOnly" model="closed">
      <b:FieldInfo/>
   </ElementType>
   <ElementType name="F61_1" content="textOnly" model="closed" d:type="date">
      <b:FieldInfo edi_datatype="DT" format="YYMMDD"/>
   </ElementType>
   <ElementType name="F60M_4" content="textOnly" model="closed">
      <b:FieldInfo/>
   </ElementType>
   <ElementType name="F60M_3" content="textOnly" model="closed">
      <b:FieldInfo/>
   </ElementType>
   <ElementType name="F60M_2" content="textOnly" model="closed">
      <b:FieldInfo/>
   </ElementType>
   <ElementType name="F60M_1" content="textOnly" model="closed">
      <b:FieldInfo/>
   </ElementType>
   <ElementType name="F60F_4" content="textOnly" model="closed" d:type="number">
      <b:FieldInfo edi_datatype="D2" justification="left" pad_char="0x20"/>
   </ElementType>
   <ElementType name="F60F_3" content="textOnly" model="closed">
      <b:FieldInfo/>
   </ElementType>
   <ElementType name="F60F_2" content="textOnly" model="closed" d:type="date">
      <b:FieldInfo edi_datatype="DT" format="YYMMDD"/>
   </ElementType>
   <ElementType name="F60F_1" content="textOnly" model="closed">
      <b:FieldInfo/>
   </ElementType>
   <ElementType name="F28C_1" content="textOnly" model="closed">
      <b:FieldInfo/>
   </ElementType>
   <ElementType name="F25_1" content="textOnly" model="closed">
      <b:FieldInfo/>
   </ElementType>
   <ElementType name="F21_1" content="textOnly" model="closed">
      <b:FieldInfo/>
   </ElementType>
   <ElementType name="F20_1" content="textOnly" model="closed">
      <b:FieldInfo/>
   </ElementType>
</Schema>
```

The Parser Code

The parser sample is not exactly short. The core file parser.cpp has slightly more than 1,000 lines of code, which is certainly a lot to chew through in printed form. Therefore, while the core parser code is presented in its entirety here, the supporting files and headers are not listed because the complete code and project files are available from this book's web site. The downloadable package also contains information on how to install this sample component.

The implementation code is also not necessarily shown in the same order as it appears in the downloadable sample files, but rather, in the order in which it makes the most sense to explain what's happening.

The Parser Class

The first file shown is, of course, the header file for the parser class, which gives you an overview of the implementation. This file is presented here to show you the big picture and to explain the elements when we look at the implementation.

```cpp
/////////////////////////////////////////////////////////////////////////////
// Parser.h : Declaration of the CParser class
// Microsoft BizTalk Server 2000 Sample Parsing Component for SWIFT
// (c) 2001 Clemens F. Vasters - clemensv@newtelligence.com
//
// All rights reserved.

#ifndef __PARSER_H_
#define __PARSER_H_

#include "resource.h"        // Main symbols
#include <bts_sdk_guids.h>   // BizTalk CLSIDs, CATIDs, and IIDs
#import  <msxml3.dll>        // Import for the Microsoft XML 3.0 parser
using namespace ::MSXML2;    // Namespace declaration

/*
     RecordInfo: consolidated BizTalk Schema information for record
*/
typedef struct tagRecordInfo
{
     _variant_t vStructure;
     _variant_t vTagName;
     _variant_t vTagPosition;
     _variant_t vDelimiterType;
     _variant_t vDelimiterValue;
     _variant_t vFieldOrder;
     _variant_t vEscapeType;
     _variant_t vEscapeValue;
     _variant_t vCountIgnore;
     _variant_t vAppendNewLine;
     _variant_t vSkipCR;
     _variant_t vSkipLF;
     _variant_t vMinOccurs;
     _variant_t vMaxOccurs;
```

```
}
RecordInfo;
/*
      FieldInfo: consolidated BizTalk Schema information for field
*/
typedef struct tagFieldInfo
{
      _variant_t vEDIDataType;
      _variant_t vJustification;
      _variant_t vFormat;
      _variant_t vCodelist;
      _variant_t vPadChar;
      _variant_t vMinLengthWithPad;
      _variant_t vWrapChar;
      _variant_t vRequired;
      _variant_t vDataType;
      _variant_t vMaxLength;
      _variant_t vMinLength;
      _variant_t vPosStart;
      _variant_t vPosEnd;
}
FieldInfo;

///////////////////////////////////////////////////////////////////////
// CParser
class ATL_NO_VTABLE CParser :
      public CComObjectRootEx<CComSingleThreadModel>,
      public CComCoClass<CParser, &CLSID_Parser>,
      public IBizTalkParserComponent,
      public ISupportErrorInfo
{
protected:
      CComPtr<IStream> m_pstmInputStream;  // Input stream that holds the
interchange
      int m_nCodePage;  // Flag indicating whether input stream is IBM EBCDIC
      BOOL m_bEnveloped; // Flag indicating whether interchange is enveloped
      DWORD m_dwTotalBytesRead; // Total number of bytes read from stream
      DWORD m_dwHeaderOffset;   // Offset of document from stream beginning
      DWORD m_dwDocumentLength; // Length of document
      DWORD m_dwRecordPos; // Current position within record (used in parsing)
      CComPtr<MSXML2::IXMLDOMDocument2> m_pDocSchema;  // XML Schema document
      _bstr_t sBizTalkPrefix; // XML namespace prefix for BizTalk Schema
      _bstr_t sDataTypesPrefix; // XML namespace prefix for data types
      _bstr_t sSchemaName; // Name of the XML Schema
      CComBSTR sSpecName; // Name of the document definition in the config db


public:
      CParser():m_nCodePage(1252),m_bEnveloped(FALSE),
                  m_dwTotalBytesRead(0),m_dwHeaderOffset(0),m_dwDocumentLength(0)
```

```
        {
        }

DECLARE_REGISTRY_RESOURCEID(IDR_PARSER)
DECLARE_PROTECT_FINAL_CONSTRUCT()

BEGIN_COM_MAP(CParser)
     COM_INTERFACE_ENTRY(IBizTalkParserComponent)
     COM_INTERFACE_ENTRY(ISupportErrorInfo)
END_COM_MAP()

BEGIN_CATEGORY_MAP(CParser)
     IMPLEMENTED_CATEGORY(CATID_BIZTALK_PARSER)
END_CATEGORY_MAP()

protected:
     HRESULT ParseHeaders(IDictionary * Dict);
     HRESULT ParseBody(MSXML2::IXMLDOMDocument ** ppDoc);
     HRESULT ParseFooters(IDictionary * Dict);
     HRESULT StreamRead(WCHAR * wchBuffer, DWORD cchBuffer, DWORD * pcchRead );
     HRESULT StreamMoveBack(DWORD dwCharacters);
     HRESULT LoadSchema(BSTR bstrDocType, IXMLDOMDocument2 ** ppdoc);
     HRESULT HandleChildren( RecordInfo & ri, IXMLDOMElementPtr currentEntry,
                             IXMLDOMDocumentPtr targetDocument,
                             IXMLDOMNodePtr currentContext );
     HRESULT ParseRecord( RecordInfo & ri, IXMLDOMElementPtr currentEntry,
                          IXMLDOMDocumentPtr targetDocument,
                          IXMLDOMNodePtr currentContext,
                          BOOL * pbRecordAdded );
     HRESULT ParseField( RecordInfo & ri, FieldInfo & fi,
                         IXMLDOMElementPtr currentEntry,
                         IXMLDOMDocumentPtr targetDocument,
                         IXMLDOMNodePtr currentContext,
                         BSTR * pbstrField );
public:
// ISupportErrorInfo
     STDMETHOD(InterfaceSupportsErrorInfo)(REFIID riid);
// IBizTalkParserComponent
     STDMETHOD(ProbeInterchangeFormat)(IStream * pData, BOOL FromFile,
                                       BSTR EnvName, IStream * pReceiptData,
                                       BSTR * Format);
     STDMETHOD(GetInterchangeDetails)(IDictionary * Dict);
     STDMETHOD(GroupsExist)(BOOL * GrpsExist);
     STDMETHOD(GetGroupDetails)(IDictionary * Dict);
     STDMETHOD(GetGroupSize)(LONG * GroupSize, BOOL * LastGroup);
     STDMETHOD(GetNextDocument)(IDictionary * Dict, BSTR DocName,
                                BOOL * DocIsValid, BOOL * LastDocument,
                                GeneratedReceiptLevel * ReceiptGenerated,
                                BOOL * DocIsReceipt,
                                BSTR * CorrelationCompProgID);
```

```
        STDMETHOD(GetNativeDocumentOffsets)(BOOL * SizeFromXMLDoc,
                                     _LARGE_INTEGER * StartOffset,
                                     LONG * DocLength);
};
#endif //__PARSER_H_
```

Before we go into the details, let's quickly look at the purpose of the IBizTalkParser Component interface methods and the sequence in which they are called so that you don't get too lost in the following explanation:

- ▼ **ProbeInterchangeFormat**   This method is the first one called in each parser component instance's life and allows the code to sniff into an incoming document data stream. If the parser determines that it is able to parse the code, it returns a positive acknowledgment.

- ■ **GetInterchangeDetails**   This is the second method called and is responsible for extracting interchange-level information from the data. The requested information is source and destination identifiers and all other data than can be extracted from the envelope of an interchange. If no envelope is present, the method can opt to do nothing.

- ■ **GroupsExist**   This method is the third in the call sequence, and the return value indicates whether the interchange has and supports groups. In the sense of this method, groups are functional groups as they exist in UN/EDIFACT and X12 and can contain multiple documents.

- ■ **GetGroupDetails**   If groups exist, each group has its own header block, which this method is required to evaluate, and it puts the extracted information into a dictionary. The method is called only if GroupsExist returned True. (Our example parser does not support groups; thus, this method is not implemented.)

- ■ **GetGroupSize**   This method must return the total size of the group section in bytes (used for document tracking), and it indicates whether the most recently parsed group was the last group in the document, which will tell BizTalk that all groups have been processed and that parsing is complete. Again, this is applicable only if groups exist.

- ■ **GetNextDocument**   When there is no support for groups, this method is called immediately after *GroupsExist*. This is the core parsing method, which must extract the next document from the input stream and place it into the transport dictionary. When the method has parsed a document and has reached the end of the stream (or the end of the group), it sets the LastDocument output argument to True, which tells BizTalk that no more documents are in the stream and parsing is complete for this interchange (or this group).

- ▲ **GetNativeDocumentOffsets**   This method is always called immediately after each call to *GetNextDocument* to retrieve the offsets of the most recently parsed document in the native input stream. BizTalk uses this information to cut the native document out of the original interchange for storage in the document tracking database.

Probing the Format

All of the following code is contained in the parser.cpp file. The first method we will look at is the implementation of *ProbeInterchangeFormat()*.

The code needs to detect the following information: find out whether the message is a SWIFT message, and figure out whether the message is enveloped and which character set is used. To do this, we will make two basic assumptions. First, if a message is enveloped, it will begin with a curly brace followed by the basic header block, as in this example:

```
{1:F01BANKBEBBAXXX2222123456}{2:…
```

Because this header is sufficiently different from UN/EDIFACT, X12, and XML, we will test only the first three characters for equality to the {1: character sequence. We will test these characters for all three characters sets that we want to support. If we find the signature in any of the three characters sets, we will flag the interchange as enveloped and remember the applicable code page.

The second assumption that we will make is that if a document is not enveloped, it will begin at a colon character (:) followed by at most three digits (of which the last may also be a letter), which are again followed by a colon character. This would match common field prefixes like :20: or :61M:. And this simple detection should be sufficient to at least differentiate SWIFT documents from the other formats.

However, note that using the ProbeInterchangeFormat message is a parser's only shot at detecting the format properly. For instance, if you wanted to write two parsers for formats that are very similar, the method would have to thoroughly analyze the stream to make sure that it will understand the format. Once a parser signals that it understands a data stream, it must be able to handle it properly, and the stream will not be passed to any other parsers for probing.

The following implementation uses the m_nCodePage member variable's state to finally decide which result to report. If m_nCodePage has been set to a nonzero value during the probing process, it is assumed that the document could be positively detected.

```cpp
STDMETHODIMP CParser::ProbeInterchangeFormat( IStream * pData, BOOL FromFile,
                        BSTR EnvName, IStream * pReceiptData, BSTR * Format)
{
    BYTE bProbingBuffer[32];
    ULONG ulBytesRead=0;
    HRESULT hRes = S_FALSE;
    LARGE_INTEGER pos;

    if (Format == NULL)
        return E_POINTER;

    *Format = NULL;

    // Reset the stream.
    pos.QuadPart = 0;
    pData->Seek(pos,STREAM_SEEK_SET,NULL);
```

```
memset(&bProbingBuffer,0,sizeof(bProbingBuffer));
// First, we'll get 32 bytes of the inbound stream to probe the format.
if ( SUCCEEDED( pData->Read( &bProbingBuffer, sizeof(bProbingBuffer),
                             &ulBytesRead)))
{
    // We have several possible scenarios:
    // (a) we have a SWIFT message envelope. In that case, the message
    // begins with "{1:"
    // (b) we have no envelope. In that case, we will accept the message if it
    // is ":xxx:", where xxx must be a two-digit or three-digit code, where
    // the third character may also be a capital letter.

    // First do the test using the ANSI/ASCII code page.
    if ( bProbingBuffer[0] == 0x7b && bProbingBuffer[1] == 0x31 &&
         bProbingBuffer[2] == 0x3a )
    {
        // ASCII/ANSI match -- prefix was "{1:"
        m_nCodePage = 1252;
        m_bEnveloped = TRUE;
    }
    else if ( bProbingBuffer[0] == 0x7b && bProbingBuffer[1] == 0x00 &&
              bProbingBuffer[2] == 0x31 && bProbingBuffer[3] == 0x00 &&
              bProbingBuffer[4] == 0x3a && bProbingBuffer[5] == 0x00)
    {
        // Unicode match -- prefix was "{1:"
        m_nCodePage = 1200;
        m_bEnveloped = TRUE;
    }
    else if ( bProbingBuffer[0] == 0x48 &&  bProbingBuffer[1] == 0xf1 &&
              bProbingBuffer[2] == 0x7a )
    {
        // EBCDIC match -- EBCDIC prefix was "{1:"
        m_nCodePage = 1026;
        m_bEnveloped = TRUE;
    }
    else if ( bProbingBuffer[0] == 0x3a )
    {
        // Leading ASCII colon detected, now check signature
        // Rule: characters 1-3 must be digits or character 3 may be cap
        // letter.  Must be terminated by colon
        for ( int i=1;
              (i<4) &&
              ((bProbingBuffer[i] >= 0x30 && bProbingBuffer[i] <= 0x39) ||
              ( i >= 3 && (bProbingBuffer[i] >= 0x41
                    && bProbingBuffer[i] <= 0x5a)));
              i++)
        {
            if ( i>=3 && bProbingBuffer[i] == 0x3a )
            {
```

```
                m_nCodePage = 1252;
                break;
            }
        }


        for ( i=1;
              m_nCodePage == 0 && bProbingBuffer[1] == 0x00 &&
              bProbingBuffer[i*2+1] == 0x00 &&
              (i<4) &&
              ((bProbingBuffer[i*2] >= 0x30 && bProbingBuffer[i*2] <= 0x39) ||
              ( i >= 3 && (bProbingBuffer[i*2] >= 0x41 &&
                           bProbingBuffer[i*2] <= 0x5a)));
              i++)
        {
            if ( i>=3 && bProbingBuffer[i*2] == 0x3a )
            {
                m_nCodePage = 1200;
                break;
            }
        }
    }
    else if ( bProbingBuffer[0] == 0x7a )
    {
        // Leading EBCDIC colon detected, now check EBCDIC signature
        // Rule: characters 1-3 must be digits or character 3 may be
        // cap letter. Must be terminated by colon
        for ( int i=1;
              (i<4) &&
              ((bProbingBuffer[i] >= 0xF0 && bProbingBuffer[i] <= 0xF9) ||
              ( i >= 3 && (bProbingBuffer[i] >= 0xC1 &&
                           bProbingBuffer[i] <= 0xE9)));
              i++)
        {
            if ( i>=3 && bProbingBuffer[i] == 0x7a )
            {
                m_nCodePage = 1026;
                break;
            }
        }
    }

    if ( m_nCodePage != 0 )
    {
        // Hold on to the stream.
        m_pstmInputStream = pData;
        // Set the result to "ok" and set the FormatString
        hRes = S_OK;
        *Format = SysAllocString(L"SWIFT");
    }
```

```
        // Reset the stream.
        pos.QuadPart = 0;
        pData->Seek(pos,STREAM_SEEK_SET,NULL);
    }
    return hRes;
}e
```

Analyzing the Headers

When the parser is finished, the next step is to analyze the headers and to figure out the interchange details. This is especially important for self-routing documents. The method that BizTalk calls on the parser component to pick up the header data is *IBizTalkParser Component::GetInterchangeDetails()*.

```
STDMETHODIMP CParser::GetInterchangeDetails(IDictionary * Dict)
{
    // This method is the first one to begin the parsing process and is
    // required to parse the headers. -- if we have an envelope
    if ( m_bEnveloped )
    {
        HRESULT hRes;

        if ( SUCCEEDED( hRes = ParseHeaders(Dict)))
            hRes = LoadSchema(sSchemaName, &m_pDocSchema );
        return hRes;
    }
    else
    {
        return S_OK;
    }
}
```

As you can see, the implementation has two separate paths. If the document has not been detected to have an envelope, the code will return a success code but do nothing more. In this case, we will have to rely on BizTalk Server to pass a document name later in the call to *IBizTalkParserComponent::GetNextDocument()*, which we can use to load the schema.

If an envelope was detected, the local method *ParseHeaders()* is called, which analyzes the headers and extracts the interchange details such as the routing information and the schema type. If the headers were valid and data could be extracted properly, the local method *LoadSchema()* will be called, which attempts to retrieve the matching BizTalk Schema from the management database.

We will look at the *ParseHeaders()* method's code first. If you are a C++ purist, you will find the use of unconditional jumps in error conditions disturbing. However, when the *goto* statement is used for error handling and a single exit point, it is typically clearer than many scattered exit points or a too-deeply nested hierarchy of success tests.

The method expects the SWIFT basic header block and an input or output application header block for the financial transactions application. In SWIFT terms, an input block is created for messages that are sent into the SWIFT service network, and output messages are messages that are received from the service network. Both headers are always strictly positional in their format and have fixed length. We will therefore read the exact number of characters from the stream that we expect for each header and will test the proper terminators before we begin extracting the data. The basic header block has 29 characters, the input application header has 25 characters, and the output application header has 51 characters. It is important to speak of characters and not bytes here. The stream-handling functions will map the character counts to bytes according to the code page.

The data extraction itself is trivial and is done from right to left in each header. All values that have been extracted are then placed into the transport dictionary. The *put_Value* method is used to place values into the dictionary. Although the data is correctly set up for the *PutMultiple* method of the IDictionary interface, testing showed that *PutMultiple* does not work right.

Notice that in the *ParseHeaders()* method, some properties are placed into the transport dictionary that are not documented in the BizTalk Server help files. That's because values like message_priority, session_number, and sequence_number are indeed specific to SWIFT. So why would you want to place them into the transport dictionary to begin with? As you will recall from the architecture discussion in Chapter 11, the transport dictionary values travel beside the documents (which are actually contained in the dictionary). Therefore, all information that you place into the transport dictionary in the parsing stage will also be available to your own application integration components, transport providers, and serializers.

When all data is extracted, the next header may be prefixed with {3:, indicating that a custom user-to-user data header exists. We will skip such headers here. The block that starts with {4: is the text block that contains the body of the message. The prefix is immediately followed by a CR/LF sequence (or a plain LF if translated from EBCDIC). The stream pointer is immediately moved past the CR/LF or LF for the body parsing code to pick up at that point later.

```
HRESULT CParser::ParseHeaders(IDictionary * Dict)
{
    WCHAR wchBuffer[128];
    ULONG ulBytesRead;
    HRESULT hRes;
    CComVariant vSenderReceiver;

    // The SWIFT headers are pretty simple to parse because they are
    // fully positional. The first header is compulsory, and we've therefore
    // used it as the signature. The total length including the delimiters is
    // 29 characters.
    // Sample: {1:F01BANKBEBBAXXX2222123456}

    memset(&wchBuffer,0,sizeof(wchBuffer));
    if ( SUCCEEDED( hRes = StreamRead( wchBuffer, 29, &ulBytesRead ) ) &&
                ulBytesRead == 29 )
    {
```

```
        if ( wchBuffer[0] == L'{' &&
            wchBuffer[1] == L'1' &&
            wchBuffer[2] == L':' &&
            wchBuffer[28] == L'}' )
        {
            LPOLESTR fields[4] = {L"application_identifier",
                                  L"application_protocol_data_unit_identifier",
                                  L"session_number",
                                  L"sequence_number"};
            CComVariant values[4];

            wchBuffer[28] = 0x00;    values[3] = &wchBuffer[22];
            wchBuffer[22] = 0x00;    values[2] = &wchBuffer[18];
            wchBuffer[18] = 0x00;    vSenderReceiver = &wchBuffer[6];
            wchBuffer[6] = 0x00;     values[1] = &wchBuffer[4];
            wchBuffer[4] = 0x00;     values[0] = &wchBuffer[3];

            for ( int j=0;j<4 && SUCCEEDED(hRes);j++)
                hRes = Dict->put_Value(fields[j],values[j]);
        }
    }

    // Now we check to see whether we can find the application header.
    memset(&wchBuffer,0,sizeof(wchBuffer));
    if ( SUCCEEDED( hRes = StreamRead( wchBuffer, 25, &ulBytesRead ) ) &&
        ulBytesRead == 25 )
    {
        // Check whether we can find an input app-header signature.
        if ( wchBuffer[0] == L'{' &&
            wchBuffer[1] == L'2' &&
            wchBuffer[2] == L':' &&
            wchBuffer[3] == L'I' &&
            wchBuffer[24] == L'}' )
        {
            // This header looks great.
            // Let's just assemble the stuff and get out of here.
            LPOLESTR fields[7] = {L"input_output_identifier",
                                  L"functional_identifier",
                                  L"Src_ID_Type",
                                  L"Src_ID_Value",
                                  L"Dest_ID_Value",
                                  L"Dest_ID_Type",
                                  L"message_priority"};
            CComVariant values[7];

            // We're doing this from back to front to make string
            // extraction easier.
            wchBuffer[20] = 0x00;
            values[6] = &wchBuffer[19];
```

```
    wchBuffer[19] = 0x00;
    values[2] = L"55";
    values[3] = vSenderReceiver;
    values[5] = L"55";
    values[4] = &wchBuffer[7];
    wchBuffer[7] = 0x00;
    m_sSchemaName = values[1] = &wchBuffer[4];
    wchBuffer[4] = 0x00;
    values[0] = &wchBuffer[3];


    for ( int j=0;j<7 && SUCCEEDED(hRes);j++)
        hRes = Dict->put_Value(fields[j],values[j]);

}
else if ( wchBuffer[0] == L'{' &&
          wchBuffer[1] == L'2' &&
          wchBuffer[2] == L':' &&
          wchBuffer[3] == L'O' )
{
    // The output header signature found. Need to read more characters.
    // The output hdr is 51 characters long.
    // {2:01001200910103BANKBEBBAXXX22221234569101031201N}

    if ( SUCCEEDED( hRes = StreamRead( wchBuffer+25, 26, &ulBytesRead ) )
         && ulBytesRead == 26 && wchBuffer[50] == L'}' )
    {
        LPOLESTR fields[9] = {L"input_output_identifier",
                              L"functional_identifier",
                              L"Src_ID_Value",
                              L"Src_ID_Type",
                              L"Dest_ID_Value",
                              L"Dest_ID_Type",
                              L"output_date"
                              L"output_time"
                              L"message_priority"};
        CComVariant values[9];

        wchBuffer[50] = 0x00;
        values[8] = &wchBuffer[49];
        wchBuffer[49] = 0x00;
        values[7] = &wchBuffer[45];
        wchBuffer[45] = 0x00;
        values[6] = &wchBuffer[39];
        wchBuffer[29] = 0x00;
        values[5] = L"55";
        values[4] = vSenderReceiver;
        values[3] = L"55";
        values[2] = &wchBuffer[17];
        wchBuffer[7] = 0x00;
```

```
            m_sSchemaName = values[1] = &wchBuffer[4];
            wchBuffer[4] = 0x00;
            values[0] = &wchBuffer[3];

            for ( int j=0;j<9 && SUCCEEDED(hRes);j++)
                hRes = Dict->put_Value(fields[j],values[j]);
        }
    }
    else
        goto fail;
}
else
    goto fail;

// Now we check what's next by probing the next three bytes.
memset(&wchBuffer,0,sizeof(wchBuffer));
if ( SUCCEEDED( StreamRead( wchBuffer, 3, &ulBytesRead ) ) &&
     ulBytesRead == 3 )
{
    if ( !wcsncmp(wchBuffer,L"{3:",3 ) )
    {
        // This is a custom header that we will purposely choose not to
        // understand here. We will scan for the closing brace and
        // proceed to the text header that begins with "{4:"
        int nCount=1;
        while ( nCount > 0 )
        {
            if ( SUCCEEDED( StreamRead( wchBuffer, 1, &ulBytesRead ) ) &&
                 ulBytesRead == 1 )
            {
                if ( wchBuffer[0] == L'{' ) nCount++;
                if ( wchBuffer[0] == L'}' ) nCount--;
            }
            else
                goto fail;
        };

        if ( SUCCEEDED( StreamRead( wchBuffer, 3, &ulBytesRead ) ) &&
                        ulBytesRead == 3 &&
                        wcsncmp(wchBuffer,L"{4:",3 ))
        {
            // Next characters must either be CR/LF or LF
            if ( FAILED( StreamRead( wchBuffer, 2, &ulBytesRead ) ) ||
                 ulBytesRead < 2 )
            {
                goto fail;
            }
            else
            {
```

```
                    if ((wchBuffer[0] != 0x0d && wchBuffer[1] != 0x0a) &&
                        wchBuffer[0] != 0x0a )
                    {
                        goto fail;
                    }
                    else if ( wchBuffer[0] == 0x0a )
                    {
                        // Put next character back into the stream
                        StreamMoveBack(1);
                    }
                }
                m_dwHeaderOffset = m_dwTotalBytesRead;
            }
            else
                goto fail;
        }
        else if ( !wcsncmp(wchBuffer,L"{4:",3 ) )
        {
            // Next characters must either be CR/LF or LF
            if ( FAILED( StreamRead( wchBuffer, 2, &ulBytesRead ) ) ||
                 ulBytesRead < 2 )
            {
                goto fail;
            }
            else
            {
                if ((wchBuffer[0] != 0x0d && wchBuffer[1] != 0x0a) &&
                    wchBuffer[0] != 0x0a )
                {
                    goto fail;
                }
                else if ( wchBuffer[0] == 0x0a )
                {
                    // Put next character back into the stream
                    StreamMoveBack(1);
                }
            }
            m_dwHeaderOffset = m_dwTotalBytesRead;
        }
    }
    else
        goto fail;

    Dict->put_Value(L"in_codepage",CComVariant(m_nCodePage));

    return hRes;

fail:
    return E_FAIL;
}
```

Stream Handling

The methods that read from the stream and that move the stream pointer always work on character counts and do all necessary length conversions immediately. If the code page is 1200 (Unicode), it is assumed that every character has two bytes; for the code pages 1026 (EBCDIC) and 1252 (ASCII), every character is assumed to have one byte.

```
HRESULT CParser::StreamMoveBack(DWORD dwCharacters)
{
    LARGE_INTEGER li;

    // Move back the stream.
    if ( m_nCodePage == 1200 )
        dwCharacters *= sizeof(wchar_t);

    li.QuadPart = -((__int64)dwCharacters);
    return  m_pstmInputStream->Seek(li,STREAM_SEEK_CUR,0);
}


HRESULT CParser::StreamRead(WCHAR * wchBuffer, DWORD cchBuffer, DWORD * pcchRead )
{
    HRESULT hRes;

    // This method reads the specified number of characters from the input stream.
    // The method is code-page aware and handles Unicode and all eight-bit CPs.
    if ( m_nCodePage == 1200 )
    {
        DWORD dwRead;
        if ( SUCCEEDED( hRes = m_pstmInputStream->Read( wchBuffer,
                                                cchBuffer*sizeof(wchar_t),
                                                &dwRead) ))
        {
            m_dwTotalBytesRead += dwRead;
            *pcchRead = dwRead / sizeof(wchar_t);
        }
    }
    else
    {
        BYTE * pbBuf = (BYTE*)malloc(cchBuffer);
        if ( SUCCEEDED( hRes = m_pstmInputStream->Read( pbBuf,
                                                cchBuffer,
                                                pcchRead )))
        {
            MultiByteToWideChar( m_nCodePage, 0, (char*)pbBuf, cchBuffer,
                                wchBuffer, cchBuffer);
        }
        free(pbBuf);
```

```
    }

    return hRes;
}
```

Loading the Schema Based on Selection Criteria

When the headers have been successfully parsed in *ParseHeaders()*, the transport dictionary's functional_identifier entry and the m_sSchemaName member will contain the functional identifier of the document definition that needs to be loaded. Because this is not directly equivalent to the name of the document definition, but rather, to the functional_identifier property of the selection criteria, we have to find and load the document definition using the document's property set (which is just another term for the selection criteria).

You will also see that the code sets the standards_version_type and standards_version_value properties in the property set. This is somewhat arbitrary because it is not really applicable to SWIFT. However, it is useful in this chapter because it illustrates how the selection criteria are used with other formats. The *IBizTalkDocument::LoadByPropertySet* method will succeed and return a result only if all criteria match fully with the definition stored in the management database. If you omit a property in the query dictionary that exists in the database, there won't be a match.

```
HRESULT CParser::LoadSchema(BSTR bstrDocType, IXMLDOMDocument2 ** ppdoc)
{
    HRESULT hRes = S_OK;
    CComPtr<IBizTalkConfig> cfgroot;

    // Load the schema from the configuration database based on
    // the property set.
    if ( SUCCEEDED( hRes = cfgroot.CoCreateInstance(CLSID_BizTalkConfig)))
    {
        CComPtr<IBizTalkDocument> pdoc;

        if ( SUCCEEDED( hRes = cfgroot->CreateDocument((IDispatch**)&pdoc)))
        {
            CComPtr<IDictionary> pdict;
            CComVariant vDocType(bstrDocType);

            pdict.CoCreateInstance(CLSID_CDictionary);
            pdict->put_Value(L"functional_identifier",vDocType);
            pdict->put_Value(L"standards_version_type",CComVariant(L"S"));
            pdict->put_Value(L"standards_version_value",CComVariant(L"1996"));
            if ( SUCCEEDED(hRes = pdoc->LoadByPropertySet(pdict)))
            {
                CComBSTR content;

                pdoc->get_Name(&m_sSpecName);
                if ( SUCCEEDED(hRes = pdoc->get_Content(&content)))
                {
                    IXMLDOMDocument2Ptr schemadoc;
```

```
                           schemadoc.CreateInstance(__uuidof(MSXML2::DOMDocument));
                           schemadoc->loadXML((_bstr_t)content);
                           hRes = schemadoc->QueryInterface(ppdoc);
                      };
                 }
            };
      }
      return hRes;
}
```

(Not) Handling Group Information

When the *LoadSchema()* method returns successfully to its caller (*GetInterchangeDetails*), the transport dictionary will contain all information that could be extracted from the headers.

Unlike X12 and UN/EDIFACT, SWIFT does not know functional groups. Our implementation will therefore return False when BizTalk asks whether groups exist; it will just return default values for the other two methods that deal with groups because those will never be called if *IBizTalkParserComponent::GroupsExist()* does not return True.

```
STDMETHODIMP CParser::GroupsExist(BOOL * GrpsExist)
{
    if (GrpsExist == NULL)
        return E_POINTER;

    // SWIFT never has groups.
    *GrpsExist = FALSE;
    return S_OK;
}


STDMETHODIMP CParser::GetGroupDetails(IDictionary * Dict)
{
    // No groups, just ignore nicely.
    return S_OK;
}


STDMETHODIMP CParser::GetGroupSize(LONG * GroupSize, BOOL * LastGroup)
{
    if (GroupSize == NULL)
        return E_POINTER;

    if (LastGroup == NULL)
        return E_POINTER;
    *GroupSize = 0;
    *LastGroup = TRUE;
    return S_OK;
}
```

Parsing the Document

At this point, we have consumed the headers, and the stream pointer has been moved just before the first data character of the SWIFT text block that contains the message data. When the *IBizTalkParserComponent::GetNextDocument()* method is called, it's time to take care of parsing the document data.

If the document was not enveloped, the previously shown method *IBizTalkParser Component::GetInterchangeDetails()* will not have loaded a schema document, because we had no header information from which to derive the schema name. Therefore, we will make it a requirement that the document name (argument DocName) is passed to the *IBizTalkParserComponent::GetNextDocument()* method. If the document name is empty for a nonenveloped document or the schema cannot be loaded based on the name, processing will fail.

The actual parsing is performed by the local *ParseBody()* method, which we will look at immediately after inspecting *GetNextDocument()*. When that method returns successfully, we will populate the transport dictionary with all additional information that we gathered on the way and finally place the parse result (an XML document) into the working_data entry of the dictionary.

```
STDMETHODIMP CParser::GetNextDocument(IDictionary * Dict,
                                      BSTR DocName,
                                      BOOL * DocIsValid,
                                      BOOL * LastDocument,
                                      GeneratedReceiptLevel * ReceiptGenerated,
                                      BOOL * DocIsReceipt,
                                      BSTR * CorrelationCompProgID)
{
    if (DocIsValid == NULL || LastDocument == NULL || ReceiptGenerated == NULL ||
        DocIsReceipt == NULL || CorrelationCompProgID == NULL)
        return E_POINTER;

    MSXML2::IXMLDOMDocument * pDoc;
    HRESULT hRes;

    if ( !m_bEnveloped )
    {
        hRes = E_INVALIDARG;

        if ( !DocName ||
             !DocName[0] ||
             FAILED(hRes = LoadSchemaByName(DocName, &m_pDocSchema )))
            return hRes;
    }
```

```
    if ( SUCCEEDED( hRes = ParseBody( &pDoc ) ))
    {
        CComBSTR bstrXML;
        if ( SUCCEEDED( hRes = pDoc->get_xml(&bstrXML)))
        {
            // Populate the transport dictionary.
            Dict->put_Value(L"standards_version_type",CComVariant(L"S"));
            Dict->put_Value(L"standards_version_value",CComVariant(L"1996"));
            Dict->put_Value(L"interchange_id",CComVariant(L"0001"));
            Dict->put_Value(L"functional_identifier",
                            CComVariant((BSTR)m_sSchemaName));
            Dict->put_Value(L"doc_type",CComVariant((BSTR)m_sSchemaName));
            Dict->put_Value(L"doc_id",CComVariant(1));
            Dict->put_Value(L"Document_Name",CComVariant((BSTR)m_sSpecName));
            hRes = Dict->put_Value(L"working_data",CComVariant(bstrXML));
        }
        ParseFooters(Dict);
    }

    *LastDocument = TRUE;
    *DocIsValid = TRUE;
    *DocIsReceipt = FALSE;
    *LastDocument = TRUE;
    *ReceiptGenerated = InterchangeReceiptGenerated;
    *CorrelationCompProgID = SysAllocString(L"");
    SetLastError(0);
    SetErrorInfo(0,NULL);
    return hRes;
}
```

The *LoadSchemaByName()* method is similar to the *LoadSchema()* method, but it uses a different method on the IBizTalkDocument interface.

```
HRESULT CParser::LoadSchemaByName(BSTR bstrDocName, IXMLDOMDocument2 ** ppdoc)
{
    HRESULT hRes = S_OK;
    CComPtr<IBizTalkConfig> cfgroot;

    // Load the schema from the configuration database based on
    // the name.
    if ( SUCCEEDED( hRes = cfgroot.CoCreateInstance(CLSID_BizTalkConfig)))
    {
        CComPtr<IBizTalkDocument> pdoc;

        if ( SUCCEEDED( hRes = cfgroot->CreateDocument((IDispatch**)&pdoc)))
        {
            CComPtr<IDictionary> pdict;

            if ( SUCCEEDED(hRes = pdoc->LoadByName(bstrDocName)))
```

```
        {
            CComBSTR content;

            pdoc->get_Name(&m_sSpecName);
            if ( SUCCEEDED(hRes = pdoc->get_Content(&content)))
            {
                IXMLDOMDocument2Ptr schemadoc;

                schemadoc.CreateInstance(__uuidof(MSXML2::DOMDocument));
                schemadoc->loadXML((_bstr_t)content);
                hRes = schemadoc->QueryInterface(ppdoc);
            };
        }
    };
    }
    return hRes;
}
```

Finally, we get to the beef of the parser. The *ParseBody()* method is the entry point for the schema-driven parsing code. Its task is to prepare and navigate to the XDR ElementType definition of BizTalk Schema that represents the root node of the XML document instances that the parser will generate. Once the root element schema type has been found, control is passed to the local *HandleChildren()* method, which will start a recursive descent into the schema hierarchy during which the SWIFT stream is being parsed.

Once (and if) the *HandleChildren()* method returns successfully, the result document's namespace is set to the target namespace definition of BizTalk Schema before the result is passed back to the caller.

The technique shown to extract the namespace prefix by using an XPath query via selectSingleNode and using the prefix later as shown with *IXMLDOMElement::getAttribute()* calls instead of using the namespace-aware methods (the serializer uses them) saves us a couple of success validations and keeps the code a bit tighter.

```
HRESULT CParser::ParseBody(MSXML2::IXMLDOMDocument ** ppDoc)
{
    IXMLDOMDocument2Ptr pOutDoc;
    IXMLDOMElementPtr schemaRoot;
    HRESULT hRes=E_FAIL;

    if ( m_pDocSchema == NULL )
        return E_FAIL;

    pOutDoc.CreateInstance(__uuidof(MSXML2::DOMDocument));
    schemaRoot = m_pDocSchema->
        selectSingleNode(L"//*[@xmlns:*='urn:schemas-microsoft-com:xml-data']");
    if ( schemaRoot != NULL )
    {
        WCHAR wszQuery[128];
        IXMLDOMNodePtr instanceRootType;
```

```
IXMLDOMNodePtr biztalkNamespace;
IXMLDOMNodePtr datatypesNamespace;
_bstr_t sTargetNamespace;

biztalkNamespace = schemaRoot->
    selectSingleNode(L"@xmlns:*[text()='urn:schemas-microsoft-com"
                     L":BizTalkServer']");
datatypesNamespace = schemaRoot->
    selectSingleNode(L"@xmlns:*[text()='urn:schemas-microsoft-com"
                     L":datatypes']");
m_sSchemaName = schemaRoot->getAttribute(_bstr_t(L"name"));

// If the BizTalk namespace was found, isolate the prefix (for later).
if ( biztalkNamespace != NULL )
{
    IXMLDOMAttributePtr attr;
    m_sBizTalkPrefix = biztalkNamespace->baseName;
    swprintf(wszQuery,L"%s:target_namespace",(wchar_t*)m_sBizTalkPrefix);
    attr = schemaRoot->attributes->getNamedItem(_bstr_t(wszQuery));
    if ( attr != NULL )
    {
        sTargetNamespace = attr->text;
    }
}
// Do the same for the data types' namespace.
if ( datatypesNamespace != NULL )
{
    m_sDataTypesPrefix = datatypesNamespace->baseName;
}

// Get the ElementType for the root element of the schema.
swprintf(wszQuery,L"ElementType[@name='%s']",(wchar_t*)m_sSchemaName);
instanceRootType = schemaRoot->selectSingleNode(wszQuery);
if ( instanceRootType != NULL )
{
    RecordInfo ri;

    // Descend into the schema tree and handle fields and records.
    if ( SUCCEEDED(hRes = HandleChildren( ri, instanceRootType,
                                          pOutDoc, pOutDoc )))
    {
        IXMLDOMElementPtr pRoot;

        // Set the document length.
        m_dwDocumentLength = m_dwTotalBytesRead - m_dwHeaderOffset;

        // Finally, set the target namespace.
        if ( ((BSTR)sTargetNamespace) != NULL &&
             ((BSTR)sTargetNamespace)[0] != NULL )
```

```
        {
            pRoot = pOutDoc->documentElement;
            pRoot->setAttribute(L"xmlns",sTargetNamespace);
        }
        hRes = pOutDoc->QueryInterface(ppDoc);
    }
}
};
return hRes;
}
```

The *HandleChildren()* method is the core method of the parser and, as such, it is a bit lengthy. The method is designed to handle all children of a given record entry. When the method is called from *ParseBody()*, the parent record is empty and the current entry is the ElementType element of the schema that represents the root element in the XML target document. The currentContext element is the last element that has been inserted into the target document, which is initially the document itself.

As its name already indicates, the method will query the list of the current record's children using the XPath element | attribute set expression, which returns a collection of all element and attribute children of the current ElementType entry in the schema.

With this ordered collection, the method enters a loop that spans pretty much the entire method body. The loop is repeated, while the loop body can produce output records from the input data stream. This is necessary for repetitive groups of multiple, sequential records. The continuation condition for the loop is that the nRecordHits value is greater than zero when the processing sequence for a group is complete.

The inner *for* loop iterates over the collection in the order it was returned from the XPath query. We assume that the SWIFT fields must occur in the given sequence independently of the XDR order attributes. (Note that the implementation shown does not support XDR grouped sequences.)

NOTE: The following discussion may be a bit confusing because we have to use the same terminology for the explanation of what is explained. Reading speed limit ahead!

For each found element, we will determine the *type* attribute that will either point to an *AttributeType* for attribute elements or *ElementType* for *element* elements within the same schema.

If the definition could be found, the handling code for *element* will test whether the content of the element type is *textOnly*, in which case, the element type represents a field. If that is the case, the attributes of the *ElementType*, the associated BizTalk Schema *FieldInfo* element, and the *element* elements are extracted into a *FieldInfo* structure that is then passed to the local *ParseField* method to extract the field data from the input data stream. A subtly different—but largely equivalent—handling code section will be used for attribute type fields.

If the element definition represents a record, the content of the element type is either *eltOnly* or *empty* (in which case, it can contain attributes but no other elements). The asso ciated BizTalk Schema is *RecordInfo*, and the *ElementType* and *element* elements' attributes will be read into a *RecordInfo* structure and handed to the *ParseRecord()* method, which will handle record parsing from the input stream.

If a record does not have a source tag identifier (called tag_name in Schema-speak), the record is treated as a loop, and the code will descend into a recursive call to *HandleChildren()* to take care of the nested record sequence.

```
HRESULT CParser::HandleChildren( RecordInfo & parentRecord,
                     IXMLDOMElementPtr currentEntry,
                     IXMLDOMDocumentPtr targetDocument,
                     IXMLDOMNodePtr currentContext )
{
   int nRecordHits=0;
   IXMLDOMNodeListPtr containedElements;
   HRESULT hRes=S_OK;

   // Get all contained elements in order.
   containedElements = currentEntry->selectNodes(L"element|attribute");

   // This loop is repeated as long as it finds any subrecord
   // for the inner iteration loop. This serves to implement
   // repetitive groups.
   do
   {
      BOOL bNodeAdded;
      IXMLDOMElementPtr newNode;
      WCHAR wszQuery[256];

      newNode = targetDocument->
             createElement((_bstr_t)currentEntry->getAttribute(L"name"));
      nRecordHits = 0;
      bNodeAdded=FALSE;

      for (int i=0;hRes == S_OK && i<containedElements->length;i++)
      {
        IXMLDOMElementPtr entry = containedElements->item[i];
        IXMLDOMNodePtr type = entry->attributes->getNamedItem(L"type");

        if ( type != NULL )
        {
           if ( wcscmp(entry->baseName,L"element") == 0 )
           {
              IXMLDOMElementPtr elementType;

              swprintf(wszQuery,L"ElementType[@name='%s']",
                    (wchar_t*)type->text);
```

```
elementType = currentEntry->selectSingleNode(wszQuery);
if ( elementType == NULL )
{
  swprintf(wszQuery,L"/*//ElementType[@name='%s']",
        (wchar_t*)type->text);
  elementType = currentEntry->selectSingleNode(wszQuery);
}
if ( elementType != NULL )
{
  if ( !bNodeAdded )
  {
    currentContext->appendChild(newNode);
    bNodeAdded = TRUE;
  }
  if ( (_bstr_t)elementType->getAttribute(L"content") ==
      _bstr_t(L"textOnly") )
  {
    // This is an element that is a field.
    IXMLDOMElementPtr fieldInfo;
    swprintf(wszQuery,L"%s:FieldInfo",
              (wchar_t*)m_sBizTalkPrefix);
    fieldInfo = elementType->selectSingleNode(wszQuery);
    if ( fieldInfo != NULL )
    {
      FieldInfo fi;
      CComBSTR fieldValue;

      fi.vEDIDataType =
        fieldInfo->getAttribute("edi_datatype");
      fi.vJustification =
        fieldInfo->getAttribute("justification");
      fi.vFormat = fieldInfo->getAttribute("format");
      fi.vCodelist =
        fieldInfo->getAttribute("codelist");
      fi.vRequired = entry->getAttribute("required");
      fi.vPadChar = fieldInfo->getAttribute("pad_char");
      fi.vMinLengthWithPad =
        fieldInfo->getAttribute("minLength_withPad");
      fi.vWrapChar =
        fieldInfo->getAttribute("wrap_char");
      swprintf(wszQuery,L"%s:datatype",
                (wchar_t*)m_sDataTypesPrefix);
      fi.vDataType =
        elementType->getAttribute(wszQuery);
      swprintf(wszQuery,L"%s:maxLength",
                (wchar_t*)m_sDataTypesPrefix);
      fi.vMaxLength =
        elementType->getAttribute(wszQuery);
      swprintf(wszQuery,L"%s:minLength",
```

```
                            (wchar_t*)m_sDataTypesPrefix);
            fi.vMinLength =
              elementType->getAttribute(wszQuery);
            swprintf(wszQuery,L"%s:posStart",
                        (wchar_t*)m_sBizTalkPrefix);
            fi.vPosStart = entry->getAttribute(wszQuery);
            swprintf(wszQuery,L"%s:posEnd",
                        (wchar_t*)m_sBizTalkPrefix);
            fi.vPosEnd = entry->getAttribute(wszQuery);

            if ( SUCCEEDED( hRes = ParseField( parentRecord,
                                    fi,
                                    elementType,
                                    targetDocument,
                                    newNode,
                                    &fieldValue ))
              && ((BSTR)fieldValue)[0]!=0x00 )
            {
              IXMLDOMNodePtr fieldNode;
              fieldNode = targetDocument->createElement(
                (_bstr_t)elementType->getAttribute(
                                L"name"));
              fieldNode->text = (_bstr_t)(BSTR)fieldValue;
              newNode->appendChild(fieldNode);
            }
         }
      }
    else
    {
        IXMLDOMElementPtr recordInfo;

        // This is a record.
        swprintf(wszQuery,L"%s:RecordInfo",(wchar_t*)m_sBizTalkPrefix);
        recordInfo = elementType->selectSingleNode(wszQuery);
        if ( recordInfo != NULL )
        {
            RecordInfo ri;

            ri.vStructure = recordInfo->getAttribute("structure");
            ri.vTagName = recordInfo->getAttribute("tag_name");
            ri.vTagPosition = recordInfo->getAttribute("tag_position");
            ri.vDelimiterType =
              recordInfo->getAttribute("delimiter_type");
            ri.vDelimiterValue =
              recordInfo->getAttribute("delimiter_value");
            ri.vFieldOrder = recordInfo->getAttribute("field_order");
            ri.vEscapeType = recordInfo->getAttribute("escape_type");
```

```
            ri.vEscapeValue = recordInfo->getAttribute("escape_value");
            ri.vCountIgnore = recordInfo->getAttribute("count_ignore");
            ri.vAppendNewLine =
               recordInfo->getAttribute("append_newline");
            ri.vSkipCR = recordInfo->getAttribute("skip_CR");
            ri.vSkipLF = recordInfo->getAttribute("skip_LF");
            ri.vMinOccurs = entry->getAttribute("minOccurs");
            ri.vMaxOccurs = entry->getAttribute("maxOccurs");

            if ( ri.vTagName.vt == VT_NULL )
            {
              hRes = HandleChildren( ri, elementType, targetDocument,
                                     newNode );
            }
            else
            {
              BOOL bRecordAdded;
               hRes = ParseRecord( ri, elementType, targetDocument,
                                   newNode, &bRecordAdded );
              if ( bRecordAdded )
              {
                 nRecordHits++;
              }
            }
         };
      }
   }
}
else if ( wcscmp(entry->baseName,L"attribute") == 0 )
{
   IXMLDOMElementPtr attributeType;
   IXMLDOMElementPtr fieldInfo;

   swprintf(wszQuery,L"AttributeType[@name='%s']",
                     (wchar_t*)type->text);
   attributeType = currentEntry->selectSingleNode(wszQuery);
   if ( attributeType == NULL )
   {
     swprintf(wszQuery,L"/*//AttributeType[@name='%s']",
                       (wchar_t*)type->text);
     attributeType = currentEntry->selectSingleNode(wszQuery);
   }
   if ( attributeType != NULL )
   {
     // This is an attribute that is a field.
     swprintf(wszQuery,L"%s:FieldInfo",(wchar_t*)m_sBizTalkPrefix);
     fieldInfo = attributeType->selectSingleNode(wszQuery);
     if ( fieldInfo != NULL )
     {
```

```
                        FieldInfo fi;
                        CComBSTR fieldValue;

                        fi.vEDIDataType = fieldInfo->getAttribute("edi_datatype");
                        fi.vJustification = fieldInfo->getAttribute("justification");
                        fi.vFormat = fieldInfo->getAttribute("format");
                        fi.vCodelist = fieldInfo->getAttribute("codelist");
                        fi.vRequired = entry->getAttribute("required");
                        fi.vPadChar = fieldInfo->getAttribute("pad_char");
                        fi.vMinLengthWithPad =
                            fieldInfo->getAttribute("minLength_withPad");
                        fi.vWrapChar = fieldInfo->getAttribute("wrap_char");
                        swprintf(wszQuery,L"%s:datatype",(wchar_t*)m_sDataTypesPrefix);
                        fi.vDataType = attributeType->getAttribute(wszQuery);
                        swprintf(wszQuery,L"%s:maxLength",
                           (wchar_t*)m_sDataTypesPrefix);
                        fi.vMaxLength = attributeType->getAttribute(wszQuery);
                        swprintf(wszQuery,L"%s:minLength",
                           (wchar_t*)m_sDataTypesPrefix);
                        fi.vMinLength = attributeType->getAttribute(wszQuery);
                        swprintf(wszQuery,L"%s:posStart",(wchar_t*)m_sBizTalkPrefix);
                        fi.vPosStart = entry->getAttribute(wszQuery);
                        swprintf(wszQuery,L"%s:posEnd",(wchar_t*)m_sBizTalkPrefix);
                        fi.vPosEnd = entry->getAttribute(wszQuery);

                        if ( SUCCEEDED( hRes = ParseField( parentRecord, fi,
                                                           attributeType,
                                                           targetDocument, newNode,
                                                           &fieldValue ) ))
                        {
                           newNode->setAttribute(
                            attributeType->getAttribute(L"name").bstrVal,
                            (BSTR)fieldValue);
                        };
                     }
                     if ( !bNodeAdded )
                     {
                        currentContext->appendChild(newNode);
                        bNodeAdded = TRUE;
                     }
                  }
               }
            }
         }
      }
      while( nRecordHits > 0 );

      return hRes;
};
```

For each record entry found, the *ParseRecord()* method is invoked. *ParseRecord()* assumes that it is invoked with the stream pointer at the beginning of a SWIFT field. The method keeps iterating over the input stream as long as input records of the same type are found. This is independent of what cardinality was specified for the record. If more records are found than the schema allows, the document validation that is performed later by the document-processing pipeline will catch such problems and record them as errors.

Records are detected by checking the record's source tag identifier (enclosed in colons) against the input stream. If the characters at the current stream position do not match the expected signature, it is assumed that the expected record is not present (cardinality zero), and control is returned to the caller reporting that no record was added to the target XML document. This is not an error condition.

If the signature is correct, the code will descend recursively into the next schema level by calling *HandleChildren()*. The record's XML tag is indeed added by the *HandleChildren()* method whenever the first subordinate attribute or element is found. If no fields or subordinate records are found for a record, the XML tag will not be emitted.

```
HRESULT CParser::ParseRecord( RecordInfo & ri, IXMLDOMElementPtr currentEntry,
                              IXMLDOMDocumentPtr targetDocument,
                              IXMLDOMNodePtr currentContext,
                              BOOL * pbRecordAdded )
{
    int nRec=0;
    DWORD dwCharsRead;
    HRESULT hRes;
    WCHAR wchBuffer[256];

    *pbRecordAdded = FALSE;
    if (ri.vTagName.vt == VT_EMPTY )
    {
        hRes = HandleChildren( ri, currentEntry, targetDocument, currentContext );
    }
    else
    {
        do
        {
            // Detect the record signature.
            if ( SUCCEEDED( hRes = StreamRead(wchBuffer,1,&dwCharsRead)) &&
                 dwCharsRead == 1 &&
                 wchBuffer[0] == L':')
            {
                _bstr_t tagName = ri.vTagName;
                size_t tagLen = tagName.length();

                if ( SUCCEEDED( hRes = StreamRead(wchBuffer,
                                                  tagLen+1,&dwCharsRead)) &&
                     dwCharsRead == tagLen+1 &&
                     !wcsncmp(wchBuffer,tagName,tagLen) &&
```

```
                wchBuffer[tagLen] == L':')
        {
            *pbRecordAdded = TRUE;
            m_dwRecordPos = tagLen+2;
            if ( FAILED(hRes = HandleChildren( ri, currentEntry,
                                               targetDocument,
                                               currentContext )))
                goto fail;

            // Next characters must either be CR/LF or LF.
            if ( FAILED( StreamRead( wchBuffer, 2, &dwCharsRead ) ) ||
                 dwCharsRead < 2 )
            {
                goto fail;
            }
            else
            {
                if ((wchBuffer[0] != 0x0d && wchBuffer[1] != 0x0a) &&
                     wchBuffer[0] != 0x0a )
                {
                    goto fail;
                }
                else if ( wchBuffer[0] == 0x0a )
                {
                    // Put next character back into the stream.
                    StreamMoveBack(1);
                }
            }
            nRec++;
        }
        else if ( SUCCEEDED( hRes ))
        {
            StreamMoveBack(dwCharsRead+1);
            break;
        }
        else
            goto fail;
    }
    else if (SUCCEEDED(hRes) && dwCharsRead == 1 &&  wchBuffer[0] == L'-')
    {
        StreamMoveBack(1);
        hRes = S_OK;
        break;
    }
    else
        goto fail;
}
while ( 1 );
}
```

```
    return hRes;


fail:
    return E_FAIL;
}
```

The *ParseField()* method extracts the data from the source stream. Each field has positional boundaries startPos and endPos, just like the BizTalk flatfile parser, because SWIFT streams are typically positional. The core difference to the BizTalk flatfile parser is that parsing will terminate (successfully) at each occurrence of CR/LF or a single LF character. The shown implementation supports SWIFT-compliant date, time, and number types. The parsing code of dates and times is pretty compact and uses a fairly unusual approach by going from right to left, matching a pattern like YYMMDD against the input data, but it does indeed do the job. When a value could be successfully extracted and converted, it is returned as a BSTR. The caller (HandleChildren) will then create the appropriate element or attribute for the output XML stream.

```
HRESULT CParser::ParseField( RecordInfo & parentRecord, FieldInfo & fi,
                             IXMLDOMElementPtr currentEntry,
                             IXMLDOMDocumentPtr targetDocument,
                             IXMLDOMNodePtr currentContext,
                             BSTR * pbstrValue )
{
    HRESULT hRes = E_FAIL;

    // The record must be marked positional.
    if(parentRecord.vStructure.vt==VT_BSTR &&
       !wcscmp(parentRecord.vStructure.bstrVal,L"positional"))
    {
        WCHAR * wchBuffer;
        DWORD dwCharsRead;
        DWORD dwCharsToRead;
        LONG lCharsToSkip;
        BOOL bScanOk = TRUE;

        fi.vPosStart.ChangeType(VT_UI4);
        fi.vPosEnd.ChangeType(VT_UI4);
        dwCharsToRead = fi.vPosEnd.lVal-fi.vPosStart.lVal+1;
        lCharsToSkip = fi.vPosStart.lVal-m_dwRecordPos-1;
        wchBuffer = (WCHAR*)calloc( (max(dwCharsToRead,
                                    (DWORD)abs(lCharsToSkip))+1),
                                     sizeof(wchar_t));
        // Now get the field data.
        dwCharsRead = 0;
        memset(wchBuffer,0,sizeof(wchBuffer));
        while ( lCharsToSkip > 0 || dwCharsToRead > 0 )
        {
```

```
DWORD dwRead;
if ( SUCCEEDED( StreamRead( &wchBuffer[dwCharsRead], 1, &dwRead )) &&
     dwRead == 1)
{
    // If the character is either 0x0d (windows/dos) or 0x0a
    // (unix,mainframe), we stop here and put the character back
    // into the stream.
    if ( wchBuffer[dwCharsRead] == 0x0d ||
         wchBuffer[dwCharsRead] == 0x0a )
    {
        StreamMoveBack(1);
        break;
    }
    if ( lCharsToSkip > 0 )
    {
        lCharsToSkip--;
    }
    else
    {
        dwCharsRead++;
        dwCharsToRead--;
    }
    m_dwRecordPos++;
}
else
{
    bScanOk = FALSE;
    break;
}
}

if ( bScanOk )
{
    // wchBuffer now holds the data element.

    // Check whether this is a decimal number. For decimal numbers,
    // we need to  replace the decimal sign from "," to "."
    // (Can occur only once.)
    // Data types in question are D0 ... D9, N0 ... N9 and R0 ... R9
    if ( fi.vEDIDataType.vt == VT_BSTR &&
         (fi.vEDIDataType.bstrVal[0] == 'N' ||
          fi.vEDIDataType.bstrVal[0] == 'D' ||
          fi.vEDIDataType.bstrVal[0] == 'R') &&
         (fi.vEDIDataType.bstrVal[1] >= '0' &&
          fi.vEDIDataType.bstrVal[1] <= '9') )
    {
        for (DWORD k=0;k<dwCharsRead;k++)
        {
            if (wchBuffer[k]==',')
```

```
        {
            wchBuffer[k]='.';
            break;
        }
    }
}
// Otherwise, test whether the data type is a date.
else if ( fi.vEDIDataType.vt == VT_BSTR &&
          (fi.vEDIDataType.bstrVal[0] == 'D' &&
           fi.vEDIDataType.bstrVal[1] == 'T'))
{
    int y,m,d,l;
    y=m=d=0;
    // Empty format; make it "YYMMDD"
    if ( fi.vFormat.vt != VT_BSTR || fi.vFormat.bstrVal[0] == 0x00)
        fi.vFormat="YYMMDD";
    l= wcslen(fi.vFormat.bstrVal);
    for (int k=0;k<l;k++)
    {
        switch(fi.vFormat.bstrVal[k])
        {
        case 'D': if ( wchBuffer[k] < L'0' || wchBuffer[k] > L'9' ||
                        wchBuffer[k] == 0x00)
                    {       k=l; break; }
                    d = d*10 + (wchBuffer[k]-L'0');
                    break;
        case 'M': if ( wchBuffer[k] < L'0' || wchBuffer[k] > L'9' ||
                        wchBuffer[k] == 0x00)
                    {       k=l; break; }
                    m = m*10 + (wchBuffer[k]-L'0');
                    break;
        case 'Y': if ( wchBuffer[k] < L'0' || wchBuffer[k] > L'9'||
                        wchBuffer[k] == 0x00 )
                    {       k=l; break; }
                    y = y*10 + (wchBuffer[k]-L'0');
                    break;
        default:  if ( wchBuffer[k] != fi.vFormat.bstrVal[k] )
                    {       k=l; break; }
                    break;
        }
    }
    dwCharsRead=10;
    wchBuffer=(WCHAR*)realloc(wchBuffer,
                        (dwCharsRead+1)*sizeof(WCHAR));
    swprintf(wchBuffer,L"%04d-%02d-%02d",
                    y<1000?(y<50?y+2000:y+1900):y,m,d);

}
// Otherwise, test whether the data type is a date.
```

```
       else if ( fi.vEDIDataType.vt == VT_BSTR &&
                 (fi.vEDIDataType.bstrVal[0] == 'T' &&
                  fi.vEDIDataType.bstrVal[1] == 'M'))
       {
           int h,m,s,l;
           h=m=s=0;
           // Empty format; make it "HHMMSS"
           if ( fi.vFormat.vt != VT_BSTR || fi.vFormat.bstrVal[0] == 0x00)
               fi.vFormat="HHMMSS";
           l= wcslen(fi.vFormat.bstrVal);
           for (int k=0;k<l;k++)
           {
               switch(fi.vFormat.bstrVal[k])
               {
               case 'H': if ( wchBuffer[k] < L'0' || wchBuffer[k] > L'9' ||
                              wchBuffer[k] == 0x00)
                         {     k=l; break; }
                         h = h*10 + (wchBuffer[k]-L'0');
                         break;
               case 'M': if ( wchBuffer[k] < L'0' || wchBuffer[k] > L'9' ||
                              wchBuffer[k] == 0x00)
                         {     k=l; break; }
                         m = m*10 + (wchBuffer[k]-L'0');
                         break;
               case 'S': if ( wchBuffer[k] == 0x00 || wchBuffer[k] < L'0' ||
                              wchBuffer[k] > L'9')
                         { k=l; break; }
                         s = s*10 + (wchBuffer[k]-L'0');
                         break;
               default:  if ( wchBuffer[k] != fi.vFormat.bstrVal[k] )
                         {     k=l; break; }
                         break;
               }
           }
           dwCharsRead=8;
           wchBuffer=(WCHAR*)realloc(wchBuffer,
                               (dwCharsRead+1)*sizeof(WCHAR));
           swprintf(wchBuffer,L"%02d:%02d:%02d",h,m,s);
       }
       *pbstrValue = SysAllocStringLen(wchBuffer,dwCharsRead);
       hRes = S_OK;
   }
   else
   {
       hRes = E_FAIL;
   }
   free(wchBuffer);
```

```
    }
    else
    {
        // Not implemented
        hRes = E_NOTIMPL;
    }
    return hRes;
};
```

Now the parser code is almost complete. The last method that we need to look at is *IBizTalkParserComponent::GetNativeDocumentOffsets,* which must return offsets into the original data stream that will allow the tracking database handler code to cut out the correct portion of the inbound data for logging purposes. The implementation is trivial because we keep track of the values on the way.

```
STDMETHODIMP CParser::GetNativeDocumentOffsets(BOOL * SizeFromXMLDoc, _LARGE_INTEGER *
StartOffset, LONG * DocLength)
{
    if (SizeFromXMLDoc == NULL)
        return E_POINTER;

    if (StartOffset == NULL)
        return E_POINTER;

    if (DocLength == NULL)
        return E_POINTER;

    *SizeFromXMLDoc = FALSE;
    StartOffset->QuadPart = 0; //(__int64)m_dwHeaderOffset;
    *DocLength = m_dwTotalBytesRead; // m_dwDocumentLength;
    return S_OK;
}
```

It is much easier to understand exactly what is happening at every stage when you run the parser in the debugger. Unfortunately, doing this with Visual C++ 6.0 is not too easy because you will have to hook the debugger into the running BizTalk Server process. You can find the complete how-to, including the MT940 sample specification and a sample data stream, in the distribution package for the sample code (on this book's web site).

WRITING CUSTOM SERIALIZERS

A serializer performs basically the same function as a parser but just the other way around. Serializers are responsible for translating XML documents into their native counterparts. As you would expect, translating from XML into a native format requires much less effort than parsing, and the required code is indeed almost exactly half as long as that for the parser. Let's go!

How BizTalk Serializers Plug into BizTalk

Serializers are configured a bit differently than parsers. Using a custom serializer requires you to use a CUSTOM envelope definition, which you configure in the management database. (This is independent of whether the serializer actually writes an envelope format or not.) The envelope definition does not require an associated envelope specification.

You must then configure the envelope definition for a port in Messaging Manager. Then on the Advanced (last) configuration page for a channel that is bound to that port, click the Advanced button, select the Envelope tab, and select the desired serializer component.

To be listed in the combo box on the configuration page, BizTalk serializers must implement the IBizTalkSerializerComponent interface and must be registered in the COM category with the identifier CATID_BIZTALK_SERIALIZER. Just like parsers, serializers must also be registered as free threaded or must support both COM threading models (free threaded and apartment threaded).

The Serializer Code

For the serializer component, we will also show only the core file of the component project. The general structure is similar to the parser in that we have special handling methods for headers, the body section, and single nodes. (Here, we use the XML terminology.)

The Serializer Class

Again, to provide a better overview on the context of the class, the header file for the class implementation is provided without much further comment, and we will drill down into the details in the following sections.

```
//////////////////////////////////////////////////////////////////////
// Serializer.h : Declaration of the CSerializer class
// Microsoft BizTalk Server 2000 Sample Serializer Component for SWIFT
// (c) 2001 Clemens F. Vasters - clemensv@newtelligence.com
//
// All rights reserved.

#ifndef __SERIALIZER_H_
#define __SERIALIZER_H_

#include "resource.h"        // main symbols
#import <msxml3.dll>
#include <bts_sdk_guids.h>
#include <biztalkobjectmodel.h>

using namespace ::MSXML2;


//////////////////////////////////////////////////////////////////////
// CSerializer
class ATL_NO_VTABLE CSerializer :
```

```
    public CComObjectRootEx<CComMultiThreadModel>,
    public CComCoClass<CSerializer, &CLSID_Serializer>,
    public ISupportErrorInfo,
    public IBizTalkSerializerComponent
{
protected:
    CComBSTR m_srcQual;
    CComBSTR m_srcID;
    CComBSTR m_destQual;
    CComBSTR m_destID;
    CComBSTR m_FuncID;
    LONG m_EnvID;
    CComPtr<IDictionary> m_pDelimiters;
    BOOL m_bEnveloped; // flag indicating whether interchange is enveloped
    DWORD m_dwTotalBytesWritten;
    CComPtr<IStream> m_pstmOutputStream;
    LONG m_PortID;
    DWORD m_dwRecordPos;
    int m_nCodePage;
public:
    CSerializer():m_nCodePage(1200),m_dwRecordPos(0),m_dwTotalBytesWritten(0)
    {
    }

DECLARE_REGISTRY_RESOURCEID(IDR_SERIALIZER)

DECLARE_PROTECT_FINAL_CONSTRUCT()

BEGIN_COM_MAP(CSerializer)
    COM_INTERFACE_ENTRY(ISupportErrorInfo)
    COM_INTERFACE_ENTRY(IBizTalkSerializerComponent)
END_COM_MAP()

BEGIN_CATEGORY_MAP(CParser)
    IMPLEMENTED_CATEGORY(CATID_BIZTALK_SERIALIZER)
END_CATEGORY_MAP()


public:
    HRESULT LoadSchema(LONG ChannelID, IXMLDOMDocument2 ** ppdoc);
    HRESULT WriteHeader( void );
    HRESULT WriteBody( IXMLDOMDocument2Ptr pdoc );
    HRESULT WriteNode( IXMLDOMNodePtr pnode );
    HRESULT WriteFooter( void );
    HRESULT StreamWrite(WCHAR * wchBuffer, DWORD cchBuffer, DWORD * pcchWritten );

// ISupportsErrorInfo
    STDMETHOD(InterfaceSupportsErrorInfo)(REFIID riid);
```

```
public:
// IBizTalkSerializerComponent
    STDMETHOD(Init)(BSTR srcQual, BSTR srcID, BSTR destQual, BSTR destID,
                    LONG EnvID, IDictionary * pDelimiters, IStream * OutputStream,
                    LONG NumDocs, LONG PortID);
    STDMETHOD(AddDocument)(LONG DocHandle, IDictionary * Transport, BSTR TrackID,
                    LONG ChannelID);
    STDMETHOD(GetInterchangeInfo)(BSTR * InterchangeID, LONG * lNumGroups);
    STDMETHOD(GetGroupInfo)(LONG * NumDocs, _LARGE_INTEGER * GrpStartOffset,
                    LONG * GrpLen);
    STDMETHOD(GetDocInfo)(LONG * DocHandle, BOOL * SizeFromXMLDoc,
                    _LARGE_INTEGER * DocStartOffset, LONG * DocLen);
};


#endif //__SERIALIZER_H_
```

Serializer Intialization

The first call that each serializer component receives is made to *IBizTalkSerializer Component::Init()*. In this call, BizTalk passes all data that it can provide for creating the envelope portion of an outbound document, which are the source and destination identifiers, a reference to the envelope definition, the output stream, the port reference, and the number of documents that need to be written in this serializer run.

Our implementation is quite simplistic in that we store the arguments in the class' member variables and only check whether the number of input documents is 1. BizTalk never attempts to serialize more than one document in the current product release, however. *Batching*, the submission of multiple documents in a simple interchange, is hinted at in the BizTalk documentation, but it is currently unsupported.

```
STDMETHODIMP CSerializer::Init(BSTR srcQual, BSTR srcID, BSTR destQual, BSTR
destID, LONG EnvID,
                                IDictionary * pDelimiters, IStream *
OutputStream, LONG NumDocs, LONG PortID)
{
    // SWIFT has only a single document inside an envelope, and the envelope
    // can be written only when we see the document. We will memorize all
    // arguments and wait for the AddDocument call.
    m_srcQual = srcQual;
    m_srcID = srcID;
    m_destQual = destQual;
    m_destID = destID;
    m_EnvID = EnvID;
    m_pDelimiters = pDelimiters;
    m_pstmOutputStream = OutputStream;
    if ( NumDocs != 1 )
    {
        return E_INVALIDARG;
    }
```

```
    m_PortID = PortID;
    return S_OK;
}
```

Writing the Document

When the serializer instance is properly initialized, the *AddDocument* method is called for *each* document that will be submitted in the interchange. Of course, "each" assumes batching support; thus, the method is only called exactly once for BizTalk Server 2000.

The document is submitted with its internal document handle (which identifies the document only during this serialization run), the complete transport dictionary (which will give you access to all the custom values that you may have put there in the parsing stage), the tracking ID (which BizTalk autogenerates), and the channel identifier. Because this component serializes outbound documents, the channel identifier will allow us to dig into the management database and obtain the output document schema that will be used to drive the serialization process.

The XML data document is contained in the working_data field of the transport dictionary. If we can extract this successfully and are also able to load the schema document (the *LoadSchema()* method is shown immediately following the *AddDocument()* method), we will stuff the schema document into an MSXML schema cache, attach the schema cache to the new MSXML document instance, and proceed to load the data document into the new object.

NOTE: We blindly assume that this action will succeed because BizTalk does exactly the same thing some split seconds before this action to perform output document validation. If that fails, this method would never be called.

So, once the document is properly loaded, we will call the *WriteHeader()*, *WriteBody()*, and *WriteFooter()* methods to write the output stream.

```
STDMETHODIMP CSerializer::AddDocument(LONG DocHandle, IDictionary * Transport,
BSTR TrackID, LONG ChannelID)
{
    HRESULT hRes;
    IXMLDOMDocument2Ptr schemaDoc;
    CComVariant vDoc;

    if ( SUCCEEDED( hRes = Transport->get_Value(L"working_data", &vDoc)) &&
        SUCCEEDED( hRes = LoadSchema(ChannelID,&schemaDoc)))
    {
        IXMLDOMDocument2Ptr dataDoc;
        IXMLDOMSchemaCollectionPtr schemaCache;
        IXMLDOMNodePtr targetNamespace;

        dataDoc.CreateInstance(__uuidof(MSXML2::DOMDocument));
        schemaCache.CreateInstance(__uuidof(MSXML2::XMLSchemaCache));
```

```
            if ( SUCCEEDED( targetNamespace =
                 schemaDoc->documentElement->attributes->
                   getQualifiedItem(L"target_namespace",
                      L"urn:schemas-microsoft-com:BizTalkServer")))
            {
                schemaCache->add(targetNamespace->text,
                              CComVariant((IDispatch*)schemaDoc));
            }
            else
            {
                schemaCache->add(L"",CComVariant(schemaDoc));
            }
            dataDoc->schemas = CComVariant((IDispatch*)schemaCache);
            if ( SUCCEEDED( hRes = dataDoc->loadXML(vDoc.bstrVal)))
            {
                if ( SUCCEEDED( hRes = WriteHeader()))
                   if ( SUCCEEDED( hRes = WriteBody(dataDoc)))
                       hRes = WriteFooter();
            }
        };
        return hRes;
}
```

Loading the schema based on the channel ID requires loading the channel through the configuration object model, getting the output document specification reference, and using that reference to obtain the document, as shown in the following code:

```
HRESULT CSerializer::LoadSchema(LONG ChannelID, IXMLDOMDocument2 ** ppdoc)
{
    HRESULT hRes = S_OK;
    CComPtr<IBizTalkConfig> cfgroot;

    if ( SUCCEEDED( hRes = cfgroot.CoCreateInstance(CLSID_BizTalkConfig)))
    {
        CComPtr<IBizTalkChannel> pchn;
        LONG lOutputDocHandle;

        if ( SUCCEEDED( hRes = cfgroot->CreateChannel((IDispatch**)&pchn)) &&
             SUCCEEDED( hRes = pchn->Load(ChannelID)) &&
             SUCCEEDED( hRes = pchn->get_OutputDocument(&lOutputDocHandle)))
        {
            CComPtr<IBizTalkDocument> pdoc;

            if ( SUCCEEDED( hRes = cfgroot->CreateDocument((IDispatch**)&pdoc)) &&
                 SUCCEEDED( hRes = pdoc->Load(lOutputDocHandle)))
            {
                CComBSTR content;
                CComPtr<IDictionary> pdict;
                CComVariant vDocType;
```

```
                if ( SUCCEEDED( pdoc->get_PropertySet((IDispatch**)&pdict)) &&
                    SUCCEEDED( pdict->get_Value(L"functional_identifier",
                                          &vDocType)) &&
                    SUCCEEDED( pdoc->get_Content(&content)))
                {

                    IXMLDOMDocument2Ptr schemadoc;

                    schemadoc.CreateInstance(__uuidof(MSXML2::DOMDocument));
                    if ( SUCCEEDED( hRes = schemadoc->loadXML((_bstr_t)content) ))
                    {
                        vDocType.ChangeType(VT_BSTR);
                        m_FuncID = vDocType.bstrVal;
                        hRes = schemadoc->QueryInterface(ppdoc);
                    }
                }
            }
        };
    }
    return hRes;
}
```

The local *WriteHeader()* method takes care of writing the SWIFT header. We will ignore some of the details in this sample implementation and will write only the source and destination identifiers and the functional identifier, a.k.a., message type.

```
HRESULT CSerializer::WriteHeader()
{
    WCHAR wchHeader[128];
    DWORD dwWritten;

    swprintf(wchHeader,L"{1:F01%s0000000000}",m_srcID);
    StreamWrite(wchHeader,wcslen(wchHeader),&dwWritten);
    swprintf(wchHeader,L"{2:I%s%sN0000}{4:",m_FuncID,m_destID);
    StreamWrite(wchHeader,wcslen(wchHeader),&dwWritten);
    return S_OK;
};
```

As you probably noticed, the output values for the dwWritten argument that is passed to both calls to the local *StreamWrite()* method are (intentionally) ignored for this sample as well. The total bytes written to the stream are counted by the stream method directly. The stream method also takes care of required code-page conversions on output.

```
HRESULT CSerializer::StreamWrite(WCHAR * wchBuffer, DWORD cchBuffer, DWORD *
pcchWritten )
{
    HRESULT hRes;

    if ( m_nCodePage == 1200 )
```

```
    {
        DWORD dwWritten;

        if ( SUCCEEDED( hRes = m_pstmOutputStream->Write(wchBuffer,cchBuffer*2,
                                                   &dwWritten) ))
        {
            *pcchWritten = dwWritten / 2;
            m_dwTotalBytesWritten += dwWritten;
        }
    }
    else
    {
        BYTE * pbBuf = (BYTE*)malloc(cchBuffer+1);

        WideCharToMultiByte(m_nCodePage,0,wchBuffer,cchBuffer,
                            (char*)pbBuf,cchBuffer,NULL,NULL);
        if ( SUCCEEDED( hRes = m_pstmOutputStream->Write(wchBuffer,
                                                   cchBuffer,pcchWritten)))
        {
            m_dwTotalBytesWritten += *pcchWritten;
        }
        free(pbBuf);
    }
    return hRes;
}
```

The bulk of the serializer's work is performed by the recursive *WriteNode()* method. The *WriteBody()* method that is called from *IBizTalkSerializerComponent::AddDocument()* is just a wrapper for calling *WriteNode()* to pass the document element (root node) of the input document.

While the parser was driven only by the schema structure, the *WriteNode()* method of the serializer is driven by the input document's structure on the record level and by the schema structure on the field and subrecord level. In the implementation, we take advantage of MSXML's capability to bind the appropriate schema definitions directly to each element of a DOM document through the *definition* property. If you query the *definition* property for an element of a schema-bound document (meaning that the schema collection is not empty), MSXML will return the ElementType definition that defines the current element.

If a node is a record, the implementation will drill into the schema and find all children in the exact sequence as they are defined and serialize them with a recursive call to *WriteNode()*. If the node is a field, it will gather the formatting information, including data types and data formats, from the schema and perform the necessary conversions on the input node's text data before it is written to the stream.

```
HRESULT CSerializer::WriteBody( IXMLDOMDocument2Ptr pdoc )
{
    return WriteNode(pdoc->documentElement);
}
```

```
HRESULT CSerializer::WriteNode( IXMLDOMNodePtr currentEntry )
{
    HRESULT hRes=S_OK;

    // Children? Schema info? Element?
    if ( currentEntry->selectNodes("*")->length > 0 &&
        currentEntry->definition != NULL &&
        currentEntry->nodeType == MSXML2::NODE_ELEMENT )
    {
        IXMLDOMNodeListPtr containedElements;
        IXMLDOMElementPtr recordInfo;
        recordInfo = currentEntry->definition->selectSingleNode(L"b:RecordInfo");
        if ( recordInfo != NULL )
        {
            BOOL bIsRecord=FALSE;

            _variant_t vStructure = recordInfo->getAttribute("structure");
            _variant_t vTagName = recordInfo->getAttribute("tag_name");
            _variant_t vTagPosition = recordInfo->getAttribute("tag_position");
            _variant_t vDelimiterType =
                recordInfo->getAttribute("delimiter_type");
            _variant_t vDelimiterValue =
                recordInfo->getAttribute("delimiter_value");
            _variant_t vFieldOrder = recordInfo->getAttribute("field_order");
            _variant_t vEscapeType = recordInfo->getAttribute("escape_type");
            _variant_t vEscapeValue = recordInfo->getAttribute("escape_value");
            _variant_t vCountIgnore = recordInfo->getAttribute("count_ignore");
            _variant_t vAppendNewLine =
                recordInfo->getAttribute("append_newline");

            // A new record begins here if the source tag identifier
            // (tag_name) is set.
            if ( vTagName.vt == VT_BSTR )
            {
                CComBSTR recordPrefix;
                DWORD dwWritten;

                StreamWrite(L"\r\n",2,&dwWritten);
                recordPrefix = L":";
                recordPrefix += vTagName.bstrVal;
                recordPrefix +=L":";
                StreamWrite(recordPrefix,recordPrefix.Length(),&dwWritten);
                m_dwRecordPos = dwWritten;
                bIsRecord = FALSE;
            }

            containedElements =
                currentEntry->definition->selectNodes(L"element|attribute");
```

```
        for (int i=0;hRes == S_OK && i<containedElements->length;i++)
        {
            IXMLDOMElementPtr entry = containedElements->item[i];
            IXMLDOMNodePtr type = entry->attributes->getNamedItem(L"type");

            if ( type != NULL )
            {
                if ( wcscmp(entry->baseName,L"element") == 0 )
                {
                    IXMLDOMNodeListPtr children =
                        currentEntry->selectNodes(type->text);
                    for ( int k=0;k<children->length;k++)
                    {
                        WriteNode(children->item[k]);
                    }
                }
                else if ( wcscmp(entry->baseName,L"attribute") == 0 )
                {
                    IXMLDOMNodePtr child =
                        currentEntry->attributes->getNamedItem(type->text);

                    if ( child != NULL )
                    {
                        WriteNode(child);
                    }
                }
            }
        }

        // If this element was a record and there was no an explicit
        // request not to  terminate it with a new line (which is CR/LF
        // in our case), we emit a new-line break.
        if ( bIsRecord &&
            !(vAppendNewLine.vt == VT_BSTR &&
              !wcscmp(vAppendNewLine.bstrVal,L"no")))
        {
            DWORD dwWritten;
            StreamWrite(L"\0x0d\0x0a",2,&dwWritten);
        }
    }
}
else if ( currentEntry->definition != NULL &&
         (currentEntry->nodeType == MSXML2::NODE_ELEMENT ||
          currentEntry->nodeType == MSXML2::NODE_ATTRIBUTE) )
{
    IXMLDOMElementPtr fieldInfo;
    fieldInfo = currentEntry->definition->selectSingleNode(L"b:FieldInfo");
    if ( fieldInfo != NULL )
    {
```

```
IXMLDOMNodePtr ndDataType;
IXMLDOMNodePtr ndMaxLength;
IXMLDOMNodePtr ndMinLength;
_variant_t vTypedValue;

_bstr_t sText;
_variant_t vDataType;
_variant_t vMaxLength;
_variant_t vMinLength;
_variant_t vEDIDataType = fieldInfo->getAttribute("edi_datatype");
_variant_t vJustification = fieldInfo->getAttribute("justification");
_variant_t vFormat = fieldInfo->getAttribute("format");
_variant_t vPadChar = fieldInfo->getAttribute("pad_char");
_variant_t vMinLengthWithPad =
     fieldInfo->getAttribute("minLength_withPad");
_variant_t vWrapChar = fieldInfo->getAttribute("wrap_char");

if ( (ndDataType = currentEntry->definition->attributes->
        getQualifiedItem(L"datatype",DATATYPES_SCHEMA)) != NULL)
{
   vDataType = ndDataType->text;
}
if ( (ndMaxLength = currentEntry->definition->attributes->
         getQualifiedItem(L"maxLength",DATATYPES_SCHEMA)) != NULL)
{
    vMaxLength = ndMaxLength->text;
}
if ( (ndMinLength =
        currentEntry->definition->attributes->
          getQualifiedItem( L"minLength", DATATYPES_SCHEMA)) != NULL)
{
    vMinLength = ndMinLength->text;
}

vTypedValue = currentEntry->nodeTypedValue;
if ( vTypedValue.vt == VT_NULL || vTypedValue.vt == VT_EMPTY )
    vTypedValue = currentEntry->text;

// Check whether this is a decimal number. For decimal numbers, we
// need to replace the decimal sign from "," to "." (Can occur only
// once.)
// Data types in question are D0 ... D9, N0 ... N9, and R0 ... R9.
if ( vEDIDataType.vt == VT_BSTR &&
     (vEDIDataType.bstrVal[0] == 'N'  ||
      vEDIDataType.bstrVal[0] == 'D' ||
      vEDIDataType.bstrVal[0] == 'R') &&
     (vEDIDataType.bstrVal[1] >= '0' &&
      vEDIDataType.bstrVal[1] <= '9') )
{
```

```
        size_t l;
        vTypedValue.ChangeType(VT_BSTR);
        l = wcslen(vTypedValue.bstrVal);
        for (size_t k=0;k<l;k++)
        {
            if (vTypedValue.bstrVal[k]=='.')
            {
                vTypedValue.bstrVal[k]=',';
                break;
            }
        }
    }
    // Otherwise, test whether the data type is a date.
    else if ( vTypedValue.vt == VT_DATE &&
            vEDIDataType.vt == VT_BSTR &&
            (vEDIDataType.bstrVal[0] == 'D' &&
             vEDIDataType.bstrVal[1] == 'T'))
    {
        SYSTEMTIME st;
        WCHAR * wchBuffer;
        size_t l;

        VariantTimeToSystemTime(vTypedValue.date,&st);
        // Empty format ? make it "YYMMDD"
        if ( vFormat.vt != VT_BSTR || vFormat.bstrVal[0] == 0x00)
            vFormat="YYMMDD";
        l= wcslen(vFormat.bstrVal);
        wchBuffer=(WCHAR*)calloc((l+1),sizeof(WCHAR));
        for (int k=l-1;k>=0;k--)
        {
            switch(vFormat.bstrVal[k])
            {
            case 'D': wchBuffer[k]=L'0'+st.wDay%10;
                      st.wDay /= 10;
                      break;
            case 'M': wchBuffer[k]=L'0'+st.wMonth%10;
                      st.wMonth /= 10;
                      break;
            case 'Y': wchBuffer[k]=L'0'+st.wYear%10;
                      st.wYear /= 10;
                      break;
            default:  wchBuffer[k] = vFormat.bstrVal[k];
                      break;
            }
        }
        vTypedValue = wchBuffer;
        free(wchBuffer);

    }
```

```
// Otherwise, test whether the data type is a time value.
else if ( vTypedValue.vt == VT_DATE &&
          vEDIDataType.vt == VT_BSTR &&
          (vEDIDataType.bstrVal[0] == 'T' &&
           vEDIDataType.bstrVal[1] == 'M'))
{
    SYSTEMTIME st;
    WCHAR * wchBuffer;
    size_t l;

    VariantTimeToSystemTime(vTypedValue.date,&st);
    // Empty format ? make it "YYMMDD"
    if ( vFormat.vt != VT_BSTR || vFormat.bstrVal[0] == 0x00)
        vFormat="HHMMSS";
    l= wcslen(vFormat.bstrVal);
    wchBuffer=(WCHAR*)calloc((l+1),sizeof(WCHAR));
    for (int k=l-1;k>=0;k--)
    {
        switch(vFormat.bstrVal[k])
        {
        case 'H': wchBuffer[k]=L'0'+st.wHour%10;
                  st.wHour /= 10;
                  break;
        case 'M': wchBuffer[k]=L'0'+st.wMinute%10;
                  st.wMinute /= 10;
                  break;
        case 'S': wchBuffer[k]=L'0'+st.wSecond%10;
                  st.wSecond /= 10;
                  break;
        default:  wchBuffer[k] = vFormat.bstrVal[k];
                  break;
        }
    }
    vTypedValue = wchBuffer;
    free(wchBuffer);
}

vTypedValue.ChangeType(VT_BSTR);
sText = vTypedValue.bstrVal;
if ( sText.length() > 0 )
{
    WCHAR wszQuery[128];
    DWORD dwInternalPads = 0;
    CComBSTR padChar=L" ";
    IXMLDOMElementPtr elementDecl;

    LPWSTR pwsz = (wchar_t*)currentEntry->definition->
        attributes->getNamedItem(L"name")->text;
```

```
swprintf(wszQuery,
         L"element[@type='%s']|attribute[@type='%s']",
         pwsz,pwsz);
elementDecl = currentEntry->parentNode->
    definition->selectSingleNode(wszQuery);

if ( vMinLengthWithPad.vt != VT_EMPTY &&
     vMinLengthWithPad.vt != VT_NULL )
{
    vMinLengthWithPad.ChangeType(VT_UI4);
    if ( sText.length() < vMinLengthWithPad.ulVal )
        dwInternalPads = vMinLengthWithPad.ulVal - sText.length();
    if ( vPadChar.vt == VT_BSTR )
        padChar = vPadChar.bstrVal;
}
if ( elementDecl != NULL )
{
    IXMLDOMNodePtr posStart =
        elementDecl->attributes->getQualifiedItem(L"posStart",
                                                  BIZTALK_SCHEMA);
    IXMLDOMNodePtr posEnd =
        elementDecl->attributes->getQualifiedItem(L"posEnd",
                                                  BIZTALK_SCHEMA);
    if ( posStart != NULL && posEnd != NULL )
    {
        DWORD dw;
        DWORD dwExternalPads = 0;
        DWORD nposStart = _wtol(posStart->text);
        DWORD nposEnd = _wtol(posEnd->text);

        dwExternalPads = nposStart - m_dwRecordPos;
        if ( nposEnd - nposStart < sText.length()+dwInternalPads)
        {
            long a;
            dwInternalPads =
              (a=(nposEnd - nposStart)-sText.length())<0?0:a;
        }
        if ( dwInternalPads > 0 )
        {
            WCHAR * pBuf=(WCHAR*)malloc(dwInternalPads);
            for (dw=0;dw<dwInternalPads;dw++) pBuf[dw]=padChar[0];
            if ( vJustification.vt==VT_BSTR &&
                 !wcscmp(vJustification.bstrVal,L"right"))
            {
                StreamWrite(pBuf,dwInternalPads,&dw);
                m_dwRecordPos += dw;
            }
            StreamWrite((wchar_t*)sText,sText.length(),&dw);
            m_dwRecordPos += dw;
```

```
                        if ( vJustification.vt==VT_BSTR &&
                            !wcscmp(vJustification.bstrVal,L"left"))
                        {
                            StreamWrite(pBuf,dwInternalPads,&dw);
                            m_dwRecordPos += dw;
                        }

                    }
                    else
                    {
                        StreamWrite((wchar_t*)sText,sText.length(),&dw);
                        m_dwRecordPos += dw;
                    };
                }
            };
        };
    }
    }
    return S_OK;
}
```

Finally, we will output the footer, which, for this sample, is just closing the text block.

```
HRESULT CSerializer::WriteFooter( void )
{
    DWORD dwWritten;

    StreamWrite(L"\r\n-}",4,&dwWritten);
    return S_OK;
}
```

The final three methods for the serializer component must all be implemented for the IBizTalkServerSerializerComponent interface and return size and counter information that must be stored in the tracking database. All three methods are trivial to implement and don't require much explanation because we support only a single document and no groups.

```
STDMETHODIMP CSerializer::GetInterchangeInfo(BSTR * InterchangeID, LONG *
lNumGroups)
{
    if (InterchangeID == NULL)
        return E_POINTER;

    if (lNumGroups == NULL)
        return E_POINTER;

    *InterchangeID = SysAllocString(L"0001");
    *lNumGroups = 0;
    return S_OK;
```

```
}

STDMETHODIMP CSerializer::GetGroupInfo(LONG * NumDocs, _LARGE_INTEGER *
GrpStartOffset, LONG * GrpLen)
{
    if (NumDocs == NULL)
        return E_POINTER;

    if (GrpStartOffset == NULL)
        return E_POINTER;

    if (GrpLen == NULL)
        return E_POINTER;

    return E_NOTIMPL;
}

STDMETHODIMP CSerializer::GetDocInfo(LONG * DocHandle, BOOL * SizeFromXMLDoc,
                                     _LARGE_INTEGER * DocStartOffset, LONG *
DocLen)
{
    if (DocHandle == NULL)
        return E_POINTER;

    if (SizeFromXMLDoc == NULL)
        return E_POINTER;

    if (DocStartOffset == NULL)
        return E_POINTER;

    if (DocLen == NULL)
        return E_POINTER;

    *DocLen = m_dwTotalBytesWritten;
    *SizeFromXMLDoc = FALSE;
    DocStartOffset->QuadPart=0;
    *DocHandle = 0;
    return S_OK;
}
```

Of course, both the parser and the serializer that were shown here are not really complete, production-ready implementations, but that was already announced at the beginning of this chapter. However, you should have learned by example that creating schema-driven parsers and serializers is nothing mysterious that only Microsoft or some dedicated BizTalk tool vendor could provide. Extensibility is one of BizTalk's strengths, and these interfaces were designed for writing custom parsers and serializers for your own formats. You or one of your colleagues can write them if you need them.

CHAPTER 23

Writing Application Integration Components

With its support for HTTP, SMTP, file-system dropoffs and pickups (through receive functions), and especially its comprehensive Microsoft Message Queue (MSMQ) transport support, BizTalk is already well equipped for many enterprise integration scenarios.

However, using these transport options also requires appropriate endpoint support in the corporate applications that you want to integrate with each other or with external partners. Quite a few enterprise systems have document-driven external interfaces and do indeed communicate asynchronously through message queues (or employ simpler data-exchange mechanisms like export and import of data through files), and they can therefore directly integrate with BizTalk Server out of the box. But even more systems exist that use vendor-specific communication interfaces, which require custom adapters to be written for BizTalk integration. To create these integration bridges, you have basically two choices.

The first choice is that you can write wrappers or extensions for your corporate applications that will allow them to expose BizTalk-compatible endpoints. Such endpoints would have to "speak" one of the protocols supported by BizTalk Server and would need to be capable of extracting the required information from XML that BizTalk delivers on these endpoints. However, this option requires that you modify or extend your various systems and tailor them to fit BizTalk Server. The software packages that need to be integrated may be from several "software generations," may run on multiple platforms, and may not necessarily have been written within your own organization; therefore, this approach could be quite difficult to organize from a project standpoint and would certainly become quite expensive.

The second choice puts most of the integration work into a single place: BizTalk Server itself. The BizTalk SDK provides two alternative ways to implement Application Integration Components (AICs). You can configure AICs to use with BizTalk messaging ports instead of the built-in transport options, allowing you to integrate virtually any application into BizTalk Messaging, as long as you can somehow access the application programmatically from the Windows 2000 platform. This should be possible for almost every major independent software vendor (ISV)-supplied enterprise application on the market today, even if the application executes on a Solaris, HP-UX, AS/400, or z/OS (IBM's new moniker for OS/390) system.

For CORBA-based systems, you will be able to use a CORBA client on Windows; systems written in Java that use the native Java Remote Method Invocation (RMI) remote procedure call technology can use a Windows-based Java bridgehead, and so on. BizTalk Application Integration Components are written in COM. However, nothing technically stops you from writing a COM component that talks to a remote CORBA server, essentially wrapping all CORBA object request broker (ORB) calls that you need to get information to and back from the remote application in a single COM method. (Hand-coded COM wrappers for CORBA clients and CORBA wrappers for COM clients are typically much more stable and cheaper than any shrink-wrapped bridging solution.)

If you plan to use BizTalk as an Enterprise Application Integration (EAI) solution, this chapter is definitely for you.

WRITING SIMPLE INTEGRATION COMPONENTS

If the previous chapter about parsers and serializers scared you because of the sheer mass of code that you must write for such components, take heart. If you choose Microsoft Visual Basic for implementation, the simpler of the two variants of the BizTalk Application Integration Components has merely four lines of BizTalk-related code.

Indeed, integration components are one of the few extensibility interfaces in which using Visual Basic is a viable option. The BizTalk product architects' choice to make writing AICs really easy was very smart. Especially when you want to create integration solutions for a specific environment—where you do not need to provide user-manageable configuration options, but rather, you can hard-code most of the integration code—writing Visual Basic components is the most productive option, especially if you want to communicate with systems that already expose COM-programmable integration interfaces.

Simple Application Integration Components implement the IBTSAppIntegration interface, and the simplicity is really stunning. The interface has a single method that accepts an input string as its only argument and may (optionally) return a response document. The response will, however, become significant only if the port that uses the integration component is invoked synchronously (IInterchange::SubmitSync).

The following code is an excerpt taken directly from the Visual Basic version of the BizTalk SDK BTSAppIntegration sample, located in the .\SDK\Messaging Samples\BTSAppIntegration\VB path of your BizTalk product directory.

```
Implements IBTSAppIntegration

Public Function IBTSAppIntegration_ProcessMessage(ByVal bstrDocument As String) _
                                                  As String

    On Error GoTo ExecuteError

    Workload bstrDocument
    IBTSAppIntegration_ProcessMessage = "ack"

    Exit Function

ExecuteError:
    On Error GoTo 0
    Err.Raise Err.Number, Err.Source, _
            "The following Error was encountered: " & Err.Description
End Function 'IBTSAppIntegration_ProcessMessage
```

In the previous code, the private Workload function is not shown, which submits to an XLANG schedule the XML document received through the string argument of IBTSAppIntegration::ProcessMessage. However, the mechanism shown in the sample does illustrate quite well how BizTalk Messaging activates new schedules if you configure a port to submit documents to an XLANG schedule.

The relevant portion of the previous Visual Basic class code (besides the method signature) is really only the Implements IBTSAppIntegration line, which indicates that you are implementing that interface in this class. Before you can implement the interface, you must add to your project a reference to the Microsoft BizTalk Server Application Interface Components 1.0 Type Library. (In Visual Basic, select Tools | References.) The type library is preregistered on each BizTalk machine and should therefore be available in the components list shown in the Visual Basic References dialog box. If you are using a different tool or cannot find this entry, you can also import the btscomplib.tlb type library directly. It is located in the root of your BizTalk Server program directory.

To allow BizTalk to detect the component as a valid AIC and make it available as an option in Messaging Manager's Port Configuration Wizard, you must configure the category of the component. Unfortunately, this task is a bit tricky in Visual Basic because it does not provide the same type of built-in support for COM component categories as ATL does for C++.

You should therefore configure your Visual Basic project for binary component compatibility (this means that the component GUIDs will never change once you have compiled the project once), and create an extra registration file that will be used to enter the two required keys into the Registry. In the SDK sample directory, a sample registration file called affinity.reg contains the necessary keys:

```
REGEDIT4
[HKEY_CLASSES_ROOT\CLSID\{C963714C-143E-46B2-9661-1A74BE71C84F}\Implemented
Categories\{5C6C30E7-C66D-40E3-889D-08C5C3099E52}]
[HKEY_CLASSES_ROOT\CLSID\{C963714C-143E-46B2-9661-1A74BE71C84F}\Implemented
Categories\{BD193E1D-D7DC-4B7C-B9D2-92AE0344C836}]
```

The string {C963714C-143E-46B2-9661-1A74BE71C84F} is the component's class ID (and must be properly replaced for your new component), and the other GUIDs shown are the category identifiers. Once you have built a new component, the easiest way to figure out your component's class ID is to use the regedit.exe tool to look it up in the Windows Registry (under projectname.classname).

An alternate way to register is to use a small Windows Scripting Host script using the following routine, which takes the ProgID value of the component as an argument and does the registration for you:

```
Function RegisterAICClass(byval ProgID)
    Set WshShell = WScript.CreateObject("WScript.Shell")

    clsCat1ID = "{5C6C30E7-C66D-40E3-889D-08C5C3099E52}"
    clsCat2ID = "{BD193E1D-D7DC-4B7C-B9D2-92AE0344C836}"

    ClassID = WshShell.RegRead("HKCR\" & ProgID & "\Clsid\")
    call wshShell.RegWrite("HKCR\CLSID\" & ClassID & _
                        "\Implemented Categories\" & clsCat1ID & "\","")
    call wshShell.RegWrite("HKCR\CLSID\" & ClassID & _
                        "\Implemented Categories\" & clsCat2ID & "\","")
    RegisterAICClass = ClassID
    set wshShell = nothing
End Function
```

Once you have added the category settings to the Registry, the component shows up as a configuration option in the transport address settings for the Application Integration Component transport in Messaging Manager's Port Wizard. When you configure a port using this component, all documents that are routed through channels connected to that port will land in your Application Integration Component.

WRITING PIPELINE COMPONENTS

Quite often, simple components that have access only to the document data, that have no other information about the interchange, and that also cannot be configured on a per-port basis, will not be sufficient for your integration needs. Especially when you need to implement additional transport protocols or other general-purpose integration components rather than specifically tailored, hard-coded solutions for a specific case, you will require a lot more flexibility than the previous IBTSAppIntegration sample above provides.

For these more complex integration scenarios, BizTalk employs the pipeline-component programming model, which was introduced with Microsoft Site Server (the predecessor of Microsoft Commerce Server 2000). As you learned in Chapter 11, *pipeline components* are COM components that are sequentially invoked and that process the BizTalk transport dictionary by modifying its data or the documents contained therein. Application Integration Components are the last components in the document-processing pipeline, and their job is to deliver the documents (and possibly additional information from the transport dictionary) to the destination. The destination may be either some internal application or a remote server.

The following example does not serve to integrate an internal application, but rather, provides a fully functional AIC transport component for the FTP protocol. Although this component is provided only to illustrate the how-to, the error handling here is significantly better than in the serializer and parser examples, simply because the component is a bit shorter and it shows how proper error checking is done without introducing too much error-checking "pollution" in the code. Remember that you cannot be neurotic enough about checking error conditions in server code. The following code is already somewhat better, but it is still not production quality in a serious system environment. However, we need to balance between robustness and brevity for the purpose of illustrating the coding techniques so that you still get the idea of what the code is doing.

While pipeline components can be implemented in Visual Basic, we will again use C++ and ATL here because that will give us more low-level control over what we are doing. Also, the complete code and Visual Studio project are available on this book's web site. Therefore, we will focus on the main implementation files PipelineComp.h and PipelineComp.cpp and leave the rest up to you to explore. Like in the last chapter, we will start with the header file and discuss the code in more detail later in this section.

```
/////////////////////////////////////////////////////////////////////////////
// PipelineComp.h: Declaration of the CPipelineComp class
// Microsoft BizTalk Server 2000 Sample AIC Pipeline Component
// (c) 2001 Clemens F. Vasters - clemensv@newtelligence.com
```

```
//
// All rights reserved.

#ifndef __PIPELINECOMP_H_
#define __PIPELINECOMP_H_

#include "resource.h"       // Main symbols
#include <bts_sdk_guids.h>
#include <commerce.h>

///////////////////////////////////////////////////////////////////////
// CPipelineComp
class ATL_NO_VTABLE CPipelineComp :
    public CComObjectRootEx<CComMultiThreadModel>,
    public CComCoClass<CPipelineComp, &CLSID_PipelineComp>,
    public ISupportErrorInfo,
    public IDispatchImpl<IPipelineComponent,
                         &IID_IPipelineComponent,
                         &LIBID_PIPELINEAICLib>,
    public IDispatchImpl<IPipelineComponentAdmin,
                         &IID_IPipelineComponentAdmin,
                         &LIBID_PIPELINEAICLib>,
    public IDispatchImpl<IPipelineComponentDescription,
                         &IID_IPipelineComponentDescription,
                         &LIBID_PIPELINEAICLib>,
    public IPersistStreamInit
{
public:
    CComQIPtr<IDictionary> dictConfig;
public:
    CPipelineComp();
    CComQIPtr<IErrorInfo> ReportError(UINT error);
    CComQIPtr<IErrorInfo> ReportWin32Error(UINT error);

DECLARE_REGISTRY_RESOURCEID(IDR_PIPELINECOMP)
DECLARE_PROTECT_FINAL_CONSTRUCT()

BEGIN_COM_MAP(CPipelineComp)
    COM_INTERFACE_ENTRY(ISupportErrorInfo)
    COM_INTERFACE_ENTRY(IPipelineComponent)
    COM_INTERFACE_ENTRY(IPipelineComponentAdmin)
    COM_INTERFACE_ENTRY(IPipelineComponentDescription)
    COM_INTERFACE_ENTRY(IPersistStreamInit)
    COM_INTERFACE_ENTRY(IPersist)
END_COM_MAP()

BEGIN_CATEGORY_MAP(CPipelineComp)
```

```
    IMPLEMENTED_CATEGORY(CATID_BIZTALK_COMPONENT)
    IMPLEMENTED_CATEGORY(CATID_BIZTALK_AIC)
END_CATEGORY_MAP()

public:
// ISupportsErrorInfo
    STDMETHOD(InterfaceSupportsErrorInfo)(REFIID riid);
 // IPipelineComponent
    STDMETHOD(Execute)(IDispatch * pdispOrder, IDispatch * pdispContext,
                       LONG lFlags, LONG * plErrorLevel);
    STDMETHOD(EnableDesign)(BOOL fEnable);
// IPipelineComponentAdmin
    STDMETHOD(GetConfigData)(IDispatch * * ppDict);
    STDMETHOD(SetConfigData)(IDispatch * pDict);
// IPipelineComponentDescription
    STDMETHOD(ValuesRead)(VARIANT * pvar);
    STDMETHOD(ValuesWritten)(VARIANT * pvar);
    STDMETHOD(ContextValuesRead)(VARIANT * pvar);
// IPersist
    STDMETHOD(GetClassID)(GUID * pClassID);
// IPersistStreamInit
    STDMETHOD(IsDirty)();
    STDMETHOD(Load)(IStream * pstm);
    STDMETHOD(Save)(IStream * pstm, BOOL fClearDirty);
    STDMETHOD(GetSizeMax)(_ULARGE_INTEGER * pCbSize);
    STDMETHOD(InitNew)();
};

#endif //__PIPELINECOMP_H_
```

Like parsers and serializers (and also like the simple AIC shown earlier in this chapter), pipeline components must be registered with the proper category settings. Application integration components are registered with CATID_BIZTALK_COMPONENT and CATID_BIZTALK_AIC. As you can see from the class declaration, the pipeline component implements five interfaces:

▼ **ISupportErrorInfo**   The COM-compliant extended error-handling interface.

■ **IPersist/IPersistStreamInit**   The interface that supports saving the component's state to a stream. (This is optional and not currently used by BizTalk—code is not shown here.)

■ **IPipelineComponent**   The main pipeline component interface.

■ **IPipelineComponentAdmin**   The administration and configuration interface.

▲ **IPipelineComponentDescription**   The description interface that tells the client which values are read from or written to the transport dictionary. (Also optional and not currently used by BizTalk—code is not shown here.)

The only member variable of the component class is the configuration dictionary, which is initialized by the constructor as shown here:

```
CPipelineComp::CPipelineComp()
{
    // Initialize the configuration dictionary.
    dictConfig.CoCreateInstance(CLSID_CDictionary);
    dictConfig->put_Value(L"Server Address",CComVariant(L"localhost"));
    dictConfig->put_Value(L"Server Port",CComVariant(21));
    dictConfig->put_Value(L"Logon Anonymous",CComVariant(1));
    dictConfig->put_Value(L"Logon User",CComVariant(L""));
    dictConfig->put_Value(L"Logon Password",CComVariant(L""));
    dictConfig->put_Value(L"Target Filename",
                          CComVariant(L"/out%tracking_id%.dat"));
}
```

The configuration dictionary contains six preconfigured entries that are specific to this component, and they reflect the properties that we will need later to establish an FTP connection to an arbitrary host. The keys for the dictionary entries are somewhat atypical in that they contain spaces, but you will see at the very end of this section, where AIC configuration is covered, that there is a good reason to choose the property names in this way. Although it is rather obvious what role the entries play, we are going to look at them in a bit more detail anyway:

▼ **Server Address**   The name of a remote FTP server. The name can either be an IP address in dotted notation like 10.1.1.1, or a DNS entry like ftp.microsoft.com. The value for this entry must *not* be prefixed with a URI protocol prefix (ftp://). The default value is set to the local machine's localhost alias.

■ **Server Port**   The port number for the remote FTP server. The default IP port for FTP is 21; thus, this is preset as the default value.

■ **Logon Anonymous**   An integer (used as a Boolean expression) that indicates whether the server should be connected with anonymous FTP. If the value is set to 1 (which is the default), logon is performed anonymously; otherwise, an explicit username and password is required.

■ **Logon User**   The username to be used if explicit logon is required.

■ **Logon Password**   The password to be used if explicit logon is required.

▲ **Target Filename**   The name of the target file on the remote server. The filename can contain the %tracking_id%" escape that is supported by BizTalk's built-in file transport.

```
// IPipelineComponent
STDMETHODIMP CPipelineComp::EnableDesign(BOOL fEnable)
{
    return S_OK;
}


// IPipelineComponentAdmin
STDMETHODIMP CPipelineComp::GetConfigData(IDispatch * * ppDict)
{
    if (ppDict == NULL)
        return E_POINTER;

    return dictConfig.QueryInterface(ppDict);
}


STDMETHODIMP CPipelineComp::SetConfigData(IDispatch * pDict)
{
    dictConfig = pDict;
    return S_OK;
}
```

The methods *IPipelineComponent::EnableDesign()*, *IPipelineComponentAdmin::GetConfigData()*, and *IPipelineComponentAdmin::SetConfigData()*, are also related to the configuration dictionary. When the component is loaded while defining a port or the advanced properties of a channel, it is put into design mode by calling EnableDesign(). This method is always the first one that is called when the component is created by Messaging Manager (or any other designer). You would typically create a fresh set of configuration settings in this method. However, because we are always doing this in the constructor, we can simply return S_OK here. Whether you always initialize a new configuration dictionary in the constructor or wait for the EnableDesign call to do that is a matter of run-time optimization. The implementation choice made here will always guarantee that a valid configuration dictionary exists.

BizTalk Server calls the methods *GetConfigData()* and *SetConfigData()* to set and retrieve the component's configuration settings. The configuration settings for AICs are permanently stored in the bts_outputcfg table of the management database either in the field pritransconfdata (if the AIC is used for the primary transport) or sectransconfdata (if it is the secondary/backup transport). Our implementation of *SetConfigData()* simply replaces the local default configuration dictionary with the one BizTalk Server reads from the management database.

The *Execute()* method of the pipeline component does the actual work. The FTP functionality is built on the Windows Internet API (WinInet), and the code should be quite straightforward to understand. The working_data field of the transport dictionary that holds the document is evaluated and streamed into a temporary, local file, which is then handed over to the FtpPutFile API for transmission to the remote endpoint.

We do error checking at all stages (WinInet initialization, connect, and transmission), and if we run into an error condition, we set the appropriate COM error information by using the ReportWin32Error utility method.

```
STDMETHODIMP CPipelineComp::Execute(IDispatch * pdispOrder,
                                    IDispatch * pdispContext,
                                    LONG lFlags, LONG * plErrorLevel)
{
    HRESULT hRes;
    CComQIPtr<IDictionary> dictTransport(pdispOrder);
    CComVariant vWorkingData;

    if ( !dictTransport )
    {
        return E_INVALIDARG;
    }

    if ( SUCCEEDED( hRes = dictTransport->get_Value(L"working_data",
                                                    &vWorkingData )))
    {
        WCHAR TempFile[512];
        CComVariant serverAddress(L"");
        CComVariant serverPort(L"");
        CComVariant logonAnonymous(0);
        CComVariant logonUser(L"");
        CComVariant logonPassword(L"");
        CComVariant targetFilename(L"");
        CComVariant trackingId(L"");
        std::wstring outputFilename;
        const LPWSTR trackingIdPattern = L"%tracking_id%";

        // Obtain configuration from the configuration dictionary.
        dictConfig->get_Value(L"Server Address",&serverAddress);
        dictConfig->get_Value(L"Server Port",&serverPort);
        serverPort.ChangeType(VT_UI2);
        dictConfig->get_Value(L"Logon Anonymous",&logonAnonymous);
        logonAnonymous.ChangeType(VT_I4);
        dictConfig->get_Value(L"Logon User",&logonUser);
        dictConfig->get_Value(L"Logon Password",&logonPassword);
        dictConfig->get_Value(L"Target Filename", &targetFilename);
        dictTransport->get_Value(L"tracking_id", &trackingId);

        // Construct the target filename.
```

```
        outputFilename = targetFilename.bstrVal;
        std::wstring::size_type tp = outputFilename.find(trackingIdPattern);
        if ( tp != std::wstring::npos )
        {
            outputFilename.erase(tp,wcslen(trackingIdPattern));
            outputFilename.insert(tp,trackingId.bstrVal);
        }

        // If the login is anonymous, we use some default values
        // instead of the configured username and password.
        if ( logonAnonymous.lVal != 0 )
        {
            logonUser = L"anonymous";
            logonPassword = L"user@tempuri.org";
        }

        // The first thing we do is write the document to a temporary file
        // that we can hand over to the protocol function later.
        if ( GetTempFileNameW(L".", L"bzt", 0, TempFile ) != 0 )
        {
            HANDLE hf = CreateFileW(TempFile, GENERIC_WRITE,FILE_SHARE_
WRITE,0,CREATE_ALWAYS,FILE_ATTRIBUTE_NORMAL,
                                            0);
            if ( hf )
            {
                DWORD dw;

                if ( WriteFile(hf, vWorkingData.bstrVal,
                               wcslen(vWorkingData.bstrVal)*sizeof(WCHAR),
                               &dw, NULL) == 0 )
                {
                    UINT err=GetLastError();
                    hRes = HRESULT_FROM_WIN32(err);
                    SetErrorInfo(0,ReportWin32Error(err));
                }
                CloseHandle(hf);
            }
            else
            {
                UINT err=GetLastError();
                hRes = HRESULT_FROM_WIN32(err);
                SetErrorInfo(0,ReportWin32Error(err));
            }
        }
        else
        {
            UINT err=GetLastError();
            hRes = HRESULT_FROM_WIN32(err);
            SetErrorInfo(0,ReportWin32Error(err));
```

```
    }

    // If everything went well, we proceed to push the document to
    // the destination using the WinInet API.
    if ( SUCCEEDED( hRes ) )
    {

        HINTERNET hInternetSession;

        hInternetSession = InternetOpen(
                            _T("Microsoft BizTalk Server 2000"),   // Agent
                            INTERNET_OPEN_TYPE_PRECONFIG,      // Access
                            NULL,      // Proxy server (default)
                            NULL,      // Defaults
                            0);        // synchronous
        if ( hInternetSession )
        {
            HINTERNET hFTPSession;

            hFTPSession = ::InternetConnectW(
                    hInternetSession, // Internet handle
                    serverAddress.bstrVal, // Server we wish to connect to
                    serverPort.uintVal,    // Use appropriate port
                    logonUser.bstrVal,     // Username, can be NULL
                    logonPassword.bstrVal, // Password, can be NULL
                    INTERNET_SERVICE_FTP,  // Flag to use FTP services
                    0,                     // Flags (See SDK docs.)
                    (DWORD)0);             // See SDK docs.
            if ( hFTPSession )
            {
                BOOL bResult;

                bResult = ::FtpPutFileW(
                    hFTPSession, // Handle from an InternetConnect call.
                    TempFile,
                    outputFilename.c_str(),
                    FTP_TRANSFER_TYPE_BINARY,
                    0);
                if ( !bResult )
                {
                    UINT err=GetLastError();
                    hRes = HRESULT_FROM_WIN32(err);
                    SetErrorInfo(0,ReportWin32Error(err));
                }
                // Close connection.
                InternetCloseHandle(hFTPSession);
            }
            else
            {
                UINT err=GetLastError();
```

```
                hRes = HRESULT_FROM_WIN32(err);
                SetErrorInfo(0,ReportWin32Error(err));
            }

            // Close connection.
            InternetCloseHandle(hInternetSession);
        }
        else
        {
            UINT err=GetLastError();
            hRes = HRESULT_FROM_WIN32(err);
            SetErrorInfo(0,ReportWin32Error(err));
        }
    }
    DeleteFileW(TempFile);
}
else
{
    SetErrorInfo(0,ReportError(IDS_WORKING_DATA_NOT_FOUND));
}
return hRes;
}
```

The error-handling methods are simple but important. BizTalk picks up the IErrorInfo error information set through *SetErrorInfo()* and records the error in the event log. If the server address could not be resolved, the administrator will want to see a proper error message, and the COM error handling is the way to relay that information. No special magic is involved, except that the Win32 version explicitly loads the wininet.dll for the call to FormatMessage. This results in the appropriate message string being loaded from the DLL if the error condition was indeed found by one of the Internet functions.

```
CComQIPtr<IErrorInfo> CPipelineComp::ReportError(UINT error)
{
    CComPtr<ICreateErrorInfo> createErrorInfo;
    WCHAR wchBuffer[256]=L"";

    CreateErrorInfo(&createErrorInfo);
    createErrorInfo->SetGUID(IID_IPipelineComponent);
    createErrorInfo->SetSource(L"PipelineAIC.PipelineComp");
    LoadStringW(Module.GetResourceInstance(),error,wchBuffer,sizeof(wchBuffer));
    createErrorInfo->SetDescription(wchBuffer);
    return createErrorInfo;
}


CComQIPtr<IErrorInfo> CPipelineComp::ReportWin32Error(UINT error)
{
    CComPtr<ICreateErrorInfo> createErrorInfo;
    LPVOID lpMsgBuf;
```

```
HMODULE hLib;

CreateErrorInfo(&createErrorInfo);
createErrorInfo->SetGUID(IID_IPipelineComponent);
createErrorInfo->SetSource(L"PipelineAIC.PipelineComp");

hLib = LoadLibrary(_T("wininet.dll"));
FormatMessageW(
    FORMAT_MESSAGE_ALLOCATE_BUFFER |
    FORMAT_MESSAGE_FROM_SYSTEM | FORMAT_MESSAGE_FROM_HMODULE |
    FORMAT_MESSAGE_IGNORE_INSERTS,
    hLib,
    (error&0xffff),
    MAKELANGID(LANG_NEUTRAL, SUBLANG_DEFAULT), // Default language
    (LPWSTR) &lpMsgBuf,
    0,
    NULL
);
FreeLibrary(hLib);
createErrorInfo->SetDescription((WCHAR*)lpMsgBuf);
LocalFree( lpMsgBuf );

return createErrorInfo;
}
```

Although the component's code is now listed almost completely except for the two interfaces IPersistStreamInit and IPipelineComponentDescription (which are not shown here for brevity and because they exist for future use), something is still missing: the configuration user interface. At this point, there is still no way for the user to enter the server address and logon information in Messaging Manager. So how is this done?

The BizTalk documentation doesn't explain how to create component configuration user interfaces, and (at the time of writing) an MSDN Online article mentions it in only five lines. We want to display a configuration dialog box in the properties of the primary or secondary transport component of a channel (hidden behind the Advanced button on the Advanced page of the Channel Wizard) that uses this component. The dialog box should look like the one shown in the following illustration:

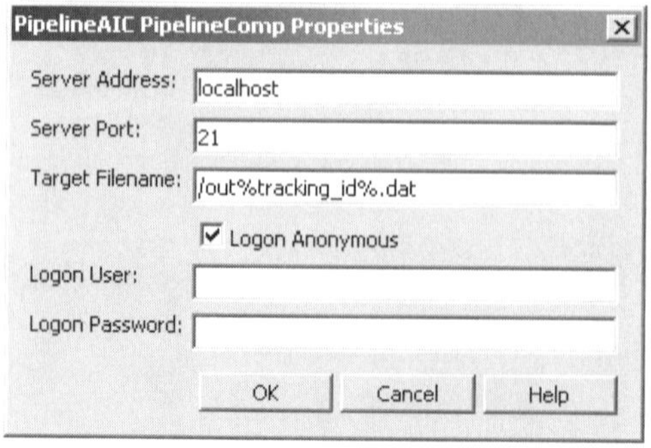

If you compare the names of the labels in this dialog box against the configuration dictionary of the component, you will find them to be identical. That is because there is indeed a direct link between those fields and the dictionary entries.

As you already know, Messaging Manager is an Active Server Pages (ASP) application whose core functionality runs remotely on the BizTalk Server machine you connect to. Therefore, the component configuration must also be executed remotely in some way. The configuration dialog box for the component must run on the server, but it must still be displayed on the client. To make this stunt work, BizTalk comes with a small ASP library that allows you to implement such hybrid configuration dialog boxes.

All BizTalk Server–configurable pipeline components that provide advanced configuration properties (this includes the HTTP, FILE, and SMTP transports) have a pair of ASP files that are located in the .\MessagingManager\pipeline product subdirectory. The name of the files reflects the component's programmatic identifier (ProgID), and by this naming convention, BizTalk is able to locate the proper file pair for the current component.

For instance, BizTalk's built-in HTTP transport component has the ProgID identifier BizTalk.SendHTTPX.1. The ASP file for the dialog box definition is BizTalk_SendHTTPX_1.asp, and the file that handles the dialog box results is called BizTalk_SendHTTPX_1_post.asp.

Our component's ProgID is PipelineAIC.PipelineComp.1; therefore, the proper names for our file pair are PipelineAIC_PipelineComp_1.asp and PipelineAIC_PipelineComp_1_post.asp.

The BizTalk ASP API is entirely undocumented and, as such, it is typically a use-at-your-own-risk thing with Microsoft products. However, figuring out the available functions should not be a problem if you browse through the ASP code in pe_global_edit.asp.

In our configuration dialog box, we need three text boxes: Server Name, Port, and Target Filename. And we need a check box for the anonymous flag, an edit box, and a password field for the user credentials.

As you can see from the following ASP code (this is the PipelineAIC_PipelineComp_1.asp file), specifying the required elements is fairly easy (once you know how). The labels must correspond exactly with the configuration dictionary of the AIC component because they are also used to set the properties. (Localization is not an option here.)

```
<%@ LANGUAGE = VBScript %>
<%
'----------------------------------------------------------------
'
'      PipelineAIC_PipelineComp_1.asp
'
'      PipelineAIC sample AIC for Microsoft BizTalk Server 2000
'      Copyright (C) Clemens F. Vasters 2001.  All rights reserved.
'
'----------------------------------------------------------------
```

```
%>

<!--#INCLUDE FILE="pe_edit_header.asp" -->

<%

        call InputText("Server Address")
        call InputText("Server Port")
        call InputText("Target Filename")
           call InputCheckbox("Logon Anonymous")
        call InputText("Logon User")
        call InputPassword("Logon Password")

%>

<!--#INCLUDE FILE="pe_edit_footer.asp" -->
```

The handling page (which ultimately sets the results) is similar, but it calls a different set of functions:

```
<%@ LANGUAGE = VBScript %>
<%
'------------------------------------------------------------------
'
'       PipelineAIC_PipelineComp_1_post.asp
'
'       PipelineAIC sample AIC for Microsoft BizTalk Server 2000
'       Copyright (C) Clemens F. Vasters 2001.  All rights reserved.
'
'------------------------------------------------------------------
%>

<!--#INCLUDE FILE="pe_global_edit.asp" -->
<%
        call GetInputText("Server Address", 0, bufsize_medium)
        call GetInputNumber("Server Port", 0, bufsize_medium)
        call GetInputText("Target Filename", 0, bufsize_medium)
        call GetCheckBox("Logon Anonymous")
        call GetInputText("Logon User", 0, bufsize_medium)
        call GetInputPassword("Logon Password", 0, bufsize_medium)
%>
<!--#INCLUDE FILE="pe_post_footer.asp" -->
```

Both files must be placed in the .\MessagingManager\pipeline directory. When the component is properly built and registered and these two files exist, you will have a working AIC for FTP.

CHAPTER 24

Writing Custom Functoid Containers

As you learned in Chapter 16, BizTalk Mapper is a powerful tool that lets you create complete mappings between virtually any pair of XML schemas. There are only a few scenarios in which you will not be able to create a mapping between two schemas by using "onboard" tools.

When mapping is difficult due to differences in schema complexity—like when you map multiple, conditional source record types to a single output record type—you can solve this problem in only one way: create specific output-only schemas and introduce redundancy replicating the output record type for each source type. However, you can easily address most problems by writing small script functions using the scripting functoid. Chapter 16 includes three examples of little scripts that helped us map codes between schemas of different document standards.

Over time, and depending on your typical mapping tasks (which depends on the document standards you work with), you will likely assemble a collection of little scripts for the Mapper. When you need to use custom scripting functoids regularly, you will find two idiosyncrasies greatly annoying: first, the script "editor" inside BizTalk Mapper is a simple edit field and, as such, is even less comfortable than Notepad; and second, you must store the functoid scripts somewhere else and copy them via the clipboard every time you need them—unless you create a custom functoid container.

Custom functoid containers are COM components that BizTalk Mapper automatically loads at startup and which extend the functoid palette. This extensibility mechanism allows you to create a collection of "canned" scripts that you can reuse for all the maps you create. BizTalk Mapper itself uses this extensibility interface for the built-in scripts, which are contained in the CannedFunctoids.CannedFunctoid.1 component that is implemented in CannedFunctoids.dll, located in the XML Tools subdirectory.

You can implement custom functoid containers in Visual Basic and C++ (and, of course, in any other language that allows you to implement COM components). This chapter shows a sample implementation for C++ using the Active Template Library (ATL). The BizTalk Server SDK contains another sample that implements a similar functoid, which is located in the subdirectory .\SDK\Messaging Samples\SampleFunctoid.

WRITING FUNCTOID SCRIPTS

Before we look at how to implement containers, we will first create a script that can be packaged as a general-purpose functoid.

If you flip back to Chapter 16 and look at Figure 16-13, you will remember that we used a group of four functoids to split a CCYYMMDD-formatted date into year, month, and day, and we reassembled them into ISO-compliant CCYY-MM-DD format with embedded dashes. We could have handled this more efficiently, of course, by using a single script functoid that implements the same functionality. However, due to the way UN/EDIFACT dates work, both variants (the group of functoids and a custom script) are potential sources for errors because they work only for the date format code 102, which represents CCYYMMDD formatting. Should the date field contain a date or time value in a different encoding, the functoid group or an equivalent script would produce an incorrect result.

It would indeed be much nicer to have a script that understands the format code contained in the third subfield of the UN/EDIFACT date/time (DTM) segment. Then we could use this code to translate the date or time information from the second subfield reliably into ISO format. And because that would be so nice to have, the code is provided right here:

```
Function ConvertEDIFACTDate( DateString, Code )
    Dim pat
    Dim c,y,m,d,q,h,mm,s,z,w,p
    Dim IL
    Dim time,period
    Dim res
    c=0:y=0:m=0:d=0:q=0:h=0:mm=0:s=0:z=0:w=0:p=0
    time=False:period=False
    res=""

    Select Case Code
        Case 101 pat = "YYMMDD"
        Case 102 pat = "CCYYMMDD"
        Case 103 pat = "YYWWD"
        Case 105 pat = "YYDDD"
        Case 106 pat = "MMDD"
        Case 107 pat = "DDD"
        Case 108 pat = "WW"
        Case 109 pat = "MM"
        Case 110 pat = "DD"
        Case 2 pat = "DDMMYY"
        Case 201 pat = "YYMMDDHHMM"
        Case 202 pat = "YYMMDDHHMMSS"
        Case 203 pat = "CCYYMMDDHHMM"
        Case 204 pat = "CCYYMMDDHHMMSS"
        Case 3 pat = "MMDDYY"
        Case 301 pat = "YYMMDDHHMMZZZ"
        Case 302 pat = "YYMMDDHHMMSSZZZ"
        Case 303 pat = "CCYYMMDDHHMMZZZ"
        Case 304 pat = "CCYYMMDDHHMMSSZZZ"
        Case 305 pat = "MMDDHHMM"
        Case 306 pat = "DDHHMM"
        Case 401 pat = "HHMM":time=True
        Case 402 pat = "HHMMSS":time=True
        Case 404 pat = "HHMMSSZZZ":time=True
        Case 405 pat = "MMMSS":time=True
```

```
      Case 501 pat = "HHMMHHMM":time=True
      Case 502 pat = "HHMMSS-HHMMSS":time=True
      Case 503 pat = "HHMMSSZZZ-HHMMSSZZZ":time=True
      Case 600 pat = "CC"
      Case 601 pat = "YY"
      Case 602 pat = "CCYY"
      Case 603 pat = "YYS"
      Case 604 pat = "CCYYS"
      Case 608 pat = "CCYYQ"
      Case 609 pat = "YYMM"
      Case 610 pat = "CCYYMM"
      Case 613 pat = "YYMMA"
      Case 614 pat = "CCYYMMA"
      Case 615 pat = "YYWW"
      Case 616 pat = "CCYYWW"
      Case 701 pat = "YY-YY"
      Case 702 pat = "CCYY-CCYY"
      Case 703 pat = "YYS-YYS"
      Case 704 pat = "CCYYS-CCYYS"
      Case 705 pat = "YYPYYP"
      Case 706 pat = "CCYYP-CCYYP"
      Case 707 pat = "YYQ-YYQ"
      Case 708 pat = "CCYYQ-CCYYQ"
      Case 709 pat = "YYMM-YYMM"
      Case 710 pat = "CCYYMM-CCYYMM"
      Case 711 pat = "CCYYMMDD-CCYYMMDD"
      Case 713 pat = "YYMMDDHHMM-YYMMDDHHMM"
      Case 715 pat = "YYWW-YYWW"
      Case 716 pat = "CCYYWW-CCYYWW"
      Case 717 pat = "YYMMDD-YYMMDD"
      Case 718 pat = "CCYYMMDD-CCYYMMDD"
      Case Else  Exit Function
   End Select

   For IL = 1 To Len(DateString)
      Select Case Mid(pat,IL,1)
         Case "Y"   y = y * 10 + CInt(Mid(DateString,IL,1)):time=False
         Case "M"   If time Then
                       mm = mm * 10 + CInt(Mid(DateString,IL,1))
                    Else
                       m = m * 10 + CInt(Mid(DateString,IL,1))
                    End If
```

```
        Case "D"    d = d * 10 + CInt(Mid(DateString,IL,1))
        Case "C"    c = c * 10 + CInt(Mid(DateString,IL,1))
        Case "H"    h = h * 10 + CInt(Mid(DateString,IL,1)):time=True
        Case "S"    s = s * 10 + CInt(Mid(DateString,IL,1))
        Case "Z"    z = z * 10 + CInt(Mid(DateString,IL,1))
        Case "W"    w = w * 10 + CInt(Mid(DateString,IL,1))
        Case "P"    p = p * 10 + CInt(Mid(DateString,IL,1))
        Case "-"    res = res & ConvertEDIFACTDate_
                      MkDate(c,y,m,d,h,mm,s,z)&"/"
                    c=0:y=0:m=0:d=0:q=0:h=0:mm=0:s=0:z=0:w=0:p=0
    End Select
  Next
  res = res & ConvertEDIFACTDate_MkDate(c,y,m,d,h,mm,s,z)
  ConvertEDIFACTDate = res
End Function

Function ConvertEDIFACTDate_FmtNum(d,a)
   If Not a And d = 0 Then
      ConvertEDIFACTDate_FmtNum = ""
   ElseIf d < 10 Then
      ConvertEDIFACTDate_FmtNum = "0" & CStr(d)
   Else
      ConvertEDIFACTDate_FmtNum = CStr(d)
   End If
End Function

Function ConvertEDIFACTDate_MkDate(c,y,m,d,h,mm,s,z)
    Dim dt
    If (y>0 Or m>0) And c=0 Then
      c=20
    End If
    dt = ConvertEDIFACTDate_FmtNum(c,False)&ConvertEDIFACTDate_
         FmtNum(y,c>0)
    If dt > "" Then
      dt = dt & "-"
    End If
    dt = dt & ConvertEDIFACTDate_FmtNum(m,False)
    If dt > "" Then
      dt = dt & "-"
    End If
    dt = dt & ConvertEDIFACTDate_FmtNum(d,False)
    If dt > "" Then
```

```
        dt = dt & "T"
    End If
    dt = dt & ConvertEDIFACTDate_FmtNum(h,True)
    If dt > "" Then
      dt = dt & ":"
    End If
    dt = dt & ConvertEDIFACTDate_FmtNum(mm,True)
    If dt > "" Then
      dt = dt & ":"
    End If
    dt = dt & ConvertEDIFACTDate_FmtNum(s,True)
    If z> 0 And dt > "" Then
      dt = dt & "."
    End If
    If z<>0 And z<100 Then
      dt = dt & "0"
    End If
    dt = dt & ConvertEDIFACTDate_FmtNum(z,False)
    ConvertEDIFACTDate_MkDate = dt
End Function
```

The function ConvertEDIFACTDate expects the UN/EDIFACT date expression from the second DTM subfield as its first argument and the format code from the third DTM subfield as its second argument.

The implementation will translate the code into a pattern string (which complies with the UN/EDIFACT S98B standard code list) and use that pattern string to drive the string translation. The implementation does not support the 8xx codes from the code list, which classify the date expression as a single number expression for counting semesters, trimesters, and other special periods. Expressions that describe time spans are converted into two ISO date expressions separated by a simple slash, time-only expressions are emitted as HH:MM:SS, date-only expressions as YYYY-MM-DD, and time stamps as YYYY-MM-DD'T'HH:MM:SS.

ConvertEDIFACTDate() uses two utility functions, ConvertEDIFACTDate_FmtNum and ConvertEDIFACTDate_MkDate, which implement the formatting of numbers and the actual date expression. The function names are prefixed with the main function's name to avoid name collisions in the map when used with other functoids.

This brings up an important issue to consider with functoid scripts: all functoid functions must be uniquely named within the scope of a document map. This makes choosing function names a bit difficult when you are using functoids from multiple sources because there is no coordination and no guideline for naming functoid script functions; also, VBScript does not support namespaces, which could help disambiguate the functions. The only real way around this problem is to use long and descriptive names, which reduces the risk of clashing with other functions. Another way is to simulate namespaces by using prefixes derived from an Internet domain name, like com_osborne_ConvertDate().

IMPLEMENTING FUNCTOID CONTAINERS

Functoid containers implement the IFunctoid interface, which is defined in the functoid.idl file located in the BizTalk SDK Include file directory. The IFunctoid interface has three methods and exposes two properties:

▼ **Version property** The Version property is implemented with the *get_Version* access method and is therefore read-only. The method must return a version number for the functoid container. If the functoid container is updated, the version number should be changed. The SDK does not specify further guidelines for the version number, so you should start at 1 and increment the number as you are adding, removing, or changing scripts. The Mapper will use the version number to determine whether the installed functoid container is compatible with scripts already existing in a map.

■ **FunctionsCount property** This property is also read-only and implemented with the *get_FunctionsCount* access method. This property returns the number of functoids that the container provides.

■ *GetFunctionDescripter* **method** This method is called by BizTalk Mapper to retrieve a detailed description about each script. The Mapper will call this method once for every function at startup time, looping *FunctionsCount* times. The first argument is the zero-based index of the script for which information is requested.

■ *GetFunctionParameter* **method** The Mapper calls this method once for each script argument and for the return value when a functoid is placed on the grid. The method returns an information flag (connection type) that indicates which type of connection is valid for that argument (or the return value). This allows you to control whether the argument can be connected to a field, a record, or other functoids.

▲ *GetScriptBuffer* **method** This method is called when the Mapper needs to retrieve the actual scripting code. The number of connected functoid parameters is passed to this method, so you can do on-the-fly adjustments of the scripting code if necessary. This is the technique by which some of the internal functoids allow an arbitrary number of input parameters to be connected to them on the mapping grid.

For the C++ version, we will place the scripting code into an external file, GetEDIFACTDate.vbs, and include the file in the component as a binary resource at compile time. This allows us to keep the script separate and maintain it as part of the project without having to embed it in the C++ code as a string. For the resource file, we use a custom resource type SCRIPT, which is introduced for this project. In the resource file that is part of the Visual C++ project (*.rc extension), the inclusion of the external file is simply expressed as the following:

```
IDR_CONVERTEDIFACTDATE  SCRIPT  DISCARDABLE     "GetEDIFACTDate.vbs"
```

Visual Studio's resource editor manages the external resource files, so you won't need to insert this line manually. Just go to the resource view in Visual Studio, choose the Import option from the context menu, select the external file, and enter **SCRIPT** as the resource type in the dialog box that appears.

Now the implementation of the functoid container is pretty straightforward. Because the ATL implementation of the container class is pleasantly short, the entire code is implemented inline in the class declaration (C# style):

```
// MyFunctoids.h : Declaration of the CMyFunctoids

#ifndef __MYFUNCTOIDS_H_
#define __MYFUNCTOIDS_H_

#include "resource.h"        // main symbols
#include <bts_sdk_guids.h>


/////////////////////////////////////////////////////////////////////////////
// CMyFunctoids
class ATL_NO_VTABLE CMyFunctoids :
   public CComObjectRootEx<CComSingleThreadModel>,
   public CComCoClass<CMyFunctoids, &CLSID_MyFunctoids>,
   public IDispatchImpl<IFunctoid, &IID_IFunctoid, &LIBID_MYFUNCTOIDCANLib>
{
public:
   CMyFunctoids()
   {
   }

DECLARE_REGISTRY_RESOURCEID(IDR_MYFUNCTOIDS)

DECLARE_PROTECT_FINAL_CONSTRUCT()

BEGIN_CATEGORY_MAP(CMyFunctoids)
     IMPLEMENTED_CATEGORY(CATID_MapEditFunctoids)
END_CATEGORY_MAP()

BEGIN_COM_MAP(CMyFunctoids)
   COM_INTERFACE_ENTRY(IDispatch)
   COM_INTERFACE_ENTRY(IFunctoid)
END_COM_MAP()

// IMyFunctoids
public:
// IFunctoid
   STDMETHOD(get_Version)(LONG * pVersion)
   {
      if (pVersion == NULL)
         return E_POINTER;
```

```
   *pVersion = 0x0001;
   return S_OK;
}
STDMETHOD(get_FunctionsCount)(LONG * plCount)
{
   if (plCount == NULL)
      return E_POINTER;

   *plCount = 1;
   return S_OK;
}
STDMETHOD(GetFunctionDescripter)(LONG lIndex, FUNC_CATEGORY * pFuncCategory,
                                 SCRIPT_CATEGORY * pScriptCategory,
                                 FUNC_TYPE * pFuncType, BSTR * pbstrName,
                                 BSTR * pbstrTooltip, LONG * plBitmapID,
                                 LONG * plParmCount, LONG * pFuncId)
{
   if (pFuncCategory == NULL)
      return E_POINTER;
   if (pScriptCategory == NULL)
      return E_POINTER;
   if (pFuncType == NULL)
      return E_POINTER;
   if (pbstrName == NULL)
      return E_POINTER;
   if (pbstrTooltip == NULL)
      return E_POINTER;
   if (plBitmapID == NULL)
      return E_POINTER;
   if (plParmCount == NULL)
      return E_POINTER;
   if (pFuncId == NULL)
      return E_POINTER;

   switch ( lIndex )
   {
   case 0:
      {
         *pFuncCategory = FUNC_CATEGORY_DATETIME_FMT;
         *pScriptCategory = SCRIPT_CATEGORY_VBSCRIPT;
         *pFuncType = FUNC_TYPE_SCRIPTOR;
         *pbstrName = SysAllocString(L"Convert EDIFACT Date");
         *pbstrTooltip = SysAllocString(
                 L"Takes the DTA segment's period expression as "
                 L"first and the format qualifier as second "
                 L"argument and formats the date as XML compliant "
                 L"ISO date");
         *plBitmapID = 300;
         *plParmCount = 2;
```

```
          *pFuncId = 1500;
          return S_OK;
      }
      break;
   default:
      return E_INVALIDARG;
   }
}

STDMETHOD(GetFunctionParameter)(LONG funcId, LONG lParameter,
                                LONG * plConnectionType)
{
   if (plConnectionType == NULL)
      return E_POINTER;

   switch ( funcId )
   {
   case 1500:

      // The return value can never point to records.
      if ( lParameter == -1 )
         *plConnectionType = CONNECT_TYPE_ALL_EXCEPT_RECORD;
      // The arguments cannot be records either.
      else
         *plConnectionType = CONNECT_TYPE_ALL_EXCEPT_RECORD;
      return S_OK;
   default:
      return E_INVALIDARG;
   }
   return S_OK;
}

STDMETHOD(GetScriptBuffer)(LONG cFuncId, LONG lInputParameters,
                           BSTR * pbstrScriptBuffer)
{
   HRESULT hRes = E_FAIL;

   if (pbstrScriptBuffer == NULL)
      return E_POINTER;

   switch ( cFuncId )
   {
   case 1500:
      {
         HRSRC resource = FindResource(_Module.GetResourceInstance(),
                                  MAKEINTRESOURCE(IDR_CONVERTEDIFACTDATE),
                                       "SCRIPT");
         if ( resource )
```

```
        {
            HGLOBAL block = LoadResource(_Module.GetResourceInstance(),
                                      resource);
            if ( block )
            {
                LPSTR script = (LPSTR)LockResource(block);
                DWORD size = SizeofResource(_Module.GetResourceInstance(),
                                          resource);

                *pbstrScriptBuffer = SysAllocStringLen(NULL,size+1);
                MultiByteToWideChar(CP_ACP,0,script,
                                    size,*pbstrScriptBuffer,size);
                (*pbstrScriptBuffer)[size]=0x00;
                hRes = S_OK;
            }
        }
    }
    break;
default:
    hRes = E_INVALIDARG;
}
return hRes;
}
};


#endif //__MYFUNCTOIDS_H_
```

Although most of the code should be quite obvious, the information returned by *GetFunctionDescripter* needs some more explanation. The script that is embedded in our sample returns the following values:

```
*pFuncCategory = FUNC_CATEGORY_DATETIME_FMT;
*pScriptCategory = SCRIPT_CATEGORY_VBSCRIPT;
*pFuncType = FUNC_TYPE_SCRIPTOR;
*pbstrName = SysAllocString(L"Convert EDIFACT Date");
*pbstrTooltip = SysAllocString(
        L"Takes the DTA segment's period expression as "
        L"first and the format qualifier as second "
        L"argument and formats the date as XML compliant "
        L"ISO date");
*plBitmapID = 300;
*plParmCount = 2;
*pFuncId = 1500;
```

The *FuncCategory* method represents the tab in the functoid palette window on which the functoid should be placed. In our case, the appropriate locations are the Date/Time functoids, which are identified by the FUNC_CATEGORY_DATETIME_FMT constant. The script category tells the Mapper which language is used for implementation. The possible options are XSLT, JScript, and VBScript, although the first BizTalk release supports only VBScript. Because our script is consequently written in VBScript, the value SCRIPT_CATEGORY_VBSCRIPT applies. The type of the functoid is a script, and this is indicated by the FuncType value FUNC_TYPE_SCRIPTOR. Don't confuse these categories with the COM categories; this is just an internal categorization of functoid types. Also, these categories are fixed—you cannot add custom tabs to the functoid palette at this point.

The flag and category values and the ParmCount value that is set to the number of arguments for this functoid are nothing special. Things are pretty hairy with the BitmapID and FuncID values, though.

The function identifier (FuncID) must be unique among *all* custom functoids. The function identifier is used for all calls to *GetFunctionParameter* and *GetScriptBuffer* instead of the zero-based index that is used with *GetFunctionDescripter*, and it also identifies the function within the document map. Consequently, this number can clash neither with the function identifiers of the built-in BizTalk Mapper functoids nor with any other functoids written by you or supplied by third parties. All internal functoids use function identifiers below 1000. Our example script has function identifier 1500, which is an entirely arbitrary choice. If you expect to have many functoid containers and want to avoid number clashes, think of some arbitrary high number like 5244917 (but don't use this one), and take that as a seed for your function identifiers. That is as much as you can do about this problem. Good luck.

Notice that the method also returns a BitmapID value, but that the class has no interface to return a bitmap reference to BizTalk Mapper. Because this is a COM component, you would expect there to be either an extra interface (like IDataObject) or a special method that the Mapper would call to obtain the bitmap for the functoid palette. Instead, the only reference that is handed out is this identifier.

What BizTalk Mapper does with this bitmap identifier is, unfortunately, a blatant violation of all rules of well-behaved component systems, and this "hack" makes it equally impossible to write custom functoid containers in .NET-managed code (Visual Basic.NET or C#). The Mapper figures out the DLL that implements the IFunctoid interface and grabs the bitmap straight from that DLL's resource table using the exported bitmap identifier. If the resource is either not present or the functoid container is not contained in a standard Win32 PE file with a classic resource table (which is not the case for .NET assemblies and, hence, poses the problem), the functoid container will fail to load.

Therefore, our project contains a bitmap resource with this identifier (300), although it is not actively referenced by the code. The bitmap is the image that is displayed on the functoid palette and the grid representing the script.

PART VII

Appendixes

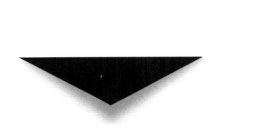

APPENDIX A

BizTalk Schema

T he BizTalk Schema language as it is implemented in BizTalk Server 2000 builds on XDR and allows you to augment document definitions with additional attributes and elements required for some advanced BizTalk features. The following table lists the BizTalk extension attributes for XDR. (BizTalk Schema is officially undocumented, so this list is not necessarily complete.)

NOTE: The BizTalk extension attributes must be namespace-qualified by using the URI urn:schemas-microsoft-com:BizTalkServer, which you must specify on the Schema element. BizTalk Schema furthermore adds two elements, FieldInfo and RecordInfo, to XDR (both namespace-qualified). FieldInfo is nested within each field definition tag (AttributeType or ElementType), and RecordInfo is nested within the ElementType tag for a record.

Attribute	Applies to Element	Description
root_reference	Schema	The attribute that defines the root element.
standard	Schema	The document standard that this schema describes. May be *XML*, *X12*, *EDIFACT*, or *CUSTOM*.
BizTalkServerEditorTool_ Version	Schema	The BizTalk Editor version with which this schema was created— 1.0 for the BizTalk Server 2000 release version.
is_envelope	Schema	Values: *yes/no*. The attribute that determines whether this schema defines a BizTalk-compatible envelope.
target_namespace	Schema	The default namespace URI for documents based on this schema.
schema_type	Schema	The schema document type. If the standard is X12 and the schema describes a variant of the purchase order, this attribute contains 850; for the EDIFACT invoice, this attribute contains INVOIC.
version	Schema	The version of this schema.

Attribute	Applies to Element	Description
standards_version	Schema	The version of the base standard. For X12, this may be 4010; for EDIFACT, it may be D98B.
def_record_delim	Schema	The default record delimiter character expressed in C-style hex code (e.g., 0xd). Applies only if the standard is EDIFACT, X12, or CUSTOM.
def_field_delim	Schema	The default field delimiter character expressed in C-style hex code (e.g., 0x3a). Applies only if the standard is EDIFACT, X12, or CUSTOM.
def_subfield_delim	Schema	The default subfield delimiter character expressed in C-style hex code (e.g., 0x3a). Applies only if the standard is EDIFACT, X12, or CUSTOM.
def_escape_char	Schema	The default escape character expressed in C-style hex code (e.g., 0x3a). Applies only if the standard is EDIFACT, X12, or CUSTOM.
edi_datatype	FieldInfo	The native data type in the EDI format described.
justification	FieldInfo	The justification of the field (*left*, *right*).
format	FieldInfo	The format specification for date/time values or other types that need type patterns.
codelist	FieldInfo	The applicable code list for the standard.
required	FieldInfo	The attribute that indicates whether the field is required.

Attribute	Applies to Element	Description
pad_char	FieldInfo	The pad character to use to fill up the field to the field length for positional structures.
minLength_withPad	FieldInfo	The minimum length of the field, including padding.
wrap_char	FieldInfo	The character used to wrap the data. This may be quotation marks for character data in some flatfile formats. This attribute is not included in the parsed data.
structure	RecordInfo	The attribute that indicates the structure of the record. May be *delimited* or *positional*.
tag_name	RecordInfo	The source tag identifier in the native document format.
tag_position	RecordInfo	The start position of the source tag identifier within a record. Counting starts at 1.
delimiter_type	RecordInfo	The type of delimiter to use. May be *inherit_record*, *inherit_field*, or *inherit_subfield*, to use the defaults specified on the document, or *hex*, to use a distinct hexadecimal character number in *delimiter_value*.
delimiter_value	RecordInfo	This attribute contains a hexadecimal number representing the delimiter character if *delimiter_type* is hex.
field_order	RecordInfo	The order of the fields relative to the delimiter: prefix means that there is a leading delimiter, postfix means that there is a trailing delimiter, and infix means that delimiters occur only within the record.
escape_type	RecordInfo	Values: *hex* or *inherit_escape* to use the default.

Attribute	Applies to Element	Description
escape_value	RecordInfo	The attribute that contains a hexadecimal number representing the escape character if *escape_type* is hex.
count_ignore	RecordInfo	Values: *yes* or *no* for whether to ignore the record counter while parsing.
append_newline	RecordInfo	Values: *yes* or *no* for whether the serializer will automatically append a newline character.
skip_CR	RecordInfo	Values: *yes* or *no* for whether the parser will skip any carriage-return character found in the input stream.
skip_LF	RecordInfo	Values: *yes* or *no* for whether the parser will skip any linefeed character found in the input stream.

APPENDIX B

ISO 6523 Codes

This table contains the ISO 6523 organization codes used for BizTalk Organizations.

Code	Authority	Description
1	Data Universal Numbering System (DUNS)	The partner identification code assigned by Dun & Bradstreet.
3	Federal Maritime Commission	Numbers assigned by the U.S. Federal Maritime Commission.
4	International Air Transport Association (IATA)	The partner identification code assigned by the International Air Transport Association.
5	Institut National de la Statistique et des Etudes Economiques (INSEE)—Systeme Informatique du Repertoire des entreprises et de leurs ETablissements (SIRET)	The French national statistics institute.
8	Uniform Code Council Communications Identifier (UCC Communications ID)	A ten-digit code used to uniquely identify physical and logical locations.
9	Data Universal Numbering System (DUNS) with four-digit suffix	The partner identification code assigned by Dun & Bradstreet with a four-digit suffix.
10	Department of Defense (DoD)	Numbers assigned by the U.S. Department of Defense.
11	Drug Enforcement Administration (DEA)	Numbers assigned by the U.S. Drug Enforcement Administration.
12	Telephone number	The partner identification code that corresponds to the partner telephone number.
13	UCS Code	UCS Code assigned identifiers.
14	European Article Numbering Association (EAN)	The partner identification code assigned by the European Article Numbering Association.
16	Dun & Bradstreet DUNS Number plus four-character suffix	The partner identification code assigned by Dun & Bradstreet with the four-character suffix.

Code	Authority	Description
17	American Bankers Association	Numbers assigned by the American Bankers Association.
18	Automotive Industry Action Group (AIAG)	The partner identification code assigned by the Automotive Industry Action Group.
20	Health Industry Number	Numbers assigned by the Health Industry Association of America (HIAA).
22	Institut National de la Statistique et des Etudes Economiques (INSEE)—Systeme Informatique du Repertoire des ENtreprises (et de leurs etablissements) (SIREN)	The French national statistics institute.
27	Health Care Financing Administration Carrier ID	Officially assigned Health Care Financing Administration Carrier identifier.
28	Health Care Financing Administration Fiscal Intermediary	Officially assigned Health Care Financing Administration Fiscal Intermediary identifier.
29	Health Care Financing Administration Medicare Provider	Officially assigned Health Care Financing Administration Medicare Provider identifier.
30	ISO 6523: Organization identification	The partner identification code specified in ISO 6523 (Structures for organization identification).
31	Deutsches Institut für Normung (DIN)	Numbers assigned by the German standardization institute.
32	U.S. Federal Employer Identification Number	The United States Department of Commerce assigned employer identification.
33	Bundesversicherungsanstalt für Angestellte (BfA)	The German social security association.
34	National Statistical Agency	The partner identification code assigned by a national statistical agency.
51	General Electric Information Services (GEIS)	The partner identification code assigned by General Electric Information Services.

Code	Authority	Description
52	IBM Network Services (INS)	The partner identification code assigned by IBM Network Services.
53	Datenzentrale des Einzelhandels	The German data center for retail trade.
54	Bundesverband der Deutschen Baustoffhändler	The German building material trade association.
55	Bank identifier code	The partner identification code corresponds to the partner bank identification code.
57	Korea Trade Network Services (KTNet)	The partner identification code assigned by Korea Trade Network Services.
58	Universal Postal Union (UPU)	The partner identification code assigned by the Universal Postal Union.
59	Organization for Data Exchange through Tele-Transmission in Europe (ODETTE)	The European automotive industry project.
61	Standard Carrier Alpha Code (SCAC)	The directory of standard multimodal carriers and tariff agent codes. The SCAC lists and codes transportation companies.
63	Electronic Commerce Australia (ECA)	The Australian association for electronic commerce.
65	TELEBOX 400 (Deutsche Telekom)	The German telecommunications service.
80	National Health Service (NHS)	The United Kingdom National Health Service.
82	Statens Teleforvaltning	The Norwegian telecommunications regulatory authority (NTRA).
84	Athens Chamber of Commerce	The Greek Chamber of Commerce.
85	Swiss Chamber of Commerce	The Swiss Chamber of Commerce.
86	U.S. Council for International Business	The United States Council for International Business.
87	National Federation of Chambers of Commerce and Industry	The Belgium National Federation of Chambers of Commerce and Industry.

Code	Authority	Description
89	Association of British Chambers of Commerce	The association of British Chambers of Commerce.
90	Societe Internationale de Telecommunications Aeronautiques (SITA)	SITA (Societe Internationale de Telecommunications Aeronautiques).
91	Assigned by seller or seller's agent	The partner identification code assigned by the seller or seller's agent.
92	Assigned by buyer or buyer's agent	The partner identification code assigned by the buyer or buyer's agent.
103	TW, Trade-van	The EDI value added network (VAN) service center for customs, transport, and insurance in national and international trade.
128	CH, BCNR (Swiss Clearing Bank Number)	The code for the identification of a Swiss clearing bank as a sender and/or receiver of an electronic message.
129	CH, Swiss Business Partner Identification (BPI)	The code for the identification of a corporate or a Swiss nonclearing bank as a sender and/or receiver of an electronic message.
144	US, Department of Defense Activity Address Code (DoDAAC)	The code assigned to uniquely identify all military units in the United States Department of Defense.
145	FR, Direction Generale de la Comptabilite Publique (DGCP)	The code assigned by the French public accounting office.
146	FR, Direction Generale des Imports (DGI)	The code assigned by the French taxation authority.
147	JP, Japan Information Processing Development Corporation/Electronic Commerce Promotion Center (JIPDEC/ECPC)	The partner identification code that is registered with JIPDEC/ECPC.
148	International Telecommunications Union (ITU) data network identification code (DNIC)	The data network identification code assigned by the ITU.
ZZ	Mutually defined	Mutually defined identifier used between trading partners.

Index

References to figures and illustrations are in italics.

7±2 rule, 263

 A

Abort shape, 159
Accredited Standards Committee (ASC) X12. *See* ANSI X12
ACID, 310, 311
acknowledgments, sending, 436–437
Action shape, 158
actions, 166
Active Directory Services, 75–76
Active Server Pages. *See* ASP
ActiveX, 14
      See also COM
AddDocument( ) method, 244
adm_Group, 208–211
administration database tables, 207–217

Administrator tool, 193–196
adm_Parser, 212–213
adm_ReceiveService, 213–216
adm_Server, 211–212
adm_TimeStamps, 216–217
ADO.NET, 72
      and XML support for Microsoft .NET Framework, 70
      and XSD, 57
Advanced Query Builder, 528–529
AIAG, 31
American National Standards Institute (ANSI) X12. *See* ANSI X12
analysis
      object-oriented, 263
      requirements analysis, 269–270
      short-track analysis principles, 263–268
ANSI ASC X.121 standard. *See* ANSI X12

ANSI X12, 6–7, 34–35
    attributes, 36–37
    composite data structure, 36
    data elements, 35–36
    data types, 36
    functional groups, 37
    interchange, 37
    loops, 37
    permissible character set, 40
    routing model, *38*
    segments, 36–37
    semantics, 38
    syntax and structure, 35–38
    transaction sets, 37, 38–40
APL, 71
Application Center 2000, 76
Application Integration Components
    (AIC), 130–131, 592
    configuring the category of the
        component, 594
    error checking, 600–603
    preconfigured entries, 598
    writing pipeline components,
        595–606
    writing simple integration
        components, 593–595
applications
    defining, 405–407
    identifiers, 127–128
architecture, 204–206
    Orchestration, 248–258
ASC X12. *See* ANSI X12
ASP, 74, 605
ASP.NET, 70, 72
ATTLIST keyword, 52
attribute, in XDR, 55–56
attributes
    actor, 111
    in ANSI X12, 36–37
AttributeType element, in XDR, 55
authentication, 472–475
    inbound transport-level sender,
        473–474
    outbound transport-level, 474–475

authenticity of data origin, 25–26
authorization, 472–475
    inbound transport-level sender,
        473–474
automated deployment, 483–486
Automobile Industry Action Group. *See*
    AIAG
axis, 59–60

 B

B2B data exchange, 18–32
    centralized data processing, 29
    digital collaboration, 29–30
    document standardization, 31–32
    failure of marketed Internet B2B
        vision, 18–22
    and flexibility, 28
    heterogeneous system landscapes,
        28–30
    and integration of mobile devices, 30
    redefining "document," 26–28
    security and electronic
        signatures, 23–26
    Web services, 22–23
bandwidth, 469
bare names, 62
batching, 578
Baudot, Phillippe, 6
Begin shape, 157, 276
binding, 253
BizTalk Framework, 108–110
    business process correlation, 122–123
    document catalog, 117–118
    document identification and
        properties, 114–116
    document source and destination,
        116–117
    messages, 113–123
    requesting and returning receipts,
        118–122
    SOAP, 110–113
    See also BizTalk.org

BizTalk Framework Specification, 108
BizTalk Framework Toolkit, 108–109
BizTalk Orchestration Designer. *See*
  Orchestration Designer
BizTalk Server 2000
    Administrator, 87, 193–196
    automated deployment, 483–486
    bandwidth, 469
    channels, 133–137
    Configuration Assistant, 191–193,
      483–486
    Configuration Object Model, 207
    Direct Integration tool, 193, *194*
    disk performance, 468–469
    distribution lists, 138
    document-processing pipeline
      components, 234–245
    document tracking database, 234
    Document Tracking tool, 87, 196–199
    editions, 86–89
    Editor, 87, 176–181, 318–320
    encryption, signatures, and
      encoding, 132–133
    envelopes, 132
    installing, 89–101
    Interchange Application, 144–148,
      477–483
    and Internet Information Server, 74
    management database, 206–233
    Mapper utility, 87, 134–413,
      181–184, 243, 360
    memory usage and processor
      requirements, 466–468
    Messaging Manager, 87, 184–193,
      404–405
    Messaging service, 5, 87, 140–144
    network performance, 469
    Orchestration, 5, 87–88
    organizations and applications,
      126–128
    performance considerations, 465–469
    planning deployments, 464–483
    ports, 129–133
    scaling systems, 469–472
    security considerations, 472–483
    shared queue database, 143, 234
    what it does and doesn't do, 84–86
BizTalkChannel object, 494
BizTalkConfig object, 490–492
    See also Configuration Object Model
BizTalkDocument object, 494
BizTalkEnvelope object, 494
BizTalk.org, 32, 107–108
BizTalkOrganization object, 494
BizTalkPort object, 493, 494
BizTalkPortGroup object, 494
bts_alias, 223
bts_application, 224
bts_channel, 224–227
bts_controlnumber, 228
bts_document, 228
bts_envelope, 229
bts_organization, 229–230
bts_outputconfig, 230–232
bts_port, 218–223
bts_portgroup, 232
bts_portgroups, 232–233
bts_xmlshare, 233
buffer overflows, 475
business-to-business data exchange. *See*
    B2B data exchange
bytecode, 13

 C

C#, 71
CanonicalReceipt.xml file, 437
cardinalities, verifying record, 445
Castrum Novaesium, 4–5
CDATA data type, 52
CDictionary object, 499–500
centralized data processing, 29
CERN, 10
certificates, support for, 431–432
channels, 133–137
    channel selection stage errors,
      457–458

creating, 411–419
defined, 133
Document Definitions Properties
   dialog box, 414–416, *417*
dynamic, 302
filters, 153
loopback, 303–305, 309–310
managing, 498–502
open-source, 151, 411
selection, 149–153
character sets, for ANSI X12, 40
COBOL, 71
CoGetObject( ) function, 252, 253
collaboration in the connected
  economy, 29–30
COM, 12, 14
    as the foundation for corporate
      development tools, 30
    monikers, 251–254
    See also COM+
COM Transaction Integrator, 78
COM+, 14, 145
    and BizTalk Interchange
      Application, 144
    See also COM
COM+ Component Services, 74–75
COM+ Transactions, 311
Commerce Server 2000, 78
commitment receipt, 120–122
common language runtime, 70–71
Common Object Request Broker
  Architecture. *See* CORBA
communities, 107–108
complexity, managing, 263–270
Component Object Model. *See* COM
components, 167
composite data elements, in
  UN/EDIFACT standard, 42
composite data structure, in ANSI X12, 36
COMTI, 78
Configuration Assistant, 191–193, 483–486
Configuration Object Model, 207, 488–490
    advanced configuration options,
      501–502

BizTalkChannel object, 494
BizTalkConfig object, 490–492
BizTalkDocument object, 494
BizTalkEnvelope object, 494
BizTalkOrganization object, 494
BizTalkPort object, 493, 494
BizTalkPortGroup object, 494
CDictionary object, 499–500
configuring transports, 498
creating and loading documents,
  499–500
IBizTalkBase interface, 493
loading and creating
  organizations, 495–498
managing channels, 498–502
managing ports, 492–498
connected economy, 19
constants, 255–257, 310, *311*
  setting as functoid arguments, *392*
context, 74–75
ContextValuesRead( ) method, 239
CORBA, 12–13
    as the foundation for corporate
      development tools, 30
    Object Transaction System (OTS), 75
crackers. *See* intrusion detection
  and defense
CryptoAPI, 467
cursus publicus, 4–5
custom preprocessors, 144

 D

data elements
  in ANSI X12, 35–36
  in UN/EDIFACT standard, 41–42
data flow mappings, 306–307
data types
  in ANSI X12, 36
  assigning precise, 444
  field data types, 327–330
  incompatible, 366

string formats for field values corresponding to, 331
verifying settings for non-XML formats, 445–446
DCOM, 14
   See also COM
Decision shape, 158, 276–278
definitions, eliminating unnecessary, 446
dehydration, 257–258, 283, 294
delivery receipt, 120–122
deployment of BizTalk
   automated, 483–486
   planning, 464–483
destination identifiers, 131
dictionaries, 237–238
Digital Dashboard, 78
digital documents
   acceptance of, 27
   increasing rate of change, 27
   information as a competitive advantage, 27–28
Digital Network Architecture. *See* DNA
Digital Signatures Act (Germany, 1997), 25–26
Direct Integration tool, 193, *194*
disk performance, 468–469
Distributed Management Task Force, 76
distribution lists, 138, 187–188
DMTF. *See* Distributed Management Task Force
DNA, 73
DOCTYPE declarations, 51
document definitions, 128–129, 190, 318
document-driven systems, 104–105
document instances, 52
Document Object Model (DOM), 11
document-processing pipeline
   components, 234–245, 595–606
   Decoder component, 235
   Decryption component, 235
   Encoder component, 236
   Encryption component, 236–237
   how the pipeline works, 239–245

   Parser component, 235–236
   Serializer component, 236
   Signature component, 237
   Transport component, 237
   Validation and Transformation component, 236
document, redefining, 26–28
document routing. *See* routing
document tracking database, 234
   dta_document_data table, 521–522
   dta_group_details table, 519–521
   dta_indoc_details table, 522–524
   dta_interchange_data table, 517–519
   dta_interchange_detail table, 514–517
   dta_outdoc_details table, 524–526
   dta_routing_details table, 527
   enabling, 512, *513*
   groups, 519–521
   overriding, 512
   structural overview, 513, *514*
   tracking field values, 524–527
   using document tracking from applications, 530
   See also Document Tracking tool
Document Tracking tool, 87, 196–199
   Advanced Query Builder, 528–529
   See also document tracking database
Document Type Definitions. *See* DTD
dta_document_data table, 521–522
dta_group_details table, 519–521
dta_indoc_details table, 522–524
dta_interchange_data table, 517–519
dta_interchange_detail table, 514–517
dta_outdoc_details table, 524–526
dta_routing_details table, 527
DTD, 50–52
   data types, 52
   defined, 49–50
   DOCTYPE declarations, 51
   EMPTY declarations, 51
dynamic channels, 302

E

E-Sign bill (U.S., 2000), 26
EAI. *See* enterprise application integration
ECMA, 31
EDI. *See* electronic data interchange
Editor, 87, 176–181, 318–320
    adding hints and annotations, 334–335
    Code List tab, 178
    completing and testing the sample, 332–337
    creating new specifications, 320–321
    creating records, 324–326
    creating specifications from templates, 337–339
    Declaration tab, 177, 323–324
    defining EDI documents, 340–355
    defining fields, 326–332
    defining XML documents, 320–340
    Dictionary tab, 178
    inferring Schema from documents, 339–340
    menus, *180*
    Namespace tab, 178
    Parse properties for EDI format fields, 352
    Parse properties for EDI format records, 353–354
    Parse tab, 178
    Reference tab, 178, 321–323
    saving the specification, 336
Eiffel#, 71
electronic data interchange
    compared to XML and EAI, 14–15
    defining EDI documents, 340–355
    development of, 5–9
    history of, 4–15
element, in XDR, 55
ElementType element, in XDR, 54–55
EMPTY declarations, 51
EnableDesign( ) method, 238, 599
encoding, 132–133

encryption, 24, 132–133, 475
    certificates for, 431–432
End shape, 157, 278
<endpoints> header, 116–117
enterprise application integration
    compared to EDI and XML, 14–15
    worries, 12–14
EntireX, 14
entities, 52
ENTITIES data type, 52
ENTITY data type, 52
enumeration data type, 52
envelopes, 132
    creating definitions for, 189
    envelope definition, 137–138
errors
    channel selection stage, 457–458
    configuration, 441
    document map, 441
    document specification, 441
    document validation and mapping stage, 458–459
    finding and isolating messaging errors, 451–459
    incorrect inbound documents, 442
    installation and transport, 441
    parsing stage, 454–457
    server run-time, 442
European Computer Manufacturers Association. *See* ECMA
European Guidelines for Trade Data Interchange. *See* GTDI
Execute( ) method, 238, 239, 245, 600
extended links, 58
eXtensible Markup Language. *See* XML
extension attributes for XDR, 622–625
external entities, 52

 F

federated services, 21
fields, 176
    available data types, 327–330

defining, 326–332
mapping, 364–368
string formats corresponding to
  data types, 331
verifying required, 445
filters, for channels, 153
firewall servers, 79
firewalls, 476
flatfile documents
  defining, 355–358
  defining fields, 357
  defining records, 357
  delimited flatfile streams,
    355, 356–357
  positional flatfile streams, 355, 358
flowchart language, 157–159
  simple workflow, *160*
  workflow with decision, *161*
  workflow with parallelism, *163*
  workflow with the While loop, *164*
  workflow with transaction, *162*
  workflow with transaction abort, *165*
Fork shape, 158, 278–279
formats, and data types, 331
fragments, 59
FuncCategory method, 617
FuncID, 618
function identifier, 618
functional groups
  in ANSI X12, 37
  in UN/EDIFACT standard, 42
FunctionsCount property, 613
functoids, 66, 373–388
  advanced, 386–387
  conversion, 381–382
  cumulative, 383, 384
  custom functoid containers, 608
  database, 383, 385
  date, 380–381
  Functoid Properties dialog box,
    373, *374*, *392*, *393*
  implementing functoid containers,
    613–618
  logical, 379–380
  mathematical, 377–378
  scientific, 382–383
  string, 374–376
  unique naming, 612
  writing functoid scripts, 608–612

G

GDI+, 72
GetConfigData( ) method, 238, 599
GetFunctionDescripter method, 613,
  617, 618
GetFunctionParameter method, 613, 618
GetGroupDetails( ) method, 241, 546
GetGroupSize( ) method, 242, 546
GetInDocDetails( ) method, 530
GetInterchangeDetails( ) method,
  241, 530, 546
GetNativeDocumentOffsets( ) method,
  242, 546
GetNextDocument( ) method, 241,
  242, 546, 559
GetOutDocDetails( ) method, 530
GetScriptBuffer method, 613, 618
globally unique identifiers, 217
group, in XDR, 56
GroupsExist( ) method, 241, 546
GTDI, 40
GUIDs. *See* globally unique identifiers

H

Hailstorm, 68
HandleChildren( ) method, 561, 563,
  564, 569
HandleConfirmationRequest method, 308
Haskell, 71
heterogeneous system landscapes, 28–30
HIS. *See* Microsoft Host Integration
  Server 2000
home organization, 127, 405–406, 496

Host Integration Server 2000, 78, 84
HTML, 9–10
HTTP, 9
    setting up HTTP receive
        capabilities, 435
HTTP/Secure (HTTP/S), certificates
    for, 431–432
hydration, 257–258, 283
Hypertext Markup Language. *See* HTML
Hypertext Transfer Protocol. *See* HTTP

I

IATA, 31
IBizTalkBase interface, 493
IBTSAppIntegration interface, 593
ID data type, 52
IEA, 37
IEEE, 31
IETF, 31
IFunctoid interface, 613
IInterchange interface, 146–147
IInterchange.Submit( ), 530
IInterchange.SubmitSync( ), 530
IIOP, 12, 14
IIS, 74
IL, 71
industry consortia, and technology
    standardization, 31
Industry Standardization for
    Institutional Trade Communications
    Group. *See* ISITC
Information Set, 11
Init( ) method, 244
installation
    installing the server, 90–101
    preinstallation tasks, 89–90
Institute of Electrics and Electronics
    Engineers. *See* IEEE
integrity of data, 24
interchange
    in ANSI X12, 37
    in UN/EDIFACT standard, 42

Interchange Application, 144–148, 477–483
    and COM+, 144–146
    submitting documents, 146–148
Interchange Control Header. *See* ISA
Interchange Control Trailer. *See* IEA
InterchangeBTM database, 207
internal entities, 52
International Air Transport Association.
    See IATA
International Standards Organization.
    See ISO
Internet Engineering Taskforce. *See* IETF
Internet Information Server, 74, 84
Internet Inter-Orb Protocol. *See* IIOP
Internet Security and Acceleration
    Server 2000, 37, 79
intrusion detection and defense, 475–483
    guidelines, 476–477
        securing run-time environment for
            BizTalk Messaging, 477–480
        securing run-time environment for
            XLANG schedules, 480–483
IPersist/IPersistStreamInit interface, 597
IPipelineComponent Description
    interface, 239
IPipelineComponent interface,
    238–239, 597
IPipelineComponentAdmin interface, 597
IPipelineComponentAdmin::GetConfig
    Data( ) method, 599
IPipelineComponentAdmin.SetConfig
    Data( ) method, 238
IPipelineComponentAdmin::SetConfig
    Data( ) method, 599
IPipelineComponentDescription
    interface, 597
IPipelineComponent::EnableDesign( )
    method, 599
IPipelineComponent.Execute( )
    method, 239
ISA. *See* Internet Security and
    Acceleration Server 2000
ISITC, 44

ISO, 31
ISO 15022 standard, 8
      See also SWIFT
ISO 6523 codes, 628–631
ISO 7775 standard, 8
      See also SWIFT
ISO 8879 standard, 58
ISupportErrorInfo interface, 597

 J

Java, 12, 13–14
      as the foundation for corporate
         development tools, 30
      Microsoft JUMP Toolkit, 71
Java 2 Enterprise Edition (J2EE), 75
Java Virtual Machine. *See* JVM
Join shape, 159, 279
JScript.NET, 71
JVM, 13

 L

links, 58
Load( ) method, 494
LoadSchemaByName( ) method, 560
loopback channels, 303–305
      generic component for, 309–310
loopback ports
      creating, 419–421
      sample configuration, 421–429
Loopback transport, 130, 131
loops, 350
      in ANSI X12, 37

 M

management database, 206–233
      administration database tables,
         207–217
      messaging object tables, 217–233

<manifest> header, 117–118
Mapper utility, 87, 134–135, 181–184,
   243, 360
      fundamentals, 360–388
      mapping fields, 364–368
      mapping records, 368–373
      Output tab, 184
      Properties tab, 183
      Retrieve Source Specification
         dialog box, 362, *364*
      Select Source Specification dialog
         box, 362, *363*
      Select Source Specification Type
         dialog box, 361–362
      using functoids, 183
      Values tab, 184
      warning message boxes, 366–367
      Warnings tab, 184
      See also mapping
mapping, 134–135
      bottom-up, 369, *370*, 372–373
      data flow, 306–307
      documents, 388–400
      examples, 400–402
      fields, 364–368
      records, 368–373
      structure flattening, 368–371
      top-down, 369–372
      See also Mapper utility
MapPOToPOAcknowledgment
   method, 308
memory usage, 466–468
Mercury, 71
message format
      business process correlation, 122–123
      document catalog, 117–118
      document identification and
         properties, 114–116
      document source and destination,
         116–117
      key features, 113–114
      requesting and returning receipts,
         118–122

message input reference (MIR), 44
message queues, receiving data from,
298–302
messages, in UN/EDIFACT standard, 42
Messaging Manager, 87, 184–193, 404–405
Channels link, 418
Messaging Ports link, 418
receiving HTTP messages, 435
messaging object tables, 217–233
Messaging service, 5, 87, 140–144
channel filters, 153
document routing, 148–154
integrating with Orchestration
schedules, 170–173
open destination routing, 153–154
preventing problems, 440–450
queues, 140–143
receive functions, 143–144
securing run-time environment
for, 477–480
sending messages to and through,
302–303
terminology, 126–138
using loopback channels for
document conversion, 303–305
Microsoft Application Center 2000, 76
Microsoft Commerce Server 2000, 78
Microsoft Distributed Transaction
Coordinator, 311
Microsoft Exchange Server 2000, 77, 84, 90
Microsoft Host Integration Server 2000, 78
Microsoft Intermediate Language, 71
Microsoft Message Queue, 75, 84
Microsoft .NET Enterprise Servers, 73
Application Center 2000, 76
Commerce Server 2000, 78
Exchange Server 2000, 77
Host Integration Server 2000, 78
Internet Security and Acceleration
Server 2000, 79
SharePoint Portal Server 2000, 77–78
SQL Server 2000, 76–77
Windows 2000 Server, 74–76

Microsoft .NET Framework, 68–69
common language runtime, 70–71
common type system, 69–70
library, 71–73
XML support, 70
Microsoft .NET initiative, 68–79
Hailstorm, 68
.NET Enterprise Servers, 73–79
.NET Framework, 68–73
Microsoft SharePoint Portal Server 2000,
77–78
Microsoft SQL Server 2000, 76–77
Microsoft Transaction Server, 74, 311
Microsoft Visual C++ with Managed
Extensions, 71
MicrosoftBizTalkServer_Group class,
505–506
MicrosoftBizTalkServer_MgmtDB class,
504–505
MicrosoftBizTalkServer_Queue class, 508
MicrosoftBizTalkServer_
ReceiveFunction class, 507–508
MicrosoftBizTalkServer_RetryQueue
class, 509
MicrosoftBizTalkServer_ScheduledQueue
class, 509
MicrosoftBizTalkServer_Server class,
506–507
MicrosoftBizTalkServer_SuspendedQueue
class, 510
MicrosoftBizTalkServer_WorkQueue
class, 510
MIME, 132–133
mobile devices, and the need for
integration, 30
monikers, 251–254
Morse telegraph, 6
MSDTC. *See* Microsoft Distributed
Transaction Coordinator
MSMQ. *See* Microsoft Message Queue
MTS. *See* Microsoft Transaction Server
Multipurpose Internet Mail
Extensions. *See* MIME

N

namespaces, 11, 48–49
  defined, 48
.NET. *See* Microsoft .NET initiative
.NET Remoting, 72
network performance, 469
NMTOKEN data type, 52
NMTOKENS data type, 52
node test, 59, 61

 O

Oberon, 71
Object Linking and Embedding. *See* OLE
Object Management Group. *See* OMG
object-oriented analysis, 263
Objective Camel, 71
OCX, 14
  See also COM
OLE, 14
  See also COM
OMG, 12
open destination routing, 153–154
open messaging source, 133
open-source channels, 151, 411
Orchestration, 5, 87–88
  architecture, 248–258
  rapid adaptation and short
    turnaround times, 106–107
  See also Orchestration Designer;
    schedules
Orchestration Designer, 88
  actions, 166
  Add Rule dialog box, 276, *277*
  components, 167
  components and communications
    elements bound to ports, 169–170
  creating programs from flowchart
    drawings, 166–173
  Decision Properties dialog box,
    276–277

defining ports, 279–310
defining the business workflow,
  274–279
flowchart language elements,
  157–159
integrating schedules with
  Messaging service, 170–173
introduction to, 272–274
long-running transactions, 310–315
ports, 168–170
Rule Properties dialog box, 278
shaping the data flow, 306–309
simple workflow, *160*
workflow with decision, *161*
workflow with parallelism, *163*
workflow with the While loop, *164*
workflow with transaction, *162*
workflow with transaction abort, *165*
See also Visio Service Release (SR-1)
organizations
  defining, 405–407
  Home Organization, 127
  identifiers, 126–127
  loading and creating, 495–498
  Organizations Properties dialog
    box, 406
  Organizations recordset, 496–497

P

paper-to-paper technology, 6
parameter entities, 52
ParseBody( ) method, 559, 561
ParseField( ) method, 571
ParseHeaders( ) method, 550–551
ParseRecord( ) method, 569
parsers, 240–242
  analyzing headers, 550–555
  handling group information, 558
  implementing custom parsers,
    534–575

loading the Schema based on selection criteria, 557–558
parser class, 543–546
parsing stage errors, 454–457
parsing the document, 559–575
plugging into BizTalk, 535
probing the format, 547–550
stream handling, 556–557
verifying settings for non-XML formats, 445–446
Pascal, 71
#PCDATA keyword, 51
Perl, 71
pipeline. *See* document-processing pipeline
PKI, 431
planning deployment of BizTalk, 464–483
ports, 129–133, 168–170
components and communications elements that can be bound to, 169–170
creating, 407–411
defining, 279–310
destination identifiers, 131
loopback, 419–429
managing with BizTalkConfig object, 492–498
messaging, 129–130, 133, 279–286
open destination, 153–154
references, 306
return, 172
transports, 130–131
predicates, 59, 61–62
privacy, 24
ProbeInterchangeFormat( ) method, 240, 241, 546
<process> header, 122–123
ProcessMessage( ) method, 244
processor requirements, 466–468
properties, 255–257
<properties> header, 115–116
Public Key Infrastructure. *See* PKI
Python, 71

Q

queues, 140–143
node, 195
receiving data from message queues, 298–302

R

rapid application development (RAD) tool, 106
See also Orchestration
raw native interface bridging technology. *See* RNI
receipts, sending, 436–437
receive functions, 143–144
Receive Functions node, 196
records, 176
creating, 324–326
mapping, 368–373
Remote Method Invocation. *See* RMI
retry queue, 142–143, 195, 196
RMI, 14
RNI, 13
rollback, 75
Roman postal service, 4–5
RosettaNet, 31
routing, 148–154
channel selection, 149–153
fundamentals, 148–149
open destination routing, 153–154
simulating, 449–450
See also channels
run-time environment
securing for BizTalk Messaging, 477–480
securing for XLANG schedules, 480–483
run-time errors, 441–442

▼ S

S/MIME, 133
scaling BizTalk systems, 469–470
    scaling out, 470–472
    scaling up, 470
scheduled queue, 142, 195
schedules, 157
    as components, 254–255
    launching other XLANG
      schedules, 287–298
    running, 251–254
    and XLANG, 248–250
Schema element, in XDR, 54
Schema language, 11, 622–625
    inferring from documents, 339–340
    repositories, 32
Scheme, 71
Secure Multipurpose Internet Mail
  Extensions. *See* S/MIME
security
    authentication and authorization,
      472–475
    considerations, 472–483
    and electronic signatures, 23–26
    implementing the receiver side of
      a secure connection, 436
    implementing the sender of a
      secure connection, 432–434
    remote channel security settings, 436
    See also certificates; encoding;
      encryption; intrusion detection
      and defense; signatures
segments
    in ANSI X12, 36–37
    in UN/EDIFACT standard, 42
serializers
    initialization, 578–579
    plugging into BizTalk, 576
    serializer class, 576–578
    writing custom, 575–590
    writing the document, 579–590
service windows, 131, 142
<services> header, 119–120

SetConfigData( ) method, 238, 239, 244,
  245, 599
SetErrorInfo( ) method, 603
SGML, 9
    and XLink, 58
shared queue database, 143, 234
SharePoint Portal Server, 77–78
signatures, 23–26, 132–133
    certificates for, 431–432
simple data elements, in UN/EDIFACT
  standard, 41
simple links, 58
Simple Object Access Protocol. *See* SOAP
SmallTalk, 71
SOAP, 11, 66, 110–113
    and BizTalk Framework, 109
    elements, 111–112
    Hailstorm, 68
    and .NET Framework, 70
Society for Worldwide Interbank Financial
  Telecommunications. *See* SWIFT
Software AG, 14
SQL Server 2000, 76–77, 89–90
Standard ML, 71
standards bodies, 31
    communities, 107–108
stencils, 88
stream handling, 556–557
StreamWrite( ) method, 581
structure flattening, 368–371
Structured General Markup
  Language. *See* SGML
stylesheets, 11
    See also XSLT
SubmitSync method, 304
suspended queue, 143, 195, 196
    See also errors
SwbemObjectSet class, 503–504
SWIFT, 8–9, 43–44
    application header block (Block
      Identifier 2), 44, 45
    basic header block (Block
      Identifier 1), 44
    semantics, 46

syntax and structure, 44–46
text block (Block Identifier 4), 44, 45
trailers block (Block Identifier 5),
   44, 45
user header block (Block
   Identifier 3), 44, 45

▼ T

telegraph, 6
Teletype, 6
teletypewriter, 6
Telex, 6
templates, creating specifications from,
   337–339
testing
   document specifications and maps,
     448–449
   in realistic deployments, 450
tracking documents. *See* document
   tracking database; Document
   Tracking tool
transaction sets, in ANSI X12, 37, 38–40
Transaction shape, 159
transactions
   adding, 311–312
   configuring transaction behavior,
     312, *313*
   failure-handling for, 313, *314*
   long-running, 310–315
   nested, 314–315
transport dictionary, 238
transports, 130–131
   configuring, 498

▼ U

UN/CEFACT, 31–32, 40
UN/EDIFACT standard, 7–8, 9
   composite data elements, 42
   D93A, 346
   functional groups, 42
   "heaven," 341–351

"hell," 351–355
   interchange, 42
   messages, 42
   S93A, 346
   segments, 42
   semantics, 42–43
   simple data elements, 41
   syntax and structure, 40–42
   and UN technology
     standardization efforts, 31–32
United Nations
   Centre for Trade Facilitation and
     Electronic Business, 31–32
   and technology standardization,
     31–32
   See also UN/EDIFACT standard
Universal Resource Identifier, 322
Universal Resource Name, 322–323
universally unique identifier, 114, 323
URI. *See* Universal Resource Identifier
URN. *See* Universal Resource Name
use cases, collecting, 268–269
UUID, 114, 323

▼ V

validation
   of custom document specifications,
     447–448
   errors, 458–459
   of standards-based document
     specifications, 443–447
   strict, 444–446
   tolerant, 446–447
value-added networks, 8
ValuesRead( ) method, 239
ValuesWritten( ) method, 239
VANs. *See* value-added networks
variables, nonexistence of, 255–257
VBScript, 71
Version property, 613
Visio Service Release (SR-1), 88, 90
   for beginners, 272–274

Visual Basic Scripting Edition. See
    VBScript
VisualBasic.NET, 71
VisualStudio.NET, and XSD, 57

 W

W3C, 11, 31, 46
WBEM. See Web-Based Enterprise
    Management
WBEM Query Language, 504
WbemObject class, 504
Web-Based Enterprise Management, 76
Web Distributed Authoring and
    Versioning. See WebDAV
web server farms, 76
Web Service Description
    Language. See WSDL
Web services, 22–23
Web Storage system, 77
WebDAV, 77, 179
While shape, 158
whitespace, 254
Windows 2000 Server, 74–76
Windows Forms, 72
Windows Management Instrumentation,
    76, 207, 502–503
        classes, 504–510
        SwbemObjectSet class, 503–504
        WbemObject class, 504
        WMI API, 503–504
wizards
        BizTalk Server 2000 Setup Wizard,
            90–95, 96
        Channel Wizard, 186–187
        COM Component Binding
            Wizard, 290–295
        Message Queuing Binding
            Wizard, 298–302
        Messaging Binding Wizard,
            280–282
        Messaging Database Setup
            Wizard, 95–97, 98–100

Messaging Port Wizard, 185–186
Method Communication Wizard,
    295–298
New Channel Wizard, 412–414,
    415, 416–419, 420
New Messaging Port Wizard,
    408–411, 412
Orchestration Persistence Database
    Setup Wizard, 97–100, 101
Port Configuration Wizard, 217
XML Communication Wizard,
    282–286
WMI. See Windows Management
    Instrumentation
work queue, 142, 195
workflow
        with decision, 161
        defining, 274–279
        instance objects, 250
        with parallelism, 163
        schedules, 5
        simple, 160
        with transaction, 162
        with transaction abort, 165
        with the While loop, 164
World Wide Web Consortium
    (W3C). See W3C
WQL. See WBEM Query Language
WriteBody( ) method, 579, 582
WriteFooter( ) method, 579
WriteHeader( ) method, 581
WriteNode( ) method, 582
WriterHeader( ) method, 579
WSDL, 70

 X

X12 standard. See ANSI X12
XBase, 11
XDR, 50, 52–56
        attribute, 55–56
        AttributeType element, 55

BizTalk extension attributes for, 622–625
element, 55
ElementType element, 54–55
group, 56
Schema element, 54
XLANG, 88
launching schedules, 287–298
ports, 129–133
and schedules, 248–250
securing run-time environment for XLANG schedules, 480–483
XLink, 11, 58–59
XML, 9–12, 46
advanced features, 11
communities, 32
compared to EDI and EAI, 14–15
core principals, 47
defining documents, 320–340
Document Object Model (DOM), 11
document syntax, 46–47
extension specifications, 57–62
Information Set, 11
as the integration technology for system connectivity, 30

namespaces, 48–49
support for Microsoft .NET Framework, 70
See also XBase; XLink; XPath; XPointer
XML Data Reduced. *See* XDR
XML Linking Language. *See* XLink
XML Path Language. *See* XPath
XML Protocol. *See* XMLP
XML Schema Definition. *See* XSD
XML Stylesheet Language Transformations standard. *See* XSLT
XML.org, 32
XMLP, 11, 66
XPath, 11, 59–62
axis, 59–60
built-in functions, 62
extraction, 286
node test, 59, 61
predicates, 59, 61–62
XPointer, 62
XSD, 50, 56–57
XSLT, 62–66
basic functional principles, *63*
mapping principle, *64*

INTERNATIONAL CONTACT INFORMATION

AUSTRALIA
McGraw-Hill Book Company Australia Pty. Ltd.
TEL +61-2-9417-9899
FAX +61-2-9417-5687
http://www.mcgraw-hill.com.au
books-it_sydney@mcgraw-hill.com

CANADA
McGraw-Hill Ryerson Ltd.
TEL +905-430-5000
FAX +905-430-5020
http://www.mcgrawhill.ca

GREECE, MIDDLE EAST,
NORTHERN AFRICA
McGraw-Hill Hellas
TEL +30-1-656-0990-3-4
FAX +30-1-654-5525

MEXICO (Also serving Latin America)
McGraw-Hill Interamericana Editores S.A. de C.V.
TEL +525-117-1583
FAX +525-117-1589
http://www.mcgraw-hill.com.mx
fernando_castellanos@mcgraw-hill.com

SINGAPORE (Serving Asia)
McGraw-Hill Book Company
TEL +65-863-1580
FAX +65-862-3354
http://www.mcgraw-hill.com.sg
mghasia@mcgraw-hill.com

SOUTH AFRICA
McGraw-Hill South Africa
TEL +27-11-622-7512
FAX +27-11-622-9045
robyn_swanepoel@mcgraw-hill.com

UNITED KINGDOM & EUROPE
(Excluding Southern Europe)
McGraw-Hill Education Europe
TEL +44-1-628-502500
FAX +44-1-628-770224
http://www.mcgraw-hill.co.uk
computing_neurope@mcgraw-hill.com

ALL OTHER INQUIRIES Contact:
Osborne/McGraw-Hill
TEL +1-510-549-6600
FAX +1-510-883-7600
http://www.osborne.com
omg_international@mcgraw-hill.com